THE AMERICAN GI
IN EUROPE IN WORLD WAR II

THE AMERICAN GI
IN EUROPE IN WORLD WAR II

THE BATTLE IN FRANCE

J. E. KAUFMANN
AND H. W. KAUFMANN

STACKPOLE
BOOKS

To all those veterans
who contributed to this project

Copyright © 2010 by J. E. Kaufmann and H. W. Kaufmann

Published by
STACKPOLE BOOKS
5067 Ritter Road
Mechanicsburg, PA 17055
www.stackpolebooks.com

Printed in the United States of America

10 9 8 7 6 5 4 3 2 1

Library of Congress Cataloging-in-Publication Data

Kaufmann, J. E.
   The American GI in Europe in World War II : the march to D-Day / J.E. Kaufmann and H.W. Kaufmann.
      p. cm.
   Includes bibliographical references and index.
   ISBN 978-0-8117-0449-6 — ISBN 978-0-8117-0454-0 — ISBN 978-0-8117-0526-4 1. World War, 1939–1945—Campaigns—Western Front. 2. World War, 1939–1945—United States. 3. United States. Army—History—World War, 1939–1945. 4. World War, 1939–1945—Personal narratives, American. 5. United States—Army—Biography. I. Kaufmann, H. W. II. Title.
   D769.K34 2009
   940.54'1273092—dc22
   [B]
                                                          2008046869

CONTENTS

INTRODUCTION

This third and final book—*The Battle in France*—in our three-volume series on the American GI in Europe in World War II describes operations in Normandy after D-Day, the Brittany campaign, and the invasion of southern France. The first volume provides the background to the United States' entry into the war, the training of the troops, and their shipment to Europe; it also details the North African and Mediterranean campaigns through the first half of 1944. The second volume covers the preparations for Operation Overlord and the landings in Normandy on D-Day, June 6, 1944.

The objective of this series is not to compile a history of individual units of the U.S. armed forces or thoroughly examine the campaigns in which they took part during the war in Europe. We included only enough historical information to provide background and context for veterans' accounts. We thought it would be interesting to follow some of these American veterans from the time of their induction and training to their participation in the invasions of Normandy and the French Riviera during the summer of 1944. We also thought it important to shine the spotlight not only on combat veterans, but also on the men who made it all possible by operating the rear echelons and supporting the troops in the front lines.

This book presents a very small sampling of the experiences of American veterans in World War II and makes no claim of being a comprehensive compendium of the war. The reader will notice that sometimes the veterans' accounts contradict not only one another, but also the chronicled versions of the events. These contradictions should come as no surprise since each veteran had his own perspective of events and because the soldiers' memories were distorted either by conditions on the battlefield or by the passage of time. It must also be pointed out that some of the veterans might have been in a position to see what others never did. It must be remembered, too, that there are as many sides to a story as there are witnesses. This does not mean that any of the witnesses intentionally lied or distorted their accounts, but it does demonstrate the difficulty—if not the impossibility—of coming up with an exact and true picture of any historical event from every point of view. This is a problem faced by most historians. It must be hoped, however, that the more witnesses and accounts there are, the greater the chance of achieving accuracy. It is our hope that the veterans' accounts in these volumes will enrich the body of data concerning these momentous events in world history.

The complete introduction, found in the first volume, includes a brief discussion of some of the problems we encountered while we interviewed the veterans decades after the fact. This work is dedicated to all those who contributed their accounts and to their comrades-in-arms.

CHAPTER 1

The Days After: The Airborne Troops

The Gliders Arrive and Divisions Consolidate

Elements of two glider infantry regiments and divisional supporting units arrived in Normandy on June 7, 1944, but no parachute drops took place. On the morning of D+1, the bulk of the 325th Glider Infantry Regiment of the 82nd "All-American" Airborne Division landed in gliders. A company from the 325th Glider Infantry Regiment of the 82nd Airborne Division, supported by a company of the 746th Tank Battalion, disembarked from landing craft in the early afternoon and pushed inland in an attempt to link up with its division. A battalion of the 327th Glider Infantry Regiment of the 101st Airborne Division scheduled to land by sea on D-Day did not land until the evening of June 7. The remainder of the glider regiment of the 101st Airborne Division also arrived by sea after D-Day.

U.S. Glider Operations in Normandy

The bulk of the glider troops of the 82nd and 101st Airborne Divisions arrived on D-Day and D+1. Two dozen additional gliders landed in Normandy between June 9 and June 13. The following missions were flown:

D-DAY, MORNING

Mission Chicago: Fifty-two CG-4, 101st A/B Division—divisional staff, two batteries of 81st A/B AA/AT Battalion, elements of the 326th A/B Engineer Company, 101st A/B Signal Company, and 326th A/B Medical Company. Landed at 3:45 A.M.

Mission Detroit: Fifty-two CG-4, 82nd A/B Division—divisional staff, two batteries of the 80th A/B AA/AT Battalion, and the 82nd A/B Signals Company. Landed at 4:10 A.M.

D-DAY, EVENING

Mission Keokuk: Thirty-two Horsa, 101st A/B Division—staff, 101st A/B Signal Company, and 326th A/B Medical Company. Landed at 8:53 P.M.

Mission Elmira (first wave): Fifty-four Horsa and twenty-two CG-4 gliders, 82nd A/B Division—over 400 troops, 13 antitank guns, 64 vehicles, and supplies for the 82nd Airborne Division in two serials. Landed at 9:04 and 9:37 P.M.

Mission Elmira (second wave): Eight-six Horsa and fourteen CG-4 gliders, 82nd A/B Division—319th and 320th A/B Artillery battalions in two serials. Landed at 10:55 and 11:05 P.M.

D+1, MORNING

Mission Galveston: Twenty Horsa and eighty-two CG-4, 82nd A/B Division—9 guns, 1st Battalion of 325th Glider Infantry Regiment in the first serial; regimental HQ with 11 guns and supplies in the second serial. Second serial landed at 7:01 and first at 7:55 A.M.

Mission Hackensack: Thirty Horsa and seventy CG-4, 82nd A/B Division—2nd Battalion of 325th Glider Infantry Regiment and 2nd Battalion of 401st Glider Infantry Regiment (attached to the 325th) in the first serial; remaining elements of the glider regiment with mortars and vehicles in the second serial. First serial landed at 8:51 and second at 8:59 A.M.

According to some historians, there were not enough aircraft or gliders available to transport both glider infantry regiments. According to others, there was a shortage of pilots and many of the gliders were flown by only one pilot and an airborne trooper as copilot.[1] Several other factors affected the decision to use fewer gliders. British Air Marshal Trafford Leigh-Mallory thought that massive landings in the checkerboard fields bordered with hedgerows would cause an unacceptable number of casualties. Most glider landings were planned for early morning or before dusk to limit the German gunners' accuracy and to prevent enemy fighter aircraft from reacting. With

---

1. Many glider pilots sat at their bases and had no mission for D-Day or D+1.

ongoing bombing missions, aircraft once again filled the skies above Normandy. The morning landings on June 7 suffered light losses.

Both airborne divisions tried to consolidate their positions while the 4th Infantry Division advanced to relieve them. However, neither of these elite airborne units was removed from the line; instead, they were ordered to hold and expand their sectors along the Merderet and Douve Rivers. Once on the ground, both divisions had to retrieve many of their scattered troops, some of whom had become attached to whatever unit they could find. The airborne divisions, unlike the infantry, were not going to receive replacements. These specialized troopers had become expendable. In the meantime, newly arrived paratrooper replacements remained in the divisional areas in England, awaiting the withdrawal of these two divisions from Normandy.

The Morning of D+1, June 7

During the night of June 6–7, the paratroopers settled in. A large number of men from the 82nd Airborne Division were isolated west of the Merderet River while the division headquarters' command radio was still in a glider that had failed to cross the Channel and remained in England, leaving the division commander, Gen. Matthew Ridgway, out of contact with higher echelons. During the afternoon, Col. Edson Raff's sea-landed detachment from the 325th Glider Infantry Regiment failed to break through the German defenses near Turqueville, which barred the way to Ste-Mère-Église.

At the close of D-Day, the 101st Airborne Division was in a slightly better situation since the 4th Division had managed to open a line of communications between it and the beach. The paratroopers failed to reach and blow up the

bridges on the road between Carentan and St. Côme-du-Mont to block a German counterattack. However, Col. Howard Johnson with men from his 501st Parachute Infantry Regiment held the lock at La Barquette, and Capt. Charles Shettle, the S-3 of the 506th Parachute Infantry Regiment, with men from his battalion held a crossing of the Douve between Carentan and the sea. Captain Shettle's men were forced to withdraw to the north bank and prepare the two bridges at Le Port for demolition. The Germans still firmly held on to St. Côme-du-Mont and the main road leading to Carentan.

As June 7 dawned, the Germans were still in control of the high ground between Turqueville and Chef-du-Pont, but they were partially surrounded by elements of airborne divisions on one side and the 4th Division on the other.[2] The Germans also controlled Amfreville and blocked the crossing of the Merderet to the east of it. German units took up positions north of Ste-Mère-Église and at Beuzeville-au-Plain, holding up the advance of the 12th Infantry (4th Division). Another German force held Carquebut to the south of Chef-du-Pont, which completed the encirclement of the 82nd Airborne Division. North of Carentan, the enemy strongly occupied St. Côme-du-Mont and also held positions along the Douve between Carentan and the coast, even though elements of the 501st Parachute Infantry Regiment (101st Airborne Division) held the locks at La Barquette. Fortunately, reinforcements for the 101st Airborne Division, namely its glider infantry, were scheduled to arrive by sea late on June 6. Although they were late, they moved directly to the front. The glider infantry of the isolated 82nd Airborne Division was scheduled to arrive by glider on the morning of June 7.[3]

Missions Galveston and Hackensack, carrying most of the 325th Glider Infantry, landed at Land-

---

2. This German position was held mainly by the 795th *Ost* Battalion of Georgian troops.

3. The remainder of the 82nd Airborne Division, mostly headquarters and support and service elements, arrived by sea after June 7.

ing Zone E and Landing Zone W before 9:00 A.M. on the morning of June 7. The regiment assembled by 10:15 A.M. and moved against the German position at Carquebut only to discover that the Germans had withdrawn. Meanwhile, the 8th Infantry attacked the Georgian 795th *Ost* Battalion, which held the high ground extending from Turqueville to Fauville. One of about two dozen captured Americans soldiers convinced his Georgian captors in Turqueville to surrender to the advancing 1st Battalion, 8th Infantry. The remainder of the Georgian battalion put up stiff resistance between Écoqueneauville and Fauville, but the other battalions of the 8th Infantry broke through and advanced on Ste-Mère-Église. The encirclement of the 82nd Airborne Division was effectively broken, and the division's glider infantry, which advanced on Chef-du-Pont, moved into reserve. However, by the end of June 7, the division still had failed to establish a bridgehead across the Merderet River, and many of its men remained isolated on the west bank.

The troops of the 3rd Battalion of the 506th Parachute Infantry Regiment under Captain Shettle continued to hold the bridges at Le Port. There was no need to blow them up since the Germans had not attacked. A German force of an estimated 300 men from the 6th Parachute Regiment advanced on his position from the north in the afternoon. Captain Shettle sent strong patrols against them, and by evening, they had killed 30 to 50 Germans and taken 255 prisoners. The Germans launched an attack from the east that night, but they were driven back.

Meanwhile, a larger group from the 6th Parachute Regiment attacked Colonel Johnson's 250 paratroopers at La Barquette. Johnson realigned his men to the north and engaged the German paratroopers. Although short of ammunition, he bluffed the Germans into surrendering. He took 350 prisoners, including the battalion commander, after killing about 150 Germans that had attacked his position. Johnson's group suffered 40

German field gun captured by troops of the 101st Airborne Division. RAY HOOD

casualties, including 10 killed. During the day, two battalions of the 506th Parachute Infantry with tanks advanced toward St. Côme-du-Mont. They were joined by a battalion of the 501st Parachute Infantry, but they were stopped outside the town. The 1st Battalion of the 401st Glider Infantry Regiment (part of the 327th Glider Infantry Regiment, which was still at sea) arrived from the beach and joined this group.

Before the gliders landed on the morning of June 7, the two artillery battalions of Mission Elmira, which had landed during the evening

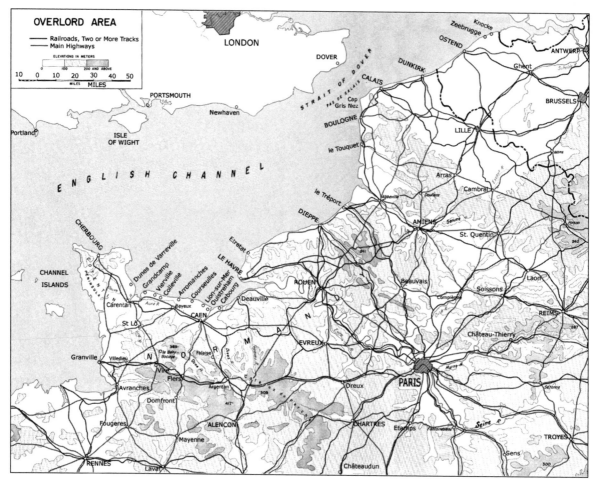

Northern France. U.S. ARMY

operations of June 6, assembled and prepared for action. Although they had taken casualties at and near Landing Zone O when they landed, most of the twelve guns of the 320th Field Artillery Battalion were recovered. This battalion's first two 105-millimeter howitzers went into action near Ste-Mère-Église at 9:30 A.M., shortly after the 325th Glider Infantry Regiment landed. The first six guns of the 319th Field Artillery were not ready until the morning of June 8 after the unit took up positions near Chef-du-Pont.

PFC Joseph Clowry of the 319th Field Artillery Battalion was among the numerous casualties of the night landing of June 6. That morning, he waited with other men from his glider for the opening of a route back to the beach. The two enlisted men who sat on either side of him had broken vertebrae in their necks. The glider pilot had a bullet in his leg, and their lieutenant, who sat in the copilot's seat, had a broken back.

When daylight came, I made my way to an aid station that had been set up at a nearby crossroad. There was a tent set up off the road marked with a red cross, a few vehicles, stretchers laying haphazardly lined up with wounded near the tent, tagged and waiting to be evacuated. I got a turn by the tent and I was cleaned up a bit and tagged. Orders were that anyone with a head wound was to be evacuated. Waiting outside the tent for transportation, not too far off in the sky I noticed a P-47 that seemed to have been hit by enemy fire and was obviously in trouble. I recall subconsciously asking myself, "Why doesn't the pilot bail out?" I was relieved when I made out a human form falling from the plane. I waited for the chute to open. The figure continued to plummet earthward and disappeared into the trees down the road—the chute never opened.

When we reached the beach, a DUKW took us out to an LST waiting off shore. Back in England, I recall being on a cot in a large circus-like tent being checked over by a nurse and having my head shaved around the slashed area. I was then sent to the 62nd General Hospital further inland where I was released a week or so later to return to Market Harborough [in Leicestershire north of London] and wait until the mid-July return of my unit.

Private First Class Clowry was lucky compared to fellow passengers in the glider, since he was a walking wounded and did not suffer from more serious injuries. His lieutenant was killed at the beach during a German strafing attack while waiting to be evacuated.

The Glider Riders of the 325th

On the morning of D+1, many of the C-47 pilots—or "power pilots" as they were referred to in their groups—who had just dropped paratroopers in the early hours of D-Day were assigned the task of towing gliders across the Channel. Some of the pilots—like Lt. William Thompson, a 1941 draftee from Pleasant Hill, Missouri, who went through pilot training in 1942—were assigned Horsas, a type of glider they had never towed before. Thompson's Horsa was one of twenty assigned to this mission. As he began rolling down the runway at Ramsbury, he

CG-4A on Hackensack Mission

Lt. Sidney Ulan's C-47 from the 441st Group towed a CG-4A glider with troops of the 325th Glider Infantry Regiment on Mission Hackensack on June 7. In his manifest were the Glider Number 43-41336 and the Tug Aircraft Number 42-101013. The passengers included a company commander, a first sergeant, a mortar squad, messengers, and a medic. The senior passenger, Capt. Herbert C. Slaughter, and his first sergeant, Edward Lobbezoo, were seated in seat 1 and 2, respectively. The mortar squad leader David W. Judson was in the rear with his mortar crew in seats 11, 12, and 13. Flight officers Lee W. Secaur and James Hall were the pilots of the glider. Each man aboard was calculated to weigh 200 pounds, and the glider carried a water can, a camouflage net, two SCR 536 radios, two sound power phones, a reel of DR-8 wire, seven boxes of antitank mines, and an 81-millimeter mortar. The total weight of crew, passengers, and cargo was about 3,800 tons.

found "it was a real task because it was heavier than the CG-4 . . . we put all the power on the airplane and pulled up at the end of the runway and hoped it was going to fly." Once airborne, it took the maximum effort of his C-47 to tow the Horsa to its destination. His 437th Group towed in the first serial of the Mission Galveston with men of the 325th Glider Infantry Regiment. Lt. Sidney Ulan from Chester, Pennsylvania, who piloted a C-47 of the 441st Group, took off about two and a half hours later from Merryfield towing one of the last fifty Waco CG-4s of Mission Hackensack, which included the remainder of the 325th Glider Infantry Regiment.

German troops captured by members of the 101st Airborne Division. RAY HOOD

The 1st Battalion of the 325th Glider Infantry Regiment assembled at Ramsbury airfield early on the morning of June 7. Its gliders and their C-47 tugs took off at 4:39 A.M. as part of the first serial of eighteen Horsas and thirty-two CG-4 gliders en route to Landing Zone E in Normandy. The second serial, consisting of the regimental headquarters and additional vehicles in two Horsas and fifty CG-4 gliders, had lifted off from Aldermaston airfield seven minutes earlier with the same destination.

First Lt. Lambert G. Wilder from Bogota, New Jersey, was at Ramsbury on detached duty from the 435th Group when he was assigned to fly one of the thirty-two CG-4As for the first serial of Mission Galveston. He had arrived a week before with twelve other pilots from his unit. At one of their briefings, the intelligence officer warned them about the hedgerows but neglected to tell them how high they actually were. He also

failed to inform them that there were posts linked by wires to hinder their landings in some of the fields. On the evening of June 5, Wilder and the other glider pilots anxiously waited in their compound for their turn as they listened to the C-47s of the power pilots roaring across the airfield with their cargoes of paratroopers. On the morning of June 7 at about 4:40 A.M., the CG-4A gliders began lifting off from Ramsbury, followed by the eighteen Horsa gliders.

I had fifteen infantrymen and was overloaded by about 2,000 pounds and it was like a half-full rowboat to control. It was misty after raining some during the night, a nasty morning. We headed for the coast and deviated a little. As far as I could see, there were streams of aircraft going over and coming back, just like a flow of ducks. Ships for miles, and when you reached the Normandy coast there were ships firing inland. You could see the flashes from their guns and [the places] where the shells landed.

As we reached the coast, the tracers were going right under us; they were underestimating our speed. After crossing the coast, they gave us the red light from the navigator's bubble in the C-47, and when we reached the LZ, the green light. If you were not off by that time, they would cut you off because they were not going to tow you back to England. We got confused because everybody was trying to get off at the same time and the gliders were going this way and that. I saw a Horsa glider try to go over two trees and they took off both wings clean as a whistle. Some of the tow ships were shot down and you could see them go down in flames.

When I came into the LZ—a pasture with horses and cows in it—I was ready to set down about fifty feet off the ground, and here comes a CG-4 right at me. It was going to be a head-on collision, so I turned to the right and, fortunately, he turned to the right. After we landed, the first mortar round came in. It was long and went over us. Then the second—it was short. They always told us in training to watch out for the third one because it would be in there. So all the troopers started crawling out of the glider, and the copilot and I threw our M-1s out the window and crawled back down through the fuselage to the door at the rear. When I reached the door to drop out, I was all wet and I said I must have been hit, but it wasn't blood when I looked. Someone had been sick and I had just crawled through it. Weapons fire started coming in, so we started crawling on the ground to the ditch on the road. My mouth was so full of cotton, I couldn't spit—I was scared. We got to the ditch when the first

shell came in and you could hear the steel singing through the trees. After that, we got up and started marching down the road to the division command post.

Once they reached the division headquarters, Wilder and the other pilots were assigned various duties such as standing guard. The men of his mission were lucky because although many of them missed their landing zone due to early releases and some were injured, none of them died during the Galveston landings.

Flight Off. Eddie Anderson, who had landed on June 6, reached headquarters ahead of Wilder. After taking some German paratroopers he and his comrades had captured during the night to a large chateau and placing them in a "rock pen," Anderson had his breakfast in a foxhole. The meal consisted of C rations washed down with coffee. After breakfast, he and a few other men went over toward a large building.

We went through a gate, and in this yard there were wounded people lying on the ground with doctors and medics working on them. In one area was a large group of Germans, including the ones we had captured. One fella was giving a pretty firm interrogation. I walked over and listened as I went to see some old buddies who had been wounded. Major Lynch of the 101st Division came through the gate. I had met him previously.

After a brief greeting, Major Lynch told Anderson that they had lost a lot of men and that the stable was full of dead people that had to be buried. He ordered Anderson to gather up his glider pilots and some German prisoners and prepare the graves. The order took Anderson by surprise, since he had not been trained to deal with the aftermath of battle and he had assumed that Graves Registration would take care of the task. Nonetheless, he obeyed Lynch, merely saying, "Yeah, major, we will do that."

Anderson took eight glider pilots on the detail. A parachute sergeant told him to remove one dog tag and nail it to the outside of a tent stake. The German prisoners, about thirty-five of them, were given entrenching tools and a shovel from a jeep and set to digging the graves. Jack Hoty, who had a movie camera, filmed the operation.

We started digging the graves, and it wasn't long before we had eight or ten dug. I don't remember who, but somebody took some of the German prisoners and when they came back they had these dead fellows wrapped up in parachutes. They gently laid them in the ground. After we got them in the ground, I had them cover the graves. Someone came over and said, "Don't you think someone should say something?" The chaplains were busy with the wounded, and there was no one around to conduct any service. So I said I would. I took my helmet off, everyone else did the same, and I mumbled something to the effect that we were here to pay our last tribute. Then it dawned on me that I had in my breast pocket a little card I picked up the night before out of a first-aid packet, which had the 23rd Psalm printed on it. I mumbled something and began to read from the psalm. As I began to read I saw that the German prisoners had their caps off and caught the rhythm and began repeating it in German.

According to Eddie Anderson, this was the first American cemetery in Normandy. However, the bodies were later removed to a larger cemetery. Meanwhile, the war raged on around them.

Twenty-year-old Tech Sgt. Harold E. Owens, the Weapons Platoon Sergeant of Company A, one of the many veterans of the Italian campaign with 1st Battalion, was ready and anxious to take part in the regiment's first assault glider landing of the war. He knew that the invasion was close when his unit was sealed off a couple of weeks before and his unit began receiving briefings. The isolation of the unit only heightened the tension; the men in the food line at the mess hall were prohibited from talking to the men serving them. Just before the invasion, Owens developed a bad toothache and he was escorted to a dentist with instructions not to speak. He almost lost control of his emotions when the dentist's drill accidentally hit his tongue, but he restrained himself for fear of missing the big invasion.

The day after his visit to the dentist (or possibly the day after that), Owens was at the airfield. Before boarding his glider, he went over to the C-47 and noticed it was *Red Dog*, the very same tug that had taken him on a practice mission in North Africa in 1943; even the crew chief was the same. The large Horsa glider Owens boarded carried soldiers but no vehicles.

We had part of a rifle platoon and I had a mortar section with three 60-mm mortars—I picked up a spare mortar someplace. We had all the mortar ammunition, boxes of AT [antitank] mines, underneath the seat on the tail where I was sitting. My job was, when we went over the coast, to get up and look out and look for the checkpoints on the ground to be oriented where we were. We took off and became part of a big air armada. Everywhere you looked were tow ships and gliders, Horsas and CG-4s. When we went over the coast, one of the gliders went down, appeared to ride on the beach, and took back off again. We were less than 300 feet and probably about 200 feet when we went over the coast. There was a flight of C-47s that flew underneath us. One had his landing gear down and a wave came up and pulled him in. The aircrew climbed up on the wing. We were all watching all this

Elements of the 101st Airborne Division assemble at Carentan for an awards ceremony late in June.

below while I had taken my seat belt off and was standing up at the window looking for my checkpoints.

As we crossed the beach, we got turbulence and our glider would go up and down. I looked out there and saw a little town called Ste-Marie-du-Mont. It had a little circle and square so I knew where we were. We picked up AA [antiaircraft] fire just before I spotted the town. Then we came into the landing zone and started dropping. They gave us the green light and we cut loose. Down we went. Finally, we hit on the skid, bounced up and over a hedgerow, and went into another field where there were

two great big trees. The pilot hit the nose between these oak trees and sheared off the wings. There was a country road there and sort of a hump where the hedgerow was. When the tail hit the hedgerow, it goes "whoop" and breaks off. The two guys sitting beside me stay in the tail while I remain in the main part of the glider's body. I did a flip and was thrown amongst the riflemen. It was about that time when the wings hit the trees. It was like someone crushing a matchbox; it all just crumpled. I was hit in the head by the AT mines and my helmet broke my nose. The AT mines underneath my seat had hit me in the back of the head, crushing my arms and body. Finally it all stopped. My only thought was, "Is this the way it feels to die?" I thought it was raining—it seemed to be damp—and I was bleeding and thought it was rain falling on me. When it stopped, I knew I wasn't dead and I hopped up. Somebody took a pot shot at me and I yelled at the men, "Let's get out of here!" I looked back in and saw that all those riflemen were twisted up in a ball. Fortunately, just a few had broken their legs. The two fellows sitting beside me had broken backs. There was nothing we could do since we had no medical help. We laid them in a ditch and pinned a note on them.

The paratroopers started coming around. I thought they were going to help us, but apparently, they lost most of their equipment. They were trying to take as much equipment from us as they could. I saw one of them taking off with my mortar and I had to stop him. I looked around in the field and I saw one of the rifle sergeants who was a good friend of mine. I ran out to him and said, "Where are you hurt?" He said it was his leg, and I took his morphine Syrette and was getting ready to stick him when a machine gun opened up on us. As I was getting ready to stick him with it, he was not there. He beat me back to the road where we had come from!

We finally got organized and the Germans did not come in where we were. The ones that could move on went, and those that couldn't we had to leave. We went on to our assembly area. We had lost about a third of our people in the landings. Our company commander and the others in his glider were killed after it flipped over.

That night, Tech Sergeant Owens began to turn black from the shoulders down and he could not move his shoulders. He was placed on a jeep and evacuated to the beach. He was soon transferred to a hospital ship and taken to Southampton. He remained hospitalized for three weeks, after which he was taken to a replacement center at Litchfield Barracks. Finally, he was allowed to return with other men from his unit to Leicester and rejoin his regiment.

T/5 Gerald M. Cummings of the 325th Glider Infantry Regiment's Service Company, a veteran of operations in Sicily and Italy, boarded his glider for what would be his first venture into the front lines in Normandy. His job as a company clerk, with the regimental sergeant major, was maintaining records on personnel. His company had arrived at Aldermaston on May 29 and set itself up in a large hangar. On June 2, the unit was briefed, and on June 5, the men loaded a quarter-ton trailer and about 450 pounds of anti-tank ammunition on a glider. On June 6,

We put on our battle clothes and rolled up our old clothes to be sent back to camp. My impregnated pants were an inch too small around the waist and my shirt was a size too small. The invasion was announced on this day, but we knew it was on because the soldiers occupying the other half of the hangar had left during the night.

At 0435 on June 7 we took off in our glider named *Mittie the Moocher* into the damp gray dawn. By daylight, we were ready to start across the English Channel. We saw several ships near the French coast and were soon over land when we heard the spat of a couple of bullets through our glider. The trees in the hedgerows of France, unlike those in England, were tall. We cut loose, tore some fabric off the tail of the glider as we tried to clear a treetop, dived toward the ground, skimmed along to the far side of a narrow field, and crashed into a hedgerow. The front of our glider caved in, and it came to rest with its wheels in one of the ditches the Germans had dug around the field. Equipment was strewn everywhere, with my rifle going in one direction and my helmet in another.

We had been taught that in the event of a crash we were to make our bodies as limber as possible. I was able to do this, and the poor fellow in front of me absorbed my weight when we crashed. Three of us were unhurt, but the other four were injured, including the copilot, whose leg was fractured in two places.

Guns were cracking as we stepped out of the glider, but no one was firing at us. Another glider carrying a jeep landed in the same field we did. We chopped part of the framework out of the side of our glider and used the jeep to finish pulling the side out so that we could get our trailer out. We soon reached a road and then hid when we heard a tank coming until we could identify it. We were much relieved to see that the tank bore a friendly star. Some minutes later we came to our CP [command post].

Wearing his green-dyed field jacket for camouflage and armed with an M-1, Cummings drove the regiment's executive officer, Lieutenant Colonel Sitler, in a jeep to locate the 1st and 2nd Battalions. The command post was moved several times during the day as they advanced on Chef-du-Pont and moved into reserve to the southeast of Ste-Mère-Église. Later in the month, on June 28, Gerald Cummings calculated the regiment's casualties from the landing and determined that 27 men had died in the operation and another 159 had been hospitalized. Of those who were injured, 125 were in CG-4As and 34 in Horsas. The 27 killed on landing were all in Horsas.

Pvt. Richard D. Weese, a nineteen-year-old rifleman in 1st Platoon, Company B, 1st Battalion of the 325th, arrived in France on the morning of June 7 in the first serial of Mission Galveston.

His glider lost its landing gear going over a hedgerow and a tree ripped off the left wing, causing the glider to land on its side. His squad poured out of the damaged glider and took cover in the hedgerow ditch. Weese later discovered a dead German soldier behind a glider who, his fellow squad members surmised, had been hit by the aircraft. After a month, "our company was reduced to 32 troopers from 120, with no officers, and the wounded stayed on the line." However, not all of Company B's officers succumbed in the landings. First Lt. Wayne Pierce, a veteran of the campaign in the Mediterranean, received, according to Weese, a well-deserved battlefield promotion to captain on June 21 to help replace some of the losses.

As Pierce remembered it, the landing zone had been changed from an area west of the Merderet to a zone near Ste-Mère-Église (Landing Zone W) and again on the day of the operation (Landing Zone E). On June 7 at 2:00 A.M., he received

a rude wake-up call by a whistle from the mess hall. It was dark at Ramsbury Airfield where we were sleeping, fully dressed, on our packs with weapons at our side. My musette bag had served as my pillow for the brief four hours of sleep on the ground near the mess hall. No one lingered; everyone got to their feet, stretched, made small talk with a buddy, and shuffled off to the latrine to wash up for breakfast. This was one meal we were not going to miss, for it would be our last hot meal for some time, and for a number of men, it would be their last meal on this earth.

Before lying down for the night, we had turned in all excess equipment and had cleared the barracks where we had been sleeping for the past five nights while sealed in at this forward staging area. Like condemned men, we were served a good dinner, took long hot showers, and pulled on the uniform that was prescribed for our regiment—wool O.D. [olive-drab] shirt and trousers that had been impregnated with an anti-gas chemical. They were stiff, cold, and clammy, but underneath we wore two-piece long underwear to keep the chemically treated shirt and trousers from touching our bare skin. Canvas leggings and a waist-length cotton-lined field jacket, recently dyed a forest green, completed our uniform. In our light packs, we carried K rations for three days (nine boxes the size of a Cracker Jack box) and a D ration of concentrated chocolate. In addition to rations in our pack, we carried a change of underwear, socks, toothbrush, shaving kit, mess gear, and cleaning equipment for your weapon. The mess kit was stuffed with toilet paper to keep it from rattling. We were also required to memorize the password for the next three days.

The basic load of ammunition for a rifleman was a full cartridge belt, two bandoliers of .30 caliber ammo, and two hand grenades. Each man carried a gas mask slung over his shoulder and a canteen of water attached to his cartridge belt. A first-aid packet containing morphine was attached to the belt, shoulder strap, or the helmet; a trench knife was strapped to a boot; and a sheathed bayonet hung on the backpack. The weapon I selected to take to Normandy was the old style .45 caliber Thompson submachine gun. This weapon was difficult to control for accuracy, but it could throw a lot of lead. Rifle company officers were armed with the .30 caliber carbine. I had little faith in this weapon, so I made an unauthorized switch to the .45 submachine gun. The enlisted men of the company did not have a choice of weapons.

The long cartridge tubes for the Thompson .45, carried in a pouch attached to my web belt, were heavy and cumbersome. In addition, I carried a map dispatch case, binoculars, and a gas mask. I placed my overseas cap in my dispatch case, hoping I might have a chance to wear it. On our right shoulder, we sewed a small American flag. Our 82nd Airborne Division patch occupied the left shoulder.

My assignment was that of executive officer of Company B, a rifle company. In this capacity, I was a backup for the company commander. Our CO, Capt. Richard Gibson from Falls City, Nebraska, was one of the finest officers in the division. First Lt. Herbert Dew, from Minnesota, had command of the Weapons Platoon and 2nd Lts. Benjamin Little and Kenneth Burgess had the two rifle platoons in Company B.

Going through the breakfast chow line that morning, I saw a lieutenant, evidently a mess officer, standing behind the serving counter, obviously to see that we were fed properly and well. As I presented my mess kit for a serving of ham and eggs, the mess officer, wanting to lend encouragement, called out, "Good hunting!" but coming from a rear echelon commando, it irritated me.

Secure equipment, form up by platoons, a quick check by squads—all present. Shortly after 3:00 A.M., our column of troops was moving out on a one-mile march to the airstrip where our gliders were lined up. It was still dark when we stopped under the huge wing of the British Horsa glider that would serve as our transport to Normandy. . . . The Horsa could carry thirty men with their equipment plus a pilot and copilot. Company B was assigned to fly in five of them.

There was a slight mist of rain in the air and the first streaks of dawn in the sky as our C-47 tow plane churned down the runway, trying to gain flying speed. The

Horsa glider after landing in Normandy.

time was about 4:40 A.M. At this moment, seated on each side of the barrel-shaped Horsa, we were concerned with the take-off. We had flown in Horsa gliders before, but never when loaded as heavily as we were this morning. In addition to our individual loads, boxes of mines, extra ammunition, and cans of water were tied to the floor in the center of the glider.

Slowly, the runway dropped away and the rumble of the wheels changed to the familiar "swoosh" of the air over the plywood structure. We were airborne!

Aboard Lieutenant Pierce's glider was another veteran of operations in the Mediterranean, PFC Clinton E. Riddle from Sweetwater, Tennessee. Although he was offered promotions, he turned them down, preferring to avoid the complications of higher rank. At the time of the invasion, he was the company clerk for Company B and served as a radioman and runner for the com-

pany. Other members from the headquarters section of the company included Lieutenant Pierce (executive officer), the first sergeant, the supply sergeant, mess sergeant, cooks, and runner, totaling about twenty men.

We loaded in the gliders, and I remember seeing the moon break through for just a moment. Then in a little while, we moved off the runway and were in the air. Men from our headquarters platoon and the rest of our company made up the number in my glider. We had a pilot and a copilot. One was from Kentucky and the other from West Virginia. I sat in the front seat near the pilot. The ride was not rough, and I was taking it easy. From the very front seat, I had a ringside view of the Channel. There were many ships in the Channel, and it was a breathtaking experience to look out.

Every man had been coached on what to do in case we went down. We didn't carry parachutes, only a Mae West life preserver. About halfway over the Channel our tow plane's engine began to miss and to sputter; then finally it just quit and we began to lose altitude. The glider pilot tried to keep the glider riding as high as was possible, and we were gliding faster than the plane. In the process, the towrope became slack and the glider overran the plane. The pilot of the plane continued to crank the engine until we were down within a hundred feet of the water. You could see the waves rushing up to meet us.

According to Lieutenant Pierce, the C-47 had difficulty maintaining sufficient power and keeping the proper altitude from the time of the take-off.

Standing between the pilot and copilot, I could see the slack in the towrope as we lost altitude and the battle the glider guider was having to keep us from becoming entangled in the 100 yards of nylon rope connecting us to the C-47. We were looking up at the tail of the C-47 and knew that it was only a matter of time until we would have to ditch.

I gave the order to open the door at the rear of the glider and to start throwing out the boxes of mines, ammunition, and cans of water we had lashed to the floor. Men were alerted and were standing by in case we ditched; they would take emergency axes from the wall of the glider and cut holes in the top of our compartment to permit us to climb out on top of the fuselage and the wings. We were told the wings were full of ping-pong balls so they would not sink.

Private First Class Riddle and his comrades checked their life preservers after laying down their equipment and prepared to ditch in the

Channel. They were at about 300 feet, remembered Riddle, and

six cases of tank mines were thrown out with six GI cans of water and anything else that would lighten the glider before contact with the water. Sergeant Stovall was standing by with an axe ready to cut a hole in the top of the glider upon contact with the water. When it looked like all hope was gone and the prayers made, at the last minute one of the motors fired up with a roar and a cloud of smoke. We had no way to communicate with the tow plane. The glider tilted up with one wing almost in a half roll. Then we knew what was going on. The slack in the tow rope had become tangled in the landing gear. The glider pilot was able to maneuver the glider about enough to get the rope from around the landing wheel. It was a miracle that our glider pilot was able to get the rope free without having to hit the towrope release lever because we still would have gone down into the Channel.

As they came within sight of the French coast, Wayne Pierce glimpsed a ditched C-47 whose crew was climbing on the top of the fuselage. Within three minutes of crossing the coast, the glider was released from its tow. Moments earlier, Lieutenant Pierce had returned to his seat

on the bench along the wall of the glider and gave the order to secure equipment. Helmets were put on, packs were adjusted, bandoliers slung over the shoulder, and weapons were held securely. As I leaned over to pick up my pack and equipment, the glider made a lurch as the pilot cut loose from the tow plane and made a steep banking turn. This sudden maneuver coming when I had my head down caught me unaware and I was momentarily airsick. Not

Members of the 82nd Airborne Division inspect a wrecked a Waco CG-4 glider in Normandy.

wanting to show my weakness, I hugged my pack and equipment, too nauseated to put it on. I hoped the men were not watching me.

At this time, Clinton Riddle had

raised up to look out the front, the pilot points towards a small field, a garden-like spot, completely enclosed by hedge, some with trees growing out of the hedgerows. The pilot brought the glider in low over the first hedgerow, and cut the top of some of the trees with the wing. The glider hit the ground, bounced a time or two, then rolled to a stop.

As the glider rolled across the field, Lieutenant Pierce moved to the large equipment-loading door across from him and

unlatched this door, kicked it open, and as the glider stopped, I jumped to the ground,

rolling on my face but holding my equipment. Looking around me, I saw a tree-lined road immediately in front of the glider, so I started running in that direction. The entire glider load of twenty-eight men exited behind me and came single file on the double after me. As we stopped briefly upon exiting the glider, I put on my pack and other equipment that I was carrying, and then I noticed that I did not have my tommy gun. While the men of Company B watched the show of crash-landing gliders all around us, I ran back to our glider, retrieved my tommy gun, and jogged back to my place at the head of our little column.

We found temporary security in the ditch along the road. It was 7:00 A.M. and gliders were crash-landing all around us. Our pilot had, with skill and luck, picked a field about eight acres in size. The top of a tree was embedded in one wing of the glider. A few mortar shells began to fall around us, but they were harassing fire only and did no damage that I could see. From a nearby road sign, I was able to orient my map, and joined by others from Company B, we started toward Ste-Marie-du-Mont.[4] The glider pilots with us were acting like school kids on a picnic. Their work was over and no doubt they were on a high, having brought most of us in for a safe landing.

Theirs was the only glider in the company to land without crashing. In at least one glider, the front wheel of the tricycle landing gear smashed through the crew compartment, cutting off the legs of several men. Luckily, the company had few casualties.

In August 1944, at a debriefing conference in England, Maj. Ted Sanford, who took over the 1st Battalion, remarked that

the gliders in Mission Galveston towed by the 437th Group and leaving from Ramsbury came in over the coast of Normandy too low. Our gliders were released at 200 feet, traveling at 120 miles per hour. Our LZ had such small fields and tall trees that the glider pilots had no opportunity to select a field or to make the proper approach for landing.

Although the C-47 pilots were supposed to climb to 700 feet after crossing the coast, most of them failed to do so or were not able to do so, leaving the glider pilots in a difficult position and resulting in many crash landings.

As Company B advanced toward the front lines, two German fighter aircraft dropped from the sky and strafed their column. Since all of the company's radios had been damaged on landing,

Private Riddle tried to install a makeshift antenna from a walkie-talkie on the large radio he carried. While he was engrossed in this task, a passing reporter took his picture, which later appeared in *Army Magazine*.

According to Wayne Pierce, the company moved through Ste-Marie-du-Mont, where most of the men came across their first enemy casualties. Captain Gibson told Lieutenant Pierce that the battalion commander, Lt. Col. Klemm Boyd, had been injured on landing and was replaced by Maj. Teddy Sanford. Pierce's friend, Lt. Jim Gayley of Company A, who sang "Beautiful Day Tomorrow" in the shower at Ramsbury the night before, had died in a crash landing.

Pierce's march through the Norman countryside was a surreal collage of peaceful everyday life and explosive war scenes. About fifteen minutes after landing, Private Riddle spotted a farmer milking a cow amid exploding German shells. Later, the same man passed through the column with a bucket of milk, stopped, and allowed Riddle to fill his canteen cup. Later in the day, as his unit marched toward La Fière along a country road, Lieutenant Pierce came across a group of about three French families hiding in a brush-covered ditch by the side of the road. Apparently, they had heeded the BBC's advice to evacuate all the villages along the coast.

Since Company B had all five of its officers, Major Sanford ordered Captain Gibson to send Lieutenant Pierce to him to serve on battalion staff since no other officers from that section were available. Early in the evening, General Gavin took him and Major Sanford to General Ridgway's command post in a farmhouse near Ste-Mère-Église for a briefing. Lieutenant Pierce did not attend the meeting but rested in an orchard until after dark. Just before midnight, they walked back down the road to their battal-

---

4. Both Landing Zone E and Landing Zone W were west of Sainte-Marie-du-Mont, and unless Lieutenant Pierce's company landed short of Landing Zone E, which is possible, they would have been moving west and not passing through that town.

ion, but halfway there, they stopped in a small field to get some sleep. Early in the morning, they heard someone firing a German machine pistol nearby. General Gavin alerted the men on guard, returned to the place where Pierce and Sanford waited, and they all went back to sleep.

Members of Interrogator Prisoner of War (IPW) Team 40 rode on gliders in Mission Galveston. Lt. Leon E. Mendel, who had been the chief interrogator of IPW Team 33 with the 1st Infantry Division, spoke seven languages, including French, German, and Russian. He had transferred to IPW Team 40 with the 325th Glider Infantry Regiment of the 82nd Airborne Division in the spring. He lost half of his six-man team in the crash landings, which left him with two NCOs. After landing, he began interrogating prisoners at Les Forges crossroads just south of Ste-Mère-Église. The first eight POWs he interrogated were Russians, possibly Georgians, from an *Ost* battalion. The next day, June 8, he joined a patrol that reached the village of Fauville, about half a mile south of Ste-Mère-Église. The captain in charge of the patrol told Mendel that three Germans were in the house ahead of them, two of whom were wounded, and asked him to persuade them to surrender. Once they reached their destination, Mendel saw four German soldiers outside the house and shouted to them to lay down their arms, since they were surrounded. After the four men quickly complied, to the astonishment of the five GIs, forty-two more soldiers came pouring out of the building, their hands in the air. The stunned five-man patrol wound up with over forty Germans who were all standing there with their hands up. That day, their spoils also comprised a dozen small German vehicles, including the small *SdKfz 2 Kettenkraftrad*, a tracked motorcycle that served as a light prime mover. Lieutenant Mendel posed for the media in the driver's seat of one of the vehicles, and his picture appeared in a newsreel that his parents saw at the theater back home.

The 2nd Battalion of the 325th Glider Infantry Regiment arrived as part of Mission Hackensack about two hours after Mission Galveston. This battalion, followed by much of the Service Company and the 3rd Battalion (formerly 2nd Battalion of the 401st Glider Infantry Regiment), was assigned to land at Landing Zone W, where twenty Galveston gliders had landed when they missed their designated objective of Landing Zone E. The first serial was greeted with heavy German fire, and both serials suffered higher casualties than Galveston, but the regiment was able to reassemble 90 percent of the men for action.

Flight Off. John F. Schumacher, a twenty-one-year-old who had joined the army in 1941, was piloting a Horsa of the 439th Group in the first serial, which departed from Upottery as part of Mission Hackensack. He carried troops of the 325th Glider Infantry Regiment. The glider operations officer had appointed Schumacher as the pilot and Flight Off. Horace Sanders as his copilot. When Schumacher reached the glider, he met with the troops he was to carry, and he was gripped by a feeling of excitement. Thirty troopers with some supplies and mortars boarded his Horsa.

We were overloaded. It was the first time I flew a glider without deliberately having the tug ship getting airborne first. We were badly overloaded and had to shift the load during takeoff. I remember yelling for them to get some men in the rear end so I could get the nose off the ground.

When we formed up, there was quite a bit of circling. It was light when we crossed the coast. We got a signal from the tug ship through the astrodome, and I cut off. I found the correct LZ and came in fairly low. I think I had time to make two 90-degree turns, and I found a spot in an inundated area, but it was the biggest one there. I landed in about four feet of water. I then heard a loud cheer from behind me after we stopped.

Troops of the 101st Airborne Division put on German helmets for a photo. RAY HOOD

Flight Officer Schumacher had landed in the flooded area near his assigned landing zone (W) with a few other gliders. Most of the gliders landed near or on the Zone, but those that hit the mark came in under enemy fire.

Capt. Joe Gault assembled his Company F, 2nd Battalion, 325th Glider Infantry Regiment, at Upottery Airfield and prepared to board the gliders lined up on the airfield. The previous day, June 6, a seemingly endless line of gliders had awaited the arrival of their C-47 tugs. On the morning of June 7, his company marched across the field, and each element moved to its assigned gliders. Gault boarded a Horsa with twenty-nine other men, including a machine-gun weapons section and his headquarters personnel. He had not been enthusiastic about the operation because many of the men had never flown in a glider before.

When they loaded the glider and took off, they didn't have any way to control the right-to-left, so they shifted the load to control it. They called for people on the left side to come over on the right side, and my runner, a young boy, came over and put his arms on my knees and laid his head on his arms. One of the machine-gun section leaders was next to me. When we cut loose, we were at about 500 feet, and we turned 90 degrees to the left to the LZ. They didn't have time to go around again.

When the glider reached the hedgerows, the pilot went between these trees in it and the wings folded back and disintegrated. I thought some type of bomb had gone off. It threw me backwards and I didn't realize it, but I landed on my back and when I looked down I couldn't see my legs. I thought they were gone! So I kicked around and kicked the plywood off of them, and when I got up I still had my seat belt on and a little piece of plywood, about eighteen inches in diameter, still strapped to my back. The runner was killed immediately, as were the four men down from me, while I wasn't even touched. One fellow had the skin on his wrist cut and peeled back like a glove. I saw him pull it back and put tape around it and heard later that he had no serious problem. I believe that five men were instantly killed and another dozen injured.

We tended to the wounded first. While we were doing that, our pilot picked up a hand grenade and pulled the pin on it. I hollered at him until I got him to throw it. These Air Corps men had no training. I told him to get attached to the rear of our column and not to interfere. We moved to our predesignated LZ, and the company reassembled there. I guess we lost between ten and twenty men to injuries on landing. We still had a pretty good-sized company left.

Joe Gault later heard that his regiment had suffered 10 percent casualties.

After assembling, they moved off with the regiment. We marched in columns on each side of the road, one platoon behind the other. We reached the area near Ste-Mère-Église where we set up a perimeter as an isolated company for the night. We were ordered to send out patrols. I sent out possibly four or five that night. They were usually a squad or possibly two squads. The company executive officer, Lieutenant Herlahy, led several of these. He was killed while on patrol that first night. This was our first contact with the Germans.

I was inside the perimeter, receiving the reports from the patrols as they came in and sending them back to battalion HQ. There were no prisoners the first night, but we didn't have instructions to take any.

Capt. Harold Shebeck, a twenty-eight-year-old reservist who had been with the 82nd Division when it was converted into an airborne formation in 1942, boarded a CG-4 glider that same morning at Merryfield. His was the last serial of gliders taking part in the invasion. He was the regiment's S-4 as well as graves registration officer. He sat in the jeep with his driver, a youth named Frank James from Pitkin, Louisiana, and the regimental transportation chief, a staff sergeant, on the floor. James succumbed to airsickness soon after takeoff and rolled retching under the jeep. Fortunately, his misery was of short duration.

It did not take long to reach the coast, and by this time one could see the skies filled with aircraft, many of them fighter planes. I soon began dozing, which I did intermittently once we were well under way. Soon after crossing over Utah Beach, we came under fire and finally our pilot cut loose. Our pilot found an open field in which I don't recall seeing any obstacles. We came across the top of a hedgerow, and it knocked the wheels off the glider. The pilot was desperately trying to slow the speed of the glider, and we crash-landed and came to a stop about five miles inland. Miraculously, no one was really hurt. As we hit the ground, I felt a terrible pain in my back and I thought surely my back was broken, but I was able to move my legs and I knew I was lucky. I was concerned that the jeep had been damaged, but luckily, it was not, and we manhandled it out of the glider. My driver had recovered from his airsickness in a hurry with the noise, dust, smoke, confusion, and small arms fire from snipers in the area.

The morning glider landings suffered lighter casualties than those of the previous day even though many gliders crashed in the hedgerows and fields. The CG-4 in which David H. Moore, a warrant officer in Service Company, was flying missed the field altogether and crashed onto the roof of a house. Moore and his companions clambered out of the craft and down the stairs to the front door.

As the 325th Glider Infantry Regiment came to reinforce the 82nd Airborne Division, most of the 327th Glider Infantry Regiment of the 101st Airborne was at sea. The attached battalion from the 401st Glider Infantry Regiment was the first to land and take up position to reinforce the 101st on D+1, while the 1st and 2nd Battalions of the 327th came ashore soon after.[5]

---

5. In the spring of 1944, the 1st Battalion of the 401st Glider Infantry Regiment remained with the 101st Airborne Division, serving with the 327th Glider Infantry Regiment, while the 2nd Battalion of the 401st Glider Infantry Regiment went to the 325th Glider Infantry Regiment of the 82nd Airborne Division until the end of the war.

The Paratroopers of the 82nd Airborne on D+1

Elements of the 507th Parachute Infantry Regiment were on both sides of the Merderet on the morning of D+1, June 7. The largest concentration of its men was on the west bank, still isolated from the remainder of the division. After the airdrop, the 508th Parachute Infantry Regiment was even more disorganized, its men widely scattered in the area. It held out west of the Merderet and managed to assemble a battalion-size force on the east bank, near Chef-du-Pont. However, like the 507th, the 508th Parachute Infantry Regiment had failed to establish a firm bridgehead with a crossing. The 505th Parachute Infantry Regiment was firmly entrenched around Ste-Mère-Église, which it took on the first day. The 325th Glider Infantry Regiment, which landed in the morning, moved into reserve south of Ste-Mère-Église by the end of the day. It was up to the glider men on the east bank to force a crossing, create a bridgehead, and relieve the units on the west side of the Merderet with the scattered units from the 507th and 508th Parachute Infantry Regiment. This did not happen until June 9. Meanwhile, the regiments of the

Children gather around troopers of the 82nd Airborne Division at Ste-Mère-Église.

82nd Airborne, after attempting to regroup on June 6, began to establish a strong position on the Merderet, while the 505th Parachute Infantry Regiment secured the northern front.

On June 6, Colonel Shanley of the 2nd Battalion, 508th Parachute Infantry Regiment, gathered his men around the dominant Hill 30, which would have been a good vantage point had the hedgerows and apple orchards not obscured the view of the causeway at La Fière and Chef-du-Pont with these men was Sgt. Zane Schlemmer, who managed to rejoin his unit on the west bank of the Merderet. Stragglers from other units came to reinforce the 2nd Battalion in its isolated position. They set up a roadblock at the end of the causeway leading to Chef-du-Pont, but according to Sergeant Schlemmer, their situation was precarious because they were unable to receive supplies or reinforcements.

Maj. David Thomas, regimental surgeon of the 508th Parachute Infantry Regiment, spent the day of June 6 with another isolated group of paratroopers, which moved out that night.

> We carried our wounded with us. We would get doors or anything else we could carry them on. We put four to six Germans and one rifleman to each litter case. Lieutenant Colonel Harrison was supposed to be in command, but he surrendered command to a red-headed major of the 507th whose name I don't remember. Lieutenant Colonel Harrison was worthless; although he was a nice guy in garrison, he couldn't hack that combat. So we had the German prisoners carrying our wounded as we moved over to this larger group where we had something like 300, and again we were surrounded. They were shooting at us and we were shooting at them and having a good time on this second day.

This second group was commanded by Col. "Zip" Millet, who was the commander of the 507th PIR. You could not get much sleep because firing was going on all the time. We had another doctor—I think maybe two—from the 507th. We were surrounded for all of the second day and I accumulated a lot of wounded, but there wasn't a lot I could do for them. We could get some food in them, but that was about it. The medical treatment was about as primitive as it could be.

The next day, this isolated group from the 507th Parachute Infantry Regiment tried unsuccessfully to move towards the Merderet where the 1st Battalion of the 325th Glider Infantry Regiment had begun to establish a bridgehead.

During the morning of D+1, Lt. Peter Triolo, the liaison officer from the 4th Division who had arrived with the glider troops of the 82nd Airborne Division on the morning of D-Day, was called to the divisional headquarters.

I was told that I would escort a patrol of the 82nd to the 12th Infantry Regiment to make contact so the officers could make arrangements for transporting their heavy equipment from the Utah Beach through the 4th Division area to the 82nd A/B. A funny thing happened on that patrol. As we were getting ready to go out, I was armed with a .45 Thompson submachine gun. A sergeant from the 82nd tapped me on the shoulder and asked if I was going to fire that machine gun if I had to. I said, "I sure will if I have to." He said that in that case I better load it. I had not realized that somewhere along the road I had lost the clip and the gun was not armed.

On D+3 Lieutenant Triolo's liaison mission was completed and he returned to the 1st Battalion, 12th Infantry.

Prisoners of War

The question of POWs was a thorny one for the paratroopers landing behind enemy lines. According to many of the enlisted men, their orders were to take no prisoners, but their officers categorically deny any such order. Whatever the case may be, many paratroopers admit to having either witnessed the execution of enemy prisoners or actually perpetrating the deed. Many, like PFC Kenneth Burch, were deeply troubled by the executions. The decision not to take prisoners, according to Major Thomas, was made by out-of-control soldiers and was not an official policy of the U.S. Army. Some groups, like Major Thomas's, took prisoners even when they were surrounded themselves, and Lieutenant Brannen took a prisoner after killing Gen. Wilhelm Falley behind enemy lines. However, other groups, like PFC Martin M. Finkelstein's and PFC Raymond Gonzalez's, summarily executed their prisoners in Italy as well as in France because they felt it was too risky to drag them along or set them free behind enemy lines. One of the interviewed paratroopers explained,

I recall a lot of boys getting hit, and one named Fick got his neck torn apart by shrapnel. I watched him die. As we were fighting forward we left him there, and the Germans started giving up. I had it in my mind that Fick had been hit that way and I would even it up by shooting all the Germans that surrendered. We couldn't take any prisoners anyway because we didn't know where to put them. I would shoot them in the head so they did not have to suffer. At that time, I believed it was right, but I do not think so now.

The Germans knew that some of their men had been killed after being captured, and in retaliation, many of the American soldiers captured in Normandy were treated harshly.

Cpl. Jack Schlegel from the machine-gun platoon of HQ Company, 3rd Battalion, 508th Parachute Infantry Regiment, and his small group ran into German armored vehicles during June 6, and they were soon captured. They had a German prisoner who helped them surrender when they were finally cornered. Schlegel heard one of the Germans say that the prisoners should be executed because they were paratroopers, but their erstwhile prisoner intervened on their behalf.[6] Instead, he and his group were taken to a farm where they joined 150 Allied prisoners. The Germans marched them to a point about forty miles from St. Lô.

There was a German interrogator who spoke fluent English at this spot. He knew more about us and our mission than we did. He told me he had lived in the U.S.A. and worked for the *Chicago Times*. He stated that the German war was just about over, but that they continued fighting to stop the Russian threat of world communism.

This German officer had a shortwave message sent (for propaganda I guess), which said, "Now here is a good German name—Jack Schlegel—who will be with us till the end." My parents in New York City got this message from a radio ham operator days later.

On June 7–8, we were transported by ten new-type German trucks with Red Cross markings on top and the sides. About forty of us were put in each truck with one guard at the rear. On the main highway to St. Lô at approximately 2:00 P.M. in bright sunlight we were attacked by two P-47s. They strafed the convoy four times. Dozens were killed and eighty Americans wounded. No Germans were hurt since they got out first.

After assisting with the wounded and piling up the dead, two men from the 505th PIR and I slipped away during all the confusion. We were above St. Lô, in a small village, when we were caught by a German MP [military police] unit. We were returned to the main prisoner group just outside of St. Lô the next day. We found out at this time that the German commander of the prison detail had sent out a warning to his forces to find three escaped prisoners.

That night, the wounded prisoners were loaded on vehicles and transported to the hospital at Rennes. Schlegel and the men with him began a forced march through St. Lô, which had just been bombed. They watched a group of B-24s pass overhead as they saw the bright glow of a burning city.

We marched in single file amidst the fire, burst water lines, and rubble from the buildings. A few French inhabitants shouted angrily at us and threw rocks at us. For two days of marching, we received no food, only water near roadside ditches. On the third day, we arrived at a walled farming monastery. It was later called "Starvation Hill." No food was available. Days later, we got a wagon full of raw milk. Everyone got several cups of milk, which gave us the runs.

Many days later, Corporal Schlegel and four of his fellow prisoners escaped from Starvation Hill when they were sent as part of a detail outside the wall. They came to railroad tracks and managed to board a freight train that took them the wrong way. The trip ended near Chartres. They continued on their way late at night, still wearing

---

6. The American paratroopers and the Germans may have executed a similar number of prisoners during the first forty-eight hours of the campaign, although the paratroopers may have considered it a matter of survival and the Germans did it for revenge.

Paratroopers of the 82nd Airborne Division take a break outside a café at Ste-Mère-Église. Note that the censor has scratched off their unit patches.

their paratrooper uniforms. Again, Schlegel ran into German MPs. This time, he told his captors that he had gotten lost after the D-Day drop. A German troop carrier took him and his companions to a *Stalag 12* outside of Rennes, but Schlegel had no intention of staying in prison.

Five days later, a British lieutenant, a 505th PIR officer, and three of us escaped from the *Stalag* and made contact with the F.F.F. in Rennes. We accompanied them on two sabotage raids only to be caught by the *SS* unit in a firefight, who turned us over to the Rennes *Gestapo*. Nine Frenchmen were shot in the *Gestapo* courtyard, and we were interrogated and tortured by the *Gestapo*.

Lieutenant Wilson had his fingers broken and wound up with a dislocated shoulder. We all ended up in the main Rennes POW

hospital. I was used in the hospital, which held over 900 wounded Allied POWs, as an interpreter working with Ober-Stab-Artz Eingsinger who was actually great to our men.

It was through his effort that I got a pass card to go to a garden and collect vegetables for our kitchen. Late in August, it gave me a chance to escape. I ran into Patton's 4th Armored and after a personal talk with General Patton, I was transported to Utah Beach, where a P.T. boat took four other escaped POWs to England. For four days, we were the guests of the OSS in London. I returned to my unit in September just in time to make the Holland jump.

Sgt. Martin Finkelstein of Company H, 505th Parachute Infantry Regiment, was also captured when his small, isolated group exhausted its ammunition around 6:00 P.M. on June 7. After he and about seven of his comrades surrendered, the Germans began searching them. Suddenly, a rifle cracked in the distance, one of the Germans was hit, and everyone fell to the ground. After a while, everyone stood up again.

They were searching us again and another shot rang out, and another Jerry was hit. Just at this time one of the Germans yelled out—I think he was an officer—"Look for knives!" It dawned on me that it must have something to do with the two officers that Stu and I killed. So when the second shot rang out and everybody hit the dust, we did too, and I yelled to the guys to get rid of their trench knives. We all had them in our boots, and it seemed like a simultaneous procedure—we all got up and threw them in the ditch. The Germans didn't notice.

We were all standing up again being searched. They took everything that we had: cigarettes, candy, invasion money. . . . I imagine it was about two or three minutes, we were almost ready to be marched away, and another shot rang out and I was hit in the shin. It was a grazing shot. It burns when you are hit.

They finally got us together and marched us off. We went down this road, and they took us to St. Lô. At a barn-type building there were some prisoners inside and some outside sitting on the ground. It was just a temporary compound, not a prison camp. This place was eventually known as Starvation Hill, mainly because we didn't have anything to eat. I mean nothing. Fortunately, we weren't there too long. I think it was more than two or three days. I can only remember getting one piece of cheese. It was a round piece of cheese about three inches in diameter and

an inch high. It was white, while actually green with mold, and also it had maggots on it. We just took the maggots off. We also had bread, which tasted like sawdust, and later we found out it was made with a type of sawdust.

One of the fellows that had been hit, Sergeant Moncksgard, who had been with us, we found in the camp. He died the next day. That second day, they brought in Stu Mulligan. His name was Ruppert Mulligan, and he was from the Chicago area. He was one of the toughest men I met in my whole life. Through our conversation, I found that he was the one who was taking pot shots at the Jerries searching us. He even knew he had accidentally hit me. It was one of the few times I saw him smile, but he would never laugh.

They finally brought trucks around and loaded us. They were fairly large with wooden sides, a gate in the back, and no canvas top—just open. We stood in these trucks. We were moving away from the coast. As we were facing forward, I was at the right side of the truck right at the rail. We were of course very hungry, very tired, and had very little to drink. There were five to ten trucks in the convoy, and a guard sat on top of the cabin of our truck facing forward towards the truck in front. The guard in the truck behind us was facing forward towards us. We were going around curved roads and a lot of U-turns. In the process of going around these turns, the front truck would disappear, as would the back truck at times. I figured this might be a good time to get the hell out of this situation and started to tell these guys that I was going to jump off when I got the opportunity. I said for them to make some kind of commotion to divert attention. They didn't say anything—I didn't know these guys.

Troops of the 101st Airborne Division near Carentan.

When he finally tried to go over the side of the truck, he was restrained by two others who pulled him back in. After a brief argument, they told him that the Germans had warned them that for every man who escaped they would shoot ten. He didn't believe it, although he had heard it himself. They arrived at a small compound for the night and received no food. The next day, about a dozen men marched out of the compound down the road.

We were given bags and told to pick potatoes. None of them spoke English, but they showed us what to do. Just pick these potatoes and throw them in the bag. We all proceeded into the field. As hungry as we were, we would pick a potato, wipe it off with one hand, while picking with the other and biting into it. Raw potatoes are an experience.

While picking the potatoes I saw this cherry tree. The guards were standing on the road smoking. I climbed the tree, grabbed one of these bunches of cherries, and started to eat it. Of course the guys down there are looking at me as I take bunches of cherries and throw them down to them. I was having a ball and couldn't get enough of these cherries. The guards started to yell at us to come back on the road. All these guys grabbed their sacks of potatoes and got up on the road. This Jerry would always count his prisoners, but for some reason he did not count them this time and just started marching them back towards the compound. They were almost out of sight down the road, and I was in the cherry tree watching. I could hear the gunfire; we were not that far from the front. I thought all I had to do was get out of this tree and cross the field and hide in the hedgerows until the Allies came up. The next thing I know, one of these Jerry guards comes running down the road and runs up to the base of the tree and points his burp gun at me telling me to get out of the tree. I did. My hands were full and red from cherry juice. He got me back on the road, marched me to the group, and began counting. A couple of guys told me later that two others had turned me in for fear of being shot if someone escaped.

Finkelstein soon wound up at a camp near Chartres, where he was subjected to his first formal interrogation. After he arrived,

a German officer was standing there, and he had two men going down the group looking at dog tags. I was the only man taken out of the group and put on the side. With a German soldier on each side of me, they took me over to this square building and we went in. The inside of the building had on one side a partition with doors that went from floor to ceiling, painted green, and with doors about three feet apart. On the other side of the building was another wall with doors, which were about eight feet apart. The middle of building was all cobblestones. The German boots really sounded horrible walking across the floor.

They took me to the side where the doors were about three feet apart, and opened a door and pushed me into a cell. It was about three feet wide and seven feet long, and it had a cot, a spittoon, and one little window at the top of the cell, which measured maybe twelve by twelve and had three bars.

There was no sound; it was daylight. I lay on the cot, and I was sobbing, feeling sorry for myself. I was frightened, but I was not

sure of what. I imagine it must have been an hour later when the door opened and the two guards took me out. They took me across the cobblestone floor over to one of the doors on the opposite side. Things got a little different. They pushed me in. As they did, I didn't expect it, and I wound up on the floor. I wasn't hurt. I stood up, and when I stood up, I was in front of the desk, which was maybe four by seven feet, a very large office desk with a glass top. Underneath the glass top, one of the first things I noticed was a big poster. On this poster were the shoulder patches of every unit in the U.S. Army, Air Force, Marines, or whatever. They were colored emblems.

The German officer was sitting behind the desk and the first thing he said, in beautiful English, was that I was to salute him as an officer. I did. He then asked my name, rank, and serial number, which I gave him. He then asked which outfit, and I refused to answer. He already knew by the outline of where my patch had been on my uniform because of the unusual shape of the 82nd patch. I made up my mind I was not going to tell him. "Where did you land, etc., etc." As we went on, I thought, This is idiotic. It was two weeks since I had been captured, and there was nothing I could tell him that was of any importance. There were two German guards, one behind me to my right, and one to my left as I faced this officer. I was at attention, and after a while, I kind of slouched down a bit to show my disgust. The guy on my right had a short Billie and shoved it into my right kidney, and that made me stand up at attention. From there on things got really bad. This officer would ask me questions, and I would still refuse to answer. This went on for about ten minutes, and then I was hit on the right shoulder. I remember that because it put me down. I didn't expect it. They grabbed me and pulled me back up, and the German officer again asked me what outfit I came from. I gave my name, and that was as far as I got when I was down on the floor again. The guy on the other side hit me below my shoulder on my back, and of course, they picked me up again. It progressively got worse.

The next thing I remember is that I woke up back in my cell. I was on the floor sobbing, crying, and I heard someone calling out. They had an English officer in the cell next to me. He told me his name and rank, which I don't remember. He was trying to impress on me not to tell them anything and that they were not going to hurt me. Here I am a bloody mess and I couldn't remember anything. They had hit me in the nape of my neck and caused a fracture that, according to army records, never healed properly.

They kept taking me back to different German officers. They beat me each time. I was there for three days. About a week after interrogation, I was put into a very large building. It had no windows and one door. When they shoved me in, I couldn't see. There were all these faces in front of me. It was loaded with other prisoners of war. There was straw on the floor. I was kept in this building with the others for about a month. The lice were so bad you could almost pick them off in groups. We had very little to eat, and when they did open the door it was usually in the late evening to feed us. There were two lights in the building. I would say about five-watt bulbs so you could just barely see. Most of us had to sleep standing up. There wasn't room enough to lie down. There were half a dozen 55-gallon drums you used to defecate. The smell was absolutely horrendous. There were quite a few men who died from malnutrition and thirst. Fortunately, I was able to survive.

Finally, Finkelstein was put on a train with about 300 other prisoners per boxcar. Two weeks later, they arrived at *Stalag 4B* in Germany. Several men died from starvation, dehydration, or illness en route.

CHAPTER 2

Operating and Expanding the Beachheads

Operating the Omaha Beachhead

Shortly after the invasion, the first blockships were sunk as other components for the Mulberry arrived off Omaha Beach. Within several days, the breakwater was in place and the large piers were in operation. The 5th and 6th Engineer Special Brigades set up a beachhead by clearing minefields and obstacles and preparing supply depots and the like. In addition to the engineers, these brigades included a variety of support troops such as quartermaster, medical, signal, military police, and ordnance units and the special naval beach battalions. On D+1, the 5th Engineer Special Brigade had opened its three beach exits.

The 37th Engineer Battalion Beach Group of the 5th Engineer Special Brigade supported the landing of the 1st Division's 16th Infantry, opened one of the exits, and helped open a second one on June 7. In addition to clearing mines and obstacles, the battalion engaged in road construction under German fire. Most of the troops of the 348th Engineer Battalion Beach Group supported the landing of the 18th Infantry on June 7. They opened Exit E-3, and at 1:00 A.M. on D+1, the first tanks rolled through. On June 8, the 348th began unloading supplies into dumps behind the beach. Finally, the 336th Engineer Combat Battalion arrived on June 7 with the 26th Infantry. These units had to open their exit under enemy fire. They cleared the road by late evening, allowing twenty tanks to move inland.

During the first days after the invasion, the bulldozer operators were vital to all the engineer operations. Although they drew enemy fire, they doggedly moved across the open beach, Athey trailers loaded with explosives and road construction material in tow.[1] In addition to clearing the obstacles planted by the enemy, they had to move abandoned and destroyed Allied vehicles blocking the exits.

By the evening of June 8, the engineers had marked all the beaches with color-coded wooden panels. They built large signs with 9-foot-high lettering and colored lights matching the name of the beach to assist in night landings because blinking lights had proved ineffective during the first few nights.

The brigade's 6th Naval Beach Battalion began operating the beaches on a twenty-four-hour basis on June 7. This naval unit set up ship-to-shore communications, handled traffic control, marked hazards, and directed the evacuation of casualties. Comdr. E. C. Carusi, until he was seriously wounded and evacuated on June 10, directed his sailors in the vital mission that earned them a unit citation.

The brigade also included the 533rd Quartermaster Battalion, with three service companies, which went into action on June 7. One of these companies was attached to each of the engineer beach groups and to the 336th Engineers. These companies provided men for unloading vessels, working at dumps, relieving truck drivers, and helping with the evacuation of the wounded.

The 619th Quartermaster Battalion, with two quartermaster railhead companies and a quartermaster company from another battalion had the mission of setting up and operating Class I, II, III, and IV dumps. Its 97th Quartermaster Railhead Company landed on D-Day and proceeded with its mission, which also included the evacuation of the wounded and even guarding prisoners.

The numerous support units included the 30th Chemical Decontamination Unit, which fortunately did not have to be used for its primary function. Instead, it helped clear the beaches. Another important unit of the brigade was the 487th Port Battalion with three port companies and two additional attached companies. It was to supply men for the ship platoons of the battalion beach groups for unloading cargo from the ships. This battalion arrived on ten coasters. Like the other units, it had to clear the mines in its own bivouac area on D+1. The coasters they came in carried ammunition and gasoline, which they also unloaded. In addition to the 487th Port Battalion, the brigade also had the 502nd Port Battalion with four port companies of black soldiers. This unit, which landed on June 7 and 8, had the same mission as the 487th.

The 112th Engineer Combat Battalion, attached to the 1121st Engineer Combat Group, was assigned to the 116th Infantry and was ordered to open Exit D-3 on D-Day. After June 7, the battalion moved inland to provide general support to the 29th Infantry Division. On June 14, the battalion was transferred from the V Corps to the XIX Corps, and it returned to the V Corps on June 21, in support of the 2nd Division. On June 7, the battalion set up a vehicle transit area in the beachhead; on June 11, it built a culvert bridge; on June 24, it erected four artillery observation towers for the 2nd Infantry Division; and on June 29, it rebuilt a road in the Cerisy Forest. In addition, it performed minor operations such as clearing roads and minefields. During the month of June, the battalion suffered about 14 percent casualties, most of them on D-Day.

After Company B of the 112th Engineer Battalion came ashore on D-Day, 1st Sgt. Raus Blondo and Sergeant Derby fell asleep in a foxhole from exhaustion at the end of the first day. Blondo slept until daybreak of June 7.

---

1. The Athey trailer was a tracked unit that had been used in rough terrain like the Aleutians earlier in the war.

LSTs arrive at Omaha Beach.

Just breaking daylight and small weapons fire was zipping over our heads. I told Derby to rise up and see what was going on. Instead he up and left that hole and ran to the hedgerow. Damn, it got lonely in that hole, so I did the next best thing and followed him. Everyone was still intact. We ate our rations, a candy bar called D ration. I checked personnel and made out reports. I learned that Corporal Wahlen had been hit and had died on the beach, and Punch Lazar had pulled him back from the water's edge. A general came strolling through our area with half a dozen MP guards. He climbed over the hedgerow and walked across the field towards the church. He made it.

I sent Bittner down the road to cover a dead GI who was alongside the house and covered with dust from the road. The Graves Registration people came later and removed him and the German dead we had around us. Then in the afternoon a half-track with multi .50 cal. machine guns pulled into the orchard with MPs. They then sprayed the house loft. The slate roof was flying off and I saw them open the loft door above the house and call in, but I never saw anybody come out.

Now we are told to march to Gouchy [sic] and set up a CP there. We did so, having to run across an intersection in the town. The Germans were supposed to have it zeroed in, but no one was hurt. We set up on top of a hill on the left side and dug in. Nice ground to dig in. Sergeant Gesche reported that he had found a lot of American equipment, packs, office equipment, etc., in a pile a short distance away. I went with him and it was true. They must have stripped for combat and left it all there. I had a guard placed on it and helped myself to a good Underwood portable typewriter. It was like gold to own one, and I used it all through the war.

Then we had a gas scare—rumors. Everyone had discarded the rubber-cased gas mask we wore onto the beach, a new issue before we left the D Area in England. This was supposed to keep you afloat just in case. It did not work all that well. Many people drowned because of that mask. Now everyone was looking for one. You should have seen them with German masks even. The scare was soon called off, and we were on the move again as our trucks had caught up to us. We watched 254th personnel moving by on their trucks on D+2, all sitting there prim and proper as though they were going to a parade. Lots of catcalls from the 112th telling them we had made it safe for them, etc.

Soon we moved right to Cérisy-la-Forêt and set up across a hedgerow from A Company. I had a sandbag CP built and dug a trench from the bottom of the CP out seven feet—a tunnel. Others were doing the same, digging tunnels into the hedgerow. Trucks all parked along the hedges. We sort of encircled a large field. These hedgerows were about ten feet wide at the bottom and tapered to nothing at the top, about six to seven feet high. Many had brush growth on them and they had little occupants such as moles and field mice. The men joined them with no complaints.

We had our mess trucks and supply trucks with us now. I always had a time training the men not to form lines waiting for mess. They were always so anxious to

eat, it became a problem. I remember a German fighter flying over and all scattered except about a dozen men who were at the front of the line. Then one evening it was starting to get dusk and a German bomber came over real low. I watched the bombs drop. Two of them, and I hit the ground in my hole and lay there with my knees knocking together like a drum roll. I just could not stop them. Sergeant Derby got hit in the heel as he dove in. The driver of a platoon supply truck had dug a foxhole alongside of his truck on the driver's side. He was hollering and cursing, and we discovered that the bomb had thrown shrapnel through the truck contents, ripping everything to shreds and also penetrating the gas tank on the driver's side. The gas was pouring into the foxhole and the driver was afraid to get out, but was trying to stop or deflect the flow with his hands while he remained in the hole. B Company suffered little damage, but three troopers from A Company had just left a tent where they had seen a movie and they all hit the ground side by side. The two outside people were untouched, but the man in the center was dead.

I had a tooth filled in this location by our dentist. I remember I had to pump the drill with my feet for him.[2]

After D-Day, PhM3/C Vincent Kordack, who was with the 6th Naval Beach Battalion, found himself at a foot of a hill where he spotted casualties.

There were all types, some had arms and legs blown off and others with shrapnel wounds on all parts of their bodies. One of them was laying there since yesterday.

---

2. The dentists were equipped with foot-powered drills because it was not practical to take heavier equipment such as generators in the field.

There was blood all over the place. . . . So I got busy and changed some of their bandages.

We had a road around five feet wide, and this was lined up with casualties. Each side the road was mined, so we did not have much room to work on. We had orders to carry the casualties down to the beach, about half a mile. So the men with slight wounds of the upper extremity walked and gave aid to help the men with slight wounds of the lower extremity. The real serious ones were carried on litters. . . .

Around 1000 (10 A.M.), the 88s opened up very close to our evacuation center and inflicted a few more casualties and some dead. Among the dead was B-6's platoon officer Lt(jg). Allison, who was hit in a few places and died instantly.

Later in the afternoon, we put a lot of casualties on a Rhino barge, but they could not evacuate until high tide, which was around 1600 [4:00 P.M.].

During the remainder of the day, Kordack had to handle wounded almost nonstop. After two days of almost constant work, he finally fell asleep at midnight.

PhM3/C Frank D. Snyder Jr., who was also on the beach with Platoon B-5 of the 6th Naval Beach Battalion, was separated from his unit on D-Day.

We stragglers were reunited with our unit early in the morning of June 7, which also happened to be my nineteenth birthday. I do not know the number of casualties of the 6th Beach Battalion at Normandy, but if those suffered by my platoon were indicative, we had perhaps 10 percent killed and 15 percent wounded. On June 7, our evacuation aid settled down pretty much into a routine, and gradually we received fewer wounded. German prisoners, some requiring treatment of wounds, were cared for and then marched aboard LSTs for their trip across the Channel.

While those LSTs and LCTs that had come ashore on a rising tide were able to back off and return to sea, those landing on a falling tide were left high and dry to wait the next flood tide. So there they sat, bow door opened, each with its own tethered barrage balloon attached.

On D+2, June 8, the local French civilians started coming to the high ground overlooking the land area, and in spite of an overwhelming spectacle of ships, guns, tanks, etc., the one thing that brought about the most amazed reaction of these people was the sight of the amphibious DUKWs, those big trucks that waddled ashore and drove unaided up the beach over the bluff and down the road. Before long, our job on the beach was finished, although we stayed about three weeks awaiting orders to be shipped back to England. On about June 19, the worst Channel storm in many years struck. Much damage was inflicted on ships, boats, and floating dock facilities.

The 6th Beach Battalion returned to England on or about D+22, and we bedded down on the large, open, weather decks of an LST while a large number of German prisoners were confined to the enclosed tank deck below. After a short stay in England, our unit returned in convoy aboard the USS *Monticello*, formerly an Italian liner. The 6th Beach Battalion was disbanded in California.

The 5th Engineer Special Brigade remained in place operating the beach, but due to the storm in late June, it had only the remnants of the Mulberry at its disposal. Although the loss of the artificial harbor greatly diminished the unloading capacity at Omaha Beach, both engineer special brigades continued to work wonders.

A number of quartermaster units landed several days after the invasion. PFC Hyman Shapiro, a twenty-seven-year-old draftee from Brooklyn, arrived with the 560th Quartermaster Railhead Company. Shapiro's situation was unusual because his basic training had been with artillery with an assignment to the 638th Tank Destroyer Battalion only to find himself sent overseas in a quartermaster unit.[3] Before the invasion, he had trained with firing rifle grenades.

Rhino barge loaded with trucks, June 11, 1944.

We embarked from Weymouth, and while we were waiting, we asked the sailors what it was like on the beach. They said, "Quiet, like your backyard." We were issued fatigues treated against gas attacks and also condoms, which the men put over the muzzles of their rifles to keep rainwater out (we were not optimistic about meeting girls). I had forty rounds of rifle ammunition for my Springfield.

My company was carried on an LCI, and it was crowded. We were jammed in like sardines, and all we saw was rough water. When we got to Normandy, we stood watching the chaos on the beach. The stuff was scattered on the beach. Our LCI ran right up to the beach in maybe a few inches of water, but we walked up that long hill which led out. The beach was strewn with athletic equipment, books, etc. I remember I found a heavy navy jacket and a paperback, *A Tree Grows in Brooklyn*. It was a bestseller that year. I remember the sailors said you could set your watch to 11:00 P.M. because that is when the Germans bombed the beach. I didn't have a watch, but those who did said it was about time and some aircraft started bombing the beach and the whole

sky lit up like the Fourth of July with all the tracers. After a while it looked like rain; the spent projectiles came raining down on top of us. Nobody was hit.

We spent the first night sleeping in an apple orchard with no food. It was strange to me because I had never been hungry in my life. But from that time on supplies were plentiful. We pushed about six miles inland and set up a supply base. Trucks dropped off rations and we set it up. Other units like the 29th Division came in and picked up their allotment. From the men who came from various units we heard more rumors and stories than those up front would. One rumor was that the infantry of the 29th Division was suffering heavy casualties and in a month only three or four men were left of the originals. Another rumor was that two of every three prisoners captured was either Polish or Russian. We also heard that there were Japanese troops sniping, but they turned out to be Mongolians from the Russian front. I did see leaflets dropped by

---

3. The 638th Tank Destroyer Battalion did not leave the United States until August and arrived in France in September 1944.

our side that were printed not only in German, but also in Polish and Russian.

Our supply base didn't look like much. It was just a clearing under a tree for cover from aircraft. In some places they were able to pitch pup tents because they were going to stay longer. It was all open storage.

I was just a guard. I had volunteered because I thought it was a good deal. It was four hours on and eight hours off. When the base was shelled, I jumped into a foxhole. I had been reading the *Readers Digest*, and I was only interrupted for a few minutes. I went out and examined what kind of splinters the shells left and was surprised to see they were very light, like aluminum. Nobody was injured.

One day shortly after landing, the company commander called for volunteers because a Frenchman had reported a German paratrooper landing. About 75 percent of the company volunteered to go only to discover that the alleged paratroopers were nothing but a loose barrage balloon that had shattered and scattered its pieces over the area.

On June 11, the 430th Anti-Aircraft Artillery (Automatic Weapons) Battalion (Mobile), formerly designated as a coast defense unit, began landing.[4] The antiaircraft artillery battalions, along with the barrage balloon detachments, provided some degree of protection to the units within the beachhead. The first batteries came ashore at Colleville and the battalion was attached to the V Corps. On June 14, the battalion was transferred to the XIX Corps under the 12th Anti-Aircraft Artillery Group. Battery A supported the 230th Field Artillery Battalion, which in turn provided fire support to the 30th Infantry Division. During June 14–15, the guns were used in a ground-

support role. Battery B supported the 58th Field Artillery Battalion and Battery C the XIX Corps headquarters. Battery D, with one platoon from Battery C, provided antiaircraft artillery defense for the 200th Field Artillery Battalion.

On June 18, Battery A moved to the Isigny sector to defend the vital bridge over the Vire River, and on June 20 it shot down an FW 190 using only five rounds of 40-millimeter ammunition. This was the first enemy aircraft downed by the XIX Corps. On June 21, the 430th Anti-Aircraft Artillery Battalion was attached to the VIII Corps and moved into the Cotentin Peninsula.

Pvt. Edward A. Trennert, then a twenty-one-year-old draftee from Chicago, who arrived with the 430th Anti-Aircraft Artillery Battalion, served with one of the 40-millimeter gun crews of Company C as an azimuth tracker. He had witnessed the loading of the unit on two Liberty ships in England and he had been assigned to one of the vessel's 20-millimeter guns as an alternate. During the crossing, his convoy was attacked and shrapnel from the bomb hit his ship, but there were no casualties since everyone had been kept belowdecks at the time. On Sunday, June 11, Trennert and his companions climbed down a rope ladder onto a Rhino barge that took them to the beach.

The ramp went down and we were ready to go. I guess I was the second truck off. We reached our assembly area, and each man was told to take his shelter half and put them together with someone else to make a tent. We were told not to leave our area because of snipers in the area. A couple of guys did see a GI hit by a sniper. It was not too good of a feeling.

---

4. Early in the war, the army redesignated many coast artillery battalions as antiaircraft units since their gunners had been trained for firing at moving targets, unlike those of field artillery units.

Units continued to arrive on Omaha Beach even after the destruction of the Mulberry in the storm. Among the supporting formations was the 978th Field Artillery Battalion, which began landing on June 26. On the next day, the battalion took up firing positions and on June 28 opened fire on the enemy. Between then and June 30, the battalion expended 911 rounds of ammunition in about forty separate missions. Small L-4 liaison aircraft hovered over the battlefield serving as aerial forward observers.[5]

Many days passed between the time PFC Maynard E. Daggett, a twenty-year-old from Waterville, Maine, who served as a machine gunner in Battery A of the 978th Field Artillery Battalion, heard the announcement of the invasion on the BBC and the time he embarked with his unit at Boermouth. Before he boarded the ship, his unit's 155s and trucks had already been loaded on the LSTs, one battery per ship. Daggett's battery included two 2½-ton trucks, a weapon carrier, and a tractor to tow the guns.

It was night when we got on the LST. By the time we got to Omaha, it was about an hour after dawn. Once we got near the landing area, the navy guys came and told us we were going into Omaha Beach and they lined us up, and we went straight in, side by side close together—the LSTs. When we came in, they had a sign that said, "Omaha Red Beach." The sign was painted with red paint on a white background. We came in about 10:00 A.M. The landing people directed us. They were up on the road and had foxholes dug in on the side of the road. From what I understand, they had handheld lights that they would direct the ships in with at night. The sea was a little rough and the battleships were still cruising out there.

We were the first battery to land and the others came in later. We followed the road and went to the left maybe 150–200 yards and then turned right on the road out. We waited for the rest of the unit to join us. On the second day, we got strafed by an Me 109. We got a couple of guys wiped out on that. He came in low and level, maybe 100 feet off the ground. He flew over us the first time and then turned around and came back. We were getting in the holes, but some of the boys didn't take it seriously or didn't recognize the aircraft. They just stood there and looked at him, and they didn't make it. We were hollering at them "Get in your holes!" Friendly air cover showed up later. The next morning, about daylight, a German patrol penetrated our position. They didn't get in, but they got close enough that we could see them. We swapped ammunition, but they got away. It was just about daylight. There were only four that we saw, but there must have been more.

During the night, three or four of us stood guard. The password was changed each day. The gun positions were over in a field with hedgerow around them. We were camped in a hedgerow field and our guns were in another. Each gun had a guard from its gun crew. During the day, nobody stood guard. The guns were not dug in because we were waiting for the rest of the battalion. They were kept by the trees for camouflage and we had foxholes dug.

According to Daggett, this was the normal security routine as the battalion moved from position to position.

---

5. Each artillery battalion had two of these light unarmored aircraft.

Operating Utah Beach

Since Utah Beach was smaller than Omaha Beach, only one engineer brigade—the 1st Engineer Special Brigade—was assigned to operate it. Like at Omaha Beach, there were restrictive exits from the beach area. At Omaha, they consisted of defiles leading through the bluffs, while at Utah they were causeways crossing the marshes behind the beach. A Gooseberry gave limited protection to the coast, but only at Omaha Beach and Arromanches[6] were there the artificial harbors known as the Mulberry. Despite the fact that Utah Beach had no such harbor, it continued to handle a high amount of tonnage during the next few months.

The engineers initially set up the supply dumps by the beaches of Omaha and Utah, but after the bridgehead expanded, they moved them several miles inland to insure better dispersion. Due to the uneven tidal flats at Utah Beach, the navy was reluctant to beach LSTs because they were in range of German artillery and the vessels could break their keels at low tide. Since the latter did not happen, they began to make beaching the landing craft routine beginning on D+3. This method delayed shipping schedules, but it was still much faster than using lighters to unload them while standing off the beach.

The 38th Engineer General Service Regiment, which joined the 1st Engineer Special Brigade on June 10, was responsible for maintaining the beach, improving facilities, and clearing mines. Instead of marking Utah Beach with huge colored-light signboards like at Omaha, the engineers painted the barrage balloons floating over the beach with the corresponding beach color. When the 531st Engineer Shore Regiment opened Sugar Red beach to the north, they used two red balloons to avoid confusion with Uncle Red. On June 12, the 38th Engineers opened a fourth beach—Roger White—along the northern coast. Before this, Roger White Beach had been used briefly by coasters, but continued German artillery had made operations there difficult, if not impossible. It was finally determined that Roger White Beach was not needed. The beach was not put back into use again until after the Germans moved.

One week after the invasion, the number of troops and supplies that came ashore on the Utah and Omaha beachheads was about 30 percent below the planned volume. At Utah, the ammunition shortage was becoming critical. Meanwhile, the Mulberry's first pier at Omaha became operational on June 16 and was beginning to function as a real port when a massive storm struck on June 18. The Mulberry was destroyed, forcing the Americans to shift the burden of supply back to Utah and Omaha on June 22. Utah had to take up the slack because the engineers at Omaha had to clear the debris of the wrecked Mulberry from their beach. The great storm also delayed shipping, creating shortages on the front. As a result, coasters carrying ammunition beached themselves at Utah Beach to unload DUKWs and trucks. The change of plans was achieved without any losses. At the end of the month, both beaches were bringing in 80 percent of the planned supplies.

Elements of the Transportation Corps 11th Port[7] (which also operated the Mulberry) and the 4th Port began to open small ports on the Normandy coast such as Grandcamp and Isigny. At the same time, other units were sent to help the 1st Engineer Special Brigade to open St. Vaast, Barfleur, and Granville. Grandcamp was opened for limited operations on June 17 and Isigny on June 23. St. Vaast and Barfleur fell on June 21 as the Germans retreated to the fortress of Cherbourg. Like all the other small ports of the Nor-

---

6. Arromanches was located between Omaha Beach and the British beaches.

7. The 11th Port was a designation for a command structure that eventually included over 7,600 men in four port battalions, five amphibious truck companies, three quartermaster service companies, three quartermaster truck companies, and a few other maintenance-type units.

Floating roadway (Whale) linked to Loebnitz Pier used as part of Mulberry off Omaha Beach.

man coast taken since the landing, they were accessible to lighters and coasters. The engineers quickly opened Barfleur by removing the naval mines and putting the port into operation within a few days. At St. Vaast, the Germans had mined the harbor and sunk fifteen ships inside the harbor. The engineers cleared these obstacles and opened the port on July 9. Although it fell relatively early in the campaign, Carentan remained too close to the front lines and the engineers could not open it until July 25, after which, it stayed in operation for only six days because access from the sea was too problematic. The other small ports, on the other hand, operated for several months.

After Cherbourg finally fell, the engineers had to perform extensive work because of German demolitions. There were forts built into the breakwaters that formed the inner and outer harbors of Cherbourg. The inner harbor was a deep-water port serviced by the *Quai de France*, which

was linked to a large railway station, the *Gare Maritime*. The *Darse Transatlantique* adjacent to the *Quai de France* was a deep-water basin. A narrow channel also led to the two basins in the center of the city. The eastern end of the harbor was an open area.

Since all these facilities were ideal for supporting an invasion force, the Germans were reluctant to leave them intact. They destroyed the two main quays, wrecked the *Gare Maritime*, and sank two ships in the entrance to the *Darse Transatlantique*. They also sank many smaller vessels in the three basins and their entrances and extensively cratered other facilities. After the Germans surrendered, the commanding officer and the staff of the 1056th Engineer Port Construction and Repair Group inspected the damage on June 26 and formulated a plan on June 28. The 332nd and 342nd Engineer General Service and 333rd Engineer Special Service Regiments, assigned to the construction and repair group, used captured German supplies and equipment. One of their first priorities was to create hards for LCTs and LSTs. On July 6, the engineers opened a bathing beach for DUKWs on the west side of the port. However, it was another week before mines were cleared from the approaches. By July 17, barges were unloading at the basins and the first Liberty ship docked on August 9. Originally, the planners had intended Cherbourg to reach a capacity of up to 9,000 tons per day, but by mid-September, 75 percent of the port was operational and it was taking 12,000 tons. By that time, the supply officers had hoped to expand its capacity to 20,000 tons because the ports in Brittany had not yet been captured. In November, the tonnage actually reached 19,955 tons, but after that it declined as the war moved east and new ports were opened.

Port Operations		
Location	Tonnage daily rate	Dates
Omaha Beach	7,500	
Utah Beach	4,500	
Grandcamp	675	June 17–Sept. 19
Isigny	740	June 23–Oct. 15
Barfleur	803	June 24–Oct. 16
St. Vaast	1,172	July 9–Oct. 16
Carentan	300	July 25–July 31
Cherbourg	12,000	Mid-July–Nov.

On D+1, Utah Beach operated more smoothly than Omaha because the landings had gone more smoothly there and the 1st Engineer Special Brigade had had more time to clear the shore. According to the commander of the 2nd Naval Beach Battalion (attached to the 1st Engineer Special Brigade), a couple of enemy batteries with 88-millimeter and 155-millimeter guns had presented the most serious problem. On D+2, one of the batteries located to the south was eliminated, but the other continued to fire sporadically, but accurately, on the beach until D+5. John F. Curtin, commander of the 2nd

Beach Battalion, assumed that the Germans brought a mobile battery that went into operation on D+9 because the beach came again under fire, this time from the north. The Germans continued to fire at infrequent intervals until the evening of June 17, when the 4th Division advanced against them and put a stop to the shooting once and for all. Nightly visitors flew over Omaha and Utah Beach occasionally dropping bombs.

At Utah Beach, the Gooseberry, consisting of a line of old Liberty ships sunk at the two-fathom line, formed a less-than-satisfactory breakwater in severe weather. The navy used one of the sunken ships as a repair shop, but the rest of the Gooseberry was worthless and only denied the use of about 600 yards of good beach. The engineers also laid out two sunken causeways made of pontoons. Each was two-pontoons wide and ran from the high-water line to about two-thirds of the distance out to the low-water line. Pontoon sections or blisters were placed along the sides of the causeways so that the LCTs could unload their vehicles.

Surprisingly, the engineer teams found fewer mines than expected in the beach area, but this may partially be due to the fact that the D-Day forces disembarked on the wrong beach. Behind the beach, the Germans had mined the area more extensively with antitank mines and many antipersonnel S mines. Like at Omaha Beach, many of the barbed-wire areas marked "MINEN" turned out to be free of mines. According to 1st Engineer Special Brigade estimates, their mine teams removed about 45,000 mines. The engineer units assigned to open the dumpsites cleared those areas of mines.

On D+1, work began on roads leading to dumps and situated in fields, and on D+2, the delivery of supplies to permanent dumps began. By D+4, the temporary beach dumps were no longer needed because the 1st Engineer Special Brigade had moved all supplies to permanent dumps. Between D+6 and D+15, the 1st Engineer Special Brigade turned all dumps over to the G-4 of the First Army, and its sole mission became the handling and delivery of supplies to the dumps.

The initial two beaches were expanded to three. A fourth was planned at Quineville, but it was never opened because by that time the 4th Division had pushed the Germans back and the other three beaches operated at a sufficient capacity to make it unnecessary.

When the engineers drained the flooded area behind the beach, they discovered that the causeways were in relatively good condition. They brought crushed rock from local barrow pits located beyond the inundated area and exposed by the aerial bombardment. Since the building material was within easy reach and in plentiful supply, construction proceeded rapidly. Within two weeks, a single battalion put about sixty miles of road in operation.

The provost marshal was responsible for the success of the road system. To speed up transportation inland, one-way roads were set up wherever possible. The MPs carefully directed traffic according to the rules. Numerous nighttime markers indicated road hazards such as road edges (stripped painted stakes), dangerous points on the road such as turns or craters (luminous buttons), dump routes, and entrances (luminous sign boxes). The trucks traveled over 24,000 miles per day along the existing 60 miles of road.

The engineers employed over 8,000 prisoners at Utah Beach to help with all this work. Prisoners of war were also routinely used to open other harbors, including Cherbourg. The POWs who were not put to work were evacuated on the first available ship.

By July 3, over 188,000 men and 119,529 tons of equipment and supplies, and 32,617 vehicles had passed through Utah Beach, and 14,802 casualties and 30,805 prisoners of war had been evacuated from there.

Men of the 1st Engineer Special Brigade

The 531st Engineer Shore Regiment was one of the most important components of the 1st Engineer Special Brigade since it was responsible for clearing and operating the beachhead. It had a wide variety of duties from clearing mines, unloading ships, to setting up water points. Its 3rd Battalion Headquarters Water Point Section established three water points that provided 20,000 gallons on D-Day. Its 24th Amphibian Tractor Battalion included DUKW companies for hauling supplies. Its 286th Joint Assault Signal Company handled communications. Its other attached units such as ordnance, transportation, military police, and medical carried out the routine operations necessary in the beachhead.

PFC John P. Gallagher's Company D of the 531st Engineer Shore Regiment consisted of three platoons and a headquarters platoon. Each of the companies of his battalion hauled in supplies by dozer on D-Day and laid out Pierce planking, interlocking matting placed over the sand.[8] On June 7, Gallagher and his comrades unloaded incoming boats and cleared mines. Having concluded that the mine detectors were rather ineffective, many of them resorted to using bayonets. They stacked the mines up and left them for the ordnance men.

Private Otway Burns of Company A of the 531st Engineer Shore Regiment also landed on the morning of D-Day. The LCT he came in also transported two bulldozers towing 57-millimeter antitank guns for beach defense. Two trucks, one of which he drove ashore, were loaded with the ammo for the whole company. Burns spent most of the first weeks of the campaign hauling

---

8. Similar types of planking (PSP) were used inland for creating a hard surface on bulldozed dirt airstrips.

ammunition to a dump not far from Ste-Mère-Église. His unit handled a large amount of captured German ammunition. One day, someone accidentally set one of the German bombs with a delayed fuse, setting off a massive explosion that destroyed the whole dump.

During the first three days of the landing, the tires of Burn's truck were shredded by shrapnel and had to be replaced at least twenty times. In some cases, German prisoners of war were given the task. One time, Burns recalled,

a German was airing up the thing—we had a truck with an air hose on it and an air tank—he was blowing up the tire and he didn't have the steel ring that held the tire on good and it blew up and popped out. Boom! That ring went off and took his head right off. It went rolling across the ground and I stood there freaking out.

Another time, I saw a German prisoner we had taking up mines. He went nuts or something and ran into the minefield. His friends kept yelling for him to stop. Finally, the guard had to shoot him while he was running.

A lot of the mines were Bouncing Bettys—three-pronged mines. A lot of the wires rusted off and didn't go off. The first night we were there, a guy went out to the bathroom, stepped on one of those in the middle of the night, and cried half the night. An officer and a couple of guys got him about 3:00 A.M. He was yelling for three hours, moaning, "Mama! Mama! Hurt! Hurt!" He was freaking out everybody. They finally got him and brought him in, but I think he died.

Soon Burns had a relapse of the malaria he had contracted during Mediterranean operations, and he was put in a field hospital.

One defense platoon from each of the three battalions of the 531st Engineer Shore Regiment was assigned for beach defense. Pvt. Howard G. DeVoe, a twenty-six-year-old volunteer from Syracuse, New York, was an antitank gunner serving with the Defense Platoon of the 3rd Battalion headquarters.

The 3rd Battalion operated on the north side or right flank of Utah. Our defense platoon defended an arc on the northern section of the beachhead. We never reached our assigned point because we landed on the wrong beach on D-Day.

Our squad worked a seventy-two-hour stretch unloading 90-mm ammo, not all our squad, just six of us. We unloaded one barge at a time. A case was ninety pounds. I don't know how many cases of ammo, but we never stopped or slept. Every time the tide went out, we would have a barge on dry sand that we would unload and it would float out on high tide. Then we would lie on a sand dune and shoot the breeze. It was the toughest seventy-two hours of my life.

Another time, we were on outpost for about three weeks, and when we came back to the company, the first job we got was to dig a hole for a new latrine that the carpenters had built. It was an eight-holer—four back to back. Jimmy said, "That is one thing I hate, so let's dig this big enough!" So we dug it eight feet deep.

Across the swamp from us was a 90-mm AA [antiaircraft] gun. Every night, it would fire a shot, and we would lock in our radar. When he fired his locking shot, the damn latrine collapsed into the hole. The ground was all sand. So we pulled the darn latrine seats out of the hole and we dug a latrine hole two feet deep. So instead of digging an eight-foot hole, we dug an eight foot by two foot and the hole held. It was all sandy there, so it was easy to dig.

We lost a destroyer to shell fire on D+1. They lost quite a few men. At our gun position near the beach, a single sailor washed ashore right near us and he was the only body I saw. That shook me because he was a very young kid, almost a child. He still had baby teeth; I never saw such small white curly teeth, no whiskers, just fuzz. He must have lied like hell about his age. I think he was 13 or 14. Anyhow, we buried him.

We had a [dead] German right nearby. An Englishmen washed ashore, we never knew how he got there. We also had an American GI. We started burying them before they started smelling. We dug one grave and put the bodies in it.

Across the road from our gun position was a minefield with signs up all around. One day, three guys came along in a weapon carrier and jumped out. There was a sidewalk going up to a camp. We hollered as loud as we could, but they paid no attention to us and all of a sudden, we heard a "pop" and one of the guy's feet went sailing up in the air. It must have gone up twenty-five feet. He came running on the stump of his leg and managed to get in the weapon carrier himself and the other two fellows got in and went like hell down the road. They must have been some greenhorns from a QM [quartermaster] unit or something looking for souvenirs.

On D+18, a guy landed and told me it was rough. He was in a QM unit that was stockpiling meat. He was eating meat, which I had never seen on the beach. I had canned corn beef for six weeks straight at one stretch. One meal I missed was canned salmon. The reason this guy said it was rough was because he was a drunkard and had a hard time finding a drink. I saw him twice on the beach and I knew him from back home. He was dead drunk both times.

Like half of his men, Capt. David D. Moore from Trenton, Missouri, the commander of the 478th Amphibian Truck Company, was a veteran of North Africa, Sicily, and Salerno. Half of his company and its DUKWs had been aboard *LST 507* during its disastrous voyage in Exercise Tiger. The remainder had been with him on *LST 289*, which survived a torpedo hit.

The invasion of Normandy was largely anti-climatic to me. Following Tiger Exercise, most of the time was spent in securing replacements in men and material. Replacements were obtained within a week to ten days. . . . But instead of fine-tuning training it was necessary to train the new replacements intensively in DUKW operations. . . .

Also, during this time, First Lieutenants Burgess and Logan were transferred to take command of two Negro DUKW companies out of four companies, which had just arrived from the States and been attached to the 1st ESB. In exchange, I received three young second lieutenants untrained in DUKW operations.

Crossing the Channel on D-Day was uneventful. I disembarked from the LST with my DUKWs in the early afternoon of D+1 about a mile from shore. As we neared the beach, an enemy plane perpendicular to us was strafing the beach. One of my staff sergeants, Nicholas Vrakas, was manning the .50 cal. machine gun on my DUKW. Tracers from his gun appeared to be on target among the hundreds of other shells from the intense cone of fire from army and navy AA guns in the beach area, and the plane was shot down.

The DUKWs were dispersed along the beach, and I reported to the beachmaster, Lt. Col. Stephen Force, CO [commanding officer] of the 2nd Battalion, 531st Engineer Regiment. We were assigned to an

Troops arriving along floating roadway.

area that had been cleared of mines that was just behind the large sand dunes lining the beach behind the seawall. Initial supply dumps were already established in the adjacent area. We went into operation promptly unloading materiel as specified from barges that had been beached and small ships that were grounded at low tide. During that night, operations had to be suspended for a period of time because troops bivouacked in an adjacent area opened fire at the sound of a motor running!

On D+2, supply dumps were set up inland. In the initial assault, a hard surface road was secured virtually intact, and it was discovered that there was another road about a half-mile north that was only covered by water to a maximum depth of about eighteen inches. Securing of these roads negated the need for bridging the artificial swamp behind the beach. This left

a number of ships loaded for the invasion with bridge equipment with very low priority, so some were still sitting there three weeks later. Circular one-way travel was established inland over the hard surface road with return to the beach over the partially submerged gravel road. In this early phase, DUKWs were used to transport the supplies to the inland dumps as they were established.

On D+3 or D+4, my company reverted to assignment to the 24th Amphibian Truck Battalion, Lt. Col. F. G. H. Smith commanding, for operations.

On D+4, the Company moved from the beach area to a field adjacent to Ste-Mère-Église and adjoining the main highway from Carentan to Cherbourg. The trees and hedgerows provided good concealment for the motor pool and maintenance area and the company headquarters and bivouac areas.

On about D+7, four Negro DUKW companies landed on Utah Beach. This made a total of seven DUKW companies. The 479th Amphibian Truck Company, which had been a truck company in the 361st QM Battalion and had been in the initial landings in Sicily operating as a truck company, and the 462nd Amphibian Truck Company, which had joined the 1st ESB in England, were the other two DUKW companies.

On June 18, there was a violent storm during which operations had to be suspended. Large numbers of vessels were driven onto the beach, and the force had been sufficient to send vessels the size of LCTs over the fifteen- to twenty-foot sand dunes behind the beach. I remember riding in my jeep along the beach at low tide and having extreme difficulty in finding a path through the debris. We were able to recommence operations at low tide, unloading beached vessels while the seas were still running too high to come alongside ships for unloading. Also, as I remember, the only shortages that occurred during the storm were for 105-mm howitzers.

In the early phases of the operation, the DUKWs transported the supplies from the vessel to the inland dumps, which limited the amount of supplies that could be unloaded because of the three- to five-mile trip involved after reaching the beach. By about June 20, cranes had been secured, which made it possible to make a direct transfer of supplies in nets or pallets from a DUKW to a 2½-ton truck. This provided a substantial increase in tonnage landed during a twenty-four-hour period, and by late June, we were handling better than 10,000 tons daily [this is about twice the official figures].

Enemy operations against the beach were minimal. During the first two weeks, there was intermittent fire from a German gun emplacement hidden in the hills northwest of the beach. The location was finally [eliminated]. . . . After D+2 there was no daylight strafing or bombing on Utah Beach to my knowledge. Occasionally there were a few nighttime attacks by one or so bombers. Damage, however was minimal. Several DUKWs had their hulls pierced by bomb fragments during one such attack, but none from my company. Also during one such attack a 2,000-pound land mine was dropped on the Cherbourg–Carentan highway adjoining my company area. Luckily, it failed to explode. The bomb disposal squad, after partially excavating it, decided to detonate it in place. A sizable fragment ripped through my tent.

I received my rotation orders on July 4, 1944, and left Normandy on an LST for England the next evening. By happenstance, the other three brigade officers on the same order chose the same LST. We celebrated by drinking a bottle of cognac liberated from Cherbourg!

T/5 John A. Perry, a draftee from Johnstown, Pennsylvania, who served as a truck driver in the 462nd Amphibious Truck Company, was also a survivor of Exercise Tiger. His company came ashore at Uncle Red Beach on the evening of June 7.

The LSTs were about five to six miles out in the Channel when we unloaded. I was the first DUKW out of the LST. All DUKWs upon arrival ashore commenced unloading cargo and started operations from ship to shore and to the dumps as well as hauling wounded from the shore to the ships. Periodic enemy strafing and bombing attacks on the beach and in the bivouac area occurred. Enemy artillery fire landed on the beach.

The 462nd Amphibious Truck Company discontinued operations on Utah Beach on November 11 and departed for Le Havre.

T/4 Hyatt W. Moser came ashore on D-Day with the 286th Joint Assault Signal Company (JASCO) to help establish communications for the 1st Engineer Special Brigade. During operations in France when radio silence was maintained, he spent most of his time working as a wireman because the company needed additional men to string telephone lines. During this time, one of his major gripes was that he had to climb French telephone poles. This was a real problem because his gear was for climbing wooden poles, and these were made of concrete. However, on his third day in Normandy, his tour was suddenly interrupted.

An 88 shell had landed in an adjacent foxhole, and the next thing I knew was that I woke up ten days later in a hospital in England without a scratch on me. During this period of unconsciousness, the malaria I had contracted in North Africa took over, and I spent another thirty days recovering from it.

T/5 Henry Sunier, of the 286th JASCO, prepared for a long stay on June 7.

I dug the most palacious foxhole any GI could dig. It was very elaborate, with a small opening, although it was large below ground. I spent many comfortable hours in there, although it was very difficult to sleep in it due to the cold and the bugs. We were

able to manage, and I am sure it was very safe because of the size of the opening.

The Expanding Bridgehead

During the night of June 6–7, 1944, the Allies secured their bridgeheads and the Germans rushed to reinforce the troops holding the line and to try to push the Americans back.[9]

On June 7, many American troops wounded in action began the slow and painful trip back to the beach where they would be evacuated. Once they reached the crowded and littered beachhead, they joined a sad procession of wounded soldiers and shrouded bodies. Several naval units and transports continuously crossed the Channel back and forth carrying troops and supplies to the invasion beaches, and the dead and the wounded to the invasion ports. Among the supplies headed for the continent were the numerous components of the two artificial harbors or Mulberries and the five breakwaters called Gooseberries, which consisted of blockships, concrete caissons, tugs, and other very specialized features. More than one regiment and supporting unit rode at anchor off the Norman coast that night awaiting its opportunity to land in the morning. As for the airmen, it was business as usual, their planes already drawn up for the next mission.

The logistical tail of the invasion force depended on the success of the troops in expanding the beachhead on June 7, as well as on the rapid development of the artificial port facilities. The vast Allied armada could not maintain the invasion force indefinitely. However, despite careful planning the Allied forces failed to secure many of their first day's objectives. The American airborne divisions occupied a precarious position, but the successful advance of the 4th Division on June 6 left the Allies in a good situation for oper-

---

9. Most of the German armored reserve was finally en route, although slowed by Allied air power and in many cases forced to rely on night movement. It was concentrated against the Second British Army on the Allied left, which was considered the greatest threat at the time.

ations on June 7. On Omaha Beach, the 1st and 29th Divisions failed to reach their objectives on D-Day, and they held a rather narrow, but firm, bridgehead. The British forces had secured many of their key objectives, including a bridgehead over the Orne to hold the eastern flank, but they were unable to link up with the Americans on Omaha Beach. The most significant German achievement on June 6 was preventing the British from taking Caen, a primary Allied objective. The fight to take and control that city lasted for over a month. As a result, the British suffered the brunt of the attack from most of the panzer divisions, the main German battle formations. Elsewhere, Carentan, which separated the two American beachheads, also became a focal battle point until it fell only to be replaced by St. Lô, which the Germans had to hold to keep the American forces bottled up.

Immediately after the Allied landings, the German and American commanders directed their attention to Cherbourg, the only major seaport between the Orne River and Brittany. Both sides realized that the Allies needed port facilities to support the invasion. On June 7, the Allies started building the artificial breakwaters or Gooseberries by sinking old ships off Utah, Omaha, and the British beaches to compensate for the lack of a port.

The Germans fired on some of the Allied blockships from their remaining coastal artillery positions, scoring a few hits and sinking at least one vessel. Since a few of these blockships were old warships, including a few French and British battleships from the last war and a Dutch cruiser, the Germans concluded that their artillery barrage had been successful, not realizing that these ships were sunk by the Allies to create artificial port facilities off the invasion beaches. Not realizing that these were makeshift ports, the Germans committed numerous troops to the Cotentin Peninsula to forestall an American advance on Cherbourg and deny the Americans its port.

LSTs beached at low tide. *LST 326* was a veteran of the invasions of Sicily and Anzio before taking part in the Normandy landings. After the Sicily operation, the navy turned the LST over to a Coast Guard crew.

The first weeks of the campaign saw both sides concentrating their efforts on the port of Cherbourg, the hedgerow country around St. Lô, and open rolling terrain leading to Caen. With the exception of Cherbourg, the majority of the Norman sectors became part of a war of attrition. After many days of bloody fighting, the British drove the Germans from Caen on July 9 and the American took the ruins of the heavily battered town of St. Lô on July 18, heralding the end of the battle for the bridgehead and the opening of the breakout campaign.

On June 7, the only new division to arrive in Normandy was the 2nd Infantry Division, which landed at Omaha Beach. The remaining elements of the original D-Day divisions—the 1st and 29th on Omaha and the 4th and the 90th on Utah—and a very large number of artillery and antiaircraft battalions that were necessary to secure the beachhead, also landed that day.

As the combat and support units landed on June 7, the artificial harbors began to take shape. The Americans at Omaha Beach began moving inland, to their left to link with the British, to their right to relieve the Rangers at Pointe du Hoc, and forward to deepen their beachhead. At Utah Beach, the 4th Infantry Division moved forward to relieve the overextended airborne divisions, which were striving to consolidate their position.

Moving Out from Omaha Beach, June 7 to 30

At the close of D-Day, since the regiments of the 1st and 29th Infantry Divisions fell far short of their planned objectives, there arose a serious supply problem. Only a little over 100 tons out of a planned 2,400 tons of supplies came ashore on D-Day. A vast majority of the materiel, from artillery to ammunition, remained offshore, delayed by the slow progress on the beachheads. June 7 was a critical day for the V Corps. On its left, the British faced two German infantry divisions and a panzer division. The VII Corps at Utah Beach moved against elements of two infantry divisions, an air landing division and a parachute regiment. The regiments holding the Omaha beachhead faced the reinforced German 352nd Division. German reinforcements were beginning to show up everywhere, including on the V Corps' front, where the

> 352nd Division represented an offensive unit which the enemy expected to use for counterattack by the second day. Employed instead in closeup defense of the beach, it had made the initial assault phase harder but had not achieved defensive success. The 352nd Division had been used up on D-Day, and lost [all] available strength for effective early countermeasures.

The phrase "used up" was an overstatement because the 352nd Infantry Division, despite serious losses, was reinforced and continued to play a key role in holding back the American forces for many days and took part in the spirited defense of St. Lô. Gen. Dietrich Kraiss, commander of the 352nd Division, informed corps headquarters late in the evening of June 6 that his division would continue to offer the same determined resistance on June 7, but that heavy casualties would require reinforcements by June 8. The German 716th Infantry (Static) Division, defending against the British landings, notified the Seventh Army's headquarters late in the evening of June 6 that a number of its strongpoints were still resisting. However, the 716th Division reported that it had lost communication with most of those positions, but that it was the army's responsibility to relieve them. The German High Command and Hitler remained split on the actual scale of the invasion. At the end of June 6, the situation on the front of the German 352nd Division remained precarious, and if the landings were a diversion, as Hitler believed, sending large reinforcements might be a mistake. And fortunately for the Americans, the German commanders were still convinced that they might be able to reach some of the isolated garrisons on the coast and eliminate what they considered the greater threat presented by the British sectors. Thus, many of the newly arriving German reinforcements moved against the British. On June 7, the 352nd's reinforcements consisted mainly of elements of the 30th Mobile Brigade, an inexperienced unit made up of three bicycle-mounted battalions that had made an exhausting trip to the front.

Gen. Clarence Huebner took personal command of the 1st Division and released the attached units of the 29th Division to Gen. Charles Gerhardt after V Corps headquarters took over command of the beachhead on June 7. General Kraiss launched counterattacks against the beachhead on that day. Early on the morning, his artillery bombarded the Vierville area and the beach exit until Allied naval fire silenced his guns at about 8:00 A.M. Meanwhile in the morning hours, German troops struck Company B of the

121st Engineers near Château de Vaumicel and tried to retake Vierville with the 916th Grenadier Regiment. The 914th Grenadier Regiment of the German division pinned the Rangers at Pointe du Hoc while Resistance Nest #76 (W-76) at Pointe de la Percée continued to hold out. It took almost six hours for General Kraiss to make the short drive to that strongpoint due to Allied airpower; the road trip normally took only about thirty minutes. When he reached the coast, Kraiss viewed firsthand the massive invasion fleet and the now uninterrupted stream of reinforcements arriving on the American beachhead. By the end of the day, his German division as well as the American forces had suffered heavy losses in the counterattacks. However, his troops could do little more than briefly contain the invasion despite further reinforcements and morale continued to sink. The ammunition supply for his artillery was rapidly dwindling and resupply was difficult. In his postwar report, Lt. Col. Fritz Ziegelmann, assistant chief of staff for the 352nd Division, wrote, "in the villages the infantry (American) fought stubbornly and skillfully. In open terrain the impetus of the attack soon came to an end when the infantry met with strong German defense. Then infantry fighting was replaced by fighting with heavy weapons, with materiel." On June 8, his forces tried unsuccessfully to hold back the onslaught of the American 1st and 29th Infantry Divisions with their tank support and the newly arriving 2nd Infantry Divisions.

The V Corps quickly had to expand the beachhead, which had a maximum depth of about 2,000 yards, before the enemy 352nd Division was reinforced. It was critical that the American regiments get across the flooded Aure Valley, cross the lower Vire River, and move deep into the hedgerow country before the Germans could set up defensive positions and prevent the troops at Omaha Beach from linking up with the British beachheads and their fellow Americans at Utah.

The fog of war favored the V Corps. On June 8, the Americans were finally able to secure their D-Day objectives. The German 352nd Division did not receive any major reinforcements until June 10 when the 3rd Parachute Division arrived from Brittany.

The American breakout began on June 7, but some of the troops had their first encounter with the hedgerows as early as June 6. When the three regiments of the 1st Division advanced, German resistance began to crack, albeit slowly, and the hedgerows would soon allow the Germans to blunt the American drive. The 1st Division had three battalions of artillery—and a fourth coming ashore during the day—to support the offensive. In addition, the five remaining operational tanks of the 741st Tank Battalion and the newly arrived 745th Tank Battalion went into action. The 16th Infantry, seriously weakened on D-Day, received reinforcements. Two battalions of the 16th Infantry, and other detached units, spent much of June 7 cleaning up German resistance within the beachhead. Headquarters and artillery units also helped eliminate snipers and round up the Germans who finally decided to surrender.

By the end of June 7, the 1st Division pushed up to four miles inland. The 3rd Battalion of the 18th Infantry and the regiment's 2nd Battalion to its left crossed the Aure River early in the evening. The 3rd Battalion of the 16th Infantry, reinforced with the 1st Battalion of the 26th Infantry, moved toward Port-en-Bessin at 11 A.M. in an attempt to link up with the British, whose 47th Commando Battalion moved toward the port from the other direction. The dominant heights of Mt. Cauvin, to the south of Port-en-Bessin, were one of the main objectives.

The 3rd Battalion of the 26th Infantry, attached to the 18th Infantry on the division's right flank, had the mission of taking Formigny, the site of one of the last battles of the Hundred Years' War. The Germans checked its advance on June 7, but the battalions of the 18th Infantry

Adm. Harold Stark inspects a German gun casemate.

outflanked them to the east and cut the main road from Bayeux.

On June 7, during the battle around Vierville, the Germans captured plans of the V Corps showing invasion objectives, but they did not have sufficient forces at hand to react during the first forty-eight hours of the invasion. The German 352nd Division failed in its attempts to retake Vierville and other coastal towns and, at the end of the day, it was no longer able to counterattack. Only the hedgerows offered the German division a chance to hold back the Americans.

On June 8, the Americans did not gain as much ground. Their main effort was directed against the left flank of the German division and Port-en-Bessin. On the right flank, tanks from the 745th Tank Battalion joined the 18th Infantry in its effort to clear Formigny in the early hours of the morning. On the left flank, the action focused on Mount Cauvin, which fell later in the day. Meanwhile, the 1st Division strengthened its hold south of the Aure, which enabled it to attack the two battalions of the German 915th Regiment of the 352nd Division standing in front of the 1st Division between Trévières and Blay. German units on the left flank of the 1st Division began to retreat from a pocket formed between British and American forces northwest of Bayeux. Elements of the 916th and 726th Regiments of the 352nd Division were identified in the 1st Division area. (The 726th Regiment was attached from the 716th Division.) The 517th Battalion from the 30th Mobile Brigade arrived from the area of St. Lô, but all these units had already taken a beating. German artillery support began to dissipate, while the Americans received close air and naval support to aid their advance.

Armor Support: The 741st Tank Battalion

The 741st Tank Battalion suffered heavy losses on D-Day. Most of the Sherman DD tanks of its B and C Companies were lost before reaching shore on June 6. Most of A Company made it ashore an hour later (at 6:40 A.M.). Early on the morning of June 7, three trucks hauling much-needed fuel reached the battalion assembly area 200 yards north of St. Laurent-sur-Mer after passing through Exit D-3.

On the morning of June 7, five tanks under Captain Thomas moved forward to support the 2nd Battalion of the 16th Infantry. Two of the tanks came from the HQ Company and each of the remaining three from the three tank companies. Soon they were directed to support the 1st Battalion of the 18th Infantry in cleaning up snipers and machine-gun nests. The 1st Battalion was taking heavy casualties until the tanks arrived and successfully elimi-nated the opposition. In the early afternoon, they passed by Engranville, but they had to return and put the town under fire when they discovered that it was still held by the Germans, who were firing at the 18th Infantry from behind. By 7:00 P.M., the tanks returned to the battalion assembly area with only five rounds left in each tank. One tank from the HQ Company was sent to the 2nd Battalion of the 16th Infantry, which was under fire from a German artillery piece. At 9:00 P.M., the tank eliminated the German gun, as the last resistance around Colleville was broken.

June 8 was dedicated to salvage and repair operations. Five T-2 tank recovery vehicles set to work on the beach in the morning. The eight operational Shermans (one more than on June 7) went to support the 1st and 2nd Battalions of the 16th Infantry near Russy and remained there through the night.

As the 1st Division advanced, the 29th Division began to move toward its D-Day objectives after beating back the morning German assault on June 7. The 116th Infantry sustained serious casualties on June 6, and many of its units were widely dispersed during the move from the beaches. The division's two artillery battalions already ashore had less than half their guns. The division's 175th Infantry, held as corps reserve, finally disembarked late in the morning of June 7 to reinforce the 115th Infantry. On June 7, the 29th Division still had to clear the last Germans from positions near Exit D-3 and St. Laurent and the area around Vierville in order to put Exit D-1 fully into operation.

First Lt. Carl Hobbs, a 1942 officer candidate school graduate from Austin, Texas, and the S-2 for the 1st Battalion, 175th Infantry, climbed down the cargo net into an LCVP on the morning of June 7. His ride on the choppy seas was rough, as it was for the troops on D-Day, but there was little to no enemy fire. The LCVP approached the shore with no problems and

the ramp was opened and we moved out. We were in water up to our hips, but there were soldiers in the water on our right because an LCVP had hit a mine and exploded. We had our gas masks on our chests, and it had enough air in it to keep a man's head above water. The shore was not sandy where I landed, mostly rocks and pebbles. We were pretty well exhausted when we got to the shore. There was rifle and mortar fire, but I don't recall any of the men and battalion HQ or my section being wounded on the beach. It did not take long for us to get from the beach to the cliffs. We moved up to Vierville and continued moving until we reached the area where our regimental HQ was established. We passed some abandoned equipment and dead soldiers on the beach and at the water's edge.

It was hard to remember how you felt, but you had the feeling you were going to get shot any second and began to realize that war was a dangerous business. Although we had practiced over and over, it took a little bit to get used to the fact that people were getting killed, but you got accustomed to that pretty fast.

As he moved across the beach, Hobbs saw ships unloading all along the shore and all kinds of vehicles and equipment rolling along. On his way inland toward the bivouac area, he noticed stockpiles of rations, gasoline, and car pools.

Lieutenant Hobbs and 1st Sgt. Ernest Lee of the I&R Platoon, who landed with him that morning, had to leave their jeeps aboard the LST, so their original recon mission toward St. Lô was scrapped. Lee had vivid memories of the beach.

I ran to the seawall and there was a cable leading into a hole with a barrage balloon at the other end. Other than the deceased soldiers on the beach piled up at random, the first two people I saw were two young black soldiers in this hole. I collected my men behind the seawall since there was still firing from several locations on the cliffs above the beach although this was the second day. I ran into Colonel Canham of the 116th Infantry, who had returned to the beach looking for stragglers. He waved us on up through the exit at Vierville and we

proceeded on towards Isigny. We spent the night at La Cambe.

According to Lieutenant Hobbs, the march to Isigny that day was slow. They moved before dark and walked all night, taking a few twenty-minute breaks. They carried two to three D rations in their packs, one K ration, and a large chocolate bar. Soon the regiment would undergo its baptism of fire.

During the morning of June 7, the 1st Battalion of the 116th Infantry moved west along the coast road with three companies of the 2nd Rangers and two of the 5th Rangers. Ten tanks from the 743rd Tank Battalion advanced in support. They bypassed enemy positions since their mission was to reach the Rangers at Pointe du Hoc. They reached St. Pierre-du-Mont at 11:00 A.M. By this time, despite limited weapons and naval support, about 100 Rangers grimly held out at Pointe du Hoc. In the afternoon, the Germans repelled repeated attacks by the relief column, but thirty Rangers and supplies delivered in two LCVPs managed to reach the men at Pointe du Hoc.

While Hobbs was coming ashore early that morning, T/4 Clifton Bitgood, Company C, 121st Engineers, and his platoon were removing 75-millimeter rounds that had failed to detonate and stacking them alongside the road. His unit joined in the advance to Isigny, but everything passed in a blur for him and his next memory was of crouching under sniper fire near a statue in the square of Isigny.

The 116th Regiment and the 5th Ranger Battalion stayed in the Vierville area during the night of June 6. In the morning, they stopped a counterattack launched by the 352nd Pioneer Battalion of the 352nd Division and elements of its 916th Grenadier Regiment. However, the Germans penetrated the town of Vierville and captured an Overlord operations map. Early dur-

The German 352nd Division Captures the V Corps' Operations Plan

In the afternoon of June 7, German soldiers of the 352nd Pioneer Battalion found next to the body of a dead American officer a briefcase that contained the V Corps Overlord Operations Plan. At about 10:00 P.M., the staff of 916th Grenadier Regiment notified Colonel Fritz Ziegelmann of their discovery.

Lt. Col. Fritz Ziegelmann, a 352nd Division staff officer, went through the approximately hundred-page document that included maps and charts and telephoned General Marcks of the LXXXIV Corps at about 1:00 A.M. on June 8, giving him the main points of the plan. Colonel Helmdach, the chief of staff of the Seventh Army, was also informed by telephone before the plan was sent to corps headquarters. According to Gen. Guenther Blumentritt, chief of staff of OB West, the plan was delivered at OB West on either June 9 or June 10, after which key parts were sent to OKW (German Armed Forces High Command), where they could not have arrived any later than June 12.

On June 8, the Seventh Army telephone journal noted a message from the chief of staff of Army Group B concerning the captured document notifying the Seventh Army of "an urgent demand for information on the situation by order of Field Marshal Rommel, since the report telegraphed this morning has not yet come through." According to the same log, the following information was extracted from the documents and sent on:

VII American Corps with four divisions.

Mission: To attack northward from the Carentan-Quineville bridgehead and take Cherbourg.

V English [actually U.S.] Corps with four English divisions and two American divisions in Calvados sector.

Mission: To take Bayeux and join up with the American VII Corps.

According to General Blumentritt, this plan confirmed OB West's opinion that this was the long-awaited invasion. Unfortunately, Field Marshal Gerd von Rundstedt still had to answer OKW. However, at OKW, Hitler was unconvinced because the plan did not account for General Patton's army group, which he did not realize was only a part of the Allied diversionary plan. Furthermore, Hitler could not believe that the Allies would be able to land as many as sixty divisions on that section of the Normandy coast, so the real invasion must not have taken place yet. In Blumentritt's opinion, the staff at OKW did not think that there would be a second landing after the end of June, but Hitler remained unconvinced.

Although the plan helped the Germans understand Allied intentions, General Blumentritt claimed after the war that his side gained no special advantage because of it, and that it did not affect Allied losses, especially since OKW attached no importance to the document. Even with knowledge of Allied schedules, General Blumentritt admitted, there was nothing the Germans could do about it.

ing that attack the Germans also took a group of engineers from the 29th Division by surprise, killing or capturing some of them. Despite heavy losses, the German pioneer battalion moved further east to stop the advance of the 1st Division south of St. Laurent.

Among the prisoners taken during the attack on the 29th Division was PFC Thomas R. Fitzgerald, a medic with Company B, 121st Engineers. He was captured at about 6:00 A.M. as several of his companions were shot. As the prisoners marched down the road, a German lieutenant waved a machine pistol, threatening to shoot them all until another officer intervened. The Germans moved Fitzgerald and about forty fellow prisoners to a building near a creamery near Isigny where they spent the night. The next day, they marched to a villager further behind the lines and locked them in a barn. During the following night, Allied aircraft bombed the area around their temporary prison, their German guards took to their heels, and the American prisoners made a bid for freedom, but several were killed by the falling bombs. The Germans rounded up the survivors within a few hours and herded them to a monastery at Tessy-sur-Vire, where they joined another 900 prisoners.

The battalions of the 116th Infantry cleared the Germans from the bluffs and advanced south of Vierville, where they encountered resistance at Louvières only a mile away. Meanwhile, the 3rd Battalion of the 115th Infantry cleared the enemy strongpoint on the west side of St. Laurent and advanced with the 1st Battalion toward Longueville but did not gain more than about a mile before the Germans held them up near Louvières. The 2nd Battalion was able to push forward less than a mile before it encountered German resistance at the village of Vacqueville, but with artillery support it broke through and reached the outskirts of Montigny, about a mile behind the German position at Louvières, where the other two battalions were held up. Early on

the morning of June 8, they found that the hamlet had been prepared for defense, but it was abandoned.

The 175th Infantry came ashore during the afternoon of June 7, got off the beach near Exit D-3, and marched through Vierville and westward down the coast road to Gruchy, where it turned southwest toward Englesqueville. Two additional artillery battalions of the 29th Division also disembarked on the afternoon of June 7. After the 9th Infantry of the 2nd Division came ashore, it was directed to take over the mopping up operations of the 29th Division near the beachhead the next day, June 8.

On June 8, the V Corps' headquarters ordered the 116th Infantry to continue its advance with the two Ranger battalions past Pointe du Hoc down the coast road to Grandcamp and Maisy. At about noon, the 1st Battalion, 116th Infantry, finally reached the 2nd Rangers at Pointe du Hoc. That evening the Germans at Grandcamp surrendered to the 116th Infantry while the 1st Battalion, which took another route, turning south from Pointe du Hoc and moving through Jucoville, reached Maisy.

The 175th Infantry with two companies of the 747th Tank Battalion had renewed its advance shortly before midnight on June 7 and reached La Cambe at 3:00 A.M. on June 8. Here, German resistance stiffened. The tank battalion finally broke the German position, but not before German 88-millimeter guns west of La Cambe put six tanks out of action. Despite encountering increased resistance, the 175th continued its relentless advance, clearing St. Germain-du-Pert by late afternoon. Later that evening, Cardonville and Osmaville fell and the 175th pushed on to Isigny, trapping the remaining German forces north of the Aure Valley. In the opening hours of June 9, the first elements of the 175th entered Isigny with naval support. When they reached the key bridge over the Aure River, the tank drivers at the head of the column refused to cross the bridge, fearing it was mined. General Gerhardt, 29th Division commander, roared up in his jeep to find out what the holdup was, and ordered the men to cross the bridge. Isigny fell at 3:00 A.M. after token resistance. The patrols of the 175th linked up with elements of 327th Glider Infantry Regiment of the 101st Airborne Division located just east of the Douve River. Thus, the Omaha and Utah bridgeheads finally established a link.

On the foggy morning of June 8, during the advance on Isigny, the 1st Battalion of the 175th was strafed by British Typhoons as it was passing through La Cambe, incurring about twenty casualties. One of the injured was Lt. Carl Hobbs who, to his disgust, became a legend that day. For decades history books reported that the doctors had gingerly removed a live 20-millimeter round that had lodged in his shoulder. Despite the fact that he repeatedly pointed out that a round of that size could not physically fit in his shoulder without causing mortal injuries, the myth persisted. He was actually wounded in the back by a piece of shrapnel from a 20-millimeter round.

Clearing the roadside of mines while heavy equipment moves off the beach. ROBERT LEHMANN

> I had on a tank combat jacket, which was heavier than the average jacket. I never saw the planes and was right in the ditch along side the road when this object hit my back and I heard it hit the jacket. It was a shell that exploded after hitting a tree limb or something and it was a piece larger than my little finger nail. It pierced the jacket and went into my body. There was no shell; somebody just built up a story. A little piece of the shell hit me in my left earlobe and it started bleeding and the blood fell into my mouth. Here I was hit in the back and I could taste blood, so I though I was in bad shape.

An aid man from Company A treated his wound with sulfa powder, and he walked back to battalion headquarters. From there, he was sent to the battalion first-aid station, and by the afternoon of June 8, he was at the beach on his way back to England in spite of his protests that he was OK. In the hospital, an X ray showed that a metal fragment buried in his flesh, just short of his lungs. Since an operation was too risky, the doctors decided to leave the piece of shrapnel in his body and kept Hobbs under observation for about a week.

On June 8, the 115th Infantry had orders to move the division's left flank toward the Aure River between Canchy and Trévières. The line along the Aure was achieved against minimal resistance that day. Holding a line along the Aure River from Isigny to Mount Cauvin via Trévières ensured the security of the Omaha beachhead along with the advance of the 1st Division on the eastern half of the beachhead. However, the hedgerow-covered terrain, the high ground to the south, and the flooded Aure Valley allowed the Germans to contain the American V Corps while the panzer reinforcements hammered away at the British positions. On June 9, the V Corps faced the remnants of the 352nd Division with its reinforcements, but the Germans doggedly continued to delay the southward advance.

On June 9, D+3, the 115th Infantry, after marching and countermarching on the previous day, moved up to the Aure River and the inundated area around it after finally taking Longueville. Each battalion was assigned a different crossing area. The troops moved out before dawn. The lead elements of the 3rd Battalion entered the muddy terrain near Canchy, but several hundred yards out, the marsh became too deep and the engineer battalion had to bring boats. Finally after dawn, the battalion crossed the river and reached Colombières before 10:30 A.M. When it tried to cross the river near Écrammeville, the 1st Battalion, which was operating in the 2nd Division's sector, was repulsed by the Germans at Trévières. The 2nd Battalion, which came close on the heels of the 1st, moved across with no opposition and reached La Carretour that very evening. Some of the troops were too tired to dig in. During the night, German troops pulling back from the Aure River line stumbled across them. The Germans soon overwhelmed the dazed Americans, who were trying to fight back. The battalion commander, Colonel Warfield, refused to surrender and died during the battle. General Gerhardt, commander of the 29th Division, who had lost contact with the 2nd Battalion, went in search of it and found the bodies of its commander and many of his men mingled with dead German soldiers. Gerhardt reassembled the remnants of the battalion and sent it back in line with the other two battalions along the Elle River on the evening of June 10.

Lt. Charlie A. Miller from Baton Rouge was a twenty-six-year-old drafted out of college and three years later was leading the 1st Platoon of Company I, 3rd Battalion, 115th Infantry, from the beach to the Aure River.

We were briefed on the inundated area and generally we knew the depth and I believed the width was about 2,000 yards. We spent the night [June 9] on the shore, and then moved out in regular combat formation with scouts out and the soldiers spread apart. This was early morning [before dawn]. We were well out into the water when some artillery rounds began to fall and at some point we returned to the same shore from which we had departed. Later, another attempt was made and we crossed. Generally, the water was less than waist deep; however, on a number of occasions there were deeper areas, which in some cases were over our heads, but these areas were not very wide.

PFC John McQuaid, who in February 1943 had enlisted in the reserves at his home in Ware, Massachusetts, at age seventeen, reported for basic training when he finished high school that summer. In 1944, he was sent to a replacement camp in southern England. On June 6, he awoke to the sound of aircraft and saw the sky filled with planes and gliders. Soon his unit was trucked to Southampton. On June 7, McQuaid and his comrades were given their farewell meal with ice cream for dessert. On June 8, they were driven to the loading docks, where they boarded a British ship at dusk. At breakfast they were served fresh eggs with lamb, a treat they had not had for many a month. On June 9, they came within sight of Omaha Beach, and they were issued ammunition before they left the transport. Once they hit the shore, they went through the Vierville draw, marched until dark, and dug in a field for the night. On June 10, they boarded trucks to reach their destination.

[We] assembled around an officer who told us we were at the front and that some of us would be dead or wounded by this time tomorrow. One first lieutenant passed out and had to be revived. It was early morning as we dug in. We were split up and taken by an NCO to the 1st Battalion, 116th Regi-

Loebnitz Piers of the Mulberry, which could be raised and lowered with the tides.

ment, and I was assigned as a radioman. We were outside of Couvain. Fighting was heavy—tanks tried to support us but couldn't in the hedgerows. Two days later, I was assigned to A Company. When I finally got to the area of A Company, there were dead and wounded everywhere, more Americans than Germans. I observed the dead Americans piled between two apple trees like cordwood—many had landed with me.

McQuaid heard rumors that some men were so shaken by the sight that they shot themselves in the foot in order to be taken out of the front lines. After a couple of days, he was put in charge of communications and rose from PFC to sergeant but managed to lose his stripes before his promotion became official.

During the days that followed, the 29th Division penetrated the Elle River line while the 2nd Division on its left cleared the Creisy Forest. The 1st Division, on the left flank of the V Corps, pushed south toward Caumont into a major gap in the German lines between Berigny and Longraye that had appeared after the collapse of the left flank of the German 716th Infantry Division after the fall of Bayeux to the British. However, the hedgerows, easily defended by the enemy, slowed its progress considerably. The Germans tried to close the gap on June 10, but only the recon battalion of the 17th SS Panzer Grenadier Division had reached the front. As a result, the G-2 of the V Corps concluded that the 1st and 2nd Divisions might expect a serious counterattack by enemy armored forces. The two divisions stopped and did not launch an attack until June 11, when the 29th Division joined the offensive. The 1st Division took Caumont on June 13. Meanwhile, the German troops facing the 2nd and 29th Divisions took full advantage of the *bocage* (hedgerows).[10] The casualties continued to mount and territorial gains became minimal. At the close of June 13, the V Corps attack ground to a halt. General Corlett's XIX Corps, which had just become operational with the 30th Division, took command of the 29th Division from the V Corps. The 1st and 2nd Divisions of V Corps were ordered to take up defensive positions since the 2nd Panzer Division was identified on the left flank of the corps. After that, no major progress was achieved along the fronts of either American corps for the rest of the month. On July 1, the V Corps front ran from Caumont to Berigny and the XIX Corps front faced St. Lô, turned at Villers Fossard and continued north, along the Vire River line.

Naval Operations after D-Day

After June 6, 1944, the navy maintained stations off the beaches providing fire support and air defense and protecting logistical and combat units that continued to pour into the beachheads. The U.S. Navy was responsible for the Western Task Force, which supported Utah and Omaha Beaches and had to be ready to defend against assaults from light German naval units stationed at Cherbourg. On the other flank, the British Eastern Task Force had already engaged German torpedo boats from Le Havre and taken losses as soon as the invasion began. The Germans did not come away unscathed either from these operations. During the night of June 6–7, the *Luftwaffe* made an appearance. The beach area became a frequent target for German aircraft despite a warm reception from American antiaircraft units.

As for the troops on shore, almost every night they spotted overhead a lone German aircraft they soon dubbed "Bed Check Charlie."

Before long, Hitler became obsessed with the desire to destroy the battleships, which, he realized, provided invaluable fire support to the assault troops and were effective against the German coastal defenses. To this end, he ordered the new German midget submarines against the Allied fleet, but once again, most of these efforts focused the British sector.

Most of the sailors on the larger warships actually witnessed little of the action outside, except for the glimpses they caught from their battle stations. The men assigned to the deck guns and observation positions got the best view of the action. Their fellow seamen on the landing craft and other small vessels, on the other hand, were caught right in the middle of the action.

Marine 1st Lt. William McDaniel, who served with the marine detachment aboard the USS *Augusta*, had a particularly good view of the operations off Normandy.

My position in the main mast was that of being a control officer for the Section No. 3, which was the starboard section from midship aft. We had one quad mount of 40-mm guns, one twin mount of 40-mm guns, and approximately six to eight single-barrel 20-mm guns. My connection with these guns was simply by telephone, and I was to give them orders as to when to fire and also what target they should select. I had very little of that to do. My partner on the No. 4 quadrant, which was the aft and port side, at that time, was a Lieutenant Markham of the U.S. Navy. He subsequently became a famous professor at Harvard. Lieutenant

---

10. The term *bocage* refers to hedgerows enclosing fields found in many parts of northern France. To the south of the coastal area of the initial Omaha beachhead, the Americans referred to that part of Normandy as the *Bocage* region, which ran from south of Bayeux to Brittany. See the next chapter for further description.

Markham and myself had most of the night watch, and we were able to arrange it so one officer could handle both sections and the other could go down to the ward room and smoke a cigarette or have a cup of coffee. So we did not have to stay up there all the time, although we were there most of the time. One of our main problems was that it was very cold. We did have occasions to need a cup of coffee, believe me; it was cold and miserable up there.

Those of us in the AA battery devised a system of twelve on and twelve off, but during the twelve [hours] off we could get a little rest. I was in the group that had the night watch. This was good in one respect, you saw all the fireworks, a sky full of tracers, but you did not have an opportunity to see what was going on on the beach. As I recall, we stayed in general quarter's positions for about forty-eight hours, although we were able to get away for a few minutes now and then to relieve ourselves. As I recall, food was brought to us in a sack, so we did stay in our positions a long time.

At night, the Germans would come in and drop mines. Our supporting aircraft would return to England at night, and I believe one reason was that we had so many trigger-happy gunners that would fire at the sound only, and the sky would be full of tracers. This was a tremendous waste of ammunition, and there was the dangerous element of these particular projectiles coming down. The 5-inch and 40-mm ammunition would explode at the highest elevation they would reach, but the 20-mm and .50 caliber did not and they came down and sometimes it would be like a hailstorm and those on topside would be exposed to it.

Sea mines were a source of great concern for the navy personnel. On the morning of D-Day, the destroyer *Corry* hit a mine and sank off Utah Beach. The next day, the minesweeper *Tide* suffered the same fate. North of Utah Beach, the destroyer *Glennon* struck a mine and was grounded in shallow water; its stern took on water the next day. The destroyer escort *Rich* struck two mines on June 8 as it went to the rescue of the *Glennon*. As a result, the little ship broke in half and lost almost half its crew. The destroyer *Meredith* ran into a mine or was a victim of a glider-bomb. All in all, June 8 was a bad day for the navy.

Seaman 1/C C. Everett Douglas, an eighteen-year-old Tennessean who had joined the navy only the previous October, was serving on the *Meredith* as it escorted a convoy to Normandy and began its fire-support missions. The *Meredith* was a new ship and had gone to sea in May, arriving in time to participate in the invasion. On June 6, 1944, the crew recovered the body of an RCAF pilot who had crashed his Spitfire off their bow. The ship screened the transport area for most of the day.[11] On June 7, the *Meredith*, like most of the other destroyers, moved close to shore to support the ground troops. Her small guns peppered German troop concentrations on D-Day. However, she ran out of luck that night.

We hit a mine at about 2 A.M. [June 8] and had to abandon ship. We were taken to the cruiser *Tuscaloosa*, where we remained the rest of the day and night. Then we were taken to Portsmouth, where we received medical attention, fresh clothes, and food. We were placed in a barracks for the next

---

11. This most likely was one of several Allied aircraft shot down by friendly antiaircraft fire on D-Day and not one that crashed due to a mechanical problem.

few days and then went by train to Glasgow, Scotland, and put on the *Queen Elizabeth* for New York.

Cmdr. George Knuepfer described the events in more detail in his report of June 11, 1944.

We stayed in this area supporting the troops throughout the day on 7 June, and on the evening of 7 June, about four minutes before midnight, we were ordered to proceed to the northward of the heavy ships in their gun support areas and screen them against E-boats. Just prior to this, a report had been received that E-boats were concentrating in that area from the Cherbourg coast. I was assigned to the northward of a position just about five miles from the Island of Marcouf and was patrolling my station along with about six other destroyers, when suddenly I struck a submerged mine. This was at 0152 [1:52 P.M. on June 8].

The ship gave a tremendous lurch forward and upward and everybody on the topside was thrown to their knees, and we were all drenched with a huge cloud of water as a result of the mine explosion. This water just seemed to fall for minutes and minutes until it appeared as if we were going down under the sea. Suddenly all abated, flying debris had stopped falling, and we stirred around to find out the extent of damage. All communications had been lost and [the ship lost all power].

We immediately investigated the extent of damage and found that the mine had struck on the port side of the keel right under No. 2 fireroom and had wiped out both No. 1 fireroom, No. 1 engine room, and No. 2 engine room, killing most of the men in that area, including those that were in the repair parties on topside just above that area. The explosion blew a hole about

sixty-five feet outward in this area, completely wiped out the main deck, the forward boat davit, the motor whaleboat, the super structure deck, and half of no. 2 stack.

The machinery in those areas was actually blown overboard, just a tangled mass of machinery was in evidence. The ship had immediately taken a list to starboard of about twelve degrees as a result of machinery missing in the engineering spaces, and she appeared to be settling. The bulkheads on each side of the damaged area were intact, and the bilges were dry. It was one of those unusual conditions of damage control, but there was nothing we could do. My forward auxiliary diesel engine was in operation, but there was no area to pump out. The ship had taken a position of static balance and nothing materially that we could do within our means could help the ship. If felt that the jettisoning of heavy weights would only upset this balance . . . so my first thought was to get hold of the salvage parties.

The salvage plan for this area was quite elaborate, and I decided to take advantage of it. I called alongside two PC [patrol craft] boats to take off my wounded and a good proportion of my crew, just to get them out of the way.

In the black of night, I didn't know when she might break in two. I felt that the keel was broken, that all that was holding me together was probably the starboard shaft and the starboard side of the ship. So I thought of the safety of the crew as being the most important thing at the time since I knew that the salvage tugs would come to me shortly, so I removed the wounded half of the crew on these two PCs and then the ship gave another lurch. I thought she might break, so I called a DE [destroyer escort] and put all my key men, about 150 of them, and key officers, and myself on this

Truck and tents of a naval beach battalion on Omaha Beach in June 1944.

DE, and I requested the skipper to lie off about 100 yards until the salvage tugs arrived.

The ship took a list of about two more degrees when I left, and the starboard rail went further under the water.

The crew throughout the operation followed the best traditions of the navy. There was no panic, everybody did their job. Men remained at their station till they were told to leave. It was about an hour and fifteen minutes before all hands were clear of the ship.

Two PCs went into the transport area to the bigger ships while I stayed off close aboard, watching the ship. Throughout the night she drifted toward the Cherbourg coast, which was another reason for my wanting the crew off, because I knew as soon as she got within range of the Cherbourg coast that she would be taken under fire by eleven-inch guns in that area.

However, at 6 o'clock in the morning, two salvage tugs appeared on the scene, and we immediately proceeded back to our ship, helped the salvage tugs secure the lines to the ship, and they took her in tow into the advanced transport area. There the salvage parties inspected her, and the decision was made to remove topside weights and to strengthen the side and have divers look at the keel. There were so many other ships at that time damaged that not much could be done on my ship.

About two o'clock in the afternoon on the 8th, they decided there was danger of her sinking, and if she sank in the transport area, she would definitely been an obstruction. So they moved me down into the fire support area about a mile and a half off the beach. We arrived there about four o'clock in the afternoon. En route to this area, we suddenly saw two floating mines about 100 yards off the starboard bow, and we immediately screamed to the tug that was towing us alongside to pull us out of the way. People had had just about enough of mines and to have hit that would have been rather a crucial moment. By the fine ship handling of the captain of that tug, he managed to pull us clear and anchored us, using his own anchors.

Salvage work continued throughout the afternoon and early evening. By this time the crew and officers and myself that had originally come aboard were rapidly reaching the point of exhaustion, so I decided to place a relief party on board of three officers, that had not been on board previously, and about fifteen men as a security watch. I gave them instructions that if at any time the ship appeared in danger of breaking up, to hail the tug, which would either be alongside or nearby to take them off.

On the early morning of the 9th, the area was heavily bombed by the enemy and one 2,000-pound bomb landed abut fifty yards off the ship's bow and it shook the ship terribly and it had indicated the first evidence of the stern working itself loose.

The break of the deck had originally been quite level and now the stern section began rising but still the bulkheads were intact, the bilges were dry, and we felt that the ship would eventually be saved and live to fight again. However, about ten o'clock on the morning of the 9th, she suddenly gave a terrific crunch and broke in two. There was sufficient time for everybody to jump clear into the water to be picked up by the tugs. The bow slid down aft and the stern slid down forward and just as the bow was about to go underwater, she turned over so that the keel was exposed and she broke in two and rapidly sank out of sight.

She sank about thirty-two hours after she was originally struck.

The *DE Bates*, *PC 1232*, and *PC 1263* were the ships involved in rescuing the crew of the *Meredith* during these operations. Thirty-five members of the crew, including two officers, were lost, and twenty-five were hospitalized. However, it is not clear if the *Meredith* actually struck a mine, since the commander of Destroyer Squadron 17 reported on July 5, 1944, that on the night of June 7–8 the *Meredith* had been the victim of a glide-bomb attack from an He 177. According to the report, destroyer *Jeffers* picked up guided missile signals five times between 1:35 and 2:00 A.M. and the last missile hit the *Meredith* at 2:05 A.M. The "*Meredith* listed and down by the stern with a large hole in port side abreast No. 2 stack." However, Samuel Eliot Morison is one of the few sources for this version of the event and other writers remain silent on the subject. According to Morison, this was the most serious damage inflicted by the *Luftwaffe* in 1,683 sorties against the Allied navy in the first week of the invasion.[12]

The smaller naval vessels had additional problems beside enemy fire. Ens. Donald E. Irwin had a great deal of difficulty trying to unload the cargo from his *LCT 614* at Omaha Beach on D-Day. After fruitless attempts, he finally dropped off the American troops on a British beach. As he looked for a place to anchor for the night, he passed one of the American battleships.

You'll never know how tremendously huge a battleship is until you look up at it from fairly close by from an LCT. Anyway, the thought entered my mind. What could offer more security than anchoring close by a battleship? And believe me, after what had happened in the preceding hours, we were

12. The *Dictionary of American Naval Fighting Ships* (published by the Navy Department) claims it was a mine.

looking for security. So we anchored far enough away from the battleship so that when it swung on its anchor chain it wouldn't hit us, yet close enough to feel secure.

As I remember, it was just starting to get dark. We were all dead tired, having been underway all night from Portland, England, then the landing itself, which left us all in a state of shock. I don't believe any of us had any appetites then or probably for a couple of days afterward. We had orders to proceed the next morning to the British D-Day invasion beaches. . . .

So we had just settled in when a terrible explosion took place between us and the battleship. What had happened was that German aerial reconnaissance had spotted the battleship's anchoring place and a German plane had passed overhead and dropped a bomb meant for the battleship, but it missed and almost got us. That German plane took several passes at the battleship, and the battleship opened fire and shot the plane down. Believe me, we got the engines started, raised anchor, and got out of there as fast as we could. We anchored by some smaller ships and thereafter continued that practice. We learned an extremely valuable lesson—the enemy was after the larger ships and we could be killed by just being an innocent bystander.

The next morning we proceeded as per our orders to the British beaches. Our assignment was to go alongside anchored British and American merchant ships (mostly Liberty ships) assigned to us, tie up to them, have them load us with vehicles and equipment, and then make a landing on the beach. . . .

For the first weeks, we operated unloading ships night and day. At night it was most difficult for we had to operate under black-out rules, making it extremely difficult to locate the ship we were to help unload and then find our way to the assigned spot on the beach. I was thankful that I had another ensign, my executive officer, to relieve me in command of the ship during all these continuous hours of ship handling.

Ensign Irwin's LCT continued to operate off the beaches throughout the summer.

Ens. Walter G. Treanor, a deck officer on *LST 58*, crossed the Channel with the invasion fleet, and late on June 7, his vessel sailed from Utah Beach loaded with wounded army personnel.

We didn't go in to unload our tanks until sometime on June 7. We sat off the beach on June 6 and, except for a couple of strafings by German planes, it almost seemed like a movie. It was hard to relate to it until we started receiving the wounded that came out to us on LCTs, LCVPs, and smaller craft. Then the horrible reality set in. We had a much better appreciation of what those people on the beach were going through. It was a revealing experience to see that it isn't like it is in the movies.

As we left the beachhead loaded with wounded, there was a column of about eight of us. We were the lead ship and had to come out through a very narrow marked channel, which was swept of mines. That was a very difficult time, and I was the officer of the deck bringing the ship out from the beach. I remember being terribly nervous with the thought—God forbid—that if we hit a mine, there was no way of getting many of the desperately wounded personnel off that tank deck and to safety. Fortunately, all the vessels made it. Some did not carry as many wounded as we did and had POWs.

The majority of the wounded we carried out were airborne troops who found their way back to the beach after their drops inland. I don't recall how many wounded we carried, but I do know our naval surgical team together with an army surgical team, which had come aboard in Plymouth with the invasion troops, were extremely busy. Many of the troopers did not survive despite the Herculean efforts of the surgeons and corpsmen on their behalf. I recall having to go down to the tank deck where stretchers covered an entire huge area and supervised the removal of the dead. We tried to treat them with tremendous respect, wrapping them in blankets before carrying them to the forward end of the tank deck where there was no choice but to stack the bodies somewhat like cordwood.

When we arrived back in England, I recall that we did not go to Plymouth, but shortened the trip by going to Portland or Weymouth. I will never forget that day as we lowered our ramp, taking the wounded, most of whom were not ambulatory, but there were perhaps several score on crutches or leaning on someone's shoulders. Most were on stretchers. In any event, we carried the wounded out before we started removing the bodies past the starboard side of the ship while the replacement troops (I don't recall what unit) entered, coming down the port side. It must have been a horrific experience for those troops coming in to see what was happening with the wounded as they boarded and the wounded departed. There were very few who could keep their eyes from the stack of about thirty dead wrapped in blankets.

On the trip to Omaha Beach on June 8 or 9, the situation was still unsettled. We were sitting on the beach, having unloaded our compliment of troops and equipment and taken on board about 500 German prisoners. We were waiting for the tide to come in so we could withdraw. I was up on the bridge at about noontime and the ship's company was at lunch when we came under fire by a sniper. We never did find out from where he was firing. He did bounce a couple off the bridge, but no one was hurt. He fired about three or four rounds and we heard nothing further. He may have been eliminated by the numerous troops on the beach.

The prisoners were on the tank deck without even elementary sanitary facilities. I really don't think they minded that much, they were seemingly happy to be out of the war. They did discover the stretchers stacked along the bulkhead, ordinarily used for the wounded. The troops that we took out were frankly not very impressive compared to some we took out later when the prime German troops were committed. They were of various nationalities and from conquered countries. A couple of trips later, we began to bring out the professional German troops, and there was a marked difference. They were extremely scary in their militarism and open defiance. To my amazement, the British, to whom we turned over the prisoners, knew how to handle them and make them straighten up and pay attention.

Ensign Treanor's LST continued to shuttle between England and Normandy, mainly Omaha Beach.

Some veterans of nightmarish Exercise Tiger, like Lt(jg). Eugene M. Eckstam, went back on duty and participated in the Normandy invasion. After Lieutenant Eckstam lost his LST during Exercise Tiger, he and the other survivors were given shore leave. Then Eckstam was reassigned as a ship's doctor to *LST 391*. His vessel carried part of the 5th Ranger Battalion headquarters to a

OPERATING AND EXPANDING THE BEACHHEADS 63

Phoenix section of the Mulberry being towed into place during the first days after the invasion.

point off Omaha Beach. This group was not to land until D+1, so they arrived after invasion fleet. His LST carried mostly field grade officers.

We remained offshore for about five days, until Omaha Beach could be secured and they could be discharged from our ship. Being a survivor of a torpedoing, I was extremely jittery on the approach to the coast and hearing the bombardment. During this time of cruising up and down the coast of France, we were being shelled by shore batteries and bombed by airplanes, so it was necessary to keep moving constantly. Raids came so frequently that I actually slept through air-raid drills in the middle of the night. We were not too far from the cruiser *Augusta*, which sent salvos ashore with great regularity.

We were not particularly afraid during this particular time except that an errant shell might hit us. After we discharged the army and its trucks onto Rhino ferries, which carried them to shore, we proceeded to Utah Beach. We again remained about a mile offshore. The DUKWs brought army casualties on litters, twelve at a time, from an army field hospital out to our ship. I made a round trip with one of these DUKWs to survey the army position on shore. I must say that it was extremely well organized. The field hospital was made of tents and located several city blocks from the sea on level ground. It looked like it was a stateside operation and very efficient. All the army casualties were very well taken care of, all medications were up to date, the wounds were cleaned and pain medications given to them. The soldiers were in as good spirits as possibly could be expected.

On board the ship, we had about 225 American casualties and around 20–25 German prisoners who were casualties. We treated our own individuals, then we treated the Germans, but they got the same treatment our boys did.

The logistics of taking care of this number of casualties was faulty. We had far too few syringes and needles for the administration of penicillin. A 120cc syringe was used to inject twenty soldiers with penicillin. This was done every three hours, and the needles were sterilized at that point of time. There was no way we could sterilize the needle between each patient or we would never have gotten around to all of them and they would have suffered possible fatal consequences from their infections from wounds. I don't know how many cases of hepatitis we caused by this particular happening.

Aboard ship, back across the Channel, the ship's company was taking photographs and other trinkets from the German POWs. I reported this to the captain, and he made all the men return these treasures to the prisoners. We are proud of the fact that these boys were treated humanely and the same as our boys. They obviously expected different treatment and showed their appreciation that they were treated in a respectful manner. We discharged our casualties in the port of Falmouth.

We brushed a British ship, which crossed our bow and damaged the bow doors. We gave the proper signals, but the ship seemed to ignore them. We went into dry dock, and our medical group was sent to study chemical warfare. It seems it was taken quite seriously that the Germans would use gas out of desperation, and our medics were trained to treat gas casualties.

According to Eugene Eckstam, many medical groups returned to the States at that time. He returned home on the seaplane tender *Albermale* and was assigned to a Seabee base in California. Later, in 1945, he was sent to the Philippines.

The Coast Guard LCIs continued operating off the beachheads after June 6. After *LCI 85* sank on June 6, BM2/C Elmer E. Carmichael and other members of the crew ended up on a tug.

The next day, they transferred us when we came alongside an LST that was going back to England to pick up the next load. We went back with them, and they put us in a survivor camp in Plymouth. They gave us a Red Cross Survivor Kit, which had toilet articles and red pinstriped trousers. I had on a blue slip-over sweater, and the only identifications I had was my dog tags. They gave us a British army battle jacket, which I still have. I was dressed in these pinstriped trousers, blue sweater, British army jacket, and white sailor hat. They allowed us to go into Plymouth and warned us not to leave the Plymouth area because the shore patrol knew who we were by the way we were dressed.

This kid off the same ship I was on had a girlfriend stationed in the Woman's Land Army about sixty-five miles from there, and he wanted me to go up there to visit this girlfriend of his. He said she had a girlfriend stationed there with her who was good-looking, so I decided I would go with him, although we knew we weren't supposed to. We caught a bus and rode it as far as it would go and hitchhiked out to this farmhouse. We got out there in the late afternoon. A woman owned this farm and she fixed supper for us, and all five of us sat there eating supper. About that time, the light sprang up. They had searchlights on the house. Somebody knocked on the door. It was a couple of English policemen. We had been reported as being German paratroopers and they took us to the jail and when we got into jail they were asking us a lot of questions. They told me I looked like I was a German and I told them I was half-German—my mother was born in Vienna, Austria, and was German. They thought we were enemy paratroopers, and they wanted identification, which we didn't have. They were asking us questions about Chicago since apparently one of the policemen had lived there at one time. I told them all I knew about Chicago, but it wasn't much. Finally, I convinced them to let me call the shore patrol down in Plymouth. They sent a jeep and picked us up. It was about 2 o'clock in the morning when we finally got back to the survivor camp and we really got chewed out, but they didn't do anything.

About two weeks later, we went up to Scotland by train and loaded on to the *West Point* [troopship] for the trip to Boston. I believe we had about 4,000 German prisoners aboard. It irritated me because they fed them three meals a day and we got one meal and complained. They said the rules of war required the prisoners receive three meals.

I was supposed to swab the long passageway every morning. I said baloney on that, so I went back on the fantail where they had a mooring line coil that was big enough that we could get inside and play poker all the way back to the States. When we reached Boston, that was the end of my LCI duty.

On June 6, S1/C Robert McCrory was fished out of the sinking *LCI 93* by the crew of the destroyer *Emmons*, and he spent that night on the destroyer. While he was on board, the crew also pulled out of the heavy seas a German flyer who had been shot down.

They rescued him, but he lived about half an hour after they picked him up. According to the doctor, this German flyer had a pocketful of rubbers and he also had syphilis! We couldn't figure out why he had all the rubbers when he already had syphilis. That tale spread all over the ship like wildfire.

We spent about five days on the *Emmons* before we went back to England and they put us in what was known as a survivors' camp. It was a large camp and consisted of people who had lost a ship. They were all dressed like I was. When I went over the side I had dungarees and a life jacket. One of the men on the *Emmons* gave me a pair of galoshes and a dungaree jumper. We stayed in the camp for two weeks. It was almost the end of the second week before we got navy clothes. We had no toothbrush, money, razor, or anything. The Red Cross came through one time and gave out little packages consisting of a plastic razor, a tube of toothpaste about as large as your finger, and a toothbrush. The first time I brushed my teeth all the bristles came out in my mouth and I had to spit them out. No razor blades came with plastic razor. We were really well off in that respect. They wouldn't give us liberty, so we made a hole in the back fence and got out on our own. Everybody knew we were dressed like that because we had lost our ships. We would go in the pub, and everybody wanted to buy us drinks. We found it hard not to accept because we didn't want to hurt relations between our countries! The MPs and SPs would pick us up and bring us back to base. While they did this, more were slipping out through the hole. Finally, they just opened the gate and told us to go on into town and quit bothering us. We moved from this to another camp somewhere in England and stayed a week or so. They passed out all the

Purple Hearts and so forth, and then they sent us up to Scotland. We caught a ship out of Glasgow, the old luxury liner *America*. We landed in Boston in the latter part of July.

Coast Guardsman GM3/C Frances L. Enlow arrived on his *LCI 326* on D-Day. For him, the most memorable event of the day happened when some soldiers tried to bring aboard an explosive-filled remote-controlled Goliath, a miniature tank they had captured. He and his fellow shipmates spent the remainder of D-Day rescuing downed pilots. Enlow is sure that on the second day he shot down an Me 109.

The events of June 7 also remained clearly branded in the mind of CMOMM Ralph Gault, serving on *LCI 88*.

We had a load of the injured we were bringing off the beaches. We inadvertently got between the battleship *Texas* and the beaches and when they let go of a salvo, they split our seams and knocked around everything. Even the bunks jumped out of their bins. We were sent out there for a few days as a communications ship, although we begged to go back to England for repairs since we were taking on water. Fortunately, our pumps kept up with it. The packing back on the shafts was blown out. It was quite an affair there.

When you brought the wounded alongside the transports, the skipper of the transport would say, "Take them back to the beach and bury them!" Those son of a bitches were never on the beach and never knew what we went through. These big transports were luxury compared to what we had and they didn't want the bodies.

I was belowdecks and I was in charge of damage control as the chief engineer, so when we had all the damage up on the bow and lost our manpower, I was called up above decks to take over and to assess damage control. Before I even had a chance at that, somebody shoved a fire hose in my hand and I had to wash all the blood, guts, and canned milk off the decks because almost all the deckhands above were wounded or sick—really sick. I don't know how I kept going, but I managed.

You could hear the explosions and I could feel the thud aboard ship when we got hit and you could hear everybody screaming back-and-forth on the intercom. We had a pair of earphones—the big earphones with a chest plate with the microphone on it. Of course you could hear everything going back-and-forth, and you were not heard until you pressed the button. When I say all hell cut loose, it cut loose. We weren't on the beach too long—probably three minutes. We bounced around out there for a while and finally took a load of prisoners after three or four loads of injured out to the ships. Finally, we took a load of prisoners back over to England. We tied up and were put in dry dock while they rewelded all our seams. I don't remember any details since I was down in the engine room. We were in dry dock for close to ten days for repairs. We had a blown engine, seams to re-weld, patch up the front end and all the holes in the side with square patches.

Lt. Ed Fabian commanded the Coast Guard's *LCI 86*. He was unable to see the Sherman duplex-drive tanks that he had watched during training exercises swim ashore on the morning of D-Day. Later in the day, he had tied up his LCI to the old British battleship *Centurion* after it was sunk as a blockship.

We stayed about a week. They started bringing all the stuff into the beach and putting together the Mulberry. It was still a little bit rough, but nothing like later on. They put it all together and the blockships were already in place. The piers went in and the floating docks so they could run up the LSTs and other vessels. We were part of the breakwater. We tied up just inside of the Mulberry and moved up and down the beach after that.

Y2/C George Gray was aboard *LCI 87*, which served as a headquarters.

On the second or third day, we bent a propeller on an underwater object, and I think it was the fourth day we landed on the beach at almost high tide to salvage a prop from a burned out LCI. The beach had been washed almost clean to the high-water mark, but I saw a torso (no head, arms, or legs) on the beach and saw that the LCI had hit a mine forward, which started a fire and killed most of the soldiers in the forward hold. Their bodies were still there.

During the repair, two or three men from the ship and I rode on a DUKW full of mortar shells to near the front. On the way, we came under fire from a sniper in a church tower. We took cover in a ditch, but in a couple of minutes soldiers manning a twin .50 caliber machine gun cut the weakened steeple off at its base. Along with the sniper, it fell to the street. Further on, we passed a large field, about twenty acres, full of dead soldiers, row on row, side by side, with Graves Registration personnel working. We returned to the beach with no intent of going inland again.

CHAPTER 3

June Days

The Airborne Troops Struggle On

After June 7, both American airborne divisions began to solidify their position as more troops and equipment arrived from the beach. The arrival of the 325th Glider Infantry Regiment by air that day helped stabilize the position of the 82nd "All-American" Airborne Division. On June 8, the 327th Glider Infantry Regiment finally moved into position after landing by sea. With these reinforcements came tanks and heavier supporting weapons. In addition, the infantry divisions began to take over larger sectors of the front.

After regrouping and securing the beachhead on June 7, the American airborne troops, and their sea-landed armored reinforcements, finally succeeded in expanding their position. The "Screaming Eagles" of the 101st Airborne Division made progress along the Douve towards Carentan. In the meantime, after a few days of hard fighting, the 82nd Airborne Division secured a bridgehead across the Merderet, opening the way for an advance across the Cotentin Peninsula. Only one major obstacle lay in front of them: the Douve at St. Sauveur-le-Vicomte. Once this town fell on June 16, the Germans were left with a tenuous hold on the peninsula and Cherbourg.

Graves Registration Officer

Capt. Harold A. Shebeck of the 82nd Airborne Division was assigned to the position of graves registration officer. According to him, the S-4 (supply officer) of the regiment was usually the one designated to perform the dismal but necessary task. Although Shebeck was an infantry officer, he wound up working closely with the Quartermaster Graves Registration units. In addition, Shebeck was responsible for gathering casualty statistics for his unit. After the regimental commanding officer asked him to calculate the ratio of Americans to Germans killed, he determined that it was two to one Germans. Later he also appraised the S-2 (intelligence officer) that twice as many Americans were killed by artillery and mortar fire than by small arms.

An hour after his glider landed in Normandy, Shebeck came across another wrecked glider, its pilot slumped dead over the controls. It was the first casualty in Normandy whose removal he had to arrange. After a cursory examination of the corpse, his men removed it from the craft and took it to a large field where a Graves Registration unit was already setting up shop in a smashed Horsa glider. Shebeck entered the Horsa in search of the unit's temporary office and found it at the end of its steeply tilted floor. Having accomplished his business, he laboriously climbed back up to leave. The setup tickled his sense of humor every time he went there on business, providing fleeting moments of hilarity in an otherwise grim activity.

After their personal information was processed in the glider "office," the fallen soldiers were loaded on a 2½-ton truck and

Dead paratroopers are wrapped in parachutes before burial.
NATIONAL ARCHIVES

taken to a large temporary cemetery set up in a large field near Ste-Mère-Église.

The first time I saw this cemetery, it was a gruesome sight to behold, with bodies laid out row upon row occupying several acres. Some burials were already taking place. One half of the individual's dog tags were left with the body, the other half stayed with the personal effects. If only one tag was found on the body it stayed with the personal effects. Bodies were wrapped in shelter halves, blankets, or mattress covers, with most of them being buried in mattress covers. Graves were dug to a depth of five feet with only one body to a grave. In hasty battlefield burials, and there were many,

continued

Graves Registration Officer *continued*

A paratrooper from the 101st Airborne stands guard as German prisoners dig graves. NATIONAL ARCHIVES

graves were often only sufficiently deep to prevent elements from exposing the body.

For burials being made hurriedly not in established cemeteries, an official War Department form, Report of Burial, had to be completed, and I accomplished some of these. There was a space on the form to provide a sketch giving the location by means of a map reference and coordinates, or by reference to a prominent permanent landmark. Information had to be specific, accurate, and complete. Personal effects taken from the body were listed on the burial report form along with information regarding the identity of the deceased, organization, emergency addressee, all of which was turned over to the Graves Registration unit wrapped in a personal

effects bag, towel, or any such available material. Government property was not included with personal effects but was turned in to a Salvage Collecting Point already operating.

In one of these burial reports, Harold Shebeck wrote that the soldier in question was killed by mortar fire near Montebourg on June 9, 1944. He had the following personal effects: "Bill Fold, one pr. glasses, two pocket knives, one ring, 5 British stamps, $27.10 French money, one shilling, 5½ pence British money, and a Soldier's Pay Card." An accompanying sketch showed map coordinates, indicated the name of the map sheet, located the burial site, and noted: "Grave marked by rifle, helmet, dog tag." The body was to be removed as soon as possible after this hasty burial to the temporary cemetery near Ste-Mère-Église by the Graves Registration unit. Shebeck kept a duplicate of the document as a keepsake and as a grim reminder of the consequences of war.

The German dead were transported separately to their own temporary cemetery near Montebourg. Captain Shebeck was there when a truckload of bodies arrived a few days after the invasion. "When the truck stopped, the front end was alongside what looked like a burned tree stump. As I looked at this 'tree stump' more closely, I realized that it was the burned torso of a human body from about midsection to the knees, which had previously been brought in for burial."

continued

Graves Registration Officer *continued*

According to Shebeck, two things were usually found on the bodies of most of the German soldiers: a head of cabbage and a loaf of dark rye bread, both partially eaten.

In the summer heat, the corpses decomposed within a matter of hours. "Faces turned a distinct green color, heads bloated, and it was not unusual to find bodies where the skin on the face and head had already burst," he recalled. The overpowering odor disturbed Shebeck the most. The bodies were buried as quickly as possible in order to prevent the spread of disease.

A number of German prisoners were ordered to unload the bodies from the trucks in the rear areas where the cemeteries were far from the front. This alleviated the problem of manpower shortage for the Graves Registration units, especially when it was necessary to the get the bodies buried as soon as possible.

Due to the nature of his assignment, Captain Shebeck often had unpleasant surprises. One day, for instance, he was informed by a French farmer that there was a dead American in the barnyard. When he went to investigate, he found a dead officer lying face down with two strips of tape on his shoulder straps to indicate his rank. It was a company commander from his regiment who had been promoted to captain just before the invasion and had used the tape to indicate his new rank because he had not been able to get a set of bars.

Sometimes, as the following incident illustrates, the Graves Registration units had very little to work with.

Chaplain Francis L. Sampson, 501st Parachute Infantry Regiment, blesses fallen paratroopers. In the background are German prisoners preparing to dig graves. NATIONAL ARCHIVES

One day, I was supervising a detail of men who were transporting bodies to cemeteries and the only remains we found of one person was simply a pile of intestines. There were no other bodies around the immediate area, which was an apple orchard, and there was a German tank still burning in a roadside ditch nearby. We had to assume the body had been blown out of the tank and the remains were swept into a mattress cover with a broom and taken to the German cemetery.

A paratrooper of the 505th Parachute Infantry Regiment on a horse he found, Ste-Mère-Église, June 7, 1944.
NATIONAL ARCHIVES

Four soldiers of the 82nd Airborne Division, June 12, 1944.
NATIONAL ARCHIVES

On June 10, Field Marshal Rommel took stock of the situation and concluded that the Allies' objective was to establish a large bridge-head between the Orne and Vire Rivers. This beachhead, he surmised, would be used for a major thrust inland. The American troops that had landed in the Cotentin would move quickly against Cherbourg and westward to cut off the peninsula. Rommel and other German commanders were also convinced that the Allies would need a port like Cherbourg to improve their logistical situation and that if the battle for the peninsula became "too fierce," they would switch to an early inland offensive from the bridgehead between the Orne and the Vire. Rommel intended to pull back most of his armor from the British front and shift it to a position where it could support an offensive against the Utah beachhead between Monte-bourg and Carentan. If the Allies advanced from their bridgehead, he would use his armor to counterattack beyond the range of Allied naval guns. Rommel still believed he had a chance to crush the Utah beachhead because the units already committed continued to withstand both Allied air and naval bombardment. Even if he failed to destroy the beachhead, he would have a firm defensive hold along the Douve and Merderet and be able to maintain control of Cherbourg. However, Hitler categorically rejected Rommel's plan and ordered him to focus the main effort of his army group on an assault against the British at Caen. Thus, even though they failed to take Caen, the British achieved their objective of drawing in most of the German panzer units.

Even though Hitler rejected Rommel's plan, reinforcements slowly made their way to the front, hindered by Allied air power. However, it proved too little to stop the Allies in the Cotentin. The troops of the "Famous Fourth," the 4th Infantry Division, had already begun their

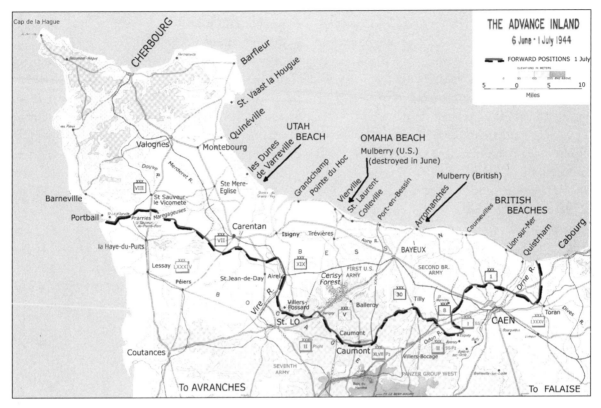

The advance inland. U.S. ARMY

push northward toward Montebourg, initially aided by the 505th Parachute Infantry. The 82nd Airborne Division expanded its bridgehead on the Merderet. These airborne troops of the "All-American" Division moved west and crossed and secured a bridgehead on the Douve River at St. Sauveur-le-Vicomte. Finally, the 60th Infantry Regiment of the 9th "Varsity" Infantry Division, advancing north of the 82nd Airborne Division from its bridgehead at Ste-Colombe on the Douve had succeeded in sealing the peninsula by June 19 when it took Barneville-sur-Mer. The division's 47th Infantry passed through the paratrooper's bridgehead at St. Sauveur-le-Vicomte and advanced on Portbail (about five miles southwest of Barneville-sur-Mer). The paratroopers and glider men of both airborne divisions held most of the southern front in the Cotentin from

the marshes of the Praries Marecageuses to the Carentan, facing the remnants of the German 265th Infantry Division and the newly arrived 17th SS Panzer Grenadier Division.

The Glider Men

On June 7, the glider pilots reported to the divisional headquarters where they were assigned miscellaneous duties, including burial details and standing guard. After a few days, Flight Off. Eddie Anderson, who had landed his glider with Mission Keokuk, marched from Heisville to Utah Beach with a group of other pilots. They took with them 365 German prisoners. When they reached the beach area, they placed the prisoners in a compound. The glider pilots boarded DUKWs, and the beachmaster directed them to the ships that would take them back to England. Anderson and his fellow officers climbed a net up to the deck of the ship where they were warmly welcomed and taken belowdecks for coffee and juice. The next morning, they were back in England at their base in Aldermaston.

Glider pilot Lt. Lambert Wilder also escorted a group of prisoners back to Utah Beach where he watched them board an LST for the trip to England and a prison camp. Wilder and a few other pilots were taken to the British monitor *Erebus*, one of two British monitors off Normandy. This World War I veteran mounted two 15-inch battleship-size guns in a turret for shore bombardment. The HMS *Erebus*, recalled Wilder, had had a "flash back" from one of its guns and was returning to England for repairs. Since the pilots were officers, they were treated with exceptional deference on the ship and shared quarters with the crew's officers.

Flight Off. Chas Gauntt, who broke his leg on landing, was evacuated sooner than his fellow pilots because of his injury. The vehicle he lay in traveled down one of the narrow country roads and came across a large shell-shocked bull that charged and almost overturned it. Around another corner, the occupants of the vehicle came face to face with a German tank, its gun pointed right at them. After a heart stopping moment, they realized that they were in no danger, since the tank had been knocked out earlier. After this last scare, they reached the beach, where Gauntt was evacuated on an LST and taken to a General Hospital in England where he remained in traction until September. After that, he was sent home for further hospitalization and was not released until October 1945.

Despite his injuries, Gauntt was lucky, because the pilot with whom he had originally flown, wanting his old copilot back, had switched. The glider in which the two men flew hit a brick wall, killing them. Lieutenant Wilder was also for-tunate. The pilot with whom he had normally flown had been detached from the group. As he came in on the evening of June 6, he hit a tree and was killed instantly with his copilot.

Back in England, a number of glider pilots who missed out on the Normandy invasion were readying for another mission in June. Hope blossomed in the breast of 2nd Lt. William Knickerbocker, a draftee from California who had volunteered to fly gliders. In Italy, he had not seen any action, and he had actually gone to the front to see what was happening. He could not bear the thought of missing another glider operation. Now, as he volunteered to fly Horsa gliders in on a mission beyond Caen, his fervent dream to see some action was about to materialize.

We were issued British uniforms and tin-pan hats and dressed exactly like the British troopers. They took us down to Welford Park for our briefings. On about the third day we had been issued uniforms and everything we needed and were ready to go. I think I was to carry about twenty troopers and six bicycles with some other equipment—all British. I don't know what unit, but I believe it was from the 1st Airborne. We were all ready to go for our final briefing. During the briefing in a blacked out room, the colonel was called to the phone and came back in about fifteen minutes. He said, "Gentlemen, I am sorry to tell you the mission has been called off, there are two panzer divisions parked on our landing zone." That was the end of that.

Despite the fact that there were numerous glider pilots who had not taken part in the invasion, the men who had were still needed back in England for future missions. They returned to England as soon as the troops they had carried into Normandy set out on their missions.

The actions of the 325th Glider Infantry Regiment on June 8 appear to be rather confusing since its battalions were operating separately for a short period of time. The 2nd Battalion was moving with the 505th Parachute Infantry Regiments in support of the 4th Division's left flank operations as that division advanced on Montebourg. The 1st and 3rd Battalions were sent to help secure a bridgehead on the Meredet in support of the 507th and 508th Parachute Infantry Regiments.

Lt. Wayne Pierce was en route to the 1st Battalion of the 325th Glider Infantry Regiment early on the morning of June 8 after attending a briefing at the division command post near Ste-Mère-Église the previous night. After sleeping overnight in a field, Lieutenant Pierce and his superiors began their trip back to the 1st Battalion.

At daylight, we were up and on our way back. . . . Major Sanford [Teddy H. Sanford, acting battalion CO][1] rode in the jeep with General Gavin. I rode on the front hood of the jeep as a lookout for whatever. The road was heavily tree-lined and the trees overhung the road so that little daylight came through. Sanford and I spent most of the day relaxing with Colonel Lewis [Harry L. Lewis, CO of the 325th] and his regimental headquarters group. The 2nd Battalion . . . was attached to the 505th for an attack north. . . . During the day, as we discussed possible commitments for our battalion, small arms fire was sporadic. At one point, bullets were clearly audible zipping through the air where we were standing. Everyone hit the ground except Colonel Lewis. He did not move. Colonel Lewis was well liked by the men . . . and over-age for a combat airborne leader. Unknown at the time, he was suffering from cancer and would die within a year.

That afternoon, on orders from Gavin and Lewis, Sanford made plans for our battalion to ford the Merderet River and attack the Germans holding the west bank of the river at the La Fière-Canquigny Church Causeway. We were to be led across the ford of the Merderet by a 507th lieutenant who had come across the ford seeking assistance for a group of 507th men under the command of Lieutenant Colonel Timmes. These 100 men under Timmes had been holed up at a farm and orchard since landing.

After a two-man patrol from the isolated paratroopers on the west bank successfully crossed the Merderet on a barely submerged road and made contact, headquarters directed the 325th Glider Infantry to launch an assault across the river to reach Lieutenant Colonel Timmes's isolated group of the 2nd Battalion, 507th Parachute Infantry. The 3rd Battalion was to force a crossing to the main causeway at Canquigny, and the 1st Battalion was to move north along the railroad embankment, across the Merderet, and into the flooded area until it turned west along the submerged road. Col. George V. Millet led a group of isolated paratroopers west of Amfreville toward Timmes's group, but Millet's force was driven back during its night move by a German position consisting of a group of buildings known as the Grey Castle. This same position also stopped the 1st Battalion, 325th Glider Infantry, when it reached the west bank of the flooded area. Clearly, the American paratroopers needed a new action plan.

---

1. The battalion commander, Lt. Col. Klemm Boyd, was injured on June 7.

Sanford's plan of attack was that we proceed in a column of companies in the order of Company C, A, and B. Company C was to ford the river, turn slightly to the right, and attack what we called the Grey Castle. . . . Company C was to make a show of firepower against the Grey Castle, then fall back to the farm orchard. Company A, next in line, was to proceed through the orchard, turn slightly to the left, and follow a country road about one half mile to a road junction. Here they were to set up a blocking action to keep German reinforcements away from the La Fière Causeway. Company B, which followed, would pass through the orchard then turn almost 180 degrees to the left and attack toward the Canquigny Church and the La Fière Causeway. After falling back from the Grey Castle, Company C was to align on the right of Company B in the attack toward the causeway.

We started moving at 11 P.M. along the railroad, which paralleled the river. The flooded Merderet was several hundred yards wide at this point. Major Sanford moved out with the lead company, and I shuttled along the column to make sure all units moved as planned. Standing at the turnoff spot where we were to ford the river, I realized that the tail of the column had passed me; no more troops were coming along the tracks in the dark. Knowing that all units had not yet passed, I ran back along the track about one quarter mile and found the tail of the column sitting on the rails resting. The man in the lead who had broken contact in the column was asleep. [He] was a Company B man whom I had disciplined several times for sleeping during training lectures. I shook him awake and got the men moving. We caught up with the rest of the column after we forded the river.

It was a dark, black night as we forded the river. Company C made a lot of noise and drew a lot of fire in their feint on the Grey Castle. Company A proceeded through the orchard and moved out on the road leading to Amfreville. Company B was making the swing to the left toward Canquigny Church and the causeway as Company C came back in line. As we walked in the darkness, I talked to Lt. Brewster Johnson of Company C. He and his men were elated. They had done a lot of shooting and felt that they put fear in the Germans. Brewster said, "They can't shoot worth ———." Brewster (or "Rooster" as we called him) was a Georgia Cracker who got along well with the men. He had joined the 325th the same day I did in November 1942. He was KIA in the next hour.

Major Sanford and I, with one or two communications men, followed behind Company C in a position that we thought would put us near the center of the two attacking companies. We crossed a road that was to be one of our guiding terrain features in the attack, moved through a wheat field, and came to a small orchard. Our little headquarters group took a German prisoner from the corner of this orchard. He was not a very alert outpost guard for his unit. It was a little after 4 A.M., June 9, and still dark.

Up ahead, about forty yards and slightly to our right, Company C got into a very heavy firefight along a sunken road. Tracer fire was heavy from both sides. As the small arms fire ahead of us turned sporadic, the first light of dawn arrived. Objects took shape and the terrain around us was visible. Our small group was stretched out in a shallow ditch along the fence row of the orchard. Sanford was up ahead with the commo men, then me, the prisoner, and a runner or two. Looking to my right I could make out a German artillery piece located only a few feet from where we were. From the sounds up ahead it appeared that a German armored vehicle was moving up the sunken road toward Company C.

The firefight died down to just an occasional shot and became quiet. Sanford passed the word back that it "looks like Company C is wiped out, we had better move back." At that, everyone in our party, except me, got up and ran stooped over along the fence row back toward the wheat field. I watched them go, but I was not yet convinced that Company C was finished. Small arms fire in the Company B area some distance to the left was slight to heavy. Looking back, I watched the bobbing heads of Sanford and the CP group go over a little rise in the wheat field. The prisoner was moving just as fast as his captors and appeared to be taking the same evasive action.

There I sat, crouched on my haunches, looking and listening, very much alone. I ran to my right, past the artillery piece, across to the other side of the orchard. Running under an apple tree, my helmet was knocked off my head by a low branch. The helmet was uncomfortable to wear, but it gave you a sense of safety. I went back and picked it up. . . . On the other side of the orchard, I looked through the hedge and all about for some sign of Company C. I could hear activity along the sunken road but could not tell if this was friend or foe. By this time it was after 5:00 A.M. and quite light. I decided that if I wanted to be around for lunch that day, I had better get moving and find some friendly troops.

I carefully placed my dispatch case and binoculars under a bush in the hedge. . . .

Then I lost no time in moving back along the orchard fence and into the wheat field. Knowing that a moving target was hard to hit I bent over and ran. Once over the small rise in the wheat field, I came upon several Company C men who told me that their company was decimated. Some men had surrendered and many were killed and wounded. With these six or eight men, I moved back to the road we had crossed while moving up during darkness. German machine-gun fire was coming sporadically down this road from the Canquigny Church area. There was a steep bank on both sides of the road where we wanted to cross. I instructed the men to go one at a time and dart across the road. . . . I went last and when I hit the bank on the other side I dug into the dirt.

Across the road, we were within sight of the farm. By now I had accumulated a total of about twenty-five men, a straggler or two from Company A, a few who had fallen back from Company B, but most were from Company C. The Company C men were very demoralized. One man, Sergeant Mason, was without a weapon. He told me that he had gone forward to meet a German officer, thinking the German wanted to surrender. When he got close enough to see the German (it was still dark), the German held a pistol on him. Mason was still white as a sheet, but he got away minus his rifle. In future action Mason was a very good and dependable combat soldier. Another man, Sgt. Reynolds Koze, had lost his tommy gun, but picked up an M-1 rifle. Koze was still carrying the case with his tommy-gun ammunition. Seeing that I was armed with a tommy gun, he tried to give me his ammo. I did not want it for it was too heavy and cumbersome to carry. He was so insistent that I finally took it from him and, when he was not looking, quietly laid it on the ground and walked away.

To get some semblance of order, I organized this little band into two squads with a sergeant in charge of each. Then I told them we were going up to help Company B. Small arms fire in the Company B area was still sporadic to heavy. Just as we were ready to move out we received small arms fire from our rear. . . . At that point, not knowing what had happened to Company A, I decided . . . to head for the farm and orchard where we could get instructions from Major Sanford.

At the orchard, Major Sanford was directing the companies of the 1st Battalion into the perimeter defense the paratroopers had set up. The barn was being used as an aid station. Sanford and I established a CP with a radio operator and runners in a corner of the orchard. . . .

Small arms fire was very heavy interspersed with barrages of mortar fire. Many colored signal flares went up from the German positions and sometimes the hostile fire would cease completely when this happened. Shortly after 8:00 A.M., Major Sanford made radio contact with the Regimental CP across the river and we were able to get some supporting artillery fire. This seemed to quiet the Germans down, for the pressure began to let up on our position.

Second Lt. Paul S. Kinsey of the hard-hit Company C received the Distinguished Service Cross for his valor in action.

While his platoon was pinned down by flanking fire, Lieutenant Kinsey, although limping badly from a leg wound, personally halted and engaged an enemy truck which was closing in along the road on his platoon. The assistant driver of the truck opened fire with a machine pistol. Lieutenant Kinsey, in spite of this fire, moved forward, seized the barrel of the machine pistol, and dropped a grenade into the cab of the truck, setting it on fire and destroying the driver and assistant driver. Although knocked down by the explosion, Lieutenant Kinsey, hearing cries and movement in the rear of the truck, completed its destruction with a rifle grenade. Lieutenant Kinsey's act kept open a route of maneuver for his platoon and enabled his unit to inflict additional damage on the enemy.

Lieutenant Kinsey was wounded in the elbow, calf, and thigh and was captured when his platoon was overrun. He spent thirteen days in a German hospital, but at the first opportunity, he relieved a sleeping attendant of a P-38 pistol and escaped from captivity. He managed to find an American patrol and returned to friendly lines.

During the predawn German counterattack on Company C, 1st Battalion, PFC Charles N. DeGlopper, the tallest man in the regiment, stood in full view of the enemy, firing his BAR against the enemy, covering his company's withdrawal until enemy gunfire cut him down. He became the first and only man of the 325th Glider Infantry in Normandy to receive the Medal of Honor, albeit posthumously.

When Gen. James Gavin, the assistant division commander of the 82nd Airborne Division, realized that the 1st Battalion, 325th Glider Infantry, had been repulsed, he ordered the regiment's 3rd Battalion with the reinforced company led by Capt. Robert D. Rae from the 507th Parachute Infantry Regiment in support to attack directly across the causeway leading to Canquigny. He did not place too much faith in the performance of the 325th, which he considered to be inexperienced. In reality, only the 3rd Battalion, which came from the 401st Glider Infantry, was relatively green. During a supporting artillery barrage, which was lifted at 10:45 A.M., the 3rd Battalion moved up from Chef-du-Pont. The glider men had to follow the paratroopers along a stone wall because the smoke cover was not sufficient to obscure their progress. Although the Germans forced most of them back, a small group from Company G managed to reach the end of the causeway. A supporting tank disabled in a friendly minefield near a knocked-out German tank further constricted the causeway. Company G, followed by E, moved across the causeway. The Germans at Canquigny were cut off and surrendered. General Gavin ordered Captain Rae's company to speed up the attack just as Company F crossed the causeway. The 3rd Battalion firmly established a bridgehead, and Rae sent a patrol of paratroopers northwest to contact Timmes's paratroopers and the 1st Battalion, 325th Glider Infantry. By evening, the bridgehead extended from Timmes's paratroopers of the 507th Parachute Infantry in the north (where 1st Battalion, 325th, had crossed) to Lt. Col. Thomas Shanley's fifty-man force of the 2nd Battalion, 508th Parachute Infantry, in the south.

On June 8, Shanley's small group had to abandon the roadblock they had set up on the causeway the previous day and pulled back to Hill 30. On the night of June 8, Shanley sent a patrol back down to clear the causeway. However, Col. Roy Linquist of the 3rd Battalion on the other side of the Merderet decided it was too risky to send a convoy across the causeway. By the time the 325th launched its assault across the Merderet, the situation of the men of the 2nd Battalion under Colonel Shanley's command had begun to deteriorate. Sgt. Zane Schlemmer agonized as he listened to the moans of the wounded soldiers who could not be treated because there were no medical supplies left. To distance himself from the suf-

fering, he volunteered for outpost duty and the dangers it presented. One night, before he and his comrades were relieved, several of his companions volunteered to wade across the flooded marshes and river. Finally, after several days of isolation, Schlemmer's unit was able to call for artillery support from across the river. The rescue did not come a moment too soon for Schlemmer, whose outpost was under German attack. "After one firing to break up a German attack coming up a sunken lane very near our outpost, we captured and retrieved two small German artillery cannons and some shells," he recalled. They hauled their spoils back to Hill 30 and used the guns to repel the next German attack.

The 325th Glider Infantry Regiment was able to relieve most of the isolated parachute units west of the Merderet, as well as Shanley's group. The Germans were on the verge of losing control of the Merderet River and opening the way for Allied troops to advance across the Cotentin Peninsula.

Company C of the 1st Battalion, 325th Glider Infantry, lost all its officers and about half of its men during the early morning assault. Lieutenant Pierce took over its command and at about 5:00 P.M. led it southward to make contact with the 3rd Battalion. As Lieutenant Pierce organized his company's new position, he came across four German bodies piled in a ditch. "As I looked at them, I could see that one man was breathing," he said. He told one of his men who spoke German to order the enemy soldier to get up. The man popped up, followed by the other three men. After that, Pierce and his men settled in for a relatively calm night only disturbed by a lot of noise on the German side.

The 2nd Battalion of the 325th and the 505th Parachute Infantry operated north of Ste-Mère-Église between June 8 and 11. The 505th moved against Montebourg Station (about 2,000 yards southwest of the town of Montebourg), and the

2nd Battalion moved on its left flank to attack toward Le Ham. After advancing past Grainville, Capt. Joe Gault's Company F was pulled back and moved toward Le Ham to join up with the battalion's remaining companies. The 4th Division's 8th Infantry directed the operations of the 505th and the 2nd Battalion of the 325th Glider Infantry in the advance north. The 325th was pinned down during the first days of the attack, and it took heavy casualties. Finally, with support from the 505th and the 8th Infantry, the 2nd Battalion took Le Ham, but casualties were heavy. Gault learned that Captain Dickerson, the commander of Company E, had been seriously wounded and that the commander of Company G had been killed. Word was that Company G was down to three men and one officer. At Le Ham, for the first time since they had landed in Normandy, Gault and his men engaged the enemy in action.

The 2nd Battalion was given the mission to move on Le Ham. At H-Hour Colonel Swenson, the battalion commander, came into our area, and at dawn we moved out and advanced down a slight incline to a small brook. The fire was spasmodic to the brook, but accurate, and upon entering the brook all types of enemy fire broke out and the brook was mined with antipersonnel mines. Sgt. Forest Nipple, a squad leader from the 2nd Platoon was hit by such a mine and died on the spot.[2] I advanced on up the slope and noticed Sgt. Robert C. McCarty had been hit in the head. He was staggering around firing his rifle up in the sky. Colonel Swenson had been hit in the stomach and was trying to get up and move on. He was a man of guts, but his war was over. The fire became so severe that we had to move forward by crawling. We advanced

on a machine gun that was giving us immense problems. Grenades knocked out the gun and its gunners, and one gunner was set afire by a phosphorous grenade. After knocking out the machine gun, we advanced on toward our objective. At a barn we captured several Germans, and before I could stop him, an unnamed sergeant dropped to his knees and killed two of them. I knocked the sergeant's gun up and ordered him to cease fire.

This man had come to us in Ireland as a replacement. He was surly, unclean, and always needing a shave—anything but a squad leader. I looked for something to reduce him in rank, but he stayed just on the border. This sergeant, who shall remain unnamed, was a combat holy terror. He loved to go on patrol and while on patrol was fatally wounded. They brought him by me on a stretcher and he said, "Captain Gault, I'll be back." In a few hours, he was dead.

We regrouped and jumped off again, not far from Le Ham. Company F was on the right of the road leading into Le Ham. Because we had been ruffled up and lost many men, the men began to run and yell as we advanced. In the only charge I ever saw or participated in, we moved into Le Ham. Sgt. Fred A. Mason led us down a hedgerow. I was second and behind me was Sgt. Albert Kost. All of Company F came rushing behind us, and as we were just through the town, an artillery shell landed very near us. Sergeant Mason was hit in the foot. Sergeant Kost, behind me, was mortally hit and died screaming as I administered morphine to him. Again, I was not hit—hard to explain. We took up defensive

---

2. Gault is probably referring to the standard German antipersonnel mine, the S-Mine, which the GIs called the Bouncing Betty. When triggered, a small explosive charge threw a cylinder in the air that detonated a few feet above the ground, throwing out over 300 small steel balls.

positions and came under the heaviest 88 fire of the Normandy offensive. We were passed through and relieved to the rear to lick our wounds.

I had about fifty men left, and the Weapons Platoon and 1st Platoon officers. The Company G commander, Lieutenant Bloom, was killed on about the third day before entering Le Ham. The Company E commander was gone and Company G commander killed, so I sent Lieutenant Jones to take Company E. Then I received a telephone and wire crew, which stayed between the two companies. Company G did not have enough men to operate with and the other companies were like platoons.

Captain Gault did not recall receiving any fire support. However, he did remember that artillery firing in support accidentally hit advancing elements of the 4th Division in his sector and that he had to call for them to cease fire. Some 75-millimeter guns were attached for support. One day, a tank unit showed up, but the tank lieutenant said that he was not able to operate in hedgerows and withdrew.

On the night of June 8, T/5 Gerald Cummings drove Lieutenant Colonel Sitler, the executive officer of the 325th, in a jeep to look for the regiment's 1st and 2nd Battalions. They joined the command post that night somewhere southeast of Ste-Mère-Église. After the 1st Battalion established a bridgehead over the Merderet on June 9, they set up headquarters in a large stone house near Canquigny.

I had been on guard at the gate in the stone wall surrounding the house. When I was relieved, I went into the house and lay down and went to sleep. I was awakened by rifle bullets bouncing off the wall of the house. We had captured two German soldiers and

guards were taking them to the prisoner compound. When they got to the gate and stepped out onto the road, the troops who were to relieve us opened fire on the Germans. They were poor shots, for they missed the Jerries. A general in our headquarters said that he was in World War I and hadn't come under as much fire as he did from his own troops during this episode.

Paratroopers of the 507th Parachute Infantry Regiment

Pvt. Edward Jeziorski and his comrades had been dropped near Hébert on June 6, and by the evening of June 8, they made their way to join elements of their regiment on the Merderet. At La Fière, they joined Company C of the 507th Parachute Infantry, which had been reduced to about half strength.

Later during the night, we were bombed by a single Jerry plane and received a direct hit upon our positions. In the early hours of D+3 we were briefed that the newly arrived 325th Glider Infantry Regiment would be assaulting over the Merderet River through our positions at La Fière bridge. We were told to be ready for anything, and if the glider troopers faltered or were held up, we would have to move out immediately to continue the attack and take the bridge.

Prior to the 325th glider men moving out there was to be an artillery barrage of around fifteen minutes and then smoke laid in to screen the attack. . . . The Jerries were dug in well behind the stone walls and had excellent crossing and supporting fire from all their positions. On the single route we could approach on, our artillery had as much effect on the Krauts as a fart would have on a hurricane. As far as smoke was concerned, we saw more from our cigarettes. When the glider men started out literally all hell broke. The glider men probably got from one-half to two-thirds of the way and then there didn't seem to be any more of them that were moving. Then came the yell, "Come on you paratroopers, let's go!" and we took off for the Germans on a dead run. I can't say how many times I fired my light machine gun during the assault. I do remember finishing standing up and firing from crouched positions. My gloved hand was scorched. How we made it to the road forks I to this day cannot comprehend. Picture 800 to 1,000 yards of enemy grazing fire, troopers moving into this without letup, bodies on both sides of the road laying almost head to foot. At one point, a pile of dirt flew up from the left road bank and knocked me down. I can only guess it was an artillery dud and the velocity of it tore the bank up and on top of me. At the left road of the second road fork, an MG-42 sent two bursts at me, missed, just got my jump jacket sleeve. He was dug in on the left side in the open. I stitched him pretty good. Things quieted down real quick after this. We outposted and dug in.

Private Jeziorski, who served in Captain Rae's reinforced company, which had assaulted the causeway in support of the 325th Glider Infantry Regiment, received the Bronze Star for this action and the advance on Le Motey.

PFC Dick Johnson of HQ Company, 1st Battalion, 507th Parachute Infantry, like many other men, wandered aimlessly after D-Day. He eventually joined a group of over two dozen men commanded by a lieutenant and was able to link up with the division after a few days. His friend Cavanaugh, the only man from his stick he came across, was finally able to receive treatment at a field hospital. Johnson also was treated for the piece of shrapnel in his wrist before he was sent on to his own regiment. He remained with the 507th in Normandy until the regiment was sent back to England.

West of Amfreville, Colonel Millet, at the head of isolated elements of the 507th Parachute Infantry, had held out for two days with a small force of about thirty men that grew to a hundred, but not enough to attack the Germans at Amfreville. His small group was separated by only about 1,000 yards from Lt. Col. Charles Timmes's 2nd Battalion of the 507th that was east of Amfreville but had no contact with them. Timmes had briefly held Canquigny, linking it with other elements of the 507th and the 508th. Col. Roy Lindquist, commander of the 508th Parachute Infantry, held the La Fière bridgehead until the Germans counterattacked on June 6. On June 8, Colonel Millet was joined by Capt. Allen Taylor with another 250 men, and Millet finally established contact with division headquarters. He was directed to move around Amfreville and link up with Timmes's isolated force while the 1st Battalion of the 325th Glider

A group of paratroopers from the 508th Parachute Infantry in a street flanked by a cemetery in St. Marcouf. NATIONAL ARCHIVES

Infantry would try to cross the Merderet and link up with Timmes (see section above from Lieutenant Pierce's account of the 325th and the Grey Castle). Millet's group moved out on the night of June 8, but his force broke up in the darkness and was dispersed, finally resulting in his capture. Only 155 men from Millet's 400-man group reached the lines of the 508th Parachute Infantry Regiment on June 10. The rest, like Millet, were captured or killed.

According to one of his men, Colonel Millet was captured in part because he had not earned the enlisted trooper's respect. During training in England, he had ridden in his jeep each morning while his men had run behind him. In addition, like other officers in the unit, he had lived in the lap of luxury in a castle while the men had had to make do with Spartan tents. Such disparity may have fostered resentment among the troops, but Millet's behavior probably was not much different than that of most other officers. Colonel Millet may have been captured simply because he was in the vicinity of Amfreville, far to the west of the Merderet, where he had only a small force that was isolated and without support, and his group had to move through difficult terrain at night, causing his formation to become scattered. Col. Edson Raff, after Millet was confirmed as missing on June 15, took command of the regiment.[3]

It was rumored that all officers who were captured were sent back to the United States when they were freed, but this does not seem to have been the case. The regimental surgeon of the 508th Parachute Infantry Regiment, Maj. David Thomas, is a case in point. Due to a bad drop, he ended up with Colonel Millet's isolated group on the second day. When on the night of June 8 they attempted to link up with the 1st Battalion of the 325th Glider Infantry Regiment, Major

Paratroopers of the 82nd Airborne in a rubble-strewn street, June 16, 1944. NATIONAL ARCHIVES

Thomas's fate was similar to that of Colonel Millet. Thomas's description gives a more realistic view on how Millet was captured and why most of the men didn't reach friendly lines.

We lit out of there heading for the Merderet and were supposed to link up with some other group [Colonel Timmes's isolated group and the 325th]. Again, we were moving in the dark, and I had to leave the wounded behind—those who couldn't walk. I had a couple of wounded medics that I left with them. Their instructions were to get the Krauts to take over the wounded. I have no idea what happened to them.

Our group got broken up during the night as a result of fatigue. We were going single file, and when we would get a break, you would fall asleep since nobody had slept for three days. When you woke up everyone was gone. I wound up with about twenty-six guys on the banks of the

3. Col. Edson Raff led a mixed force of glider men and artillerymen from the 82nd Airborne Division ashore on Utah Beach on D-Day. With tank support, his group advanced on Ste-Mère-Église but was unable to clear one of the landing zones for gliders that were to land that evening, according to Gerard Devlin in *Paratrooper*. Although Millet was captured on June 8, it was not until June 15 that Raff took over as battalion commander (Devlin, 1979, 406–7).

Merderet, and again we were catching a lot of shooting and we occupied ditches along the hedgerow. Since the Krauts knew right where we were, they were trying to drop mortars in on us, but they never did hit a thing. People would try to escape by getting over and into the waters of the Merderet. This was all flooded country—shallow flooding—and then a machine gun had enfiladed the area and quite a few people got shot.

I was digging in deeper in the ditch when a round just barked the tree, and it went into the bank where I was digging. By shooting a back azimuth, I could tell it came from this one tree. So I sat and stared until finally I could make out a pair of German jackboots and from that you could figure out where the body was. I got a guy with a rifle and tried to get him to see, but he couldn't see him. So I said, "The hell with it! Give me the goddamn M-1 and I will knock this guy off!" I took careful aim and fired, but nothing happened. His gun was so damned dirty it wouldn't fire, so I chewed on him awhile and gave him some instructions. I took a carbine from another guy and shot several rounds up where this Kraut had to be and jumped back down in my hole. I came back later (after I was captured and escaped) and there he was lying under that tree.

The day wore on and people just ex-fil-trated one way or the other trying to get out of there. I wound up with another medic from the 507th, S. Sgt. Roy Perkins. We had a lot of dead people around there—Americans. I was down in a ditch with several dead around me, and I could see a German coming along the ditch. I thought all I could do was play it cool, so I lay down alongside a dead guy and breathed as shallow as I could, and stayed as still as possible. This Kraut came along and looked at me—I guess he was looking at me—and he placed his boot under my ankle and jerked it up. I just let it go and continued to breath shallow. He stood a little while and just walked along. That was the longest moment of the day. At the same time, I policed [sic] up an M-1 rifle. I must have been in the rear area of some German unit because here were four Krauts sitting out in the field relaxing, enjoying themselves. I could have killed every one of them, but I felt if I did that others would soon find me. Roy and I managed to hang around there without getting caught until dark.

I said to Roy, "Jesus, Roy, I hate crossing the Merderet; it is so damn cold!" He said he didn't want to cross either, so I said, "Why don't we just get in the middle of the road as if we own the place and see where we end up?" He agreed, and we began walking toward the town of Amfre-ville. Then we started crawling across a field and hit a rope, which was apparently tied on to some German machine gunner's wrist because he began to lay down a field of fire. So we retreated from there. We tried several other ways of getting out of there, but we were not doing very well. So I said, "We just walked into this town, so why don't we see if we can't just walk on out?" We are walking down the middle of the road and a German challenges us from under a tree where we can't see him. He gives us the "Hander Hook" and that was the ball game.

So we were taken prisoner, and I was separated from Roy, who escaped twenty-seven days later from Cherbourg (he lost much weight because they weren't feeding him).

According to Major Thomas, the Germans were amazed to see that such a high-ranking officer was a medic serving with combat troops. In their army, no medical officer with a higher rank than a captain served in the field. The German captains were merely doctor's aids and not actual doctors.

So they took me and made me surgeon for a *Kampfgruppe*. When I arrived, along comes the commander of the *Kampfgruppe*, riding in a Volkswagen. He throws up his hand and says, "Heil Hitler!" and all the rest of these clowns return the salute and respond, "Sieg Heil!" I said to myself, "Holy Christ! It is just like they told me."

The HQ of this group was at a Y in the road in a house. Down in defilade was a stone barn, and this was made our aid station. I had a great staff, which included a German staff sergeant who had been with Rommel in Africa and was often shot at. He was really goosey. Periodically, the 90th Division, which was opposite this group, would lob in a few shells, and it would land on the defilade past our stone barn. This German sergeant would scurry for cover.

We had a few supplies, which did not amount to much. We would also get in occasionally a few captured American guys from the 90th. I would try to pump them for where the front line was and what was the best way to get out of here. They wouldn't talk to me; they figured I was a plant. They were good soldiers.

Finally, after a few days, Major Thomas found his opportunity. As the Americans began to apply pressure, the German battle group was forced to fall back. The headquarters moved to a stone manor. On his arrival there, Major Thomas was greeted by an old Frenchman who kindly patted

A radio operator from the 82nd Airborne. NATIONAL ARCHIVES

him on the back, offered him a cup of milk, said, "Américain, Bon Ami!" and declared that the Germans were "swine." The gift of milk was a mixed blessing.

There were six or eight dead flies in it and I thought, "Hell, I can't let this old boy lose face." So I drank the milk through my teeth and spit the flies out.

A German with a *Schmausser* guarded me, and like a good soldier, he was interested in staying alive, so he began digging his hole. He began to pick up some of the bundles of shrubs, which the farmers cut and leave lying along the hedgerow to use for heating and cooking, to put across his foxhole. He then began throwing the dirt back on top of it. Nobody was paying much attention to me, so I stepped through a gate into a field. I took a few steps down and urinated. Then I slowly walked down the hedgerow, went along to the next hedgerow, and dove into the ditch. By that time it was getting to be dusk, and I just waited for dark. While I am laying there a whole bunch of Krauts on bicycles came down this country lane and took a ten-minute break right on the other side of the hedgerow. So I waited till dark. I fished out my compass only to find it was non-operative. While I had these patients around I had stolen a little bread from them, hardtack and that sort of thing. I had that with me, so I had a little to eat. I followed the stars and went the direction I had to and lay down to sleep awhile.

I do not know where I was, but I could hear the firing and I headed north by using the stars. That first night I walked up on a German sentry—they carry these little flashlights with a red glass on them. I walked right up on this guy before I saw the red glass. He must have been standing there sleeping because I tiptoed back and he didn't do anything. Then I damn near fell into a mortar pit. It must have been a big mortar because they had a ladder to get down into the damn thing. Then I walked up on some sort of a headquarters because there were wires coming into this tent all over the place. I thought, "Jesus! If I cut these wires I will get these guys all screwed up." I also thought I would let them know I was around. I didn't do that. Then when it got dusk, I holed up in a shallow foxhole, more like a ditch of a hedgerow. There was a *Schmausser* at either end of this hedgerow and our guys were on the other side, so every once in a while, they would fire the *Schmausser* and then a machine gun down this hedgerow—it would just clear my butt. That is where I found out about nervous polyuria—I would pee about every 15 minutes and make mud out of the stuff and smear it on my Red Cross [on the helmet].

I spent the day there and when it got dark I started out again. I hadn't got very far when I saw a poorly dug foxhole where the guy had left his spoil around. I sneaked up on it and here was a rifle, a raincoat, some C rations, and nobody. I opened the C ration and ate. I waited for the squad leader to show up, but he never came, so I moved out to the rear. Along about dawn I saw a 105-mm howitzer and encountered a boy from Arkansas with a carbine who wanted me to give the password.

To his great relief, Major Thomas's odyssey behind enemy lines was at an end. He was taken to the headquarters of the 90th Division, from where he was sent to the headquarters of the 82nd Airborne Division. After giving a report to the G-2, he was driven to the 508th Parachute Infantry.

A few days later, a trooper who came to his aid station told him that one of their artillery rounds had hit a German chow line, scattering food and men all over the place. The Germans had been giving out toothpaste in the chow line, said the man between chuckles. Thomas got a jeep and drove to the site to "liberate" the alleged toothpaste. It turned out to be tubes of cheese paste, which he had seen when he had been a prisoner.

For many of the soldiers involved in the Normandy invasion, the hours and days of combat merged into one long jumble of noise, explosions, flying bullets, running, dodging bullets, and firing at the enemy. Time was momentarily suspended in their minds, and though they clearly remembered individual events, many were never able to piece together their precise sequence. Pvt. Kenneth Burch of the 507th is a classic example of this phenomenon.

One morning, we were pushing against German bicycle troops trying to break through us to reach the beaches. It was close warfare—fixed bayonets. Stumbling over bicycles and German artillery exploding among us, the ground was strewn with torn bodies. I was upright, advancing, as were all of us, when an artillery shell exploded so near me that it tossed me like a rag doll.

I felt my head expand and shrink from the concussion and I was knocked unconscious. I could see only fuzzy white dots floating around. I was on my knees feeling for my rifle and trying to clear my head when a beautiful red and dull green began to float into the fuzzy white. As my vision cleared, I saw that I had crawled over a German soldier. Like myself, he was young and had blond hair. He was torn in half. He lay there with a content look on his face. I was directly over his midsection and there were his lungs, stomach, intestines and then he was whole again with legs intact. His being torn apart at the middle had also torn his belt open, and there before me embossed on the back of his belt buckle was "Gott Mit Uns."[4] I quickly searched his pockets for food.

One day [early in the campaign], we were clearing the hedges along a small road leading up to a bridge over a small creek. The Germans held one side of the creek and the bridge. I was in the roadside ditch near the bridge waiting for the word to go across with the others. By then we had learned that the French drink wine and usually had barrels full in their barns, and some soldiers preferred to die drunk. They had filled their canteens with wine. Some were drunk that day, but not me. We were ready to go across when from the rear

came, "Cease fire!" It was a surprise to hear, and then strangely enough, from the Germans' side (cease-fire). Being suspicious, but not knowing what it was all about, no one exposed themselves. Then from behind us, on the road came the sound of hobnailed boots, and about 100 yards back came a French farmer walking down the middle of the road. He passed and crossed the bridge, and on into some woods on the other side. A couple of minutes passed, and the Germans soldiers left their protection as did we. Each side standing around looking cross at the other and then the farmer reemerged herding some cows ahead of him. Seems it was milking time. He and the cows passed through us to the rear and took cover and the war started again. We did not attempt to cross the bridge that evening.

Sometime during the advance from the Merderet to the Douve after June 8, generals Ridgway and Gavin were with Kenneth Burch's unit, which was ahead of the main force and partially isolated. As they prepared to repel a German attack, Burch stated that a German officer on their right flank surrendered his men to a medic named Madlock.

On June 16, after watching the Germans withdraw from St. Sauveur-le-Vicomte, the paratroopers of the 82nd Airborne Division were ordered across the Douve River. The 325th Glider Infantry Regiment crossed the river to the southwest of the division to cut off the Germans, and Burch's group forded the river during the night.

We were told the engineers had built a pontoon bridge for us to cross on. It was

---

4. *Gott Mit Uns* translates to "God with us." The old Imperial Army belt buckles had the same inscription, but those of the Third Reich era had replaced the imperial crown on the buckle with the eagle and swastika emblem.

pitch black and each tied a white rag on one arm to be seen by those following. About thirty of us-most of Company A-loaded down like mules, were to infiltrate, take a road junction, and hold it until the glider troops could fight through to us in the morning. We took off—"Splash!" The damn engineers had built the bridge only halfway. It was a struggle getting across and up the river bank on the opposite side. We were soaked and double heavy with water.

We came upon the road junction quietly—a crossroads sunken between hedgerows with woods around. A German tank sat in the middle of the crossroads. We each carried Composition C and we had a bazooka man with us. He fired from close to the target and the round went into the tank. Out of the tank came one German soldier who could hardly speak and shook as a dog with a St. Vitus dance. We had one man in our company who spoke German, and he asked this poor soul what or who was defending the crossroad. He broke down and cried—the only one I ever saw break. It seems the thirty of us were to defend against two companies of German infantry and one tank.

We deployed as much as we could in a circle around the crossroads while it was still dark. As dawn broke, they came on us but we held. Our lieutenant called for our artillery to fire on us in the hope of doing some damage to the Germans. Our artillery for once was accurate, it along with the German fire landed among us. One shell landed close to me, throwing up dirt all over me. I did not wait for the reload, but moved over the hedgerow out into the road. I felt the presence of someone above and behind me in the hedgerow. Burp gun slugs began to skip the road (paved, but nar-

row) past my head. I heard the gun jam, the bolt being pulled a couple of times and then a potato masher [grenade] went off about a foot from my head. I was fortunate to be in a half-turned position as the tin went into my left shoulder and neck below the helmet. The left side of my head went numb—I thought it was blown away. I could still see from my left eye and felt my face with my hand. It was still there. I went up looking for the German, but never saw him.

After being hit and going numb on the left side, Sergeant La Pine saw me in the road going to look for who threw the grenade. He hollered, "Get out of the road or you're gonna get hit!" I answered, "I'm already hit and looking for who did it!" He said, "Go to the aid station," which had one medic—Madlock. I said, "Where the hell is he?" We were in a tight little circle holding the crossroads and La Pine motioned in a direction. I went there and found a lieutenant, Madlock, a radio operator, and a friend named Lavers, who was guarding five German prisoners. The lieutenant asked, "How badly are you hurt?" I said, "Who knows, I don't feel nuthin'." Madlock said, "You want a shot of morphine?" I said, "No." As Madlock put a bandage on, the lieutenant said, "Take a position over there in that gully guarding the one with the holes through his lungs." At that moment, one of our artillery shells landed very close. Two German prisoners were nicked with shrapnel and began to squeal like little pigs. Lavers and I began to laugh at the pig-like noise. The lieutenant began to holler over the walkie-talkie, "Cease fire! Cease fire!" I went over to the gully to protect my fellow soldier with the holes in his lungs. The Germans kept attacking and my fellow soldier kept screaming, "Don't let them get me!" I then saw a scout for the glider troops and took him to the lieutenant. That day was over for me. The next day every speck of me hurt!

Paratroopers of the 505th Parachute Infantry Regiment

First Lt. Jack Isaacs of Company G, 505th Parachute Infantry, operated behind enemy lines for two days. Of the small group he had assembled, only two men were left. On the morning of June 8, he continued to make his way back to friendly lines with an artilleryman from the 101st and Corporal Echols, who hobbled along with a broken ankle. Late in the afternoon, they heard small arms fire.

Eventually, we did see what appeared to be an infantry squad moving towards us. They were firing over our heads, for that matter; they had chased Germans on our flank and the Germans were now actually behind us. The Americans to our front were in the field of fire of the Germans and took cover as best as they could. We avoided being hit by both sides. Shortly, I heard the American squad leader say, "Bring the son of a bitch BAR up here!" and the men did and drove the Germans from the area. Then we made known our presence to the American unit. The sergeant informed me he was a member of the 4th Infantry Division and they had come over the beaches and were attacking to the north. He told me where his battalion HQ was and directed me there. With the help of the artilleryman, we managed to get Corporal Echols down the hill into the road and on to the farmhouse where the infantry battalion HQ was located. I told the battalion CO of our experience and he

evacuated Corporal Echols. He directed me and the artilleryman to sack out in the barn at the field HQ and we could go back to our unit the next day.

That was how Lieutenant Isaacs spent his first night in relative security since the airdrop. The next day, when he came out of the barn, he came across his battalion executive officer, Maj. Bill Hagen, who was speaking to the infantry battalion commander. A little later, they returned to the 3rd Battalion, 505th. Lieutenant Isaacs rejoined Company G, where he learned about the action around Ste-Mère-Église. He also found out that Captain Follmer had broken his hip on landing and that Lt. Ivan Woods, the executive officer, had taken command of the company. Isaacs took over his platoon, while Lieutenant Orman and Lieutenant Mastrangelo led the other two platoons. The next day, June 10, Lieutenant Woods assembled his platoon leaders for a meeting, but no sooner had he arrived than a German 88-millimeter round burst in a nearby tree, inflicting several casualties. Lieutenant Woods was severely wounded and evacuated from France. Lieutenant Isaacs suffered a shoulder wound and went to the battalion aid station, where he was quickly patched and returned to duty. Corporal Moniee, the company mechanic, lost an arm, and others were also injured. Lieutenant Orman took over the command of the company, which promptly returned to action.

PFC Raymond Gonzalez of Company C, 1st Battalion, 505th, went through many memorable days of fighting and witnessed several of his comrades loose their nerve.

We were on the front lines and this one man, whose name I won't mention, started going back. I asked where he was going. He said, "I'm going to get some fresh water, I saw a well back there." I told him that I had fresh water, and he said that he wanted to fill his canteen. I knew that his canteen was full, but he went back and he never did come back. Another boy I knew stuck his two feet underneath a jeep so he would be wounded in action and sent back.

These men were burned out, he believed, because of the merciless slaughter they had been part of over a period of so many days. Rumors that the beachhead had not been successfully established and that they were surrounded, added to the fact that they had to scavenge for ammunition from the bandoliers of their dead and wounded comrades, further sapped the men's morale. Finally Gonzalez got a chance to verify the situation for himself when his lieutenant sent him back to the beachhead to get rations.

We walked most of the way to the beach and hitched a ride also. I recall one soldier say when we walked into the supply depot, "Who the hell are you guys?" because we

Capt. Robert Abraham of the 508th Parachute Infantry Regiment and a group of French civilians in St. Marcouf. NATIONAL ARCHIVES

had different uniforms. It is ironic to me that the majority of the foot soldiers didn't know what a paratrooper uniform looked like with the big pockets on the side. So I said we were paratroopers. He replied, "They said you guys are in no man's land and I wish I could go up there." We got a hold of him and told him he was going to get us a bunch of supplies and drive us to the front line. This soldier had just come from England, and he had a weapon carrier loaded with ammo and supplies. We told him which way to head. When we reached our lines, the Germans saw our truck coming up and started throwing shells. This soldier saw the shells hitting around his truck and put it in reverse and took off like a bat out of hell. About 500 feet back, he turned around and took off back to the beach and we never did get our supplies.

On another occasion, Gonzalez sat in his foxhole when Gen. James Gavin came up to him and said, "Hi, soldier, how is it going?" Gonzalez looked up, saluted, and replied, "OK, sir!" The general declared, "You are doing a good job!" and walked off. Such personal interest and concern won General Gavin the loyalty and respect of Gonzalez and others.

Another time, Gonzalez was on a recon with Lieutenant Browning when his group came across a large haystack.

All of a sudden, a machine gun went off and we jumped in the ditch, full of mud and crap and everything. I turned to Browning and said, "Should we keep going?" and he said, "Fuck you, Gonze! Let's get back!" We crawled back about 500 feet and went back down the road about a mile and a half. We heard some noises on this crossroad we were coming to. We crawled up on a hedgerow to see what it was. It was Americans trying to get a truck out of the road. They pulled out their guns and said, "Who the hell are you guys?" We said we were paratroopers, and they said they had never seen a paratrooper with a uniform like that. We almost got our ass shot off because a lot of foot soldiers didn't know what a paratrooper looked like. We asked where their HQ was and went up there and found out how far they had advanced, and then went back to our outfit.

The 82nd Airborne Division's Last June Offensive

By June 16, after advancing from its bridgehead west of the Merderet River, the 82nd Airborne Division, with the 9th and 90th Divisions on its right, reached the Douve River at St. Sauveur-le-Vicomte, where it established a new bridgehead. The 325th Glider Infantry held a defensive position on the east bank of the river south of Rauville. The glider units were tired and depleted. According to Captain Joe Gault of Company F, the 1st and 3rd Battalions were engaged in a frontal attack while his battalion was ordered to cross the Douve River in small boats with the remnants of Company E and G abreast and his company in reserve.

They were some type of little square-looking boats. The best I can remember was that they held maybe four or five men. We had to get in some swamp because after the engineers who handled the boats took us as far as they could, we had to disembark in water about waist deep. One man was night blind, as I discovered later, so they tied him to the man in front of him because he couldn't see a thing. My company crossed, but was in the rear.

They crossed the river, turned when they hit the road at the crossing, and moved back towards the river to catch the Germans at the crossing and attempt to annihilate them. When the Germans discovered that we were attacking in their rear, they came pell-mell down the road on foot and on bicycles. The firing was terrific, and as they drew abreast of Companies E and G, the firing was ceased for fear of firing into each company across the road. The Germans completely withdrew.

During the crossing of the Douve, the commander of the 325th called in an air strike against a bridge, but the air corps did not respond until twenty-four hours later, after the regiment had already taken it and while airborne troops were still crossing it. Luckily, there were no casualties.

At the end of the month, the 2nd Battalion, 325th Glider Infantry, took up defensive positions near La Haye du Puits. The weather was bad and Joe Gault's Company F took a rest, only sending out patrols. By this time, Gault's men were tired and dreaded those patrols. The artillery fire inflicted more casualties, but they hung on. Finally, at the beginning of July, Captain Gault received orders to take about a dozen men and return to England. He was to help prepare for his battalion's return to England. The regiment withdrew from the front lines in Normandy on July 12 after thirty-one consecutive days in action. For Gerald Cummings, the four-mile march to Utah Beach seemed interminable, but to his relief, he had to spend only a few hours on the shore before they could board the LSTs that had unloaded their cargo. Once they boarded their transports, they had to wait for the tide to come in late that evening before they sailed back to England. For the first time in over a month, the survivors of the 325th were served a warm meal and got a chance to clean up, protected from the elements. The next day, the rested veterans disembarked at Southampton and got a ride back to their base. Joe Gault's company returned with only about forty-five men (less than a third of its authorized strength of over one hundred and fifty men). In another company of the regiment, only thirteen men remained fit for duty. The depleted units of the regiment received replacements in England.

On June 16, the parachute regiments of the 82nd Airborne Division also crossed the Douve and the 505th Parachute Infantry Regiment seized St. Sauveur-le-Vicomte, pushing back the disorganized enemy troops. Company G, 3rd Battalion, 505th, was ordered to attack through the town and take the high ground to the west. Lieutenant Isaacs led his platoon of Company G during the attack.

> We launched our attack without any recon—very little information about what we might encounter. We were attacked by five German tanks, two of which G Company managed to knock out with one bazooka and three rounds of ammunition. We were strafed by two of our own fighter planes and seriously opposed by several German machine-gun positions. The night fell and we continued the attack in the dark. By this time I had been appointed company commander. I was talking to Lieutenant Orman when he was killed. Lieutenant Mastrangelo was wounded while trying to cross the railroad embankment during the day. Our other officers had all been wounded, captured, or missing. I was the sole officer left, out of eight we started with in G Company.

The attack continued all night long. Dawn came with our company having worked its way behind the enemy positions, but I only had seventeen men left.[5] The others were lost, strayed, or became casualties. We were in a strategic position running alongside the road that ran west from St. Sauveur-le-Vicomte. We were actually 200 or 300 yards ahead of I Company, and when our position became known to the Germans, they started withdrawing in front of I Company. We were in an excellent position to deliver flanking fire while I Company sent frontal fire and caused a great many casualties among the retreating Germans. Also, at point-blank range in this position we observed an 88-mm gun being towed down the road towards us, and it was accompanied by two or three other vehicles with about twenty-five men. With my seventeen men lying just alongside the road in the hedgerow, we delivered very rapid fire when they approached and took them completely by surprise and wiped out everybody on the German side, including the vehicles. This created further problems for the Germans, who were attempting to defend themselves against I Company.

The next day the company was able to reassemble and our seventeen-man company grew to about seventy-five men.

After this action, we moved toward La Haye du Puits and took the town and road junction. Eventually we were relieved by the 8th Infantry Division and prepared to return to England in July.[6]

---

5. A parachute company had an authorized strength of over 125 men.

6. On June 19, the division moved south of the Douve River and then held a large part of the south front until the VII Corps took Cherbourg and the VIII Corps took up the western part of the south front. The offensive action against La Haye du Puits took place early in July and was the last action the 82nd Airborne Division saw before it was withdrawn from the front on July 8–11 and sent back to England.

The 82nd Airborne Division was engaged in Normandy for thirty-eight days from the early hours of June 6 and spent most of that time on the front line. The division had an authorized strength of over 8,500 men but went into campaign with more than that. While paratroopers were dropped into Normandy early on June 6, gliders and ships ferried about 3,000 men from the glider regiments of the two airborne divisions on June 6–7. The 82nd Airborne lost 1,282 men either killed or who died from their wounds later. Another 661 men were missing but accounted for at the end of the war. Of the 3,077 wounded or injured in action, 2,056 returned to duty, leaving about 3,000 vacancies, or the equiv-alent of about one-third of a division's strength. The 101st Airborne Division sent 6,928 para-troopers into Normandy. In June, the division had 4,670 casualties, of which 868 were killed or died of their wounds, over 2,300 wounded, and over 660 captured. This includes more than 500 casualties from the 327th Glider Infantry. The total is less than the official figure of 4,670, but since the numbers are similar to those of the 82nd, the difference may be troops wounded that returned to active duty in England. Normandy had taken a heavy toll on both airborne divisions, and the fact that they did not receive replace-ments in Normandy like regular infantry divi-sions made the situation worse.

CHAPTER 4

From Utah to Cherbourg

The 4th "Ivy" Division Advances

The 4th Division continued to advance inland on D+1 to widen the bridge-head and keep the paratroopers linked to it. At about 10:00 A.M. on June 10, Lt. Col. Charles Jackson, at the head of the 1st Battalion, 12th Infantry, was held up by enemy machine-gun fire coming from a group of houses to the south of Bandienville, just north of Beuzeville.

I, with a small command group, was waiting in a lane when I happened to look to the rear. There, I saw Brig. Gen. Theodore Roosevelt saun-tering down the lane toward me wearing a wool knit cap. He was famous for his dislike in wearing a helmet liner or the liner with the steel helmet. He came up to me and said, "Well, Chuck, how are things going?" After I had explained the situation, he said, "Let's go up to the front." I replied, "We're in the front line. See those two men (about fifty yards away). They are the leading scouts of Company A." He came back with, "Let's go talk to them." And we did!

A little later, Jackson heard the droning of an engine, looked up, and spotted a fighter with German markings on its wing come in at treetop level.[1] It was the last enemy aircraft he saw for many days.

The 4th Division was still actively engaged against the German forces, which kept receiving additional reinforcements. On June 8, a German machine-gun battalion counterattacked Jackson's 1st Battalion, stopping his advance and inflicting heavy casualties. Jackson called for artillery fire directly in front of his troops, a decision that exposed his men to friendly fire. However, he believed he had no other choice. The counterattack was eventually broken up. Col. Russell P. Reeder commended Jackson and his men but ordered them to delay their advance so they could take a break, allowing the companies to regroup. Jackson, however, would have none of it. He asked Reeder for permission to continue to push the Germans back while the momentum was in his favor. Reeder relented, telling him to do what he thought best. The advance from Utah Beach was going well, and further reinforcements were coming ashore, allowing the bridgehead on the Cotentin to expand.

PFC Harper Coleman, a member of a six-man machine-gun squad of Company H of the 2nd Battalion, 8th Infantry, had left Utah Beach with one man left behind, Richard Keiffer. He saw his first dead German at Pouppeville on June 6. After that, his unit seemed to be constantly on the move, with little time to rest as they progressed toward Cherbourg.

By the end of June 7, S.Sgt. Jack W. Carter, a communications man with the 44th Field Artillery, reached Ste-Mère-Église, where he spent the night.

> . . . I woke up the next morning, raised my hand behind my neck, and felt something cool and metallic. I looked around to see what it was. It turned out to be an unexploded 16-inch shell from one of our battleships. Needless to say, after that I was more careful as to where I slept![2]

On June 8, Sgt. William H. Buell, regimental ammunition sergeant of the 12th Infantry, awoke in a German foxhole where he had slept during the night. He discovered the remains of an American parachute nearby and—of more immediate interest to him—a can of evaporated milk.

> I don't think anything ever tasted so good. The nights were cold sleeping on the ground, and we had no blankets. It was on that day I believe we all abandoned our gas masks. Several days later, there was a gas scare and at least one other on the night of July 25.
>
> At the CP [command post] before we moved to Joret was where we lost Colonel Reeder. Red Reeder was a tremendous inspiration the first few days after landing. He would come back from the front with his retinue to the CP standing up in the jeep with an M-1 over his shoulder almost like a Wild West star and always with encouraging words. He lost his foot.[3]

The first regimental CP that lasted for several days was at a French farm chateau in

---

1. He actually described it as a swastika on the wing, but that type of marking would have been on the tail and the German cross on the wings.
2. The heaviest guns on the warships at Normandy were 12 to 15 inches. The only 16-inch guns on warships that took part in the bombardment were on the British battleships *Rodney* and *Nelson*, which did not arrive off Utah Beach until June 11. However, a 12-inch or even 14-inch shell may look like a 16-inch, especially if it is not fully exposed to the observer.
3. Col. Russell Reeder believed in leading by example and told his troops they would not find him back at the command post. He received a citation from the First Army (dated June 20, 1944) for his leadership and heroism in moving among his men on June 7, encouraging them in their assault on a German position at Beuzeville-au-Plain. After the advance stalled, he moved into the open, exposing himself to enemy fire to help lead his men in driving the enemy from Bandenville.

Joret outside of Montebourg. The commander was still leery of everything and locked up the poor residents in the cellar at nighttime. There was one young quite attractive girl there. One day, which happened more than once, the assistant division commander, Gen. Theodore Roosevelt Jr., breezed in as always informal in his fatigues. He noticed this beautiful sweet thing feeding the animals, and as he passed the guard he said, "Soldier, are you getting any of that?"

Another time at that CP, General Roosevelt was in the chateau talking with Colonel Luckett, who he apparently liked a lot, and to others when the warning sounds for the arrival of some screaming-meemies went off.[4] Everyone lay down on the floor except the general, who never moved from his chair saying, "I'm too old to die."

Just before we got to Joret, apparently the 70th Tank Battalion surprised thirty to sixty Germans on bicycles on a side road across the way from Joret and mowed them all down. It was quite a mess. At Joret, I saw the first sizable bunch of German captives.

For Lt. Thomas Cortright of Company I, 12th Infantry, the gas alert on the morning of June 8 was a replay of June 7.

It was a fake [gas alert] and only the morning fog starting to come in. Now it was the morning of the 8th and Company I was again given a special assignment. This time, we were to go out on the left flank a thousand yards or so as security against a flanking attack, as the 8th Infantry was not abreast of the 12th Infantry as they were supposed to be. We were moving up a blacktop road, which I believe was the main road to Montebourg, with the 2nd Platoon leading, and I was right behind them in front of the main body of Company I. There were hedgerows on either side of the road, so I couldn't see the men over there. I was talking to a lieutenant from the engineer special brigade who was there to direct the fire of the battleship *Texas*. On the horizon, I thought I saw a man and sat down on the road with my feet in the ditch and raised my binoculars to confirm when a terrific artillery barrage came in, and I was hit across the back in the first burst. Obviously, the fellow I saw was an FO [forward observer]. The barrage was devastating, as I found out when I called the lieutenant I had been talking to as I wanted to give him coordinates to fire his guns. I called several times and finally the voice that answered me was that of our weapons platoon lieutenant who had crawled up to assess the damage. He said, "Tom, this is me; they are all dead over here, and the radio is ruined." So I gave him the coordinates and told him to go back and contact the battalion to fire the mission. Then the men passed upward and our captain told them to pull back, so we all scrambled back to the next crossroads, where the captain was counting his effectives as we came around the corner. We had around eighty KIA and wounded. I took the two half-tracks from the AT [Anti-Tank] Company that were with us, loaded the wounded, and set out to find the battalion. We had a sharp little firefight on the way but reached the CP, which was also the regimental CP. I gave the coordinates to fire the mission to the regiment's S-3 and turned into the aid station.

They gave me a shot and strapped me to a jeep with some other guys, and the next

---

4. Col. James Lockett took command of the 12th Infantry after Colonel Reeder was wounded on June 11 during the advance on Montebourg. Reeder was wounded by a fragment from a German shell, resulting in the loss of his leg.

thing I remember is someone was trying to take my gun away. The voice said, "Come on, Tom, you won't need it in England." I opened my eyes, and fortunately for him, I recognized the doctor from the 4th Clearing Company. I had been to his wedding recently. I was put aboard an LCT lying on a stretcher on the deck with lots of other guys. Arriving in Southampton I was sent to a hospital where I was operated on. The doctor told me that had I been flown over that he probably would have removed my left kidney, but time and youth was on my side and by the time he saw me, the healing was taking place and he elected to close me up and let nature take its course.

Capt. Herbert M. Krauss, a twenty-nine-year-old draftee from Chicago and 1942 graduate from an Officers Candidate School class at Fort Benning, was the regimental communications officer for the 8th Infantry, but his position with the headquarters staff was not much safer than the front lines. On June 10, his section was hit by artillery, and he lost four of his men. Captain Krauss was also seriously wounded—losing one eye, breaking a leg, and receiving other shrapnel wounds—and was sent back to England where he spent the remainder of the war in a hospital. While in the English hospital, he watched a slightly wounded Ranger go AWOL in order to rejoin his unit in France. Some could just not get enough of the war or had to get back to their buddies.

Capt. John E. Galvin, 8th Infantry, was present when the wounded Captain Krauss was brought in.

His jeep pulled into the CP. Captain Krauss had been hit by a shell. He was hurt pretty badly. Three of his men were killed—pretty much annihilated with the tops of their bodies gone.

I had thrown away my gas mask and that night there was a gas attack and I went back to take the gas masks off of those bodies that had been brought back so a couple of us would have gas masks.

CWO-2 Larry Knecht, assistant adjutant, 8th Infantry, went through a similar false gas attack when he went to pick up replacements and came across an old-timer who had served with him at Fort Screven, Georgia.

I went down to the repple-depple to get the men.[5] I was down there taking these men to the Service Company when I was told that there was a gas attack. So I put the gas mask on, and when they called the all clear we took the masks off. Those men in the 2½-ton trucks had not been in combat of any kind; they were raw recruits and had hardly any training. When they got to the Service Company, they had jumped out of this truck and put the gas masks on. One of these guys was so frightened that when the all clear signal came he stayed in the hole. He jumped in that hole and stayed with his gas mask on. They immediately made a guard post around it. In the meantime, the Service Company commander had these men walking by and all of a sudden, he sees this monster come out of the hole with his gas mask on. One of the men hit him over the head with a rifle. That is how the story was told to me.

We had a Charles Ratteree who was a private in Company C of the 8th Infantry at Fort Screven who in 1942 went off to OCS [officer candidate school]. We heard nothing from him until D+14. At this time, some person gave me a note. It was from First Lieutenant Ratteree telling me that he was in the 2nd Replacement Depot on the

---

5. Repple-depple is slang for the replacement depot.

beach. I went to the depot and saw him. I got him out of the depot and tried to talk him out of going to Company C, but instead I could get him in the 4th Division HQ because at one time he was Gen. Raymond Barton's orderly. Ratteree told me that he would like to see General Barton but still wanted to fight with Company C. I took him to division HQ, and he saw the general. Capt. John Galvin told him they needed a platoon leader in Company B, but he wanted to go to C. In a few days, he got his wish and was assigned to Company C. My friend, 1st Lt. Clyde Epeniger, was the CO of Company C at the time. Clyde was the first to tell me that Rat was KIA sometime later.

Two or three weeks after the invasion, to his great surprise, CWO Larry Knecht ran into his brother-in-law, Clay Brooks, who had joined the army in June 1940 and was a paratrooper in the 82nd Airborne Division. This had been his third combat jump (Sicily and Salerno were the others), and he had injured his foot when he landed on a rock. When Knecht found him, he was still unable to fully lace up his boot and had to walk with his shoelaces loose. Apart from that, he had come out of the weeks of combat virtually unscathed.

Sgt. Clarence P. Faria led the 2nd Platoon, Company L, 3rd Battalion, 12th Infantry. After June 7, he found himself in the thick of it. One night, the regiment had to pull back (probably when it advanced to the east of Montebourg, and "we got all mixed up and lost on our way back. . . ." During these operations, a German machine gun began firing from the rear at his platoon.

I spotted the smoke from the gun the second time he fired at us and immediately fired my M-1 at the spot of the smoke. I then took over firing a machine gun at the spot because our men manning it could not see the target. When I moved up on the tar-

get, after I stopped firing the machine gun, I discovered an MG–42 with ammunition left by the men who took flight. I retrieved the gun and ammunition and dumped them in an empty foxhole back a ways from the hedgerow. I believe it was where the CO had his CP.

On June 14, I was wounded in the upper right arm by a mortar while in a firefight outside of Montebourg. This happened because I was exposed while standing upright behind a hedgerow trying to observe the fire of a 60-mm mortar I was trying to direct at the enemy who was only about 100 to 150 yards away at the next hedgerow in the front of us. The enemy must have spotted our gun and fired at us. I observed the explosion as I had just turned to give more fire orders to the gunner of the 60-mm mortar. This happened about 6 or 7 P.M. We had always told the men, when hit, if you can walk, you must evacuate yourself to the aid station. After being wounded, a wounded officer helped me bandage my arm with the first-aid kit we all carried. I ran into the medics following in our rear and was tagged wounded and given directions where the aid station was located. Upon reporting in at the aid station, I was given a shot for tetanus, put on a jeep with other walking wounded, and evacuated to the beach area. I stayed there overnight and I was put aboard an LST. Sometime during the night, we sailed for England.

The 90th Infantry Division

On D-Day, one regiment of the 90th Infantry Division was ready to land in support of the 4th Infantry Division. The bulk of the division came ashore on June 8. Many of its troops came from Texas and Oklahoma when it had formed during World War I—hence the T and O on the patch. When the division was reactivated in 1942, the troops often said the T and O stood for "Tough 'Ombres." The division's 2nd Battalion, 359th Infantry, and Company C of the 315th Engineer Battalion were aboard the *Susan B. Anthony* when it hit a mine and sank on the morning of June 7. Fortunately, none of the men was lost, but they made it to shore without their weapons.

On June 10, the 90th Division assembled and was ready for operations. Its first mission was to support the 82nd Airborne Division and push across the Merderet River. This allowed the 4th Infantry Division to attack northward at Montebourg and Valognes where the German 709th Division and elements of other units were concentrating to protect Cherbourg. A German counterattack a little to the north of Pont-l'Abbé brought advance of the 90th Division to a sudden halt.

The German 91st Air Landing Division and the hedgerows proved to be quite a challenge for the green American division. Although the 90th Division had a bad reputation early in the campaign, acts of bravery were not uncommon among its leaders. Company B, 359th Infantry, led by Capt. Donald B. Hutchens, was among the units that were pinned down. Since the situation was untenable, Hutchens decided to direct friendly fire from a nearby tree. As he started to climb, a limb gave out and he went crashing to the ground. Undeterred, he got up and started again since someone needed to act as an observer for the artillery. On June 12, on the left flank of the 359th, the 358th Infantry also came to a stop and it was S.Sgt. Warren Snider who took it upon himself to direct mortar fire from an exposed position for over an hour to break the stalemate.

In the late afternoon, P-47 fighters bombed Pont-l'Abbé, and the 358th Infantry moved into the ruins by evening of June 12. Units of the 90th Division encountered fierce resistance all along the front. Gen. J. Lawton Collins, commander of the VII Corps, and Gen. Omar Bradley, First Army commander, concluded that the leadership of the division was unsatisfactory, and they pulled it out of the line; they even considered breaking it up altogether. The 9th Division was chosen to replace the 90th and to continue the advance across the Cotentin Peninsula. On June 15, the 9th Division took over the offensive, and the 90th Division was left to mop up. The 90th Division was soon switched from the VII Corps to the newly formed the VIII Corps.

The 9th Division had unloaded across Utah Beach on June 10 and moved into position shortly after that. In late April 1944, Lt. Col. William Westmoreland,[6] several other senior officers, and Lt. Charles Scheffel had been ordered to give lectures on their combat experiences in North Africa and Sicily. Soon after the lectures, Lieutenant Scheffel became the executive officer of Company D, 1st Battalion, 39th Infantry. The 39th Infantry loaded and crossed the Channel during the night of June 9–10. The crossing did not go without incident. Scheffel was on deck with his company commander, Captain Thomas, when "looking forward on the port side of the ship, directly under the bridge, suddenly I saw something taller than our ship headed directly toward us without lights." The two officers fled to the starboard side; "the ship shuddered and rocked with the terrible shattering sound of part of the ship tearing apart." The ship's captain later told Scheffel that they had been "sideswiped" by a battleship. Eventually the ship anchored off Utah Beach, but damage from the incident prevented its passengers from disembarking. Scheffel and Thomas watched other elements of the regiment unloading from other ships. About twenty minutes before nightfall, a group of German aircraft flew over, strafing the ships. Scheffel was one of the casualties and saw

an aircraft's flashing guns and an explosion on the deck in front of us. I must have

6. Westmoreland became the commander of U.S. forces in Vietnam in the 1960s.

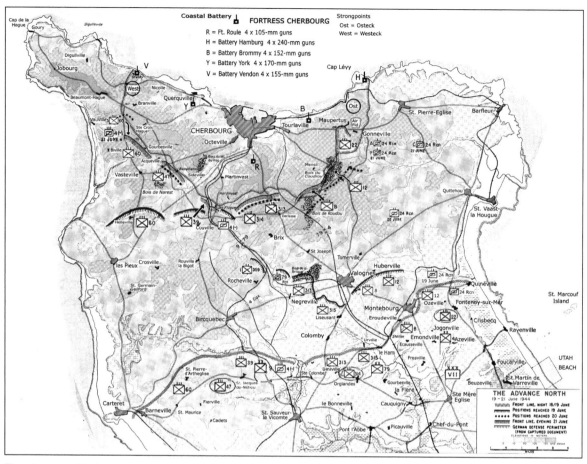

The advance on Cherbourg. U.S. ARMY

crumbled as I was hit from fragments as his 20-mm bullets exploded on the deck. Next I recall one of the ship's medical people coming to my side. I had been hit by many small fragments on the right side of my face, my right arm, in my legs, and somewhere in my groin area.

Scheffel was transferred to an LCT bound for England loaded with prisoners. During the trip, he glanced down to his Swiss watch he had purchased at Camp Robinson and realized that a fragment had shattered it, stopping its hands at

11:20 P.M. The convoy, according to him, was attacked by E-boats, which were driven off. When his ship docked at Weymouth, he was put on a British hospital train.[7]

On June 16, the 9th Division and the 82nd Airborne Division took the Douve at Ste-Colombe and St.-Sauveur. Before long, the 9th Division reached the west coast of the peninsula, isolating the German forces to the north. The German 77th Infantry Division and the 91st Air Landing Division moved south and broke through the position of the 90th Division, giving that American unit another bad day.

7. After recovering, on July 10 he was sent to the 10th Replacement Depot near Southampton. There he was put in charge of a platoon of replacements for the 4th Division. On July 21, he crossed the Channel once again. This time, he landed at Omaha Beach and then was taken to the 92nd Replacement Battalion near Carentan. On July 23, he was reassigned and taken to the headquarters of his 39th Infantry.

The 70th Tank Battalion

During all these advances, the American forces were accompanied by armor. The 70th Tank Battalion—the first to come ashore on D-Day—continuously took active part in operations inland even as fresh tank battalions landed on the beaches. On June 7, Companies A, B, and C, in support of the 1st and 2nd Battalions of the 8th Infantry and the 3rd Battalion of the 22nd Infantry respectively, drove through to Ste-Mère-Église and overcame heavy resistance. Company D, which supported the 101st Airborne Division, lost two of its light tanks. The next day, the battalion pushed northward against Azeville and the high ground at Ozeville and Company D lost another light tank, still in support of the 101st Airborne Division. On June 9, the 22nd Infantry, elements of the 899th Tank Destroyer Battalion, and all the artillery of the 4th Division continued the attack on the Ozeville strongpoint. Heavy enemy artillery fire, including *Nebelwerfers*, slowed the operation and destroyed two Shermans. As the battle continued into June 10, Company A, which supported the 8th Infantry southwest of Montebourg, lost four more Shermans. On the next day, the 22nd Infantry finally succeeded in taking the high ground at Ozeville. After that, the 70th Tank Battalion went into reserve for the 4th Division, but its Company D continued to operate to the south.

Company A went back in action on June 12 in support of the 12th Infantry advancing on Montebourg. It was not until June 15 that the 70th Tank Battalion fell out of contact with the enemy and it was again briefly placed in reserve. Its remaining elements arrived from England on June 17. On June 18, with Company D back from the south, the battalion returned to action in support of the 4th Division near Joganville, to the northwest of Azeville. The advance on Cherbourg was underway. On June 26, the battalion's tanks, accompanied by infantry, entered Cherbourg from northwest of Tourlaville. On June 27,

the battalion, in support of the 22nd Infantry, moved against strongpoint "Hamburg," a heavily defended coastal battery east of Cherbourg. Late in the evening, the combatants called a cease-fire and waited for the enemy to surrender. The strongpoint finally capitulated at 1:30 P.M. the next day. On June 30, the battalion began preparations for its move south to support the 82nd Airborne Division.

T/4 Charles J. Myers, the driver of the battalion commander's tank in the headquarters section, took part in most of these battles.

On June 7, we went into battle [after joining the battalion the night of June 6]. We fought through several hedgerows, and later in the afternoon, we strafed several hedgerows, overran a bicycle battalion, and captured many prisoners. During this attack, only the .30 and .50 caliber machine guns were used, except for my tank. The CO spotted an ammo dump and had me hit it with a 75-mm HE [high-explosive] round, which blew it up. He then directed the driver across a hedgerow at an oblique angle, and the tank rolled over on its side. We had to come out on foot, fearful of enemy and friendly fire. The next day, we retrieved the tank, despite occasional sniper fire. We later captured two infantry squads from the adjacent field. I recall that we knocked the steeple off the church at Montebourg in the belief that it was a German observation post. Then we routed out some snipers in Valognes. We also went looking for wine and Calvados in the tunnels and caves around Cherbourg.

The Front on the Cotentin Peninsula, June 10–July 5

The newly arrived 90th Division and the 9th Division as part of the VII Corps joined the 4th

Division during the first week after D-Day. The 82nd Airborne helped hold the bridgehead over the Merderet River, and the 101st held the southern section of the front along the Douve River to Carentan.

The Germans tried to contain the American bridgehead on the Cotentin Peninsula with the 709th, 91st, and 243rd Divisions reinforced with the arrival of the 77th Division. The German 265th Division was south of the Douve River, and the 17th SS Panzer Grenadier Division arrived to contain the paratroopers of the 101st Airborne in the vicinity of Carentan.

After the 9th Division reached the west coast of the peninsula, the German 77th and 91st Divisions broke through the cordon to establish a defensive position on the south side of the peninsula. On June 21, the 9th Division of the VII Corps moved against the western defenses of Cherbourg, the 79th Division on the town's southern front, and the 4th Division against its eastern front. At the end of June, the Germans held the southern end of the peninsula with the 243rd, 353rd, 77th, 2nd SS Panzer, 17th SS Panzer Grenadier, and the Panzer Lehr Divisions facing the two American airborne divisions and the newly arrived VIII Corps with the 79th and 90th Divisions. The enemy units that had originally defended the peninsula on D-Day were reduced to shattered remnants of the original formations on the southern front, aside from those who had been eliminated at Cherbourg altogether.

American troops had had little training with hedgerows in England, which were much less formidable than those in Normandy. Hedgerows were first encountered by the Americans as they moved inland from Omaha Beach in the Bessin region and also in Cotentin. The infantry troops involved in the hedgerow fighting not only had to overcome the enemy situated in sited positions in the *bocage* country, but they also had to play a dangerous game of hide-and-seek. Once they penetrated one hedgerow, they had to face the next.

The narrow passageways between hedgerows with their irregular shapes formed a veritable maze in which it was easy to get disoriented. When the defender counterattacked, he faced the same problems. Thus, achieving a breakthrough in this type of terrain was almost impossible, especially in the face of a resolute opponent.

The 9th Infantry Division

The 9th Division had come ashore at Utah Beach on June 10, followed four days later by the 79th Division. The 39th Infantry of the 9th Division was assigned to the 4th Division for operations on the coast on the way to Quineville, while the remainder of the division was not ready for operations until June 14. On June 15, the 9th was to replace the 90th Division and join the 82nd Airborne Division for the drive across the peninsula.

PFC Earl Duncan, a nineteen-year-old draftee from Humbolt, Tennessee, attached as a medic to Company D, 39th Infantry, 9th Division, soon after he landed at Utah Beach. His company moved north when his regiment was attached to the 4th Division.

This was my first battle and it was June 12, 1944. I was assigned to the 1st Platoon, which was the machine-gun platoon, and it was attached to Company C. We were making an attack on some pillboxes there on the beach. We were having lots of casualties and one of the platoon leaders of Company C said that some of his men were wounded up close to one pillbox and he wanted me to try to see about them.

I made my way to them. There were three or four shot up pretty badly, and as I started to treat them, I was feeling nervous with fear and shock for seeing all the blood and the wounds for the first time. Then one of the soldiers said, "Doc, you are going to take care of me." Then I began to realize

A Special Type of Hell—The *Bocage*

The Norman *bocage* or *boscage* region is the site of much heavy fighting that took place during the Normandy campaign between June and July 1944. It was bounded to the north by the Cotentin Peninsula and the coastal plain of the Bessin beginning near Lessay, on the west side of the peninsula, and extending eastward, just to the south of Carentan and Bayeux, until reaching the vicinity of Caen. The eastern boundary of this region runs from a point west of Caen ending just north of Flers, and then it extends south to the west of Avranches. St. Lô and the large towns of Coutances, Villers Bocage, and Vire are within this region. Both the Cotentin and Bessin Peninsulas also included hedgerows. This partially natural and partially man-made environment consists of rolling, wooded hills that were cleared centuries, if not millennia, ago to form a checkerboard of small fields, each surrounded by a talus and often a ditch to control runoff and erosion and drain excess water during particularly rainy periods.

The taluses vary in thickness from one to four feet, providing excellent cover for a defender. Long ago they were overgrown with bushes and trees that form thick three- to twelve-foot-high hedges that serve as windbreaks that protect the fields and orchard from the fierce Atlantic winds. The hedges in Normandy consist mostly of brambles, hawthorn, vines, and various species of trees up to three feet thick and up to fifteen feet high that form an almost impenetrable wall. Every field requires one or more openings in the hedges to give access to the farmers. Often a narrow, sunken lane between hedgerows leads from one field access to the other. Except in the winter months, the trees and bushes form a leafy tunnel. The entire checkerboard thus forms a veritable maze, which throughout history has provided excellent cover to highwaymen, *chouans*, and combatants.

In 1944, the *bocage* was the scene of some of the fiercest combat between the Germans and the Allies. The defenders only need hold the few access points. If one hedgerow fell, they fell back on the next. When the tanks tried to drive over the hedgerow, they exposed their lightly armored bellies to the enemy's antitank weapons. The Americans developed various methods to breach the hedgerows, ranging from planting explosives in their base to using bulldozers. In June and early July, the ordnance section of the First Army tried to install dozer blades on Sherman tanks, but only forty of these modified tanks were ready for Operation Cobra on July 25.

The 121st Combat Engineer Battalion, 29th Infantry Division, with the help of the 747th Tank Battalion, placed explosives in the taluses. In June, Lt. Col. Robert Ploger, the battalion commander, calculated that each tank battalion needed sixty tons of explosives to cover a distance of one and a half miles for a total of thirty-four hedgerows, an amount far in excess of the supply available to any engineer battalion. The 29th Division also tried installing pairs of timber prongs—"salad forks"—on the front of tanks. A vehicle thus equipped rammed the device into the earthen talus of the hedgerow and pulled it back, leaving holes in which the engineers placed explosives. The tactical policy of the 29th

continued

A Special Type of Hell—The *Bocage continued*

Division became "one squad, one tank, one field." In July, the 747th Tank Battalion began welding pieces of rail tracks onto their tanks. One solution came from Sgt. Curtis Culin Jr. of the 102nd Cavalry Squadron, who welded pieces of German anti-invasion obstacles on tanks, forming a set of steel prongs known as "Culin cutters." About 500 Sherman, called Rhinos because these devices looked like rhinoceros horns, had the ability to tear their way through hedgerows, but none went into operation until Operation Cobra, which began on July 25, because General Bradley wanted to keep their presence secret.[8]

8. Steve Zaloga's extensive research on the use of these devices during the campaign has shown that despite glowing reports, the Rhinos' performance had mixed results and that they most likely did not prove to be a very decisive element in the campaign

what I was there for and I had to give my best. I was still afraid of the small arms fire and the shelling, but I realized I was not the only one up there risking his life and then I began to feel good as I looked at the brazen young riflemen. They had risked their lives and they had already been shot; I was there to treat them, and so it was until the war ended.

Once the Germans attacked us early in the morning and some of the soldiers could not get out of their sleeping bags in time and some were killed while in their bags because their zipper would not unzip.

Texan Pvt. Sam L. Burns, a rifleman in the 1st Squad, 1st Platoon, Company F of the 39th Infantry of the 9th Division, crossed the Channel on an English ship. His last warm breakfast in many a day consisted of fish, oatmeal, and tea—horrible stuff in his opinion. By midday, he was on the beach, which was still littered with weapons, barbed wire, and wrecked vehicles. His regiment was attached to the 4th Division as it moved up the coast. His company's first mission was to take a large pillbox on the high ground that had been bypassed by earlier units.

We attempted to take it with the squad, but we were driven back by intense fire. We had tried to knock it out with satchel charges, but to no avail. We called for air support and P-51s dropped 50-pound bombs on it. The concussion put the pillbox out of commission. We moved up and relieved part of the 4th Division and headed for Quineville. We remained with the 4th Division until we returned to the 9th Division and went into reserve for a couple of days on June 16.[9]

Sgt. Herbert Stern from Cincinnati, a veteran of operations in the Mediterranean, served as a G-2 interrogator and was assigned to the 9th Medical Battalion of the 9th Infantry Division. He crossed the Channel on a small New Zealander freighter. He and his comrades waited for many hours off Utah Beach before they slid down chutes from the freighter into the waiting landing craft.

9. The 39th Infantry remained attached to the 4th Division while the 9th Division drove across the peninsula with its other two regiments.

We waded ashore, but I noticed that the engineers were already building huge pontoon bridges into the channel to allow for heavy equipment to be brought on shore. We quickly moved inland to a point near Ste-Mère-Église and noticed numerous gliders that had been damaged on landing and camouflaged parachutes hanging from trees. We were introduced to the dead bloated cattle lying in every field—we never got used to the stench.

Many of the early prisoners our unit took were conscripted Poles who barely spoke German and every prisoner carried brand-new 250 Francs, just printed. Resistance after the first two days became more severe. Our casualties in the first two weeks became quite heavy.

Sergeant Stern was usually with his battalion but worked closely with the G-2 in the interrogation of the prisoners.

During our stay in England, I was assigned to a British intelligence school in London for one week. I attended lectures in "interpretation of enemy documents."

German prisoners often carried more than their service record. Occasionally, written instructions and crude maps of combat situations were handed over to us. Personal paper such as letters from home, photographs, etc., were often also of value. Often wounded prisoners (slightly wounded) would be sufficiently discouraged and talked freely. In the early stages of combat, we often encountered the well-trained professional soldiers who were usually uncooperative and sometimes quite arrogant. If the prisoner was perceived to have important information we attempted several things:

1. Have him dig a six-foot trench and let him know he might end up in it.

2. If we were in a building, we would have him escorted to a room where he was surrounded by several football-player types—intimidation did not always work.

Probably the most successful interrogation was that of wounded prisoners, since they were confused, frightened, and of course hurt, and if we spoke in their native tongue, they became cooperative.

Many of the Germans Sergeant Stern interrogated suspected he was German-born, but most did not realize he was a German Jew.

PFC Ernest J. Botella, a nineteen-year-old volunteer from Olive Bridge, New York, was an ammo bearer with a machine-gun platoon of Company H, 47th Infantry, 9th Division. He crossed the Channel in an English freighter whose holds were modified to take on bunks. He was quite pleased with the food he was served on board. His company was transported from the freighter to the beach on LCVPs. By the time he landed, the beach was well organized and litters of casualties and quite a few German prisoners were awaiting evacuation.

The Germans were in company-size formations with MPs carrying .45 Thompsons, but they weren't trying to get away. They were happy to go. Quite a few of the prisoners were very young or very old.

We actually set up in the afternoon of June 10 when the rifle companies in front of us got into a blind position. They moved rather rapidly and on June 10 we fired no rounds. The first night, we got to bivouac around 11:00 P.M. All of us were told how deep to dig our holes, but most of us were too tired and I don't think I went down more than six inches.

We went in with our gas masks and impregnated clothing that had been issued in Portsmouth. I would say within four days they picked up all the gas masks. I think I kept my impregnated clothing up until the time I was wounded. I was wounded on the 22nd or twelve days after landing.

June 11 was the first day we fired. Captain Zesser, our company commander, had put out the word that every man in every squad would have the opportunity to fire when the situation permitted. In a heavy weapons company, you are normally delivering primarily overhead fire while a rifle company moves up. I only know of about three occasions where we delivered true offensive fire and that was quite a ways out, usually when we were on high terrain and could look down towards the Germans—not too much of that. I happened to be on the machine gun, it was my crack at it when the people I was firing at fired back. Any bad feeling I had about shooting anybody went away real quick when I figured they were shooting at me too. We were on high ground on the forward slope of a hill, and they were shooting back at us with I guess the MG-42s. We were out in the open. This was on either June 12 or 13 and it was my first occasion to fire.

Every fifth round was .30 caliber tracer and you could see where it was going. I was firing at a German column of troops with three or four of the Volkswagen equivalents of our jeep. The gentlemen who fired before me stopped their movement. I guess they were trying to regroup. These Germans knew where they were falling back to and they generally leapfrogged. Each of us had several minutes on the gun, and we did it on several occasions. On this occasion, the Germans were about 800 to 900 yards away. I don't remember even using the sights, just the tracers. We were up high and they were on a flat pasture that extended about half a mile forward. The first man

caught them while they were driving. When I was firing, they were shooting at us. The first vehicle, the lead one, was still on the road and the others had pulled over and got partially into the ditch alongside the road. This was an unpaved farm road. I remember seeing about three jeeps and fifty or sixty Germans—everybody on foot. Most of them dropped down into the ditches facing us and were firing at us. You could see the bursts of their machine guns, a short burst of five or six rounds.

They weren't interested in coming at us; they were going their own way. I don't believe anybody in my platoon was wounded, but I think the 2nd Platoon, off to my left, had some casualties. At that location our first section of two squads was firing. The 2nd Platoon was on the left and I don't know how many were firing. I think the mortars got into it about the time we finished firing. The Germans moved. Company E was in front of us and advanced on them as they high-tailed it out of the area and left their casualties behind.

Each rifle company had air ID panels. The HQ Company for some reason had lost theirs, so they borrowed ours because Company H was suppose to support the rifle companies. On one of those days we were between two rifle companies and the pilots saw the big empty space with no panel—they were about two by six feet and HQ company still had ours. We got bombed. They dropped a couple of 500-pound bombs in there. My platoon leader was later killed in a similar situation.

I was used mostly as a platoon runner, so I never had to pull guard duty. I was usually with the platoon leader or company commander and carried the SCR-536 radio.

On June 15, I ran into my company commander from basic training. He had tried to jump into the same ditch during a German mortar attack. We bumped heads and I recognized his voice and we talked about 30 seconds. I never saw him again. He was not in our division and was on a recon or something. I recognized him by his voice.

On the morning of June 18, our regiment cut across the peninsula and we made a right turn towards Cherbourg. On the morning of June 22, we were close enough to Cherbourg where, through field glasses, you could see the taller buildings and Fort du Roule. I would say about five minutes after I got a look at it, just shortly after dawn, I was wounded by a German 50-mm mortar round that landed about five feet behind me. I survived because I had a pack on that protected me. I was accompanying the platoon leader and the 1st Section was about ten yards behind me. The platoon leader and I were too close together. I don't know if I was in the process of going up to him or he was coming back to me, but we were about five feet apart when I got hit and he was saved from shrapnel because I was between him and the round. He bandaged me up. Another round hit in the section behind me and the medics were taking care of them. When Lieutenant Zesser saw my pack, he said it looked like it had saved me. He took my pack off and saw where the holes were. He took off my jacket, my shirts and put my first-aid packet with the sulfur powder on it. I put my shirt back on backwards. When I met my company commander a few minutes later on my way back, he thought I had been shot through the heart because of the position of the hole in my shirt. Zesser said, "You go on back to the company aid station and we will see you. Lots of luck!" He got killed on July 12, and I never saw him again.

The aid station was between the company headquarters and battalion about 400 yards. I went back alone, and that is when I met our company commander. At the aid station, they checked my bandage, said I was fine, and told me I could go to the collecting company because they had other people there more seriously hurt than me. The aid station had a tent fly (it was just a cover with no sides to it and would cover maybe half a dozen litters). From there, I went in a weapon carrier to a collecting company. I don't believe it was part of the 9th Division. It consisted of a series of four or five tent flies, but no surgery. I went back with the walking wounded. Litter people went in a different type of vehicle. I went direct to a field hospital and they performed surgery on me and I was evacuated by air to England the following day on a C-47. We departed from a temporary airstrip made of metal panels and no litter patients were carried. I was ready to return to duty in August, but they had other ideas in the hospital where they put me to work. I tried to get back to my unit anyway but was brought back to the hospital and court-martialed.

Private First Class Botella was kept at the hospital for "rehabilitation," a term they used to keep extra help around "to push the mops," according to him. He was broken to private and fined $30 a month for six months. Eventually, Botella managed to rejoin his unit, never paid the fine, and finished the war as a captain.

First Lt. Henry G. "Red" Phillips from Burbank, California, was with Company M, 47th Infantry of the 9th Division. He served with the Heavy Weapons Company of the 3rd Battalion, which included two machine-gun platoons, a mortar platoon, and a company headquarters with twenty-nine men. The machine-gun platoons numbered forty-four men each, and each platoon was divided into two sections, each section into two squads with a .30-caliber water-cooled machine gun per squad. The mortar platoon consisted of fifty-seven men divided into three sections of two squads each with an 81-millimeter mortar per squad. Lieutenant Phillips's battalion crossed the Channel on an LSI and reached the shore on a landing craft on June 11. Unfortunately, the ramp of the landing craft was let down too soon and he and his company disembarked in deep water. The first thing he noticed on crossing the beach was a Goliath, a miniature remote-controlled German tank, turned on its side at the edge of a crater. Aside for the booming of a naval gun and his unexpected dunking in deep water, he and his men had a rather uneventful landing.

As they moved inland, Phillips and his men were rather surprised to see the numerous wrecked gliders. As they reached the assembly area, the battalion was greeted with intermittent enemy fire. Recon Sgt. Victor Albert was the first man in the company to fall in action, only a couple days after landing. During the march inland, Sergeant Albert had distinguished himself in action when he fired a clip from his M-1 into a German jeep that raced down the road, killing the driver while everyone else in the unit had ducked for cover.

PFC John D. Gregory, a twenty-year-old draftee from Franklin, Kentucky, transferred from the 8th Armored Division in the States and arrived in Great Britain as a replacement. Late in May, at the replacement depot in Wales he sprained his ankle sliding into base while playing baseball. He spent the next three weeks in the hospital, where he heard on the radio that the invasion had taken place. Before long, he too was wading ashore at Utah Beach, praying all the while that he did not step into a hole because he couldn't swim.

He was assigned as a rifleman to the 3rd Platoon, Company C of the 47th Infantry. He was appointed as the first scout because, he was told, he was fresher and more alert than the veterans.[10]

My first full day in France brought me face to face with the reality of kill or be killed. I crawled on my belly to join my unit. Small arms fire was going full blast. Being new, I was very confused. I had never heard the enemy guns firing before. Later, I could tell theirs from ours. This made things much easier. It did not take long to recognize incoming fire and outgoing shells. You could soon tell by the sound how close it was coming.

I was introduced to my new squad leader. I asked him, "What should I do first?" "Learn to pray," he replied, and I soon found out what he meant. The hedgerows were a terrible place to fight. I was told to go out front to a shell hole and to watch when the troops in front of us moved out. When I got in this hole I was the only one there. When we moved up there, there were five or six larger ones. Whew! I heard the cry "Medic!" much too often here.

The fighting in the hedgerows was slow or not moving at all. The Jerries had the hedgerow positions mapped out. They could spot us, look at their maps, and zero their artillery in on us real quick. This caused us lots of casualties. One day, when the shellfire was at its worst, this young French girl was riding on a bicycle up and down the road near us. The officer in charge ordered, "Stop that girl!" We did and the shelling let up real soon. She was their eyes. I don't know what they did with the girl.

The 47th Infantry began its advance across the peninsula on June 15, moving toward the Douve

---

10. In the twelve-man rifle squads, two riflemen were designated as scouts.

River. In his book *Heavy Weapons* Lieutenant Phillips wrote,

Resistance was fierce in the hedgerow country, or "*bocage*" as the French called it. This area was broken up into small farms with tiny fields, apple orchards, or pastures for what were now mostly dead cows. Each field was surrounded by a stone wall heaped over with dirt and topped with a thick growth of hedge. In such a position a few defenders with automatic weapons could easily fend off many times their number. Mortar and artillery fire bursting on contact with the hedges overhead played havoc with the unprotected attackers. . . .

The key to the hedgerow defense was to closely follow supporting mortar fire, which could be adjusted relatively safely with limited observation. Then one had to bring his own automatic weapons to bear before the enemy recovered from this barrage. The magic lay in keeping up the fire while moving forward and maintaining momentum. But attacks had to be methodical and closely controlled. If a unit got ahead, it had to be watchful of its flanks. The defenders would sometimes give way just to lure the unwary off guard. Also, one could get killed by friendly mortar fire as fast as the enemy's. This game was not for beginners.

The close hedgerow country was entirely different from what we had fought over in Africa and Sicily where usually the tactical problems were just the opposite, that is, unlimited observation and opportunities for supporting weapons, little concealment, and not much fierce resistance. On the other hand, Normandy's "*bocage*" was not all that different from the terrain on which we had exercised in England. Happily for us, the planners had anticipated the particular problems of Normandy and rehearsed us in their solutions over and over . . . in its first combat in France, the 9th Infantry Division blitzed through the Germans.

The commanding officer of the 3rd Battalion was in his glory in Normandy. Stocky and heavily mustached, Lieutenant Colonel Clayman walked pigeon-toed in the way that John Wayne would make famous in his cowboy movies. . . . The colonel was enamored with the idea of the night attack, belittling its attendant problems or the notion that one should have a pretty good idea of the enemy's situation before going in. . . . He was a master in the coordination of fire and movement. . . .

. . . M Company had its orders for an advance after dark on June 17. These included having the machine gunners leave their crew served weapons behind on the squad jeeps to be delivered on the objective. They would move with the riflemen armed with their pistols and carbines. The battalion's assault would be made in a column of files with Clayman's "Thugs" leading. The battalion commander had learned from a local French Resistance source of a narrow gap in the enemy's lines. Through it a trail led to a crossing of the Douve River and the German's rear. . . . Walking along in the dark in absolute silence, with sporadic halts of the column, was hairy, especially for a small party of spanking brand-new M Company replacements whose eyes stood out in the darkness. At one point the Germans could be heard calling to one another and moving vehicles about in low gear. At another time a hand grenade exploded at the head of the column, then silence and nothing more until the column moved again. The column broke once and the rear peeled off on its own track until someone realized what had happened and had the wayward element retrace its steps.

Thomas J. Morgan [a recent replacement to 2nd Platoon] remembered:

". . . I was carrying the platoon's sniping rifle with its telescopic sight which made the situation even more frightening. . . . I had a cold and was coughing very badly. Everyone in the outfit kept passing back sugar cubes for me to eat to arrest the coughing. We could hear the Krauts talking. I was sick from all that sugar but it worked. At daylight the first shot fired at us killed my closest friend at that time, Eddie Stanton, who had joined the battalion with me. . . .

. . . The battalion was in a German tent camp which turned out to be a division command post. German staff officers and clerks went flying. We were on our objective. The coastal road was cut. The machine guns and the mortar platoon joined up and we began to dig in for an expected counterattack. Soon, however, we were relieved by another unit and on the road again, north towards Cherbourg."

T/5 Aaron D. Lubin, a draftee from New York City and a veteran of the North African and Sicilian campaigns with the 9th Division, had been an antitank gunner but never had a chance to fire a shot during the Mediterranean campaign. During the Normandy campaign, he served with HQ Battery of the 84th Field Artillery Battalion. After landing at Utah Beach, his unit got lost and passed through Ste-Mère-Église several times before it found the right direction. His most vivid memories were of the attack in the Cotentin Peninsula.

The Germans counterattacked at St. Jean de Haye, and we were awakened by a tremendous explosion in our position. A shell, probably from an 88, struck in the center of the field. The previous night, the officer's two orderlies had dug a foxhole, which was so deep that an officer walking past said, "You have got nothing to worry about down there!" As you can guess, they were dug in at the base of a tree and right where the shell hit and they were killed instantly. My closest friend was severely wounded. A fragment of the shell whizzed through his helmet and into his head. When I heard he had been hit, I ran to his tent and bandaged his head.

I have often wondered why the two orderlies had dug in at the base of a tree, the worst possible spot, and why we were sleeping on the ground instead of foxholes since we were a veteran group and should have known better. Three deaths caused because of our own stupidity.

Unfortunately, Lubin's friend died at the hospital a few days later.

The Battle of Cherbourg

The divisions of Gen. J. Lawton "Lightning Joe" Collins's VII Corps closed on Cherbourg by mid-June. This was the GIs first battle for a fortress. The 4th Division advanced into the northeast end of the peninsula, moving against Cherbourg from the east, while the 9th and 79th Divisions approached the fortified city from the south.

PFC Joseph M. Foye from Sioux City, Iowa, a veteran of the African and Sicilian campaigns, served as a rifleman in Company C, 60th Infantry, 9th Division. Even though he had suffered severe hearing loss in Sicily when an enemy round had exploded near him, he continued to serve with his company in France. Not long before the invasion, his brother, a crew chief on a B-17, had bailed out over the Cotentin Peninsula and had been rescued by a French family. His rescuers had moved him out of the area by train, telling the Germans who inquired that he was deaf and

Underground position near Cherbourg. The city was surrounded by both old and new fortifications.

dumb. After the breakout in August, Foye's brother made his way to the 3rd Armored Division and was soon on his way back to the States. Meanwhile, Joseph Foye was fighting in the same region where his brother had been hiding before the invasion. During the advance toward Cherbourg,

I went down into a large courtyard where there was a château. I stood in front of the château; all the shutters were closed and I felt something was wrong. Then all of a sudden, a small German half-track marked with a Red Cross entered the courtyard about 300 feet from me. I put my M-1 on it and it stopped. The driver was German and the passenger was an American GI medic. They walked to me. Then all the shutters and doors opened up on the

château and a sad group of our glider people came rushing to me. By that time, the rest of our platoon was there. One major looked like he had gone fifteen rounds with Joe Louis. He told me he went through the windshield of his glider when it hit a hedgerow. Another fellow had his arm off at the shoulder and wanted my Lugar to kill the German doctor. All he got was my cigarettes. Then we moved on.

Another time, our squad was on line behind a low hedgerow. On the enemy side was a secondary gravel road and it made a full left turn. I don't know where I had been but someone came and told me a German jeep was down the road with its motor running. It was about 100 yards from us and turned at an angle into the hedgerow right by a gate. I went down through a field, opened the gate, got in the jeep, and put it in gear, and all I did was hit the bank. I noticed a map and bottle of wine between the seats. I got out and worked the damn thing crossways in the road and was going to take it up to our CP. All of a sudden, there came a German major and his driver. The driver had a machine pistol and the major had his pistol out. I made the wrong decision. I grabbed the map and the wine and ducked down and used the vehicle for protection. I got through the gate and headed for our CP. I gave the map to Captain Hardage. I drank the wine. I have felt many times since then that they may have wanted to give up, but when I raised my rifle at them they did not drop their weapons.

Captain Hardage said, "You go back down there and fill that machine with plenty of armor-piercing bullets." We did it and the Volks kept right on running. I guess we finally realized the motor was in the rear and it finally died. What made me mad was the next day here comes one of the jeeps pulling the little Volks that wouldn't die with Colonel Kaufman sitting on the hood.

Another time, air and tanks softened some town and we were to go in on the left flank. We were on a narrow road with high hedgerows. Sergeant Coffey said, "Foye and Givoniene, get up on the hedgerow and look around." We did and moved forward. A Russian or Polish fellow stood up. I knew he was put there for a reason, maybe trouble ahead. Guess I was starting to get battle-wise. A replacement raised his rifle to shoot him, and I said no. Givoniene took him and I went on alone. In about 300 feet a sergeant came out with his hands up. I yelled, "Achtung!" and about twenty Germans came out of the trenches and lined up. I motioned for the sergeant to take his pistol out of his holster. He did and so did the rest of them. There were P-38s and Lugars all over the ground. I got the sergeant's P-38 and his 10 x 50 field glasses. When the rest of our fellows got there, they had easy pickings for pistols. Then I wondered why they gave up since they could have given us quite a little battle. I saw their antitank gun and then I looked towards the town and saw one of our tanks 200 yards away and the barrel was pointed right at their position. The German antitank gun was in a shallow ravine, pointed the way our platoon came at them. I felt we took them by surprise or they might have planned to surrender.

Pvt. Sam Burns, 2nd Battalion, 39th Infantry, 9th Division, advanced across the peninsula and then turned northward to take part in the battle for Cherbourg.

The company I was with moved to a small town of Octeville[11] and my squad was assigned to secure a final line of departure for the final attack on Cherbourg. We were led by a sixteen-year-old FFI [French Forces of the Interior, i.e., the French Resistance] man named "Louie" through the German lines at night. This fellow knew the country very well, so we had no trouble getting to the location we wanted and the balance of the battalion joined us there the next day. Louie's picture soon appeared in *Yank* magazine. While we were in Octeville, several of us were on the second floor of a building fronting on the main road into Cherbourg and we were getting small arms fire. I noticed a white flag waving from a thatched emplacement in a three- to five-acre field. I

---

11. A town on the southwest side of Cherbourg.

hollered to the squad leader that there was a white flag, but none of the others would admit they could see it. So I was told to go out of the building and cross the road and go through a gate and turn right and move around to the emplacement. As I went through the gate and turned right, the Germans opened up on me and I hit the ground and froze for what seemed hours before I received help in the person of my friend Monroe Broome. Broome caught my foot, dragged me back through the gate, and behind the hedgerow. He told me to never do that again unless someone was with me. Immediately, one our half-tracks pulled up to the gate and started firing at the emplacement. At that time, an 88 opened up on the half-track, knocked the turret [?] off of it, and killed all inside. I cleaned my pants out and found a new location to operate from.

Our platoon leader, Lieutenant Bennett, took several men with him and started down the road to Cherbourg. Lieutenant Bennett was hit bad and called for a medic. The medic going to his aid was killed and Lieutenant Bennett bled to death. Two other men were also hit. We finally broke through and started down the road to Cherbourg, but had to stop to blow up huge concrete traps in the road between two buildings—room for only walk-through traffic—and also we had to blow a round sentry building. We had to search all buildings on both sides of the street. As we were moving down the street, we heard a large explosion on the right side and smoke came out of the second-floor windows. We sent three men to check the situation out and found Bundy Zaglow with a bazooka had blown a wall safe that was empty. We had been worried that someone had been shot or booby-trapped. We continued down the street and took several prisoners on the way until we

German prisoners taken from one of the forts in the harbor after the city was taken.

came to an underground tunnel with a huge maze of complete living quarters and provisions for several hundred men. We got more prisoners out of these rooms and from here we moved on down to *Gestapo* headquarters and spent the night there.

I went into a large bedroom suite—a lavish bed with red satin sheets and pillowcases and red velvet spread with gold fringe—and lying in the bed was Lyle Hendren with a bottle of champagne with all of his gear and clothes on, including muddy boots. We were moved to a rest area for a couple of days.

Private Earl Duncan, also in the 39th Infantry, served as a medic with the weapons company of the 1st Battalion during the battle for Cherbourg.

As the company medical-aid man, it didn't seem that I would get all of the wounded treated and their wounds bandaged for the machine gunners and riflemen, and the attached tank battalion had suffered many casualties. The street fighting was wicked. To make it more difficult for me, one of the rifle platoon medical-aid men had been wounded and had to be evacuated.

A young German medical lieutenant made it through the 39th Infantry lines to ask that the Americans not shell the hospital. He asked that plasma be given to take care of 150 wounded Americans that were in the building.

On June 24, Lt. Henry "Red" Phillips's battalion of the 47th Infantry, 9th Division, approached Cherbourg,

K and I Companies each attacking on parallel ridges that led down to the harbor. In his inimitable way, the battalion commander was leading from in front of one of his companies. . . .

On this day [Lieutenant Colonel] Clayman, a couple of his messengers, and I were huddled in a bomb crater a couple of hundred yards in front of I Company. The radio was out and we were pinned down by a very determined German who was firing from a water tower a few hundred yards to our front. He was a good shot. One of the messengers was winged through the buttock as he dove into the crater.

"My ass! My ass! He shot me in the ass," he cried. The fellow was still in the sniper's sights. Bang! "First my ass and now my heart!" the wounded man yelled. "I'm dead!"

The second shot had creased the soldier's breast as neatly as the first had stitched his fanny. Clayman sympathized: "Take care of the kid so I can think."

The colonel decided to sit tight and let I Company overtake us. . . . K Company was moving well but had become spread out. No one was checking out the wooded draw that extended between the two ridges. Out of this suddenly appeared about fifty grayclads [Germans] who charged into K Company's right flank. After a few minutes firing, those getting the brunt of it fell back . . .

into a farmyard providing some cover and a bit of elevation on the enemy. We watched the Germans crawl up and throw their potato masher–style grenades at the farmyard. A GI ran out of a building, scooped them up and threw them back.

The battalion commander and I watched this through field glasses. It was soon over because someone with high explosives at their disposal began laying it into the draw and the Germans backed off. . . . Later that day, Clayman told me that . . . the guys in the farmyard were M Company machine gunners. The one throwing back the grenades was Pvt. Dick Kinkennon of the 1st Platoon. . . .

. . . Taking the city was no pushover. Sgt. John B. Knight, then a 2nd Platoon squad leader . . . recalls: "We had just taken over a German position. The machine gun was set up and manned by Henry Via and Harold Venem. It was almost immediately destroyed by a German 88 and I remember these men being evacuated in a double-decker stretcher jeep. I later learned that Hank died and Harold was critically hurt...

When he discovered a warehouse loaded with liquor, Lieutenant Colonel Clayman ordered the ammo platoon from the battalion headquarters to drop everything, get down there, and haul everything out before someone learned of their discovery. The last two days of the month, the men of the 3rd Battalion, 47th Infantry, finished the clean up and enjoyed a well deserved rest with copious libations from the loot their commander had confiscated. Meanwhile, Lieutenant Phillips learned that the mortar platoon of Company M had literally burned out its weapons during the artillery duels and that new weapons had to be flown in from England.

The 79th Division arrived on Utah Beach on June 14, followed almost a week later by the 83rd

DUKWs unloading a Liberty ship at Cherbourg in July 1944.

Division.[12] The 79th Division had earned its distinctive Cross of Lorraine patch when it was last in combat back in 1918 in the Argonne sector of France. The division assembled and moved north with the 9th Division to join the 4th Division in the Battle for Cherbourg. The original arrival schedules for the divisions on both beaches had changed so that the 3rd "Spearhead" Armored Division did not land until after the 83rd Division. The 83rd Division was sent south, largely to relieve the paratroopers of the 101st Airborne Division. The 79th Division and the remaining divisions of the VII Corps moved south to join the 83rd Division at the end of the month, after the fall of Cherbourg.

The medical battalion of the 79th Division, the 304th, assigned teams of medics to each of the regiments of the division. First Lt. John A. Kirchner, a doctor with Company A, went with the 314th Infantry. He had commanded the company in the States until shortly before its departure for Europe when replacements had arrived from Attu, Alaska. One of the replacements, a doctor who had a few months seniority, took over the command, and Kirchner had become the executive officer. Company A backed up the three-battalion aid stations of the 314th and always set up camp far enough behind the lines to be out of the range of German small-arms fire, but not enemy artillery.

12. The 83rd Infantry Division was also returning to France, but in 1918, it had served only as a depot division and few of its units saw any action in the Great War. Known as the Ohio Division because of its origin in World War I, its unit patch consisted of the letters O H I and O superimposed. Early in 1945, the 83rd Division took the nickname Thunderbolt.

I believe we left from Tiverton and we had a rough trip across with over half the men seasick and hanging over the edge of the vessel throwing up. It was the closest I ever came to getting seasick. We waded ashore in the morning. There was still sporadic shelling or bombing, but it was relatively light. I waded ashore with the gas mask overhead as all of us had to do. Then we had to get our ambulances and vehicles out of these landing craft and through the water. Many of them had to be winched up on the beach because they would get bogged down in the surf. On the beach, there was some guy up on the high ground with a bullhorn saying, "Don't stay on the beach! Move off the beach!" I thought at the time that was the most useless advice I had ever heard; I had no intention of hanging around there to start up a card game or anything! That day, I had to dig a slit trench. I got halfway through digging and one of the men had to finish it for me. After about a week, I could dig as fast as the next guy.

Our first contact with the enemy was June 19, when the 314th Infantry was ordered to move up around Valognes. The regiment had been in reserve. We were ordered at 7:20 A.M. to move up to the line and attack. That night, our advance was successful, and we had captured the objective. We had five casualties; the first five we had to take care of in our station were noncombat casualties. There were three shot by their own men and two self-inflicted wounds. One of the men shot by his own unit was Captain Martin. This fellow was a company commander of one of the rifle companies and he was a very strict person. I knew him because we were in Camp Blanding, Florida, together. We had set up our tent and they carried in Captain Martin on a stretcher and he looked at me and said,

"Doc, how do you like that, after two years, the first night in combat I had just posted my guards around the field in the dark and went around to check them. As I approached the first one, all I heard was 'Halt!' then Bang!" He was shot through the abdomen and he of course never saw any combat since that was it for him. I think he survived. It was funny in a way because the sergeant who worked with me also knew him. When we got him back to the clearing station, the sergeant said to me, "The man who shot Captain Martin either didn't know him or he did know him."

In Normandy, one of our first casualties was the battalion chaplain, Father Teraney. When we were in the hedgerow country, one of the men had been hit going between hedgerows. Father Teraney volunteered to go out and get him. As he got near the wounded man, he was shot right through the head by a sniper. He may have been our first casualty.

We didn't get much artillery fire, but occasionally the Germans used counterbattery fire that would come in over our heads. We would push off in the morning in Normandy—you would be sleeping in the slit trench and the whole ground would start to shake with our own artillery starting up. The Germans thought it was an automatic system—automatic artillery.

We took care of our own casualties, but as we got in toward Cherbourg, there were as many German wounded as Americans that came through. We had two of our medical officers that took care of casualties and one or two sergeants and I guess a couple of PFCs with them. One of the PFCs was a German fellow who had come to the United States, become naturalized, and then joined the army. His name was Walter Norack. Walter could speak German to these guys [wounded prisoners] and would ask them where they were from. As we were moving up the peninsula towards Cherbourg, a lot of the casualties we saw from the German side were not German; they were Polish, Lithuanian, and Italians assigned to labor units that dug trenches and helped build pillboxes, but they were all in uniform and fought the advancing Americans.

As we worked our way up the peninsula towards Cherbourg, we had a lot of casualties, even in my company. I don't know exactly how many, but during the war, of the ninety-six EM [enlisted men], from my company five were killed and twenty-five wounded. One of them, Private Crittenden, an ambulance driver, was sitting in his ambulance outside the battalion aid station, which was in a stone building. He was eating his lunch, which was kind of a stupid thing to do. An 88 shell hit and cut him right in half in pieces.

Our regiment was the one that captured Fort du Roule. Colonel Robinson, our CO, found that it was stocked with liquor. He saw to it that each officer in the regiment got a bottle of Three Star Hennessy.

We weren't far from the coast and there was a battleship offshore that on occasion fired. One of our men had been captured by the Germans and taken north towards Cherbourg was telling us that as a prisoner he heard this tremendous blast. One of the ships offshore had thrown in what must have been 14-inch shells; it demolished a couple of buildings in the street, and the Germans scattered in every direction. He took off south and made it back to our own lines.

The first so-called combat fatigue casualty we encountered was one of our own infantrymen who was in a line walking up a road in Normandy. They kept a good ten yards or so between men walking along the road and a mortar shell hit in the middle of the road. The man ahead of him had his head taken off right at the shoulders. It was apparently this guy's buddy and he just went berserk. He was trembling and couldn't move. They got him back to our truck and we loaded him up with [methadone].[13] He was crying and yelling that he wouldn't go back to his unit. We just loaded him up and he slept a couple of days. We would wake him up and give him some food and drink. After two or three days, he had settled down, but swore he was not going back. His CO stopped by and talked to him and they took off together for his unit. We didn't have a lot of this.

One of the worst types of casualty we received, other than bodies blown apart by artillery fire or mortars, were victims of flamethrowers. As we worked up towards Cherbourg, I went into one of these pillboxes, which had just been taken, and there were still dead soldiers laying around in it. Some of them had been burned by flamethrowers and you could smell the flesh—it was awful.

We didn't get clothes and shoes for about two weeks. I remember when they brought in shower trucks. This was a unit with four overhead nozzles on each side of an overhead pipe. Four men could go in on each side after they took off their clothes and then they would give a squirt and you would soap up. Then they would give you

---

13. The spelling he used did not match any known drugs. He may have actually been referring to methadone, which was a drug the Germans developed and used in the same way the Americans used morphine.

another squirt and you would run out and dry off while another eight would go in.

One thing not to be appreciated about war is the smell. There were many horses and cows killed by artillery fire and often you could smell what you were coming to long before you reached it. The partly rotted carcasses that had been hit a few days before smelled terrible.

The first strafing we received came from our own air force. It was near a town named Brix. Our unit had laid down a smoke line to show our front line and the German had thrown a smoke line behind us. When the P-38s came over they just strafed everything in sight. We had set up our tent in a field behind a hill. There was a road at the bottom of the hill. There was an engineer truck that had stopped just across the field from us. Of course, when these planes came over we all got down in our holes and it didn't bother us too much. They hit the engineer truck and since it had some ammunition in it, it blew up. A couple of men had gone into the truck as protection against small arms fire, and of course they never found their remains. We had a company clerk, a little guy named Sommerville, who was a Seventh-Day Adventist, and we always had problems with him in the States because he wouldn't work on Saturdays. He kept our company records. When this truck blew up, I could feel a concussion even in the slit trench where I was and the next thing I knew I heard Sommerville running across the field yelling, "Sergeant Morgan! Sergeant Morgan!" Morgan was our top sergeant. I thought Sommerville had been hit. He said, "My file box was hit and all my papers and everything." The poor guy was so conscientious of keeping all the records in a box and now all his records were gone, they were just all over.

Later in the day, they started bringing in casualties. One of them was an American aviator with a broken leg. I don't know how he survived the crash. They brought him into the station, and one of my men said to him, "Were you one of the boys strafing around here today?" He replied, "Not me, friend, not me!"

One of the worst jobs was the Graves Registration units. They would pick up the dead after we advanced, load them on their trucks, and take them back. I remember on one occasion, one of these trucks had pulled up in a field opposite the one we were set up in. It was filled with bodies and they had dug a huge hole in the field and were starting to throw these bodies into the hole. An officer drove by, maybe an infantry colonel; he looked at what was going on and said, "I don't want my men thrown in there with those goddamn Krauts!" The chaplain had prayed over the group and said: "Well, colonel, sir, they are all children of God. . . ." There wasn't much he could do because they had to bury them.

During the battle for Cherbourg, the 79th Division played a key role in assaulting Fort du Roule, a stronghold on the southern side of the fortress. First Lt. Carlos C. Ogden, an April 1941 draftee from San Jose, California, and a November 1942 graduate of officer candidate school, led the 4th Platoon of Company K, 314th Infantry. His landing at Utah Beach was nothing out of the ordinary. The night march into Normandy and the artillery fire were the only events that stood out in his memory until he reached Cherbourg where he took over command of Company K on the morning of June 25 after its commander and executive officer were wounded. He stated that during the battle to take Fort du Roule:

When I came forward, both the 1st and 2nd Platoons were tied down by an 88-mm gun emplacement and two machine guns. Armed with an M-1 rifle, a grenade launcher, and several hand grenades, I was able to work my way up the hill and destroy the 88 and two machine guns, which allowed my company to advance and occupy the hill, which was to the left of Fort du Roule. This allowed the 2nd Battalion of the 314th Regiment to take the fort.[14] I was wounded three times and evacuated on the night of June 25.

Lieutenant Ogden advanced alone against the enemy positions. He was slightly wounded in the head by a round from the German machine gun, but he eliminated the 88-millimeter gun position with a rifle grenade and took out the two machine guns with hand grenades. He was awarded the Medal of Honor for this action. He returned to the front lines on July 4 but was wounded again on July 6 and returned to England.

As Lieutenant Ogden climbed toward the fort to take out those positions that held up his unit, Cpl. John D. Kelly from Venango, Pennsylvania, of Company E, used a ten-foot pole charge against a German bunker that had pinned down his platoon. After one fruitless attempt, he took another charge, climbed the slope again, and destroyed the machine guns that protruded from the bunker. He went back a third time, blew open the armored door of the position, and threw in grenades until the Germans finally surrendered. Like Lieutenant Ogden, Kelly was awarded the Medal of Honor. He later died of wounds sustained in another action after five months of combat. Ogden and Kelly were instrumental in

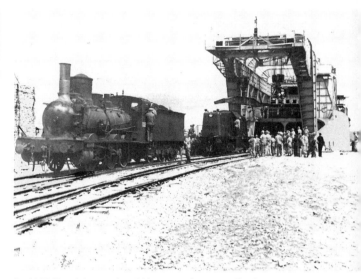

An 1882 French locomotive picking up equipment at Cherbourg and using a railway system army engineers had restored, July 1944.

opening a chink in this key German position, which dominated the city of Cherbourg. By that afternoon, the Americans occupied the upper works of Fort du Roule. However, the four guns in the cliff position below the fort continued to fire on other American troops. At the captured fort, Col. Warren Robinson, commander of the 314th Infantry, tried unsuccessfully to drop explosives on the German gun positions. The next day, June 26, Capt. Paul A. Hurst of Company E led a team that lowered demolitions into the German casemates from above while antitank guns from below fired to divert the enemy. The assaults silenced the German battery permanently. In the meantime, Pvt. Thomas B. Smith of Company M entered a tunnel below Fort du Roule and brought out 159 German prisoners. Eventually, a total of 500 Germans serving in the fort surrendered to the Americans.

Second Lt. Robert T. Dove, a Californian, commanded the 3rd Platoon of the 79th Recon

---

14. Fort du Roule was on a dominant position overlooking Cherbourg and the harbor area. Just below the old fort, the Germans had carved out a gun battery position with four casemate positions for 105-millimeter guns and a gallery linking them. This battery covered the city and port area. The area around the fort was well defended.

Troop[15] of the 79th Division. During the Channel crossing, most of the men with him, including the guards he left on the vehicles, had slept on the LST. They awoke to the sound of cannon fire on shore. A Rhino barge came to ferry them to shore. His platoon's vehicles were among the last to leave. After they landed, they de-water-proofed their vehicles and moved off the beach at a speed of about 20–25 miles per hour. The troop drove to Picauville through Ste-Mère-Église and bivouacked west of the town.

I saw car commanders ahead saluting, so I called attention and got ready to salute. Maj. Gen. Ira Wyche had been our lead vehicle and was directing our troop down a far road. Everyone I saw had a big grin for the general, and he was giving us nods.

The 3rd Platoon was the southern most unit in the field of less than an acre. We had a field or two south of us and a hedgerow enclosed the area. We were a field away from the buildings of Picauville. After out posting our field I walked through the other platoons to the HQ's field holding the command section. I told our commo section where we were and our executive officer that we would soon patrol dismounted to the south and due west of our field. On the way back to my field I told the 1st and 2nd Recon Platoons of our intentions to patrol. The 2nd and 3rd Sections were facing south and the 1st Section of our platoon faced west in our field.

About six of us went on patrol. We first went to the walls of Picauville. It wasn't a walled city, but the house and bar walls gave that impression. We found an abandoned 82nd Airborne trench covering the gully approach to Picauville. The hole was a foot deep and a square big enough for four men to sleep comfortably in. We decided it was a poor spot. It had signs of first aid and lots of empty brass. We discussed why the loose dirt was not camouflaged. There was no overhead cover, and if you sat up, your chest and head would be exposed. There was no "pot hole" in which to drop incoming hand grenades before they exploded. Worse still, there was no "back door." The west wall of Picauville was unpierced for 100 feet in each direction. Still, the position was high and had a great field of fire.

In the gully to the west, we found the bodies of three Germans. There were also casualty signs beyond the bodies. The bodies were off-color, and I saw no one go within three feet of them. This was the first time I realized our maps showed each hedgerow enclosed field. I was able to locate the bodies to an "eight figure" grid location.[16] The bodies were the basis for the first message I wrote in France—it was to the QM Company of all things. We were around the bodies more than wanted and one of my "quick lips" asked to move on as he was getting hungry.

We saw other signs of combat, mostly empty brass. I was told of other German dead to the west, but we saw nothing but empty fields for about 600 yards from our field. June 17 was our first day in France, and it was very routine. We could hear cannon fire to the north, but no small arms fire.

Our second day was duller yet, at least until midafternoon. The lieutenants were called to the CP tent. HQ Platoon was well set up in their field. We must have had a

---

15. Every infantry division had a company-size recon unit called troop, a cavalry term for company.

16. The military grid on the maps issued to American troops made it easy to pinpoint a location without using latitude and longitude. This also allowed forward observers, including those in L-4 aircraft, to quickly radio in the coordinates to the artillery fire.

land line phone to division, as Lt. William C. Miller, our executive officer, briefed us on the mission for June 19. We were heading north to Cherbourg as fast as we could go. We were to go around the Germans that we "couldn't push or wouldn't leave." We were told many things, but three days of rations and extra ammo seemed more important than the rest. Our troop commander, Capt. James F. Beaver, arrived from his briefing. He only had to emphasize speed and "follow our SOPs [standard operating procedures] as long as they fit." Our command section gave us our June 19 frequencies and three copies of our brevity code. We had a two letter code for all letters, numbers and words like "Wilco" and "Roger" and phrases, i.e., "road cratered at," "bridge blown at," "continuing on mission," etc.

I went back to the platoon, gathered all the 3rd Section so that their two guards could hear, and we talked a long time. We went over every subject we could think of. We couched that even though we weren't slated for the first mission, we would prepare for it as "it was the only war we have right now."

When we broke up many had jobs to do. I asked my radio operator, T/4 John Adank, to quickly change all radios to the new frequencies, but to have one 510 and one 506 on current listening silence. He reminded me that would be a violation of radio security and procedure. So I said, "So tap it in." My guys loved to play code and had a tap-to-mike code. We called it "jungle radio." For the next hour or so one vehicle at a time would leave for a spot up to a thousand yards away and enter the "jungle net." So far as we knew we did not get caught. That violation gave an added benefit as all drivers were previously starting engines every hour as they were sure listening silence would drain their batteries. With the new arrangement, only my M-8 motor was started every hour.

As I had called, "Up and ready!" on June 19 at 0400 hours, many were fed and bunked down with the late afternoon sun in their face. Yes, I heard a few "hurry up and wait" comments.

Except for guard duty in place (no walking to or fro in combat) the night was just more cannon fire in the distance. I was in the CP tent by 0345 on June 19. I was studying the situation map when Captain Beaver came in bright and cheery five minutes later. He sent for all officers. I stayed at the CP as the 1st and 2nd Platoon leaders left. Soon after 0350, the 1st Platoon leader returned to say he wouldn't be able to make the IP (initial point) on time since his men weren't ready and his radios were not on mission frequency. So the 2nd Platoon got the assignment. They reported soon after 0430 that they too wouldn't make the IP on schedule. As Captain Beaver blew steam, I signaled one of my men at the HQ field gate to relay the "mount up, start engines, and move out" signals. I told Captain Beaver that "we have got it." He tried to give me some late reminders. I walked away with "No more time; I have seven turns and seven miles and nineteen minutes." He was following me and yelling, "Boy, I'm going to love you!" when my scout sergeant, Willie Medonal, asked, "What's that all about?" I said, "It's the exuberance of youth." I rode sidesaddle on the lead jeep and we moved out fast.

By repeated double-time signals, we were soon going very fast at 30 mph on country roads in early light, which is dangerous. We went faster! Slowing down is tough too, and we had to slow to about 8 mph so as to cross the IP at 12 mph. Two division HQ captains were at the IP with two 313th Infantry officers. One division officer gave us the boxer victory sign and the other put his finger on his nose as he looked at his watch. I was the wiser and the 3rd Platoon guessed what had happened at troop. We entered the radio net and reported the crossing of the IP—now called "start point." The message was coded of course. We had been told that Colombe was unoccupied, but we skirted south and west of the village as I didn't want the chance of being stopped in town. We took a road leading northwest toward Nègreville, which was just outside the division boundary. I stopped the column west of Colombe when I knew we were well in front of the infantry and out of sight. I got off the lead jeep and joined my M-8. This first mission was loaded with tension and I kept wondering if we were doing things the best way. I remember being very watchful and wondering what I should think of next. We reconnoitered by bounds and used our binoculars often. There was no "egg hunting" on contact with French civilians. So far as I know, we spoke to the French for the first time on June 24, north of the battle area, but within sight of it. A good father type wheeled a load of bread across the road to his outdoor oven. He had eight to twelve loaves to bake and he was going to do his chores—war or no war.

On June 19, we had a few things to grin about. We shot up the east side of Nègreville with only the .50 cal. jeeps and the 1st and 2nd Section M-8s firing machine guns and cannon. As we fired, the 3rd Section .50 cal. jeeps opened up full automatic, but 200 yards to the rear. When the front of the column quit firing to reload, the 3rd Section's .50 cal. remained quiet. At least I knew we weren't surrounded. I jogged to the rear about 170 yards to see what the firing was

all about. The .50 cal. gunner had fired into a hedgerow to the east while Nègreville had been to our west. I don't remember my question to the gunner, but the answer was "The Germans didn't know I couldn't see anything." I thought better of talking to him, so I stepped behind the jeep and spoke to Sgt. Edward Dolpak, saying, "Did you give the order to commence firing?" He answered, "No, sir!" "Sergeant, did you give the order to cease fire?" I asked. Again, "No, sir!" "Well", said I, "you just keep doing what you think is right till we decide different." I grinned at them all, but they all laughed at me as I walked away. They knew damned well I had evaded a situation.

After leaving Nègreville, we soon found an abandoned German trailer-mounted 88-mm flak cannon. The tiller man was dead in his seat. The prime mover was disconnected and pulled back on the road and left. We checked for mines and booby traps, and then I opened the breach, threw in an ignited thermite grenade, and closed the breach. We reported the location and went on.

We passed the Bois de la Briuq—the 1st Battalion objective—to the west before noon and continued on to the northeast for another 2000 yards. We then moved slowly across the objective front watching north, east and south. We didn't want to be shot up by anyone. We claimed we could see and control. We went slowly and drew our second grin. The NCS (Net Control Station) sent an encoded message: "Can you move faster?" T/4 John Adauk, my M-8 radio operator, decoded and answered for me as I was with the 1st Section at the time. He quickly answered, "No!" No encoding, no use of the procedure word "negative"—just flat "no!" All could hear NCS laughing when he got "Roger and out." NCS had bugged us all morning—SOP. They asked for progress reports every 15–20 minutes. They were doing as told, but HQ was tense too!

We returned due west to clear the front of the 1st Battalion of the 313th Infantry and moved slowly south cross country. The infantry was exactly where we expected to find them. We came in from the west and dismounted. The infantry sergeant was irate that his watchers hadn't reported before they saw three vehicles moving in.

We moved south, possibly 300 yards, and found battalion HQ. The platoon halted along their west flank as I reported and was debriefed. We got lots of complaints as Lt. Col. Van Bibbor was informed of our progress hourly. He asked us to stick close and add protection to his CP. I told him our mission was to continue to recon to the north and that we would be moving over our present tracks at first light. He said he would personally inform all guards of our proposed movement.

We moved 100 yards to the rear south to block the road the battalion CP was on. We could also fire across their west flank. We soon became aware of a German machine gun ripping off bursts of twenty to the southeast of us. The range was 800 to 1,200 yards, and we concluded their fire blocked an east-west road to our rear. Soon the infantry battalion S-4 in a jeep with a driver pulled up to our orchard gate. We talked over the situation. He was going back for his supply trucks to bring them up for resupply of the forward companies. Our last words warned him of the German machine gun to the east. Minutes later, we heard the machine gun go full automatic for many seconds. We hoped it wasn't for the battalion S-4, but it was. We heard his jeep before we saw him. When he came into view, he was

sitting high, on the body of his driver. We stopped him and recovered the driver's body. I gave him a driver and the 3rd Section. My instructions to Sergeant Polsak were simple: "Take the captain to his supply point, help him load, and return with him here as soon as you can." I told him to follow this phone wire and if he didn't like where it led to go around to the west and rejoin the wire. While they were gone, we talked over the tragedy and wrapped the body in a shelter half. I then asked the two sections who wanted a pistol as a side arm. The platoon wanted seventeen pistols.

Sergeant Dolsk, with his section leading, was back within an hour and a half. Following the phone wire had done the job. The S-4 had another driver and three 2½-ton trucks. He and I talked. Soon the captain was back to our position with his empty trucks. He now had an M-1 rifle on his lap. Before his personal weapon was a pistol. He and I went to the side again and I asked for seventeen pistols for the platoon. His first reaction was explosive: "My God! I've only seven in the battalion." His next action was to give me the pistol, magazine pouch with two magazines off his belt. He said, "From here on I dance with the dame I know—an M-1." We spent minutes planning delivery of the other sixteen pistols, knowing they would be short-stopped, as all GIs are thieves. We stopped the order on July 10 as some found the pistols weighed more than they wanted. I carried my pistol and carbine until December.

On June 25, Dove's 3rd Platoon had breakfast at about 3:00 A.M. and then got into its vehicles and drove to the battalion of the 315th Infantry farthest to the north. Lieutenant Dove's platoon numbered twenty-eight men and an attached medic. Dove left several men with the vehicles and took eighteen on a foot patrol carrying mostly ammunition, but no radio or food. They first went to the battalion command post tent.

I went in with one eye closed to save night vision and explained our mission to six standing officers while they grinned at me. I was filthy and wore no insignia. One lieutenant colonel said, "I've got to see this!" I followed him outside and stayed beside him. He spoke in a low voice about the mission until his vision improved. When he realized we were armed to the teeth and all were equally dirty, he stopped talking and walked the line. None of us had had a bath or real cleanup since England. He went back to the front and center and said, "I would hate to be out there in German boots today." He left us laughing. Neither Patton nor Ike could have made a more inspiring speech or made us feel top rung. I still don't know who the officer was.

We walked quietly to the right flank of the battalion. When well clear, we turned west. We were on a fair road when we captured the first German. It was morning at dark-gray light. We sent him back to the CP with one [man] since we thought he might be of real value. With the prisoner gone, we bypassed to the right about 150 yards. At first light, German mortars began firing on both our right and left. We were traveling west once again. We encountered about six field telephone lines and knew they were German. Eight of us pulled all the slack from the lines and cut 300 feet from each line leaving a gap of 100 feet. Some of the wire guys were looking north until I called them back. The mortars to the north never resumed firing to our knowledge.

We soon turned southwest, then south. The first Germans we saw were trailing at quite a distance. Our rear men waved them back as I didn't want to chance anything before the battalion jumped off.

We were west of and ahead of the battalion when the firing started. The three Germans we killed were members of the *Nebelwerfer* team. They were walking north when we saw them. Four of us fired. As we were looking for more targets, return fire, etc., the screaming-meemie fired six rounds toward east-southeast, not toward us, who were 150 yards due west. The noise was awesome! The *Nebelwerfer* team then destroyed the launcher. We could get glimpses of the action, but they offered no targets.

Generally, we kept pace with the battalion advance. We went by sound only. We soon captured three Germans and took their bottle of cognac. I then made contact with the right flank infantry company. I met with and talked to the first sergeant and one man. I sent for the three prisoners and gave them to the infantry. Then we drifted south and a little west and never fired another round all day. Sometimes we surprised the enemy and they surrendered. At times they saw us first and then surrendered. By late afternoon, there were seventeen of them and seventeen of us. The area had been quiet for three to five hours. We headed toward the area when the last firing was heard. We were quite a mob and we went slowly. To the question, "Where the hell have you guys been?" I said, "Have any of your guys some extra rations?" Then followed the most dangerous part of the day when C rations rained on us from all directions. Those clowns fired in volley trying to hit the Germans, I hope. At 40 mph a can of wienies and beanies hurt if not caught. We sat down in the road and had a picnic. We had to show the Germans how to use the little folding can opener. They thought the opener a marvelous invention.

Soon two officers came over and I told them the situation to the front. We ate in twenty minutes and left the prisoners with the infantry company. We had a long walk back to our vehicles, then a fair ride to the Troop CP in the dark of June 25. I reported to the Troop CO who listened to my account. He said, "Colonel McMahon is a real gentleman. He is new to the division, so he gets credit for all those Germans."

Our NCS was always busy. The Germans must have considered our NCS a likely target. All six rockets from the *Nebelwerfer* had the range, but landed 150 yards to the south of their M-8 armored cars.

On June 25, the 79th Recon Troop suffered its first casualty at Tollevast when Tech 5 Nordfleet of the 2nd Platoon went on a three-man foot patrol and was hit by small-arms fire when he approached a camouflaged bunker. He was seriously wounded and was finally rescued by his sergeant. The platoon slept until noon on June 26. Dove and his platoon not only destroyed a *Nebelwerfer*, but also killed three Germans and captured seventeen prisoners. One of these prisoners gave information that helped an infantry patrol capture forty more men in a bunker who were waiting for the opportunity to shoot up advancing American troops.

On June 26, the 1st and 2nd Platoon fought into sections of Cherbourg. During the preceding days, few in the platoons had time to wash and shave. All looked tired, ugly and were dirty with sweat-streaked faces. Captain Beaver thought at least one in the troop should look victorious. He was clean and in his best pink and greens and had shined cavalry boots. All who saw him said he was ready for a parade or fit to kill. His personal weapon was an ivory handled .45 revolver with extra ammo across the top

of the open-style holster. He went into town with one of the platoons. In the heat of the battle, a German with a machine pistol jumped from concealment and took on Captain Beaver at 70 yards. We called his weapon a "Schmiesser." Captain Beaver drew and leaned against a building to steady his aim. The German fired full automatic but quit when Captain Beaver hit him the second time. Beaver's order was to "patch him up and get him to a doctor." A few minutes later, one of the platoons saw signs of blood on the captain's back. A German bullet had passed between Captain Beaver and the wall. The wound was more of a red welt than a cut. The shirt had a nine-inch cut, which caused Captain Beaver to slip into a kill-all attitude. He was in a rabid mood for at least a day. So we didn't turn in any prisoners to the troop. On about June 28 or June 29, I saw him for the first time in nearly a week. He questioned me about turning two prisoners over to the infantry. I told him yes and that I gave two more away to an engineer team and that until he got over his torn shirt I wasn't going to turn in any. He laughed and said, "Shirt—shit! I've got other shirts; it's prisoners we want because when we do the work, we should get the credit!"

The 4th Division, the first ashore at Utah Beach, also took part in the battle for the fortress while clearing the northeast part of the Cotentin. T/5 Fred R. Tannery, a messenger from the 4th Signal Company with his own jeep and driver, was attached to division headquarters throughout the entire war in Europe. In June, during the battle for Cherbourg, he received the only message he delivered during the war.

I had to deliver a message from division headquarters to a forward command post just outside of Cherbourg. While driving down the main road into Cherbourg, nearing our drop-off point, a German shell landed in front of my jeep. My driver stopped the jeep and we jumped out and crawled into a ditch. While hugging the ground, the Germans continued to shell the area. I finally crawled to the jeep and drove it behind a stone wall. Then I ran back into the ditch. My driver, Pappy Sloan, was ahead of me in the ditch. A shell landed in some hedge growth above me. Then something told me to move and when I did, a shell landed in the spot I had moved from. Luckily, we were not hurt. Finally, the shelling stopped and I was able to deliver the message. At times, my driver and I drove into some very tight quarters even driving under mortar fire, that's how close we were to the front lines.

For the remainder of the campaign, Tech 5 Tannery and his driver simply watched the war go by and were more what he considered to be GI tourists.

Sometime after June 21, Pvt. William E. Finnigan, who also served in the 4th Signal Company, advanced on Cherbourg with his division.

We were shelled by friendly fire and lost a couple who never returned. At a small village square, we were strafed one sunny day, but no one was hit. We were bombed another night. We sat on the hillside above Cherbourg and watched our artillery pound the breakwater forts where the Germans were holding out.

In Normandy, everything was squeezed together so you heard the screaming-meemies at night and, when quiet, the "wosh-wosh" sounds of our shells going over above us.

According to Finnigan, most of the German equipment was of little use to the Americans.

The only German army equipment we used were their field telephones, as they worked fine on our system. One of the largest groups in our company consisted of Indians from Oklahoma with names such as Elgin Red Elk. They said they had been brought in to write their language, which could be used as a coded communication, but it seems code machines ended the need for that.[17]

When we left the LST, we "liberated" quite a few gallon cans of fruit cocktail. The ten-in-one ration was highly desired. I always looked for the D ration chocolate bar! K rations were barely acceptable and C rations required too much preparation.

For S.Sgt. Murphy Chustz, 42nd Field Artillery, 4th Division, the food was unsatisfactory. "The kitchen caught up with us on D+7 and we had a few hot meals, but mostly it was C and K rations. . . . Before D-Day, I was 185 pounds, but when we got to Paris I weighed 165 pounds, although I picked it up later!"

Private Ralph Brazee was a gunner in an anti-tank company of the 22nd Infantry whose 57-millimeter antitank guns were towed by half-tracks. His company also included jeeps and a supply truck. Their first mission came as the regiment advanced up the coast.

We first fired our gun from the hedgerow right behind an infantry company. Our target at that point was a church steeple the Germans were using as an observation post.

---

17. The Native Americans sent and translated messages in their own language, which was unknown to the enemy and faster than a normal message that had to be encoded.

I don't recall the number of HE [high-explosive] shells we fired at that target. During this first firing, the Germans spotted our position and gun flashes and they retaliated with their *Nebelwerfers*, which we called screaming-meemies. They had concussion and some shrapnel, but weren't very accurate. Our jeep was in the middle of a field and never was hit, except for minor shrapnel marks.

We did not fire many more times because we were on the roads to protect against tanks, which the Germans did not have on the way to Cherbourg. On the advance to Cherbourg, late one day, we moved our gun into position along a road behind the front line when I noticed five German aid men on the other side of our hedgerow. I went to get a buddy to help me and by the time we got over the wall, they had vanished.

Another time, we had placed our gun by hand on the top of a small open hill. Before we were fully operational, an 88 tried to knock out our gun. The gun was way off near Cherbourg and never made a direct hit. They were either too short or over, which was good for us.

During the advance on Cherbourg, Capt. Robert B. Kaye of Company I, 3rd Battalion, 12th Infantry, was wounded on the outskirts of Tourlaville probably on June 24.

Teddy Roosevelt visited our CP outside of the town of Tourlaville. I was given the dubious honor of controlling the mass fire of VII Corps artillery to support us to our front prior to attacking a wooded position and taking the high ground. I remember very vividly calling in and correcting the shellfire as it whizzed over us by lowering it a 200-yard adjustment and creep it up. We

Trucks being loaded at Cherbourg. Note the truck in the foreground loaded with Jerry cans.

were able to move up after, although shrapnel was coming back close to us as it dropped in close. The massing of artillery was a concentrated firing problem in which I think each weapon from behind was to fire ten or seventeen rounds and having adjusted on 200 yards down it came in closer and I walked it back up. I think this contributed to the fact they we were successful in taking the town of Tourlaville shortly thereafter that night and the next morning. Unfortunately, I was wounded shortly thereafter that night and I did not see the final result of capturing Cherbourg.

On the other hand, Sgt. Leonard F. Herb, a draftee from Philadelphia who served in the Intelligence and Reconnaissance Platoon of HQ Company of the 12th Infantry, got to witness the battle for Cherbourg.

Our platoon entered Cherbourg after it was captured by our rifle companies [on June 26]. Several of our men were still lying in the streets with a covering of flowers. The local citizens appreciated our presence. We occupied the high ground and watched as our cannon company fired on the outlying fortified islands.

We ate extremely well as the German garrison departed hurriedly: jellies, butter, bread, fish, wine, etc.

For 1st Lt. Peter Triolo, an officer on the staff of the 12th Infantry who had served as a liaison with the 82nd Airborne Division on D-Day, the assault on the Cherbourg forts in the harbor was one of the most memorable operations of the campaign.

When we captured Cherbourg on or about June 25, in the harbor, about 1,000 yards out, was a reinforced fort, which held three large naval guns. The navy informed us they could not come in and occupy the harbor of Cherbourg until this outer fort was neutralized. The 4th Division, along with the air force, had two air raids: one with 500-pound bombs and the other with 1,000-pound bombs, which had no effect on the outer fort. Lucky as the American soldier is sometimes, in one of the last air bombardments, they wounded the commanding officer and some of the other officers and men, and they knocked out their radio contact with German HQ.

They [the Germans] contacted us by flag signal asking us for medical services, which our regimental commander refused unless they surrendered. At first, they refused to surrender, and finally did so with the understanding they would get medical attention if they surrendered to us.

What we discovered to our surprise was that the harbor was magnetically mined and that a steel-bottomed ship could not get out from the harbor to the fort, so we had to find the harbormaster who informed us where the lanes were and helped us get a wooden-bottom boat. So I took a squad from one of the rifle companies and my sergeant and sailed out to the fort and accepted the surrender of the troops out there.

It is amazing what we found there in the outer fort. Some of the walls were twenty to thirty feet thick, solid concrete and the gun emplacements were behind solid steel walls ten to twelve inches thick. The guns would go out and shoot and retreat back and this solid steel door would close in front of them. We found in the fort a hospital, living quarters equal to the Holiday Inn, canned food, cakes, and anything the troops needed to live on there for months.

My problem with the German soldiers was that they did not want to leave the fort. So we had them all surrounded in one of the gun emplacement positions, which was a circular area about twenty-five to thirty feet in diameter, under machine-gun protection.

My problem was that I was left out there with about 24 men to guard about 150 to 160 Germans. The thing that caused the most excitement was that at about 5:00 P.M. a line of American DUKWs came into the harbor. When the Germans saw them, they came out of the fort and refused to load onto them, yelling, "Magnetic mines! Magnetic mines!" So I instructed the sergeant that unless they loaded right away we were going to shoot them all and leave. When we fired a burst of machine gun fire over their heads, they all started running down the stairwell and got into the DUKWs and we sailed to land.

All the forts surrendered, including the one with the control panel for detonating the mines. The approaches to the harbor, already badly damaged by German demolitions, finally fell to

The Rear Area of a Combat Division

In addition to the divisional headquarters, there were regimental headquarters that served the frontline battalions in various capacities ranging from distribution of personnel to supplies. According to CWO-2 Lawrence "Larry" Knecht, Capt. John Galvin's assistant adjutant, their operations in Normandy were only slightly different from their personnel office in England. Knecht, who alternated his duties with Captain Hollis at the personnel office, was in charge, among other things, of battlefield promotions. Upon the recommendation of the regimental commander, Galvin, Hollis, or Knecht swore in the newly promoted officers. Since they were not located near the regimental headquarters in the field, either Hollis or Knecht made the trip there. They handled all the recommendations for medals and awards in the personnel section.

Two burial grounds had to be opened near the 2nd Replacement Depot in the vicinity of Ste-Mère-Église. The first, Mohawk 1, filled so quickly that the second, Mohawk 2, soon replaced it. It was here at the 2nd Replacement Depot that Knecht met his friend from prewar days at Fort Screven, Charles Ratteree, who had gone through officer candidate school and was waiting to be assigned to his former Company C. After trying in vain to convince Ratteree to take a position at headquarters, Knecht took him to the division command post, where they met General Barton, the division commander.

General Barton was sitting and another officer on staff said, "General, I have a paratrooper here that would like to speak to you." While I was standing right there with Lieutenant Ratteree, this paratrooper came up to this general and saluted him. I could see something was wrong mentally with the man with his eyes jumping around in his head and all that. General Barton was sitting on a stool and they stood right in front of him. Paratroopers had lots of pockets and this man had been operating alone like some of them did for days and he evidently had been lost. I think he suffered from shell shock and all that it sort of made him deranged. He started pulling ears—German ears—out of his pocket and he was putting them on the ground in front of the General. The general kept looking and couldn't believe this. This man was pulling ears out from all those pockets. He said, "General I decided I would bring you these ears to show you what we have been doing, to see that we did our job." General Barton called over one of his staff and told him to take this man to an aid station. That is the last I heard of that because I went back up to the regiment.

Lieutenant Ratteree received the assignment he wanted to Company C, 1st Battalion, 8th Infantry. Not long after, Larry Knecht visited the grave of his old friend at Mohawk; he had been killed shortly before the battle for St. Lô.

Much of the work at the cemetery was done by African-American troops.

continued

This was dangerous work, according to Clay [Brooks], because some paratroopers that had pulled pins on grenades and put rubber bands on them.[18] What actually happened was that when the bodies of the paratroopers started coming in down on the beach, a paratrooper cemetery was established called Mohawk. Several men had been severely hurt and some killed on the burial details. I remember that because of this business of paratroopers putting these grenades in their jacket. The people burying them instead of opening their pockets and reaching in and taking the grenade out, used long pocket knives to slit the pockets open and reach in and pull the lever on the grenade and pull them out that way because they didn't know whether the pin was pulled or not.

I talked to one of the men doing the burials. They would have a little cloth bag that would hold maybe a pound and they would get any items from the body; rings off the fingers, etc. When men died, their hands would swell, so to get the rings off and put them in the bags they had short knives and they would cut to the bone to take it off and put it in the sack with anything else, such as a watch. They would put these in the bag and attach the dog tags for ID. One of them would lift the body up. They had mattress covers to bury those men in. After they got all the personal effects, they would tie up the end of the mat-

tress cover and throw them in the hole. Putting these bodies in there and seeing how it was done just shocked me and I will always remember it.

At the replacement depot, Knecht reported to the major in charge and gave him a requisition form from Captain Galvin for officers, NCOs, and others. During the night, he escorted the replacements to the regiment's service company where the men received different-colored tags before they were sent on to the battalions.

Just as in England, paperwork for court-martials had to be prepared. Knecht drew up the specifications or charges for either a special or general court-martial. Early in the war, they tended to be general court-martials and involved several officers charged with "misbehaving before the enemy." Although the phrase usually refers to cowardice, Knecht denied that this was always the case. However, there were few such cases, and none involving the older officers, only the replacements. One of Knecht's own friends, a company cook, sought solace in the bottle to relieve the stresses of war. One night, bottle in hand, he went to the home of young girl and her mother. When the women locked the door to keep him out, he started shooting through the door, killing the mother. After a court-martial, the man was sentenced twenty years at Leavenworth. The only man Knecht remembered being executed after a court-martial was a soldier in England who had shot the first sergeant in the head in the barracks with a .45 pistol.

---

18. Clay Brooks, Knecht's brother-in-law, was a paratrooper in the 82nd Airborne Division.

continued

The Rear Area of a Combat Division *continued*

One enlisted man, who had been in trouble in the United States, where he had been court-martialed several times, went to Normandy with the division and deserted. A few days later, Knecht received a report the man had turned up at division headquarters. Knecht went to retrieve him and turned him over to the MPs.

He tried to tell me he did not know what he was doing, but he was in deep trouble. He took off his helmet and there was a hole in it, somebody had shot through it and I asked if it was on his head when they shot. He said yes. So I put the helmet back on his head and where the hole reached to his ear.

There were few court-martials among officers, but it was not very long before the army started reclassifying them. If an officer became too shaky at the front, he was sent to the rear and was reclassified at the personnel office, which involved sending him back to England to a special unit. Knecht also knew of a very brave officer he had known for many years, who broke and ran back past the beach into the water during the invasion and was subsequently reclassified.

American control so that repairs and reconstruction could begin.

When Cherbourg fell, CWO-2 Larry Knecht was in a jeep, approaching the city when he came across a group of Germans.

There were about seven to eight Germans and some of them were lying down, but most of them were sitting up. Some of them were propped up against an apple tree. One of them had a rifle across his legs. They were white as sheep, but I looked at them and there was not a mark on them, no blood or nothing. I remember taking my foot and lifting it up and kicking one of them on the shoulder and he just fell over. They were stiff, just as if they were made out of wood. What actually happened, or the conclusion I came to, was that the big shells that the battleships fired evidently burst high enough to cause enough concussion to kill them, but I don't know.

I remember when Cherbourg fell and the Germans gave up. I went into the city and the first thing I saw was an island with what looked like German ack-ack being attacked by American planes. I stood up and watched this for a while, but the next thing I saw was one of the most terrible explosions I have ever seen in my life, just a mass. . . . It wasn't until a few years ago I talked to a former captain of the 29th Field Artillery who was a spotter for the artillery. He was the one that fired those shots.

While at Cherbourg, I remember a humorous incident when a German officer, all dressed up in a parade uniform, was standing on a corner. I understand later that he was a field marshal in charge of the whole thing.[19] He had two suitcases, one

---

19. This was Major General von Schlieben, who commanded the troops defending Cherbourg.

on each side, and he looked like he was waiting for some taxicab or something to pick him up. He had a full uniform with medals on and everything.

I went into this mountain inside the city and it had all kinds of supplies, cases and cases of Norwegian sardines, big round cheeses—they had everything. After the soldiers got inside that mountain position, all that food disappeared.

There were also a lot of whorehouses in Cherbourg. The girls were French and after the town fell, the French Resistance gathered all these girls up and shaved their heads. What a sight!

During the fighting around Cherbourg, Knecht spotted Lt. Earle Dooley in a field, sitting under a tree, his back against the trunk. He told his driver to stop the jeep and pull over. Seeing that Dooley seemed very depressed, Knecht went over to talk to him to see what was wrong. Pointing to a black hole about fifty feet from the tree, Dooley told him that the night before he had been separated from his platoon and heard Germans talking so he had frozen in his tracks and tried to find the source of the voices. He had crawled over to the hole where he heard Germans talking beneath the ground. He had taken two grenades, pulled the pins, and thrown them into the hole. He said, "You should have heard the sound coming out, the men screaming—then I took my automatic and stuck it down the hole and fired three or four bursts until I heard no more sounds." Knecht went over and peering into the hole saw a nightmarish scene of carnage. A few days after this encounter, Knecht learned that Dooley was killed.[20]

Pvt. William C. Montgomery, a litter-bearer with Company A of the 4th Medical Battalion,

passed through Fresville, Montebourg, and Valognes with his unit on the way to Cherbourg late in June.

As the infantry fought its way up to Cherbourg, we came under sniper fire a number of times. Once, some paratroopers stopped, searched the perimeter of the field where our aid station was, drew fire, and flushed out and killed two snipers in trees [in the advance on Montebourg]. We found a cache of their ammunition nearby and were astounded to find they were using wooden bullets in metal cartridges. Some of the bullets were stained in blue, some red.

I never actually saw Cherbourg, but in the rolling country at the rim of it we came under fire from 88s that ringed the city below as antiaircraft guns. They were mounted on pedestals, which I saw some of later. They fired air bursts low above us and took a hellish toll.

From Cherbourg, we moved to the base of the peninsula to relieve paratroopers who had been fighting in the swamps and hedgerows there since they had landed. I think it was the 82nd Airborne. The foxholes and fortifications the Germans had improvised in the hedgerows were amazing.

PFC Harper Coleman's machine-gun squad of Company H, 8th Infantry, was engaged numerous times during the advance on Cherbourg, including when it was ambushed while moving through a wooded area along a road up a hill. An enemy machine gun opened fire from their rear, and they had to "run the gauntlet up the hill for some hundred yards or so." Not everyone made it, and "I passed one person holding his insides

---

20. Knecht's perception of time was, understandably, somewhat distorted. An article in the *New York Times* reports that Dooley died months later in the Hurtgen Forest. In the early 1950s in Saigon, Knecht met a famous navy doctor named Tom Dooley III, who served a on a ship carrying refugees from the north. He was Earle Dooley's half brother.

with his hands and begging for help, but there was no stopping."

After the surrender of Cherbourg, Coleman's 2nd Battalion was put in a deserted German naval barracks on the edge of town. For the next few days, they did police work, but the large shower tents arrived; they received their first new set of clean clothes since leaving England as they exited the shower. The field kitchens also began serving hot meals, the first Coleman remembered since disembarking. A few days later, they loaded onto trucks and moved south to take part in the battle of the hedgerows in the St. Lô area.

PFC John A. Plonski, a volunteer from New York City, was a BAR man with an infantry platoon of the 8th Infantry. He was sent on many combat patrols and miraculously went untouched until he was wounded in January 1945. He considered himself extremely lucky but complained that many of the reinforcements his unit received were not well trained. Some, he claimed, "couldn't even load their M-1 when a new clip had to be put in, but they always volunteered to go on patrols—mostly the American Indians who were my best replacements and not afraid of anything."

Payday

Lt. Luther Richard Underwood splashed ashore at Utah Beach late in June at the head of his 21st Finance Disbursing Section, carrying heavy metal field safes filled with invasion currency. Underwood and his men moved off the beach in a "liberated" German *Opel* truck, which they used throughout the campaign. They spent the first night in the hedgerows off the beach. The unit was subsequently attached to the First Army Headquarters (Rear) and moved into Cherbourg behind the 4th Division.

Lieutenant Underwood had many friends in the 4th Division, whom he met from time to time since he and his unit were responsible for army- and corps-level finances.

I looked up my former buddies of Company B, 8th Infantry, including Sgt. Homer Dixon, who later lost a leg in the Hurtegen Forest. Right after entering Cherbourg, we saw some Rangers riding some of the "liberated" horses about Cherbourg. We set up operations in a downtown building in Cherbourg and it seemed like we were an international bank as we began supporting the multitudes of military personnel that began assembling there and passing through: British, Dutch, French, etc., mostly for exchanging or converting currency. Our unit stayed in Cherbourg until St. Lô fell.

When the dead soldiers were placed at Collection Points, the Graves Registration units that identified them and gathered their personal effects turned in the money found to the Finance Section—us—for proper accountability and credit. We received money stained with blood and some with bullet holes. Such money could not be reused so we had to list it by denomination and serial number and then burn it. The witnessed list was sent to the U.S. Treasury Department.

At one of the collections sites, it was sad to see the miscellaneous personal effects scattered about the area, which were not part of the accountable effects. I saw countless little packages of rubber condoms scattered all about the site. Apparently, this was an item of issue along with the French francs that was a morale booster for the troops, or at least that was my opinion.

CHAPTER 5

Operations in Normandy

Summary of June Operations

The British achieved most of their objectives on landing, but they soon faced most of the major German armored formations so that, instead of taking Caen during the first days of the invasion as planned, they had to fight for the city for several weeks.

The V Corps of the U.S. First Army established itself on Omaha Beach with unexpected difficulty, but after it finally secured the beachhead, its divisions advanced inland, pushing deep past the Cerisy Forest and denying the Germans the chance to turn it into a major obstacle. However, German resistance stiffened and the V Corps was unable to take St. Lô, a pivotal position. The American VII Corps landed on the wrong beach, but turned the Utah beachhead into a success with the help of the two airborne divisions that made it virtually impossible for the Germans to drive the infantry back.

By June 17, the American V Corps had advanced as far south as Caumont, but had come to a stop before St. Lô. In the meantime, the newly operational XIX Corps secured the area between the two American beachheads as early as June 10. A British offensive of mid-June had failed to encircle Caen. The British XXX Corps was repulsed by the newly arrived 2nd Panzer Division at Villers-Bocage on June 13. The next day, the artillery of the American V Corps came to support the British corps in a battle that ended on June 19 when the German 2nd Panzer and Panzer Lehr Divisions succeeded in driving back the British force.

In the meantime, the American V Corps faced the German 3rd Parachute Division and the remnants of the 352nd Division and its reinforcements in front of St. Lô. The V Corps made little progress for the rest of the month. The XIX Corps, with the support of 101st Airborne Division, stopped the early counterattacks of the German 6th Parachute Regiment and 17th SS Panzer Grenadier Division in the direction of Carentan. The American V Corps was becoming mired on its front.

The situation on the V Corps' front unfolded as follows:

June 19: On 2nd Inf. Div. front, enemy continues defensive operations. Enemy is making extensive use of stone houses as MG [machine-gun] positions, firing from holes through walls.

June 21: On 1st Inf. Div. front, enemy is generally inactive and well concealed. On 2nd Inf. Div. front, enemy activity is limited to sporadic mortar fire. Patrols attempting to pierce enemy defenses are met by MG, machine pistol, rifle fire, grenades, and flares. On 29th Inf. Div. front, enemy continues resistance to patrols. Salient (Villers–Fossard) area between 175th and 115th Inf. Rgt. strongly resisted an artillery concentration at 0500 and a Bn [battalion] attack, and is still held by enemy. Sniping continues.

June 27: In 1st Inf. Div. area, enemy continues arty and mortar fire, attacks forward OPs [observation posts] and attempts ambush of patrols. In 2nd Inf. Div. area, enemy continues resistance to patrols. Some 2nd Inf. patrols penetrate enemy lines 400 to 500 yards. In 29th Inf. Div. area, enemy activity generally defensive in nature. No marked increase in patrol activity. Reports indicate enemy using antipersonnel mines more extensively than in past.

Early in the campaign, the VII Corps began two drives: one to the west across the Merderet and Douve Rivers in an attempt to cut the peninsula and a second to the north toward Cherbourg with the 4th Division. The 82nd Airborne Division played a major role in the move west. The newly arrived 9th Division had to take over from the 90th Division to complete this operation, which effectively sealed the peninsula by June 18. Meanwhile, the 4th Division, joined by the newly arrived 79th Division, advanced on Cherbourg by mid-month. Five German infantry divisions proved unable to halt the advance of the American VII Corps. In the end, the 709th and part of the 243rd Division were all that was left to defend Cherbourg while the other German divisions struggled to set up a defensive position across the peninsula, taking advantage of the huge expanse of flooded areas and the hedgerows.

The American VII Corps pushed north while the 4th Division cleared the eastern side of the peninsula, the 9th Division concentrated on the western side, and the 79th Division moved up the middle. On June 22, these units launched the assault on the fortress of Cherbourg. The VIII Corps took command of the remaining divisions and occupied the southern front on the peninsula.

The British navy maintained a strong presence off the coast, hammering German positions with its battleships and a monitor. By mid-month, the

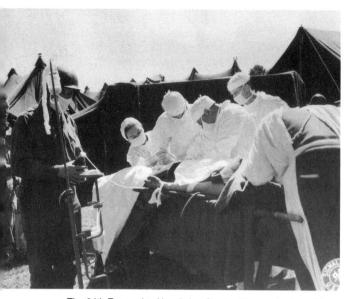

The 24th Evacuation Hospital at Cambe, Normandy, June 17, 1944.

front of the American First Army had advanced beyond the effective range of supporting ships in most sectors, freeing the large warships to move north along the Cotentin Peninsula and support the VII Corps' attack on Cherbourg. On June 25, the battleships *Texas* (with 14-inch guns) and *Arkansas* (with 12-inch guns) and five destroyers took on the strongly defended Battery Hamburg (with four 280-millimeter guns), east of Cherbourg. The big naval guns were relatively ineffective against the German position, but the Germans scored some hits. One round from the *Texas* destroyed a 280-millimeter gun position, but the remainder of the German battery remained in operation. On June 27, all resistance at Cherbourg ended. Within a few days, the 9th Division eliminated the last opposition: several thousand German troops who had retreated into Cap de la Hague. Next, the 79th Division moved south to take up a position on the right flank of the 82nd Airborne Division and join the VIII Corps. A few days later, the remainder of the VII Corps and the 83rd Division took over the east part of the Cotentin Peninsula. The 101st Airborne Division was already on its way back to England.

On June 19, the great storm of the century hit the Normandy coast, destroying the American Mulberry at Omaha Beach and battering the British one at Arromanches. The British Mulberry was repaired and kept in operation, but Admiral Hall decided that the American artificial harbor, which was about 60 percent wrecked, was not worth maintaining. Parts of the American Mulberry (Mulberry A) were used to repair the less severely damaged British Mulberry (Mulberry B). Supply operations at Omaha Beach temporarily slowed, increasing the importance of Cherbourg. The planners of the invasion had assumed that Cherbourg would become operational as quickly as the ports taken in North Africa and Italy, but it turned out that they had miscalculated. The Germans fought from many strong defensive positions that might have held out longer if their commander, von Schlieben, had not been isolated so early in the campaign and if he had had more troops to man his landward positions. Even so, von Schlieben had time to destroy most of the port facilities.

Although they captured the harbor of Cherbourg at the end of June, the Allies were unable to use it because of the damage. The entrance to the main basin was blocked by two large sunken ships. One of the inner harbor breakwaters was pierced and there were scattered mines everywhere. Plans to put the port back into operation within three days turned out to be optimistic. It took almost a month to sweep out most of the mines and ready the port for limited operations, and more work was still needed. Fortunately, effective beach operations made it possible for the two invasion beaches to maintain the logistical support needed until Cherbourg could function properly.

As the main American effort directed at Cherbourg came to a conclusion, the British launched a major offensive to break the stalemate on their front and take Caen. The British Second Army had eleven divisions in Normandy, including two armored, the day before the offensive known as

Operation Epsom. The assault began on June 25. The British made some headway by June 29 as they pushed forward in an attempt to encircle Caen. However, at the end of the month, the British offensive had stalled in the face of determined resistance from the Germans 12th SS, 1st SS, and 2nd SS Panzer Divisions, which had been reinforced by the 9th SS and 10th SS Panzer Divisions. The British faced the bulk of eight panzer divisions and three infantry divisions. The Americans, on the other hand, faced elements of ten divisions and a panzer grenadier division on a much longer front. Thus, the Allied forces were bottled up in Normandy, but they continued to build up and were ready to break the front open at any time.

S1/C Myron Parsons on board *LCT 851* had already had a chance to exchange shots with the Germans when his vessel was beached on Utah Beach on D-Day. Several days later, he visited the transport *Susan B. Anthony*, which had struck a mine and sunk on June 7.

My skipper pulled up to it and ordered us to go aboard to see if anything was there. I went down the gangway hatch and it was all flooded and I didn't see any bodies. I opened up a locker and found a cross on a chain, which I took and still have. Most everything was empty. We were there about ten minutes and I told the boatswains mate to tell the skipper there was nothing here and it was crazy to look with half the ship sunk—half was underwater. The skipper told us to come back. I have never seen a ship with the bow sticking up and the other half underwater. The anchor chain was tighter from the bow. It was there until the end of July.

When the great storm hit the Channel, it ripped out the pontoon causeway of about 600 feet length at Utah Beach. We headed for a small channel, which led up to

Carentan, and rode out the storm there. We were about a mile up that channel, and our mast took down a bunch of wires hanging over it when we entered about a quarter of a mile up the channel. We were the only ship up there during the storm and were carrying equipment and supplies.

Ens. Walter G. Treanor continued operating between Omaha Beach and England on *LST 58* during the month of June.

Several weeks after the invasion, the Mulberry's effectiveness was destroyed in the storm and most of the supplies had to be taken in by the LSTs, which would land right on the beach without a pier for unloading.

On the Fourth of July our ship, *LST 58*, was anchored about a quarter of a mile or less off Omaha Beach awaiting to get some space on the beach to unload. The ships off the beach began firing all the 20-mm, 40-mm or anything that had a tracer, to celebrate the Fourth of July. It didn't last long. The senior officer present, I don't know who, apparently went into a rage over this because it was kind of stupid because of the danger of fragments from AA fire sent in to the air. It was amusing.

On one of our trips, we loaded up with Long Toms [155-millimeter guns]. I was told I would be getting a very special piece of equipment at the last minute and it had to be carefully handled. I didn't know what we were going to get, but all of a sudden it was driven up the ramp. It was a green Packard sedan, a car for General Patton, who was not on the ship. I think it was a replacement automobile for him. There was a driver and I guess a mechanic responsible for fixing it. I remember lashing it down right behind the unloading ramp and dreadfully afraid there would be a scratch on it. This seems stupid looking back at it, but we treated it as if it were a crown jewel. I was never so relieved when we got to the beach and it was driven off the ramp. We had to get up high on the beach and make sure the tide was out before we unloaded the Packard. Meanwhile, everything else had to sit on the tank deck before it could get off.

On what I believe was our first trip to Cherbourg, we were moored out and a tremendous explosion occurred inside the port about a quarter of a mile away. It was a small ammunition ship that had exploded. There was no suggestion about sabotage, probably just a tragic action in handling ammunition.

The ships had elevators to take the equipment from the upper deck to the tank deck, where all loading and unloading took place through the bow doors. *LST 58* did have an elevator, as did *LST 31*, which I went to later, but the more modern models substituted a ramp for an elevator, which made it much quicker for the movement of vehicles and equipment. When operating between England and Cherbourg, we had railroad tracks welded into the tank deck so we could carry a number of locomotives and boxcars, which were moved directly from the tank deck up to a connecting track on the hards.

One of our main problems was to keep enough welding rods in the supply of the deck division because the ships were welded together and frequently the welds would fail. I learned early on what to do, and this is from a guy who knew nothing about the mechanics of keeping something like this afloat. If you took an acetylene torch and burned a hole about the size of a quarter about a foot below where the seam

was splitting, it would stop splitting. When the seas were too rough, that is when the seams would generally split, you would secure the compartment and stuff rags or anything to keep the water out until you could weld it shut. After sealing them up, you generally would not have a split on the same seam again.

When the Germans launched the Buzz Bombs [V-1 Flying Bomb] we were not hampered because the main target was London. We did see them going overhead, particularly in the evening, and that was a sight to see. I was in London on leave for about four or five days during the Buzz Bomb attack and I can say that was probably one of the most frightening experiences of the war for me. You were helpless—the bombs would come over and the engine would stop and then an explosion.

Walt Treanor transferred to *LST 311* sometime in September and to *LST 290* in December. After V-E Day, he returned to the United States, where he was given command of an LCM and was sent to take part in the planned invasion of Japan.

Lt. Ed Fabian, commanding *LCI 86* of the Coast Guard flotilla, was off the Normandy coast during the great June storm.

It had been blowing from the same direction and it started increasing. There were big swells. With the current and the waves, it would start undermining part of the breakwater system and it started coming apart. The breakwater was not so effective and when it started letting the waves into where the piers were, then their anchors and everything started letting go. Pretty soon it was all going up on the beach and it really piled up. It lasted for it seems a couple of days. It increased slowly and decreased

Gun crew of a 57-millimeter antitank gun in Normandy, July 31, 1944.

slowly. Then they lost the use of the piers and everything else they desperately needed to get ammunition ashore. There was this ammunition ship that came in and anchored fairly close to the beach at high tide and wasn't too far from us. The tide went out, and they started unloading it with DUKWs. The DUKWs were the most successful part of the whole amphibious operation since they could do everything. They started going out and unloading this ship, a small British coastal freighter. They were unloading with booms, king posts and slings and dropping ammunition with nets into the DUKWs. They would take off, and by that time they had bulldozers that had plowed through the cliff embankment and they had a regular valley and ran a road up there. The amazing thing to me was how quickly they got things going inland.

We went back to Weymouth and unloaded the communications group we had carried since the invasion. They put us to work convoying troops back and forth with us as the convoy leader. They put a LORAN (Long Range Aid to Navigation) on board. It was the type of equipment pathfinder aircraft used for bombing. You could get an accurate location within fifty feet. The largest convoy we led had about thirty ships. We went back and forth across the Channel. My ship carried troops and put them on the beach—always back to Omaha. This was after the storm and lasted about two months.

When Cherbourg was taken, we carried the first troops there by sea. I think there were about eight LCIs. We loaded at Weymouth for this mission, but I don't think they were all combat troops. We were cautious at Cherbourg because we figured it was mined. I am sure that the minesweepers had evidently been in there before us. We used the swept channels and went through the outer breakwaters. They had these big impressive forts on the ends of the breakwater. We came directly in and went alongside one of the piers. I remember the dilapidated cranes, docks, and sunken ships and all the debris. There was a place where we could get ships ashore and we did. I don't remember if we used our ramps on the dock or not. Everything was shot up, blown up, or bombed. We made just that one trip in July.

We then continued our runs back to Omaha Beach. Later we were in a large convoy out of Omaha and hit a tremendous gale with poor visibility [either June 28 or July 11]. Since the swept channel paralleled the coast and I knew the Channel would be really rough, we ducked into Cherbourg harbor inside the breakwaters. We went up there and anchored thirty ships until the next morning. That was my second trip to Cherbourg, but we didn't go ashore. The place was still a mess. Our last mission was in October.

Lieutenant Fabian next returned with his ship to the Charleston Navy Yard where he was reassigned to a lighthouse tender.

LCI 88 made a run to Cherbourg soon after it opened in July. CMOMM Ralph Gault left his engine room to go ashore with his skipper. They were picked up by an LCVP, and when they came ashore, they went off in different directions.

Being considerate of the crew, I was going to bring back some fresh vegetables. I met these two guys delivering *Stars and Stripes* in an army jeep. They were going to go up towards the front to deliver the newspapers. On the way up, we passed a little French cottage and the driver said, "Let's stop in here, this used to be the HQ of *Stars and Stripes* before we got pushed back." We went in, and one guy crawled up in the attic and came down with three bottles of red wine they had stashed there before the Germans arrived. We each took a bottle and toasted. As I lifted it up to take a good swig, the bottle exploded. They guys hollered something like, "Duck! Let's get the hell out of here, there's a sniper." My khaki uniform was red all over the place and my hand was bleeding. We got in the jeep and left; I had my hand bandaged up the next day by a medic on the beach. I ended up sleeping with a great big bunch of scallion onions underneath my arms in a haystack that night. The next morning, after seeing the medic, I hitched a ride on a DUKW back to the ship and received a good tongue-lashing from the skipper.

Ens. Donald E. Irwin skippered *LCT 614* along the British sectors of the Normandy coast for several months, unloading larger vessels. The month of June was the most harrowing, as far as he was concerned.

A terrible storm that lasted three days and nights swept across the English Channel. The only chance we had of keeping our landing craft from being beaten to bits was to anchor a long way off the beach out in the Channel and hope we could ride the storm out. The strong winds and huge waves buffeted us day and night, and although our anchor did drag, bit by bit, we rode the storm out successfully. I was so fearful that the anchor cable might snap, I recall sleeping on the floor of the chart house during the nights so that if it did give way I would have a better chance of not drowning as I was up considerably higher than if I was in my bunk. Besides, I was responsible for the security of the ship.

African-American 155-millimeter "Long Tom" gun battery in action near St. Lô. This was one of the few African-American combat units.

We were fortunate the storm ended when it did because our anchor had dragged so much we were very close to a line of sunken ships that had been put a distance from the beach as a breakwater. If we had smashed into them, our ship would have taken a terrific pounding and probably have sustained great damage. There is no manner in which we could have gotten underway successfully, as the huge waves and breakers would simply have thrown us up on the beach and probably pounded us to pieces.

One more incident took place in Normandy. As I recall, it was one rather pleasant French morning. We were beached and I think waiting for the tide to go out so we could get ashore to do some souvenir hunting when we heard a tremendous explosion closeby on the beach. We ran over to it and came upon a pitiful sight. Three British soldiers had been walking abreast, one of them with a mine detector looking for German mines on the beach. One of the soldiers had apparently stepped right on a mine and set it off. He was pretty well blown to pieces, and there was no doubt he was dying. Another of the soldiers had chunks of flesh missing and of course was in great pain. The third, as I recall, didn't appear to be wounded but was more shocked and dazed than anything else. There didn't appear to be any help for the soldiers nearby, so I sent our cook, who was in charge of first aid on the LCT, back to the ship to obtain some syrettes of morphine. We administered them to the soldiers to make them as comfortable as possible until their own medical personnel arrived.

Irwin returned to the United States in January 1945. He was assigned as a gunnery officer on an LST in preparation for the invasion of Japan.

SM1/C Ed Matousak of *LCI 84* was concerned about his brother, whom he hadn't seen for three years.

I was down in the bunk on D+10, and I was given the message that my brother was ashore. I went right into the captain's cabin and asked permission to see my brother Jimmy. The captain said no, but I said I was going anyway and he agreed. I hailed a DUKW, which was passing by, and they took me to the beach. It was getting dark. I saw a figure in the distance and ran up to him, and it was my brother. I told him to contact me from the front. After a week there was no message. Fourteen days went by and I was very worried, so I went back to the captain for permission to go ashore. I went ashore looking for the 137th Infantry of the 35th Division. I hitchhiked in my navy uniform. The last guy I approached was carrying ammunition. I asked if he knew of my brother, and he directed me to a clearing about 200 yards away. There I found my brother and 8 others with 150 German prisoners standing in a circle. I called to him and he replied, "You dumb SOB, what the hell are you doing here?" He gave me the password and a carbine from a dead comrade. I didn't see him again until the end of the war.

Our ship carried infantry into Omaha Beach for fifty-seven days, and we also did some salvage work.

Y2/C George L. Gray, a Coast Guardsman aboard *LCI 87*, was assigned the task of bringing in supplies.

During the first week, it seems to me we cruised just off the beaches taking calls from shore for materials needed, keeping track of arriving cargoes, and passing on requests. There was a call one night, which caused us to require a cargo ship to put on its cargo lights and pass ammunition to an LCM for transfer to the beach. The commodore's rank and authority was required to get the cargo ship commander to do this. Luckily, no German bombers were there as the cargo ship lighted up at night.

During the storm, we too tied up to the ships in the sunken breakwater with the monitor [probably HMS *Erebus*]. We broke our lines and finally rode the sea using engines to stay off the beach. We continued the monitoring of arriving cargoes, buildup of troops and materials, repairs to Mulberry harbors, etc., and then returned to England to continue orders for use of the amphibious forces assigned to Commodore Imlay.

View from the Top

The month of June 1944 turned out to be the most critical of Operation Overlord, as the stage was set for the great Allied victory that followed. For the commanders of the Allied armies, these events and chief concerns determined the outcome of the campaign that month. The southward advance against the Germans unexpectedly bogged down in the hedgerow country when the U.S. First Army on either side of St. Lô and the British Second Army engaged many of the German armored units concentrated in the vicinity of Caen.

General Eisenhower, who was in overall command, was mainly involved in the big picture rather than the tactical operations. Air operations became critical to the overall operation. After June 15, he decided to divert heavy bombers from the Eighth Air Force to supply the French Resistance forces in south central France and in the Jura area of eastern France. These operations tied down German units and contributed to the aerial campaign against lines of communications. A more costly decision had to be made about the threat of V weapons against England. Eisenhower, more for political than military reasons, had to divert both his air forces in England to future Crossbow missions. Although these missions may have affected the Germans' attempt to the use their rockets against England, they in no way helped the overall campaign in Normandy.

An even more serious problem faced Eisenhower in the form of logistical support for the invasion. Ammunition shortages became one of the key problems in June. In addition, the navy refused to beach its LSTs while the shoreline was still under enemy fire, which aggravated the situation because transferring troops and equipment from LSTs to lighters at sea was time consuming. The British, on the other hand, decided to beach their LSTs on D-Day. After the destruction of Mulberry A at Omaha, the navy had little choice but to give in; however, this presented Eisenhower with a second problem. He had to prepare to send landing craft to the Mediterranean for Operation Dragoon, the proposed invasion of southern France. As he became committed to this operation, he found it necessary to push for the capture of Cherbourg in the hopes of alleviating the supply problem and reducing his dependence on LSTs.

As it turned out, Cherbourg's German garrison of over 30,000 troops was able to hold out for several days and completely devastated the port facilities before it surrendered. As a result, it was months before the port was able to operate at full capacity. Fortunately, neither Field Marshal Rundstedt nor Rommel was keen on wasting troops for the defense of this city once its port facilities were destroyed. Hitler had wanted a more determined effort, but von Schlieben, the commander, was unable to offer a prolonged defense. According to some critics, the Americans wasted too many lives in pursuit of a useless port. However, they are quite mistaken. If von Schlieben had been able to hold

The 320th Barrage Balloon Battery moving through a partially cleared minefield after have landed on D-Day. This was an African-American noncombat unit. When he came ashore on D+1, Sgt. Ernest Lee noticed that those troops manning the balloons on the beach had to dig in for protection.

out until July or until the end of the war, like the commanders of the Biscay ports, the Allies would have had to attack another heavily defended port and spend months repairing it since the beaches were not expected to operate past the fall. No Allied advance was going to push the Germans out of France without a solid, secure logistical lifeline, and the beaches were not suitable for that during the harsh winter months. Cherbourg, even with its devastated port that had to be rebuilt, was important to the success of the campaign. In the weeks to come, the Allies concentrated their efforts into putting Cherbourg's massive storage facilities back in service. PLUTO (Pipe Line under the Ocean), was laid across the Channel from the Isle of Wight to Cherbourg and began pumping oil to the Allied forces in early August.[1] LSTs ferried locomotives and rolling stock from England in order to restore the French railroads for use as part of the logistical lifeline. Cherbourg became a key to the Allied victory over Germany on the Western Front after the breakout began.

Bad weather not only hindered naval and supply operations, but it also seriously hampered ground operations. As Gen. Omar Bradley, commander of the First Army, directed Gen. Lawton Collins's VII Corps against Cherbourg, he ordered Gen. Troy Middleton to push his VIII Corps (temporarily attached from the Third Army, which had not arrived yet) south beyond the marshy terrain of the Cotentin. Shortage of ammunition and bad weather prevented Middleton's corps from achieving success and allowed the German infantry to strengthen their position.

The Second British Army of Bernard Montgomery, commander of the 21st Army Group, spent the whole month held in check outside of Caen, its D-Day objective. It appeared that the British achievement was rather limited, but that was not the case. Although they failed to take Caen, in comparatively open terrain compared to the American sectors, the British succeeded in drawing in most of the German panzer divisions in Normandy as well as those that arrived later. The American commanders were concerned with the fact that their main battle tank, the Sherman with a 75-millimeter gun, was not an equal to the German Panther with its 75-millimeter gun or the Tiger with its 88-millimeter gun. As a matter of fact, most of the British tanks could not stand up to them either.[2] Luckily, however, not all the German tanks were Tigers or Panthers. The British faced 725 German tanks while the Americans, on a wider sector, had to contend only with 140 at

the end of the month. In July, that situation slowly began to change, but by then, the American First Army was firmly established on the continent.

July Operations

July opened with an apparent stalemate. Field Marshal Montgomery was still intent upon launching additional assaults to take Caen and break the German position. Montgomery, as commander of the 21st Army Group, which included the U.S. First Army at the time, had intended to use his thrust in the vicinity of Caen to tie down large German formations to allow the Americans to launch a breakout on the western side of the Allied front. General Bradley, on the other hand, could not attempt a breakout until he advanced south and established a jump-off line that required taking St. Lô. Once that was achieved, his army could launch the breakthrough attack in an operation to be known as Cobra. To gain the jump-off positions for Cobra, Bradley planned to push the VIII Corps down the coast road from La Haye du Puits to Coutances while the VII Corps advanced on Periers. The XIX Corps, with support of the 3rd Armored Division, was to push south and take St. Lô.

The first couple of weeks showed slow progress. The VIII Corps was fighting in hedgerow country, and the VII Corps began pushing through the marshes to the hedgerow country, where the American forces became mired for a while. According to many critics, the excellent training of American divisions proved to be no substitute for experience. In many cases, the American soldiers encountered more German and veteran troops and the uninspired recruits of the *Ost* battalions. Slowly, the Germans began to shift their armored forma-

---

1. PLUTO consisted of undersea cables that were flexible and protected by a rubberized coating. It took only ten hours to lay the pipeline the seventy miles across the Channel, but storage facilities at Cherbourg and other locations had to be built or repaired before it could be put into use. As the Allies advanced across France, the pipelines were extended and an additional undersea pipeline was laid from England to the Pas de Calais.
2. British armored units were equipped with Cromwell and Churchill tanks and a number of American Shermans. All these tanks were armed with a 75-mm gun and none were much of a match for the German heavy tanks.

tions, such as the Panzer Lehr Division and 2nd SS Panzer Division, to reinforce their infantry in the Cotentin Peninsula. The American infantrymen were becoming worn down by the hedgerow fighting, which involved taking one field after the other. Although they developed various techniques that allowed them to advance, the pace of the war was slow. Casualties continued to mount until, on July 14, Bradley ordered Middleton, whose corps was outside of Lessay, to end his offensive. The VIII Corps suffered over 10,000 casualties after advancing a mere seven miles in twelve days. The 90th Division lost 2,000 men in clearing Mount Castre to the east of Le Haye du Puits. The 79th Division suffered 2,000 casualties in five days in taking the Montgardon Ridge on the other side of the town by July 7.

The VII Corps was also brought to a halt after the 4th Division suffered over 2,300 casualties by July 15. On the first day of the operation, on July 4, the 83rd Division lost 1,400 men, and at the end of twelve days, on July 15, it had taken over 5,000 casualties. Soon the 4th Division took over the attack, and on July 7, both divisions faced troops of the 2nd SS Panzer Division and German paratroopers. The action of the VII Corps prevented the Germans from moving armor against the VIII Corps on the coast road and drew troops away from the St. Lô sector.

On July 7, Gen. Charles Corlett, at the head of the XIX Corps, launched his attack across the Vire-Taute Canal and the Vire River. The 30th Division was directed against the high ground west of St. Lô. The division engineers were to support the crossing of the river and canal and set up bridges. When the attack began, most of the German reserves in the immediate area had drawn away to the fronts of the VII and VIII Corps. After the crossing, Bradley sent the 3rd Armored Division to the XIX Corps to push through the 30th Division. However, problems cropped up when the armored division tried to move across the bridgehead, coordination became

A two-man mortar team dug in near St. Lô.

difficult, and confusion took over on July 8. One of the companies of the 743rd Tank Battalion attached to the 30th Division was destroyed in an ambush on July 9. The 30th Division commander was reluctant to use CCB (Combat Command B) of the 3rd Armored Division because of the congestion and confusion, but CCA passed through this bridgehead to support the 9th Division. On July 10, CCB helped spearhead the drive on Haut-Vents and Pont-Hébert, but the advance soon ground to a halt. The Panzer Lehr Division launched a counterattack against the 9th and 30th Divisions on July 11. After making penetrations, the Germans met stiff resistance and the Americans beat them back. On July 11, CCB of the 3rd Armored Division claimed twenty Panzer IV tanks and the VII Corps another thirty tanks, while the Air Corps accounted for approximately twenty tanks. The Panzer Lehr Division lost 25 percent of its effective strength and went on the defensive the next day. The 35th and 29th Divisions of the XIX Corps opened up attacks

Infantry-Tank Hedgerow Tactics

The following material is extracted from Memorandum No. 1, "Armored Notes," published June 19, 1944, by U.S. First Army headquarters.

1. Terrain in Normandy is low, rolling, and in some places flat and marshy. The usable tank terrain is cut by many hedgerows and occasional woods. Hedgerows grow on earth embankments with ditches alongside. Often the hedge is interspersed with stout trees. Roads are narrow, sunken and numerous. Observation is difficult. There are frequent towns and groups of buildings. The German defends the hedgerows and towns. He uses small arms, machine guns, mortars, bazookas, antitank grenades, bombs, mines, obstacles, and a few antitank guns to cover main routes.

2. A successful combination adopted by our troops has been to put a company of M-4 tanks with an infantry battalion. Infantry battalion and company commanders are provided with SCR-609 radios.[3] These are fixed on infantry pack boards and provide effective communication with infantry and tank commanders.

3. Some of the tanks move along the hedgerows running in the direction of attack, using the bow gun and coaxial machine gun to flush out the Germans who are dug in. These tanks are followed closely (sometimes ridden) by infantry, which mops up.

4. Other tanks, supported by infantry heavy weapons, cover the hedgerows crossing the direction of advance. As the tanks reach a crossroad, the infantry mops up, occupies the hedge, and protects the tanks from attack by hostile bazooka and grenade men.

5. Tankdozers are used to open passages in the hedges for the tanks. Some tanks must watch the other hedges while this passage is made. Infantry must protect dozers and tanks from hostile foot elements.

6. Crossroads and road junctions are shelled by artillery or mortars and tank fire to eliminate possible antitank guns before tanks advance toward them.

7. Some of the infantry must be constantly on the alert for snipers who hide in trees and buildings. Tank cannon fire against buildings usually clears them rapidly.

8. The rate of advance is slow. Infantry and tanks must stay close together to permit mutual support. Tank blitz action has proved generally unsuccessful. If tanks advance too fast, they have to return to mop up and relieve the pressure on infantry pinned down by pockets of resistance overlooked in a hasty advance.

A G-2 Report from the 2nd Armored Division dated July 31, 1944, reported that

continued

---

3. The infantry used the SCR-536 handie-talkie, a small hand-carried AM radio, but at company level, a radioman carried on his back the SCR-300 walkie-talkie, an FM radio for short ranges. The SCR-609 was a field artillery radio and a portable FM unit for short ranges. Armored vehicles generally had an FM radio.

Infantry-Tank Hedgerow Tactics *continued*

captured German artillery officers divulged, after interrogation, that they had noticed that American infantry soldiers did not advance under heavy artillery fire. In addition, if the Germans concentrated their fire on an area, the Americans almost always withdrew. However, they admitted, the American tanks and armored vehicles advanced with such force and speed that it was impossible to stop them because the Americans paid little heed to blown-up vehicles and whizzed past them. At the very moment the German officers were making these confessions, the breakout had begun.

---

against St. Lô on July 11 as the 2nd Division of the V Corps advanced on the critical Hill 192. The 35th and 29th Divisions continued to push slowly forward toward St. Lô until July 15, when Bradley stopped the advance of VII and VIII Corps. On July 18, the 9th and 30th Divisions reached their objective, the St. Lô–Periers highway. The 29th Division continued its push along the Martinville Ridge toward St. Lô as the 35th Division approached the town from the north. By the evening of July 18, the 29th Division took the heavily damaged town of St. Lô.

At the end of the first week of July, the British Bomber Command launched the first carpet-bombing attack in Europe, devastating the city of Caen. However, the operation did little to remove the Germans from the city. The British continued to hammer away with attacks designed to cut off the remaining German forces holding Caen. Operation Goodwood, which began on July 18, resulted in heavy losses for the British but allowed the occupation of the remainder of Caen and strengthened the British position east of the Orne. The British, at heavy cost, had tied down the bulk of the German panzer divisions as the Americans prepared for Operation Cobra.

On July 20, the U.S. First Army was lined up from Lessay to St. Lô in preparation for Operation Cobra, but it would not be ready to launch its attack for a few more days. This delay may have been quite unfortunate, because on July 20 the failed assassination attempt on Hitler in his East Prussian headquarters left the German command in a slightly confused state for almost an entire day. The V Corp secured the left flank with the 2nd Division and 5th Division from Hill 192 to Caumont. Ten American infantry divisions and three armored divisions (the 4th Armored Division arrived in July) prepared for the breakout. Between St. Lô and Lessay, this American force was faced by two panzer divisions, one panzer grenadier division, one parachute division, and the remnants of six infantry divisions. However, the hardest and most bitter fighting was over.

Operation Cobra began on July 25 as virtually the whole of the American First Army front advanced from Lessay to Caumont. Two British corps moved into the Caumont sector at the hinge of the American left wing. The Panzer Lehr Division was destroyed on the first day by the second carpet-bombing attack of the campaign, which also caused some American casualties when bombs fell short of the target. By July 31, the VIII Corps had taken and passed Avranches with the 4th Armored Division and the newly arrived 6th Armored Division. The First Army, at the end of the German left flank, was poised to break out in a massive battle of encirclement. The VIII Corps was about to return to George Patton's Third Army headquarters in preparation for the big breakout.

CHAPTER 6

The Air War

Allied Air Power in June

The Normandy campaign forced the Allied air chiefs to alter the strategic bombing campaign of Germany. The pre-invasion bombing occasionally forced the RAF Bomber Command and the U.S. Eighth Air Force to divert their efforts from their strategic objectives for crippling the German war machine. The invasion required the two organizations to concentrate virtually all of their efforts on supporting operations in Normandy, mainly destroying railroads, bridges, communications, and transportation hubs as well as military targets.[1] During the month of June, once again they directed their efforts against the Reich's oil and transportation centers as well as the *Luftwaffe* and its factories. The RAF continued its night operations, but on several occasions, it took part in daylight attacks. However, in many cases, bad weather interfered with operations, which were often postponed, canceled, or aborted en route. In spite of this, the *Luftwaffe* got little respite since fighters and fighter-bombers from the U.S. Eighth and Ninth Air Forces and the British Second Tactical Air Force continued to roam over northwest France engaging ground targets and enemy aircraft.

---

1. This also included bombing targets outside the Normandy invasion area to divert the enemy's attention.

The *Luftwaffe* began the month of June 1944 with almost 1,000 fighter aircraft, 700 of which were operational and ready to defend the Reich. After D-Day, 300 Germans fighters flew to Normandy to challenge the Allies. The best German bases in and around Normandy had been destroyed, and the German fighter pilots had to operate from airfields that were poorly equipped or far from the front. By the end of June, there were 425 *Luftwaffe* single-engine fighter planes in France and the Low Countries. Only 370 single-engine fighters remained to protect Germany, and the *Luftwaffe* had to deploy 425 additional fighters from Greece to the Baltic to protect the oil resources and the troops on the Eastern Front after the collapse of Army Group Center in the face of a massive Russian assault in June.[2] In June, the Germans lost 931 aircraft in operations over France, 250 in the skies of Germany, and 250 due to noncombat causes.

The U.S. Ninth Air Force and the British Second Tactical Air Force continued to hammer Normandy, interdict transportation lines, and attack German ground units arriving as reinforcements. Meanwhile, the strategic air forces began to direct operations against Germany. The U.S. Twelfth Air Force in Italy, which had medium bombers and fighters, continued to direct most of its operations against German forces on the peninsula. The U.S. Fifteenth Air Force, on the other hand, continued its strategic campaign against Germany. Early in the month, the B-17s of the Fifteenth Air Force flew shuttle missions to the Soviet Union and struck at targets, mainly oil, in the Balkans. The RAF Bomber Command and the U.S. Eighth Air Force struck at centers of synthetic oil production in Germany, while the Fifteenth Air Force directed a number of missions against oil fields in Rumania, Hungary, and Austria. By the end of June, the *Luftwaffe*'s aircraft fuel production was reduced by 70 percent and synthetic fuel production was down by 60 percent.

On June 13, the Germans briefly succeeded in diverting the strategic bombing forces of the Allies from the Normandy area and Germany by launching the first ten V-1 flying bombs against England. These attacks on civilian populations were mostly meant to break the morale among the Allies. The Eighth Air Force and RAF Bomber Command responded by implementing Operation Crossbow, the destruction of German secret weapons and their launching and supply sites.[3] The British dropped huge 12,000-pound Tallboy bombs against some of the hardened V weapons sites in France, like Wizernes (V-2), Watten (V-2), Siracourt (V-1), and Mimoyecques (V-3, a special multitube gun site). On June 18, the medium bombers of the Ninth Air Force joined these missions, but returned on June 20 because its bombers were needed in the Normandy area.

Air force activities during the month of June included Operation Frantic, a scheme to shuttle bombs between American bases in England and Italy and bases in the Soviet Union. The Russians agreed to allow U.S. aircraft to land at Poltava, Mirgorod, and Piryatin, east of Kiev. The Fifteenth Air Force sent over 100 B-17 bombers and seventy P-51 fighters, which bombed the marshalling yards at Debreczen and landed in the USSR on June 2. Additional operations took place until June 21 when almost 150 B-17s and

---

2. The Soviet offensive (Operation Bagration) that opened against German Army Group Center on June 23, 1944, three years and one day after the German invasion of the Soviet Union, virtually tore the front apart in a matter of days. In just over a month, more than sixty German divisions were destroyed or left as remnants as the Soviets advanced over 300 miles in some sectors. The Anglo-American force in Normandy engaged fewer enemy divisions (thirty-seven divisions) and took longer than two months to shatter the German Seventh Army and about another month to advance the 250 miles toward the German border.

3. Operation Crossbow actually began in 1943, especially with the bombing of launching sites in December.

P-51s landed at the Soviet bases after having bombed a synthetic oil plant south of Berlin. That night, about seventy German He 111 and Ju 88 bombers launched a surprise attack on the seventy-two B-17s at Poltava, destroying forty-four and damaging twenty-six. The remaining B-17s at Mirgorod and P-51s at Piryatin moved to Zaporozhe, 150 miles further away. On June 26, those aircraft took off from the Soviet bases, bombed the oil refinery at Drohobycz, flew on to Italy, and returned to England on July 5. Operation Frantic was a spectacular diversion that allowed the Allies to strike at faraway targets and take the Germans by surprise. However, the Germans' ability to strike at the Soviet bases negated the value of the operation and inflicted heavy material losses.

The British also carried out operations almost nightly against German-held ports from the Bay of Biscay to the Netherlands, which helped restrain the limited enemy naval forces already in the Channel. On June 14, Bomber Command launched a daytime raid with over 200 bombers on the E-boats and their pens at Le Havre. One Tallboy bomb penetrated the roof the E-boat pens. Supposedly, thirty-five naval vessels were sunk, reducing the naval threat to operations off the Norman coast. On June 15, Bomber Command sent almost 300 aircraft on another daylight raid.

The missions against bridges, railroads, vehicles, and supply depots in northern France, which continued to isolate the battlefield and wore down German forces, proved decisive in the Normandy campaign.

Even though the *Luftwaffe* took heavy losses in June, the Allies did not come back from their missions unscathed as the flak and enemy fighters continued to take their deadly toll. Despite the losses, the American bomber crews were informed that the number of missions they had to fly had increased.

Fighters and Medium Bombers

The VIII Fighter Command of the Eighth Air Force performed tactical missions similar to those of the fighters of the Ninth Air Force, but also escorted the heavy bombers on missions over Germany. On D-Day, the VIII Fighter Command undertook over 1,870 sorties and downed twenty-six enemy fighters. On June 7, the fighters continued escort and fighter-bomber missions and shot down twenty-three enemy fighters. On June 8, the Germans lost thirty-one fighter planes. However, on each of the three days the VIII Fighter Command lost an average of twenty aircraft a day. Within a few days, the *Luftwaffe* put up stronger opposition as the Americans strafed and bombed tactical targets with their fighters. In less than two weeks, the fighters were again flying escort missions over Germany.

The Ninth Air Force devoted most of its effort toward supporting the operations in Normandy with its medium bombers and fighters. If bad weather prevented bomber operations, the fighters of the Ninth Air Force and British Second Tactical Air Force usually flew in the Norman skies.

First Lt. Frank Gallagher, a bombardier on a B-26 Marauder in the 450th Squadron, 322nd Bombardment Group, flew into Normandy on D-Day and later.

Sometimes in June we flew four missions a day with a briefing at 4:00 A.M., a take off at 5:00 A.M., and back by 11:00 A.M. On June 7, I think we hit marshalling yards in the Normandy area, but the night of June 14 stands out. Oh, God, that was hairy! I am surprised I am here or any of us survived. It was to Cherbourg and led by Pathfinder—the British unit that drops flares over the target. It was navigation from target back to base, time and distance, and it was staggered. Two groups were involved. We went in at 4,500 feet and I think one at 3,500 feet and maybe 500 feet apart. We were to drop our bombs and hope we didn't drop them on one of the aircraft underneath us. Immediately after dropping, we were to turn right and come back between the Jersey and Guernsey Islands and return to England all in the dark. This was individual release; it was saturation, with no bombsights, dropped on time and distance with British flares to light up the target. You just dropped on the area they pinpointed with flares, I think it was the wharf and harbor. We had to take off after 11:00 P.M. because it was still light in June. It was dark when we crossed the Channel and got to Cherbourg. We were staggered and individual at different altitudes, about eighteen aircraft in the 450th—the whole squadron up to 12,000 feet. No navigators—the bombardier navigated—and I hadn't had a great deal of navigation expertise and knew only a little about time and distance. I saw the flares at Cherbourg—they started a few fires. We were about 4,000 feet or 4,500 feet, and we were the second plane over the target. The others followed in if their navigation of time and distance was right. No flak over Cherbourg. Near the Channel Islands I noticed small gunfire down there off Guernsey. We returned at the same altitudes. The worst was navigating without a whole lot of proficiency. We lost one or two aircraft and I think through navigational problems. It was still dark when we got back.

My next mission was later in the morning of June 15 after returning from the night mission. This was mission seventy-three of my seventy-five missions. My last mission was on June 17. We were always running into flak that you could practically

An aerial view of the effects of the bombardment near Bretteville-sur-Laize, south of Caen. B-17s of the U.S. Eighth Air Force participated in the bombing. NATIONAL ARCHIVES

walk on. The worst I remember was around Rouen and Dieppe.

Lt. Graydon K. Eubank, a Marauder pilot from Throckmorton, Texas, was in the United States on leave from the 322nd Squadron when the invasion started. After he returned to England at the end of July, he was assigned to a B-26, and he received a new crew on August 4.

On August 9, we went in at 500 feet on a low-level attack on the sub pens at Brest. We were afraid the fragments from the bombs would hit our planes and bounce us around when the bombs exploded because I wasn't the first man on the target. I believe we carried 2,000-pound bombs. When we came in, the fragments were already coming up in the air. There was a lot of flak around there.

On August 12, we had a mission to Falaise to attack the escaping Germans. I was flying in the No. 6 position. The No. 3 got hit and caught on fire, and what I remember is pulling the throttle back and putting the gear down and lowering the flaps and trying to back away from him because I knew he was going to blow up. I got out of there as fast as I could. He blew up and everyone on board was killed.

Since the medium bombers usually flew at lower altitudes than the heavies did, Eubank encountered German flak on every mission. On August 13, he went after a railroad bridge and on August 16, after another bridge, which he returned to bomb the next two days. His squadron hit the sub pens at Brest on August 25, September 3, and September 6 and a gun position at Brest on September 14. On August 26, he was sent against fuel dumps near Paris. On September 10 and September 11, his unit attacked German positions at Nancy and Metz. During August, he trained for night missions, but his seventy missions were completed before he could put his new skills to the test. All of these missions reflected the advance of the Allies from Normandy into Brittany and eastern France. After Lieutenant Eubank completed his combat missions, he began ferrying aircraft until December. Then, as the Battle of the Bulge began, he was sent on his seventy-first combat mission against a bridge at Trier. On Christmas Day, as he flew his last combat mission, his aircraft was badly shot up and he had to make a belly landing.

On an interdiction mission on June 13, Capt. Jack Ilfrey led his 79th Fighter Squadron to Angers. After completing his mission, the unthinkable happened to interrupt his routine as his P-38 named *Happy Jack's Go Buggy* was hit in the starboard engine.

Our mission this day was to dive-bomb the railroad bridge over the Loire River at La Poissonière, not far from Angers. Our P-38s were loaded with two 1,000-pounders, and I led sixteen ships of the 79th Squadron. We took off at 1848 [6:48 P.M.] and arrived in the target area at 2030 [8:30 P.M.]. We came in out of the west with the sun on our backs and successfully dive-bombed the bridge.[4] Several direct hits severed the tracks and inflicted serious damage on the bridge structure. We were then to strafe rail and motor traffic and any other targets of opportunity from the Loire north into Normandy.

We had just reassembled at about 8,000 feet when I spied a locomotive with steam up in the village of Le Lion just north of Angers. The Germans had become pretty wise to our attacks on trains and usually had several flak cars on the trains, especially one behind the engine. Therefore, in order to do a complete job of knocking out the locomotives, we planned coordinated attacks on them. The leader, as a rule, went after the engine while his wingman went in after the guns on the flak car, and the others in the squadron provided cover.

I dived down towards the engine, and while taking aim at it, caught a glimpse, out of the corner of my eye, at some tracer bullets coming up at me from the flak car behind the engine. Just after I opened up on the locomotive, saw the boiler explode, and pulled up, my whole right engine burst into flames and smoke, and somebody

---

4. The sun does not set until late in the evening during the summer at these latitudes.

yelled over the radio, "Bail out, Jack! You're on fire!" My cockpit immediately filled with smoke, blinding and choking me. I jettisoned my canopy and the smoke cleared momentarily, and I could tell I certainly wasn't very high above the ground. However, without any hesitation, I released my safety belt and went out over the left side, opening the parachute immediately. I had just looked up and yelled, "That S.O.B. works!" when I hit the corner of a farmhouse and bounced off into the yard.

According to another pilot, Jesse Carpenter, Ilfrey's chute only oscillated once before he hit the barn. Art Heiden, another pilot, saw that some camouflaged 88s in the next field "were just snapping at your ass" as Jack attacked the engine. Heiden tried to land in an attempt to rescue Ilfrey, but there were too many obstacles. Once on the ground, Jack Ilfrey pulled in his chute and piled it up with his other flying equipment before trying to escape. While he was trying to erase all evidence of his presence, a Frenchman with a pitchfork showed up and pointed him northward as his wrecked P-38 exploded. After removing his flying suit and insignia, Ilfrey, wearing a gray sweater and olive-drab trousers, put the items from his escape kit in his pocket. As he headed north, he came across two boys on bicycles who took him to the cafe owned by one of their fathers in the next village. The family gave him shelter, provided him with a bicycle and some clothing, and sent him off to the north in the direction of Caen where he hoped to make it to the Allied lines. On his northward trek, Ilfrey came across German units more than once. A German troop-truck camouflaged with branches passed him as he ate lunch on the side of the road. Fortunately, the Germans took no notice of him, thinking he was French. During the afternoon, he passed many vehicles

parked on the side of the road. He even passed through a German airdrome where he was stopped by a sentry, but he produced a doctor's note indicating that he was deaf and they let him go. The installation was wrecked, two wrecked P-38s lay on the ground, several Me 109s were warming up on a camouflaged revetment under some trees, and there were further signs of damage inflicted by his fellow pilots. When dusk fell, Ilfrey pulled over in a barn where he spent the night because the Germans enforced a strict curfew during the hours of darkness.

The next morning, Ilfrey met a French priest, who took him to his church to help him repair the bicycle and gave him more supplies. However, Ilfrey had to leave quickly when a parishioner who hated Americans came to see the priest. Ilfrey pedaled north through another German roadblock where he used his doctor's note. Again, he met a couple of helpful French boys. Before long, he left the flat country for the rolling hills of Normandy.

A few miles after he passed another troop convoy, six P-38s swooped in and launched an attack. Ilfrey pedaled as fast as he could and reached a height from which he could watch his comrades bomb the convoy. Near Domfront, a German tried to commandeer his bicycle, but luckily for Ilfrey, a passing German truck gave the soldier a ride. Later, he heard the rumble of B-17s and felt the vibrations from their bombs. When he passed through the town of Flers, he beheld the devastation they left behind. As he approached the town of Condé, he came across civilians fleeing south and German troops moving north. During his trip, he had been lucky to meet cooperative French civilians, but now the number of Germans was increasing. After spending the night with a French family in a village, he pedaled north toward Fontenay. He encountered two German soldiers carrying a wounded comrade who commandeered his bicycle and searched him. After that, as he continued on foot toward Fontenay, he noticed that the number of German troops was dwindling. Apparently they were pulling back.

> I heard voices over to my left and saw some Germans entrenched in the tall grass. . . . I could tell they were yelling at me and motioning for me to get down. I promptly fell to the ground and one of the soldiers crawled over my way and motioned for me to follow him back into the grass. We crawled a few yards and came up to a group of them lying around in holes. Several near me started asking question in German, which . . . I didn't understand. . . .
>
> We lay there for a while until one of the soldiers near me was hit in the leg and stomach with shrapnel. Others motioned to me, and I readily caught on they wanted me to put the wounded soldier in a wheelbarrow, which was out in the ditch by the road, and wheel him back to a first-aid station . . .[5]

Ilfrey obeyed their command and took the wounded man to a German aid station where a medic came out to tend to the wounded man and gave him some cigarettes and a candy bar. After this close encounter, Ilfrey continued his northward journey. Finally, he came across some British vehicles—burned-out tanks and trucks—at an intersection. A quarter of a mile farther north, he finally heard English voices and made contact. He had made it to the Allied lines. The British soldiers, however, refused to trust him and strip-searched him. It was not long before he was on his way back to England. On June 24, Ilfrey was back in the air, flying escort to Bremen and eleven more missions until July 24, when his unit converted to P-51 Mustangs.

Captain Ilfrey was promoted to major and continued flying missions until December 6, when he completed his 142nd mission. One of his missions was Operation Frantic VI, another shuttle flight to Russia, on September 11. Amazingly, Major Ilfrey was reduced to the rank of second lieutenant for breaking the rules, but he remained in command of the squadron and missions remained just as dangerous as before. On November 20, he landed behind enemy lines to rescue his wingman near Maastricht; it was quite a feat for two men to fit into a Mustang.

The Bomber Crews on D-Day and After

T.Sgt. Alvin J. Anderson, a flight engineer and top turret gunner on a B-17 of the 525th Squadron, 379th Bomb Group, had been quite excited about the D-Day mission. However, the cloud cover and fog made it impossible for him and his comrades to complete their task, and their aircraft returned without having dropped any of its bombs. Normally, they released their ordnance in the Channel when the mission was cancelled, but that day too many ships were plying those waters. Anderson got his best view of the fleet on June 7, when the cloud cover broke up. By June 10, he had completed thirty missions. His commander, Colonel Elliot, asked him and his pilot, Lieutenant Smith, to stay on for another tour. However, Anderson, who had a surfeit of combat, declined and returned to the States with the remainder of the crew. Lieutenant Smith, on the other hand, decided to stay on for another tour. For Sergeant Anderson, who had had plenty of excitement during his previous missions, June turned out to be anticlimactic, and for him, the only memorable event of D-Day was the glimpse he caught of the invasion fleet.

---

5. See *Happy Jack's Go Buggy* for additional details.

S.Sgt. Bonnie Skloss from Stockdale, Texas, a flight engineer on a B-17 of the 562nd Squadron of the 388th Bombardment Group, underwent his baptism of fire on a mission over Bergen, Norway, in July 1943. He spent the next eleven months flying some of the most dangerous missions of the war over heavily defended targets in Germany. The raids on Regensburg in 1943 and Berlin in 1944 were the roughest for him. The situation improved in 1944 when P-51 fighter planes were able to escort them over Germany. Curiously enough, he never had occasion to fire his machine gun during any of those missions. He finished his service after his twenty-seventh mission, which he flew over Normandy on June 6. While the air war raged on, he was sent to Southampton where he remained from June until September with two other crews, waiting to find a berth on a ship bound for home. "We had a big barracks all to ourselves for six months and nothing to do," he remembered. Finally, in September, he and his comrades boarded the *Santa Paula*, where they remained for twenty-one days until they reached the States in December.

S.Sgt. Byron C. Cook, a B-17 gunner with the 388th Bombardment Group, had flown a mission to Caen on June 6, 1944. The next day, his squadron bombed Nantes; on June 11, Pontaubault; and on June 12, Amiens. Meanwhile, the Eighth Air Force strove to isolate the battlefield. On June 25, Cook flew on a mission to supply the French Resistance. In his personal log he recorded,

June 7th, Mission #25 (7 Hours) Nantes

Bad weather held up the air support of our ground forces half the day, but in the late afternoon we were briefed on a rush job to Nantes. All the way across the Channel, we caught glimpses of the small craft carrying troops and equipment to the landing forces. . . . We passed over the coast at Caen and could see hundreds of ships. . . . The group's target was a railroad bridge at Nantes. Flak was accurate but not heavy. Little damage was done to our ship, but many others were shot up, although I didn't observe any going down. The bridge appeared to be well hit by the group, although the bombs in our plane hung up and failed to release. Pohl received permission (via VHF) to bomb a target of opportunity, so we made a run on another likely-looking railroad bridge. Hervy came very close with his salve and probably would have had a "shack" if the bombs hadn't momentarily hung up again.[6] Near Rennes, we finally caught up to the formation again and departed the Brest Peninsula near Lannion. . . .

June 11th, Mission #26 (7¼ Hours) Pontaubault

Again, we were scheduled to hit a railroad bridge. . . . We took off in terrible weather and flew to the target through squalls even worse. We made one run on the bridge but held our bombs, circled around into position again, and flew down the alley on a second attempt. This time we let the eggs drop, but with unobserved results.

June 12th, Mission #27 (7¼ Hours) Amiens

A super-fort at Amiens was to have been the recipient of some of our high explosive calling cards, but upon reaching this objective, we discovered it to be totally obscured by cloud coverage. Our B and C targets were likewise 10/10, so we flew all over

6. "Shack" means on the target.

northern France searching for targets of opportunity. All vital ones were covered. . . . We finally returned with our bomb loads intact. The lead plane brought us out right over Ostend and they blasted us. . . . When we climbed out of the ship back at Knettishall, it was leaking sunlight like a sieve; so many holes had been ripped through it.

June 24th, Abortion (2 Hours) Paris

Dirty weather had played hob with heavy bomber missions for better than a week and a half. . . . Our crew was scheduled to fly the old junker, "Red Cross Darling," notorious for its many abortions due to mechanical failure. We took off and climbed through ragged clouds toward our rendezvous point, but before reaching it, Navigator Young complained of sharp pains in his chest. He told Pohl to continue for a while, but before long he said that they were becoming unbearable and so we returned to base. . . .

A D7 armored bulldozer removes the wreckage of a German Messerschmitt Bf 109 B-1, which was a model no longer in use in 1944. NATIONAL ARCHIVES

June 25th, Mission #28 (10:00 Hours) Supply Mission Secret Area 5 in Southern France

Since this was a secret mission, I kept no notes of any kind. . . . We were about to undertake the dropping of supplies to a small group of French partisans . . . called "Maquis," which were holding off an entire German infantry division some distance southwest of Bordeaux. . . . The planes were loaded with rations, arms, and radios, and we took off in the dark. . . . We flew at normal altitude until near the target and then let down to within about three-hundred feet of the ground. We soon passed over three columns of smoke forming a large triangle, which was our "go ahead" signal, but made another approach to make certain. We lessened our altitude to about fifty feet and kicked the bundles out the waist opening where the door had been removed.

As we left the drop point, we could see the Maquis wildly waving their berets in jubilation.

On his July 13 mission to Munich, he noticed little enemy resistance until over the target. The next day his squadron flew another supply mission to the Maquis, this time in Area 4. He noted that it was somewhere in the mountains near Switzerland and several of the aircraft dropped OSS men. On July 17, he flew a memorable mission over Calais.

About ten second after "bombs away," we caught several close bursts that threw us up on one wing, just as the formation was swinging left in evasive action. We continued on course, unable to turn, while the other ships in the group slid off to the left in front of us, some pulling up and others diving beneath, in an effort to avoid collision. When I finally dared breathe again, we were still flying on into France with one wing high. Pohl and Etter finally managed to get us fairly well leveled out, but the aileron controls were useless for a banking turn. By skidding the ship through the air by means of the trim tabs, engines, and rudder, they finally managed to get us turned around and heading for England. On the way back we took a vote on whether to try and crash-land the fort (with wheels up), or to bail out of it. It was settled for us when we passed in over the field, for Pohl received instructions to stay aloft while the group landed, and then to bail the crew out. The last of the forts landed in the gathering dusk; as we made our final approach to the field I pulled the emergency handle on the waist door, which removed the hinge pins. I kicked the door out, and the lessened pressure almost sucked me out with it, before I had snapped my chute on the harness. That bit of carelessness gave me a good scare. We all checked each other's chutes and harnesses and then awaited the signal to jump. I was to be the first out, Carney second, Babicky third, and then Keltner. Hervatine was next, and then a replacement R.O. taking Galson's place was to follow. Hervatine plugged his earphones into the waist intercom outlet, in order to get the signal. . . .

Finally, the signal came, and I stepped upon the door ledge and kicked back with both feet. The rest happened so fast that it was a little bewildering. Although I had no sensation of falling, I did realize that I was getting quite a buffeting around—probably due to being tumbled by the slipstream. I jerked hard on the ripcord handle, the chest pack flew apart, but the bundle of silk stayed on my chest and lap. I must have

been falling with chest down, body parallel to the ground, for the chute remained in that position until I pushed it away with my arms. By that time I must have been upside down for the chute suddenly shot straight between my feet, and with a terrific jerk that tore the breath from me, I suddenly found myself floating underneath the broad canopy. The first sensation I had after regaining my wind was that of pressing silence. One moment the deafening roar of four engines, and the next, only the flapping of the chute, and the rapidly diminishing sound of the fort. . . . As I looked up towards it, I could see the rest of the crew bailing out, the chutes blossoming out like white flowers above the tiny black figures. One of the others pulled his cord while upside down, as I watched, for the snap of the parachute opening, jerked him around like a tiny pinwheel.

I looked down at the ground, in order to see which way I was drifting, but was unable to tell. . . . I then tried to pull in the shroud lines of one side of the chute, in order to collapse that part of the canopy. According to our instructions, that is supposed to steer the chute in that direction, but I couldn't see that anything was accomplished. . . . I could see another chute descending near me, which turned out to be Babicky. The others were spread out for miles. On the road toward the field, a jeep was kicking up dust while racing my way, while several farmhouses seemed to be rapidly getting larger as they slowly passed under me. I could see several tiny dots that were people watching us from the road. I commenced to try and pick out the spot where I thought I would hit. . . . I got a quick impression of a hedgerow coming at me; I just cleared it, smacked the ground, and went into a double back somersault. I was a little dazed for a moment, then jumped on the billowing silk in order to spill the air out of it so that I wouldn't be dragged across the ground. I had landed in a plowed field. . . . A moment later, I heard Babicky calling from some distance away. He had landed in the same hedgerow that I had missed and was being helped out of it by some Limey farmers. . . .

A jeep picked us up and transported us back to the briefing room where we learned that Pohl and Etter had decided to bring the ship in to a landing and had succeeded. After interrogation, the public relations sergeant took a few notes and snapped a picture of Frank and myself, which afterwards was sent to our hometown newspapers, unbeknownst to us. The rest of the crew was picked up and brought back with comparatively minor injuries. . . . This parachute jump, which caused the ankle injuries, later proved to have been the cause of saving our lives, for instead of flying a mission in Little Boy Blue the next day, we were given a three-day pass. That morning another crew replaced us—Lieutenant Malanuak's crew—and shortly after takeoff, the airplane was involved in a collision, with only traces of the crew and *Little Boy Blue* ever being found.

Only the tail gunner of *Little Boy Blue* survived the collision. Miraculously, the other plane was able to land. On his next mission, Sergeant Cook flew over Munich, where one of the B-17s was destroyed by a ground rocket before his eyes. Several other bombers were hit by flak and turned off, heading for neutral Switzerland. Cook flew his last mission on August 1. It was another supply mission to the Maquis, this time to Area 12 in south France. After completing that mis-

sion, he was assigned to the S-2 Office of the 3rd Scouting Force until the end of the war.

S.Sgt. Melvin F. Larson, a toggalier with the 560th Bomb Squadron of the 388th Bomb Group, flew his twenty-eighth and most memorable mission on July 14.

It was my tenth and last mission. I flew as a toggalier with Lt. George Montgomery and his crew. Our target today was Area #4, in Southern France, to drop supplies to the Maquis. Today we carried specially constructed C-3-type bombs. These "bombs" were large canisters that contained guns and ammunition, medical supplies, or food. The canisters, when dropped, released a colored silk parachute to aid in softening the landing. The color of the parachute indicated to the Maquis what supplies were in the canister. We had a very early briefing that was held at 1:30 A.M. Thirty six B-17s took off from Knettishall by 3:40 A.M., and this time there were no aborts. The takeoff and formation was a nail-biting situation, as it was performed in pitch darkness. Miraculously there were no air-to-air collisions.

To reach the drop zone, we had to fly through a mountain pass. It was fascinating, as we were able to look up the sides of the mountains. We had been briefed that we would not drop our canisters unless certain signal fires were observed burning in a large field that was designated as the drop zone. On our first pass, we received a fly-off signal because the Maquis were engaged in a confrontation with some German soldiers. On our second pass, the signal fires were lit. The bomb bay doors were then opened and we released our canisters. We were flying the B Group and when we dropped our canister, the ground was already a rainbow of colors. We made a third fly-by over the drop zone, and this time I observed a bustling of human activity as the canisters and silk parachutes were being rapidly removed. Some of the Maquis waved up to us, and one attractive woman stood in the middle of the field throwing kisses up to us. We learned later that the Maquis women went wild over the silk colored parachutes and made dresses and other garments out of the silk. We saw no enemy fighters or flak that day. All our aircraft returned back safely at Knettishall by 1:30 P.M., and all crews were physically and mentally exhausted from the long mission.

The 388th Bomb Group performed three supply missions to the Maquis. The first was on 25 June 1944 to Area Number 5 with thirteen fortresses. The second mission was conducted on 14 July 1944 to Area Number 4 with 36 fortresses, which I took part in. The final mission was on 1 August 1944 to Area Number 12 carried out by 31 Fortresses.

Sergeant Larson completed two more missions to attain his required thirty and was fortunate to have missed the mission that resulted in the loss of his original crew over Bordeaux in early 1944.

First Lt. Douglas G. McArthur, a B-17 pilot of the 561st Bomb Squadron, 388th Bomb Group, had completed half of thirty-five missions after June 6. On June 17, after a bombing mission against a German airfield at St. Trond, France, his aircraft had a minor collision with another B-17. Although almost six feet of his right wingtip was bent like a spoon, both planes made it back safely. The next day, McArthur flew against a V-1 storage area at Beauvoir in the face of "very accurate flak." "McFarland's plane, flying on our wing, was hit bad—lost two engines, all oxygen out, all hydraulic out, etc.—top turret operator badly injured." In spite of the damage, McFarland

dropped to 10,000 feet so his crew could breathe, and he made it back to England, where he had to make a belly landing. On June 21, the bombers took off for the big mission over Russia.

We carried ten 500-pound bombs. The target was a synthetic oil plant at Ruhland, Germany. Got a "shack" (direct hit on plant), tracking flak and German Me 109 fighter planes hit us on the way to Poltava. I flew the 1st Squadron lead—low squadron on lead group of lead wing. Capt. Bob Davis (561st operations officer) flew copilot with us on this mission, and Lieutenant Zades, our regular copilot, flew observer copilot. Our bomber, which was almost brand new, had "Inside Man" painted on the front side. This was our longest mission of over twelve hours.

After landing at the Poltava airstrip, a German recon spotter plane flew over about 4:30 P.M. We wanted to refuel and fly farther east into Russia to another base, but our colonel was outvoted by a two star Russian general, who said that they would protect us in case of a German attack.

That night, about 11:00 P.M., the Germans came and wiped us out. They dropped parachute flares so they could see and hit us for about forty-five minutes and came back a short time later for another twenty- or thirty-minute strike. I watched the German bombers for as long as two or three minutes at a time in the Russian searchlights, but the Russian ground gunners, many manned by women, never brought any of them down. The ground guns were all manual, no radar control like the Germans had.

The Russians had slit trenches dug around the area but didn't show anyone where they were before the fireworks

Aerial shot of bombs exploding near Rocquancourt on July 18, 1944. The town near the bottom is Fontenay le Marmion. The aircraft is a B-24 Liberator from the Eighth Air Force, which was bombing in support of British and Canadian forces in Operation Goodwood. NATIONAL ARCHIVES

started. So everyone was on their own that night. About a dozen of us ended up in the garbage pit about twelve feet square, and Tex, our radio operator, ended up in a latrine trench with two or three other guys landing on top of him—imagine his comments later. Fortunately, only one man was killed outright and one man badly wounded. He died later.

The next morning, we found the airfield covered with parts of B-17 bombers— mostly engines and tail sections because the rest had been burned up by incendiaries. There were just sixteen bombers out of over seventy that could be made flyable with little trouble. Our Inside Man was one of them; however, the Germans had also dropped antipersonnel bombs on the area, and by the time the Russians were done blowing these with quarter sticks of dyna-

mite, there were only six bombers left that could fly on to Italy and then back to England. After they were done, our Inside Man had all its tires flat, a big hole blown through the right inboard wing and gas tank inside it, along with much more shrapnel damage.

Once they got the field clear, the six bombers could take off. They loaded them with fuel and bombs, and they took off. The rest of us had to stay until the ATC (Air Transport Command) planes could be brought in to carry us back to England via the North Africa route.

The Russians moved those of us who had to stay out to a bivouac area in the brush and away from the airstrip. We found later, just before flying out of Russia, that one side of our bivouac area was a fuel dump and the other an ammunition dump. We spent about five days sitting there.

We flew out of Poltava on June 27 to Teheran in a C-46 via Rostow. Our pilot was Maj. R. H. Talbott. We finally landed in Cairo. On June 28, we left Cairo for Morocco in a C-54 piloted by Captain Lane. This was the same aircraft used by President Roosevelt on his first conference with Stalin at Teheran. We stayed at Casablanca for two days because of bad weather. We left Casablanca on June 30 for Scotland in another C-54. On July 1, we left Prestwick, Scotland, for Huntington Air Base in a C-47.

On July 14, McArthur was flying again, this time on Zebra missions to drop off supplies for the Maquis in southern France. On the last day of the month, he flew against Munich, where his plane was hit, and after dropping out of formation, he was able to make it back. At this point, he only had three more missions to go.

Like Lieutenant McArthur, T.Sgt. Javis J. Roberts, a flight engineer/gunner with the 561st Bomb Squadron, 388th Bomb Group, took part in Operation Frantic, the shuttle flight to Russia on June 21. This was to be his last mission.

We bombed an oil refinery at Ruhland, Germany, south of Berlin, while most of the Eighth Air Force bombed Berlin. We continued over Poland and landed at Poltava. Plans were to bomb Germany on the way to Italy and then bomb Germany on the way back to England. However, on the night of June 21, the German air force bombed the B-17s on the line, which destroyed eleven of our planes, including our I'll Get By. They also dropped some antipersonnel butterfly bombs all over the base. The Russian demolition teams blew up these all day on June 22.

On June 23, we flew via ATC to Teheran, Iran; Cairo, Egypt; Tunis, Tunisia; Casablanca, Morocco; and back to England. Upon return to England, we were offered to complete our tour. We had twenty-nine missions and six missions short, or we could sign up for another tour and be sent home for thirty days R and R, which we did. After thirty days R and R, we were sent to Atlantic City, New Jersey, to be reassigned to our group in England to complete our second tour as planned. This was September 4. On September 5, we were notified we were not being sent back overseas. At that time, I signed up for Cadet Flight Training.

First Lt. Chester Pietrzak was a bombardier with the 563rd Squadron and also took part in the June 21 mission to Russia.

We were to leave the next day for Italy (bombing on the way) and then the following day back to England. On the night of our arrival at Poltava, the German air force gave us a resounding welcome. Bombs away, strafing, mines—the whole bit. Our crew was the last to leave. We flew a patched up B-17 on July 14 back to England via Teheran–Cairo, Benghasi–Casablanca, and Ireland. Our plane had 100 holes in it. We came home alone on this long trip.

Pietrzak flew his thirty-fifth and final mission on August 8.[7]

First Lt. Jack R. Sargeant, a B-17 pilot of the 326th Squadron, 92nd Bomb Group, had flown two missions on D-Day. On June 11, he was hospitalized, and he did not return to flying until July 11. He participated in two missions that his unit flew over a period of four days against southern Germany.

They were not a piece of cake by any means, and they all ran ten hours or better. Remember, we didn't have anything to eat from the time we left.

If we had breakfast—which was usually horrible—that orange marmalade I can do without. About the only time we went for breakfast was when they had pancakes. I watched the chef prepare those powdered eggs one morning. They came in a long can, maybe three feet long. He would lay this can down, hit it with an axe on he floor, cut it in half, take the two pieces, empty their contents in a greased skillet with baking grease, lard, or whatever he had, and prepare scrambled eggs in this fashion. Right then

---

7. The number of missions required to complete a tour of duty was established by Gen. Ira Eaker in the spring of 1943 to improve morale in the Eighth Air Force. He set it at 25 combat missions for bomber crews and 150 for fighter pilots. Those who completed the required number of tours received the Distinguished Flying Cross. By August 1944, the number of missions was increased to 35 for bomber crews. The number of missions for bomber crews in the Mediterranean Theater was 50 to 60.

and there, I got a queasy stomach, so I didn't participate in breakfast.

Sargeant continued flying with the squadron until he completed his last mission in December. For T.Sgt. William F. French, a twenty-year-old Californian who served as a radioman gunner on a B-17 of the 729th Squadron, 452nd Bomb Group, the week of the Normandy invasion was anticlimactic. On the morning of D-Day, as the aircraft neared the target, he went to check the bomb bay doors to see if they were open and noticed that the bombardier had forgotten to remove the safety pins on the bombs.

I went back and told him and then put on a walk-on bottle and strapped my chute on. I was pulling the pins when the bomb bay doors opened, and I could look all the way down and I was hoping they would not say, "Bombs away!" We were over the Channel.

After two more missions—the second one on June 7—French and his comrades got a three-day pass. At the end of the month, after a few more missions over France, French participated in a raid on the synthetic oil plants at Whittenberg, Germany. On one of his last missions, he was flying with a new crew when he was presented with the rare opportunity of actually using the radio and attempting to get fixes to find the plane's location when the pilot got lost. However, as soon as he turned on the radio, the pilot ordered him to turn it off; as a result, they flew aimlessly for what seemed like hours. Needless to say, their mission was aborted. After landing back in England, French recounted his experience to the operations officer, who chewed out the pilot, telling him that he the reason he was given a radioman was to help find their location when necessary. After his last mission, French went to Preston, England, where he waited a couple weeks before he went home.

T.Sgt. Herbert J. Beatty, a twenty-one-year-old draftee from New York City, was a flight engineer on a B-24 of the 702nd Squadron, 445th Bomb Group, Eighth Air Force. He was with a lead crew that flew less often than the others did. He asked his commanding officer to appoint him to a regular crew because all the men who had come with him to Europe had already rotated back to the United States. In the summer of 1944, he was assigned to a regular crew.

They were a bunch of rookies who came over from the States and thought it was all milk runs now. I told them not to believe it; they are still shooting at us. I had a hotshot pilot who had to have more training in formation flying. He could not hold formation. I had to keep setting his controls as flight engineer. When you get in formation and take off, full rich is taken off and set on medium to conserve gas. If I didn't get out of my upper turret once, I got out of it five times cautioning this first lieutenant that, "If you don't hold formation, you drop back and give it a full rich mixture to get back in formation, you are using up my gas, and gas is vital on a trip." I cautioned this pilot a few times, and I told him when we go into the target, "You will notice the black flak. When they are not black flak and it changes to orange or green, that is the signal for their outlying fighters to come in. So pay attention to the flak because I cannot have eyes all over the place. You must realize flak color change is the signal for fighters." My tail gunner said to me, "Look at this beautiful green flak behind me! How do you like this?" I turned around, an Me 109 right up my tush, and I said, "You stupid ass! It's a fighter pilot shooting a 20-mm cannon at us! Shoot that son of a bitch!" Well we got through that.

As a lieutenant in late 1941, Capt. Robert J. Hahlen of Brodhead, Wisconsin, had flown with a B-26 group, but at the end of the year he suffered from a collapsed lung and he was taken off flying status. After recovering, he helped form the 312th Air Base Group, a headquarters squadron, and two service and supply squadrons, which performed third-echelon service and supply for two air combat groups.[8] The service and supply squadron included a full sheet-metal shop, a carpenter shop, and a technical shop for aircraft supplies. His 331st Service Squadron (one of the 312th's squadrons) was sent to Bournemouth, where it serviced the P-47s of a fighter group of the Ninth Air Force. From there, his unit moved east to Lymington to work with another P-47 fighter group.

We had a wire mesh runway there, and after the fighters kept using it for a while, this wire mesh would roll up ahead of them and restrict them on takeoff, especially if they had a large bomb load. They had everybody on the base including cooks and clerks out to put in a steel planking runway. They started one morning when the engineers came in with bulldozers, pulled out the wire, and hauled in the steel planking. They finished at midnight and did it all in one day. At 3:00 A.M., the P-47s took off for the invasion of Normandy.

Hahlen, whose squadron shipped out for France, landed on Omaha Beach on the morning on June 18.

I was in the advance party of the 312th Service Group. I carried a .45 pistol, but I could not hit anything with it, so before we left England I went to supply and got a car-bine. We got off on the beach and started to move on, and at about every quarter or half mile there was an MP. We kept walking, and every time we came to an MP, we asked, "How much farther?" They would reply, "Just a little ways." Soon we started seeing infantry that had fallen out along the trail because they could not hack it. We kept going until we reached a field where we stayed that night in shelter halves we brought with us. We dug a slit trench. As we set up, it started raining, and it rained like hell for some time. About 11:00 P.M., we had another rain and Bedtime Charlie came over and dropped a few bombs not too far away. At 3:00 A.M., I went down to one corner of the slit trench to get some coffee. The next morning they had trucks take us to Ste-Mère-Église, where there was a field behind the village next to an apple orchard. There was a big storm right after we landed, so the rest of the outfit didn't get over for another two or three weeks. Every morning at 5:00 A.M., there was a battery of 155-mm guns right behind us that fired three rounds so that was our alarm clock. We just sat around and waited for the outfit to arrive.

Every bush and tree had a tank, truck, or something sitting under it. The Germans shelled us a couple of times. The other groups were operating, and when the B-26 came in and moved to the end of the runway, it was a full ten minutes before the Germans started putting shells into it.

After a meeting in an office once used by the Germans, we started outside and heard a "burrrppp" and everyone knew it sounded different and dived for cover. An

---

8. Combat groups did their own first-echelon maintenance, the Service Squadron was supposed to handle second- and third-echelon maintenance, and the depot performed fourth-echelon work. If repairs took over three hours, the aircraft was sent to depot.

The wreckage of an Eighth Air Force B-17 near Cherbourg.
NATIONAL ARCHIVES

Me 109 came right across us followed by a Spitfire. The Messerschmitt must have been after the P-38 sitting on the hard stand since it hit it in the center of the fuselage. I don't know if the Spit got it or not.

Our work serving this fighter group did not get much cooperation. This type of operation did not work well in Europe because they did not want to go to the service group because they could go to the depot for repairs.

Several days after the bombing near St. Lô on July 25, Captain Hahlen's squadron moved to Avranches and from there to Orly (outside Paris) for about six weeks.

First Lt. William Denham from Racine, Wisconsin, flew a B-17 bomber with the 452nd Bomb Group and, like many other pilots who survived, he had a number of close calls. All his combat missions took place in the months before D-Day and ended on May 31. He observed the reports of the invasion until he received orders in July to start ferrying aircraft, but on July 15, after a few missions, he received new orders.

We fell into the best deal you ever heard of. It was to replace a couple of pilots in London. We got our bags packed and thumbed a ride with some general. They had half a dozen airplanes and a ground crew and were to take people anywhere they wanted from the air staff SHAEF. We were Flight A and had a C-45 with the general who committed suicide. He was a one star with an aide. The twin engine C-45 for seven or eight passengers he could call up at any time and so we would be gone for so long. We had a couple of UC 78, the same type I had in advanced training, a C-51, an L4, and an L5. There were several older aircraft including a UC 61, UC 64, and an A-29. We could travel anywhere in the ETO, but could not return to the U.S. with the orders we had.

We moved over to France to a site near Mt. Saint Michel in late July where we had a dirt strip and lived in tents. We moved up to Versailles from there. I took trips across the Channel before the move to France. The expression was "Safe with SHAEF."

Both the Eighth Air Force in England and the Fifteenth Air Force in Italy operated B-24 and B-17 bombers. The B-24 had a bad reputation compared to the B-17, especially since it had to fly at lower altitudes (from 28,000 to 32,000 feet compared to 35,600 to 38,500 feet). The B-17 was reputed to take incredible damage and survive. However, the B-24 had a faster cruising speed than most B-17 models and the capacity for a heavier bomb load, and it was assigned to carry out many difficult missions, including raids on Ploesti in Rumania. The ball turret was one of the bad features of the B-24 since it had to be retracted into the fuselage for landings and takeoffs. The turret could be retracted from only one position, and the gunner could not exit it unless it was retracted. If the turret jammed, the gunner was trapped inside.[9] Furthermore, it was so small that unless the gunner was a very small person, he could not fit inside with a parachute.

S.Sgt. Kenneth F. Potter, who was a ball gunner on a B-24 of the 851st Squadron, 490th Bomb Group, arrived in England in May. His first mission against Jammel, Belgium, was particularly memorable for him.

We were all green when we went in. When we got into the overcast, we were told to return. I was in the ball, and all I could see was the other ship coming towards us. I remember hitting the switch and telling the pilot we had to get the hell out of there. He banked in 25 or 30 degrees and when you bank a B-24 too much, there is no controlling it, but we were lucky.

I stood back with the side gunners until we reached a certain altitude. At that time, they would lower me. I would go down and it felt like you wouldn't stop until you turned your guns up to see if the aircraft were there. You sit on a little piece of armor plate and the window is pretty thick. You sit there for about eleven hours. I normally got out of there at about 11,000 feet because you could light a cigarette as you began to come down. I had a relief tube down there, but I never used it. In combat, I normally had my guns rotated. The only thing they have in there to stop you from shooting your propellers is a cam. It was not a comfortable place to be. Normally, when I got into heavy flak I would turn that thing as fast as I could 360 degrees in my mind hoping that if a piece of flak hit, it would

ricochet off. When we dropped the bombs I would normally count them going out and make sure they all left and tell the bombardier the bay was clear (in both B-24 and B-17s).

On another mission to Brux in a B-1, my electrical controls for the ball went out with my guns facing forward, which means my exit from the ball was at my back. My heated suit went out and it was cold, very cold. I got my foot on the mike switch and called the people up there to crank me up so I could get out, and they did. The B-17 also had a crank that lifts the ball itself, the part you sit on, not the turret. We had a safety precaution, which was periodic crew check every five to ten minutes and someone next to you would check to see if you lost oxygen or were hit. We had heated suits in both the B-24 and B-17 with an electrical outlet in the ball to plug into in both aircraft.

During his tour, Potter never witnessed a fighter attack, but he saw an Me 262 jet make a pass once during the autumn of 1944. He never fired his guns, except to test them over the Channel, and once he placed the two guns in the wrong positions when they prepared the aircraft so he couldn't have fired them if he had to.

One B-24 crew of the 851st Squadron, 490th Bomb Group, departed the States on the very day of the invasion and did not fly its first mission until August. The pilot, 2nd Lt. James C. Williams, flew a couple of missions over France early in August while his crew was training but saw little flak. His squadron changed to B-17s when his crew was ready to fly.

S.Sgt. Ralph D. Rickles, a waist gunner on Williams's aircraft, described the procedure.

9. The ball turret of a B-17 also had to be properly aligned in order for the gunner to exit, although it did not retract.

The first time, I remember, the wind sock that flew over squadron HQ was to let us know if we would fly the next day. Then you would load up and go down to eat breakfast. You would have fried eggs instead of powdered because they didn't know if you were going to come back, I guess. Then the gunners would go to a different location than the officers. We would go to a briefing where they would pull a curtain away, give us a speech, and show us where we would bomb. Then we would load on a truck and take our guns and ammo out and arm the plane. Then they would come out and we would take off.

Another member of the Williams crew was S.Sgt. James W. Henkel, who had a rather brief career as a ball gunner.

This AA would pop out there with all this pretty smoke and [it was] real exciting to watch it. You weren't scared of it; it was like fireworks with all this shooting around. It was on the fifth mission, after about twenty holes through my ball turret, that a piece came through, ricocheted around, and hit me in the leg so that I was ready to go home to Texas. No more AA for me.

Sgt. James Ross, the tail gunner for Williams's crew, remembered the flak on the first mission also.

We were told we would be fascinated by the AA fire and I found it to be true. I looked out and thought, "Look at those bursts! Aren't those beautiful?" I suppose it wasn't a very eventful mission because we were recalled. I remember the first firing at Hess in anger and I saw AA bursts and it was true, you just stood there and gawked at them a while, but after you saw what they could do, you didn't gawk at them anymore. Instead, you would get behind armor plating or squash down in your helmet.

Flight Off. Douglas N. Morilon on Williams's aircraft also had indelible memories of the first mission:

The bombs were armed when they were loaded. The wires that released pins to arm them were pulled out when the bombs dropped. I had to make sure they were loaded right and had to pull a cotter key after we were airborne and at altitude. I retained the cotter pins as a safety factor.

I was in the nose and we were moving around real fine. I believe the target was Bremen. It was just like a training mission. We loaded the live bombs and made sure they were armed. We knew that we were going into battle and we had our Mae Wests on, flak suits, and helmets. It was about four hours before we got to Heligoland and they started shooting at us. We had a recall because of the weather conditions over the target area, so this whole mass exodus looked like we chickened out at the first shot.

Williams's bombardier, who also operated a machine gun turret on the B-17, like other officers, had less gunnery training than an enlisted man did. According to the navigator, 2nd Lt. William Laahs, the routine seldom varied.

I remember the same procedure on every mission, just like the first. Usually our take-off was at predawn, in the dark with several hundred to a thousand aircraft taking off at about the same time. The air bases were only about five miles apart. I was standing up front with my head in the astrodome watching for aircraft. Also, we had a procedure on when to form up on our lead ship—they would fire different color flares; possibly they would fire red, yellow, or green. We would look for those and watch that we didn't collide with another aircraft at the same time. We were scheduled to form up at a certain altitude on our lead plane and we kept circling after take off. There were quite a few midair collisions if I recall correctly. I also operated both cheek

guns on the B-17, while Morilon and I each had one on the B-24.

On the Meresburg raid, a shell exploded close to Sgt. James C. Ross, the tail gunner. The shrapnel pierced a hole the size of his head near his position, three in the vertical fin, and one in the stabilizer. During combat, the airman was in as much danger as the foot soldier, but he had no place to hide when the firing started. However, if he made it through, the airman spent the night in safe, comfortable quarters instead of a foxhole on the battlefield.

CHAPTER 7

Buildup and Breakthrough

In early July, after the conquest of Cherbourg, the 4th Infantry Division moved south to rejoin the VII Corps in operations aimed at extricating the American forces from the marshlands and hedgerow country. However, having sustained heavy casualties in the north, the division was first pulled out of the action to rest. The American bridgehead in Normandy had been bursting with men and equipment by the end of June with over 500,000 tons of supplies and 150,000 vehicles disembarked, not to mention new infantry and armored divisions and thousands of troops that passed through replacement centers to keep the fighting divisions at full strength. The two exhausted airborne divisions, which received no replacements while in France, soon departed for England to prepare for their next airborne operation. It was pointless to allow these two elite formations to take further losses in the ground campaign that had become costly as the Germans turned the hedgerows into field fortifications. Besides, by the end of June, there was an ample supply of men and vehicles in Normandy.

The German Side of the Hill

When the invasion began, Col. Gen. Friedrich Dollmann commanded the German Seventh Army defending Normandy and Brittany. Field Marshal Erwin Rommel, who had prepared the coast to meet the invasion for many months, was on leave in Germany, away from his Army Group B Headquarters. Field Marshal Gerd von Rundstedt was at his OB West command post near Paris. Gen. Wilhem Falley, the commander of the 91st Air Landing Division with 7,500 men in the Cotentin, was killed by American paratroopers in the early-morning hours of June 6.[1] The loss of leaders and Hitler's personal intervention finally brought the Germans to the breaking point, but not without weeks of dogged resistance.

Two divisional commanders assumed key roles in the German resistance against the American invading forces. At Utah Beach, it was Gen. Karl-Wilhelm von Schlieben, commander of the 709th Infantry Division with 12,320 men, who led the northward withdrawal and was appointed commander of Fortress Cherbourg, which Hitler wanted held to the last man. Von Schlieben assumed command of the remaining divisions in that part of the peninsula until he was forced to surrender late in June.

Facing the Americans at Omaha Beach was Gen. Dietrich Kraiss with his 352nd Infantry Division (with 12,734 men) and attached elements of the 716th Infantry Division (with 7,771 men). Even with additional detachments from other divisions, his forces were pushed back, but finally managed to take full advantage of the *bocage* to protect St. Lô for weeks. His front was reinforced with the green troops of the 3rd Parachute Division (17,420 men), which came under the command of General Meindl's II Parachute Corps. According to American intelligence reports, at the end of May, the 352nd Division consisted of remnants of the 383rd Infantry Division, which had been destroyed on the Russian front and had a high percentage of foreigners. The division's morale was low. However, the Allied intelligence sources must have underestimated Kraiss's division because it gave a good account of itself holding between the beaches and St. Lô, despite taking heavy losses. Kraiss was killed in combat near St. Lô on August 2.

The 3rd Parachute Division originally came from Brittany with a battle group to reinforce the 352nd Division. The full division finally took over the sector to the right of the 352nd Division on June 18. Gen. Richard Schimpf, who commanded this division since it was formed at the end of 1943, reported that he entered the campaign with 100 percent troop strength. However, he only had 70 percent of his authorized weapons, lacked machine guns and antitank guns, and had only 40 percent of his transportation. His troops marched from Brittany in almost record time without interference from Allied aircraft, but the situation prevented him from giving them even a day's rest. The 3rd Parachute Division, which faced the American 29th Division in

continued

---

1. Unit strengths are for June 1, 1944.

169

the battle for St. Lô, was as green the American division, but became battle-hardened early in the campaign.

SS Gen. Joseph "Sepp" Dietrich led his I SS Panzer Corps from Hitler's OKW Reserve near Paris to Caen, which he reached on June 8. He was instrumental in preventing the British from breaking out in June. SS Gen. Paul Hausser led the II SS Panzer Corps (9th SS and 10th SS Panzer Divisions with 16,800 and 15,800 men, respectively) on the Eastern Front. His plans for an offensive at Kowel (on the Russian Front) had to be cancelled when Hitler ordered him on June 12 to move his corps west to join with the I SS Panzer to keep the British in check. Late in June, General Dollmann died of a heart attack before he was informed that he was relieved of command because of the loss of Cherbourg. Hauser took command of the Seventh Army.

On June 13, the XLVII Panzer Corps of Gen. Hans von Funck moved from Army Group B reserve to Caumont to prevent the American 1st Infantry Division from breaking through. On June 17, at conference in Soissons, Hitler authorized Panzer Group West to counterattack in the Bayeux sector on July 5. Panzer Group West took command of the forces, including 250 medium and 150 heavy Panther and Tiger tanks and 75 percent of the 88-millimeter guns of the III Flak Corps. On June 28, Panzer Group West faced the British, which left the Seventh Army with 50 medium and 26 heavy Panther tanks to face the Americans. There were approximately 35,000 Germans soldiers on each of these fronts. On July 2, Hitler ordered the replacement of General von Geyr, commander of

Panzer Group West since before the invasion. In early July, both Rommel and Hausser suggested pulling back to a better position, but Hitler refused and even forbade the preparation of any rearward defensive positions between Normandy, the German border, and the old West Wall fortifications.

When the invasion began, the LXXXIV Army Corps was holding the front facing the Americans. Gen. Erich Marcks was in command until he died in July and was replaced by Dietrich von Choltitz. In July, with the arrival from Brittany of Gen. Eugen Meindl's II Parachute Corps, the LXXXIV Army Corps shifted its position to cover only the area west of the Vire River. Meindl controlled the divisions on the St. Lô front, including the remnants of Kraiss's 352nd Division. His own 3rd Parachute Division reinforced the divisions already in the area.

On July 18, Rommel's car was shot up by a British Spitfire, and the field marshal was wounded. He was replaced by Field Marshal Günter von Kluge. On July 3, Gerd von Rundstedt was replaced by Hans Günter von Kluge as OB West, who, after Rommel's removal, controlled both higher headquarters on the Normandy front. Through the month of July, Hitler refused to release the Fifteenth Army from its coastal defenses between the Seine and the Belgian coast for fear that Normandy was only a secondary invasion. As a result, the German divisions on the Normandy front were forced to remain in continuous action and could not be withdrawn to rest and refit according to normal procedure.

continued

After the failed attempt on Hitler's life on July 20, 1944, a number of high-ranking German officers, including Rommel, either were executed or committed suicide, which further reduced the military leadership's ability to control the campaign.[2]

On the Normandy front, Allied air superiority kept the Germans at a severe disadvantage logistically, even though many Allied soldiers on the front lines were unable to appreciate it because of the hard fighting. The German frontline units received less than one fifth of the daily-required ammunition and other needed supplies. Battle groups had to be formed and sent forward to fill in gaps and prop up the front. German armored units moving into Normandy were largely restricted to nighttime travel because of Allied airpower.

The German tanks proved to be superior to the Allies' and prevented the British from breaking out. However, on the American front, where the bocage dominated the landscape, they had limited value and the mortar was king. The American 2.36-inch bazooka was a deadly weapon in the close quarters fighting among the hedgerows. According to some estimates, the German artillery was able to fire a fifth to a tenth of the rounds of the Americans due to the German supply situation. In addition, the small American liaison aircraft made up for the lack of direct observation through the hedgerow country by helping

The German Side of the Hill *continued*

direct artillery fire. Chances of the Germans driving the Allies back to the beaches were more remote than an Allied swift break through the hedgerow country. While German armored units kept the British penned up, the lynchpin of the entire German front was St. Lô. If this city fell, the troops of the LXXXIX Corps holding the front between the Vire and the west coast of the Cotentin would be in jeopardy north of Coutances.

The nemesis of the American 1st and 29th Divisions was the 352nd Division, which continued to hold that key road hub with the help of the 3rd Parachute Division and reinforcements until late into July. The addition of the American 2nd Division on the left (east) of the 29th Division in June, and later the 30th and 35th Divisions on its right, forced the Germans to bring reinforcements. These included regiments of the 17th SS Panzer Grenadier Division (17,321 men), the Panzer Lehr Division (14,699 men), elements of the 2nd SS Panzer Division (18,108 men), and the 275th Infantry Division (10,768 men) to hold the front to the west of St. Lô between the Vire and the Taute Rivers. By the end of July, the German situation was becoming untenable. Only the Americans' failure to launch surprise attacks, their fear of taking excessive losses, and inability to exploit success may have staved off disaster for a few days longer, according to General Schimpf.

---

2. In the summer of 1944, SS General Dietrich had informed Rommel that, if so ordered, he would surrender, but Rommel no longer commanded Army Group B after July 18.

Souvenir Hunting

Many soldiers collected souvenirs from the battlefield for various reasons. In some cases, they traded the battlefield souvenirs for money, food, equipment, or any little luxuries that made their lives on the front more bearable. When it became known that some soldiers were stripping prisoners of personal items, including ribbons and decorations, a directive was sent out forbidding this kind of behavior. When the Germans learned of American soldiers' interest in collectibles, they began to booby-trap such items. According to a 2nd Armored Division G-2 report of July 5,

A German *Mauser* rifle was picked up in a collecting point where it had been carried by U.S. personnel for storage. When attempt was made to cock the rifle or otherwise move somehow the parts of the firing mechanism, a violent explosion broke the gun in half and severely injured a soldier. From study of parts it seems evident that small penthrite charges have been made which can be introduced into the firing mechanism of small arms such that when parts are disturbed detonation will occur. It is important to note that no visible signs of this booby trap were left on the exterior of the gun. Any rifle, however harmless in appearance, may contain one.

Of course, many American troops, especially those in the airborne divisions, were trained to use German weapons—when operating behind the lines they might need them. American troops were warned of enemy booby-trapping as early as the North African campaign as demonstrated in one of the Private SNAFU animated cartoons shown to the troops as a training film.

A constant flow of replacements and equipment kept the American divisions at full strength. American intelligence was well aware that the Germans were not able to do the same. According to a G-2 report, prisoners and captured documents revealed that "German officers and enlisted men were becoming disorganized. The ammunition shortage in the 3rd Parachute Division was so acute that the Heavy Weapons Companies had to be used as rifle companies."

Hedgerow War, June 8 to July 20

Before Operation Cobra, the breakout operation in early August, Gen. Omar Bradley's First Army swept through most of the Cotentin while General Gerow's V Corps and General Corlett's newly arrived XIX Corps, which had become operational on June 14, tried to push south through the hedgerow country leading to St. Lô and Caumont during June. The German 352nd Division was reinforced and stubbornly clung to the area in front of St. Lô. To the west, General Collins's corps tried to clear the Germans from the high ground across the Douve between the marshes and west coast of the Cotentin early in July.

The 90th Infantry Division was once again encountering command and leadership problems during combat operations, which were not noticed by the average rifleman of the "Tough 'Ombre" Division. Pvt. William A. Biehler, a draftee from New Jersey, boarded *LCI 1711* from the replacement depot at Weymouth, but his trip was delayed because of the big storm and his group did not land until June 22. From the beach, Biehler and his comrades went to a replacement center near Ste-Marie-du-Mont, where they slept on the ground. Their barracks bags were taken away, and they never saw them again. On June 23, Biehler and his group were driven to the regimental headquarteres near Ste-

Mère-Église, where they were assigned to Company K, 357th Infantry, 90th Division, which was at about half strength at the time.

During the next fifty days, they ate nothing but K or C rations. The small can openers that came with the C rations became a prized item. It was well into August before they finally got a hot meal, a shower, new uniforms, and even a USO show.[3] During his first night in combat, Biehler slept in a foxhole, took off his glasses, and shot at anything that moved thereafter. After that first night, he wised up and "from then on I slept with my helmet and my glasses on and my loaded M-1 rifle cradled in my arms." The soldiers kept an organized watch system in the foxholes. "Each of us had a buddy in the same foxhole or next to us so that we were awake two hours and then slept two hours and a buddy took over alternating at night and during the day when we were under threat." No one checked the guard at night for fear of getting shot. "We had one new second lieutenant who tried it and gave up after three foxholes." The lieutenant quickly learned that, after a few days of combat, an infantryman had a good chance of surviving and quickly developed a sixth sense for danger.

Private Biehler's first major engagement was at Hill 122 on the ridge by the Forest of Mont Castre (to the east of La Haye du Puits) early in July when his regiment failed to take the position.

> My platoon went through a notch in a hedgerow, and in the middle of the field, about halfway to the next hedgerow, the Germans opened up with 88s, machine guns, and rifles. They were dug in and well camouflaged behind the next hedgerow. The 1st and 2nd scouts were killed immediately. They were both replacements with me and were eighteen years old. We did as we

Sgt. Paul Lutick in German tunic displaying a trophy. PFC Ed Rutkowski (on the left) and 1st Lt. Jay H. Mehaffey (on the right) of the Company C, 5th Rangers. The flag was found in a German bunker of the Maisy Battery. JAY H. MEHAFFEY

> had been trained and kept advancing past the dead scouts until none of us could go any farther. As I went past the two scouts, somebody was already yelling for a medic. The rest of us were pinned down. I found myself along in the middle of the field and prayed. There was no order to retreat; none of us could go any farther. When I discovered that I was the only one in the field not dead, I decided I had waited long enough. I then ran back through the notch to join the others who had beat me there. They said they had seen bullets kicking up dirt all around me and were amazed that I had not been hit. We recovered the bodies of the dead that night, and as I remember, the Germans did not bother us. The battle lasted several days. Later in the battle for

---

3. Biehler also mentioned that while they were shown the film *Destination Tokyo*, someone jumped up, yelling, "Screw the navy!" and shot up the screen with his BAR. Apparently, it was not a good idea to show a war film to combat soldiers so near the front.

nearby Beaucoudray they cut off and captured two companies of the 90th Division.

The 8th "Golden Arrow" Division began landing on July 3 while the 90th Division was recovering. PFC John B. McBurney, a draftee from Jennings, Louisiana, and a mortar man in Company D of the 13th Infantry, disembarked from the Liberty ship *Porpoise.*

We landed early on the morning of the Fourth of July, offloading into landing craft. The landing craft carried us to shore. The night sky was filled with tracer fire and aerial bursts, and I never was sure if the display was wartime combat action or a 4th of July celebration.[4] We relieved the 82nd Airborne after a thirty-mile forced march near the village of La Haye du Puits. During this march, I fell asleep walking with all of my equipment plus an 81-mm mortar base plate. I woke up after falling in a ditch with the 40-pound plate on my neck. This walk was pretty scary, for all along the roads from the beach, long rows of dead American soldiers were lined up with their gray dead bodies covered with dust and waiting to be loaded on ships we had just departed. There is a distinct smell of mass death, a sickeningly sweet odor, and the air was heavy with this aroma. Mixed with this was the smell of cordite hanging in the air. The combination of these odors added much to our feeling of uneasiness.

Shortly before we went into battle for the first time, my captain, a man named Morgan, decided to go on a reconnaissance and hollered for me and another guy to go with him. We went over the top of a hill in an orchard, and a German machine gunner dug in on the downslope opened fire on us. We all three took off up the hill when Captain Morgan, running full out and head down, rammed helmet first into the trunk of an apple tree and knocked himself out. The other two of us each grabbed him under an arm and dragged him with us back over the top of the hill. This ended the recon job. (Later, in Germany, I was with Morgan when he bravely led two rifle companies in a seemingly suicidal attack across open fields into a wood where the enemy lay in wait, while the officers who were supposed to lead the attack declined the honor).

Almost immediately, we were thrown into the wild confusion of battle. A red-headed sergeant and I started through a small field surrounded by hedgerows to the forward lines to establish an OP [observation post]. We were both carrying rolls of wire and were stringing it out as we went, for communications back to our guns. Of course, the front line was all around us, as fierce fighting was going on for the possession of each such little field. Unknown to us, a German machine gun was placed on the opposite side of the hedgerow, dug into its side with just a small opening for the barrel to protrude on our side. A burst of fire from this gun caught him [the sergeant] and he fell dead. We had been taught to not stop and try to help in this situation, so I ran across to safety. This machine gun nest was quickly eliminated.

Near the village of La Haye du Puits, all of the vital telephone lines were strung along the surface of a sunken road, which ran between hedgerows, and near which stood a church with a tall bell tower. Unknown to

---

4. When McBurney disembarked on the Fourth of July, in spite of ammunition shortages, General Bradley ordered all the First Army's artillery weapons to open up in celebration, and many troops probably joined in with small arms all along the front.

us, there remained in the steeple an enemy mortar observer. The lines to our own mortars were among these so laid, and we kept losing contact from our OP back to the guns, so I was sent to repair these [wires]. When I got opposite the church, I saw many wires that had been blown apart and proceeded to patch them together, checking each end to be sure I was splicing the right ones together. The job was slowed down, for as I began splicing, I heard the sound of incoming mortar shells, and would dive into the nearest shell hole in the road. The holes were quite shallow in the hard surface. I would scrunch down as tightly as possible to the bottom until it would quiet down and then dash out to put another together until the next bunch of shells came in. I patched several units' wires together other than my own, and then there was one wire left. A soldier from my outfit came along and asked if he could help me and I told him he could splice the last one. He checked both ends and made the connection and when he did, they asked his name and unit. He later got a Silver Star and a battlefield promotion to sergeant for this since the last line happened to be to the Division CP.

At some point, someone finally realized there was an enemy observer in the church tower and he was eliminated. Recently, I was told by another veteran that this observer was a woman.

Luckily, I made it through the hedgerows without a scratch with the help of a few bottles of wine from local farmers.

PFC John F. Troy of Company E, 13th Infantry of the "Golden Arrow" Division, a draftee from Gary, Indiana, landed at Utah Beach and moved into line with his unit between the 79th "Cross of Lorraine" Division, which was on the coast, and the 90th "Tough 'Ombre" Division.

I don't remember the date; maybe 17 or 18 July, we started to make unspectacular, but decent, gains until we finally came to a small French river called Ay.[5] A couple of days before this they moved us up to plug up a hole in the line between two battalions. We were to take one hedgerow, then get on top of a road going east-west. We were attacking south and the Jerries let us pass the hedgerow and let us get on the north side of the road. We started to dig slit trenches, but before we could finish they dropped over a dozen rounds on us. We had four casualties in our platoon: two dead and two wounded. Later we found these enemy rounds were not more than twenty feet from each other.

The guy next to me received a large amount of shrapnel. It looked to me like fifteen to twenty small holes, each bleeding through his ODs [olive drabs]. The two medics with us shook their heads—meaning too rough. They thrust two rifles through the sleeves of my raincoat to carry him. Another fella and I carried him to the battalion aid station. We got there wringing wet with sweat and our lungs heaving and wheezing. We put him down outside the house, which served as the aid station. He was still alive when we left and I hope he made it. It was just another terrible day in the hedgerows.

The 4th Division, which had taken heavy losses during battle for Cherbourg, suffered again in early July in the battle of south of Carentan. Replacements continually flowed from England

5. The Ay is a small stream that runs through Lessay.

to the camps set up near the Normandy beaches to the various divisions as needs arose.

On the American southern front, fighting was probably even more vicious in the hedgerows where German resistance continued despite their lack of replacements and other shortages. On July 4 on the 1st Division front near Caumont, two deserters from the 2nd Panzer Recon Battalion of the 2nd Panzer Division confessed

[their] strongpoint consisted of 7 or 8 LMG [light machine guns] sited for all-around defense. It was manned by the reinforced 3rd Platoon containing approx. fifty men. The MG's were emplaced behind a hedge on both sides of the road. The strongpoint was surrounded by S and T mines, about twenty yards from the position. Mines covering the path were not taken up during the day. Tripwires were attached to the mines. The 4th Company, which was part of the MLR [main line of resistance], was in position 200 yards behind the strongpoint. It was protected by S and T mines, placed forty yards in front of position, and barbed wires.

The use of mines and hedgerows made overcoming German resistance on the southern front very slow and difficult. The German soldiers put covers on their foxholes and even dug into the hedgerows so that only a direct hit could create casualties. To prevent their mines from being removed by American engineers, they put anti-handling devices on some so that the American engineers were warned that the only alternative was to destroy the mines in place and not try to deactivate them.

German prisoners complained of the shortage of food and mentioned that they had to purchase eggs and vegetables from farmers. A few even decided to surrender when several nurses were returned to their lines and they heard about how

well they were treated. Some prisoners complained of the constant American shelling that almost drove them crazy since they felt the concussion even in the foxholes. For weeks American intelligence reports found morale poor among many of the foreigners serving in the German army and even many Germans in the static infantry divisions. Elite paratrooper and panzer units were rushed into the critical areas to stiffen the resistance, and although they suffered from losses and similar shortages, it took weeks for the front to crack.

The 29th Division had taken many casualties by the end of June, and T/4 Clifton Bitgood was one of them. On June 18, his company of the 121st Engineers was ordered to join up with an infantry unit during the advance on St. Lô.

We were moving along a hedgerow that bordered the road when I was hit in the right arm. The bullet missed the artery and the bone but hit the radial nerve. I was given a shot of morphine and taken back to the beach. I was in a hospital tent all night with lots of wounded. German bombers came over during the night, and the next morning I was loaded onto a C-47 and sent to England. When we took off, I could see the craters the bombs made; they were large enough to drop a house in. In England, I was put on a train and sent to a hospital somewhere in northern England. On the train a doctor came around to check the wounds but did nothing to my wound. Later a nurse came around, and she was going to change the bandage. I said the doctor had just looked at it, and she replied that he doesn't know anything about that as he is an eye, ear, and nose doctor. A few days after reaching the hospital, I was operated on. Next day, the doctor who performed the surgery told me he grafted in about eight inches in the radial nerve and said that my arm may never improve and I could be paralyzed for the rest of my life. He then said they were sending me back to the States.

PFC John McQuaid enlisted in the reserves in Ware, Massachusetts, at age seventeen, and as soon as he finished high school that summer, he went to basic training. In 1944, he was sent to England, and in June, he joined Company A, 116th Infantry, as a replacement for the 29th Division, where he soon underwent his baptism of fire.

During an attack on a German position, McQuaid found himself near Lieutenant Colonel Metcalfe, who was hit and died soon after. Maj. Tom Dallas, who had helped get the troops off the beach on D-Day, took over the command of the unit. After the fighting around Couvains, the unit pulled out of the line to the Forest de Cerisy and McQuaid and his comrades received a helmet full of hot water to wash and new clothes. Then they moved back to Couvains to train their new replacements in hedgerows warfare with tanks. They also practiced new tactics in the hedgerows. Unfortunately, an unexpected heavy artillery shelling killed many of the replacements.

General Gerhardt came to the location the next morning ripping mad about the losses. The first time I ever saw him, I had my back to him and when someone yelled and I turned around I bumped into him almost knocking him down. He gave me hell for not wearing my stripes and I never got my promotion or money.[6]

We went back to the front line and now the attack for St. Lô began. First light and on the move again to the Martinville Ridge. While on the ridge, one of our men came over the hill with a German prisoner, stopped, spoke for a couple of minutes, and left. We were being shelled heavily; everyone was running along the hedge. "Boom!" One hit and four men dead and eight wounded. I was one of the wounded. God was with me, my helmet saved my life. The shrapnel hit the helmet liner and was diverted to a point between the helmet liner and the steel helmet, landing right on top. If this had not happened I would have been hit right between the eyes. I received wounds in both legs, arms, my right hand, and face. All were shrapnel and all small.

After I was wounded, I was able to climb over a couple of hedgerows to the aid station. There were many wounded men being handled by the medics. A Father Kelly was right there helping and consoling the wounded. He gave me the last blessing, put me on a stretcher onto a jeep, and I was off to the field hospital, arriving a few minutes later. At the hospital, when they lifted me onto the operating table, the tag with the information about my wounds slipped down under me. The doctor couldn't find it, and just then they brought in another very seriously wounded man. I told the doctor I was all right and to take care of the other fellow. The doctor ordered me taken out and sent to the hospital back at the airport. When I arrived there by ambulance, we were all put into a large tent. After a while, a doctor and nurse came in, and he said, "What the hell is this country coming to, sending kids over here to fight!" (I was nineteen years old.) He told them to get me on a plane back to England, and I was taken out to a C-47. I was scared to death; I had never flown before. The nurse came in,

---

6. Many officers and NCOs removed their insignias of rank after it became obvious the enemy snipers were targeting unit leaders.

took one look at me, and asked what the matter was. I told her—she smiled and went and got the pilot. He came over to me and told me everything was going to be all right. I asked him how long he had been flying and he looked at the nurse and she gave me a shot that put me to sleep. All I saw was the runway on takeoff and the runway when we landed in England.

After he recovered in September, John McQuaid was assigned to the Judge Advocates' Office in the Ninth Air Force.

Sgt. J. R. Slaughter, 116th Infantry, 29th Division, survived unscathed through the entire month of June. On July 5, after he was grazed by a bullet fired by a sniper, he was awarded his first Purple Heart, but things went downhill for him after that.

Standing in our quest for St. Lô was an ordinary Normandy village, Couvains. We were attached to one of the rifle companies and moving cautiously, single file, as we approached the outskirts. The dirt road was narrow and flanked by hedgerows. There were German communication ditches, about three feet deep, on each side of the road. Those ditches protected the German multicolored communication wire from artillery. The day was hot in more ways than one. The village was conspicuous by a church steeple that dominated the skyline. As we got closer to the steeple, the 88s became all-seeing. The only part of the town visible was the church belfry.

The frightful banshee-scream sounded like it had my number, and I dove head first into the roadside ditch. My helmet separated one way, and I went the other. I landed on my head and thought I had nearly broken my neck. The exploding 88

somehow missed. Upon brushing myself off, I was shocked to see the arm of a German soldier lying on the parapet of the trench. Part of his uniform sleeve was there with just the arm about where the elbow should be. The thumb and four fingers were intact and the arm inside the sleeve. What could have happened to the rest of that unfortunate young man?

Twenty minutes later, I heard moaning sounds coming from the undergrowth off to the right of the road. Cautiously I inspected the area and found a young German paratrooper with a serious leg wound. The leg was almost severed by shrapnel. Remembering my vow taken back at the beach [not to take prisoners], my first reaction was to put him out of his misery and keep going. . . .

The German said tearfully, "Bitte!" (please). He was an impressive-looking soldier, and I just couldn't do it. Instead, I made sure he was unarmed, and then I cut away his trouser leg and applied a tourniquet. He had an ugly wound that had torn away most of the meat from his thigh. I gave him a shot of morphine, a drink from my canteen, and then I lit an American Lucky Strike cigarette for him.

As I was leaving, he smiled weakly, and said in understandable English, "Thank you very much, may God bless you. Good Luck!" That changed my mind about not taking prisoners. I still hated the German soldier, but I couldn't kill one at close range if his hands were over his head. As we entered the outskirts of Couvains, an apple orchard appeared. Up ahead, Sergeant Norfleet and some officers from a rifle company were reconnoitering the area. A short round from our friendly artillery killed one man and wounded three. Norfleet caught a

Stuart light tanks in Normandy, July 1944. Note the hedgerow cutter on the lead tank.

piece of shrapnel in his right elbow. That ended the sergeant's combat duty the hard way. It was no million-dollar wound, because it severed the nerve, disabling his right arm.

Sgt. Romeo B. Bily . . . was also shot by a sharpshooter entering Couvains. His wound was a bullet between the eyes, killing him instantly. PFC Tony Carusotto was also killed in that orchard. The snipers were deadly but the 88s were much more frightening. We couldn't move without the boom-swish-boom! Boom-swish-boom! "Medic!" Then some smart GI realized the culprit was that church belfry tower. Battalion sent engineers with explosives, which they planted at the base of the steeple. Ka-boom! That ended our misery for a while.

Slaughter also described the effects of being under constant enemy bombardment.

After surviving twenty-four hours under . . . shelling, the infantryman is an unbelievable sight. He is, of course, filthy dirty. The dust from the tops of the slit trench has been falling on the occupants and the perspiration causes dirt to adhere to the skin. Around the eyes mud has caked and the eyeballs are red from irritation and lack of sleep. Sleep is hard to come by, even though one is dog-tired. When nature calls, it must be performed in the safety of the slit-trench, lying down.

During the bloody fighting for the Martinville Ridge in the battle for St. Lô, many in Slaughter's unit hoped for the million-dollar flesh wound that would give them a ticket out of the front. Replacements continued to pour into his company, but the battle of attrition took a heavy toll. Some soldiers had their own self-inflicted wounds and one soldier even committed suicide with a Springfield rifle. Sergeant Slaughter finally got his wound, a sliver of shrapnel in the back on August 7 at Hill 203 overlooking the Vire. This earned him a trip back to England for a two-month rest while his 29th Division advanced on the Vire. He rejoined his Company D as it advanced on Aachen, Germany, in September.

Pvt. Robert Hardesty, rifleman, 1st Platoon of Company A, 115th Infantry, had arrived as a replacement a month before the battle. Before the 115th and 116th Infantry launched a new assault against St. Lô on July 11, Sergeant Murphy, his platoon sergeant, picked thirteen men for a recon patrol behind German lines in St. Lô. "At that time," said Hardesty, "our lines were about three miles from St. Lô and our patrol got to St. Lô and back with no problems and based on these patrols."

The front of the 29th Division was shortened when the 35th Division took over its right flank. The 30th Division had advanced to Pont Hébert from the Taute-Vire Canal during the first two weeks of July, presenting a new threat to the German hold on St. Lô. However, on July 11, before the 29th Division could attack the high ground and drive the Germans from St. Lô, the German 3rd Parachute Division launched its own assault in the predawn darkness. Although the Americans were thrown off balance, General Gerhardt ordered his men to go ahead with the attack. The 115th Infantry was delayed until late morning, but the 116th attacked at about 6:00 A.M. along the Martinville Ridge to outflank St. Lô with tank support. The fighting raged for days. Meanwhile, on July 11 the 2nd Division on the left of the 29th Division was able to capture Hill 192. Finally, the German Seventh Army commander,

SS Gen. Paul Hausser, realizing that his position was untenable, withdrew all but a rear guard from St. Lô. The 29th Division finally occupied the war-torn town on July 18.

The 2nd Infantry Division with the attached 741st Tank Battalion moved inland as it prepared to assault Hill 192. The subsequent events were recorded in the following letter, which was recovered from a fallen young German paratrooper and was dated July 24.

Dear Struppell,

For the third time I am trying to get in touch with you by letter; I hope that it will reach you. . . . I made my ten jumps. Then I came to my regiment and to my CP. We were stationed in Brittany near Brest. When the invasion started, we moved and marched approximately thirty to forty km daily, but only at night. During the day, American fighter-bombers controlled the area. Then we were put in the line east of St. Lô. . . . When we were committed, our company strength was 170. Then the eleventh of July arrived and the most terrible and most gruesome day of my life. At 0300 hours, our company sector got such a dense hail of artillery and mortar fire that we thought the world was coming to an end. In addition to that, rumbling of motors and rattling could be heard in the enemy lines—*tanks*. It scared the pants off us. We could expect a very juicy attack. If we thought the artillery fire had reached a climax, we were very much disillusioned at 0530. At that time, a tremendous firing started, which continued until 0615, then tanks arrived. . . . These hedgerows are winding and crisscross through the fields. We dig in behind these walls and the Americans do the same. It is a regular hedgerow war. Well on 11th of July the tanks were rolling towards us. They shot through the hedgerows as if they were made out of cake dough. Sharpshooters gave us a lot of trouble. You must know, however, that the Americans are using HE ammunition, which tears terrible wounds. Around noon the order came to withdraw, as our positions could not be held. I had one wounded in my machine-gun position. When I wanted to get him into my position with the help of someone else, a shell landed two yards away from us. The wounded fellow got another piece of shrapnel in his side and the other fellow was wounded. . . . Anyway, on that day I escaped death just by seconds a hundred times. . . .

At 1135, I left my platoon sector as the last man. I carried my machine gun through the enemy lines into a slightly more protected defile and crept back again with another fellow to get the wounded. . . . The tanks were moving in thirty yards from us.

On our way back, we were covered again by intense artillery fire. We were lying in an open area; just then the inevitable happened because I have been expecting it right along. The tanks kept breaking through the hedgerows and they broke through the one near me and traveled along the hedgerow strafing and shooting its big gun. It buried most of the men alive in their holes, I shall never forget this, it was terrible right along. . . . At that moment I lost my nerves . . . and acted almost like a madman. The others acted just like me. No one ever knew how gruesome war can be. When one hears the whining, whistling, and bursting of shells and the moaning and groaning of the wounded, one does not feel too well. Although it was hell, I've never figured out how those American tanks ever got through the hedgerows.

Our company had only thirty men left. . . .

Your Friend,
Helmut

As this letter shows, the Germans were suffering as much as the Americans were. Cpl. Walter Jutkins of the 741st Tank Battalion took part in the action at Hill 192.

We were attached to the 2nd Division and were supposed to have rolling artillery, but we got ahead of the artillery. I was the tank commander. When we went up and over the hedgerows was when they hit us. The infantry followed behind us.

We got bazookaed, the driver lost part of his arm, and I never heard from him again. Sergeant Riggins said he saw us get hit. The tank was knocked out, the control panel destroyed, and the driver, Bishop, was wounded. They put my crew and me in another tank.

In July, Pvt. A. B. Mirmelstein of Company H, 115th Infantry, recorded the pace of events for the 29th Division and the trials and tribulations of the typical infantryman in his diary.

July 1—Came off the lines for a twenty-four-hour rest. Saw my first robot bomb [V-1] while on guard duty that night.

July 2—Returned to lines and relieved 3rd Battalion of 115th about three miles from St. Lô.

July 12—About 3:00 P.M. in the afternoon, during an intense artillery barrage by the enemy, I left my foxhole to render first aid to a rifleman who had been wounded and was calling for help. With the aid of others, I helped carry him back to the aid station. At 7:00 P.M. we counterattacked, but because of the intense enemy fire, could not gain any ground.

July 13—After another unsuccessful attack at dawn I cracked up and my lieutenant sent me to the aid station where I

Citation for Private Abraham B. Mirmelstein for July 12 Action

On August 2, 1944, Private Mirmelstein was awarded the Silver Star.

. . . for gallantry in action against the enemy in Normandy, France. On 12 July 1944, during an intense enemy barrage, the foxhole in which an enlisted man had sought protection received a direct hit burying him beneath the supports and earth used for overhead cover. With complete disregard for his personal safety, Private Mirmelstein rushed to the aid of the entombed man and with the assistance of an officer and several enlisted men uncovered and rendered first aid to the wounded man. The gallantry and high degree of courage exhibited by Private Mirmelstein reflects great credit upon himself and the military service. . . .

Signed C. H. Gerhardt

was evacuated. I woke up at the 622nd Evacuation Hospital.

July 17—After three days of twilight sleep, I recovered and was sent to U.S. Correspondence Press Camp where I pulled guard duty and light KP [kitchen police] duty. Saw Ernie Pyle, General Patton, General Bradley, also saw all important AP Press men.

July 24—Visited port of Cherbourg.

For over forty days, the 29th Division struggled to advance to its first major objective, St. Lô,

which was just about twenty miles from Omaha Beach. The last ten miles were the most difficult, locking the division in heavy fighting in the hedgerows for over thirty of those forty days. PFC Albert J. Bartelloni of HQ Company, 3rd Battalion, 175th Infantry, who had become a naturalized citizen of the United States only a year earlier, participated in the entire operation.

Before we took St. Lô, we were constantly patrolling into enemy lines. This one particular day we formed two combat patrols of twenty men to probe the enemy to see how strong they were in this area. We made contact with the Germans and took some heavy losses and returned to our company. The second patrol got a few hundred yards into enemy territory when a heavy firefight occurred. One of my buddies, Robert Walker, was hit and left for dead. After repeated questions about what happened, I decided he might be alive and started to go where he was supposed to have been killed. Just before I started to go into the German lines, he crawled back by himself. He was hit in the chest, both arms, and legs, but managed to crawl back to his own lines. He was evacuated and had many operations to help him get back the use of his arms.

His expertise as a scout on patrols and his willingness to face danger earned him the Oak Leaf Cluster to his Bronze Star in December 1944.

The fighting in the 29th Division sector was so heavy that even its rear-echelon troops had to be thrown into the battle for St. Lô. On July 20 after the town fell, the division pulled out of the line for a week in order to rest and receive replacements. As Sergeant Slaughter put it, "After the fall of St. Lô, we received a seven-day rest that included close order drill, hedgerow tactics, arms inspections, and other chicken-shit directives."

The division had incurred about 2,000 dead and 5,000 wounded since D-Day and was now truly a battle-hardened veteran formation. The 35th Division took over their section of the front on July 20, and the division was pulled off the front for the first time in forty-five days.

Early in July, while the 29th Division prepared for its assault on St. Lô, the 30th Division, with the help of the 35th Division, was given the task of creating a bridgehead over the Vire to expand the front and to reduce the front of the 29th Division. The engineers of the 30th Division led the way in forging a link with the 9th Division (VII Corps). Twenty-seven-year-old Maj. John A. Allison from Biloxi, Mississippi, was the S-3 for the 105th Engineer Combat Battalion of the 30th "Old Hickory" Division at the time.

As operations officer, it was my job to prepare the engineer plan in the crossing of divisional troops across the Vire River. Through the study of available maps and aerial photographs I determined possible crossing sites for the assault waves, bridge sites (foot bridges) for the follow-up waves of infantry assault troops, and bridge sites (vehicles and tanks) for supporting services.

I directed the reconnaissance by engineer troops of said sites and on numerous occasions led reconnaissance patrols myself. I prepared schedules for and monitored when possible the training and rehearsal of infantry assault teams with engineer guides and storm boat crews. I monitored the rehearsal of engineer troops in prefabing footbridges, and I ordered, in the CO's name, the building of scaling ladders and foot bridges by the engineer units. Once the sites to cross were selected, the location of infantry assembly areas were located, hedgerows to the river were cut through for passage and ditches spanned with temporary walkways prior to H-Hour.

I made one plan after another, it seemed, and submitted them to higher headquarters for approval, only to have the Division G-3 change their plan of operation, and I had to go back to the drawing board and start over. Timing and scheduling of events were of the utmost importance in each of the engineering plans. During this period of preparation, engineers with rubber boats ferried infantry combat patrols across the Vire on almost a nightly basis. Final reconnaissance of the chosen crossing sites were made in each regimental sector on July 5 and D-Day was set for July 7 and H-Hour at 0420.

On D-1, Lt. Col. Carrol H. Dunn [commanding the 105th Engineer Battalion] moved in to a forward CP with Brig. Gen. William K. Harrison (Asst. Div. CO) where he could observe the launching of the assault waves and installation of the footbridge for the following waves of 117th Infantry. Major Stuba was assigned to monitor and assist C Company that was to cross the 120th Infantry over the Vire-et-Taute Canal in the afternoon.

I, in turn, was attached to the Forward Division Command Post near the last hedgerow with Maj. Gen. Leland Hobbs [division commander]. I could observe nothing from this position but maintained contact with our forward company command posts at A and B Company by radio and managed to keep General Hobbs abreast of the engineers' situation. Upon my release by General Hobbs about 0800 on D-Day morning, I crossed the Vire in my jeep to catch up with the attacking battalion of the 117th and ascertain casualties amongst A and B Companies of the engineers and what if any tools or equipment they might need to further their defense of their objective—a counterattack being expected.

My driver and I came under artillery fire upon our return on approaching the permanent concrete bridge over the Vire, and we hit the ditch. I immediately fell asleep from exhaustion. Upon awakening some thirty minutes later, the barrage had lifted, and we climbed back in our jeep and headed across the bridge, casually noting the headless body of the MP who had directed us across the bridge an hour and a half earlier, and had been caught in the same enemy's artillery barrage. After that, my friend, Major Craig, made all his MPs dig vertical holes in which to stand when directing traffic and/or slit trenches nearby, when stationed near defined objects readily found on maps, i.e. bridges, crossroads, etc.

That afternoon, I caught up with C Company and Major Stuba to determine how the 120th Infantry made out in their crossing of the canal, only to learn of the many problems encountered by the regiment in crossing. As a result, our C Company's commander was relieved of command and transferred to a replacement depot, I surmised for failure to make adequate reconnaissance of proposed crossing sites and construct suitable bridging of the canal.

Major Allison described the operation.

The scaling ladders were built for use on the steep west banks of the 117th Infantry area and the catwalk bridges to span the steep-walled sides of the canal on the division's north shoulder, defended by the 120th Infantry. At 3:30 A.M. on July 7, 1944, the division's artillery, supported by three battalions of corps artillery, opened fire on our proposed crossing sites. Half an hour earlier, the assault battalions of the 117th Infantry were met in their assembly area behind the last hedgerow by engineer troops of Company A, 105th Engineers, carrying rubber assault boats and scaling ladders. They moved across the 400-yard open area to the east bank of the Vire River and crossed the first wave at 4:20 A.M. without incident. Thirty minutes later, during the crossing of the second wave, enemy artillery and mortar rounds found the range and were crashing into the river. Further north in the 117th Infantry Regiments sector, the 3rd Platoon of Company B began carrying to the river bank preassembled infantry foot bridge sections as the second wave of the assault battalion of the 117th Infantry crossed. Six bays of the bridge were in the water when a direct hit destroyed it. Another concentration of enemy fire killed four engineers and wounded four others who were carrying footbridge sections from the preassembly area. The remaining members of the platoon grimly began rebuilding the footbridge, which was still under observed fire. The last bay had been just put in place when enemy fire again made a direct hit, tearing the bridge loose from its moorings and wounding several more engineers. Forty percent of the 3rd Platoon of Company B were now casualties. Several remaining engineers dove into the fourteen-foot-deep stream and swam across to the far side and secured the bridge. By 5:30 A.M. it was open and ready for use. At 7:30 A.M., an infantry five-ton support bridge was ordered into place at a cost of fifteen casualties to supplement the damaged stone bridge that had been hastily repaired, following the removal of a shot up ¾-ton truck with its two occupants that had been parked on the Airel Bridge since before the 30th captured the town. At 8:30 A.M., work began on the damaged stone bridge and four hours later work was com-

Stuart light tank equipped with makeshift hedgerow cutter or plow.

plete and tanks from Company A, 743rd Tank Battalion, moved across in support of the 117th Infantry. At 1:45 P.M., the 120th Infantry jumped off along the Vire-et-Taut Canal. In places, the canal was shallow enough for the infantry to wade across, climbing out on assault ladders furnished by C Company of the 105th Engineers. The engineers found their catwalks too short and had to double them up before the infantry could cross the deeper sections. By nightfall, all units had reached their objectives. The 3rd Platoon of Company B of the 105th Engineer Combat Battalion was later awarded the Distinguished Unit Citation for this action.

For Cpl. Floyd E. Brooks, a nineteen-year-old draftee from Los Angeles who was with the Survey Section of HQ Battery, 230th Field Artillery, 30th Division, the days on the front were not uneventful.

When we first went to France, we were on C and K rations. Then we got the 10-in-1 rations, the result being everyone did their own cooking. The only thing I could not stand was the cooking from English-style stew. All the kitchen did was provide hot water to wash the mess kits in. One PFC was sent back to the beach area to pick up supplies and picked up half a cow. We were anticipating steaks to go with our 10-1.

Bailey [the mess sergeant] gave us what he called stew—it was boiled cow. In about three weeks, the Class D [B?] rations started to come in, so the kitchens had to go to work. In less than ten days, HQ and HQ Battery had the GI's [diarrhea]. This time, Bailey couldn't say it was something the men were getting in town. The morning after this occurred Bailey was standing in the mess line dishing out breakfast. He had not shaved in several days and no one knew when he last washed his face or hands. The colonel looked at him and told him to get cleaned up by noon. When noon came there was Bailey just as cruddy as ever. Colonel Beaman took one look at him and said, "Private Bailey, get out of the serving line!" Arthur Schultz became the new mess sergeant and Bailey was sent to one of the wire parties.

The first time I went on the water detail it made me sick. The water that was being pumped into the purifiers had just been used by the French women for the laundry. Also, the kids were wading in it.

While we were gone, a P-47 came straight down into the HQ Battery area. The pilot had bailed out and when it hit, it exploded and was scattered all over the whole area, but no one was hit by the debris.

It did not take very long to standardize my slit trench. I dug a hole about six-and-a-half feet long and two-and-a-half feet wide. It was three feet deep, and I covered it with scrap lumber. I also used 105-mm ammo boxes for the roof and all the dirt that I dug out went on the roof. I used a shelter half as a roof over the entrance opening. When I slept, I was as safe as possible, and I was dry when it rained. I removed my boots at night and changed my socks. We didn't have any

means to take a bath, so we forgot about that. I slept with my carbine in my bedroll.

I always carried toilet paper, two hand-kerchiefs, and a pair of socks in my helmet and also an extra package of toilet paper, a first-aid kit, and a clip for my carbine in my pants pocket.

On July 8, the recon party crossed the Vire-Taute Canal, and we ran our survey about 200-300 yards south of the canal. The Germans had had plenty of time to mine the area south of the canal, and they did a thorough job. The engineers were out probing the shoulder of the road and stringing a white tape to indicate the safe areas. They had not had time to check the fields, so we had to take our chances. I decided then that if I had to step on a mine it would be a small one and it would be my right foot. I had a case of athlete's foot on that one. I cut through a field and crossed the road in front of some guys who were probing. One looked up and asked what good it did to clear the road and then for us to cross where it was not clear. Sergeant Fisher told him, "Sorry, but we had to work here." Late in the afternoon, the engineers stacked the mines they dug up and then detonated them. I was behind a hedgerow across the main highway at the time. This one apparently had been a mass of vegetation and I don't think it stopped any of the junk from the mines. I sure must have been standing in the right place for it was a sight to behold when those fragments came through.

On July 9, when our attack was going south, the Germans made a counterattack, and it got rough and confusing. A column of tanks from the Combat Command A of the 3rd Armored Division made a wrong turn and engaged in a twenty-minute fight with units of the 823rd Tank Destroyer Battalion [M-10 Wolverine Tank Destroyers].[7] HQ for 2nd Battalion, 120th Infantry, was cut off. Corps artillery removed all restrictions on rate of fire. Everybody that was not throwing shells in the guns lined up behind the hedgerows. We were waiting for the infantry to cave in.

The battalion displaced on down the road to our next position at St. Jean de Daye. While we were running the survey, we came across the remains of a German Mark IV and an American Sherman that had fought it out on a curb at about a range of forty yards.

The survey party got a nice barn behind the farmhouse. Fisher and Nichols tested the wine barrels and found the good ones. About two hours after moving into the barn, the German that was hiding in the church across the street shouted, "Kaput!"

The 823rd Tank Destroyer Battalion was stationed on the dirt road behind the barn. Two guys took from the TD crew a five-gallon gas can down the road for about 150 yards. If any German tanks came through, they were to let the first one or two come through and throw the gas can on the next one and run like hell. The TD crew left after a couple of days so that our next neighbor was a 155-mm howitzer outfit in the field behind us. They set the guns up with muzzles through the hedge and running over the sunken road. Soon thereafter, a major we did not know and his driver drove directly under the muzzle of one of the guns when the battery fired. He came into our barn to find out if we were part of that outfit. We said, "No, sir!" and he charged out the door. The next thing we saw were two check points—one on each side of the battery—which would stop traffic when there was a fire mission.

The ordnance tank retrievers hauled wrecked American and German tanks and SP [self-propelled] guns back to a wide spot in the road opposite our barn, leaving them for tank transporters to pick up. Gray, Shelton, Evans, and I went across the road to look over a junked German SP gun. I climbed up on the deck and looked down into the machine. That was something I would never do again. I knew that there was something in that seat that I just could not recognize. Then it dawned on me: I was looking at the remains of a driver. A bazooka shell had hit the vehicle directly at the driver's location.

While running the survey for the next position, we ran across one of the largest fields I ever saw in the hedgerow country. Just as I started to cross it, a bullet snapped by just above my head and I hit the ground. As I lay there, I heard more go by. I crawled back to the hedgerow where Evans was, and we talked it over. We both got into the field a short distance and listened to the bullets go by. We decided they were from a firefight and not from someone aiming at us. There were too many of them, and they all seemed to be about six feet off the ground. We decided we could chain the distance across the field if we walked stooped over. That was about the longest 600 feet we ever chained.

---

7. The 823rd Tank Destroyer Battalion was attached to the 30th Division. The armament of its M-10s was a 3-inch antitank gun, which has less penetration power than the German 75-millimeter PaK or the British 17-pounder. Late in July, many battalions had M-10s upgraded to a 17-pounder antitank gun.

Later, Tom and I were on guard early in the morning. At about 3:30 A.M., we heard a noise behind us. We turned, and there was S.Sgt. Sidney Stroger. He passed the word that a German patrol had killed several men in the 113th Field Artillery. The rest of the guard period, I saw the shrubs and bushes moving!

At our next position, we ran a survey about 300 yards from where C Battery was to go into position. The survey ran through a crossroads that had a small herd of cattle lying around that had been killed by artillery fire. I got my turning point set and moved through this mess but was almost sick. A hundred yards or so farther on, I set a turning point. As I was pulling the distance, I glanced at a red pile and saw that the rags had been the uniforms and the shattered remains of a German soldier. A shell had hit almost on him. Before I really got settled down from that, I was going over a ridge when a German in the hedgerow directly in front of me opened up with a machine pistol. His shots went by on my right, and I hit the ground at the foot of the ridge. Evans hit the ground behind me and asked if I was OK. I answered yes, and he moved up to where I was and checked to the side to see where the fire had come from. We did not see the German.

Some parties used TNT to dig gun pits. My first experience with this was when a TD company parked on the road below us. When the blast went off, they all bailed out of the trucks and into the ditches. If the fish in the streams were as plentiful as the worms in the ground, then fishing must have been good.

In July before the breakout, as Lt. Luther R. Underwood, 21st Finance Disbursing Section, traveled to the front from his unit's office in Cherbourg, he beheld the scars of war everywhere along his path.

The miserable hedgerows were behind; the land was pock-marked with huge craters from the aerial bombs and the shells from the naval bombardment. Many horses, oxen, cows, and pigs were innocent victims and lay rotting in the fields, giving off a horrible nauseating stench. The Germans still held St. Lô, and at Carentan, I saw an unforgettable sight.

My driver and I were returning to the rear from a mission near the front. We had to pass through Carentan where the Germans were lobbing in occasional shells. Their object was to destroy a bridge, which we had to cross on the outskirts of town. Although the bridge was still standing, the immediate area was a scene of desolate devastation. Most of the population had fled to God knows where, buildings were crumbling ruins, streets were torn up, trees were shattered and upended, and debris scattered everywhere.

As my driver and I approached the bridge in our jeep, we became increasingly nervous. We had just passed a dead German soldier lying in a ditch. We also saw a hand, swollen and purple, making a gruesome sight lying off to itself with a body attached. The ditches on each side were filled with land mines and all types of discarded equipment. Nearby, our own army engineers were blowing up land mines to make safe corridors for our heavy equipment.

We crossed the ridge as a German shell whistled overhead, and we saw the building it hit and exploded. We were scared and in a hurry to get through Carentan, but we had to pass that building. As we drove by, a

An M-2 treadway pontoon bridge built in lowland area of the Cotentin Peninsula. A Belgian gate can be seen on the right set near the abutment of the destroyed bridge.

woman came running out. She was crying and shouting hysterically and was carrying a small child in her arms. The pitiful little child was beyond help; the whole top of its head was completely blown away. Have you ever seen a toy doll with its plaster head crushed with only a shell remaining? This child's head had a similar appearance. There wasn't even any blood. The concussion of the explosion had blown away the complete insides of the head and left the ragged edges of what was left of the head a blackish pur-

ple tinged with red. There were no eyes or nose; the little mouth and chin, and what remained of the little face, were swollen and purple beyond recognition. This was war at its worst, and a scene I shall never forget.[8]

When the 9th Division took part in the assault on Cherbourg, 1st Lt. Charles Scheffel was not there. He was wounded by shrapnel from the guns of a German fighter that attacked his transport just as it sighted the coast of Normandy on June 10. He was sent back to England and hospi-

---

8. Lieutenant Underwood's unit became known as the 21st "Fighting" Finance Section when it narrowly escaped capture with the First Army's rear headquarters during the Battle of the Bulge. Near Liege, one of the trucks in the convoy was hit by a V-1 Buzz Bomb.

talized before he had a chance to reach the beach. He received his Purple Heart a month later, on July 8, and he reported at the 10th Replacement Depot near Southampton on July 10. He took charge of a replacement platoon with men mostly from the 4th Division. On July 21, he landed at Omaha Beach and took his replacement platoon to the 3rd Replacement Depot.

I was immediately transported to 92nd Replacement Battalion near Carentan. I stayed there until July 23, when I was given order to immediately report to the 9th Infantry Division. I was no longer what is called a "casual officer," but at my request I was assigned to my old 9th Division. When I arrived at the 9th Division HQ near St. Lô on the evening of the 24th, I found out that Colonel Flint had been killed and Lt. Col. Van H. Bond now commanded the 39th. I reported to him in his tent HQ, and he welcomed me back and told me that I would be going back to Company D as executive officer as soon as I did a little work for him. As I had been in all the companies of the battalion and a former Battalion S-3, he gave me a fairly good map and told me to go out and pinpoint all the units down to platoons and then get back to him.

It was in the middle of the afternoon, after I had gotten my gear somewhat assembled, before I got on with my mission. It was dark by the time I got back, which, because of double daylight savings time, was about midnight. I had found the exact location of all the rifle companies and pinpointed for Colonel Bond the exact location of Company D's Heavy Weapons Platoon.

The 35th "Santa Fe" Division was involved in the heavy fighting for St. Lô, but its front had

become rather static since it made few gains. During the weeks of intense fighting, life was rather routine for the men who were not committed to the front like PFC Robert Lehmann, a twenty-two-year-old draftee from New York City who was a switchboard operator in the communications section of HQ Company, 1st Battalion, 320th Infantry.

I laid commo wire to the forward company and one line to a forward observer during July. It was the same routine: lay wire, repair broken lines, and tend to the switchboard. Our CP relayed all telephone lines to all forward companies. I was pretty busy those days; some of our lines crossed over hedgerows, and they were scary going over them at night because you wouldn't know what's on the other side until you got there. No one from our section was killed or wounded.

PFC William A. Lawrence, a twenty-five-year-old draftee from Pittsburgh, spent the entire month of June in replacement camps in Wales and England. On July 7, he crossed the Channel as a replacement. When he and his companions moved inland, their sergeant told them to pitch their tents and dig foxholes.

The man I was with said, "Let's dig a foxhole!" We did and then we laid down to rest. Just about dusk, we heard a plane overhead and our ack-ack opened up on him. The plane dropped a few flares but no bombs. You should have heard the sound of shovels digging foxholes! We were not bombed that night.

On July 16, I joined Company B, 137th Infantry, 35th Division, near St. Lô. I carried a New Testament with me, which had been given to me by my church pastor before I left home. A new man came in the outfit and was assigned to my foxhole. He saw me reading the book in the evening just before dark. He said that he noticed I was reading the Bible, and said he was a Catholic, but didn't go to church. He said, "If I get out of this alive, I am going to go every Sunday with my wife and small son." He did not go home because he was killed in an ambush a few days later. He saved my life because it was my turn to be where he was, but he did not fall back and let me take his place.

When Pvt. Richard Stewart from San Antonio, Texas, joined up at age seventeen in 1943, he was full of visions of glory and medals. When he was assigned as a replacement to Lt. Murray Pulver's Company B, 120th Infantry, 30th Division, he quickly found out that reality did not measure up to his dreams.

When I joined the company, all you could see was the artillery the first night; it was like lightning. I didn't sleep that night. You don't look when a barrage comes in. The guy with me was looking, and he got hit, fell back into the hole, and bled to death. I had to stay with him. I remember he looked white—he was already a white man—but what was happening hadn't hit me. He was also a replacement, and this was one of his first days.

I must have fired my M-1 a couple of times in the first few days. It jammed up on me, and I must have used two or three rifles in combat. I would throw them away and pick up another since there were a lot of them on the road.

A new lieutenant came in and warned us there was a sniper. He had made a cup of coffee, looked at me, walked outside the barn door, and got hit in the back by the sniper. We dragged him back inside, and we never saw him again. He hadn't been with us more than half an hour and was wearing his insignia because he wanted to be known as a lieutenant. We got another lieutenant and must have gone through half a dozen before taking St. Lô.

First Lt. Murray S. Pulver had joined New York's 27th National Guard Division in 1939 at age twenty. After the attack on Pearl Harbor, his unit was transferred to the West Coast and from there to Hawaii. As a sergeant he was sent back to Fort Benning for officer candidate school in 1942 and then assigned to the 75th Infantry Division.[9] In April 1944, two officers from each company in the division were sent to Boston and in mid-May put on a ship bound for England. Pulver was put in charge of two groups of replacements identified as G-52 and G-53, totaling about 110 men. When they landed in Normandy on D+7, he was surprised to see bodies still floating in the surf. Pulver and his men stayed in a replacement camp behind Utah Beach near many wrecked gliders, one of which was being used as a kitchen. They lived on K rations until July 2 when he, eleven other officers, and sixty enlisted men were assigned to the 120th Infantry of the 30th Division.

We soon passed the big guns blasting away. Then we could hear the chatter of machine guns and the crack of rifle fire. We were not in the hedgerows and close to the front. The fields were torn up with shell holes and bomb craters. Dead cows were scattered everywhere. The air was full of the almost unbearable stench of death.

---

9. The 75th Infantry Division formed in April 1943 but did not deploy to the ETO until November 1944. A number of its troops departed earlier as replacements.

Engineers construct a treadway and truss bridge over the Vire River. In the combat zone, the engineer battalions used light foot bridges, the M-2 treadway bridges (for truss or pontoons), and the British Bailey bridges. Here components of the M-2 are being emplaced over a ford in the river using an M2 crane.

Pulver and his companions were led to a farmhouse where the regimental commander, Col. Hammond D. Birks, briefed them on the Vire Canal crossing and their objective, St. Jean de Daye. Pulver was assigned to the 3rd Platoon of Company B, and another replacement officer, Lieutenant Hare, took the 2nd Platoon. As they ate their C rations, Lieutenant Hare was wounded in the hand and Lieutenant Pulver took over both platoons. The next day, he took a squad on patrol to make a body count of dead from both sides and pick up any wounded. The only casualties they encountered were twenty dead Americans. On the way back to camp, some Germans opened fire on them, and two of his men were wounded. After they reached their camp, the sergeant who led the squad went out in a field and started firing a BAR in all directions. Apparently, he had known the twenty dead men they had spotted, having trained with them, and the sight of their mangled bodies over-

whelmed him and sent him over the edge. Lieutenant Pulver cautiously approached him, calmed him down, and managed to wrestle the BAR from him, burning his gloved hand on the barrel in the process. Eventually, the sergeant was sent to a hospital. This was Pulver's first encounter with shell shock, but he saw many more cases of it as the campaign went on.

On July 16, Pulver's battalion attacked along the highway to St. Gilles. His platoon was in reserve as the company advanced with four tanks. The lead tank, equipped with a dozer blade, smashed through the first hedgerow. The tank following it knocked out a German tank in the next hedgerow. Five minutes later, three of the American tanks were hit and the company took some losses.

On my left I observed an enemy tank, all guns blazing, edging along the road toward us. I yelled for the bazooka team. Pvt. Werner G. Goertz rushed up with a bazooka, informed me that his buddy, the gunner, had been wounded, and that he didn't know how to fire the thing.

I had had dry-run practice . . . in England but had never fired a live round. By the time I was ready to shoot, the enemy tank was about 100 yards away. German foot soldiers were moving along both sides of the tank, firing their rifles at us.

I took careful aim and sent the missile on its way. Bull's-eye! Lucky me, for I had hit the right spot. The tank exploded and began to burn. Some of the enemy soldiers close to the tank were killed. We took care of most of the rest with our rifle fire. . . .

I was ordered by the CO to attack the next hedgerow. Company C would be moving up at the same time. I quickly informed all the men. On signal, I yelled, "Let's go!" I jumped over the hedgerow and landed in a hole with three Germans in it. To my amazement, they had been in that hole within ten feet of me for the past half hour. They meekly surrendered. . . .

Four more Germans came out of another hole about twenty feet away with their hands up . . . while my two platoons rushed to the next hedgerow under heavy fire. . . .

Company C was now along a hedgerow on our right. We heard a desperate call from some men there for a bazooka team. Private Goertz and I responded and encountered Captain Hobgood, the company commander, who pointed out a German tank behind a stone wall fifty yards to our front. I was about to fire the bazooka when the tank's machine gunner opened up, the bullets just missing me a few feet to the left. . . . I then rose up, aimed, and fired. My second direct hit of the day!

As the Germans continued their counterattack, Pulver called his commander, Captain Greer, who got artillery support from the 230th Field Artillery, which broke up the assault.[10] Captain Hobgood had been killed by the tank's machine gun. For his actions on July 16, Murray Pulver was awarded the Distinguished Service Cross. The citation read

When intense enemy fire inflected numerous casualties and wounded the leader of another platoon, Captain Pulver, commanding the reserve platoon, moved forward and assumed command. The platoon was on the verge of panic due to the murderous enemy onslaught when Captain Pulver fearlessly exposed himself and urged them to remain steadfast. With a bazooka he personally knocked out two enemy tanks and killed a

large number of infantry with rifle grenades. He then rescued a wounded man from an exposed position. . . .

T/4 Dale K. Kearnes, a thirty-year-old volunteer from Pittsburg, Kansas, was with the headquarters battery of the 35th Division's 219th Field Artillery Battalion. His unit was behind the front about 400 yards from the gun positions.

We were surrounded by 105s, but we did our own security. Each of us had a carbine. We set up near an apple orchard, and there was a big hedgerow where on the other side the colonel and his men were. I remember they fired off some dynamite to make their holes, and we thought it was a bomb and we were all scared.

One of our command cars had a radio in it, and I would listen to them giving fire directions. When we got ready to move out, one of our units had moved into St. Lô. When we came around, we saw the debris. We came down that hill on the side of St. Lô and moved towards Vire. I remember the first time we came across dead Germans— there were these horse-drawn carts, but there weren't any horses, only four or five Germans in there and they were getting swelled a little bit. Everybody shied away from them. We were in that area about two days. The next time we went through there, the GIs were in there going through their pockets. Some of those GIs were our guys who got used to the sight of them, but after a while it didn't bother us any longer, unless it was one of our guys. The Graves Registration unit would come in and take them out on a trailer with sideboards.

---

10. The 230th Field Artillery Battalion was one of the 30th Division's three field artillery battalions.

First Lt. Kenneth K. Jarvis, a twenty-nine-year-old National Guardsman from Alhambra, California, was the S-4 of the 1st Battalion, 137th Infantry, when the 35th Division disembarked. The division came ashore near Colleville between July 5 and 7 and then moved inland to a site west of Columbières. From there, the division moved into position between the 29th and 30th Divisions for the assault on St. Lô. Jarvis's unit, after taking up positions, began sending out patrols to make contact with the Germans. The assault began on July 11 as the division advanced after an artillery barrage and the division suffered its first fatalities.

The Regimental Commander, Colonel Layng,[11] had received reports from the S-2 that there was nothing in front of us. He didn't believe us and came up to the front to find out for himself. There was a perfectly straight narrow road about a mile long that went up to the 1st Battalion front. It had a small church steeple at the far end. Colonel Layng brought his whole staff and marched up the road. You could see land mines on the road and in the ditches from the bridge at the friendly end of the road. The Germans let him advance to about 100 yards from the church and then opened up with snipers. The colonel was hit in the jaw and the knee. The colonel's driver drove down the road, picked up the colonel, turned around, and got out of there. I understand he received a medal for that action later.

I received a message from the battalion commander on the field phone. He said, "Jarvis, get your ass up here and evacuate these dead bodies; they stink like hell!" I replied to him that I couldn't do that because my trucks were brand-new kitchen trucks and if I used one of them for this purpose, it would have to be replaced before I could use it again as a kitchen vehicle. He said very politely, "The hell you can't! You are supply and evacuation, are you not?" I said, "Yes, sir!" I picked up the first truck I came upon and told my driver to get the tarp off and fold and remove the bows. I took off with a detail and started down the above-mentioned road. We had to cross a small bridge near the intersection at the beginning of this road. As soon as we hit the bridge, the German 88s came flying in; we backed up and around the corner behind cover. I talked it over with my men, and we agreed that if we backed in down that narrow road, we could get the hell out of there in a hurry if we had to. The road was too narrow to turn around on, and we could see the land mines. So we backed around the corner, over the bridge, and all the way up to where the colonel's staff was hit. There were no 88s, we never did figure out why. We picked up a lieutenant colonel, a West Pointer, artillery staff officer with one bullet hole in his forehead exactly between the eyes; Captain Kurr, another West Pointer artillery staff officer with a bullet in the same place. One private runner to the regimental commander, a conscientious objector, an "unarmed," also with one bullet in the forehead, was picked up. We continued on and filled the 2½-ton truck with bodies both of American and German dead. Some of the bodies, I am sure, had lain there for thirty days and were badly

11. Col. Grant Layng, commander of the 137th Infantry, advanced to a place dubbed "Purple Heart Corner" by the GIs in order to drive a German contingent from Château St. Gilles, an ancient seigniorial residence. After he was wounded by machine-gun fire, he was evacuated from the battlefield and replaced by Col. Robert Sears.

decayed. We had to use K ration slats to scoop the bodies on to a stretcher we had brought along. I reported to the battalion commander, and he told me to pick up a lieutenant of ours who had been killed in a small house. I went to the house and immediately ascertained that he had been killed by a booby trap. He had pulled a table over under a cabinet that was high up on the wall and when he opened the cabinet the booby trap exploded. In OCS, we had been taught never to enter a booby-trapped area until it had been cleared. I left him there. We went back to the service company in the rear area. We arrived just when everyone was lined up for chow. I told the driver to pull his truck across the road in an open field. The bodies had been covered with the tarp. The word got around in a hurry and all the curious rushed across the road to the truck. There was three quarters of the meals not eaten. I couldn't eat for two days.

They replaced my truck and immediately the chaplain was detailed and given a crew and a ¼-ton trailer for his jeep. The chaplain's crew was made up of fellows who just couldn't cut it on the front lines. Their nerves just went to pieces up there, but were OK in the rear area. Two days later, we came upon Max Schmelling's body in a German uniform.[12]

One time, the battalion commander called me up to the front. My driver and I went up through the hedgerows as far as we could and then we walked up. As I approached the CP, I was talking to all the men in their foxholes along the way and I realized they didn't have any foxholes for visitors. Just about that time the 88s started coming in. I dove over a hedgerow and found a hole to crawl into. A rabbit crawled into the hole with me and snuggled into the cavity of my neck and shoulder. We laid there and shook together. It was still there when I left.

Another time, I went up to the front and the 88s came in again. My driver, Corporal Lucas, floored the gas pedal, and we passed another jeep coming the opposite way. I swear we clicked door handles as we passed with both of us wide open. The other jeep was driven by Avie Hunt, and he had the colonel with him.

Every night at 11:00 P.M., we received a visit from Bedcheck Charlie. He dropped small bombs that exploded above the ground. When they exploded on the ground, they left black burned spots about the size of an orange with straight lines extending out in every direction. The next thing I knew, my neck stung and was all wet. I had been hit with a piece of shrapnel on the left side of my neck. Then I was notified that one of my cooks had been badly hit. I gathered up my jeep driver, Corporal Lucas, and we took off for the field hospital. I asked for an ambulance, but the doctor said, "I better take care of your neck first." I told him about my cook and he released the ambulance and we headed back. When we got back, I couldn't believe how many casualties we had, there was standing room only in the ambulance and my jeep was loaded. We had to put the cook on a stretcher and scoop some of his brains onto the stretcher. He died at the hospital during the night. When the doctor came around to me, he told me that if the shrapnel had been over one quarter of an inch it would have killed me. It just wasn't

12. This cannot be correct since Schmelling survived the war.

General Eisenhower visits the troops in Normandy. The soldier on the right carries a bazooka, and all the troops have an entrenching tool on their packs.

my time. They kept me in the hospital overnight, and we could hear the planes above—it was kind of scary. I reported back to my outfit the next morning. That is how I got the Purple Heart.

On one occasion, I was riding in my jeep and went around a corner, and along the right side of the road was an open suitcase with a human head and a pair of hands in it.

Second Lt. Charles W. Bell from Valentine, Texas, was only twenty years old when he assumed the commanded of the 2nd Platoon of Company A, 320th Infantry, 35th Division. His experiences during the attack on St. Lô were different since he led a platoon of infantry.

When our ship anchored off Normandy, we stood at the rail looking at the beach, and that night, July 4, we watched gun flashes and heard their rumble in the direction of Caen. Sleep only came with exhaustion, as was to be the case for months to come.

The next morning, we scrambled down rope ladders into landing craft, and after walking ashore, we quickly assembled and moved off the beach through sand dunes and the debris of the earlier battle. We moved into assembly areas near St. Clare to wait. Our first incoming fire, an artillery round, hit us as we moved into this area, and we heard our first cry, "Medic!"

During the night of July 9, we moved into positions on the front occupied by units of the 29th Infantry Division. Teams of guides from the 29th and our units led us by platoon and squad into the foxholes occupied by the 29th, and their units were led back to the rear to go later into position on the left of the 35th. When the last whispers, jingles, and crunching footsteps died away, the silence became deafening, and the realization that we were at last in contact with the enemy with only ourselves to depend on was almost overwhelming.

Later that night, a sergeant brought two former occupants of our forward listening post to my foxhole. They reported sounds to their front that indicated many Germans were advancing on us. I quickly led the men back to the listening post, and it only took us a few minutes to determine that the "Germans" were really a Holstein milk cow quietly grazing her way across a field. This wouldn't be the last time nighttime sounds almost panicked us.

We held our positions until receiving our first attack order the night of July 10. Our ultimate objective was the Vire River south of St. Lô. Our artillery (200 guns) opened up at 0500, July 11, and we jumped off at 0600.

One incident to note here—a team from my platoon advanced and blew us an opening through our barbed wire entanglement and then the rest of the platoon ran through the opening to the cover of the next hedgerow. But one of my men became petrified with fear and refused to leave the safety of his position. I realized that if I left him there I would have to turn him in for court-martial and a ruined life. Also, if other men saw him left in relative safety, they might also try it later.

I moved to his side, and spent probably two minutes talking to him. I got him to rise up and look, and then pointed out that he could run to the safety of a large rock, then through the opening in the wire to a little ditch, then on to the men waiting at the hedgerow. Then I shouted, "Let's go!" and he came right with me. He made a descent soldier, although later wounded too badly to return.

We obtained our initial objective, but the unit on our right failed to join up, leaving us badly exposed. They had to attack forward, and then swing left 90 degrees to join us because of the way the Germans had dug in. We held our objective all day while they made repeated attempts to move up, with no success.

Finally, we were ordered to withdraw on hedgerow so that massive artillery fire could be directed on our positions and those to our right, after which we were to launch a continued attack.

After we withdrew, one of my platoon sergeants advised me he had left a wounded man at the advance location because he couldn't walk. Knowing the man would be killed by our own artillery, I directed the sergeant to bring a strong man and follow me. We raced back to the wounded man, and I saw he was shot through the hips, and one testicle was hanging out of his scrotum. I told him we had to carry him out or he would be killed and to brace for terrible pain. Two of us took his arms and one his legs, and we broke into a run.[13]

The artillery caught us as we were attempting to lift him over our hedgerow, and we had to roll him over. The shells completely destroyed two or three

---

13. Bell was awarded the Bronze Star for this action.

hedgerows to our front and short rounds covered us with dirt and wounded two or three men.

The hedgerows proved to be the worst part of the entire war, being ideally suited for defense and presenting every possible problem for offense.

The 6th Armored Division landed at Utah Beach on July 19 and proceeded to move inland to join the 2nd, 3rd, and 4th Armored Divisions for Operation Cobra. The division passed through the lines of the 8th Infantry Division on the western side of the peninsula, but was unable to take part in Operation Cobra until after it was underway.

First Lt. Rodney F. Mortensen, 212th Armored Field Artillery Battalion of the 6th Armored Division, moved to Southampton in mid-June.

We went down to Southampton, and they put us in a little caserne with the vehicles outside and us behind the wire. The guards were Scottish pipers. The big thing that happened everyday was that they went to the colors with bagpipes. They wouldn't even allow us to use our own shaving gear since it was packed, but they gave us temporary stuff. This was right after the invasion for about a week. Our boats finally arrived, and we left in July.

First Lt. James M. Crutchfield of the 86th Mechanized Cavalry Recon Squadron, 6th Armored Division, did not get tied up at the port as long as Mortensen did.

We went directly to Southampton and onto the ship without going into a holding area in the latter half of July. We had been alerted in the middle of the night, and that was when I started looking for parts for a

bunch of vehicles in the battalion that wouldn't run. So I had to go all over England to various depots and I got back and the unit was cranking up and getting in line to move out at night. We drove from Blocky, which wasn't too far from Stratford-on-Avon, down to the port, and boarded the ships. Every vehicle ran except for one guy who had to pump the fuel pump by hand to get it aboard ship. Everyone ran on except the last tank, which ran through the fish market. He must have turned going around the curve and went over an embankment and went right into the fish market. It didn't hurt the tank all that much, but it tore up the fish market. One of my duties was the claims officer all through the war. If anybody lost something, I put in the claim. This guy put in a claim for his fish market against the government, and I had to investigate. SHAEF HQ kept requesting additional information. All that happened was that the driver just missed the turn and went over the embankment, destroying the fish market. I didn't have much time to spend on it because we were embarking. All the way down through Brittany on the way to Brest I would get requests for more information. Finally, I had enough of it so I endorsed that all the individuals connected in the incident had been killed in action and that was the last I heard of it.

Lieutenant Mortensen's unit

loaded on Canadian LSTs—two of them. Two took the service battery, trains, and so on. They took us across the Channel, and we landed at Utah Beach. We spent a considerable time in England waterproofing so we could run through the water. We had snorkels and everything, and we didn't hit a

A two-and-a-half-ton truck carrying a load of German prisoners back toward the beaches passes by an M4 Sherman tank. A censor has removed unit markings. Also notice the cover over the front of the Sherman tank, which may conceal a hedgerow cutter.

hole or anything. We had about four inches of water on the tires—not much. We pulled up on the beach and a guy came up and said, "You see that hole in the sand?" I said I did. There were still shell fragments and stuff flying around on the beach, and they were still shooting on the beach with shells going in the water. We pulled in and he said to go through that hole. I started to ask him a question and he was gone. I started through this hole and saw there was engineer tape, but when I got on top of these dunes, the wind had blown the tape to where it was laying and you didn't know which tape was which. There was one of those ton-and-a-half jobs that had an extra

set of bogey[14] on the back of it like a weapon carrier, and it had been full of troops. They hit these stacked land mines, and it blew that damn thing in half and threw the eighteen or twenty guys all over the area.

We pulled up to Ste-Mère-Église and a bunch of French women came by with an old man who was probably sixty. He said something to them, and they all stopped and waited. He turned his back and pissed against a fence. We thought this was something.

We ran into one of our 6th Armored Division MPs, who gave us the high sign to go. I looked down and we had run over this

14. This usually refers to the bogey wheels which the treads run over on a tank or other tracked vehicle.

German soldier. He was spread-eagled and when we ran over him, the tracks of the tank squashed him out and . . . bah! That is the first and only time I almost got sick during the war. We went on and the MPs picked us up there and we went through Ste-Mère-Église and into an apple orchard. They had walls and rows of hedges. We went in and cut engines, and I heard this guy hollering at the top of his voice. I went over and he had one foot up on the running board of his truck and one on the ground and right between his legs were the prongs of an antipersonnel mine and he wouldn't move. That was my introduction to France. We got him taken care of and back to his truck.

There were these beautiful little apples, the ones they make cognac out of. They looked good—they were red—but they were the bitterest things you ever put in your mouth.

Lieutenant Crutchfield's unit consisted of lighter vehicles.

As I remember, we sat offshore for seven days waiting to be unloaded. The weather wouldn't cooperate. We came ashore and had no particular problem. We went directly into an apple orchard.

Because the Germans would stretch piano wire across the roads as a booby trap, we welded a piece of armor plate on our jeep to deter this.

Breakthrough, July 25 to July 31

The 120th Infantry of the 30th Division held part of the front opposite the sector, which was to be carpet-bombed on July 24 and July 25 to begin the general offensive to break through German lines. S.Sgt. Charles B. Herndon was a member of the 2nd Platoon of Company E and describes the action.

We were told when the planes would be over, that we would follow up soon after they dropped the bombs and keep going. We were told the planes would not bomb the road. My company was on the road when the planes came over and ready to move out. The planes came over as planned, but dropped short and our company was hit so badly we had to go back to the assembly area. We could not go forward—not enough men and equipment. A bomb hit close by and I was covered with debris—wire, tree limbs, dirt. The attack was called off until the next day [July 25] at the same time, when the same number of planes came over again. Knowing what they did the day before, we hoped it would not happen again, but it did-we were bombed again, but not as bad. I could see the bombs coming down when the planes came over. We survived that.

Although the American forces took some losses from the bombing, the enemy forces were shattered. The 9th Division held most of the front targeted for the carpet-bombing attack of July 25. PFC John D. Gregory was a rifleman in the 1st Battalion of the 47th Infantry when the German positions were bombed.

This was something to see. The planes started early, first fighter-bombers, then medium bombers, and then the heavy stuff. Wave after wave they came. The ground shook like an earthquake. The leaves fell from the trees and my pant legs shook. We got out of our holes and shouted, "Give them hell." I saw some bombers hit—what a sad sight! Soon we began to advance while the bombing continued. Can you believe the Germans still fired at us? As we moved up, we saw some of our troops were hit when the bombs fell short.

We punched a hole in the German lines. The tanks came through us, and they were out of sight by night. We were put in reserve to get a well-deserved rest. That morning, about 2:00 A.M., I awoke to a wild experience. The German planes dropped flares, and it was light as day. Bombs were falling everywhere. A bomb exploded between my hole and the next one. I didn't realize at first that I was hit. Then my shoe filled with blood. I had a piece of shrapnel in my right thigh. The man in the next hole lost both legs. We lost about forty men in just minutes. We waited what seemed like hours for ambulances to haul us to hospitals. The ambulances carried four GIs each. I was placed on the bottom. The blood from the man above dripped on me to the hospital. I got what we called a million-dollar wound. It was only enough to get me out of this hell for six months.

Pvt. Sam L. Burns, Company F of the 39th Infantry, who had landed with the 9th Division in Normandy, was slightly wounded in the fighting early in July but quickly returned to duty to participate in the fighting for the St. Lô–Periers road.

We crossed the road several times and were repelled several times, but we finally held as much ground as possible until we got additional units and armor moved up to help. On July 23, Col. Paddy Flint was hit in the head and killed by a sniper.

On July 25, the operation began, and the largest air bombardment started the break-through at St. Lô. We had color-identification panels out on the ground to note our locations, but the smoke from the bombs drifted back over us and bombs started to fall on and around our positions. We had to move to new positions, and I selected a solid-wheel oxcart for my cover. This did not work too well, for a concussion blew the cart away. Luckily, I survived this encounter as the ground rumbled as in an earthquake while the bombs were being dropped.

We immediately started our push across the St. Lô–Periers road and headed toward La Butte. Most of the German army and equipment was in disarray, so we had it pretty easy for this day. On July 26, we advanced toward Potigny and ran into a mortar barrage that lasted for several hours, and I was wounded in the right arm. We were between Potigny and La Buissonnerie, and I was evacuated to the aid station and treated, then sent to the evacuation hospital, where I was operated on and shrapnel was removed from my arm. We were then loaded on a hospital plane and flown to England. While we were in flight, we were strafed over the channel by a German fighter, which made only one pass. We landed in the south of England and were transported to the 55th General Hospital by train. I stayed there a couple of days and was put on a train for Scotland, where I was operated on and six weeks later loaded on the *Queen Elizabeth* for return to the States.

S.Sgt. Jack W. Carter, a wire chief in HQ Battery, 44th Field Artillery, 4th Infantry Division, was sitting on top of a hill less than a mile away from the German positions when the Eighth Air Force bombers flew over to carpet-bomb the positions of the Panzer Lehr Division.

The 4th Division was given a grandstand view of the breakthrough . . . [when] the German position was bombed by over 3,000 bombers and fighter planes, perhaps one of the greatest air attacks known to man. We were told that some planes would come over and drop smoke bombs along the enemy front lines and later the bombers would come over and drop their bombs. Dust rose to the skies, the ground shook even where we were sitting. Unfortunately, the wind shifted and some bombers dropped their bombs short of the enemy lines, killing some of our own troops, including General McNair.

Gen. Lesley McNair, Commander of Army Ground Forces, received much of the credit for building up and training the U.S. Army. He was assigned to the diversion plan for Overlord, and on July 25, he had gone forward to watch the bombing and died with over 100 other American soldiers. Close to 500 more were wounded when a number of bombs fell short. Over 900 B-17 and 647 B-24 bombers of the Eighth Air Force and 380 mediums from the Ninth Air Force, took part in the bombing. The artillery fired smoke markers, which proved of little value because of the wind and the bombardment itself. Due to an error by the lead bombardier, one formation dropped its bombs north of the St. Lô–Periers highway, causing the above-mentioned American casualties. However, most of the 3,395 tons of bombs were on target and virtually obliterated the German Panzer Lehr Division. Since General McNair commanded FUSAG, replacing George Patton, who had taken over the Third Army, his death was kept secret to maintain the myth of Fortitude. Actually, Cobra was to begin on July 24, but Air Marshal Leigh-Mallory recalled the aircraft because of the weather conditions. Most of the heavy bombers in the first wave were already on

the way when poor weather forced them to turn back, but the 315 bombers of the second wave and the 300 of the third wave dropped their bombs. By the time the abort message finally reached the remaining waves, 25 men of the 30th Division had been killed and 131 wounded by bombs that fell short.

On July 25, Lt. Murray Pulver, Company B, 120th Infantry, 35th Division, and his platoon were right in the path of the falling bombs. In Pulver's company, four men were killed and five wounded. The 4.2-millimeter mortar battalion to his rear lost half its men. General McNair had stood only about 200 yards from Pulver's position.

Pulver and his men encountered a great deal of resistance during their eventful advance. They came across an abandoned German tank, inside which they found a ring that turned out to be booby-trapped—fortunately, Pulver left it for the engineers to destroy.

Cpl. Floyd Brooks with the Survey Section of the 230th Field Artillery, 30th Division, also watched the fateful bombing.

Finally on July 24, the big day arrived. By 0930 hours, the infantry had pulled back 1,200 yards from the front lines in case there was an error. Our artillery positions were about 4,000 yards from the highway. H-Hour was 1500 hours. Almost all of the bombs landed north of the highway. Battery A lost a truck—they were all out in the open. Our telephone network was destroyed. The wire teams worked all afternoon and most of the night relaying the wire. The word then came down that another bombing would take place on July 25. Corps stated the heavies would fly east to west. Captain Blaine, the battalion communications officer, sent the wire crews out in the morning so they would be handy in case the wire net was destroyed. At the scheduled time, the B-17 and B-24s came from the north heading south. Each flight came in endless numbers. It was a sight that was unbelievable. We could see the bombs when they left the aircraft. The bombs crashed to earth on both sides of the highway. Two of the B-17s blew up in huge fireballs. A couple of B-24s went down, trailing long columns of black smoke.[15]

Two of our batteries had bombs fall in their positions. We had no injuries, but it scared the hell out of us. When the wire parties got back, Tech 5 Dokes got off the truck with a blank stare on his face, and he walked through the battery area into the woods behind us. We found him sitting on a log staring off into the distance. He sat on that log all night and most of the next day until someone was able to talk him into getting onto a truck and move out. He never went out on a wire truck again. He became the officer's orderly, and his main duties were getting their equipment on the truck when we moved and setting it up when we got to the new location. A corporal told me later that when the bombs had fallen short, he was laying on the ground one moment, and the next a round would be five feet below him. We had over 800 casualties in two days of bombing, with 662 on July 25.

When we passed through the bombed area, it was the biggest mess I ever saw. It looked like a World War I battlefield. The destruction was terrific; there were no branches on the trees, no plants, no hedges, no buildings or roads. The dust was so heavy and thick you needed a mask to breathe through it. That night, the *Luftwaffe* was out in force and some outfit behind us really got blasted.

Our next position was near Bon Fossi. Captain Blaine had the idea of setting up telephone service. He established a switchboard in the frontline infantry unit. The switchboard personnel were very lucky in that none of them were injured by this stupid idea. As the captain was leading the troop forward, he was stopped by an engineer and told that mines had not been cleared beyond this point. The captain told his driver to go on and that the engineer did not know what he was talking about. The captain established a location for the board, and as he was returning, his jeep hit a Teller mine. The mine removed the right front corner of the jeep, and Captain Blaine got a Purple Heart; his driver got shook up and almost lost his hearing. HQ called the switchboard back, and we never had that type of operation again.

S.Sgt. William L. Conrad, who had been wounded on D+1 and sent to England to recover, returned to join his Company F, 8th Infantry, 4th Division, on July 20 and in time for the big offensive of July 25.

Company F was one of the last of the units pulled off the front line just prior to the bombing. We were on our way off the line when the planes started to appear. The bombing was so intense and we were so close that we were bounced around like rubber balls, so deafening that it hurt many of us and left us with hearing problems.

As soon as the last wave of planes passed overhead, we started back to the front in pursuit of the enemy. There were tanks on fire and some on their side in bomb craters and corpses hanging from trees. What a mess!

---

15. Records indicate that only one B-17 was lost and four B-24s.

Troops take a break in a wine cellar in Vire.

The next day, we were going through open ground with patches of trees and scrub growth. About 3:00 P.M. or soon after, we were going along a fence with trees for protection and there 250 yards to the front and right was a contingent of two or three Germans on their way back. I gave my men the hit-the-ground signal and opened fire. For five to ten minutes, we laid down fire along a tree-lined ridge. We halted fire and took surveillance of the area. When we got to the ridge, there were between 500 and 1,000 Germans waving white flags. We immediately searched for weapons and pertinent information and then sent them to the rear. Then we moved forward and came to a small, uninhabited town where we dug foxholes for a possible counterattack. We stayed in the area for a couple of days regrouping and receiving supplies. While in the area, we were under constant shelling and mortar fire.

On the fourth or fifth day, a command was sent down for me to take my men down a certain road to a junction and observe. In the town there were about 500 to 700 people in their homes. We met no resistance, nor did we see any Germans, so we took a break, sitting on the steps of a church and under some trees for about half an hour before making the journey back to our lines.

PFC Harper Coleman, Company H, 8th Infantry, 4th Division, took part in the weeks of fighting in the hedgerow country near St. Lô and observed what he called the "total destruction" of just about everything. He commented that the "roads and fields looked like junk yards, dead animals in all the fields." He witnessed one of the heaviest artillery barrages of the campaign and saw a battalion command get killed as he stood near his machine-gun position. While Coleman manned the machine gun, a member of his squad was killed by a sniper and "a sniper bullet came across my shoulder and cut the top of my hand." During the breakthrough, he passed the terrible sight of a column of German troops shredded by an artillery barrage and then saw an out-of-control lieutenant execute a wounded German pleading for water. Soon thereafter, Coleman was in a field hospital for a few days since "I guess I used poison ivy for toilet paper."

Pvt. Gerald Putman, Company A, 22nd Infantry, 4th Division, was in a foxhole surrounded by an apple orchard during the bombing on July 25.

We were told tanks would come at dawn. The tanks would pass over our foxholes, and we were to follow them as infantry support. When dawn came, no tanks showed up. They decided to run spearhead columns down the road with the infantry protecting the flanks, and finally the orders came to move out.

We were not prepared for what we saw. Trees were chopped off inches above the ground and there were blood-soaked spots everywhere. We were sure no one could have lived through the Cobra bombing. Imagine our surprise when a head popped up out of the ground and said, "Get down! The Germans will shoot at you!" We said, "No, the Germans went home yesterday." He didn't believe us and would only come up two inches at a time. Finally, we had him standing on top of the ground. He had lived through the bombing. It turned out there were three more men in the foxholes, and all three could not speak or understand anything we said—they were in a vegetable state. My two friends took the four Ameri-

cans back to the American lines and I continued on.

A German fighter dived at me and I raced the bullets to the nearest bomb crater. I ran for better cover, as did ten other guys, and we ended up with one sergeant and ten privates in a ravine. I spotted a German recon car the bombs had blown into the ravine; it was lying on its side. My friends and I had never seen any German equipment up close, so we headed for it. The sergeant said, "Don't bother with that, there is nobody there." He was wrong; we took our first German prisoner. The German dropped his helmet on the ground as a sign of surrender. My two friends took the German POW back to the American lines, and the rest of us continued.

We passed a German ammo dump, which was on fire, and shells were exploding in it. We searched it for Germans and discovered an 88-mm gun. We rode on our tank support through the German lines and early in the morning of July 27 stopped to resupply our tanks in the darkness. My buddy and I were assigned perimeter guard. I was assigned to guard a tank, and I could not get anyone water until dawn or rejoin my buddy who waited for me. The Germans had dropped one shell during the night, which hit dead center on our foxhole while I was guarding the tank, and my buddy, Pvt. Norman Renninger, was killed. I was then assigned with another private to protect an artillery officer who was a spotter for a gun battery.

We crawled up near a wooded area where we thought the Germans were. The lieutenant pointed to a small tree and said he was going to fire a marker shell, which would drop a flare in front of the tree. It dropped where he said it would, and we were impressed. He then got on the radio and ordered an HE. When the shell impacted in the wooded area, a huge fireball erupted. Even the lieutenant was surprised. This proved the Germans were in the woods, and the lieutenant ordered on the radio, "Fire for effect!" Salvo after salvo impacted in the wooded area until it disappeared in a cloud of smoke and dust. We watched the area with glasses for over twenty minutes. There was no sign of life.

When we returned to the tank column, we were welcomed back as heroes. In the afternoon, we were told we had wiped out an entire German gun battery and only three Germans, who were captured, were left.

As the tanks began to move, bright-colored plastic panels were mounted on top of them. Late in the afternoon, we cut through a German column, and as soon as our vehicle moved out of the way, our fighters came in and attacked the Germans for about twelve minutes. It was getting dark at the time, and we took up defensive positions. The next day we found many burned-out German vehicles bumper to bumper. Guys on motorcycles still had their hands on the handlebars and those in side cars sat in a natural position while trucks loaded with infantry were still full and all were charred black. We were shocked at the sight and no one spoke.

On July 29, our spearhead column moved ahead until midmorning, and suddenly the Germans were hitting one tank after another. We knew there was a spotter nearby, but couldn't figure out where he was. One of our sergeants kept pointing at an American artillery spotter plane and hollered, "The German's up there!" The officers figured the sergeant had been in combat too long and ignored him. He kept insisting the German was in the American spotter plane. Finally, we shot down the aircraft and the Germans seemed to be unable to hit anything after that. The sergeant was right.

For the breakthrough, the 22nd Infantry of the 4th Division was attached to Combat Command A of the 2nd Armored Division on July 26. The unit encountered its first serious resistance north of St. Gilles, but tanks and aircraft destroyed four German Panzer IVs and the remaining opposition. As this column advanced down the Canisy road, craters and minefields became the main hindrance. In addition, the Germans began to respond with mortar and artillery fire. As the 6th and 4th Armored Divisions advanced down the coast road toward Coutances, and the 2nd "Hell on Wheels" Armored Division, with the 3rd "Spearhead" Armored on its right, raced south and southwest, the Germans attempted to break out to the southeast. On July 29, the Ninth Air Force fighter-bombers destroyed over 100 tanks and 250 vehicles around Roncey. Private Putman witnessed part of the destruction, as many Germans abandoned their vehicles and fled on foot. Remnants of several German divisions escaped southward to form a new line that they would not hold for long.

On July 31, the 12th Infantry was advancing on Villedieu-les-Poêles, when it stopped just north of the town. Sgt. Leonard Herb, a draftee from Philadelphia who served in the I&R Platoon, was on a reconnaissance patrol for the S-2 at the time.

My squad was to reconnoiter the town of Villedieu. We made an uneventful entry to the town hall, and I radioed the colonel that we had reached our objective. He sent tanks next, which were promptly knocked out.

The enemy let us pass, waiting for larger game, and they got it. We were lucky again.

In most places, the enemy forces became disorganized, and the American armor quickly overran their positions. In several cases, tactical air support had separated the enemy soldiers from many of their weapons.

Like many of his comrades, PFC Ralph Brazee of Anti-Tank Company, 22nd Infantry, 4th Division, was in a good position to observe the aerial bombardment on July 25.

[My gun was set up] in a path between two hedgerows, camouflaged with branches. We were ordered to get ready for another division to replace us. The replacement gun crew set up on the other side of the hedgerow in the field, but they used net camouflage. An air force plane strafed their position and never touched our location.

When the breakthrough came, we went with the armored vehicles early in the evening and drove like hell through burning villages and around bomb craters. Going around one of these craters only one track was on solid ground and the gun slid down into the hole before we got past.

Pvt. Robert M. Hardesty, a nineteen-year-old draftee from Baltimore, had arrived in Normandy in June as a replacement for the 29th Division. He joined Company A of the 115th Infantry just as the division began to move from St. Lô to Vire.

The fighting became extremely heavy around St. Germain. Companies A and B had forty men between them, and it was here I came across an old barn in the middle of a field. I got up close enough to hear voices from inside. I remember we were right in the thick of things. I made sure I

Temporary cemetery with soldier labeling the body bag of PFC Fredrick A. Smith.

had a full clip in my rifle and held a grenade as I kicked the door open. Thank God I didn't throw the grenade because there were six to eight French schoolchildren with their teacher. Fortunately, they could speak English, but they were scared and when they saw me, they begged me not to hurt them. So I took my pack off and gave them some chocolate and gum.

Lt. Charles Scheffel was waiting to report to Company D of the 1st Battalion, 39th Infantry of the 9th Infantry Division, but Lieutenant Colonel Bond still held him at headquarters after the bombing of July 25. He suspected that the colonel meant to give him another assignment.

I went over to see if I could find Lt. Bill Butler, my medical doctor friend. Couldn't find him, but did find the dental tent so I went in to see if all my fillings were OK. While there, Lt. Col. Bob Stumpf came in. I believe at the time he commanded 2nd Battalion. He had a toothache that seemed to have him in great pain. The doctor told him that he had a tooth that needed pulling right then, but it seemed that putting the colonel to sleep for a lack of a deadening agent kept them from doing the pulling right at the moment. The colonel started to go out of the tent, and I guess back to his battalion, when all of a sudden, he turned around and in effect said to pull the damn thing right now without any painkiller. I believe they gave him a good drink of either Scotch or Calvados and he sat down in the portable dental chair in the Dental Office. The colonel wobbled out of the tent and back to duty. I thought to myself, that there was a man with a lot of guts.

The 8th and 79th Divisions followed the 4th and 6th Armored Divisions down the coast in the direction of Avranches as the 2nd and 3rd Armored Divisions and the supporting infantry to their left attempted to cut off several German divisions between them and the coast. PFC John Troy of Company E, 13th Infantry, 8th Division, recalled how he saw it all begin.

On July 24 and July 25, the Eighth Air Force treated us to a mass bombing. They were bombing near St. Lô, but from where we were, it was a show to watch. B-17s and B-24s, wave after wave of them, flew over, with a few going down from Kraut antiaircraft. Something went wrong, for they repeated the same bombing the next day [July 25]. Later, on July 27, with the 121st and 28th Regiments of the 8th Division on line, the German front was withdrawn

under pressure from our division. According to military histories and the army, it was the 4th Armored Division breakthrough. They came through with the recon units, but there wasn't a shot fired at them. We (the 13th Infantry) were marching down the road from Lessay and along came the tanks of the 4th Armored. The credit should go to our 121st and 28th. A day or two later, they put some of the 13th on 4th Armored tanks and some in trucks to accompany the 4th Armored. The Germans had withdrawn temporarily; they saved their forces. We captured very few prisoners, only stragglers. This day I saw the greatest amount of American tanks. I guess they were always there, firing as indirect artillery. We were with the 4th Armored until I guess August 1; then we were released back to the 8th Division. We were sent by truck to attack Rennes, but the Germans withdrew that night as the 4th Armored swung around it.

Lt. Herman F. Byram was with the Service Company of the 2nd Battalion of the 9th Infantry when the 2nd Division held part of the front east of St. Lô during the breakthrough after the bombing of July 25 and even made some advances.

The first night, I took a hot meal to the frontline battalion after the jump-off on July 25. I had to go through a huge apple orchard where the engineers had cleared a road for the supply train to go up with tape marking it. There was so much German artillery and mortar fire they just tore the supply route up. They had a company of engineers assigned to each regiment. They had marked the road, and I went through at night and the German artillery had torn this tape to pieces. I was driving through

Sherman Tank Gunner in Battle

Cpl. Wardell Hopper, a tank gunner on a Sherman tank, described how he and his comrades operated in Normandy.

We had a crew of five: driver, assistant driver, gunner, assistant gunner, and tank commander. The assistant gunner loaded the gun, while the gunner took his commands from the tank commander, and he was second in charge of the tank. He took his orders on where to shoot, what to shoot, and how often to shoot.

The main duty of the gunner was to aim and fire. He was given a target, and he would judge the range and try to hit it. We didn't have any fancy gun sights, just a standard gun sight—a periscope that was aligned with the gun that I used to aim with. We could gauge the yardage. As I can remember, we could gauge the amount of yards we had to shoot and fire on one round to see how close we were.

We didn't have any special uniforms other than a helmet that was more like a football player's helmet. We lost them most of the time and didn't like them, so most of the time we wore nothing. I don't remember any coveralls; we wore our fatigues, regular army issue. We had nothing special in the way of protection.

It was very close inside the tank, but we had enough room to move. You could move around in the gunner's seat, sideways and around a little—the seat didn't move, you did. The seat was attached to the turret. The assistant gunner had the same accommodations. He was on the left side of the gun and I was on the right side.

The driver was in front of the assistant gunner. You could holler up and down to him. If you turned the turret around, you could get down to the driver's seat because we used to change. One time, someone got hurt in the gunner's seat, and the assistant gunner slipped down into the driver's seat, which was easier than the assistant driver getting over there because he was separated by the transmission and that stuff in the front. The assistant driver was to help the driver and to man a machine gun. I operated the radio, as did the tank commander. I don't think the assistant driver had a set of controls to take over the tank.

The turret had two hatches. The tank commander sat right above me. I used the tank commander's hatch. The assistant gunner was on the other side and had a hatch through which we lowered down ammunition and stuff to him. Cleaning of cannon was done every time we got a chance. If we were laid up for a few days, we cleaned everything; swabbed the barrel out and took the breach apart. The machine guns were taken apart and cleaned. We had .30 cal., but did not have any .50 cal, although most other tanks did. On the turret, we had a place to put it, but we never issued it. The assistant driver had a .30 cal. in the hull and I had a .30 mounted next to the cannon.

continued

Sherman Tank Gunner in Battle *continued*

During the evening, we would dig in, making foxholes that would be underneath the tank. We slept under the tank and put stuff around the sides to keep the light of day out [the hours of darkness were short during the Norman summer]. We also used a little light from the tank motor to relax at night and play cards. Four guys would sleep and the fifth was on guard. The infantry pulled back, but we would stay and hold the ground.

I would say we had hot meals often but not every day. We had a field kitchen with us. Each company had its own service platoon that did the cooking and stuff like that. Each company had their own kitchen group as a separate platoon.

The main gun used mostly 75-mm arm or piercing rounds and some incendiary and high explosive rounds. The Service Company handled reloading and maintenance. Companies A, B, and C were medium companies. Vitamin Baker referred to the Battalion. Later on, sometime after landing in Normandy, we received a Company D with light tanks mounting 37-mm guns. As far as I remember, the Service Company brought up the ammunition in 2½-ton trucks. They came up next to the tank, we would load the rounds into our tank, and they would get out of there.

By the time we got into Germany and thought we had the Germans whipped, we threw out ammunition and put booze in there using the shell holes. Soon we were sorry for that when the Battle of the Bulge began, since we couldn't throw Cognac into the guns. Fortunately, we still did have some ammunition left in our tank and got rid of the cognac.

---

with the cat eyes on the jeeps, and there was no way you could see the road. I hit one of these craters with the jeep, and the jeeps behind me had to pull my jeep out. I just couldn't find the route. I finally turned my battalion train around with the chow on the jeeps and the trailers with supplies. I got on the radio, contacted the battalion executive officer, and gave him the situation. He contacted the CO, and the CO said for me to stay where I was, keep the food hot, and serve it to them for breakfast. So we had pork chops, mashed potatoes, and gravy for breakfast. At 3:00 or 4:00 A.M., I loaded the train, and the engineers remarked the lane. I got there at between 4:00 and 5:00 A.M. They had a guide from each company to lead the jeeps in. When they got through feeding, they came back and we were ready to return to the rear area. I had my jeep ready to go when they came out and said, "Wait don't go!" One of the men had been hit by a sniper, and they had me evacuate him to the rear aid station. I was waiting for them to get the man, and I could hear people talking out there about one hedgerow in front of us—about a hundred yards or less. I asked if they were sure they fed everybody, and they replied yes. I asked about the people out in that hedgerow, and they said they did not because they were Germans!

The 90th Infantry Division with the 712th Tank Battalion attached also took part in the advance of the VIII Corps. Pvt. William Biehler's platoon, H Company, 357th Infantry, was riding on the tanks on July 26. At one point, Biehler "was sitting alone on the front of the tank by the gun when the gunner spotted a German tank off to our right. . . . He swung that gun so fast he knocked me off the tank." This happened quite often, but most of the riflemen did not suffer from the mishap because they were young and in great physical condition. At this time, Biehler's platoon also received a new lieutenant who took over as platoon leader. He stood up waving an American flag during the advance, and he was shot during his first ten minutes in combat.[16]

The 741st Tank Battalion was still operating in the area when Cpl. Wardell Hopper of Company B was present with another Sherman tank. His Sherman duplex-drive tank had sunk during the invasion, but he returned to action with a new tank shortly after the landings. In July, his battalion was fully committed to the battle of the hedgerows south of Omaha Beach. By the time Operation Cobra took place, the tanks were better prepared for breaching the hedgerows.

They took these German obstacles and welded them to our tanks. We welded these spikes onto the front of the tanks so we could plow right through the hedgerows. All the tanks had them on. We just hit the hedgerow and the dirt flew everyplace and we busted through. The turret was above the hedgerow. It caused a small jolt, but we scooped it right up and threw it aside. The infantry would follow behind us.

I remember once in Normandy it was one of the few times I got confused as the gunner. We had to shoot all the way down to the end of a farm yard—maybe 200 or 300 yards away or maybe more—at full speed, firing the whole time, turn around, and come back, firing the whole time again. The turret made an almost complete turn, or halfway at least, and I got back and stood up out the back of the tank and didn't have the faintest idea where I was. Firing and turning all the time I lost all concept of where we were. Our target was German infantry across the hedgerow.

I shot at a machine-gun position with German infantry and remember seeing the bodies fly. An infantry man picked up the phone on the rear of our tank and pointed out a command post that they thought was directing fire on them. I placed a few shots in there and that was the end of that. That is what I got the Bronze Star for.

I remember, when our tank got hit in Normandy, we all got out. I was watching our driver. We shot the guy that got us, a German bazooka man. His rocket hit the transmission. The driver, I thought, climbed out dead because his helmet was filled with oil and he put it over his head and it was all running down his face. I thought surely he was dying. That German had snuck up along the hedgerow to bazooka us. We got another tank pretty fast, and it also had the cutter welded on it.

There was a French town near St. Lô where we stopped in a field. The people were very nice there. A woman cooked us a chicken dinner. In France, it seemed, they stuffed a whole clove of garlic under the wings and thighs and I bit into it. My, that gets your attention, and to this day, I don't like garlic.

---

16. Biehler never learned if the lieutenant was killed or wounded.

According to Corporal Hopper, not everyone in Normandy rolled out the welcome carpet for the victorious American troops.

> I remember taking one little town in Normandy where we are going down the main street of the town, our tank was second or third, and I saw a woman lean out with a gun to shoot the tank commander in front of us. I remember shooting her with my rifle, and watching her fall out of the window. I had a Garand M-1 rifle that I kept in the tank, but we didn't all have them. I picked this one up during the invasion, and it was not a standard weapon issued to us.

The 6th Armored Division moved into position as the breakout began. Lt. Rodney Mortensen of the 212th Armored Field Artillery Battalion spent a good deal of time doing recon for his outfit. He commented that the men of his division hardly noticed the big bombing on July 25. His division pushed forward down the coast until it was ready for the big breakthrough at the beginning of August.

As the breakthrough began to turn into a breakout, both the newly arrived 28th and the veteran 29th Divisions were alerted to prepare to move into action.[17] The 29th Division began moving out from its rest area on July 28 and was at the front the next day, following the advance of the 2nd Armored Division's Combat Command A and engaging elements of the 2nd Panzer Division.

Earlier in July, as the 29th Division continued to take heavy casualties, PFC John "Jack" P. Montrose joined it in Normandy as a replacement. After he had been drafted, he had volunteered for pilot training, the Rangers, and the paratroopers, but his poor eyesight made him ineligible for the elite units. He was assigned to the radio section of HQ Company, 2nd Battalion, 175th Infantry, after July 20, while the unit was in a rest area after the fall of St. Lô. To pass the time, the men of his unit played football in a relatively unobstructed field enclosed by hedgerows. Montrose threw a pass, and the man running to catch it tripped and broke his leg, which infuriated General Gerhardt, who forbade any further football games. On July 26, when the division prepared to return to the front line, Montrose served under Sgt. Hayden Ward.

> [Sergeant Ward] told me where to dig in. Normally, you were paired up, but we had an uneven number and I was by myself. Shortly after dark, Sgt. Ward returned to apologize and told me he had located me in the wrong place, and I had to move and dig another hole. This didn't make me too happy, but I moved and dug a second hole, not nearly as deep as the first. Somewhere around midnight, German planes showed up and dropped bombs. Falling bombs produce a very unusual, never-to-be-forgotten sound. One landed close enough to completely cover me with dirt. The next morning at daylight, we found two fellows dead in my original foxhole. They had been killed by concussion. These two were also replacements with whom I had been playing poker a few days earlier.
>
> My first taste of serious combat occurred at daybreak one late July day [on or about July 30] near Villebaudon.[18] The Germans were launching a counterattack. One other fellow and I were on the corner of our defense, somewhat separated from the rest of

---

17. The 28th Infantry Division spent only about three months in England and arrived in Normandy on July 22, just in time to move forward as the big offensive began. The commanding general was killed soon after and replaced by Gen. Norman Cota from the 29th Division.
18. Villebaudon is about ten miles south of St. Lô.

The work of the 3047th Graves Registration Company in Normandy. EMMETT BAILEY JR.

the company. There was a general, probably General Cota, in the main company area firing a .50 cal. machine gun from a jeep. When my unknown companion mentioned that perhaps we should vacate the area, I told him, "As long as we have a general with us, there should be nothing to worry about." We did not notice that the general and the entire company left the area by way of a sunken road. After a while, my companion called my attention to the fact that we were alone. We discussed the situation and decided to cross an open field to the next hedgerow. I took off, giving it my best zigzag open field run and sure enough dived over that next hedgerow to land among other members of the company who had set up another perimeter defense. I had been separated from them so long that I was reported dead. Some faces turned white upon seeing me. My companion apparently didn't make it, and he did not follow me across the field.

We had a problem evacuating wounded, so three wounded men were put on the back of a 2½-ton truck headed for the rear. We found them the next day still lying in the truck where they had been sprayed by a burp gun. The driver was nowhere to be found.

The 29th Division advanced to the city of Vire by August 6, with the 28th "Keystone" Division on its right flank moving on Mortain, where both divisions began taking up positions to secure the left flank of the breakout of the U.S. First Army. Patton's newly formed Third Army was racing south, east, and west to eliminate the German Seventh Army's positions in Brittany and help encircle its main forces in eastern Normandy.

CHAPTER 8

Breakout and Encirclement

The breakout began along the front of the 9th Infantry Division on July 25, 1944, with a major offensive led by the Eighth Air Force's carpet-bombing of a sector that virtually destroyed the German Panzer Lehr Division. Gen. Lawton Collins's VII Corps, reinforced before the breakthrough that led to the breakout, received much of the First Army's nondivisional artillery battalions. The concentration of the 2nd and 3rd Armored Divisions, with the 1st and 4th Infantry Divisions in reserve, helped spearhead the advance. At the same time, the 9th and 30th Infantry Divisions of the VII Corps broke through the shattered German lines, brushing aside the German 275th and 352nd Divisions and the remnants of the II Parachute Corps. The intended goal of the 3rd Armored Division was to drive toward Coutances, while the 2nd Armored Division fanned out and pushed south. The XIX Corps with 35th and 29th Infantry Divisions also moved against the German 2nd Panzer Division east of St. Lô. On the right flank, the VIII Corps with the 79th Infantry Division and 6th Armored Division made the first significant advances, taking Lessay. By July 28, the German left wing facing the VIII Corps was collapsing. The American divisions advanced to Coutances, and the 4th and 6th Armored Divisions, with their supporting infantry, reached the area ahead of the 3rd Armored and 1st Infantry Divisions from the VII Corps. However, the German units they had hoped to trap with the help of the 3rd Armored escaped southward.

Meanwhile, the remainder of the VII Corps, where the breakthrough had started, advanced past Marigny and St. Gilles. On July 31, the American forces were about to break out of Normandy as the 79th Infantry and 6th Armored Division and the 8th Infantry and 4th Armored Divisions converged on Avranches and pushed farther south.

In the meantime, the British applied pressure on the eastern part of the Normandy front. After July 24, the Canadian II Corps launched Operation Spring, advancing southward from Caen. On July 30, the British Second Army opened Operation Bluecoat as 1,200 bombers targeted the sector of the German 326th Infantry Division on the eastern part of the Normandy front, bringing added pressure on the German defenders.

On August 1, 1944, the American Third Army led by Gen. George Patton was activated and poured through Pontaubault, the gateway to Brittany. Patton's army took control of Gen. Troy Middleton's VIII Corps, which included the 4th and 6th Armored Divisions and the 8th, 79th, and 83rd Infantry Divisions. In addition, Gen. Wade Haislip's XV Corps (5th Armored and 90th Infantry Divisions; the 79th Division was added on August 3) and Gen. Walton Walker's XX Corps (5th Infantry and 2nd French Armored Divisions) were attached to the Third Army.[1]

As Patton activated the Third Army, Gen. Omar Bradley turned over the First Army to Gen. Courtney Hodges while he activated and took command of the 12th Army Group. The armored divisions of the VIII Corps moved through Pontaubault on their way to the Brittany Peninsula. The 6th Armored Division drove toward Brest and the 4th Armored Division toward the Loire River. In the meantime, the Germans did not sit idle as their front in Normandy crumbled. Panzer Group West, redesig-

nated as the Fifth Panzer Army, held the front against the British while the shattered Seventh Army regrouped and prepared to launch a major counteroffensive with four panzer divisions on the night of August 6. Their objective was to seal off the American breakthrough at Avranches. The Americans were forewarned by Ultra intercepts, but they did little in preparation.[2] The 30th Infantry Division, which had relieved the 1st Infantry Division on August 6, found itself in the path of the onslaught. One of its battalions was soon surrounded on the high ground east of Mortain, at Hill 317, as the German armored offensive swept around it. This "lost" battalion held out for several days as the German counterattack stalled. Hitler refused to allow his panzer units to take a step back until it was too late.

On August 11, Field Marshal Bernard Montgomery ordered the launching of the British and Canadian Operation Totalize. At the same time, the American XV Corps took Argentan to the south. As Patton's troops pushed in the German left flank at Argentan, the Canadians pressed against the German right flank at Falaise, trapping much of Field Marshal Günther von Kluge's Army Group B in the Falaise Pocket. On August 16, Hitler finally agreed to a withdrawal. On August 15, the Allies launched Operation Dragoon in southern France. Kluge committed suicide on August 18 and was replaced by Field Marshal Walther Model. On August 22, the Allies destroyed what German forces remained in the Falaise Pocket, leaving a scene of carnage. The Normandy campaign came to an end.

Next, the Allies began their drive across France. Since Hitler had forbidden the preparation of defensive lines in France, the defense of the Seine failed miserably and the Allies continued their unrelenting advance on the German border.

---

1. The XII Corps included the 80th Division, which moved to the XX Corps on August 7. Some divisions assigned to corps often changed corps assignments as the offensive unfolded.

2. The British had been reading German signals for a couple of years, after capturing the German Enigma encoding machine and other items needed to break various German codes. Deciphering the huge number of messages intercepted, though, caused a significant time lag.

Soldiers of the 79th Infantry Division during an attack near La Haye du Puits, July 9, 1944. NATIONAL ARCHIVES

Contrary to Hitler's instructions, the German commandant at Paris refused to defend the city, declaring it an "open city." The French resistance rose up, and Patton sent General LeClerc's 2nd French Armored Division to liberate the city.

The Soldier's View

At the beginning of August, Sgt. William Conrad of Company F, 8th Infantry, 4th Division, was setting up defensive positions around an abandoned town his company had taken earlier.

We were ordered to set up mines on all the roads leading in and out of this little town. While we were preparing to set up the mines, we came under fire from two fronts. In an effort to get in our foxholes, we got hit by a tree burst from artillery. I got hit in the right thigh, which forced the medics to send me back to a general hospital for surgery.

This was the second time Sergeant Conrad was wounded, and this time he was sent back to

England. Within three months, he was back with 4th Division.

The time the German front began collapsing was etched forever in the mind of Pvt. Frank Catalano, an antitank gunner in the 22nd Infantry, 4th Division.

We captured 108 German prisoners, and we were only eight men. This went on for months and my squad captured a total of 408 German prisoners. On another night after this, a group of German bombers dropped flares, which were followed by other bombers that dropped bombs, and we lost our halftrack and jeeps. Out of eleven men, I was the only one to crawl out of that mess—we had a direct hit on our halftrack, which was only fifty feet away.

I always carried a pen and pencil set in my left pocket. One day, a piece of shrapnel hit between the set, which put quite a dent in them, but of course saved my life. I remained on the front lines for six months and I was not wounded because I was just lucky, I guess, and I said a lot of prayers.

During the breakout, Lt. Peter Triolo, the S-2 for the 1st Battalion of the 12th Infantry, received instructions from Colonel Jackson concerning supplies.

We got the word about this famous 10-in-1 ration and how good it was. Each box had meals for ten men. Colonel Jackson told me to go back to the supply area and get some of these 10-in-1 rations. I asked how I would do that, and he said he would write out a requisition. He did that for I guess enough boxes to feed the whole battalion. He also told me to take some souvenirs in case I needed some persuasion to support the requisitions. So I took some German helmets and things from the men who were willing to contribute. I then located a big supply dump. When I got there, I gave the requisition to this sergeant at the gate and he said, "This is no good." He said 10-in-1 rations were only for the hospitals. Then I reached back and uncovered some of the souvenirs in my jeep. He said, "Let me think about it. Why don't you put your jeep over here and load your trucks?" We loaded our trucks and left.

By August 1, the 4th and 6th Armored Divisions were passing through Avranches and breaking out deep into German lines. As the 6th Armored Division made a right turn into Brittany and proceeded westward, Lt. James Crutchfield was with the headquarters of the 86th Mechanized Cavalry Recon Squadron.

We lost the first two people in the 6th Armored Division in A Troop during the breakout. We were screening while the division was formed into task forces.

Vehicles were lined up and you didn't know what you were doing. They were bumper to bumper. I was traveling the first night and did not see a lot. I ran into a lot of dead horses and people. You ran right over them.

We passed through Avranches during the night, and the columns came to a stop. I had been back to Division HQ at that time and some of the trains were coming up. You didn't go out by yourself because you would have been a damned fool if you did. The lead unit or the spearhead, if it hit resistance, just passed it and moved on towards Brest. You could get held up two or three days if you wanted to get into a firefight. In the middle of the night, the column I was with stopped. One of the rules was that you went to the head of the column to find out what was going on. I did, and here was the Jewish chaplain all by himself at the head of the column. I asked what happened. He said it got dusty and he had pulled back until the dust cleared and now he didn't know where we were. Then I became like a bird dog and I picked up a rock. There was a foxhole by the side of the road. I threw the rock in and here comes a guy with his hands up. So I knew I was not in friendly territory. Somebody's tank was off on the skyline. I didn't know if it was friendly, and I wasn't going up there to find out. Finally, we went down into this little village and the French were so scared they wouldn't talk to us, so we knew that the Americans hadn't gone through there. So where did they go? Here I had gone from nothing to convoy commander. I felt like I could have shot the chaplain.

We put the German prisoner on the front of the jeep and rode all night long. Somebody, I didn't known who it was, said the Germans had gone through the town. Early the next morning, the guy who rode the German on the front of the jeep got mad, for the German had lied to him, so he took him in the woods and shot him. There were a few little atrocities. I didn't know he was going to shoot him until I heard the gun. The guy who shot him is dead now.

During the night that the 4th and 6th Armored Divisions crossed, there was a guy standing alongside the road, and I could tell he was American. He was all by himself. It was my battalion commander and he had got out of his command half-track and was going to catch his jeep, but it never came down the road. There he sat out in the middle of nowhere. This was just after passing through Avranches. I picked him up, and we rode on out and finally established communications with HQ and found out where we were supposed to go. Boy, what a night that was! All on account of the chaplain who just didn't like the dust.

Sometimes, we didn't have maps and went right off of the ones we had. The FFI [French Resistance] were just like worms coming out of the woodwork. They were everywhere.

A girl came pushing a wheelbarrow and she got up to my armored car when three Free French grabbed her. My armored car driver, a Frenchman, explained to me what was going on. Two of these Free French were going to hold her while the other shot her. What bothered me was that they were waving these damned guns around in the air and I thought they were going to shoot me. She had shacked up with the Germans and must have been a good one. They were going to shoot her there. I didn't have time to fool with them, and maybe she deserved it. One of the blackest blacks you ever saw walked up, a great big man and good looking, maybe Senegalese. He read the riot act to these guys and told them to give her a trial and then, if necessary, shoot her legally. So they led her off with one of them kicking her in the rear end and the other two pulling her. In some towns, we saw that they shaved the heads of these women who had collaborated.

Lt. Rodney Mortensen's 212th Armored Field Artillery Battalion also advanced with one of the task forces.

We busted out and ran all night that first night. After the recon ran into something, somebody else would come along. All I remember is that we went all that day and they had a big firefight on a river, which I was not near, but I could hear it from a mile or two away while eating and sleeping. I was loaded for bear. We took off, went across the river, and ran all day and night. In the middle of the night, the Germans stopped, and we hit them and knocked over an HQ.

When I was there, I saw the gasoline was still burning in the big half-tracks. We had to stay back because they blew up. We found some tanks—one or two at a time. I think it was the second day we turned into Brittany.

We would come into a town and liberate it. We didn't know where we were, but we tried to figure out where we were. I remember one guy came out with a green tuxedo on and a beautiful big fancy tray, a big bottle of Calvados, and fancy cut glass. He was bowing and handing out glasses. He came up to me because I was the guy with the map, I guess. He greeted me and gave me a shot of this stuff. I didn't know much about it, but smoke must have come out of my ears. He went right down the line and nobody would say a word until it damn near killed everybody.

We ran out of our military maps; they gave us Michelin road maps, and finally we ran out of them too. After that, we played follow the leader.

We had these FFI, which none of us thought too much of. They wanted gas and food and would turn around and sell it to somebody. They had these people that were supposedly knowledgeable about the roads, and they were up in the lead tank at the head of the column. They followed the leader. Supposedly, a village might have a big garrison, and they would take us around it. By the time I would get up there, I didn't know about it and I would go right through the village and get into a hell of a fight. There might be a squad of Germans in there and we would have to knock them off, and we were only the trains. I didn't have any infantry or tanks assigned to me. I had 2½-ton trucks and nothing from division HQ because they were too busy protecting division HQ.

I came to a point where the blacktop road turned and there was a fork to the left and it was kind of open. The moon was out, but going in and out of the clouds, and you couldn't see too well. I was feeling around and found some tracks that turned to the left. It was from a recon tank that came up there going about 35 mph and went to the left and all the rest of them went to the right. I didn't go over to check the other side. I had half a dozen truckloads, if I am not mistaken, and another ten or fifteen loads of ammunition—everything explosive as hell. I didn't have much in the way of support equipment. I had a bunch of .50 calibers on jeeps and three Sherman tanks. The main column had gone to the right; I went to the left for a few miles, and all of a sudden, here was a big wall—it was a textile factory at a dead end. There was a big gate that went across this corridor on the inside. We got to this place and a guy comes running out. They had a guard post or guardhouse and the German soldier in it disappeared. Somebody came running out, gave me a spanking new PK Walter, and said there was a platoon of German soldiers inside. This guy was a slave laborer; he had been a French officer in the army and could speak good English. He told us it was a textile factory. He said the Germans were overage and gray types, but they still had a Panzerfaust and so forth. I brought up one tank since you couldn't turn around on the road, but you could in this big courtyard. The tank knocked the gate open and moved over into the corner, and the tank commander got up there on the .50 caliber so he could squeeze this area on the second story in case anyone wanted to shoot from there. Then I brought up another tank and put it over in the other corner. We started bringing in the stuff and turning it around. All told, it took me two hours to do that. We had a little firefight with these Germans. A few of them would run out on the balcony and try to shoot, and we would get them. Just when we were ready to peel out, a German colonel came down. He got about twenty yards away, and I yelled in German for him to give up. Instead, he tried to grab for that damn Walter, and he kept digging for it. You had to push the thing down and lift up and pull. I was carrying a .45 with a lanyard around my neck. I kept telling him and he kept digging. The moon kept going behind the clouds, and it was like a showdown at Dodge City. He was standing there by himself, and I had three tanks. Finally, he got it, and I shot him sure as hell. He got it out, and there he stands, an overage, fat, and graying man, so I let him have it. I don't think his pistol would have fired with so much crud in it.

After the 29th Division became a motorized division at the end of July, it advanced on Vire on July 29. In August, while units of the Third Army began to break out of the peninsula, it was involved in heavy fighting. Before long, it held part of northern Mortain in the vicinity of Vire and faced the 116th Panzer Division as the Germans launched their counteroffensive on the evening of August 6.

Second Lt. Charlie A. Miller was in Company I of the 115th Infantry during the operations in August.

We had moved in trucks until we made contact with the enemy. Then we dismounted and began advancing on foot. The resistance was vicious near Vire, and our unit was stopped and was under heavy German armored attack. Finally, friendly fighter planes began bombing the enemy forces just a few hundred yards away. I was walking alone, crouched behind a hedgerow, when all of a sudden, I felt a tremendous blow to the head, and I went flying through the air with my helmet in one direction and my rifle in another. I thought I might have been struck in the head by the butt of a German rifle. I looked to see what had been a large explosion on the hedgerow, which was not too far away. It was either a bomb or an artillery shell. I hit the ground, and it seemed that I was dying. I was not afraid; it was sort of peaceful. I wondered how my wife would react when she heard the news that I had been killed, but I was not hurt badly. I had a broken right arm, shrapnel in the back of the head, and fragments through my helmet. I also had wounds to the left leg.

After evacuation to England and a series of hospitals, I was loaded on a ship for home on 23 December 1944, my fourth wedding anniversary.

During its advance, the 1st Division passed between the 9th Division, which had faced part of the sector carpet-bombed on July 25, and the 30th Division. The 9th Division shifted to the right and advanced on the left of the 83rd Division. The 2nd and 4th Divisions passed through the sector of the 30th Division, facing the other part of the bombed area. At the beginning of August, the 9th Division followed the 2nd Armored Division and 4th Division to Villedieu and the vicinity of Sourdeval, not far from the German counterattack north of Mortain. Lt. Charles Scheffel spent several days at the headquarters of the 39th Infantry, awaiting reassignment to Company D.

The German 2nd SS Panzer Division surrounded the 2nd Battalion of the 120th Infantry at Hill 314 at Mortain and penetrated west, passing south of the remainder of the 120th Infantry. Elements of the 2nd Panzer Division and the 116th Panzer Division advanced north of Mortain, past the 117th and 120th Regiments of the 30th Division. The spearhead reached as far as Le Mesnil-Adelée, leaving the 1st Battalion of the 39th Infantry at Chérence-le-Roussel north of the Sée River and the 3rd Battalion to the north

of it to hold off any thrust of the 116th Panzer Division. This move ran the risk of opening the front and giving the Germans a main road west. The 39th Infantry was on its own, trying to hold this important section of the front to contain the German advance. Scheffel was given command of the 1st Battalion's Company C.

The period of August 4 through 10 was one of the roughest periods of being a company commander. The Germans had launched a heavy armored attack against the 39th Infantry Regiment's 1st Battalion to crash through to the coast to cut off the penetration. Company C had been cut off and surrounded for three days. Again, the Germans attacked at night led by tanks and penetrated the company defense area after setting a haystack on fire, which lit up the night as if it were daylight, giving the entire battle area surrounding the nearby farmhouse and its orchard an eerie illumination. While I was taking my rifle and beating on the buttoned up hatch of one of the Sherman tanks that had been attached to the company for direct support to get the tank commander to move to a better area within the company defense area, a shell hit the front of the tank and knocked me to the ground. Dazed, ears roaring from the explosion, and on the ground in front of the tank, I thought, "I have been hit again." Thoroughly shaken, trembling, yet I couldn't detect any wounds. To top it all, my trench shovel had been blown off my .45 caliber pistol belt. Looking at my left arm, the underside of my combat jacket had several fragment holes. This sure didn't help my composure.

As I continued to shake all over, one of the medics thought that I had been severely wounded. He just couldn't believe I had even survived. He recognized my ability to command the company had been effectively reduced by this frightening condition of trembling. So, doing his duty, he started to lead me back to a little safer area inside the defensive perimeter. Moving slowly on his arm and with his help, I noticed some of my own soldiers running past in flight before the attacking enemy. At that moment, realizing the importance of "The Old Man," as the infantry commanding officer is known to my company, I somewhat gathered my wits, turned around, and yelled at the retreating men that we were here to stay. I returned to my command post in the forward area of the defensive position. The company repulsed the attack with heavy casualties on both sides. The defensive responsibility of the company across the main road held back the German panzer divisions. Company C was included in the Presidential Citation for the action with the other four companies of the battalion.

For his actions in this battle, which lasted several days, Lieutenant Scheffel received the Silver Star.[3] His division and the 30th Division to the south held their sectors. On August 8, Combat Command B of the 3rd Armored Division dispatched a task force, which included elements of the 119th Infantry of the 30th Division, to drive the Germans out of Le Mesnil-Adelée. After this force finally succeeded, it moved north to the Sée River and made contact with the 4th Division on August 9. However, it took until August 11 for this force to break through to Scheffel's battalion of the 39th Infantry at Chérencé-le-Roussel.

The situation was much worse for the 120th Infantry, 30th Division, located at Mortain. Lt. Murray Pulver had replaced Capt. Howard Greer as commander of Company B, 120th Infantry, on August 2.[4] His first duty as company commander was to get out the payroll. This was the troop's

A soldier inspects a jeep destroyed by a mine, August 4, 1944.
NATIONAL ARCHIVES

first pay in three months, and the men had no place to spend it. The unit spent a couple of days at the village of Tessy, where it rested and received replacements, including three lieutenants. In the steeple of the town church, Pulver's men also captured three German snipers who had been reluctant to do their duty. On August 6, his company moved out in trucks for the first time. Its destination was Hill 285 on the west side of Mortain, where they relieved a unit of the 1st Division.

When the 1st Division turned over its positions to the 30th, it also left behind the few maps in its possession. The 2nd Battalion, 120th Infantry, took up positions on Hill 314 rising to the east of Mortain and 2nd Battalion, including Pulver's Company B, on Hill 285 to the west of the town. Pulver's 1st Platoon put up a roadblock on the left. In the predawn darkness of August 7, the Germans destroyed the roadblock with a captured Sherman tank and took a few of Pulver's men. Next, they advanced with tanks on his company's positions with a surety that seemed to

3. In September 1944, Scheffel was again wounded, apparently more severely than on his first trip to Normandy, and sent back to the United States by November 1944. His wife later joined him at Brooks Hospital in San Antonio, Texas, where he remained until February 1945.
4. Geer was transferred on August 2 and soon promoted to major. He also received the Distinguished Service Cross.

indicate that they knew where everything was located. The regiment's cannon company and antitank company destroyed the three leading German tanks. Lieutenant Pulver destroyed another German tank with a bazooka that he had carried since the battles of July 16.

During the skirmish, Pulver's SCR-300 was destroyed and his telephone communications with battalion headquarters were cut. Undeterred, Pulver followed his last orders to hold at all costs. In the early evening, a British Typhoon came to his rescue by destroying Germans tanks. It was followed by other planes that fired on his men, killing one of his drivers. Before long, Lieutenant Franklin, who led Company A, suffered a serious head wound, and told Pulver to take over his company. When Pulver reached Company A's position, he found the men in near panic in the face of the approaching enemy. Pulver quickly rallied them and directed their fire against the Germans who were about to attack. As a result of his quick intervention on August 7, Lieutenant Pulver was awarded the Bronze Star. According to the citation, his company

> received a determined enemy counterattack consisting of at least three platoons of infantry and twenty armored vehicles. Throughout the action Lieutenant Pulver performed courageously. Through his outstanding courage and leadership his men were inspired to hold their positions against a numerically superior enemy . . . inflicting heavy casualties on the hostile forces while suffering only minor losses in their own ranks.

Maj. John Allison, executive officer of the division's 105th Engineers, summarized the events before and after the German assault.

On the evening of August 5, following the breakout of July 25 and continuous bitter fighting in the hedgerow country in its drive south, the 30th Infantry Division was ordered to the vicinity of Mortain to replace the 1st Infantry Division, where it was to protect the lines of communications with Patton's Third Army.

The following day, Sunday, August 6, the 30th moved south in motorized columns that clogged the single-lane roads from shoulder to shoulder. The roads were lined with French civilians, the girls throwing flowers and the men offering the GIs sips of Calvados (a powerful local brandy distilled from apple cider) from small flasks tucked in their waistbands. It was more like a celebration than a forced march into defensive positions. The relief of the 1st Division was accomplished by the evening of August 6 with no warning of the pending firestorm that was about to erupt—other than the strafing of the truck columns by German fighters.

At 1:00 A.M. August 7, the first indication of serious trouble appeared with the approach of enemy tanks accompanied by infantry all along the 30th's front. Soon thereafter, roadblocks were overrun by the panzers and/or bypassed, and they deeply penetrated the 30th's positions. The 2nd Battalion of the 120th Infantry was completely isolated on Hill 314 overlooking Mortain. The battalion was cut off not only from their regiment, but also from their battalion headquarters, which was overrun and captured the following day.

The letter companies of the 105th Engineer Battalion were relieved of their support missions with their respective infantry regiments and attached to them and thereafter assigned defensive sectors in each regimental zone fighting as infantry. Despite its casualties, lack of sleep, and continuous close in combat, the main body of the 30th held, and on Friday, August 11, the units of four German panzer divisions began their retreat.

S.Sgt. Charles B. Herndon was with Company E, 120th Infantry, 30th Division, which was part of the battalion surrounded on Hill 314.

Sometime in August [August 6], we got to Mortain where we went on Hill 314 to relieve another outfit. When we got there, everything was quiet; we thought we would get a little well-deserved rest. Cool nights and warm days, we would lie out in the sun sleeping a little and resting the first day. The second day, the Germans started pumping artillery, which ended our rest. They wanted the hill to split our army so they could drive to the Channel. If they had succeeded, things would have been different, but we held the hill for six days and did not give in, although we had several demands to surrender.

The city of Mortain was bombed by the Americans, then the Germans, and then the Americans again. We were completely surrounded during the six days on the hill, and my position was an outpost, where I had a good view of a road junction three-quarters of a mile away, where the Germans passed through. I was given a field telephone, with wire strung on top of the ground up to me. As the Germans would come to the junction, I would call back (I think my code was "Checkpoint Five") and our artillery would fire over our heads and hit them. I was kept busy calling in; sometimes during a slack period I would crawl out and repair the phone line until I was ordered not to take the risk, but I kept the line in operation until I ran out of tape.

We ran out of supplies, so our planes flew over on the fifth day and dropped food, water, and medical supplies by parachute,

Unloading the more than 5,000 items that comprised the medical assembly of the 5th General Hospital at Carentan, France, July 24, 1944. SIGNAL CORPS

which landed out front, between us and the Germans. The next day, they tried again, but still most of it landed out front. I started out to try to get one of the packages and one of my men, Lavern Erickson, asked, "Sergeant, where are you going?" I told him to keep me covered. I looked at him peeping up out of his foxhole about twenty feet from mine, his eyes sunk back in his head, hollow cheeks, plus being dirty in the August heat. He was a pitiful looking sight, but on the other hand, he was a good soldier. I threw my rifle down, sneaked out through small scrub oaks, and retrieved a case of K rations. No, I didn't eat any; I was too thirsty. Late evening of the fifth day, we could hear guns firing at a far distance across the valley and were told that was some of our American soldiers were coming to rescue us. I never thought I would like to hear guns fire, but after learning it was Americans fighting their way to us, it sure sounded good. The next day after noon, we were freed from Hill 314. When we got off the hill and got water, I asked one of my men for the packet of bouillon from his K ration. Even though the water was not hot, it was good. We thought we would have sometime to recuperate from this, but no, on the move again on foot. We were still fighting through hedgerows, but later they came farther apart.

Along the route we observed German equipment that they had to leave behind in the retreat: rifles, large guns, tanks vehicles, half-tracks, and command cars—some intact and some not.

On the morning of August 8, Lieutenant Pulver left Company B's position and was slightly wounded during a mortar barrage as he worked his way back to the battalion command post. The battalion commander had been informed that Pulver's company had been captured and was surprised to see him. That afternoon, Col. Hammond D. Birks, the regimental commander, told Pulver that the 2nd Battalion was cut off and that his company was to break through enemy lines and deliver supplies.

As he advanced toward Hill 314, Pulver came across the 30th Recon Troop of the 30th Division. The captain leading the unit told Pulver that he was on an impossible mission because enemy troops were swarming the area. From this position, Pulver realized that Colonel Birks had ordered him to break through at a point where the hill became a steep cliff, while over 300 Germans occupied the only possible line of advance. Pulver informed the battalion commander of the situation by radio and received the order to bring his company back that night.

The 30th Division stopped the German assault at Mortain and saved the advancing troops of the Third Army from a potential disaster. The 1st Battalion, 120th Infantry Regiment, encircled and trapped on Hill 314, held out despite the fact that attempts to supply it by land and air largely failed. The division's 230th Field Artillery Battalion fired rounds filled with medical supplies into the area occupied by the encircled battalion. On August

12, the battle came to an end; the 2nd Battalion, over half of its 700 men still alive, was relieved after days of close combat and after refusing an offer to surrender by an SS officer.

On August 12, Lieutenant Pulver was relieved of his two greatest worries. A letter from home announcing that his wife had safely delivered a child finally reached him and put his mind at rest. His other worry, which involved serious doubts about his ability to act with honor on the battlefield, had been laid to rest almost a month before and during the breakthrough, when he put on a stellar performance.

Richard Stewart, a private in Pulver's Company B, participated in a couple of four- and five-man night patrols. He and his comrades captured prisoners, sometimes bringing back one or two POWs. He was fortunate never to be detected. Stewart noticed that the heavy fighting affected each of his comrades in a different way.

We had a guy that went around and opened up mouths of the dead to get the gold out. Then one day, he disappeared and I don't know what happened to him. Another guy couldn't take it any more; he put his arm on a stone and hit his arm attempting to break it. I watched and saw his arm come back up and all he did was blacken it. We had a guy in another squad that shot a couple of Germans for being smart. He would take them back and shoot them. I didn't agree with that, but you are not going to argue with a guy with a gun. He did not do this until after the breakout.

Private Stewart, only seventeen years old at the time, received a Dear John letter from his girlfriend. According to him, letters from home were more than a means of keeping in touch with loved ones. A man in his squad had stuffed a bunch of folded missives in the chest pocket of his jacket. Later, he was knocked down by a bullet that got lodged in the wad of paper in his pocket. The letters from home quite literally saved his life. Another of his comrades was hit in the chest, and he would have surely died if the bullet had not struck his combat badge, bending it out of shape. During this period, Stewart and his comrades collected souvenirs, which they sold to the men in the rear area. Stewart had fond memories of his captain.

Captain Pulver wasn't afraid. He was a tall man and knocked out a tank by himself, although I didn't actually see it. When he said, "Sergeant, you go over there!" I said, "Me a sergeant again?" He sent me over to this house, and we killed a bunch of them as they came out of there. I said, "Hey, I am already wounded!" and he replied, "That is OK, you can still walk!" and that was why they gave me the Silver Star, but I wanted to go back.

The battle turned into a struggle for survival for the German Seventh Army, which attempted to escape from Normandy after the failed offensive and allied armored divisions smashed in both flanks of the salient it occupied. On the first day of the enemy counteroffensive, the Germans had attacked with over 120 tanks in the 30th Division sector. However, many of the vehicles were knocked out on August 7, so that about 100 lay abandoned and wrecked around Mortain by August 12. In spite of a few initial problems, the Americans reacted well and held out until the 2nd and 3rd Armored Divisions and the 9th and 30th Divisions broke the German spearhead with the help of smaller formations.

As the Germans failed in their bid to cut off the breakthrough, they drew back their forces. Gen. Leland Hobb's 30th Division, later nicknamed "Roosevelt's SS" by Axis Sally on Berlin radio, moved out again on August 14, advancing towards Domfront.

On August 22, Lieutenant Pulver came across a German wagon that his men had shot up. It turned out to be a paymaster's wagon that contained over $30,000 worth of French money and five cases of champagne, and it was sent back to division headquarters. As Pulver's unit advanced, the French came out to greet the triumphant soldiers.

The French people who had collaborated with the Germans didn't fare so well. Many of the men were shot and the women had their heads shaved and painted with swastikas, and were paraded, or kicked, through the streets. We did not get involved.

Most of the wells throughout the area carried skull-and-crossbones signs. When we came along, the civilians would run out to take away the signs and assure us that the water was safe. They said they had marked all the wells as poisoned to worry the Germans.

Murray Pulver was promoted to captain, and on August 29 his company was in the heat of battle once again. He personally led a supply party through enemy fire to deliver ammunition to one of his platoons and later returned with litter bearers to rescue two wounded men under intense enemy fire. He had to carry out one of the men on his back. He received the Silver Star for this daring rescue. In February 1945, he was cited once more for the Bronze Star. In July 1944, Pulver's trusted sergeant, Werner Goertz, a German American, helped him with the bazooka with which he took out his first panzer. Goertz was badly wounded outside his hometown of Aachen a few months later.

The 90th Infantry Division, reassigned to the XV Corps of the Third Army, helped close the Falaise Pocket when elements of the 1st Polish Armored Division (part of the British Second Army) met with it on August 20. The horrendous stench of dead German horses was etched forever in the memory of Pvt. William Biehler, who served in the 357th Infantry, 90th Division. Since he had entered combat in July, he had participated in several patrols. During the elimination of the Falaise Pocket, he was leading a three-man patrol when he came across a number of maps showing the location of German units, a feat that earned him the Bronze Star. He was not wounded until the campaign in Lorraine, when he was sent to a hospital in Wales. After he recovered, he was dispatched back to the front in time for the Battle of the Bulge. This time, however, he was assigned to the MP platoon of the 90th Division because he could speak German.

PFC Frank Beetle, who served with the Cannon Company of the 16th Infantry, 1st Division, was with his unit as the Falaise Pocket formed. The 1st Division had taken up position northeast of Domfort and was holding part of the southern side of the pocket. During a routine operation, he experienced the most frightening event of his life.

> The company was out of the line and had dug foxholes. I was sitting on the edge of the foxhole, reading letters from home. We were not under fire, and then I heard a shell, which, by its sound, I figured out was a large one coming from the rear. I knew from experience that it was going to be close, so I dove into the foxhole. Seconds later, the shell landed exactly where my correspondence had been, destroyed it, throwing dust all over me. Fortunately, it was a dud. Other men and officers came running to see if they could assist me. I was not injured but scared to death. I was ordered to leave the vicinity immediately, and the demolition squad was ordered up by the captain. I heard later that it was a 240-mm Canadian artillery shell and nobody ever figured out how it came to land there.

Frank Beetle was wounded later in October 1944 as the division approached Aachen and spent most of the next year in various hospitals.

The G-2 section of each division included a military intelligence interpreter (MII) team, an interrogation of prisoners of war (IPW) team, and an aerial photo interpreter (API) team for handling military intelligence operations, interrogating prisoners, and photo interpretation. First Lt. David G. Speer served with the MII team (French) of the 30th Division, which was headed by a captain and included an interpreter with the rank of first lieutenant (Speer's assignment), a master sergeant, a sergeant first class, and two tech 3s. Speer's team was to work with the local population. When his commanding officer was wounded, Speer took over the team. He arranged for crossings of French agents into enemy territory to assess enemy strength, emplacements, etc. Once, a French farmer identified a German headquarters, and his team worked with the API team to identify the actual farmhouse, "and within minutes, corps artillery had placed twelve shells on the house." Before the German counteroffensive at Mortain,

> I had, with my master sergeant, interrogated a terrified French civilian who gave me detailed information about tank buildup (apparently hundreds) east of Mortain. I got the information to my G-2 about 10:00 P.M.—but apparently, the G-3 wasn't concerned. The attack by enemy tanks toward Avranches began about 1:00 A.M. Enemy tanks approached the Division CP to within several hundred yards, and we were ordered to prepare to defend the HQ. It was a close call, but reinforcements drove the tanks back.

Speer's team also contacted several British agents dropped behind German lines who returned with codes, documents, and 134,000 francs, which were turned over to the G-2. In addition, his group, with the help of the French Resistance, recovered the bodies of several Sussex agents who had been murdered by the SS.[5]

---

5. Well before the invasion, two-man teams of French agents—probably consisting of over 100 men—had been parachuted into France.

"Acting on information from the Resistance," recalled Speer, "we dug them up (not a pretty sight), photographed their bodies, and turned them over to Graves Registration."

Lt. Kenneth Jarvis was the supply officer for the 1st Battalion, 137th Infantry, 35th Division, during the breakthrough.

One morning, I walked into the battalion CP, and the colonel looked like he had been run through a wringer. I asked him what was wrong, and he said, "I was ordered to jump-off and take a small village at the bottom of a hill." We could see German Tiger tanks moving around down there, and he said, "I delayed for two days, asking for tank destroyers to support our attack, but they finally told me to attack or I would be replaced." He said that he thought the battalion would be better off with him rather than some new man, so we jumped off. We took the village, but lost both frontline company commanders and half of the battalion doing it. Later that day, I personally saw Captain Stone with half of his side blown away from a direct hit by a tank shell. The other company commander was a first lieutenant, and he was missing in action. We never heard of him again.

Lt. Charles W. Bell, Company A, 320th Infantry, 35th Division, continued to lead his platoon during the breakthrough after surviving a full month in combat as a platoon leader.

As I remember the events of August 2, our company was moving without resistance astride a road leading to the Vire River. We descended a steep hill protected on our left by a rock wall alongside the road. The wall ended at a road intersection some 200 yards from the river. Seeing the bridge was blown,

as the lead platoon, I took my men forward to reconnoiter a crossing, while the balance of the company held fast behind the wall. Our approach was across a field of oats or barley, with the last decent cover about halfway to the river. I left my men concealed there and proceeded with a scout to the river. It looked like you could cross without swimming, so I left the scout to cover me and waded in above the blown bridge. When I got about armpit deep, I heard the scout call out, "Something is coming!" I then heard tracks clattering on the other side of the river. Knowing I couldn't make it back, I raised my carbine and froze as a German half-track pulled up to the opposite bank. The Germans stood up to look at the bridge and the road leading up the hill. One of them suddenly saw me, pointed, and yelled out. I shot him and as many others as I could when they bailed out of the vehicle.

I flipped my feet up and began swimming downstream on my back toward the bridge while firing at the half-track to hold the Germans down with one hand on the carbine and the other paddling. The scout met me at the bridge, and we took protection behind the pillars at the end of the railing. Suddenly, a German machine gun opened up on us from high up on a wooded hill across the river. He proved to be an excellent shot, pinning down my men in the field as well as us at the bridge.

During one of his bursts, I heard the half-track accelerate and looked up to see it back up on the hill, turn on the road, and start leaving. The driver had slipped into his seat, and made this maneuver without exposing himself. However, he couldn't steer without peering out, and I began firing at his helmet making it so hot he decided to abandon the

Several GIs in a jeep stop for a view of Paris's most famous landmark.

We put fire on the hill across the river, and I got the men out by crawling on their bellies in the protection of the barley.

We crossed the river after dark in a different place and moved across the face of the hill without encountering Germans. When we reached the far side, we lay down beside the trails to sleep until dawn—our first sleep in thirty-six hours.

Lieutenant Bell's quick thinking and valiant action earned him the Silver Star. The citation for the award gave a slightly different version of the events, but no less heroic.

Reconnoitering for a river crossing in advance of his platoon, a group of enemy soldiers de-trucked from a half-track vehicle within twenty-five yards of his position. Lieutenant Bell opened fire with his carbine, killing two and wounding at least one of the enemy. When the enemy returned fire and charged with fixed bayonets, Lieutenant Bell jumped into the river and, swimming on his back, continued to fire at the enemy to cover withdrawal of his scouts. After reaching the safety of the opposite bank and informing his company commander of the situation, he returned to his platoon, which had become pinned down by heavy fire from a concealed enemy machine-gun emplacement, and repeatedly exposing himself to enemy fire, skillfully led the platoon from the danger area.

moving vehicle, but when he threw open the door to jump, we got him and the half-track crashed.

We watched litter bearers under a white flag make several trips up and down the road, but the machine gun kept us still. I told the scout that the next time the gun switched from the bridge to the barley field, I was going full out up the road to the rock wall so I could start getting my men out. He wanted to go too, so we tore out. The machine gun switched back to us before we got there, and when we took stock later, the scout had a bullet hole through the crotch of his pants, and I had one through the knee of mine.

On September 24, Lieutenant Bell was cited for running through friendly artillery fire, which was falling on his company, and though wounded, radioing to have the fire lifted. He was awarded the Oak Leaf Cluster to his Bronze Star. At the end of November 1944, while still in command of Company A, he led an attack at Uberkinger, France. This time, he jumped into the water to supervise the construction of a foot-bridge and directed his men against German tanks and troops, constantly exposing himself to enemy fire. Next, he successfully deployed his men to repulse a German counterattack, destroying four vehicles, killing twenty Germans, and capturing fifteen without suffering a single loss to his unit. He received the Oak Leaf Cluster for the Silver Star for his actions.

PFC Buddy Mazarra of the 16th Infantry, 1st Division, was surrounded with his unit but found out that the firing mostly involved two American units firing at each other. On August 8, he volunteered with two comrades, Whitey Whiteside and Blackie Covotssos, for a patrol led by Lieutenant Jennings. As one of the platoons in his unit was pinned down by mortar fire, the patrol, trying to outflank the enemy, entered a small village where the inhabitants said there were no Germans. Suddenly, however, the Germans opened fire on them. They had walked into a trap. "I felt a bee sting in my right arm and didn't realize I was hit until I went to reload my gun and saw blood running down my arm," recalled Mazarra. He now had the coveted million-dollar wound, but his patrol was surrounded and there was no possibility of evacuation. Somehow, Mazarra and his companions made it back to their unit, and he was transported to a hospital in England where, three weeks later, he came face to face with his brother George, a gunner on a B-24 who had also been wounded. The wound was not enough to keep Buddy Mazarra out of action, for within a few months he returned to the front lines in time for the Battle of the Bulge.

On to Paris

Eventually, over 50,000 Germans were killed or captured at the Falaise Pocket; however, upwards of 100,000 men managed to escape before the pocket was finally closed and eliminated. Nonetheless, most of the German divisions that broke out were in poor shape and had lost a great deal of the equipment. Before long, the Allies reached and crossed the Seine River. Shortly after that, French and American troops were parading through Paris, but before they reached the capital, the German commander, Gen. Dietrich von Choltitz, was ordered by Hitler to turn the city into rubble. He refused and, by August 25, surrendered with 12,000 of the defenders shortly after. Sporadic fighting broke out between the German garrison and the FFI days before.

Lt. Thomas Cortright, wounded in June, returned to duty from England in August. Around August 14, he was assigned to Company L, 12th Regiment, 4th Division—his old unit.

We were in a rest area somewhere near the Falaise Pocket and a couple of days later we were committed, but I don't remember firing a shot. My company was the lead one and we did pick up a few prisoners, but beyond that, there was no action until August 23, when the regiment was ordered to enter Paris with the Palace of Justice as our objective. On the morning of August 25, the 3rd Battalion led the regiment, and my company was in reserve, since we had led for the last two days. We were loaded into trucks, and I mean loaded—you couldn't get another soldier and his gear onto any truck they were so full. The closer we got to the center of Paris, the more people there were lining the roadway. The trucks had to push their way through, and by the time we reached Notre Dame Cathedral, there was a girl on the truck for every guy.

Pandemonium and joy were prevalent. My company was assigned a street from Notre Dame to the Seine River facing the City Hall where there were a few Germans holding out. That didn't last long, and the city was surrendered to the French 2nd Armored Division.

We stayed in position all night with the French people milling around, and it was very difficult to control the men. The bars were open and the women free. It was tough duty, but somebody had to do it. Early on the 26th, we moved to a wooded area, and the kitchens were sent up. Shortly after noon, my company was sent out to support a group of Free French who had some Germans cornered in a manufacturing area. We did this and came back with the French parading the prisoners we had rounded up. I managed to get a flesh wound in my right upper arm, and I had several men wounded, including the 2nd Platoon sergeant.

While I was at Battalion HQ reporting on a successful mission, the Germans bombed the entire bivouac area, but I don't think there were any casualties. The next day was spent cleaning up, and I remember taking a helmet bath with the French people walking around and through the park entirely unconcerned.

Leaving Paris the next day, my company was again in the lead, and we were moving so fast I couldn't keep up. My legs turned to lead, and I would go down. We didn't have much action, and I remember it raining that first night while trying to get some rest sitting under a tree with a wet blanket wrapped around me. We continued through town where the people would be out with flowers to throw and wine to drink. This kind of war was great, but I still had my physical problems so I asked to be relieved of my company command and went to the battalion S-2 where I could ride in a jeep.

Sgt. Leonard Herb, I&R Platoon, 12th Infantry, was also among the American troops that entered Paris. "I was in the third or fourth jeep to enter Paris and proceed to Notre Dame early in the day

of August 26, 1944, and I saw De Gaulle the next day."

Lt. Peter Triolo, S-2, 1st Battalion, 12th Infantry, also took part in the occupation of Paris.

The 4th Infantry Division was parked along the main highway headed into Paris, waiting for the Free French Division [2nd French Armored Division] to pass through and enter first. After a few days, we realized what a dangerous position we were in due to the fact the French division was slow in moving forward. It was decided the 4th Division would go into Paris. As I recall, the 12th Infantry was the lead regiment going into Paris. I was assigned to duty with a patrol in front of the regiment. I had a patrol of two jeeps with my French-speaking corporal and German-speaking sergeant. So we were the first vehicle of the 12th Infantry to enter Paris. Upon entering Paris, we observed a photographer taking pictures of the troops coming in. We observed him and after an hour, I tapped him on the shoulders, and he surrendered his camera because he was taking pictures that were not authorized. Standing behind me was a major who performed the same operation on me and said, "Thank you, lieutenant; I will take that and turn it over to the general." So I had a prize souvenir for just a few minutes. I feel I was the first soldier of the 4th Division to enter Paris on August 25 or thereabout.

During the race through France, Lieutenant Triolo was wounded on a patrol that came under heavy bombardment from friendly artillery. He was hospitalized and returned to England.

According to PFC Ralph Brazee, Anti-Tank Company, 22nd Infantry, the 4th Division was moving so fast that on August 24 he "was pressed into service as a driver that night. It is not fun keeping sight of the vehicle ahead—just two red dots through the slit of our metal windshield. I had never driven a track before this, and it was the last time."

Lt. Kenneth K. Jarvis, supply officer for the 1st Battalion, 137th Infantry, 35th Division, and some of his men finally got a rest after the breakout.

> My men asked me for transportation into a nearby town, and I obtained permission and a pass for myself. In combat, we did not wear our bars signifying rank. I did not want to spend my time alone, so I went along as one of the guys. We were sitting in a bar that just happened to be in a house of ill repute, when the MPs rolled in and picked us all up. It went through my mind to drop out of the back of the 2½-ton truck while they were transporting us. However, the MPs had a jeep with armed men following. They took us into a hotel lobby for interrogation. It was rather dark in there, so I stole back into a corner and put my bars on and ran. I then contacted the sergeant in charge and told him my tale of woe. He released me, and I then proceeded to get my men released.

Troops take part in a parade in front of the Arc de Triomphe in August before continuing the pursuit of German forces withdrawing across France.

Days before the liberation of Paris, another Allied invasion force undertook Operation Dragoon, landing American and Free French troops in southern France on August 15. The race across France was on. As Paris fell, so did Marseille to Free French troops operating alongside Gen. Alexander Patch's Seventh Army, as part of Gen. Jacob Dever's 6th Army Group that advanced up the Rhone to the gates of Grenoble. In less than a month, the 6th Army Group linked up with Bradley's 12th Army Group. The airborne divisions in England had prepared for and cancelled planned jumps behind German lines as the front rapidly moved east, and it was not until mid-September that a major airborne operation could

be launched. As the advance to the Rhine finally slowed, the 82nd and 101st Airborne Divisions with the British 1st Airborne Division took part in Operation Market Garden. These divisions formed the First Allied Airborne Army, and their aircraft filled the sky on the morning of September 17, as they made a daytime drop behind German lines in the Netherlands in a bold and risky attempt to breach the Rhine, which failed. Meanwhile, elements of Bradley's 12th Army Group remained in Brittany to reduce the port of Brest and also to isolate the remaining German held ports, all well fortified, along the Atlantic coast.

The Brittany Campaign: August to September 1944

At the beginning of August, as the breakout began, the 6th Armored Division moved into Brittany not only to cut off German forces, but also to storm the coastal fortresses and take the port of Brest. On August 9, the division, having destroyed a German force at Plouvien, reached the outer defenses of Brest. According to Lieutenant Crutchfield, the division was given the sobriquet of "Brazier Boys" because it was sent to pin the Germans in Brest.

Meanwhile, Combat Command B of the 4th Armored Division advanced on the ports of Vannes and Lorient, which the Germans were determined to hold to the bitter end. When the offensive began, the 4th and 6th Armored Divisions represented half of General Bradley's total number of armored divisions. The diversion of the 6th Armored Division into Brittany was not as costly as might seem at first glance because the 5th Armored Division, reassembled after garrison duties in England and landed at Utah Beach the day Cobra began, compensated for it. On August 8, the 5th Armored Division passed through Avranches and took up positions at Le Mans. At the same time, the French 2nd Armored Division joined Bradley's 12th Army Group, further increasing the armored forces available for further penetrations. The 7th Armored Division landed on August 11 as the Battle of Mortain was drawing to a close, and two days later, it was racing toward Chartres. It was the last armored division to arrive before the Normandy campaign came to a close. The 10th Armored Division disembarked at Cherbourg on September 23 while the advance of Allied armies across France had begun to slow and efforts concentrated on Operation Market Garden.

The 2nd, 8th, 29th, and 83rd Infantry Divisions followed the 6th Armored Division into Brittany. The first three divisions went to Brest while the 83rd Division attacked St. Malô and held the base of the peninsula. The 6th Armored was the first to press the Germans back around Brest. Lt. Rodney Mortensen was at the head his artillery battalion of the 6th Armored Division as the division prepared to lay siege to Brest even before the infantry divisions arrived.

This general who got relieved of CCA [Combat Command A] had put us on the wrong side of the hill and everybody hollered about it, but he said this was where we will go. So we sat in there, and I was on one side and the infantry battalion was across the field on the other side of the road. We got in about midnight—it got dark after 11:00 P.M. and light by 4:00 A.M. That next morning, it got light, and it was foggier than all hell. At about 10:30 or 11:00, the Catholic chaplain came over to us and had mass in my unit. He had this deal on the back of his jeep, a traveling altar. All the Catholic kids went over there, and he had mass. When he finished, he came over and was talking when all of a sudden this hole appeared in the fog down to the naval defense guns at Brest. The 300-mm [280?] guns had a 360-degree traverse, and they spun them around. This first thing the Germans could see in this hole in the fog were the half-tracks sitting there that belonged to the 9th Armored Infantry Battalion. The CO of this outfit told the guys to clean their weapons. I couldn't understand that either because nobody ever pulled down all of their weapons at once, but this guy did it. Anyway, just as he did, they started shooting direct fire into the half-tracks. This is the only time in my life I stood there and watched a whole half-track go up in the air higher than a telephone pole and start to disintegrate. It looked like a great big invisible plow had gone through the field. This was our first morning and that general got cashiered. These guys came out and luckily,

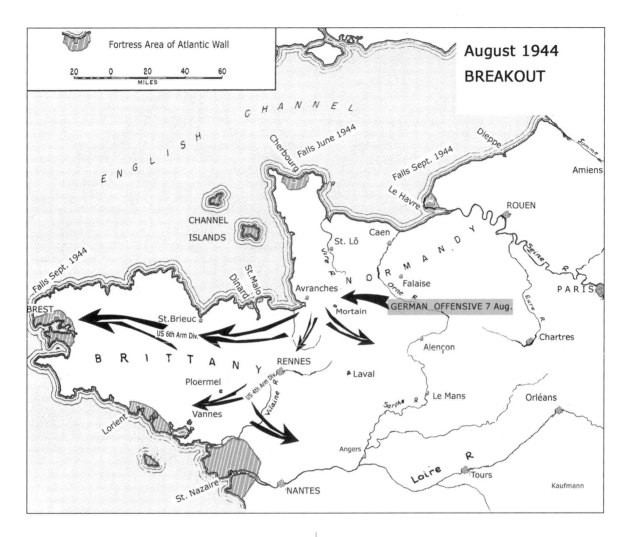

the fog didn't lift, so they couldn't see my unit or they would have got me too. We started calling fire from anything we had. The 105s gave them something to worry about, but they were all in hardened positions at Brest.

The 6th Armored Division was the only unit at Brest on the first day and then two days later we were taking eighteen tanks and split them into [groups of] six tanks and shot them like artillery. It wasn't good artillery, and it wouldn't hit much, but the Germans thought we had artillery batteries at several points. Then came the air force with 2,000 planes to soften this place up, and everybody else arrived.

When the air force came over, I went to the area I was supposed to watch on top of this big wall around Brest that was about forty feet thick. I was lying on my belly with my glasses there. I was supposed to suppress flak. When we saw flak coming, we would put artillery on it. It worked well. They started dropping 2,000-pound bombs, and it chipped the damn wall so bad I couldn't see through the glasses. It was a couple of blocks away—pretty close. This is part of the game. Anybody in artillery could calibrate with their hand. That is what I did because I couldn't see through my glasses. I called in artillery fire on the flak.

Lt. James Crutchfield of the 86th Cavalry Recon Squadron also participated in the engagements with German artillery and the aerial bombing at Brest.

I was in the HQ for a while outside of Brest, and we would get the fallout from the explosion of those big guns at Brest. During the air attack on the city, we were close enough to get a lot of the fallout from the German flak shells. We could see our aircraft making their bomb runs.

Pvt. A. B. Mirmelstein, having succumbed to combat fatigue in July, was hospitalized and later put in the rear echelon. After the breakthrough began, he was pronounced fit for action again, but he had not yet reached the 29th Division, to which he was assigned, when it fought for Vire in early August. In his diary he recorded,

August 1—was sent to 86th Replacement Depot
August 8—rejoined my old company near Vire . . . The company went into a rest area until August 15.

Four soldiers from the 79th Infantry Division enjoy a drink at a sidewalk café. NATIONAL ARCHIVES

August 15—motored to Brest on the Brittany Peninsula where we fought with the 2nd and 8th Divisions until its capture on September 20.
Sept. 26—was visited in rest area by Captain S. H. Mirmelstein, MC, had located me when he performed an operation on my wounded platoon leader.

On September 30, Mirmelstein wrote that after the fall of Brest his division loaded on boxcars and headed to Belgium via Le Mans, Paris, and Namur, reaching its destination on October 5.
First Lt. Carl A. Hobbs returned to duty with the 29th Division after recovering from the wounds he suffered in June.

The movement from Normandy to Brest was done at night with mostly the personnel arriving in 2½-ton trucks. Throughout the night of August 22, we started moving toward a new mission in a slow motor march. The convoy was miles long and included jeeps, ambulances, weapon carriers, and all kinds of vehicles. The vehicles were driven without lights; each vehicle had a rear night-light that you could see only if the vehicles maintained a close distance. The road was paved but full of artillery shell fragments, which caused a major problem—many flat tires. Driving at night single file was a maddening experience even though there was no enemy action.
We began the attack on August 25–26 about four miles northwest of the city of Brest. There was heavy fighting for five to six days, and Companies E and F had heavy casualties. Company F was involved in the fighting at Plouzane and to the south of Hill 103. After Hill 103 finally was captured, Companies E and F were again the leading companies. We were moving "aggressively" against crack German soldiers who were very skillful in fighting delaying actions.

Company F would move forward 100 to 150 yards to the next hedgerow. Captain Stevens, Company E commander, would then leapfrog forward one hedgerow. I can remember that during this time, a new officer reported to Company F, and he was assigned as a platoon leader. He was given his first order—to get ready to move his platoon forward one minute after supporting artillery and mortar began. The other forward platoon was prepared to rake the next hedgerow with rifle and light machine-gun fire. He froze. He could not give the order, and the situation was critical. Ordering him to follow me with a couple of riflemen, we jumped the hedgerow and raced to the next, followed by the men in his platoon. As we got there, we saw the Germans retreating beyond the next hedgerow. News of this incident got back to Colonel Melancon, and he gave me a hard chewing out and threatened to relieve me of F Company if it happened again.

Outside of Brest, I commanded Company F of the 2nd Battalion and was ordered to attack Fort Keranroux on the late afternoon of September 2 across a mile of open ground. We had no artillery or mortar support, and we got within rifle range of the fort when we started receiving machine-gun fire from the fort. There was a deep AT ditch about 200 or 400 yards from the fort. That is where we got when the machine guns started firing. An adjacent fort, several miles away, fired huge artillery shells. These were artillery guns designed to protect the Brest harbor. The shells didn't do a lot of damage, but they were scary because you could see these large shells at a distance, as they would come towards you. We had to wait until darkness. A routine check showed that one man was missing. He was identified, and I went with three of his buddies to search the area where they

knew he had been. We could not use a light and went through a barbed wire entanglement, crawling in the mud, until our low shouts reached him. With our raincoats and rifles, a litter was made, and we got him back to Company HQ where first aid was given and he was carried by stretcher back to the battalion aid station. It was a blow to learn the next morning that he had died.

Early the next morning, I was ordered to report to battalion HQ along with the other 2nd Battalion company commanders. Colonel Melancon and Major Wolff told us they had been ordered to lead the attack on Fort Keranroux at 0830 that morning. With the fresh knowledge of the soldier's death and the foolish attempt to take the fort the previous afternoon, I can remember asking Melancon what kind of artillery preparation and support we would have. He said he had been told it would be up to the battalion to prepare for the attack with their own smoke and mortar fire. Both Captain Stevens and I were bitterly critical, and Stevens said it was stupid and that it would be a crime to have men killed without better support. I can remember sitting on the ground cross-legged, eating cold beans out of a can, and agreeing with him. Colonel Melancon picked up the telephone and asked to speak directly with Regimental Commander Purnell. He told Purnell that he would refuse to order an attack without artillery preparation. I can remember his saying, "Have me court-martialed if you will, but you know that I am right." With good artillery and mortar preparation, including mortar smoke, the fort was captured with few if any casualties.

We spent the night in real comfort in the luxurious bunks in the fort, in greater security and comfort than we had enjoyed at any time since the beginning of the Brest campaign. I wrote a letter home that evening.

During the first day of the siege of Fort Keranroux, S.Sgt. Sherwood Hallman of Company F

ordered his squad to cover his movements by fire while he advanced alone to a point from which he could make the assault. Without hesitating, Sergeant Hallman fearlessly leaped over a hedgerow into a sunken road, the central point of the German defenses, which was known to contain an enemy machine-gun position and at least thirty riflemen. Firing his carbine and hurling hand grenades, Sergeant Hallman, unassisted, killed or wounded four of the enemy, then ordered the remainder to surrender. Immediately, twelve of the enemy surrendered, and the position was shortly secured by the remainder of the company. Seeing the surrender of this position, about seventy-five of the enemy in the vicinity surrendered, yielding a defensive organization, which the battalion with heavy supporting fires had been unable to take. This single heroic act on the part of Sergeant Hallman resulted in the immediate advance of the entire battalion for a distance of 2,000 yards to a position from which Fort Keranroux was captured . . .

Sergeant Hallman, who fell shortly after this action, posthumously received the Medal of Honor, and Lieutenant Hobbs the Silver Star. Not long after, Lieutenant Hobbs was also wounded.

On September 13, I was wounded from a burst of fire from a German submachine gun. You could recognize what it was by the sound. I received six different wounds but was still conscious. The company aid man was with me in just a matter of seconds. Litter carriers ran me to the battalion aid station, which was about a quarter of a mile behind the front. I was given morphine and strapped to a litter on a jeep and at that

point, I passed out. When I came to, I was in a field hospital; after surgery, I was evacuated to an American hospital in England for further surgery.

When I was wounded, there were about 57 men left of 187 that comprised Company F on August 25.

Lt. Robert Rideout, the commander of Company G, received a Silver Star for his actions during the battle at Fort Keranroux, and Lt. Roderick Parsch, commander of Company E, a Bronze Star. An officer candidate school graduate, Lieutenant Parsch had arrived in England in April 1944, and by September, like Rideout, he was commanding his own company. The tactics these two officers implemented to take Fort Keranroux became the textbook model for other division officers.

After taking Vire, the men of the 29th Division, including Robert Hardesty of Company A, 115th Infantry, took a short rest before they moved on.

We loaded on trucks and moved to Brest. All along the way, the French people greeted us with the V for Victory sign. Once we reached an area about eight to ten miles outside of Brest, we were unloaded and put on the right side of a three-division attack on Brest. By this time, I was a staff sergeant and pretty much in control of a platoon. There was heavy, fierce fighting right from the start.

On one occasion, we were advancing down a dirt road to attack an old farmhouse. All of a sudden, a P-51 Mustang, apparently returning to base, broke formation and laid a burst of MG [machine-gun] fire about 50 yards to our front. Figuring he did not realize we were American troops, I told everyone to take cover. We put out ID panels only to have him come back again, and this time he started firing about 100 yards to our front. All of a sudden, we heard an explosion and saw black smoke. We owe that guy our lives because he saw from the air what we could not see from the ground. It was a German tank waiting right around the bend of the road. After we got past this point, we moved on to the farmhouse only to find it was heavily defended. We lost a good second lieutenant and several men to take that place, but finally we took it with a lot of artillery and air support.

We came to an old fort called Montbarey [on the outer defenses of Brest near Fort Keranroux]. We had a difficult time taking this place. There was a sniper in there that got three men in my platoon and shot the trigger housing right out of my rifle. He had us pinned down all day until they brought in a flame-throwing tank and brought the whole place down. Once this fort was gone, we moved right along. We did not see the surrender of the fort.

What Hardesty was not aware of at the time was that troops of the German 2nd Parachute Regiment held Fort Montbarey and that additional defenses beyond the stronghold consisted of trenches, bunkers, and an antitank ditch. When the 115th Infantry attacked these outer defenses on September 13, it achieved limited success. The 121st Engineers, 29th Division, created a breach in the antitank ditch the next day as the 116th Infantry was replacing the 115th. A British squadron of Churchill Crocodile flame-throwing tanks crossed the breach made by the engineers, approached the fort, and swept it with their flamethrowers. Although the spray of flame choked the inside of the fort with heavy smoke, the Germans held out thanks to their gas masks and continued to hold back the 116th Infantry, whose men had accompanied the British tanks to the fort's moat. During the month of September, as the tanks blasted away at the fort, they partially exposed a tunnel leading from the fort to the outer side of the moat, allowing the infantry to penetrate the stronghold. During the hours of darkness on the night of September 15–16, the

engineers moved into this tunnel to a point under the wall where they placed a ton of TNT. The next morning, they detonated the charge, collapsing the fort's northern wall and forcing the Germans to surrender.

S.Sgt. William H. Lewis, HQ Company, 1st Battalion, 116th Infantry, was with his antitank unit at Vire, but as usual, he and his comrades never got a chance to use their 57-millimeter gun. When they arrived at Brest, it began to look like they might finally see some action.

[At Fort Montbarey] there was this little German paratrooper we called "Herman the German," who was always carrying his little white flag. He would go back and forth with messages.

We were firing 155-mm at the embrasures, but we never received fire from them; they just wouldn't give up. This was about midway through the battle. Eventually they surrendered. German officers with their boots all shining came out, and one of them demanded to be treated like an officer and gentleman. Somebody got killed by a booby trap down there, and Major Dobbs said that the German son-of-a-bitch who wanted to be treated like an officer and gentleman should go down there and neutralize some booby traps.

Robert Hardesty, on the other hand, witnessed the surrender of the German garrison of Brest.

After Brest fell, the German POWs rode out in a truck to a POW camp, and we had to walk. We went into Brest to search for weapons and also to see what damage our bombs had done. Much to our surprise, there were no weapons and very little damage to the sub-pens. I saw little damage done to the surface of the pens, but I didn't go inside. Two of my men had been held captive in there, and they said that with all the bombing and artillery you could hardly hear more than a thump. These men were captured in the battle of the farmhouse.

When the campaign against Brest ended and soon after the division moved into Belgium, Sergeant Hardesty was hit by mortar fire and he spent two months in a hospital in England. After he recovered, he was reassigned to the U.S. Army Air Forces' 33rd Photo Recon Group, where he worked with aerial photos.

Sergeant Lewis's memories of the surrender of Fortress Brest were somewhat different.

At Brest, they had these big guns that sounded like locomotives and *Neberwerfers*. At night, they looked like fireballs and in the day puffballs.

After the surrender of Brest, there were many prisoners. It seems they all wanted to go to America. We had a sergeant who spoke German and told them all no and that we had a deal with the Russians to send them there.

Everything was blown to hell. I saw my friend Ernest Lee again over there, and we drank a bottle of pink champagne out of canteen cups. I remember Tim Balinski had found a bunch of German 25-mm pistols and everybody thought they were harmless. One of the guys was fooling around with one, and it went off and hit Balinski right in the heart. Old Tim turned blue in the face and said, "You son of a bitch, you killed me!" He was a fine man, and we hated to lose him.

PFC John P. Montrose was with the radio section of the 2nd Battalion, 175th Infantry, 29th Division, at the time.

I was normally one member of a small group consisting of the battalion commander, Claude Melancon, Captain Dinnerman, and an artillery captain with two or three artillerymen operating radios and a fellow radioman, Ambrose Hartman. We were normally positioned somewhere immediately behind the rifle companies, but sometimes found ourselves with the rifle companies and, on a few occasions, actually ahead of them. The bulk of HQ Company was normally farther to the rear. Our wiremen, of course, normally kept up with us, providing telephone communications. Hartman and I shared carrying an SCR–300 radio, which weighed 38 pounds. The artillery people had a different type of radio. Our contact was normally with E, F, G, and H Companies, Battalion and Regimental HQ.

I recall once talking with some Rangers who had a prisoner and one man was escorting him to the rear.[6] I asked what they did with their prisoners since they seemed to be widely dispersed. They told me they traded them to the French farmers for fresh eggs, and the farmers put them to work on the farms. The going price was one dozen eggs per prisoner.

We were on the outskirt of Brest when I first noticed this unusual GI. I never learned his name, or his outfit, though I suspect he was from Company E. He was coming up a trail escorting three prisoners, and he had been wounded in one arm. The prisoners were interrogated, then sent to the rear. Medics bandaged the GI's arm, and he headed back down the trail toward the city. A short while later he appeared again, coming up the trail with a larger group of pris-

---

6. The 5th Ranger Battalion operated on the right flank of the 29th Division during the attack, and it advanced against three of the coastal forts, which fell on September 3 and 5 with few problems. After that, the battalion joined the 2nd Ranger Battalion, reducing the German positions on the nearby Le Conquet Peninsula and eliminating the German 280-millimeter coastal battery named *Graf Spee*.

oners. He had again been wounded, as I recall, this time in the leg. The same story, interrogate the prisoners and bandage the GI's wound. About this time, the colonel was trying to organize a small party to go into the city and discuss surrender under a white flag. He had it pretty well organized except the FFI guys refused to go. The colonel asked me if I knew where he could get a bottle of cognac. I told him our wounded GI with all the prisoners apparently had a supply somewhere and I could work on him. Sure enough, he left for a short time and returned with a full bottle. I gave the bottle to the colonel who started priming the FFI boys. The GI once again went down the trail toward the city. He was gone a little longer this time but returned with about twenty prisoners. He had again been wounded, this time in the shoulder, and by now could hardly navigate. He again turned over his prisoners. He was going to make another trip when the colonel ordered him to go to the aid station and told me to take him to make sure he was evacuated to the hospital. I never saw him after that day.

When I returned from the aid station, the cognac bottle was empty and the FFI boys were ready to go. They went down the trail with a couple of white flags but accomplished nothing.

Immediately after the surrender, our battalion was loaded on trucks and moved out. Some may have wandered through the city collecting souvenirs, but not our group. We were taken to the coast. It was a treeless sandy area with dirt trails and thousands of German signs designating minefields. Our company was deposited near some sort of old fortification with a moat. I don't know why we were directed to the moat; however, it was dry, never intended to hold water, and provided some protection in the

Self-propelled 105-millimeter howitzer on the moved.
JAMES M. CRUTCHFIELD

event of an unlikely air attack. About fifteen of us had descended into the moat single file and keeping our distance. I passed a window at ground level and was tempted to walk over and look through it, but the fellow ahead of me had already rounded the corner of the building, so I hurried to catch up. A little fellow from the wire section followed me. As I rounded the corner, there was a large explosion. The fellow behind me had gone to look in the window and detonated a mine. He would live but had lost a leg from the knee down and had other injuries. What a waste, after the shooting had stopped! We all retraced our footprints out of the moat and then we were transported to an area, which was supposedly clear of mines.

Like the others, PFC Albert Bartelloni, 3rd Battalion, 175th Infantry, remembered well the operations of the 29th Division against Brest.

My duties were, as always scout, patrols, and observation post. For about one week, I was a member of night patrols between our division and the 8th Division. There was a gap between our divisions. It had to be patrolled to ensure no German infiltration. We had a couple of Free French guiding us through the countryside because of their knowledge of the area. Our positions were constantly pounded by the German coastal guns, which were turned from seaward to attack our positions. These huge armor-piercing shells left some really large gaping holes in the ground. We had some heavy casualties because of this shelling.

One funny incident happened the same night we took Brest. Four of us took up residence in one of the hotels in town. We actually got hold of a fine-looking bed. Of course, we left our clothes on, and all four of us used the one bed. We all had a very restful and peaceful sleep. One catch, the next day, we realized we had to pay a dear price for having the comfort of that bed, we were eaten alive by bed bugs and had to use DDT powder that whole day. We departed the next day on trains for Belgium.

What T/5 Walter Condon, 121st Engineers, 29th Division, remembered best about Brest were the supplies at the submarine pens.

We liberated a lot of German supplies; beautiful gallon cans of dates and figs, which we found excellent to eat because we were on K and C rations since the invasion. We got gallon cans full of cigars, and I remember sending some home to my father. Then we also liberated pieces of big canned herring in tomato sauce, and that was good. All these things came from Spain. We also got cases of sardines in regular sardine oil, and we tried eating them in different ways. Eventually, we got to the point we tried cooking them in their own oil over a campfire and that was the most God-awful thing—we only tried that once.

The 8th Infantry Division moved into Brittany to join the 29th and 2nd Divisions in the attack on Brest, taking up a position between those two divisions. It began its advance on Brest on August 24, and on September 10, it lay siege to Fort Bouguen, one of the of the city's oldest forts, dating back to the seventeenth century.

Brest was the last campaign for PFC John F. Troy of Company E, 13th Infantry, 8th Division. On about August 18, his company was trucked from Rennes to Brest. The 13th Infantry stood before Hill 88, near the town of Keranchosen, a key point on the drive toward Brest. As the 2nd Battalion first tried to infiltrate the German lines, the 1st and 2nd Battalions engaged in close fighting for Hill 88 (named for all its guns, not its elevation), which they took on the night of August 26. During the night of August 29, the battalions attempted to infiltrate the enemy positions. The fighting got heavy the next morning as the Germans threw in tanks, including a captured Sherman. Companies E and G became isolated and Company F, in reserve, could not break through to them. Most of the troops were captured. Private First Class Troy was among the few men who eluded capture.

We started the attack on August 24 and left the line of departure at about 10:00 without any kind of artillery or support. I don't think the Jerries saw us or expected us that night, but when it got light, we were far from the main line of the Germans. If we had an hour more of darkness to infiltrate, we could have been right below Hill 88 where Jerry had his trenches and pillboxes.

When the firing started, we knew we were seen. We came up to a farmhouse and a barn and moved right of the buildings because there were some young trees and other wooded growth to sneak through. We came to the edge of the wood line. I had to make about a ten-yard dash across a stone path running to our right. There was a fair-sized ditch on the other side of the path, and if I could make that, I would come up to the right on a pillbox in front or on top of the hill. But there must have been another machine gun covering this one farther to the right, which should have been the 29th Division sector. He must have fired just as I was ready to jump in the ditch. The bullets hit the stone path and ricocheted up, one hit me in the thigh and followed my hip bone, cutting the tendons of my right thigh muscles. It then cut a path to my rump, exiting my ass. If those bullets had hit me straight on, I would have been a hopeless cripple. One other hit the inside of my forearm and another smashed my finger on the right hand. It was what they call a million-dollar wound. I couldn't get up because it was like getting hit with a baseball bat. I looked over and saw my rifle stock must have caught one too; it was torn up just back of the trigger. I started to crawl back on the stone path towards the farm building. A sniper picked me up, and every time I would crawl, he let one fly. He was either a crack shot playing with me, or he was the worst shot. I believe the former. I got back to the barn; a guy from 1st Platoon carried me into the barn. It was nearly full.

I was sent back to England eventually, where I had two operations to tie up my tendons. The doctors marked me limited service, so I wasn't sent back to the 13th. I had had enough after fifty-five days.

PFC John McBurney was with the mortar platoon of Company D, 2nd Battalion, 13th Infantry, during the campaign.

We had been told it [Brest] was lightly defended and would be taken in about

three days. We fought over a month to take the place. Our mortars were limited to a maximum of three to six rounds a day because, so we were told, the Longshore-man's Union of Harry Bridges was on strike and refused to load ammunition on our ships. Since then, I have had no use for unions. They placed their greed ahead of our urgent need for ammunition.

The enemy did not seem to have such shortages, especially in 88-mm ammunition. This was a most terrible weapon. If you heard the sound of the gun firing, you knew you were safe, for the shell itself flew on a flat trajectory faster than the speed of sound, and the thing had either hit you or was past you when the sound reached you.

One morning, I was relieving a man named McQuarrie in an OP located in the second story of a farmhouse when an 88 round came through the wall and killed the man I was replacing. As our names sounded somewhat alike, it was reported back to our company HQ that McBurney was the man killed. I happened to get back just as the report was about to be sent back to my family that I was KIA. When I returned to where our guns were set up, my buddy Dave Minton was white as he could be when he saw me and exclaimed, "Hey, McBurney, you're dead!" He then explained the situation to me, and I went to the CO and straightened things out.

Once, when we were moving forward to make an attack, the man in front of me was hit through the chest area, making a hole that I saw through for an instant as he continued walking a couple of steps before he fell dead.

We had a problem with our own air force. We were repeatedly strafed and dive-bombed by our own fighter planes, even though we had bright recognition panels laid out. I will never forget the sight of the nose of a fighter plane headed my way, and the bomb sliding away from its belly, seemingly right at me. A foxhole could never be deep enough for one to feel safe under this. Life in the area during the battle was one terror after another.

The 2nd Infantry Division also took part in the Brest campaign, operating on the left flank of the 8th Division, and completing the land encirclement of the city. PFC A. J. Hester, Service Battery, 12th Field Artillery, ran supplies for his unit.

When I was the command car driver with HQ, I drove into exposed areas like crossroads to draw enemy fire, hoping to get the CO killed because he was worthless. He would try to hide under the seats. At Brest, I was put back in the ammunition section. They had different ammo dumps. Sometimes you would go twenty-five miles. They were run by the QM [quartermaster]. They had gasoline by the thousands of drums, ammo, just a mass of supplies. I remember, during the breakthrough, we couldn't keep up with the guns for supply. We loaded the trucks. There was a driver and assistant driver in each truck, and we had a sergeant who didn't do anything. When you had your truck loaded, you moved away and the next one came in, and you went back and helped load the other guy's vehicle. There might be ten men loading.

My brother was a gunner in Battery B, and they were busy firing. They didn't do any of the unloading, we did.

T/4 Alex J. Ziese served in the orderly platoon of the headquarters of the 2nd Infantry Division.

Our normal routine was unloading trucks and stuff like that when they set up the HQ, but we didn't set it up. The clerks and others did that. We took care of the officers' things: clothing and like that. In HQ, about every four or five officers would have one man assigned to put up his bed, shine his shoes, and things like that. We cleaned out buildings and even the latrines, but we never did guard duty. During the breakout and drive to Brest, no one picked up souvenirs because we were afraid of booby traps—kick a can, and it might be mined! Most of the time we slept in a foxhole while the officers slept in a tent. We never had any casualties because we were ten to fifteen miles behind the lines, and the only time they ever called us up to fight was during the Battle of the Bulge.

The orderly platoon was not part of the table of organization and equipment for a division, it was created for the convenience of the officers, using enlisted men that should have been assigned elsewhere in the division.

In mid-September at Vannes and Lorient, the 6th Armored Division relieved Combat Command B of the 4th Armored Division, which rejoined its own division. In late August after the 83rd Division captured St. Malô, it took over the siege of St. Nazaire. In the meantime, the remaining divisions of Middleton's corps replaced the 6th Armored Division in the assault on Brest. The 6th Armored Division moved back to take over the siege of Lorient. Lt. Rodney Mortensen's artillery battalion found itself in the thick of this action.

We moved to Lorient after other divisions took over at Brest. I got in a hell of a firefight in an apple orchard when I arrived at Lorient. It was the only time I ever saw anybody shot where he had a piece of his gut out the front. It came out of his front side and looked like a bicycle tube, and I didn't know what to do with it so I rolled it all up, laid it on top, put it back, and sprinkled lots of sulfur powder. We called for an ambulance, and damned if he wasn't back for duty in three months!

I got a big flag there and all kinds of medals and other stuff, but in the meantime, we got a mortar hit, which peppered the hell out of us. We looted the hell out of things, and we had to walk about ten miles carrying old Pritchard who got hit in the leg. Somebody had to walk alongside because you couldn't put a tourniquet on him; it was too high up. So all we could do was put a finger up there and squeeze tight, and it still leaked like a sieve. Boy, did he bleed! He must have leaked gallons. We finally got him back, and he went to somewhere in England. He was one of our officers in the 212th.

Lt. James Crutchfield served in the Recon Squadron of the division's 86th Cavalry during the battle for Lorient.

Later we moved down to Lorient, which had become a training ground—a baptism of fire for people moving up to the front. They would shoot at the Germans and the Germans would shoot back and neither side would hurt each other, but it would give the Americans a baptism of fire.

This scenario was repeated time and again as the Americans laid siege to the German fortresses along the Atlantic coast. After they took Brest, the Allies lost interest in capturing any of the German-held ports on the Atlantic seaboard because they realized that the enemy did not surrender before laying waste to the facilities. The qualified victory did not justify the number of casualties.

From Lorient, the 6th Armored Division moved on to Orleans on the Loire, and Lieutenant Mortensen drove into Blois.

We hit the Loire at Blois, and I liberated the city and got twenty-seven truckloads of liquor. We hit the Loire at Blois, and there was a railroad track. The Germans had left a man with one round of AP [armor-peircing], and he had an 88 over in a field, waiting for something to come by. My boss, Bill Colton, was going up over this track in his command track; he got on top of the railroad track, and this guy cut loose and hit the rear idler just as square as could be on the back of the half-track. It knocked out the tracks, and everything just stopped. I was dawdling along half asleep—I was about a quarter of a mile behind him—when all of a sudden, I looked up at this thing and I heard this round go off. I didn't pay too much attention to that because it didn't explode or anything, it just stopped. Guys came out of the vehicle like jacks out of a box. I mean when they jumped out you never saw anybody jump out faster in your life.

I sent trucks with liquor to everyone's outfit. I liberated Blois and slept in the Duke of Blois's bed that first night. We stacked the liquor two cases high on the side.

CHAPTER 9

Normandy and Beyond

July–August: Nondivisional Combat Units

The supporting nondivisional combat units, which advanced with the combat divisions, were usually attached to them from the corps or army command. These units, which served in the frontlines, included a variety of units from Ranger battalions to armor and artillery units. Among these units was the 86th Chemical Mortar Battalion, one of several nondivisional mortar battalions sent to Normandy. It was a corps-level unit whose companies attached to other units on numerous occasions. Immediately after landing in Normandy on June 29, the battalion was attached to the VIII Corps. It supported the 2nd Infantry, 8th Infantry, 29th Infantry, 79th Infantry, 82nd Airborne, 83rd Infantry, and 90th Infantry Divisions during the following month. On July 6, the battalion was reorganized so that its men could be rotated to the rear for rest. During the breakout, the battalion moved into Brittany, where it supported actions at St. Malô, Dinard, Rennes, and Fortress Brest.

Weeks after the invasion, the trip across the Channel to France was still a risky business. For 1st Lt. Warren B. Hinchcliff, Company B, 86th Chemical Mortar Battalion, a Mississippian commissioned from ROTC, the crossing was not devoid of excitement.

Company B was selected to take the ammunition that was available and leave first. The whole battalion didn't leave at the same time. We loaded at Southampton on the Liberty ship *James A. Farrell* and sailed in a convoy of over a dozen ships. We were two-thirds of the way to Utah Beach when we received an alert of an air raid, and everyone went belowdecks when we learned it was a submarine alert. About that time, two of the ships in front of us were hit in the stern, and we could see this happen since everybody came piling out of the hole as quickly as they could to get back on deck. Before the last people cleared the hold, our ship blew. We got hit in the stern by a torpedo or an acoustic mine right in front of the screw. It blew the hatch covers out and into the sea. One of our people dropped back into the hold, and another was critically hurt belowdecks. The three ships were all hit astern. An LST came alongside and they lashed a companionway across from the railing and we began passing the wounded over; then we crossed. This leaky LST was our transport back to Plymouth. The *James A. Farrell* was hauled back in by the navy about a day and a half later with the stern down. All the equipment was taken off and put on the beaches. We had to go back to army depots and get everything again from scratch. That took about two weeks. Meanwhile, the rest of the battalion had gone out the following day.

We finally loaded on an LST and went back over. All our equipment was loaded so we could drive off the boat. We got in at about 11:00 at night. They rammed it up at high tide. We sat and waited until morning until the tide went out so we could drive right onto the beach. They rushed us inland as fast as they could, and we only had one guy take the wrong turn. The MPs wanted him to abandon that truck, but we defied them and took the time to turn him around. We eventually got to Ste-Mère-Église and joined them.

Second Lt. John B. Deasy from San Francisco, drafted two years earlier at age thirty-one, was serving with HQ Company, 86th Chemical Mortar Battalion, at the time.

We sailed just like Company B. About 4:00 in the afternoon, I was down in the no. 5 hold on a bunk sleeping, and something half woke me up, like an explosion. Then a second explosion woke me all the way up and I heard running around up on the deck and hollering, so I ran up to see what was going on in time to see the third ship get hit. Six ships in the convoy got hit. The next day when I was up on deck, I met the mate of the ship and got to talking to him. He told me our captain saw the mine in the water and shut off the engines and coasted over it. We were lucky!

So we spent the night off of Utah Beach, and the next morning, I went ashore by LST. They loaded all our equipment. My jeep was loaded onto an LST, and I was on it with all my people. We just drove ashore and kept on going until we found our bivouac area. One or two days later, we went into action. The first day, the first sergeant of Company D came in and gave me a list of casualties: four dead and eight wounded. Soon our men learned to get down in their foxholes, and we had only

246 THE AMERICAN GI IN EUROPE IN WORLD WAR II

forty deaths in the battalion in the whole war.

Second Lt. Fred F. Assmann from Buffalo, New York, served as an assistant platoon leader in Company B, which meant that he served as a forward observer on an alternating basis with the other assistant platoon leaders. When his battalion went into action early in July, his men fired a few rounds at the Germans, who reposted immediately, often killing a couple of men. After those first weeks, life on the front became more bearable. At the time of the breakthrough, Assmann was still a forward observer. "We were trying to keep up with the forward people and we kept laying mile after mile of wire, but you could never keep up with them because they were moving fast."

First Lt. L. Benjamin Jr. from Darlington, South Carolina—another draftee and graduate of OCS of the same age as Deasy—arrived as a replacement for 1st Lt. Ralph Vigliotti's Company D, the 86th Chemical Mortar Battalion.

I was a replacement from the U.S., and it was the best thing that ever happened to me. I had the heavy weapons mortar platoon in an infantry company—a 90-mm mortar.

Before we went into combat, we had to have a physical exam. They got us up—a whole packet of lieutenants—and asked us to stand there. I was first in line. I walked in; there was a colonel sitting down there, and I saluted him. He said, "Good morning, lieutenant, how do you feel?" I said, "Fine, sir!" I stood there, and he said to move on since there were others to be examined!

We crossed in a convoy of over 100 ships. When we landed, I remember everyone was throwing their gas mask away. At Ste-Mère-Église, they had a meat market with flies flying all over and long loaves of bread stacked on the floor. I went to a replacement depot

somewhere out of town. They called me in one night and asked if I knew about the 4.2-mm mortar. I said I had never seen one, but they said I should be able to handle it. Lieutenant Deasy came down, picked me up, and took me to the battalion.

During the breakthrough at Avranches, the 86th fired over 11,500 rounds in support of five divisions of the VIII Corps. After the massive bombing at St. Lô, which launched Operation Cobra, Lieutenant Deasy "wondered how anything could stand up to it, but when we went through St. Lô you saw it didn't get flattened." According to Lt. Warren B. Hinchcliff of Company B,

Prior the bombing of St. Lô, things were pretty tight. When St. Lô occurred, the whole battalion just began to move. We moved in about three streams of traffic down the main road to Avranches, bumper to bumper. The Air Corps did kill an enormous number of horse-drawn artillery units heading south to Avranches. We came across a lot of dead horses. The horses that were not dead were in the French farmers' homes hidden away so they could use them later on.

Lieutenant Vigliotti "was astounded by the amount of horse-drawn equipment the Germans had in Normandy." Apparently, many American officers did not realize how heavily the German army relied upon horse-drawn units because war films, including the informational films of the Signal Corps, always focused on the Germans' highly mechanized army. Hinchcliff's unit "went to Rennes and then back up to Dinant–Dinard area, where a mad colonel held the little island off the coast of St. Malô."

The 86th Chemical Mortar Battalion took part in the bombardment of Dinard and St. Malô.

An M1 40-millimeter automatic gun from the 430th AAA AW Battalion. FRED BEWERSDORF

Colonel Bachere, in charge of the defense of Dinard, ordered his troops to fight to the end. However, the bombardment, which included napalm bombs, forced the garrison to surrender on August 14 after only two days of engagement. The fortified island of Cézembre under the command of Lieutenant Seuss, did not give up until September 2. The 86th Chemical Mortar Battalion also took part in the bombardment of the Citadel of St. Malô, firing white phosphorus rounds on August 15 as aircraft dropped napalm. The fort surrendered that day. A party of two officers and two enlisted men from the battalion were sent to accept the surrender of Colonel Andreas von Auloch, the "mad colonel," at the Citadel. During this campaign, between August 1 and August 15, the battalion fired over 7,000 rounds. By August 17, it reached the city of Rennes.

We spent a couple of days there and then headed out for Brest. The trip to Brest was uneventful except for people hitting us with onions on the way. They were just hilariously happy, and that was all they had to shower us with. We did not take part in the Brest Campaign, but Company C did. We were only strafed one or two times by German planes when we got to Brest.

When Brest surrendered, we drove in and went down to the sub-pens to take a look. They were massive concrete fortifications, and we were intrigued by all the supplies in them. We helped ourselves to hundreds and hundreds of blankets since it was beginning to get cool.

During operations, we had an assistant in each platoon and that served as the FOs [forward observers] for the company on a rotation basis. They were second lieutenants and generally assigned as FOs. Occasionally, they had an enlisted man with them.

During combat, we used small amounts of white phosphorus and only for things like a smokescreen or to deliberately burn up a target. My company knocked out two American tanks at Brest, which the Germans had captured and were using. One was hit with white phosphorus[1] and the other with HE. The one was set on fire, and we blew the tracks from the other. At Brest, we lost some people to land mines in my company.

During the attack on Brest, Lieutenant Vigliotti and his men "were bogged down; the 2nd Rangers came through our company area, crawled in, and attacked the Germans with hands and grenades." Meanwhile, the Germans used their heavy artillery for coastal defense to fire on American positions.

Some of the ammunition of these big guns was faulty. I remember quite a number of their shots ricocheting off the slope and not going off, but tumbling through the air. One of them landed next to an ammunition pile of Company B. We dragged it into a hole so we could go back and move our ammunition elsewhere.

HQ Company included the mess sergeant and cooks and provided the only hot meals, but the mortar companies were usually too far away to receive the fruit of their labors. During the Brest campaign, "HQ Company was located in a cow pasture near the village of Le Drennec for what

seemed to be about six weeks. . . . We didn't worry about anything, we just pitched our tents out there and occupied the place like we were on vacation and made friends with the people in the village."

For Lieutenant Assmann, the Brest campaign was no vacation because, as a forward observer, he was up front. One day, as he was trying to locate a German position, an enemy shell fragment gouged out part of the stock of his carbine and inflicted minor scratches to the men around him. A German officer calmly walked out of the position and stood, looking about him, yet no one from the American side took a shot at him.

Lieutenant Vigliotti, whose company was supporting the 8th Infantry Division when truce was declared, was surprised at the large number of women the Germans employed. As Lieutenant Hinchcliff was passing a POW stockade, one of the prisoners called out in English, "Lieutenant, have you got a cigarette?" Surprised to hear the man speak such good English, Hinchcliff stopped to find out about the man. It turned out that the prisoner was a taxi driver in New York who had been trapped in Germany when the war began and who had been drafted willy-nilly into the German army.

The companies of the 86th Chemical Mortar Battalion, which had also supported the 2nd and 29th Divisions at Brest, received a well-deserved week of rest after the battle. They had taken casualties at Brest, mainly from land mines. After that week of respite, the battalion joined the XII Corps and reached the vicinity of Metz and Lunéville in Eastern France by October. From there, it proceeded to Belgium.[2] The battalion shuttled from one part of the front to another and joined the Battle of the Bulge in December.[3]

Among the many types of nondivisional units that filled important combat-support functions

1. The German prisoners called white phosphorus the "Whispering Death."

2. During the Battle of the Hurtgen Forest, it was, for the first time, assigned to support a single division.

3. During the Battle of the Bulge, Lieutenant Benjamin's company commander pulled the company out of the unit to which it was attached, transferring it near the 2nd Division headquarters, a move that spared it from being captured.

were the automatic antiaircraft weapons battalions that were assigned to antiaircraft artillery groups, attached to corps, or sometimes directly to divisions. Several times during the campaign in July and August, their weapons were not only turned against infantry, but also against enemy tanks.

One of these battalions, the 430th Anti-Aircraft Artillery (Automatic Weapons) Battalion, sailed for Omaha Beach on June 9 and finished unloading on June 13. On June 14, its four batteries were deployed near Isigny to provide support for the XIX Corps. The battalion first engaged the *Luftwaffe* on June 20 when it shot down an Fw-190. The next day, it was attached to the VIII Corps. It was hit several times by German 88s. Battery A shot down an Me 109 on July 14 and another on July 19. On August 2, the battalion moved from Carentan to the St. Lô area, where it was attached to the 18th Anti-Aircraft Artillery Group. Battery D defended three bridges near St. Lô.

The 430th Anti-Aircraft Artillery (Automatic Weapons) Battalion landed at Omaha Beach on D+5, a Sunday morning, and was soon attached to the V Corps. While its 40-millimeter towed guns with .50-caliber machine guns came ashore on the same day, its half-tracks did not arrive until two weeks later. Among the men of the battalion was Pvt. Edward A. Trennert, a twenty-one-year-old draftee from Chicago who came ashore on D+5, after transferring from his ship to a Rhino barge. His truck was the second to drive off the ramp and was greeted by sniper fire during the next few days.

After June 14, the 430th Anti-Aircraft Artillery (Automatic Weapons) Battalion was transferred to General Corlett's XIX, which had just been activated, in order to provide it with field artillery protection. Private Trennert and his comrades, who did not realize that the enemy guns were so close, "almost jumped out of our skins" the first time they fired. Although the *Luftwaffe* brought additional aircraft to Normandy after the invasion, it did not provide much support for the German

The 86th Chemical Mortar Battalion

The 86th Chemical Mortar Battalion was organized into four lettered companies (A, B, C, and D). Its headquarters supported all four companies even though they were usually assigned to a different division. Each company operated almost like an independent company. Each mortar company consisted of three platoons, whose assistant platoon leaders served as forward observers for the company on a rotating basis. In addition to the six lieutenants in the platoons, there was a lieutenant who was the company executive officer and a captain who was the company commander. The battalion's headquarters company usually set up near corps headquarters and supply depots since the battalion's mortar companies could be with a different combat division.

The men of the unit had no training with chemical weapons and never fired white phosphorus rounds until they were stationed in Wales, where they had to fight moor peat fires that they accidentally started. In France, they had no chemical shells with them.

The battalion's fire missions were always in support of a battalion or regiment in preparation for an attack. The effective range of the 4.2-inch mortar was about 5,500 yards, so a platoon or the entire company had to advance virtually on the heels of the attacking infantry. Each platoon of the battalion had to provide for its own security.

troops on the ground. Few sorties actually broke through the Allied air umbrella and reached Allied lines from June through August. According to Edward Trennert, the enemy's aircraft were seldom able to strike the vehicles, equipment, supplies, and men, on the terribly congested roads of Normandy, and the antiaircraft artillery (automatic weapons) battalions had few opportunities to demonstrate their firing skills.

The 430th AAA AW Battalion was located at Beuzeville-la-Bastille.

The village of Beuzeville-la-Bastille was on top of a cliff. The Germans had flooded the valley below.[4] There was only one causeway the Allies could cross in the area. We were right on top of the cliff there, overlooking the valley to give protection. I remember the small field overlooking the causeway, and next to us the little church and a cemetery. The church bell was ringing. After a while, we became suspicious because we were there for several weeks and nothing was moving; we were at a standstill, and nothing was moving up. You could hear the enemy 88 when the shells were coming in with a whistle. Eventually, the enemy shells started coming closer to our positions. We had our gun about fifty feet away from our slit trenches, and some of us slept on top of the ground. Some were in the tent [tents that were made from the shelter halves each man carried]. The MG [machine gun] was in a vegetable garden on the side of the hedgerow and our 40-mm overlooked the causeway.

On June 29, Private Trennert was at his gun and Pvt. Henry Kozar was assigned to the belt when they came under attack.

That morning, I was on duty. All of a sudden, on June 29 the Germans started shelling us and came very close, and the shell stopped whistling. It must have had our name on it. We knew it was coming in and knew it hit because we could see the smoke and smell the gunpowder. What had happened was it hit right on the hedgerow and shrapnel usually goes upward and this time it came down into the tent and the foxholes. We didn't know what happened for a few minutes. Then we heard a scream and a cry, and it was a man named Kenneth McClure; he was one of our regular guys. He was in his foxhole and was hit in the groin by shrapnel. He was screaming. We were wondering about Cpl. Richard L. Nason and went to his foxhole. He got hit by a small piece of shrapnel in his head, and he didn't have his helmet on because he was sleeping. He died instantly. I did help carry him out, put him on the weapon carrier, and went with him to our Battalion HQ where a lieutenant took him.[5]

When Private Kozar reached the gun, his back was bloody from shrapnel wounds. He had been hit in the tent where he had been sleeping when the first 88 rounds began coming in. When Private Trennert returned to the tent after the bombardment, "it was full of shrapnel holes, the tent pole was cut in half, and the gas masks we used as a pillow were full of holes. The good Lord was with me." There were more shellings during the early part of the campaign. Trennert survived them all, remaining with the battalion until the end of the war.

Private Trennert's unit routinely manned the guns from dawn until dusk.

---

4. A causeway crosses the flooded area on the north side of the Douve River and joins the causeway leading to the Merderet River and Chef-du-Pont. This is in the area where the paratroopers of the 82nd Airborne Division fought so hard after their night landing.
5. Pvt. Henry Kozar, Pvt. Kenneth McClure, and Pvt. Carleton Williamson were seriously wounded, and Cpl. Richard L. Nason was killed. All belonged to Private Trennert's gun crew, 1st Platoon, Battery C.

American infantry entering St. Malo.

We never fired at night because every one of our shells was a tracer and you couldn't see anything at night, so we were up at the break of dawn. The *Luftwaffe* would come in at dawn or dusk and were hard to see at that time. The Me 109s usually came in at higher altitudes and the Fw 190s at lower. Then there was Washing Machine Charlie, who would come in at night.

PFC Fred W. Bewersdorf, who had joined the army in 1943 and had turned down the opportunity for a deferment at a critical job, was also with the 430th Anti-Aircraft Artillery (Automatic Weapons) Battalion, serving Battery A.

Prior to daybreak on June 8, I found out we had anchored at the wrong beach-head—Utah. The anchor was stuck, and the merchant seamen were placing a tent over the anchor chain in preparation to torch cut the chain. We finally arrived at Omaha Red Beach, but we were waved off. I guess we missed our unloading time. We remained aboard ship in the harbor under some shelling and night air attacks. On or about June 11, I observed Navy gunners shooting at planes that I identified as British Spitfires and Hurricanes. The next morning, a large yacht cruised in the area, berating personnel on the misidentification of aircraft. On June 12, equipment was offloaded to a Navy LCT. There was a problem about not having a crane operator, so a soldier who had done this type of work in civilian life took over.

I clambered down a landing net with a full pack. We lost two soldiers who fell and injured themselves. We then went to the beach and drove ashore. It was raining, but I could see many American and German casualties waiting to be evacuated. One soldier went souvenir hunting, and he was injured by a booby trap. For the invasion, our gun crew was reduced to nine from twelve personnel. The residue left behind in England caught up with us on June 26.

Two men were wounded by snipers after landing, and they were evacuated. One of them, PFC Helmkamp, later died in a hospital.

I was in gun crew Helen, no. 8.

On June 14 at Isigny or St. Pellerin our crew was under sniper fire from the far corner of a hedgerow. We fired rifle grenades and had our machine gunner spray the area but did not investigate the results. Just before dark, I noted infantry troops moving up on a narrow road between hedgerows. They were young, cocky, talkative, and seemed self-assured. I saw these same depleted troops returning from the line three days later, and they appeared haggard, morose, and very quiet.

On June 15, I was crawling on my stomach next to a hedgerow, probing with my bayonet ahead for mines prior to moving the gun to a better position. That evening just after dark, the crew became aware of muffled German voices coming from the road on the other side of the hedgerow. We chose not to intercept the patrol. Gun crew no. 7 intercepted them and suffered two casualties.

On June 16, enemy aircraft were active over our area most of the night. They dropped antipersonnel butterfly bombs[6]— no sleep that night!

On June 18, while moving our gun to a new position, a jeep with General Bradley sitting in the passenger seat drove up behind the halted convoy. I was standing by the gun carriage and had a heavy beard because of the face rash I received from the impregnated clothing. He asked me how it was going, how I felt, and if we could see anything. I mentioned a shortage of ammo and rations and that the 10-in-1 rations were getting tasteless and monotonous. The next day, we were delivered a burlap sack containing twelve loaves of round GI white bread and ammo.

We also apprehended two oriental, very nondescript soldiers who had been firing at us. I turned them over to our staff sergeant, who happened to come by in a jeep. We placed one on each fender, and he and I hauled them to the MPs. The MPs refused to accept them and said, "They are your Allies," so we released them. I told the MPs, Allies or not, if they come back and harass us again, they had it.

We had plenty of hard cider, Calvados, and cognac on June 21 at Pont-l'Abbé. Our position on the riverbank was near a bridge, and when subjected to intense shelling, the guards and medical attendants at a nearby asylum let the mental patients freely roam the area. Cows roaming freely in the area caused communication problems by chewing on the ground lines. Checking the lines one day, I had the line in my hand when I spotted a booby trap. The line was attached

---

6. This was the *Luftwaffe's* SD-2A (or the SD-2B), a small 4.4-pound bomb that had a case that opened when dropped to form wings. The bombs were carried in various size containers that held from 6 to 108 of the bombs. They were classified as semi-armor piercing.

NORMANDY AND BEYOND 253

to the pin of a buried German potato-masher hand grenade.

Another time, I was in a small rowboat at this position using German hand grenades and blocks of TNT to stun and collect fish. I became the subject of mortar and rifle fire—German I assume—and I went over the side and swam mostly underwater to shore. I then crawled to my slit trench.

On July 15, at Ste-Marie-du-Mont, the section shot down an Me 109. I was knocked unconscious at this position by concussion when sitting alone in the gun pit with telephone equipment to my ear. It was dusk and raining hard and the next thing I remember was getting up from the mud in the pit. My steel helmet with liner had been knocked off, and I was bleeding from a cut in my head. We had been and were being shelled heavily here. I still do not know what happened.

On July 25, after the big American air attack, we experienced a gas attack scare when a civilian on a bicycle came pedaling by yelling, "Gas! Gas!" I never did find a gas mask since I had discarded mine on the beach.

As we advanced on August 2, we saw many dead German soldiers and heavy destruction. Most of the farm animals were milling around and chickens had basically gone wild. Cows were in need of milking and mooing plaintively.

I shot many cows that had suffered injuries—I suspect from antipersonnel mines. They were unable to eat and starving. Our battery captain was removed from command here. We had three captains during eleven months of combat. The first cap-

tain was lost when he opened fire with a captured German machine gun on a light colonel's [a lieutenant colonel] tent on the other side of the river. When a lieutenant and sergeant tried to restrain him, he proceeded to beat both of them up. He was evacuated. The second captain we lost had his leg shattered by a booby-trapped household faucet that he turned to see if water would come.

On August 11, we moved to Balleroy in the British sector and set up as an antitank protection for a British airfield. We saw no action, but from a hillside vantage point nearby, I noted rocket-firing British Typhoons or Mosquito aircraft attacking German mobile and horse-drawn equipment with deadly effect.

On August 13, the crew was deployed at St. Hilaire-du-Harcourt and then La Loupe until September 1. We missed the liberation of Paris. Our mission was to defend Orly airfield [outside of Paris] late in August, but that was changed and we returned to our positions. We engaged German aircraft many times at this position, and Helen, my gun crew, received credit for an Me 109 destroyed.

After the Normandy campaign and the fall of Paris, Bewersdorf's battalion moved on to the Netherlands in October. Bewersdorf came down with pneumonia, and he was nursed back to health by a Dutch family. He refused to go to a hospital because, according to rumor, soldiers who entered an army hospital and recovered were sent to a replacement depot upon recovery, where they were assigned to the infantry.[7] In March 1945, Fred Bewersdorf went on to Germany with

---

7. This was not just a rumor, but a fact, since infantry replacements were in short supply in the last quarter of 1944, and apparently some anti-aircraft units were also used as infantry replacements.

Organization of the 430th Anti-Aircraft Artillery (Automatic Weapons) Battalion

The 430th Anti-Aircraft Artillery (Automatic Weapons) Battalion included a headquarters and a headquarters battery to support four batteries lettered A through D. Each battery consisted of a headquarters section and two gun platoons, which included four 40-millimeter guns, four .50-caliber machine guns, and two half-tracks mounting a quad .50 caliber each. The 40-millimeter guns of the 1st Platoon were numbered 1 through 4 and those of the 2nd Platoon 5 through 8. Each of the platoons' four gun sections numbered twelve men, which included one sergeant, two corporals, one tech 5 truck driver, and eight privates. Each section also included one truck carrying tools and spare parts, the 40-millimeter antiaircraft artillery gun mounted on a four-wheel gun carriage, a spare 40-millimeter barrel, and a pedestal-mounted .50-caliber machine gun with a spare barrel. The men carried M-1 rifles. Communication was ensured by phone lines. Each battery was color-coded—A was red, B white, C blue, and D brown—and each numbered gun given a female name. The battalion averaged 825 men, and it was authorized by its table of organization and equipment to have a total of thirty-two .50-caliber machine guns, thirty-two 40-millimeter guns, and sixteen quad .50 calibers mounted on half-tracks.

his battalion, which crossed the Elbe into the future Russian sector of Germany but pulled back as the war came to a close.

Sergeant J. B. Smith was with the 463rd Anti-Aircraft Artillery (Automatic Weapons) Battalion when it was attached to the 79th Infantry Division. His battalion landed about a week after D-Day and stayed with the 79th Division all the way to Cherbourg and through the breakout in August. Since he was always close to the action, Smith was wounded twice and several men in his company were killed by snipers.

Numerous nondivisional artillery battalions served as corps artillery during the campaign. Such was the case for the 196th Field Artillery Battalion, where Pvt. George Lockett Wood, a twenty-year-old draftee from Tyler, Alabama, served with the Service Battery. He was not only an ammunition handler but also a bazooka man in his unit. Even though they landed in Normandy well after D-Day—in July—Wood and his comrades were issued impregnated clothing for gas protection. Wood's battalion of about 600 men sailed in LSTs and landed at Utah Beach on July 8. A great deal of equipment was still scattered around the area. The battalion's twelve 105-millimeter howitzers came ashore with no incident, and they were quickly moved off the beach. On July 23, Wood's outfit was at Les Déserts near St. Lô.

> We had a false gas alarm. One soldier who had thrown away his gas mask remembered having seen one on a dead German, so he ran barefoot over rocks, thorns, and hedgerows back to where the body lay, took the German mask, and put it on. He couldn't walk back until someone took him his boots.
>
> We also had one soldier [later in the campaign] who feared the buzz bombs so much that he threw up every time he heard one—once in his gas mask.

Private Wood's job was to transport ammunition to the gun batteries in 2½-ton trucks, which

155-millimeter ammunition being unloaded at Roscoff. Troops of an African-American quartermaster unit were given many dangerous noncombat assignments like this. Most African-American troops did not receive a chance to fight until later in the war when a shortage of replacements arose and a call for volunteers was made.

had landed with a full load. Most of Wood's work was mostly done under the cover of night. His routine consisted of driving to the ammunition dump, picking up ammunition that he found piled high on the ground, loading the trucks, and returning with the ammunition to the batteries. Each box of ammunition contained two 105-millimeter rounds; the fuses came in a separate box. A rack for bazooka rockets was affixed to the left side of Wood's truck.

During the carpet-bombing of July 25, Wood's battalion fired smoke rounds to mark the target area. However, the atmospheric conditions must have been unfavorable because the bombers were unable to spot the targets accurately. On August 19, the 196th was attached to Combat Command

L of the French 2nd Armored Division and marched with it into Paris on August 25.

It was rainy and muddy. We spent the night on the Avenue de la Grande Armée, which leads to the Arc de Triomphe. When we saw the Eiffel Tower, we knew we were in Paris. People were jubilant as we drove down the streets. They threw flowers and tomatoes. One Frenchman gave me a fish sandwich, which was much appreciated because we had gone without for three or four meals. We moved out of Paris on August 28.

We fired so rapidly that a captured German infantry officer asked me in English to see our automatic field pieces!

PFC Maynard E. Daggett was a machine gunner with Battery A of the 978th Field Artillery Battalion. When Operation Cobra began, Daggett had already been in action.

We moved up to support operations during the attack on St. Lô. We moved to a place near Port Herbert. We had a vehicle with a dozer blade to bust through the hedgerow so we could set up a position. We stayed here most of the time. I was reporting the coordinates for the fire missions at the Battery HQ. I operated the field telephone. We had two telephones; one was hooked to the battalion fire control and the other to the gun positions. I had the phone for the gun positions, sometimes for the fire control, and would relay the information. We did not get any counter-battery fire until St. Lô.

They took one gun, moved it up to a point near St. Lô, and fired point plank at a target. One gun crew pulled into the edge of St. Lô, firing on open sights directly at a couple of tanks and some other vehicles. There was a cemetery there—northwest corner of St. Lô—and we dug the gun in there. I used the range finder. We would fire one to get the range and then a few more for effect. You never hit the same place twice, so you had to fire several rounds.

We were in this position for about four hours. We next moved to a point overlooking the river. Some German patrols penetrated at night, and there was some small arms fire. A few guys were wounded. We remained here for about a week.

When we advanced later from St. Lô, we went through an area the Germans had mined. We lost one tractor to those mines. We figured the infantry or engineers had swept the place for mines, but either we got there before they did, or they did not clear the area. We would usually be a mile or less

from the infantry for direct support. We ran into a bunch of land mines and Bouncing Betties along the hillside of that town. We couldn't go around this one village with vehicles. One of our men got pretty well done in by one of those mines. The Germans had not picked up their dead—they were still lying around. That is the last time we ran into a bunch of dead people lying around with busted up equipment (theirs and ours): trucks, personnel carriers, etc. We hadn't seen any infantry or engineers, and our captain had all the spare guys who were with the gun crews sweep the town and find out if there were any Germans still in it. We did find a few. They were shot if they resisted. One of them was a German officer who had gone to Harvard. He spoke perfect English and demanded transportation—a jeep or something. We didn't have time to fool with him. He was executed.

We moved fast after Normandy and went almost into Paris. We waited for the French to take Paris. Halfway to Paris, we found a bunch of replacements. They did make it. They set up in an open field in pup tents. We were less than a mile from the German positions. We got up and told them not to put up those tents and to dig in. They set up the tents and sleeping bags anyway. Bedcheck Charlie showed up and after a couple of days, he returned dropping flares again and German aircraft followed, which wiped them out. I guess there were about eighty or ninety men in that field and a bunch of them got killed. Some of them jumped in with us and others took off.

Construction and combat engineer battalions were important nondivisional units with a wide variety of responsibilities that ranged from restoring roads and railroads to clearing mines and restoring installations to service or opening new

978th Field Artillery Battalion Gun Section Operation

According to Maynard Daggett, fire control sent over the information for the mission. For example, it might be "adjust fire HE, fuse delay." Possibly, a six-second delay when we did not use the quick fuse for detonation on impact. The powder charge came in two types: normal and super. Most of the time, the mission required a normal charge. Two men would hold the shell up on a tray, and then two or three others pushed it into the gun with a ramrod the same size as the shell. The two men holding it were the loaders. They pushed it into the gun, and one or two men would alternate putting the powder charge in and closing the breach. One man stood ready and closed the breech, which had an adapter that screwed it into the breech. It had the firing pin in it, and when the lanyard was pulled, a flapper would hit the shell and fire it. Everyone moved way back as the man closest pulled the lanyard at about arm's length. Everyone had cotton in their ears, and we had lots of hearing problems.

It took about a minute or more to load and fire. Each gun crew had additional men who went back for the ammunition from the trailers and trucks. Everyone would help dig in the guns and camouflage them. Each gun crew had one machine gunner for a .50-caliber antiaircraft machine gun.

Unlike the old French GPF that the Long Toms replaced, the new weapon gun could be set up faster. It took about forty-five minutes to set up a Long Tom, not including the time to dig it in. A tracked vehicle was the prime mover; it carried the entire gun crew in it plus a driver and assistant driver who manned the .50-caliber machine gun mounted on it. The vehicle carried some ammunition, but the main supply was in a truck and trailer.

ones. The divisional combat engineer battalion was able to perform these functions to a limited degree, but it also had to move with its division. Over forty engineer combat battalions landed in Normandy before the end of July. Some were organized into engineer combat groups. Since the first engineer construction battalion did not disembark until September, the combat engineers had to perform its functions as the front moved forward.

More specialized units, such as the 1055th Engineer Port Construction and Repair Group, landed in mid-June and a week later were followed by the 1056th. Other specialized units included six engineer heavy pontoon battalions, two engineer camouflage battalions, and topographic battalions. The 660th Engineer Base Topographic Battalion operated in England, preparing maps for the army until it moved to France in October. The 654th Engineer Topographic Battalion landed in Normandy late in June, and it was followed in mid-July by the 652nd. These units were not intended for frontline service like the engineer combat battalions. Without these topographic units, the combat troops would have little more than Michelin travel maps to operate with, and they were not equipped with the type of grid reference system needed for calling in or directing artillery and air support.

Capt. Donald McConnell enlisted in March 1941 at York, Pennsylvania, and a year later, he was commissioned a second lieutenant in the Corps of Engineers. He took command of Company A of the 44th Engineer Combat Battalion, and he was

The city of Brest in ruins after the battle. GORDON H. MASON

promoted to captain on June 15, 1944. His company contained the standard three platoons and a headquarters. Each platoon consisted of three squads and a platoon headquarters. The squads numbered about thirteen men and had a 2½-ton dump truck that served as their primary means of transportation and carried their hand tools, such as picks and shovels. Each squad also had a trailer that carried construction material for building or repairing small bridges. The platoon headquarters tool truck carried large items, such as power tools and heavy equipment. The company headquarterse included dozers and graders, according to Captain McConnell. Thus, these nondivisional battalions had greater construction capabilities than similar battalions organic to the combat divisions.

McConnell's company was ferried to Utah Beach in an LST on July 5. During the crossing,

his men ate C and K rations. After landing on July 6, the 44th Engineer Combat Battalion moved to Étienville, about eight miles away, where the men de-waterproofed their vehicles. Next, the battalion was ordered to patrol the road for mines and remove them, build a road for a hospital, and remove wrecked vehicles from the road. All the troops carried M-1 rifles and wore helmets, except when they had to perform physical labor far from the front. At these times, the helmets were replaced with fatigue caps. When they bivouacked in hedgerow-enclosed fields with one exit, McConnell ordered a dozer crew to open an additional outlet.

Thirty-four-year-old S.Sgt. Gordon H. Mason of Flint, Michigan, had enlisted in 1944 and served in the H&S Company of the 44th Engineer Battalion. For many days after arriving in

France, friendly artillery fire prevented him from sleeping. After a while, he, the S-2 captain, and a driver were sent to the 2nd Infantry Division for liaison duty, where they received and delivered intelligence reports from their engineer battalion. Enemy artillery fire kept them in their foxholes every night. While they were with the 2nd Division, the three men went on a recon to see what they could find.

> We captured a chicken in a farmyard, took it back to one of our line company's kitchens, had it cooked, and returned to the 2nd Division to eat it. We put it on the command car fender, but before we could touch it, German 88s opened up and drove us to our foxholes. When the fire lifted, we went back to the chicken and again the 88s opened up. This time, we had sense enough to take the chicken with us.

During his time near the front lines, Mason noticed that as soon as the Allied liaison spotter planes flew away after 6:00 P.M., the German artillery became more active. During interrogation, German prisoners confessed that they had refrained from firing when the spotters in those light aircraft were up because they did not want to be targeted.

On August 4, as the 44th Engineer Battalion moved through Avranches, Captain McConnell's company had to clear from the road a convoy of German vehicles that had been destroyed by Allied aircraft. He and his men removed a variety of vehicles, including horse-drawn artillery units and dead horses. At Periers, they had to replace a blown bridge. When they reached the village of Leluot, they were bombed and strafed nightly in the bivouac areas and had to dig foxholes. Occasionally, after building a bridge, the battalion had to leave men to guard it and direct traffic. Sporadically, this was done under sniper fire. As the Allies entered Brittany, McConnell and his men

received a royal welcome. "Everybody became preoccupied with liberating these towns because the townspeople would holler, 'Les Américains!' and they would bring out the booze. Everybody would stop and have a drink of wine or something until they got to the next town." However, the journey toward Brest "wasn't all gravy because we did continue to repair roads and bridges." McConnell's company spent most of the time working on drainage to protect the roads, and on one occasion, it was ordered to install a Bailey bridge. "We went down to the location of the site and found it would be just as easy to put in a culvert—some people had a peculiar idea of how a Bailey bridge should be used."

During the battle for Brest, the 44th Engineer Battalion was not far from the action.

> We sat outside of Brest and watched the city being attacked daily by P-47s dive-bombing and strafing and heavy artillery shelling. After the city was captured, our line companies cleared the streets. We suffered our casualties when a wall fell on several of our men—our first casualty was on the first or second day on the beach when the officer of the day was shot in the leg by one of his sentries.

After the fall of Brest, Captain McConnell and his men "spent a good bit of time in the town clearing up and cleaning up the roads and knocking down buildings that were dangerous to trucks or civilians." During this time, he wandered downtown.

> I got into an underground German officers quarters. It was a sizeable underground activity, and it appeared somewhere between eight or ten officers lived in that complex. There were a couple of Chinese plates that I absconded and packed up and sent home.

The 44th Engineer Combat Battalion

The 44th Engineer Battalion, a nondivisional combat unit assigned to the 1102nd Engineer Group, worked behind the lines. The records of Company A's operations were maintained by 1st Sgt. Foster S. Probst.

The battalion had departed the U.S. on March 24, 1944. Company A with 5 officers and 168 enlisted men arrived on Utah beach during the night of July 6 in the rain on *LST 1366*, but did not disembark until 5:00 A.M. the next morning. On July 10, the company worked on road repairs and maintenance at Neuville and moved east that evening. The next few days they did the same until July 18, when they also had to begin clearing minefields in addition to roadwork. The first few days they were shelled by German artillery each evening. During those days before Operation Cobra, it often rained, and the mud made engineer operations more difficult. When the offensive began, Company A was taken off the work duty and provided security for the battalion HQ for the next few days. On July 28, the 2nd Platoon was sent out to replace a blown bridge, which was finished the next day before the battalion moved out for Periers.

Casualties were light, with one private injured by shrapnel at the bridge site and another sent to a field hospital to be treated for combat exhaustion. On August 2, another private broke his arm when he fell off a truck. On August 3, the company engaged in more road repairs and removing wrecked German vehicles. The next day the company moved to Avranches and continued roadwork. In addition to roadwork, the company dispatched guards for bridges, and one squad was sent to hunt snipers. On August 8, the company was trucked 48 miles to Le Rhen after losing another man to combat exhaustion. The next day they moved to Dinge, another 27.5 miles. Sergeant Probst wrote that the most exciting event was that "Heweth fired his Tommy gun and got everybody on the ball" on August 9. The next few days, the company rested and cleaned up. On August 12, the company was again providing security on the main highways and repairing roads and bridges; otherwise things were quiet. The next few days were more road patrols and bridge construction. On August 19, the company was trucked 131 miles to La Féville. On August 20, they sent four dump trucks to work on a landing strip, and the next day the 1st Platoon was directed to prepare a Bailey bridge, but later that order was cancelled. On August 22, the company was trucked 35.5 miles to Kevrdnennec and given more security duties. On August 24, they moved 11.7 miles to Ménezléon, where they witnessed a lot of fire on Brest that night, which seemed to continue in the days that followed. The next day, they were repairing roads, and that continued until August 31 when that work stopped because the rain from the previous three days made it impractical. That was also payday, and after the morning rain stopped, they were back on road repair. This was the routine that continued.

continued

The 44th Engineer Combat Battalion *continued*

On September 11, they received news that the Allies had invaded the Reich, but they continued with the same routine in western Brittany in the days that followed. On September 17, they were ordered to remove Third Army identification from vehicle bumpers and replace it with Ninth Army. On September 18, Brest surrendered, and the company was sent in to clean the streets. They remained, working in Brest for the next week, and everyone in the unit was given typhus shots, but the forty-eight cases of liberated wine helped relieve the stress of work. On September 25, guards were placed at the entrances to the camp to keep prostitutes out, and the next day the company was issued overcoats and overshoes and given a "short arm"[8] inspection because they were moving out the next day. The unit was on the move and trucked to Rennes and then Chartres and finally reached Chalons on September 30. From there, on October 1, they entered Belgium and were transferred to the 1107th Engineer Group and were back in the war.

8. This referred to an inspection of a male's genitals for venereal disease.

One of the squads ran across a cache of wine and brought home forty-eight cases. We used that for our victory party a little later. After we finished our work in Brest, we were waiting to move through France, and I gave some of our men passes for R&R.

Later, the battalion was involved in the Battle of the Bulge, where it suffered heavily, losing about 400 of its 630 men.

July to August: The Communications Zone

As the combat troops advanced through Normandy and finally broke out, not all military formations followed them. Many units stayed behind to operate the beaches and lines of communications. The engineer special brigades continued to operate Utah and Omaha Beaches while additional units put Cherbourg in operation. On July 22, the Communications Zone headquarters was set up at Valognes.

Survivors of Exercise Tiger (April 1944) were placed with various units, but many with the 1st Engineer Special Brigade.[9] T/5 John A. Perry was assigned to 462nd Amphibious Truck Company, 1st Engineer Special Brigade, and continued to operate his DUKW on Utah Beach until November 11, when his unit moved its operations to Le Havre, which had been captured one month earlier.[10]

---

9. Exercise Tiger was one of the last major practice landings before the invasion, and German E-boats broke into the convoy of LSTs. The incident was kept secret for a long time.

10. Perry did not receive a Purple Heart for his injury during Exercise Tiger in September 1944.

Surrender of Brest in September 1944 by General Ramcke.
GORDON H. MASON

Sgt. Stanley Stout, also a survivor of the Exercise Tiger disaster, was placed in the 557th Quartermaster Company of the 1st Engineer Special Brigade. During the invasion, his unit remained at Cardiff where it was being rebuilt.

In Cardiff, Wales, they started putting men in the company and filling it up before D-Day. We thought we would go back to where we were, but we didn't. We ran warehouses and unloaded ships at Cardiff. We had the prisoners unload it. D-Day came, and we found out we were not going back to the 1st ESB. There were nine survivors of the whole company and no one left from my squad.

When Cherbourg fell, we were shipped across the Channel to Cherbourg. We came in through Utah Beach. Cherbourg was an excellent port, but they had sunk ships and destroyed all those that were docked, and the place was a mess. There were huge forts built there—huge concrete forts. We were lucky because we got billeted in there. It was just concrete rooms, but it beat the hell out of being outside.

We stayed there and again we had a bunch of PWs and we unloaded as soon as they got the dockside clear. We had the prisoners unload the ships. In August, they were still clearing the port. In the meantime, they had the breakout at St. Lô, and Patton moved so fast they couldn't keep the supplies moving. So they organized the Red Ball Express with all the trucking companies they could find. They would pull in, we would load them from the ship, and then they would take off.

The men worked until they dropped. It took three or four days to unload a ship, and you just wondered where all that stuff was going. The city was dirty and dusty, and we saw very few people. The PWs were eager to take the job because they got better food and treatment. The same thing happened at Le Havre. We had no problems with the PWs. We always wanted them and asked for them. We had Irish nationals at Cherbourg in companies, but these civilians were not worth a shit. The French were fair workers. The Germans did the best work because they had discipline.

PFC Hyman Shapiro, who was serving with the 520th Quartermaster Railhead Company, was in a depot behind the lines. He had not been warned of the arrival of the massive bomber force of July 25.

After a night of guard duty, I was awakened by the ground shaking under me. I crawled out of my foxhole, and everywhere I could see planes bombing the Germans. Our guys were laughing and hollering, "The Krauts are really getting it!" When we met the infantry guys later, they told us that when they stormed ahead, the Germans came out of their foxholes with blood running from their ears and noses from the concussion and had bayonets fixed—they had to fight it out.

We were behind the 1st and 29th Divisions initially. When the infantry moved, we moved. The last time, before I was wounded, at the battle near Vire, I saw three young French girls who would go out with empty sacks and return with full sacks everyday. The GIs threw away a hell of a lot of their stuff. I wrote to a friend that the GIs were throwing away enough to equip the French for another twenty years, and the captain who censored our mail called me in and told me I was insulting the U.S. Army. I was punished by being ordered to dig three slit trenches, which I never dug.

In August, I was wounded because I was in the wrong place at the wrong time and was injured because I didn't do what I was ordered to do. I was sent to a hospital with large tents and cots inside. What impressed me was that among the patients was a little boy who had shrapnel and superficial flesh wounds on his chest. His parents spent the whole twenty-four hours with him with the father replacing the mother and so on. The father told me in World War I he fought the Boches and then made the French symbol of cutting the throat. On the other side of me was a French gendarme who stepped on a mine and got his leg blown off. The nurse came around, offered me a sponge bath, and commented on how dirty I was. I hadn't

changed my clothes in two months as well as sleeping and eating in them.

I was flown by C-47 to England. On that plane were Poles who fought for the Germans. Our American Poles on the planes asked why they fought for the Nazis, and they claimed they were conscripted. From August 15 to past Thanksgiving, I was in a hospital with a wound to my chest and wrist. After recovering, I was sent back to the States.

In the hospital, Shapiro met a number of wounded GIs and noticed that the paratroopers were a breed apart. They were exuberant and "battle happy," boasting about how they had killed their foes. The infantrymen, on the other hand, tended to focus on how scared they were and how rough life on the front was.

Each division had its own MPs who handled traffic, prisoners, and matters pertaining to law and order. Although the MP battalions were mainly rear-echelon troops, on occasion they wound up on the front lines. The first MPs in Normandy came ashore on D-Day.

Cpl. Francis J. Aleksandrowicz, Company B, 769th Military Police Battalion, arrived in England with his battalion shortly before the invasion. On June 17, he and his comrades left Bristol for Southampton, where they embarked for Normandy in the evening of June 23. They crossed the Channel on a landing craft after the storm. Since the seas were still rough, many of them succumbed to seasickness on their way to Omaha Beach.

We had been held back on our departure from England due to the storm, which damaged the Mulberry facilities in Normandy. Anyway, we all were apprehensive as to what to expect over there. Our platoon sergeant kept us informed as to his meager knowledge about what was going on. We cleaned our rifles onboard ship. We were taken ashore by smaller craft, and then we made that long walk up the hill in single file with officers keeping us well spaced and moving quickly.

We did a lot of walking until we gathered in one of the hedgerow-encircled pastures where cows and horses were lying, slightly bloated and dead. We picked out foxholes along the hedgerows for the time being. We were attacked by a mobile 88 artillery unit, which most likely was a large Nazi tank. They lobbed a few shells in, and we moved out beyond their range. On coming back from a wooded area, we were informed that one unit across from us suffered casualties. One soldier was literally blown away. His left hand was up in an apple tree. There was a wedding ring on the finger—one never forgets that. During the darkness, there was a Nazi recon plane and all the ack-ack were firing away. All I, and most likely the others, could do was to rest my head on my pack, helmet over my face, rifle at the side, and tried to sleep—which I did. When you are twenty-two years old, sleep comes easily.

I awoke next morning and could scarcely open my eyes. This frightened me, of course. Seems that I was bitten by mosquitoes quite badly, and this caused the swelling of both eyelids. I had time to take a picture of my face that morning.

Our platoon then moved to Katz on June 26. I met Jules Grad, a sergeant with *Stars and Stripes* and former reporter on my hometown newspaper, on June 30.

We then moved to Barfleur. In a large stone building, we set up and had an armored vehicle with a .50 cal. machine gun on it under camouflage netting. While in Barfleur, PFC Donald Hathaway and I took a captured German rifle to an isolated beach area, placed a bottle on a huge rock, and

tried the rifle out. Soon thereafter, a combat squad encircled us thinking we were the enemy. They told us not to do this since there were pockets of enemy they were seeking out. I was embarrassed and thought about my stripes being taken away, but nothing happened.

Then some civilian came to our billet and talked about strange activities of pigeons on their roof. The buildings were around the corner from where we were located, so I was dispatched to the building and led up to the attic where there was a covered exit to the roof. I did get up through the exit and surveyed the pigeons on the roof. None had a message attached to their legs.

We placed people at important road junctions, did some directional signing, patrolled in jeeps—normally, a corporal drove and a private or PFC was with him to check movements of units and to prevent any misdirection of these convoy units. We also checked eateries, since there was a directive that Allied forces were not to eat food at these places since the French were to be given priorities in food. We came across a fine establishment just outside of Barfleur overlooking the sea where the correspondents were eating. Seems the word about lobster and steak was being passed around, and this group we found was asked to desist from ordering food. In fact, they were told to leave and use their military issued rations. They seemed to get better rations than most GIs anyway.

We had an experience where we were called to an area in Normandy where some drunken combat engineers were shooting up a town. They were brought in, around Katz as I remember, and our platoon sergeant checked them out and asked that my cohort and I take the men back to their commanding officer down the road. As soon as the fellows were in the backseat of the jeep and we were in the front and ready to drive away, a blast behind my helmeted head went off. They did not check the chamber of the rifle and a round was in it. I grabbed the rifle, used a polite reprimand, and took the guys back to their CO.

While I was placed at a traffic intersection near St. Jean-de-Day, outside of St. Lô, on August 7, a fellow came up to me saying that he had information about the "Boches." I checked with my platoon leader, and they told me to take the fellow on to St. Lô to intelligence while they replaced me on the post. I went into St. Lô. I delivered the person to a cellar where intelligence of either the corps or First Army was located. The town was badly damaged. There were some bodies of dead German soldiers about, and I remember the one across the rim of the turret of a tank, which had its tracks off and was scorched black on its side. It sat near a large puddle along the debris of bricks and wood of what was a nearby home. Wires were down and newly strung wire hung above.

At the crossroad of St. Jean-de-Day, I saw three vehicles arrive almost all at once, and three men whom I recognized as Eisenhower, Montgomery, and Bradley unfolded a large map on the hood of Eisenhower's jeep and discussed things in a rather animated way. At the time, I feared that they would come up to me and ask me a lot of questions, which I probably would not be able to answer.

During July, I was at Valogne, where I saw a man accompanied by a special services officer in a jeep. When they stopped to look at the rubble of the town, I recognized the man as Edward G. Robinson.

During July and August, our unit moved about N-13 (a main supply route). Once Cherbourg was secured, members of the 707th and 769th MP Battalions routed the traffic. This later became the Red Ball Express route from Cherbourg to Paris.

While moving about Normandy, we did make a stop in Tessy-sur-Vire, where the locals were cutting hair off the heads of females and some men who were collaborators. This was a civil affair, and we just soberly watched their "fun."

After a short stay in Villedieu, we made a long ride in August to Le Mans, where we stayed until November. From here, we not only worked the red-light district below the cathedral, but traffic escort and control as well. We were to keep the GIs from the off-limits brothels below the cathedral. The girls were lonely and talked to the MPs. On Mondays, the local doctors came to inspect the girls. Many of the girls went to church each morning. I was not on duty there, but some of my squad were and I had to check on those who were checking on the girls . . . sort of a tricky proposition in days of my youth. Much of our time at Le Mans was spent furnishing freight train escort from Le Mans to the front. Two or four people, usually with a noncom, would ride the 40&8s with coffee, cigarettes, rations, fuel, and ammo. We had to dismount from our boxcars each time the train stopped to keep GI black marketers and civilians from robbing us blind.

General Eisenhower was displeased with the fact that soldiers were not getting cigarettes while on the frontline positions due to massive pilferage in the rear areas. . . . Later our battalion and another MP battalion along with the C.I.D. got enough information to arrest an entire Railroad Operation Battalion for massive sales of American military supplies. We learned later that they were tried and convicted.

Quad.50-caliber M2 air-cooled machine guns mounted on an M16 carriage. FRED BEWERSDORF

The Red Ball operation was a twenty-four-hour run of vehicles of all types moving at high rates of speed through towns and villages. These vehicles carried supplies of all types for the troops at the front. Large white signs with a big red ball and a route number were all along the route. Any vehicles having trouble were pulled off the highway by wreckers. It was a one-way route to the front and back to Cherbourg. Our men on traffic control duty made sure nobody got in the way. Our jeep patrols and Harley-Davidson motorcycles kept up the pace through heavy dust storms churned up by the fast-moving trucks. Everything was coated with a sand-colored patina, including wires, trees, homes, etc., and the MPs constantly had to wipe glasses and goggles.

In July and August, trucks carrying supplies shuttled back and forth between Cherbourg or the invasion beaches and the front at a rate of over 1,000 vehicles per hour, tearing up the secondary roads in the area, which were also under artillery fire. The army engineers worked around the clock maintaining the roads during these months. The high volume of trucks was necessary to maintain an average flow of 500 tons of supplies per day per division. At the beginning of July, there were already twenty-two divisions in Normandy, all needing additional supplies. After the breakout, the situation changed, as supply lines expanded exponentially as demands increased.

Hauling Supplies

Opening up ports was important to the Allies in order to efficiently and rapidly unload the various supplies and equipment needed to wage war in Western Europe. The Mulberries achieved success until the great storm in June, but even after that the delivery over the invasion beaches proved sufficient before the breakout in Normandy. The capture of Cherbourg offered the first major harbor, but much work was needed to repair it. By September, the supplies could reach Normandy by sea, but once placed in depots and after the breakout in late July, an efficient method of delivery was needed until the railroads could be put back in order. The Red Ball Express helped fill the gap in moving the needed cargos from the depots to the forward areas as Allied forces advanced to the Seine and then on toward the border of Germany.

As Rouen and Le Havre came into service on October 6, 1944, the White Ball Express operated from those ports and delivered to rail transfer points at Paris, Beauvais, Compiègne, Soissons, and Reims until January 1945. The Red Ball Express closed in November, since rail transportation was operating more efficiently out of Cherbourg. Before the rail lines in the Cotentin could operate sufficiently to meet the demand, the Green Diamond Express was set up to run supplies from the depots about 100 miles to the railhead at Avranches and Dol. This operation lasted only a few weeks, from October 14 until the end of the month, using fifteen truck companies.

From September 16 and through the next four weeks, the Red Lion Express was set up to support the British in Belgium and the First Allied Airborne Army in Operation Market Garden. American truckers delivered over half their cargo to British forces, with eight truck companies in use. Other routes had to be set up as American forces moved up to the German frontier in November and then later in 1945 as the advance into the heart of Germany was underway.

The Red Ball Express, which was put in operation by the Transportation Corps in the Communications Zone in late August, numbered sixty-seven truck companies totaling over 3,300 trucks. In a matter of four days, the number of truck companies almost doubled to meet the demands of the advancing armies. An estimated 60 to 75 percent of the drivers were African Americans. The proportion was similar in most of the quartermaster truck companies. At its peak, the Red Ball Express had 132 truck companies with 5,958 trucks, but the average number of truck companies used was 83. The drivers were armed with M-1 rifles, which they had to use on occasion. In fact, during the Germans' August 7 counteroffensive, four trucks were ambushed in Mortain, one of the African-American drivers was killed, and one truck was destroyed. The remaining truckers returned fire and escaped.

Two military police battalions controlled the traffic, and two engineer regiments maintained the roads and bridges. The drivers stopped at bivouac areas en route where they were relieved by another driver. Red Ball operations continued until mid-November, keeping the rapidly advancing American forces supplied. The truckers, who had to maintain operations twenty-four hours a day, became targets for the *Luftwaffe*.

U.S. Army Transportation Truck Company Operations in Western Europe

Truck Routes	Dates	Average/Maximum Number Number of Truck Companies Used	Total Tons Delivered	Average Daily Tons
Red Ball Express	25 Aug. 1944 16 Nov. 1944	83/132	412,193	5,088
Green Diamond Express	14 Oct. 1944 1 Nov. 1944	15/?	15,590	800 (?)
White Ball Express	6 Oct. 1944 19 Jan. 1945	29/48	140,500	1,614
Red Lion Express	16 Sept. 1944 12 Oct. 1944	8/?	17,556	650
ABC Express*	30 Nov. 1944 26 Mar. 1945	14/?	250,000	2,670

* The Antwerp-Brussels-Charleroi Express formed to haul supplies out of the port area of Antwerp.

Before the Red Ball Express went into operation and after it ceased its activities, the American armed forces relied on alternate transportation services.[11] The damaged rail lines and rail facilities in Cherbourg were repaired and put back into service. The Military Railroad Service of the Transportation Corps, most of whose contingent had worked on American railroads in civilian life, went into operation in Normandy. The first detachment of the Military Railroad Service landed on D+12 at Utah Beach under the command of Brigadier General Clarence Burpee. His small group surveyed the condition of the French rail system and the yards at Cherbourg and assessed the damages. Burpee's 2nd Military Railway Service, which numbered over 12,000 men, took over the operation of the existing facilities at Cherbourg on D+26. The general directed the Corps of Engineers in repairing facilities and the rail line between Cherbourg and Carentan. When the 729th Railway Operating Battalion, the 757th Railway Shop Battalion, and the 707th Railway Grand Division arrived in Cherbourg on July 11, the first train was operating between

Cherbourg and Carentan. American locomotives and rail cars arrived at Cherbourg on specially designed LSTs with tracks on their decks.

Allied bombers had inflicted a great deal of damage to the French rail system, virtually halting all traffic at important rail centers. At Vire, where fighter-bombers struck before the breakthrough, the damage was particularly extensive. The bombs struck a German ammunition train trapped next to a German troop train in the rail yard. In the resulting explosion, over 1,000 German soldiers lost their lives. Before the MRS could take up its mission of supporting the advancing troops, the army engineers had to repair the main line centers like Vire.

The 729th Railway Operating Battalion included a headquarters company for administration, Company A for maintenance, Company B for shop repairs, and Company C for train operations, with fifty railway crews of five men, each divided among four platoons. Each platoon was led by a lieutenant and each crew by a staff sergeant who acted as a conductor. Most of the men had railroading experience from civilian life. The

11. While the Red Ball Express was still in operation, the White Ball Express, with up to forty-eight truck companies assigned at its peak, began operation on October 6, 1944, when the ports of Le Havre and Rouen became available to shorten the distance to transfer points in the Paris Basin.

battalion was placed under a Railway Grand Division that supervised all operations. In July when the route from Cherbourg to Carentan was extended to Lison, the trains often came under attack from German artillery and sometimes even friendly bombers since they operated close to the front lines.

T/4 John R. Iggens had been a railway worker in the rail yards of St. Louis when he was drafted in the summer of 1943. In 1944, he served in Company C, 720th Railway Operating Battalion.

In Normandy, we were under the 701st Grand Division, which later moved, and then the 707th Grand Division. They handled three battalions and sometimes a shop battalion, which was for heavy repairs. In England, we operated the switching in the supply depots that supplied American material for the invasion. You might have two operating crews: a telegrapher and somebody else in one place and five crews someplace else, depending on the size of the depot. Our battalion was scattered. We were the only ROB operating trains. We replaced the 728th, which took administrative duty at Kirkham.

The four-man crew consisted of an engineer, a fireman, a conductor, and a headman or hind man. In switching, you had a conductor or pull man and a short-field and long-field man. The engineer was in charge of the engine and operated it. The fireman shoveled the coal and kept the steam up. The conductor or foreman was in charge of any switch list or any assignment received from the yardmaster. He had two helpers: one was the head brakeman or short-field man and the other was the rear brakeman or long-field man, and their duties were to uncouple the cars, align switches, couple air hoses, and general operations in yard work.

Our unit left England about four weeks after the invasion in July. We rendezvoused in Southampton and went by train. There were members of port battalions. We were taken by train to port, and we boarded the ship to cross the Channel. Company B didn't go with us; they came later. We had a backpack and blankets. The 729th ROB arrived prior to our arrival, and they were stationed at Cherbourg. We disembarked the ship by rope net into landing craft and had to wade in from the landing craft. We arrived at Utah Beach and stayed in a field. We were trucked to Cherbourg through Ste-Mère-Église and assigned to Cherbourg with the 729th doing cleanup work and trying to pick up cars to rehabilitate. We stayed there about a week cleaning up buildings and gathering up rail equipment that could be used. HQ moved to Lison, and the company bivouacked in an apple orchard a short distance from the railroad. We were doing more or less nothing but waiting. We pitched tents in the field and dug foxholes. Every night, Bedcheck Charlie came over. One night, the AA batteries picked him up and knocked him down.

During this time, I was called by the first sergeant and sent to Bayeux with two other engineers to instruct the British railroad people on how to use the Westinghouse Air Brake because English trains didn't have them and the French did. The English trains had a brake on the side you mash down with a pole.

American equipment began arriving after the port of Cherbourg opened. The engines were American and the cars French. On August 13, I was called back from the detachment to my own unit and assigned KP duty. At noon, I was called out on August 15 by the first sergeant because I knew how to operate a diesel.

On August 15, our unit began operations. The train I was assigned to had a diesel engine on the head end, five boxcars between me and the second engine, which was five cars deep to prevent both engines from being blown up by booby traps. I asked the conductor how far to take the train, and he replied, "As far as there is railroad." We started out on the 15th and got to St. Lô on the left hand track. Had it not been for a French boy, we would have gone up to the city of Vire, which was still held by the German Army.

I was in the seventh train; six in our battalion were ahead of me. The 729th ROB was still working up in Cherbourg, bringing supplies off the ships. Our battalion was the first on road trains in the peninsula. Patton ordered that he wanted a train consisting of forty cars, one train of rations, one of gasoline, and another of ammunition in that order. He asked for thirty trains by the end of the week.

Near Argentan, where they reached level land, we were told two engines were not necessary, so my engine was detached and sent off while the other went to the front. My engine stopped and had to refill with oil. An army 6 x 6 delivered the oil in Jerry cans, but when they poured it in, they lost four or five gallons. I got a bucket from them and filled it with oil (capacity was 680 gallons of oil). We proceeded back to a point where trains were having difficulty getting over a hill and helped pull them over.

The German air force never made an appearance after we began operating in Normandy.

Sgt. Robert B. Seeley from New York, who had been drafted about the same time as Iggens, had also worked on the railroads before he joined the 722nd Railway Operating Battalion in 1944.

We landed on Utah Beach. Our lieutenant got injured as we disembarked. The trucks took us inland to Chef-du-Pont, and we camped in a field. The first night, we went into town looking for something to drink, and they had cider. We stayed there a couple of weeks and went by truck to Le Mans. Two days after the Germans were chased out of Le Mans, we were there, and they were still shooting Germans. We set up in town at an old school that the Germans had used for a barracks. We split up after a few days and I went with Andy Anderson up to Cherbourg and the 729th.

We went to Coutances and joined the 729th ROB. My job was yardmaster. The army had an ammo dump there where they unloaded ammo for the Air Corps and took it by truck to their supply point. They also had rail tracks in there and sent it by rail, then unloaded it and sent it on by truck. They also serviced the 720th and 722nd ROBs there. I was to make sure the men from the 722nd were fed before they went on and the engines were supplied with coal and water. When I was with the 722nd, this was what I did most of time. Every train stopped there before going on and stopped at the water tower where there was a crane to put coal on the tender while the engine cooled as they went to eat. There was an engine to push them uphill.

PFC Chester Saeger, another draftee from New York, served in the 722nd Railway Operating Battalion.

When our unit split at Le Mans, I went to the 720th at Cherbourg. We went to Lison where they went "around the world," and our quarters were in an apple orchard. The trip was a circle that went from Coutances to Lison where crews were changed. If you went one way, you went through Bayeux and Caen. Le Mans was not in the circle. Later we went up toward Paris.

We had American, German, and French cars and also used flatcars to move tanks (one to a flatcar). Port battalions loaded the cars.

PFC Julius I. Koenig, a draftee from Jackson, Mississippi, was with the 757th Railway Shop Battalion when it landed at Utah Beach in late July. He and his comrades took a French train from Chef-du-Pont to Cherbourg. At Cherbourg, he went with some members of his company to look at the gun positions at Fort Roule and found the tunnels still stacked with ammunition. The men played with the guns, aiming them at the ships in the harbor near which lay large amounts of German ammunition and torpedoes. Before long, however, a group of trucks loaded with troops surrounded the hill. Soldiers cautiously moved toward the entrance of the gun battery that was actually located just below Fort Roule and cut into the hillside. Other troops moved up the road to the fort itself. There was only one entrance into the battery, and that was next to one of the hairpin turns that led up to Fort Roule, so it only took a matter of minutes before Koenig and the others were quickly identified. The railroad men had been mistaken for an enemy contingent when someone in the town observed the guns were moving and apparently coming back to life. After the misunderstanding was cleared up, Koenig and his companions got back to work.

We started working the first day. We operated a roundhouse. The outfit that brought us on the train was gone. It was damaged, but we were getting it back into operation.

We used shovels for coal since the coal chute was down. We put the coal on the engines. The place had about twenty stalls, and we serviced the locomotives for whatever repairs were necessary, but for the first month, we had nothing to do with rail operations. We had three coal cranes in operation, but we were inexperienced in their use. The railcars were all over the railroad like most railroads. They were building a new railroad yard called Terreplein NE of Cherbourg.

The engines had a lot of wear and tear on them, and we did a lot of greasing and oiling. They brought locomotives from England to replace the French engines. They did blow up an ammunition train out of Cherbourg in August or September.

They knew I was afraid of guard duty, so they put me on it all the time.

Koenig was placed on guard duty numerous times at a place called the Selecte, a bordello. His duty was to keep all military personnel out except sailors of the merchant marine.

There was a bench out back where the GIs would wait and the old madame would come out and get them. Once, before the unit was getting ready to move, we wanted to see what type of operation was going on inside, so with a couple of others we went around back to the bench and the old madame took them in. It was a large building with a great hall, and you could see there were some beautiful women. We also saw MP officers sitting inside, and apparently they were running the whole operation.

CHAPTER 10

From Anvil to Dragoon

Events Leading to the Invasion of South France

The year 1944 dealt the Third Reich overwhelming blows that should have led to its collapse but failed to do so. By the end of the year, the Allied armies stood at or near the borders of Germany but had to wait another four months before they could declare victory. For most of 1944, the U.S. Army Air Forces and the British Royal Air Force attempted to bomb the enemy into submission. From early 1944 through April, Soviet forces drove the *Wehrmacht* from the Ukraine and reached the Hungarian and Rumanian borders. The Allies followed up by resuming offensive operations in Italy in May and driving the Germans from Cassino and their Winter Line. The Allied forces trapped in the Anzio beachhead finally broke out and drove on Rome. By early August 1944, the Germans had retreated to the Gothic Line, which ran from Massa on the west coast to Rimini on the east coast. The next major blow against the Reich fell in June 1944 in Normandy, even though the Germans managed to tie up the Allied forces in the *bocage* until the end of July. On the evening of June 22, 1944, three years to the day after the German invasion of the Soviet Union, the Soviets launched their largest offensive of the war, tearing up the Eastern Front from the Pripet Marshes to the Gulf of Finland. Within weeks, the German Army Group Center was practically destroyed, losing more men than at Stalingrad and leaving most of Army Group North isolated. By August, the Soviets had reached the Vistula

River and East Prussia, triggering the Warsaw Uprising. Also, late in August Rumania quit the Axis and joined the Allies as Soviet troops tore open the Rumanian front and encircled and trapped most of the "new" German Sixth Army.

In early August 1944, the Germans still retained control of most of France, but as their own recon missions revealed that the Allies had built up their forces in Italy and Corsica, the High Command realized that the situation in Normandy was dire and that their hold on Southern France was slipping. If the Allies landed in Southwestern France, the Germans would have to pull back toward the Rhone and prepare to withdraw from Normandy to positions east of the Seine. If the Allies landed in the French Riviera, Axis forces could hope to contain them on the narrow coastal strip and duplicate the situation in Normandy. However, in late July, before the second invasion actually took place, the Allies began to break out of Normandy. Shortly before the South France landings, the German offensive at Mortain failed to cut off the Allies, who were only days away from closing the Falaise Pocket, where most of the German Seventh Army was trapped. As the Allied forces rapidly pressed toward the Loire and Seine, the Germans were no longer able to contain a second invasion because their forces in the south would be soon cut off.

Planning for the invasion of south France started in May 1943 after the Allies smashed the Axis forces in Tunisia and gathered at the Trident Conference in Washington, D.C., to discuss their options for the future. The American Joint Chiefs of Staff suggested possible operations against southern France, southern Italy, Sardinia, Corsica, northwestern Italy, the Axis-occupied islands of the Aegean, the Balkans, and even neutral Spain. Any of these operations would be restricted by mountainous terrain. On the plus side, however, these same restrictions made it possible for a small force of several divisions to operate without drawing away forces from the massive buildup needed for the cross-Channel attack. However, Spain was no longer considered a threat. South France, which offered restricted terrain, had the drawback of allowing the Germans a broad area to build up their forces, which could force the Allies to commit more divisions than desired. It would also expose the Allied forces to aerial and naval assaults from the Italian coast. The British agreed with the Americans, and south France was dropped in favor of eliminating Fascist Italy in 1943.

After Sicily was taken in August 1943 and preparations were set in motion for the invasion of the Italian mainland, the Joint Chiefs of Staff turned their attention back to planning an operation in south France, code-named Anvil (renamed Dragoon in August 1944). In the fall of 1943, Eisenhower concluded there was not enough amphibious lift for both Overlord and Anvil and decided to postpone the latter until the Allies had advanced north of Rome. On January 23, 1944, Allied Forces Headquarters asked the planners to prepare for a three-division landing, but the next day it was down sized to a single division operation. A few days later General Patton departed for England, which drew the attention of the Germans away from the Mediterranean, since they believed he would lead the spearhead of any new offensive action.[1]

In March 1944, Eisenhower recommended dropping Anvil because the shortage of shipping made it impossible to satisfy the needs for Overlord. Nonetheless, the plan for a second amphibious operation did not die. The British as well as the Americans continued to propose new plans of action. When Rome fell on June 4, 1944, the Allies felt they were in a position to launch a second operation, especially since the Normandy invasion

---

1. Patton was assigned to FUSAG to help deceive the Germans into believing an invasion of the Calais area would take place in the spring or summer of 1944.

appeared to be bogging down on the southern front. Some shipping and amphibious forces could soon be released for a second operation. The British, including Churchill, favored renewing the offensive in Italy, landing a major force at the head of the Adriatic, and advancing through the Ljubljana Gap, which would present a new strategic threat to Germany. The Americans saw this as a major diversion of forces from the main Allied front. The other choices were landing either in the Bay of Biscay to secure ports to support the SHAEF forces already in France or in south France to help roll up the German front and open two of the largest French ports. Eventually, south France was selected, and the 3rd, 36th, and 45th Divisions and Gen. Lucian Truscott's VI Corps were pulled out of the line in Italy between June 15 and 27 and sent back toward the Naples-Salerno area to prepare for the operation. The airborne units in the Mediterranean were so few in number that they did not even make up one division. Eventually, the 1st Airborne Task Force, a division-size unit, coalesced under the command of Gen. Robert Frederick.[2] When a parachute regiment arrived from the United States in June, some ad hoc units got glider training, and a parachute battalion came in July. In addition, SHAEF sent two troop carrier wings, the 50th and 53rd, from England to join the 51st stationed in Italy. The IX Troop Carrier Command sent 375 glider pilots to join those in Italy, so each glider had two pilots. The Allied glider force numbered 50 Horsas and 130 Wacos; an additional 350 were on order and began arriving in July. Additional specialized units for the invasion included the 1st Special Service Force of about 2,000 men and two French commando units.[3]

For the invasion of south France, Gen. Jacob Devers commanded the 6th Army Group con-sisting of the American Seventh Army under Gen. Alexander Patch (a veteran of the Guadal-canal campaign) and the Free French Army B under Gen. de Lattre de Tassigny. The French forces initially consisted of the French II Corps (1st Motorized Infantry and 3rd Algerian Infantry Division) and elements of the 1st French Armored Division and were intended to land on D+1. These forces were designated as French Army B (and in late September 1944 became the First French Army). British general Henry Maitland Wilson was the overall commander of these forces, which came under Allied Forces Headquarters until they could be transferred to SHAEF after landing in France and establishing logistical support. Adm. John H. D. Cunningham of the Royal Navy, who commanded the naval forces in the Mediterranean, put Vice Adm. H. Kent Hewitt in charge of the amphibious operation with the reformed Western Naval Task Force. Hewitt commanded the Eighth Fleet in the Mediterranean, which only consisted of a couple of cruisers and smaller craft. He requested the addition of more fire support craft, including battleships, for the invasion. The Western Task Force serving in the English Channel was dissolved on July 10, and many of its ships were sent to Hewitt, where the Western Task Force reformed under his command.

Gen. Ira C. Eaker commanded the Mediterranean Allied Air Forces, which included Mediterranean Allied Tactical Air Force, Twelfth Air Force, and the Fifteenth Air Force. The Western Naval Task Force included nine escort carriers (CVEs), each with twenty-four aircraft including Hellcat, Wildcat, or British Seafire fighters. Seven of the CVEs were British and two American. Each carried only one type of aircraft: the two American CVEs had Hellcats, and four

2. Frederick had formed and commanded the 1st Special Service Force, a unit consisting of both American and Canadian troops that trained for mountain fighting and commando operations in the United States.

3. These French commandos invaded and took Elba on June 17 in Operation Brassard.

of the seven British CVEs had Seafires while the others had Wildcats or Hellcats. The Seafire was a modified naval version of the Spitfire.

Once again, LSTs proved to be a critical element. Eisenhower sent twenty-four from England, and twenty-eight new ones arrived from the United States during the summer. The planners wanted ninety-six LSTs but made do with the eighty-one. SHAEF also dispatched troopships and LCIs. This made it possible for the desired three divisions to land on a front of about forty-five miles using many of the sixteen selected numbered beaches varying from 500 to 4,500 yards in length and divided into three assault areas: Alpha, Delta, and Camel. According to the first plan, the first Allied forces would land in the Hyères Roadstead just to the east of Toulon, and two or three divisions and the Ranger units would take the Hyères Islands before the main landings. In January 1944, the plan was changed because it was too risky. The next version of the plan called for a main landing between St. Tropez and St. Raphael, an area closer to air support from Corsica and farther from the main German coastal defenses. The 1st Special Service Force was to neutralize the Hyères Islands and a key coastal battery before the main landing took place south and northeast of St. Tropez and near St. Raphael. This plan was also modified so that a third division would land near Cape Cavalaire.

After the Allied invasion of French Northwest Africa, German troops had advanced into Vichy France and taken over the French coastal defenses, which were especially strong in the Toulon–Marseille area, where some batteries included 120-millimeter, 138-millimeter, and 164-millimeter guns. After the surrender of Italy in 1943, the threat of invasion increased, so the Germans began work on the South Wall, the Mediterranean counterpart of the Atlantic Wall. German national labor units, *Organization Todt*, and the German youth national work service organization (known as RAD or *Reichsarbeitdi-*

enst), sent detachments to restore French positions and build new defenses under the direction of the army's fortress engineers and naval construction units. At first, the area between the Rhone River and the Pyrenees was given priority since the region consist of relatively open terrain compared to the area east of the Rhone River and along the Riviera, where the mountains virtually come down to the sea. One of the batteries the Germans restored to service was Battery Cépet near Toulon, which mounted 340-mm guns with a range of 18,000 yards in two twin naval gun turrets, making this the best-protected area. The Germans also used a number of railway spurs for long-range rail guns that the French had added for at least two 380-millimeter and four 280-millimeter railway guns. The Normandy invasion underscored the fact that any invasion of south France would probably be east of the Rhone in order to cut off German forces still in Western France. Realizing this, the German army commander put more effort into erecting defenses on the Riviera. Work on many of the bunkers in this region began mere months before the invasion.

Although not as numerous as on the Atlantic Wall, the battery positions were similar, consisting both of open and casemated gun emplacements and surrounding defensive positions. Well-camouflaged concrete bunkers sprouted at key points where they could cover vital areas or give enfilading fires across possible invasion beaches. Strongpoints very similar to those encountered in Normandy—consisting of groups of bunkers, trenches, wire, and minefields—were built on possible invasion sites. In addition, the Germans evacuated the sea front in the coastal towns and turned the buildings there into defensive positions. Beach obstacles, like those on the Atlantic Wall, began to appear along the Riviera coast, between the Giens Peninsula and Nice, only shortly before the invasion, since it had been a low priority area. At Beach 264—Camel Red—

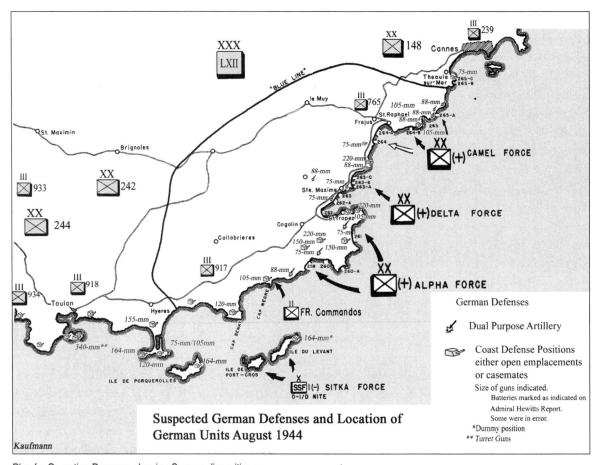

Plan for Operation Dragoon, showing German dispositions.

and the adjacent 264a, work on the concrete tetrahedron obstacles began only in mid-May, and the first row was finished on July 25. The second row was well underway. Work on other beaches in the invasion area had not moved forward as quickly. At Alpha Red, the Germans only began work in late July. Camel Red turned out to be the most heavily defended beach during the invasion.

The Germans placed underwater obstacles similar to those in Normandy in the bays with possible landing beaches. On the beaches of south France, the difference between high and low tide was not as great as in Normandy, so many of these obstacles remained submerged at all times. The gradient of the beaches, however, varied considerably from place to place, providing both advantages and disadvantages for the Germans and Allies, depending on the particular beach. Where the gradient was slight, the Germans were able to place the obstacles far out from the beach while the shallow water made it impossible for the larger Allied landing craft to reach the beach; the Allies would have to build floating causeways for the LSTs. Where the gradient was steep, on the other hand, the Germans could not place underwater obstacles very far out from the beach and the Allies had fewer obstacles to clear. Concrete pyramids (tetrahedrons) and wooden rails were the main types of underwater obstacles, but on a number of possible invasion beaches sandbars also helped the defenders.

Heavy and medium coastal batteries formed the main element of the German defensive system. They were emplaced on headlands and in positions where they could flank the coastal indentations that formed bays and gulfs and dominate the seaward approaches. Between Cavalaire Bay and Agay, the enemy had a total of eighty-eight guns formed into twenty-nine batteries, which included some 75-millimeter and 88-millimeter guns in concrete casemates. This was less than 20 percent of the 199 batteries totaling 647 guns, ranging from 75-millimeter to 340-millimeter guns with 107 casemates, emplaced between Marseille and Nice. The St. Mandrier Peninsula protecting the approaches to Toulon alone had fifteen batteries with forty-three guns (including four 340-millimeter guns in two turrets of Battery Cépet).

The Germans used nets and booms to protect Marseille, Toulon, St. Raphael, St. Tropez, Ste-Maxime, and even the small inlet of Agay, but these devices were of little value since the Allies did not plan any frontal assaults against ports. Sea mines also played a role in covering harbor entrances, as the German navy laid minefields off the coast to protect inland shipping lanes. The Germans began laying many small GZ-type[4] shallow water anti-boat contact mines in the Gulf of Fos and to the west at possible landing sites at about 50 to 100 feet apart when the invasion brought their work to a halt. German ships also laid a minefield of ninety moored mines, fifteen magnetic mines, and devices to hinder minesweeping efforts off the Gulf of Fréjus.[5] A smaller minefield was laid in the Bay of Cavalaire. Landmines were usually attached to many of the underwater obstacles, laid on the beaches, behind the beaches, and on beach exits. These mines included antipersonnel and antitank mines. There

were also many dummy minefields staked with warning signs and markers but containing no mines. In general, the German engineers placed single rows of Teller mines (circular antitank mines that came in a couple of models); however, in some places, such as Camel Red Beach, they deployed as many as four rows. They also added *Schu* mines (antipersonnel mines in wooden boxes), which were difficult to detect, in some minefields. Finally, they set up large-caliber shells with detonators and tripwires inland, mainly in fields, and wooden anti-glider stakes in places where they expected landings to take place. At St. Raphael, they drove twelve-inch-high iron stakes into the streets leading to the harbor and attached TNT charges to a third of them.

In the meantime, the Allies finalized their invasion plans. They decided to land the 36th Division on the Camel Beaches near St. Raphael. When intelligence sources discovered that the beaches near St. Raphael, 264 (Camel Red) and 264a, were quite formidable, it was decided to postpone the landings there until the afternoon of D-Day, when additional land and sea support from the other invasion beaches would be available. Camel Green, 264, southeast of St. Raphael, was selected as the main landing site for the 141st Infantry minus the 1st Battalion. Camel Yellow, 265, was on the other side of Cap Drammont, in the Rade d'Agay, but was too well defended for an amphibious assault. Plans were to open it after the initial landings. The 1st Battalion of the 141st was to land on the other side of the Rade d'Agay at Camel Blue, 265a, a small beach at the head of Anthéor Cove dominated by steep cliffs. At the head of this cove, a railroad viaduct and the coast road passed behind the beach area. (An air attack took out a section of the viaduct before the invasion, making it unusable.) Both beach areas

---

4. GZ may have been an American code or identification for these German mines.
5. A submarine on reconnaissance detected a single row of mines across the Gulf of St. Tropez.

The Invasion Beaches

THE 36TH DIVISION CAMEL BEACHES

Blue Beach (#265a)—Anthéor Cove: Inside a small inlet, a sandy beach 80 yards long—unsuitable for vehicles. According to intelligence estimates, the beach and its approaches were not mined and had *no* obstructions. Defenses consisted of several bunkers and machine-gun positions. Only one battery of 149-millimeter guns near Cannes was considered to be a threat to the right flank.

Camel Yellow (#265)—Rade d'Agay: Inlet to the half-mile long sand beach closed by a net and boom. Antitank wall on the beach, according to intelligence estimates; both the beach and inlet were not mined. The soft sandy beach was difficult for vehicle traffic. Inlet and approaches dominated by positions that included a battery of 88-millimeter guns.

Camel Green (#264b)—Cap Drammont: Only about 230 yards of the 840 yards of sand and shingle beach was useable. Most of the area backed by a steep cliff. *No* obstacles and no mines, only wire on the beach. Matting needed for vehicles to cross the beach. Only one exit, but the main coastal road and railroad less than 200 yards away. A battery of five casemated 150-mm guns controlled the approaches.

Camel Red (#264)—Golfe de Fréjus: Several hundred yards of beach. In front of the northeast part of the beach, about 400 yards of concrete tetrahedra placed in two and three rows in 5½ to 9 feet of water (the tetrahedra were 6 feet high) 30 to 165 yards offshore and 13 to 15 feet apart. In front of the southwestern part of the beach, the tetrahedra were more closely placed—only about 4 feet apart. Only the tetrahedra on the sections of the northeast half had mines.[6] A pillar-type wall backed the entire beach and formed a barrier to exiting the beach.[7]

THE 45TH DIVISION DELTA BEACHES

Baie de Bougnon (Red, Green, Yellow, and Blue): Each of these sand and shingle beaches spanned about 400 yards. The coastal road was located just a few yards behind the beaches on the other side of a line of dunes. According to intelligence estimates, the enemy had emplaced demolitions to block the road. Also, *no* obstacles other than wire and mines on the beaches. Between Cap St. Tropez and Pointe Alexandre, the area was heavily defended with five strongpoints covering the beaches and its approaches. One battery of three 220-millimeter guns was sited at Pointe Alexandre and one battery of five 220-millimeter guns (actually they were 164-millimeter guns) near Cap St. Tropez. Two batteries of 155-millimeter guns at the base

---

6. The lines were secured with wires to the seaward side, some in a one-foot cubical container but the majority in a rectangular cement shell about one foot square by two feet long. Each possessed a cylindrical wooden contact maker about four inches in diameter and four inches in height.

7. The miniature Goliath remote-controlled explosive tanks were found in underground shelters facing the beaches with runways of logs leading out of the shelters. Four Goliaths were at Camel Red.

of the Gulf of St. Tropez and a 105-millimeter howitzer in the citadel of St. Tropez. Many other smaller caliber guns (including 75-millimeter and 88-millimeter) and machine guns in casemates and bunkers near strongpoints, which also included trenches and tunnels.

Delta Red (#263a) and Green (#263a): Adjacent beaches that included a continuous concrete reinforced antitank wall 8 to 10 feet high and 3 feet thick that blocked the only beach exit. Sand bars in front of both beaches prevented dry landings and rocks flanked the approaches.

Delta Yellow (#263b) and Blue (#263c): Adjacent beaches backed by a steep embankment with only one exit that led off Yellow. *No* obstructions, besides submerged rocks off Yellow. Coastal road only a few yards behind.

THE 3RD DIVISION ALPHA BEACHES (BAIE DE CAVALAIRE AND BAIE DE BON PORTE)

Two sandy beaches 6 miles apart and about 2 miles long, backed by a narrow belt of tree-covered sand dunes. Beach defenses included mines and barbed wire covered by bunkers and machine-gun positions. Several exits led off the beaches to the coastal road. According to intelligence, the soft sand of the beaches would present a problem for vehicles. Sandbars off the beaches and offshore waters mined.

Alpha Red (#259)—Baie de Cavalaire: Tetrahedral pyramid obstacles in a single row, about 15 feet apart, spanning about 2,000 yards in front of the beach in water 5 to 6 feet deep. The tops of the tetrahedra just above the surface of the water. Most included a Teller mine. About a dozen bunkers and an estimated four gun casemates covered the beach. According to intelligence, the area was heavily defended by coastal guns that included 150-millimeter gun batteries located inland from Cap Camarat and a 164-millimeter gun battery on the Isle du Levant that could cover the approaches.[8] Two companies of about 100 men each defended the beach.

Alpha Yellow (#261)—Baie de Pampelonne: The beach consisted 4,500 yards between two rocky headlands. A double row of wooden pilings of 12 to 14 inches in diameter formed two rows spaced 20 to 25 feet apart, covering about 3,400 yards. Each piling was 15 to 20 feet from the next. The tops were sawed off so that they remained covered by about 2 feet of water. According to intelligence, they were mined. A 220-millimeter battery was located behind the beach area.[9] The shallow gradient was sufficient for LCVPs and LCIs, but not LSTs, which would require pontoon causeways to unload.

---

8. The battery at Isle du Levant turned out to be a dummy position.
9. Four Goliaths were found in shelters at Alpha Yellow.

Paratroopers drop into south France during Operation Dragoon.

assigned to the 141st Infantry appeared to be lightly defended because of the difficult terrain associated with them. The 142nd Infantry was to land on Camel Red early in the afternoon of D-Day after naval forces had time to clear the way, but that operation had to be cancelled on the afternoon of D-Day.

The 45th Division was to land north of St. Tropez in Bougnon Bay on the Delta Beaches with its 157th and 180th Infantry Regiments leading the assault at Delta Red Green (263a), Yellow (263b) and Blue (263c), east of Ste-Maxime. The 3rd Division was to land its 7th Infantry in Cavalaire Bay at Alpha Red Beach (259) and the 15th Infantry on Alpha Yellow (Beach 261) south of St. Tropez.

The night before the invasion, the French Naval Assault Group was to land northeast of Anthéor Cove, block the roads leading to Cannes with demolitions, and withdraw to the west. A French Commando Group was to land near Cap Nègre and secure the western flank by blocking the coastal road. The Commandos and 1st Special Service Force were to go in during the night of D–1 or the early hours of D-Day before H-Hour. The main landings of the assault divisions were to take place at about 8:00 A.M. so that the naval and air forces had sufficient time to bombard the beaches.[10] The Normandy landings finally convinced the Allied leaders that the surprise achieved by landing in the dark or at dawn did not allow enough time for accurate bom-

---

10. During the planning in July, some consideration was given to pushing H-Hour back to 9:00 A.M. to give the air and naval forces more time to neutralize the defenses.

The 8th Beach Battalion in Operation Dragoon

The navy's beach battalions once again served as the marines of the European theater, but their role was mainly operating the beachhead rather than storming it. One of the units involved was the "Eight Balls" 8th Beach Battalion, which formed at Camp Bradford, Virginia, on October 16, 1943; trained at Fort Pierce, Florida, in October; and sailed April 21, 1944, for Arzew, Algeria, where it disembarked on May 10. The unit, which numbered 37 officers and 415 enlisted men, consisted of a headquarters squad (14 men) and four companies with three platoons each. Each of its companies included three officers who served as beachmaster, assistant beach-master, and doctor. The platoons were divided into sections that included a hydrographic section of seventeen enlisted men, a boat repair section of eight enlisted men, a communications section of eight enlisted men, a medical section of seven enlisted men, and a rear echelon of three enlisted men.

At Arzew, the battalion trained with the 91st Division and the 40th Combat Engineer Regiment. Naval Combat Demolition Units 58 and 59 instructed members of the battalion in underwater demolitions and experimented with the new Reddy Fox until May 31. Regular amphibious training, which continued through the month of June, included traffic regulation, salvage, communications, gas drills, and rifle practice. The battalion sailed on the transports *Elizabeth Stanton, Lyon,* and *Florence Nightingale* to Naples, where it landed on June 20. It bivouacked at Salerno, where it continued training. Early in July, the battalion moved to Battapaglia, where it bivouacked and trained with the 540th Combat Engineer Regiment. Both units took part in the amphibious exercises of the 36th Division. At

the end of the month, the "Eight Balls" Battalion moved to a site north of Naples. On August 10, after a final rehearsal on August 7–8, the battalion embarked on Liberty ships, APAs, LSTs, LCIs, and LCTs and sailed for France.

The 8th Beach Battalion was assigned to the Camel assault area, and some of its elements landed in the second wave at H+10. All elements of Company A were ashore on Camel Green by H+185. By midafternoon, all three companies had come ashore. On D-Day, the battalion helped bring in the entire 36th Division through Green Beach, except for the battalion that landed on Camel Blue. The only casualties between D-Day and D+2 were six enlisted men wounded by mines. The battalion opened Camel Yellow on the evening of August 15 and had it in full operation by August 16 after the naval combat demolition units cleared the approaches. Camel Red One and Red Two were opened when St. Raphael and the mines and obstacles on the beaches were cleared on D+3 and D+4. After D+4, Camel Yellow and Green were closed and the battalion continued to operate the Red beaches and the port of St. Raphael. The attached Seabees of the 1040th Naval Construction Battalion set up twelve pontoon causeways on the Red Beaches. The naval combat demolition teams, which also operated at the Camel beaches, completed their mission by D+5 and were detached.

During the first six days, the 8th Beach Battalion evacuated 7,000 prisoners through Camel Green. Army hospital units that set up operations inland treated and evacuated 1,400 casualties through the 8th Beach Battalion.

continued

The 8th Beach Battalion in Operation Dragoon *continued*

The battalion continued to operate the Camel area through September, while Company B was detached for service at Marseille on September 10. Company C was transported to Bizerte, Tunisia, to be joined by Company A early the next month and Company B a few days later. The battalion returned to the United States in November.

Sources: War Diary of the 8th Beach Battalion for June, July, August, September, October, and November 1944; Clifford L. Leggerton, former S1C of Platoon A-2, 8th Beach Battalion.

German Defenses of South France

Minimal German naval and air units remained in south France throughout August 1944. The naval force consisted of one destroyer and a few smaller craft including E-boats. Five U-boats remained at Marseille and Toulon. Of the *Luftwaffe*'s 200 aircraft, most were earmarked for recon or anti-shipping operations.

The strength of the German Nineteenth Army, which was responsible for the region, had been sapped after the Normandy invasion to provide reinforcements for Army Group B north of the Loire. The units that moved out of the region included the 9th Panzer Division and the 271st, 272nd, and 277th Infantry Divisions, which were replaced by the 11th Panzer Division from the Russian front, the 198th (also from the Eastern Front), and 716th Infantry Divisions. The 716th, which had defended the beaches of Normandy, had taken heavy losses; its contingent had been reduced to 8,000 men, and its firepower had been halved. It was stationed in the southwest of France at Perpignan. The 198th Division, which was stationed north of Narbonne, numbered 10,500 men, many of whom were Czechs of questionable loyalty. The weak 189th Reserve Division, consisting of only four infantry battalions and some artillery, was stationed at Montpellier. The 338th Infantry Division, whose men were only fit for limited service, defended the Rhone Valley and the mouth of the river. Its headquarters was located at Arles, and four of its battalions had already been dispatched to Normandy.

Hitler insisted that Marseille and Toulon be well defended and assigned the job to the 244th and 242nd Infantry Divisions respectively. Each division was at about 85 percent strength but lacked veteran troops. In August, the German army commander, having concluded that the Allies would land east of Toulon, moved the 242nd Division into the area. In the meantime, the 11th Panzer Division began to move eastward toward the Rhone. The only other large German formation near the invasion area was the 148th Reserve Division holding the Nice–Cannes sector. Farther to the north, the 157th Reserve Division with headquarters at Grenoble was deployed against the French Maquis units. Both the 148th and 157th Divisions were estimated to be at full strength.

The Germans began construction of underwater obstacles and minefields along the

continued

German Defenses of South France *continued*

coast in early April. Several fortified gun batteries were already in the area, and laborers
began adding bunkers and roadblocks to isolate beach areas. The Germans also put back
into service old French coastal battery positions. Inland, they placed stakes in open fields
to deter airborne landings. In the drop zone

and landing zone, these obstacles were poorly
emplaced—sunk less than two feet into the
ground and spaced at thirty to forty feet
apart—and they presented only a minor problem.[11] The defenses included positions and
obstacles similar to those of the Atlantic Wall,
but not as densely spread or as well defended.

11. Beyond the actual drop zone in the Fréjus area, another type of antiglider obstacle consisted of sharpened three-foot-high stakes
well emplaced and connected with wire

bardment and did not justify the risk. For Dragoon, only the commando-type units would land
in the dark; the paratroopers would jump early in
the morning after the quarter-moon appeared.
The paratroopers of the 1st Airborne Task Force
were to land in the vicinity of Le Muy, clear the
way for the dawn glider landings, and block the
road between Le Luc and Fréjus, forcing possible
German reinforcements to use the coast road.

The dominating terrain in the invasion area
was the Massif des Maures, a large mass of hill
spanning thirty-five miles from Hyères to Fréjus
and up to ten miles in width with elevations
varying between 1,000 and 1,500 feet. Parts of
the massif were heavily wooded with pine and
cork oak, and most of it was inaccessible even to
foot traffic. The invasion beaches lay at the base
of the massif and, in some cases, were sheer cliffs
rising from the sea. Behind the massif, a corridor
created by the river valleys of two rivers linked
Toulon with St. Raphael. Beyond that rise the
formidable Maritime Alps, which become less of
an obstacle to the west. Within the Mediterranean climate, the region was landscaped with
vineyards and fruit trees, And the coast was dotted with the small coastal ports and towns of the
Riviera.

The Allies hoped that the beachhead would
span in an arc of about forty miles from the

Hyères Roadstead to a point west of La Napoule
and reach a depth of up to twenty miles by D+2.
This was marked on maps as the Blue Line, which
encompassed most of the Maures Massif, the
highway from Fréjus to Le Luc, and part of the
Estérel Massif to the east. From the Blue Line, the
assault divisions, reinforced by the French Army B
on the left flank, were to advance on Toulon and
Marseille, their first major objectives, since there
were no artificial harbors and the Allies needed a
major port thirty days after the invasion to handle
the required logistical support.

Preparations for Operation Dragoon

The Invasion Training Center in Algeria moved
to the Salerno area in the spring of 1944. After
the fall of Rome, the 3rd, 36th, and 45th Divisions were pulled from the front and moved back
to the Naples–Salerno area in the latter part of
June. The commanders of these divisions, John W.
O'Daniel, John E. Dahlquist, and William W.
Eagles had varying degrees of experience. The
3rd Division went into training in the Pozzuoli
area while the other two camped between
Salerno and Paestum. The VI Corps headquarters
of Gen. Lucian K. Truscott also moved to the rear
to prepare. General Patch's Seventh Army trans-

ferred, with Wilson's Allied Forces Headquarters, from Algeria to the Naples area, where the naval command was also concentrated. The various commands set themselves up in palaces and castles in the Naples area, including a castle on the Neapolitan sea front.

The three assault divisions were to receive about three weeks of day and night amphibious training at battalion level and then go through a final rehearsal. In July, training was concentrated on the artillery units. Sherman duplex-drive tanks were to be used again, but this time, the training of the crews was built upon experiences acquired in Normandy. Innovations that were tested in late June at Salerno included the radio-controlled Apex boats[12] loaded with explosives to destroy obstacles, LCMs converted to special rocket ships known as Woofus, a new type of aerial bomb, and other novelties to help clear obstacles on and near the beaches.[13] The 3rd Division trained between July 6 and July 27. On July 31, Exercise Shamrock, the final rehearsal for the 3rd Division, involved 146 vessels and took place in the Bay of Gaeta at Mandragone. The 36th Division conducted its training between July 8 and July 22. Early in August, it conducted its final exercise, Cowpuncher II, at Mandragone, at the mouth of the Garigliano River. Finally, the battalions of the 45th Division underwent amphibious training between June 24 and July 14 and held their final rehearsal, Exercise Thunderbird, on August 7–8, in conjunction with the 36th Division's Exercise Cowpuncher II. The troops boarded the LCIs and LSTs in the vicinity of Pozzuoli on August 7 and landed between

Salerno and Agropoli on August 8. The 157th was on the right and the 180th on the left. The exercise was called off that afternoon, and the troops boarded ship for the return to Pozzuoli. During this final two-division rehearsal, realistic beach obstacles and mines with reduced charges were set up. The assault forces fired live ammunition, naval gunfire, rockets, and did everything else necessary to make the experience as realistic as possible. Even the aircraft carrier force participated, but only a small element of the 1st Airborne Task Force was available to simulate landings five miles west of Albanella.

The 1st Special Service Force trained at the Invasion Training Center at Salerno[14] between July 5 and 20. The training included the use of rubber assault craft and loading from fast transports. The French Commandos also trained here at about the same time. The final rehearsal, Exercise Bruno, took place on the nights of August 7–9. The troops landed on the islands of Ponza and Zanona, which had sheer cliffs that the troops had to scale. After the exercise, the planners recommended using more PT boats and a different landing procedure with rubber boats if they came under enemy fire. On August 11, the 1st SSF sailed out of Santa Maria Castellabate for Corsica, the staging area, in a convoy of five APDs (fast destroyers converted to troop transports) and two troopships. The troops rested on Corsica, where they were briefed for the assault, and departed on August 14.

An additional element was added to the invasion force in July: the naval combat demolitions units. Comdr. Herbert Peterson brought the ten

---

12. Apex were radio-controlled boats, normally towed in pairs by a landing craft, released, and directed to offshore obstacles where they were detonated.

13. The Reddy Fox, a type of bangalore torpedo to be used under water after being towed to the beach. Although present during the invasion, none were used for clearing the beaches for fear they might hit an obstacle and detonate while being towed. The Woofus was an LCM(R) with short range 7.2-inch demolition rockets intended to help clear obstacles, including mines, on the foreshore. They should not be confused with LCMs and LCTs carrying rockets with a greater range that were also present.

14. In 1944, the center moved from Arzew, Algeria, to Salerno. It handled everything from training naval shore fire control parties to medical personnel. One section was set up for artillery units.

Gliders after landing in fields near Le Muy during Operation Dragoon. ELMER D. RICHARDSON

units that had cleared the way at Utah Beach from England to Italy, where they were joined by a group of men freshly arrived from Fort Pierce, Florida. SF1/C Angelos Chatas was among the Normandy veterans called to serve one more time.

Those of use who survived were put aboard a destroyer, the USS *Butler*. We boarded the *Butler*, went to Northern Ireland, down the Atlantic coast of France, through the Straits of Gibraltar, and on to North Africa, making stops every so often. We went to Alexandria, Egypt, turned around, went to Naples harbor, and prepared for the second invasion of France.

By July, forty-one naval combat demolition units were available. Each six-man team (one officer and five enlisted men), joined by five army engineers, practiced on the beaches in the Salerno area, where obstacles similar to those found in Normandy had been set up. Commander Peterson's men were to operate the Apex boats. The naval combat demolition teams assigned to the Apex boats included four experienced boatmen (one for the Apex male control boat and three for the Apex females—each loaded with 8,000 pounds of explosives). The control boat carried 2,000 pounds of tetratol in 20-pound packs, diving gear, and two rubber boats that the team would use to clear the obstructions the explosive boats failed to destroy. Other teams manned the twenty-one Woofus rocket boats and LCM(R)s mounting 120 7.2-inch rockets.

Between August 11 and 13, convoys carrying the three assault divisions sailed from the Naples–Pozzuoli area. The 157th Infantry of 45th Division boarded the landing craft on August 11 and sailed on August 12, passing between Corsica and Sardinia between August 13 and 14. Some units departed earlier, others later, depending on the type of vessels they were on and their destinations. By the evening of August 14, all the troop convoys had sailed toward the transport areas off South France to prepare for the morning landing.

Long before the amphibious operation and even until shortly before the landings, the army air force flew mapping and photo recon missions over the invasion area. Before the winter of 1943–45, the aerial photography and mapping of the Anvil invasion area had been almost completed, but additional missions were needed when the weather cleared early in 1944. Some pilots had to fly the high-risk dicing missions, during which they skimmed the ground at altitudes of a few hundred feet, taking oblique photos to help identify enemy positions.

Capt. Elmer D. Richardson, S-2 for the 5th Photo Recon Squadron, 3rd Photo Group, 90th Photo Recon Wing,[15] moved to Borgo airfield in northeastern Corsica with his Photo Recon Group in July with plans to move into south France on D+30.[16] The aircraft in his squadron flew low-level missions at three to four hundred feet to identify German gun positions and defenses shortly before the landings. Lt. Col. Thomas Barfoot was the commander for the 3rd Photo Recon Group at the time.

In relation to our mapping of south France just prior to the invasion, the army wanted to look at the coastline of southern France and Capt. Karl Polifka was selected to take a dicing mission. It is a mission you fly constantly three hundred feet above the water and about that far away from the coastline. You have two cameras, both oblique, shooting out the side. He had his mission all figured out. He would take right-hand camera, go from the coast of Italy, fly the coastline as far as the film would last, turn around, and go to the other end using his left-hand camera.

This was all preplanned by Polifka. He got about half a mile or mile using his right-hand camera, and they [enemy ground fire] shot out his right engine. In actuality, in those circumstances a conservative pilot would throw up his hands so to speak and return home, but Karl Polifka didn't. He feathered the engine and continued on, taking the pictures with his right-hand camera. Again, a conservative pilot after running out of film would have come home, but he didn't. He proceeded on, went out to sea, came back, took the photos, and returned home on a single engine. All of the oil pressure gauges were off the board; they were overheating. He had a hell of a time getting his gear down and all that sorts of stuff, but he finally made it and landed. That was another type of mission not flown frequently, but not infrequently. This may have been a week before the invasion.

---

15. The 90th Photo Recon Wing consisted of the 3rd and 5th Photo Recon Groups, with three squadrons each. The 3rd Photo Recon Group consisted of the 5th, 12th, and 23rd Squadrons. The 23rd also comprised a few Free French pilots, including the famous French author Antoine de Saint-Exupéry who disappeared on a mission over South France and whose plane was recently found showing signs of having been shot down somewhere near Marseille.

16. The success of Dragoon led to such a rapid advance that Richardson's squadron was sent back to Italy.

Two weeks prior to the invasion of southern France, as a group commander, I was called to the Twelfth Air Force, Gen. John Cannon's HQ. I was briefed from a great big guy from Texas; he was the operations officer for Twelfth Air Force. We sat around and had coffee, and he said, "Barfoot, I want to brief you on what is going to happen here in the near future. In fact, it is going to happen on 15 August." He outlined the entire air plan and ground plan for the invasion of France. When we got through after about four or five cups of coffee . . . he said, "Barfoot, you are an operational pilot, but I would suggest very strongly that you do not fly any more missions until the invasion. . . . I had all the information of what was going and if I were shot down, they could interrogate me to a point where I would have to give them some valuable information.

CHAPTER 11

Preparing for Dragoon

Lt. Ruben D. Parker, a product of officer candidate school, joined the 141st Infantry, 36th Division, in late January 1944 as a replacement in time for some of the worst days of the Italian campaign. After the breakout from Anzio, the fall of Rome, and a period of rest, the Texas Division pulled back near the Avalanche landing beaches in the Salerno–Paestum area, where the T Patchers bivouacked in their tents under the Italian sun, far from the battlefield. As soon as they were rested, the troops began amphibious training. In early August, the division's regiments encamped in the fruit orchards near Pozzuoli, several miles to the northwest of Naples.

I remember one incident in the Bay of Naples[1] [after it began raining] when the LCVP landed too soon, and the lead soldier stepped off into the water a foot over his head. He had his helmet on and his arm at sling arms, so immediately my first sergeant and I shucked our packs, dove in, and grabbed him until he could tread water and get to the beach. I remember I was wearing a GI Hamilton wristwatch that was supposed to be waterproof, but it wasn't. It stopped shortly after. What amazed me about practices was that when it came to the real thing, the terrain was almost exactly like where we practiced. So when we got to Southern France, there didn't seem to be any confusion, at least not in my mind or my platoon leaders', as to where we were going to go. That was the only thing that impressed me in training.

Lt. Martin J. Tully, another OCS graduate, who joined the division earlier than Parker, was in time for Operation Avalanche. He took over Company C, 141st Infantry, in August 1944.

We were pulled back, and we had some dry runs on territory that approximated what we would have in South France. In addition to that, C Company, which I was in at the time, received some added assault training because we were going to be the first wave in on this eighty-yard beach. That entailed Bangalore torpedoes to destroy wire, various pole charges, and TNT to blast the pillboxes.

According to Cpl. Art John Zalud, a truck driver in Service Battery, 155th Field Artillery Battalion, 36th Division, the men who served with the artillery received little special training,

just waterproofing the vehicles, the engines, and extending the exhaust pipes up. Otherwise, there was nothing interesting, just laying back and having fun. We didn't make any amphibious practices. Our unit was well organized and stayed together all through. We were told it would be practically the same as Salerno. The firing batteries were first in [the service battery followed later].

Our field artillery battalion was organized with three firing batteries, and one section from the service battery was to supply each firing battery. The service battery was commanded by a captain, and we had two lieutenants and several sergeants. My section supplied C Battery. Then they had other units to supply the firing batteries with food and other supplies. In our section there were three trucks commanded by S.Sgt. Schuman. Each section had two drivers and a sergeant in charge, about eight people to a section. The truck I was on had a .50 cal. MG mount for AA. I was the gunner on it. We each had carbines, and we always carried a load of fifty to sixty shells—each shell weighed 100 pounds. Besides the shells, we carried boxes of fuses, plus containers with the powder charges with charges of one to seven. Seven was the most powerful for the longest range. They came in separate little powder bags; with charge seven, you threw all the powder charges in. The powder was in cases with seven different-size bags.

Carl Strom, another officer candidate school graduate, had joined the 36th Division in time

1. There seems to be some confusion as to where the veterans thought they were, and many do not distinguish the Gulf of Naples from the Gulf of Pozzuoli or the Gulf of Salerno. Lieutenant Parker is not sure if this was during practice in the Gulf of Salerno or possibly additional training just before embarkation at Pozzuoli.

Troops disembarking from LCIs during the landings in south France on August 15, 1944.

for the disaster on the Rapido River. By the conclusion of the Anzio campaign, he had been promoted from the position of 3rd Platoon leader to company executive officer. His Company B would land in the second wave of the invasion.

They pulled us out of line in Italy, north of Rome. I took a week's leave with Lieutenant Tully in Rome, and we stayed drunk for the entire week. Then they sent us down to Salerno area, where we made practice landings for the invasion of south France. We went on the ships and came down the sides on rope ladders into the landing craft. The area at Salerno was similar to the area in south France, but at that time, we still didn't know where we were going. There were rumors we were going to Yugoslavia as well as south France or to the north of our lines in Italy. We made several practice landings in the same mode we would have them in south France, and there were no accidents. Everything was real smooth for Company B. Each of the companies was well separated, and we didn't see each other until before the landing. The [landings] were regimental in size, done in battalion increments because the regiments and battalions were landing on different beaches. The 1st Battalion had its own little beach on the extreme right flank, and it was only eighty yards wide. Our landing area was different from the rest of the division's and the regiment. They were landings in different terrain than we were trained on.

No change in the organization of the platoon; however, we were given added ammunition and equipment, so each man was more heavily loaded than under normal combat circumstances. We were different companies and near each other, but we didn't work together in training. This was July and August.

Our company had about five LCVPs. There was no change in the basic structure of the unit. We had the same training with the Bangalore torpedoes as C Company. I don't believe we were at full strength. I had not recovered full strength from the previous battles. I was company commander for the practice landings, and then they brought a captain in, that was Alf Mackins.

The division was moved to just north of Naples to Pozzuoli. We were all camped in pup tents[2] by the port. The day before the invasion, we boarded the ships at the port of Pozzuoli, the various LSTs, and sailed late that afternoon.

Lt. Ruben Parker's Company E, 141st Infantry, loaded onto a single ship, which he believed was an LCI.

I don't think we found out where it was going to be until we landed. We knew it was France because they gave us French script after we got on the ship, but there was always the possibility of further up the Italian Peninsula. I think, from the first, we knew what our assignment was, and I don't think anybody worried after being in combat nine months. We took it one day at a time. I think we were happy it was not Italy because Italians were somewhat two-faced. They were all smiles when you came in, but when your back was turned, that smile might turn to a grimace.[3]

PFC Arthur P. Rodgers of Oklahoma City, a machine gunner in 2nd Platoon D Company (weapons company), 1st Battalion, 141st Infantry, had mobilized with the division in 1940.

They sent me back just after the invasion of Salerno. It was ten days after the landing when they found out that I was under seventeen because my dad wrote the Red Cross, and they notified the division. They shipped me back to the U.S., and I had to wait six months. I rejoined them when they pulled back for amphibious training.[4]

They did the same thing as the preparation for Salerno. We practiced getting on the LSTs and off shore. We never knew until they gave us the company orders. I remember several guys getting a broken arm or leg, like in Africa. Williams . . . the armorer got crushed between two LSTs in Africa and killed. The rumor was we would be sent home if we took and held the beaches of south France for three days.

The fourth company in each battalion is heavy weapons. You have two platoons of water-cooled .30 cal Browning MG Model A-1 and one platoon of 81-mm mortars. The MG platoons were always attached as a platoon or section of one of the attack elements or given to a reserve company. We were always attached out to one of the rifle companies and seldom with our company. During the invasion, my section was attached to C Company. There are four machine guns to a platoon, a section of two squads with one MG in a squad, twelve men in a squad, and twenty-four men to a

---

2. The term "pup tent" refers to two shelter halves buttoned together. Each man carried half, and when two were put together, the result was a small two-man tent.

3. Ruben Parker's views about Italians were not those held by all GIs. Experiences varied from location to location. Wartime conditions for many civilians were not the best, and their future was uncertain.

4. He claimed he returned to the same platoon. NARA records show that after he was returned home before the invasion of Salerno, and apparently released from the service, he was drafted in 1943, although some NARA records have transcription errors.

section, plus a section sergeant. The machine gun had a no. 1 gunner—me—and the no. 2 gunner. I carried the tripod, and the no. 2 man carried the gun. When we went into action, I put my part down and he put the gun on. He fed the belt while I fired. We had a squad leader, assistant squad leader, and eight ammo bearers. The no. 1 and 2 gunners had .45s, and other men the same, because they carried two tins of 350 rounds or total of 700 rounds per man.

At the time of the fall of Rome, twenty-three-year-old Capt. Kenneth P. Stemmons, a veteran of all the campaigns of the 45th Division from Sicily to Anzio, commanded Company B, 1st Battalion, 157th Infantry. The breakout of Anzio was one of the most memorable moments of his wartime experiences.

For 200 yards out of the line, my legs would not support me. I had to crawl physically up the ditch for a long way before I regained control of my legs, but we continued to take the fight to the enemy. After Rome fell, on 6 June the 157th Infantry was moved to a rest area, filled up to strength and started training.

At the Rome area, we trained in attacking fortified positions. At the Naples area, we trained for an amphibious assault, where we received new replacements with no previous amphibious training. We loaded and unloaded assault boats for practice assault landings.

Stemmons was never able to shake off the memories of the grueling fighting in the mountains and at Anzio, the daily casualties, and the lack of rest that were the lot of the combat

infantryman. He was also troubled by the fact that there were more troops in the rear areas than on the lines.[5] His main gripe was that "if you were an infantry soldier in a combat division, you would become a casualty. In my rifle company of approximately 200 men, not one man went the entire way without becoming a casualty, some of us more than once." For the infantrymen, there was no tour of duty followed by a return home after so many missions, like in the air force. Instead, "you stayed in the infantry until you became a casualty. If you didn't go home from your wounds, you went back to your unit for another chance. It was the combat soldier's great fear on how bad he would get hit."

In the staging area for Southern France, again we needed good boots, weapons repair, knives, and GI watches. However, decent food was the number one item wanted. All troops were issued new clothing, boots if needed, all weapons were checked, and, yes, some of the replacements needed basic M-1 rifle training. We were issued the new type gas masks that stored on top of the pack, out of the water while wading ashore. Additional flamethrowers and Bangalore torpedoes were issued and used in training. We practiced an assault against a seawall using an eight-foot ladder that was carried in each first and second wave assault boat. All of the training was useful in the actual invasion.

PFC Ralph Fink, Company D, 157th Infantry, was a veteran of the campaign in Italy like Captain Stemmons. The months of constant action had left him physically and emotionally depleted, and he welcomed with relief the respite his unit got after it was pulled out of line after the fall of

5. He noted some facts from other sources that stated that of the 11 million men serving in the army, only 2 million—less than 20 percent—were assigned to combat divisions and only 700,000 (35 percent of 2 million) of those were assigned to infantry companies.

Rome. The period of rest in the rear lines was a time of spiritual and physical renewal after the heartbreak of watching his comrades die from combat wounds or illness and suffering from trench foot and battle fatigue.

Many of us had, and still do, guilt feelings because we somehow survived and so many other good men didn't. There was apprehension about the future. Although we acted with braggadocio, I'm sure I was not the only one that dreaded the thought of going into combat again at some time in the future.

We needed numerous replacements to get back up to strength. We were living in pup tents, but I remember it was easy living. Kitchen was set up and serving hot meals, we played some softball, just loafed around and out of danger for the present.

Fink was not particularly impressed with the training for the veterans. The practice beach landings were low-key because there were not enough available ships for a full-scale rehearsal, so the battalions were forced to practice their landings one at a time. The men boarded the ships in the harbor at Naples, sailed a few miles south, scrambled down nets into the waiting LCVPs, and stormed the beach. When the practice was over, they returned by truck to their bivouac area. However, the practice assaults were not all so dull that they faded from memory, as the following episodes will attest.

Our officer was a decent man, but extremely anxious for our practice landing to go well. As we sailed south, our officer gathered us together and stated something like this: "This will be a piece of cake. The sea is calm; the beach is level with no obstructions. We'll run through this exercise easily and should be back in bivouac in time to play softball before dark."

All went well until we were in the landing craft. For some reason, the second ship was late in arriving, so we just kept circling for about an hour at a slow speed. Even though the sea was calm, that small craft seemed to rock in many different directions, and many of us got violently seasick. Finally, when all was coordinated, we made our gung-ho charge across the beach, directly into a field of ripe watermelons. Discipline broke down at this point. There was no softball played that evening, but we probably had the greatest orgy of watermelon eating in the history of mankind.

The only special training Fink could recall was for scaling a beach wall that was expected to be in their sector. When the time to embark for the invasion finally came, Fink and his men were trucked to the port of Naples and joined

an extremely long line of soldiers, double file, heading toward the ships. The following is a little vignette that has stayed with me all these years. As we were shuffling along toward our ship, there was a small Italian bakery on the street with a cake with white icing displayed in the window. Still having Italian money in my possession and without thinking, I dropped out of line and ran into the bakery expecting to make the deal in a few seconds. This was not to be. Speaking no Italian whatsoever, I kept throwing money on the counter, and the baker kept signaling for more. To this day, I think he really took me for a ride. When I finally came out, the column had moved ahead quite rapidly, and I was a bit disoriented because everyone looked alike. In a moment of panic, I thought my outfit had already boarded one of the ships and I would have to latch on with some other group. However, my friends were watching for me;

Elements of Alpha Force (3rd Infantry Division) coming ashore in LCVPs on August 15, 1944.

when they saw me carrying that cake they let me know, loud and clear, exactly where they were. My decision to drop out of that line to get the cake was so spontaneous that our officer was not aware that I was missing until the guys started calling to me. Need I say that that cake was quickly eaten, on the run. As the incident was retold in weeks to come, there was always raucous laughter, and it was amplified each time it was retold.

I recall getting aboard ship. Each unit was kept together in their own group right up on deck. Only now were we told exactly where we were going. We were given all information available. A few maps of our landing area were given to key people, and strategies were discussed and rehashed. We were issued numerous ropes to be used to get over a seawall, which would be in our zone. I think we sailed from Naples prior to

dark on the evening of August 14th [13th?], and I distinctly recall sailing between Corsica and Sardinia sometime during the night. The night was clear, and these islands were plain to see.

Incidentally, for this operation we all had American flags sewn on our uniform shoulders in place of our divisional patches. We also had each been issued gas masks.

Along about midnight, all planning was completed. The landing was scheduled for shortly after daybreak, so we were told to flop down on deck and try to get some sleep. Although there was some fitful dozing, no one really slept well. We had all read and heard about the tremendous losses at Normandy, and we assumed this was the type of operation into which we were heading. The remaining hours seemed endless, as we each lay awake with our individual thoughts and fears.

I should mention here that little was known to us about he overall scope of the operation. I recall seeing numerous ships in Naples harbor and then in convoy as we headed north, but we had no clue if this was a major, medium, or minor operation. We had no idea if ships would be joining us on convoy from other ports. Incidentally, this was our situation many, many times in combat. We were all very concerned about what was happening on our little turf, but most often had no idea as to the big picture. Combat always had a way of bringing the focus of things right down to the individual or squad level.

PFC Isadore L. Valenti, a medic assigned to Company K, 7th Infantry, was another veteran with the 3rd Division.

Early May 1944, when in Naples area, I was busted and shanghaied to a replacement depot because of some personality quirk of my company commander. A week later, since I was a trained medical technician, I was assigned to the 7th Infantry since there was a severe shortage of medics there. I arrived at the 3rd Battalion Aid Station at 3 A.M. while it was under fire by German mortars. This was during the Anzio breakout.

The medical officer, Captain Donnelly, told me to report to Company K, which was short of medics. He didn't tell me what happened to the other medics. I learned later that several medics had been either seriously wounded or killed. I was assigned to 3rd Platoon of Company K. On the push to Rome, I was wounded, but not seriously. I treated myself and remained with my platoon.

After ten days of occasional duty in Rome, we went back to the Naples area. For the next eight weeks, we prepared for the invasion of France.

Social Problems

In Italy, familiar problems grew serious. Long weeks of combat or the boredom in the rear areas greatly sharpened the soldiers' appetite for life, food, drink, and women. In war-ravaged Italy, where the population suffered from hunger and poverty prevailed, it was easy for the relatively well-paid, well-supplied American soldiers to find a surcease for their needs. Many a young woman and even girls on the cusp of puberty were only too eager to trade sexual favors for luxuries like chocolate, cigarettes, and food. Thus, according to PFC Isadore L. Valenti, the bivouac area of 7th Infantry was surrounded by pimps and their girls. That summer, while the soldiers prepared for the invasion of France, the MPs brought the women into the camp to be inspected for VD. If they were disease-free, they received a document they could carry with them. If they were not, they received treatment. Valenti, who spoke Italian, was recruited by the medical officer, Capt. Frank Syladek, as a translator, and he had to inform the women that they must have a clean bill of health or ply their trade elsewhere.

The situation was so bad in the Naples area that troops on pass received a kit that included not only prophylactics but also six sulfa tablets to be taken after sexual activity. Unfortunately, many of the soldiers failed to use these tablets and contracted sexually transmitted diseases.

On one occasion, near the bivouac area, Valenti saw soldiers lining up at a few pup tents containing one woman each. Some of the GIs collected the money from their comrades and ran the operation without any interference from the MPs.

During the advance on Rome, about the time Valenti was wounded, a citation reveals that he was also taking many risks.

Isadore L. Valenti, 6 851 805, Sergeant, Medical Detachment 7th Infantry Regiment. For meritorious achievement in actual combat. On 1 June 1944, while leading a litter squad across a grain field towards a wounded soldier near Rome, Italy, Sergeant Valenti came under machine pistol fire at 75 yards range. Instructing the litter bearers to return to cover, he ran and crept for about 65 yards to the casualty. After rendering first aid, Sergeant Valenti crawled back to his company CP. At dark, he evacuated the casualty with the help of the litter squad.

On August 3, 1944, after their training finally came to an end, the men of the 7th Infantry assembled to hear a speech from their commanding officer, Col. W. H. O'Mohundro, who stressed the importance of their upcoming mission. The next day, the entire 3rd Division was put on review for Gen. Alexander Patch, who gave the troops some words of encouragement. Finally, on August 7, the tents came down and the 7th Infantry moved to its embarkation port. Before boarding the ships, each battalion was inspected for contraband alcohol. On August 10, the regiment was aboard ship and ready to depart. The deck of Valenti's troopship was loaded with trucks and half-tracks; the soldiers slept wherever they found enough space, if they were not assigned quarters below deck. During the trip, they ate two meals a day. Soon the convoy reached Ajaccio, Corsica, and the men were briefed for the upcoming invasion.[6]

PFC Robert L. Zahradka served in the message center as a runner for D Company and later for the 1st Battalion, 7th Infantry. After the division pulled back from Rome,

We went to an area near Pozzuoli and took vigorous training in and around the Bay of Naples. We were marched about five miles to the dock, waited for a boat—LCVP—ride to a ship, embarked, rode around, then went over the side into the LCVP and made a landing on a beach. We then ran into some sort of problem and ended up marching about five miles back to camp.

The staging area, as I remember, was the same docks where we had trained. The only problems were the continual foul-up between commands. As an enlisted man, I was never privy to the reasons; all I could do was hurry up and wait. In all, it took about four to six weeks of training. We were issued full equipment, emergency rations, a day's field rations, bandoliers of ammo, and anything they thought we might need.

Sgt. Frank Andrews, another veteran of the war in Italy, was with the HQ of the 1st Battalion, 7th Infantry, 3rd Division, during the breakout at Anzio.

We got hit rather hard and had a lot of replacements and new personnel. We lost our first sergeant, so being one of the few old-timers, I wound up with that job, and that was my first time in administrative work. It had its advantage, but it was new to me and different from what I had done before.

---

6. According to Admiral Hewitt's Report on the Invasion of South France, the troops of the assault divisions embarked on August 10. The dates Valenti gives for breaking camp and the speeches may be off a day or so, although the 3rd Infantry Division History mentions that the troops loaded on August 8.

The fall of Rome ended our campaign in Italy. We stayed there in one of the beautiful parks in downtown Rome in pup tents. Then back to Pozzuoli, Naples, and a training period. We didn't know what was going on. South France would be our fifth landing operation. We were far better equipped with landing craft and everything. The main roads leading to the docks at Naples were occupied with tanks and heavy equipment. If you took a side street, they were rather narrow with balconies that would keep big trucks out. They had to unload us quite away from the dock, and we had to march, I don't remember how many blocks, to the dock. It was quite a ways. What we didn't know was it was the red light district. Here came all these big brave American soldiers with a column on each side of the street with all their gear and everything. Next thing you know, all these chippies [slang for prostitutes] come out grabbing guys, trying to drag them in doorways and anywhere else. Within a block distance, everybody was in one line down the center protecting everybody's rear and flank.

We loaded up that afternoon, and the next day the ship was milling around finding its way into the convoy. It was the only chance I had to see old Churchill waving his big V for victory sign and smoking a big stogie. We spent a few days on the ships, which were loaded heavy with equipment on the top deck. For the trip from Naples to Southern France, it was more like time on a luxury cruise with beautiful weather with everyone laying around, playing cards, or listening to radios, and Sally [Axis Sally] telling how easy it was to surrender anytime we wanted to. She named all the units in the convoy and told us where we were at and sure enough, you could see we were passing between Sardinia and that makes your hair stand on end.

I was first sergeant and connected with admin work, so it was the first landing in which I was not involved in tactical part like the other landings.

PFC Louis Sumien was a runner in the headquarters of the 3rd Battalion of the 7th Infantry when the division pulled back from the front for rest and training. His unit was stationed at near Piano di Quattro, the same place where his unit had prepared for the Anzio landing.

In Pozzuoli, the boys of the 3rd Division rescued a young lady who is still, I understand, the division's mascot. She is now the movie actress Sofia Loren.

For the invasion of southern France, we trained at Gaeta, which supposedly resembled the next area to be invaded. We were bivouacked in pyramidal tents. The area was gloomy, and we trained and trained with amphibious training and had little else to do and nowhere to go. I understand that accidents happened at Gaeta and some men were killed. Every day, the same monotonous routine. The men hiking back from the beach area in the rain at night, falling dead asleep after chow only to be awakened early by the stinking bugle. Breakfast and back on the road with the same routine, wearing wet socks from the previous night most of the time. Credit has to be given to those fine young men, who, although they complained, bitched, cursed everything including the stinkin' army, and still always did their duty when the time came. Some of the many problems included rashes from wet and stinking clothes, tents all smelling of mildew, the rain, the mud, and the stupidity of it all.

We were dressed in olive drab. Except for Anzio, we dressed in what was called tank men's uniforms, which consisted of a khaki sort of combat jacket that zipped up the front and the same type overalls, like a farmer's with straps going over our shoulders. For Anzio, we had our leggings taken away and combat boots issued and it was goodbye forever for leggings. For southern France, the men still kept the combat jacket, which they all liked, but wore olive drab, carried packs, extra bandoliers of ammo, grenades, some bazookas, and perhaps a mortar shell, which was to be dropped on the beach. The equipment was no different than at Anzio.

We boarded LSTs on which we were assigned the usual pull-down chain-link bunks like seen in many movies. I volunteered (I don't know why) to help out in the bakery, and each night our group baked, I think, 100 loaves of bread for the men in two batches of fifty. For doing this, we received a steak dinner, which we dug out of the ship's hull. Nothing much happened during the trip. I heard the French actor Jean Pierre Aumont was aboard, but I never saw him.

S.Sgt. John B. Shirley, a latecomer to the Italian campaign but a veteran of Anzio, found it a relief when the 15th Infantry was pulled out of the line when the 3rd Division began preparing for its next amphibious invasion. His 3rd Platoon, Company I, 3rd Battalion, was restored to full strength.

I Company was a typical infantry company, and we were at full strength for the southern France invasion. I was a squad leader of the 3rd Squad of the 3rd Platoon. We had two scouts, a BAR man, an assistant BAR man, and an assistant squad leader (usually a corporal). The rest of the twelve men were riflemen.

We had left Rome after two weeks of occupation and returned to Pozzuoli for training and preparation for the southern France landing. We were in bivouac for about six weeks. We made several practice landings off LCVPs in the Nisida harbor, coming ashore among Italian bathers. I remember the final practice landing was a full-scale assault about thirty-five miles north of Naples onto a beach with a considerable bluff we had to climb. We used live ammunition for our marching fire training, and live mortars and artillery were fired overhead. One mortar round fell short and exploded very near me. No one was injured, but it was close. After reaching our objectives on the top of the bluff, we marched the thirty-five miles back to our company area. It was a hot and difficult march, but typical of many to follow in France.

Our staging area was on the side of a hill, and we had to cut scrub and brush away for tents, etc. There were no particular difficulties with it. We did get passes to Naples occasionally. We had our field kitchens set up, and we stood formation morning and evening, with the days spent in typical training activity with lots of extended order drill.

Our battalion, aboard a navy transport, moved out of Naples Harbor on August 12, 1944, and joined a convoy of similar transports.[7] As I stood at the ship's rail looking at the sights, I counted nine hospital ships as we moved out of the harbor. Although I didn't see him, I learned later that Winston Churchill moved about the harbor on a

7. The only two attack transports in the convoy for the Alpha force were the *Samuel Chase* and *Henrico*. Shirley thought the name *Samuel Chase* sounded familiar.

small craft waving his famous victory greeting at passing ships. We sailed north past Corsica and arrived off the coast of France in the dark morning hours of August 15, D-Day.

PFC Robert M. Gehlhoff, a veteran of the North African, Sicilian, and Italian campaigns, was assigned to the headquarters of the 3rd Battalion of the 15th Infantry. The regiment had just endured the many months of the Anzio campaign.

Our section was fortunate, but the division was hard hit with casualties. Now we were back at rest, thankful and relieved. So relieved were the troops that they were silly and jubilant that we had gotten through that bloody winter.

Our life of comfort and safety was cut short when they decided we go back into beach landing training. After intensive invasion training for weeks, we loaded on ships near Naples and lived with the navy for days. We lived like kings, with real beds or bunks, excellent chow, and even ice cream.

The day we set sail, we got our orders about what we were to do. We were to make a dawn beach landing at St. Tropez. We spent the afternoon getting our material ready. The Higgins [LCVP] landing craft we were to use were swung overhead on the ship, about twenty-five feet above the deck. Two of us had to climb up and store our gear (radios and other equipment) aboard these smaller craft. I'm not crazy about climbing to any heights, and going up these rope ladders on a dipping, swaying ship was a nightmare. The sea wasn't a bit smooth, so one minute you would be looking up at the clear blue sky and the next about fifty to eighty feet down at the deep blue sea. Not many slept the night before

German human torpedo found on the beach at Menton near the Italian border.

the landing; everyone was too keyed up. The navy gave us coffee and sandwiches at midnight, but not many took advantage.

On their third day at sea, 1st Sgt. Sherman W. Pratt, of the 7th Infantry's antitank company, was with his new company commander when their convoy rendezvoused at Ajaccio, Corsica. Sergeant Pratt had risen from the ranks and served with the 3rd Division from North Africa until the end of the war and was awarded the Silver Star for his actions at Anzio. In a briefing, Capt. Cheshawgwa Henry Goulette, an American of French and Indian ancestry, explained that the landing would take place in the morning at 8:00 A.M. on Red Beach.

Preparation and Air Operations for Operation Dragoon

Events leading up to the invasion of southern France

AUGUST 11

87th Fighter Wing (410 sorties): attack gun positions in Toulon and Savona areas. Radar installations at Marseille, Cap Bénat, Cap Cammarat, and Agay.

Medium bombers (144 B-25s): bomb gun positions at St. Tropez and east of St. Raphael.

AUGUST 12

German reconnaissance aircraft report concentration of shipping at Ajaccio, Corsica. Enemy recon intensifies in Corsica area and could report concentrations of shipping at Ajaccio.

Four assault convoys en route from Italy to the invasion area and one staging at Ajaccio. Other convoys completed preparations for their departures.

Strategic Air Force: Missions against the three areas outside the assault area—Genoa–Savona coast, Sète, and gun positions at Marseille.

87th Fighter Wing (386 fighter-bomber sorties): air interdiction that results in the bridges at Arles, Tarascon, and Avignon being destroyed.

Medium bombers (B-25s and B-26s): gun positions in assault area, mainly Île de Porquerolles, Cap Nègre, and Cap Cavalaire.

Aircraft carrier force of 4 anti-aircraft cruisers, 9 escort aircraft carriers (CVE),[8] and 13 destroyers departed Malta.

AUGUST 13

The remaining convoys sailed from Italian and North African ports.

87th Fighter Wing (100 P-47s): attack airdromes of the southern Rhone Valley . . . destroying installations and many enemy aircraft.

Strategic Air Force (626 heavy bombers): bomb guns positions, bridges, and communication sites.

AUGUST 14

Enemy night reconnaissance locates invasion shipping in the Ajaccio area.

All assault convoys were en route to the assault area. The Sitka assault convoy in position by the late evening.

Medium bombers (62 B-26s and 144 B-25s): bomb gun positions from Rade d'Agay south to the Giens Peninsula.

Light bombers (36 A-20s): bomb fuel dumps and motor transport.

Fighter-bombers (414 sorties): attack Wurzburg, Freya, and coast watch stations at Nice, Cannes, Cap Bénat, and Cap Camarat. No enemy air opposition.

AUGUST 15

C-47s drop Window over each diversion unit until 4:00 A.M.

All convoys arrive in designated assembly areas in the hours of morning darkness and later, on time.

Diversionary operations on eastern and western flanks begin early in the morning.

Troop Carrier Command arrives with Pathfinders at about 1:00 A.M., followed an hour later by paratroopers.

8. Each CVE had 24 aircraft and several replacement aircraft stationed at Malta..

Operation Dragoon Assault Forces

The U.S. Seventh Army and attached units carried out the landing operations in conjunction with 853 ships from the Eighth Fleet's Western Naval Task Force under V.Adm. H. K. Hewitt. This force included 5 battleships, 4 heavy cruisers, 18 light cruisers, 9 aircraft carriers, 85 destroyers, 20 large transports, 370 large landing ships, and 1,267 small landing craft. Of the total, 505 were American ships, 252 British, and 19 French. From the *AGC 5*,[9] also named the *Catoctin*, Hewitt also commanded the Control Force of 178 ships, which included 43 destroyers and a minesweeping division. Hewitt's flagship carried other senior officers, including Gen. Lucian Truscott, who could direct his assault divisions from the ship's command center.

The Special Operations Group consisted of two diversionary units, the western force, one destroyer, and a number of small ships under Comdr. John D. Bulkeley,[10] the eastern force, of several gunboats and smaller ships under Lt. Comdr. Douglas Fairbanks Jr., the Hollywood film star who received the Croix de Guerre for his participation in Operation Brassard.

The Special Operations Group was to simulate an attack. The main assault was to be carried out by Kodiak Force, consisting of the VI Corps headquarters, which was to land the 3rd, 36th, and 45th Divisions and a Combat Command from the French 1st Armored Division between Cape Cavalaire and Agay.

The French unit would follow after the beaches were secured. The Alpha Attack Force, 3rd Division, was carried and supported by R.Adm. Frank Lowery's[11] TF 84, which consisted of the assault groups of four transports and landing craft and the gunfire support group, which included the British battleship *Ramillies*, five light cruisers, several destroyers, and a minesweeper group. The Delta Attack Force, 45th Division, was transported and supported by TF 85 of R.Adm. Bertram Rodgers. Its transport group consisted of five transports, one British LSI, and landing craft, protected by several destroyers and destroyer escorts. The gunfire support group included the battleships *Texas* and *Nevada*, six light cruisers, and several destroyers. TF 85 also included a minesweeper group. Camel Attack Force, comprising the 36th Division and a French armored combat command, was carried by TF 87 under R.Adm. Spencer Lewis. The assault groups included four transports, landing craft, and an escort and screening group that included destroyers and smaller craft. The bombardment group consisted of the battleship *Arkansas*, a heavy cruiser, five light cruisers, several destroyers, and a minesweeper group.

The 3rd Division and Alpha Force loaded onto 122 troopships in the Pozzuoli–Nisida–Naples area shortly before D-Day and sailed for the invasion area while the follow-up forces of the French II Corps departed

---

9. Amphibious Force Command (AGC) ships. *Catoctin* displaced 12,690 tons, reached a speed of seventeen knots, and carried two 5-inch guns, four twin 40-millimeter guns, and ten twin 20-millimeter guns. The AGC ships included an impressive array of radar and communications equipment as well as quarters for the headquarters staff of the ground forces commander. It also directed offensive air operations.

10. John D. Bulkeley was famous for his PT boat command in the Philippines and the rescue of Gen. Douglas MacArthur before the surrender there. He led a PT boat group at Normandy, protecting Utah Beach from E-Boats.

11. Lowery replaced Admiral Moon, who after Normandy found the pressure too great. He did not believe the Western Task Force was ready and wanted the operation postponed. Frustrated, he committed suicide before the operation.

Operation Dragoon Assault Forces *continued*

southern Italy to assemble off Corsica. The 45th and 36th Divisions also loaded in the same staging area as the 3rd Division. The 45th Division and the remainder of Delta Force used 22 large transports and 106 landing craft. As Delta Force loaded, their escort of warships departed from Taranto to join them in forming a 189-ship convoy. Camel Force, with the 36th Division, loaded onto 20 transports and 91 landing ships, while its follow-up force from the French 1st Armored Division embarked 5,000 men in 5 transports and 6 LSTs at Oran and sailed with the escort of warships to rendezvous with their convoy off of Corsica. All the Kodiak Forces loading in the Naples area departed on August 11, 12, and 13, with the slowest vessels leaving first.

TF 88, commanded by British R.Adm. T. H. Troubridge, was an aircraft carrier force that included nine escort carriers (two American, seven British),[12] protected by 4 antiaircraft cruisers, destroyers and destroyer escorts, and smaller vessels. This force departed Malta on August 12. The aircraft carriers were used for fighter protection, anti-submarine duty, close support missions, and spotting.

Rugby Force was the Provisional Airborne Division consisting of 2nd British Independent Parachute Brigade and the 517th Parachute Infantry Regiment, the 509th and 551st Parachute Battalions, and the 550th Glider Battalion. Dropping in darkness at Le Muy, the paratroopers were to eliminate enemy troops and clear the area for glider landings. These units were to be carried in 415 aircraft from 32 troop carrier squadrons.

Garbo Force, consisting of HQ of the French Army B and the French II Corps with the French 1st Motorized, 3rd Algerian, 9th Colonial, and 1st Armored Divisions, landed in the St. Tropez–Cavalaire area on D+1 and after.

Sitka Force was the 1st Special Service Force (1st SSF) that was to land in the morning darkness and neutralize Port Cros and Levant. Next, it was to move to the mainland and become Stan Force before it captured the island of Porquerolles. R.Adm. Lyal Davidson aboard the *Augusta* led TF 86 that supported this operation as well as Romeo Force, the French Commando group that was also to land in the dark, neutralize the positions on Cape Nègre, and cover the left flank of the VI Corps. Davidson's command consisted of a gunfire support group consisting of the *Augusta*, a British heavy cruiser, the French battleship *Lorraine*, three light cruisers, and a few destroyers. A transport group included destroyer transports, British LSIs, a screen of PT boats, and a minesweeper group. On August 11, the troops of Sitka Force from Italy arrived in Corsica, where they remained for two days before traveling on. Rosie Force, the French naval assault group, was to land near Pointe des Trayas at night and protect the right flank by destroying points on the road system.

12. Each carrier had twenty-four fighter aircraft that included British Seafires, American Hellcats and Wildcats, some equipped with rockets for ground support missions.

It is known that there are pillboxes and coastal bunkers with heavy guns the German have moved from the Maginot Line in northern France. There will be beaucoup air bombings from daylight until we land, and our warships escorting us have been assigned the mission of neutralizing the enemy land-based artillery and the coastal guns. There doesn't seem to be any enemy sea forces around here.

Captain Goulette told his men to watch for colored flares from the beach or other vessels. If any troops or boats ran afoul of underwater obstacles that could hinder the operation, they would fire green parachute flares. Red smoke grenades would signal that there were no problems, yellow smoke would indicate friendly troops, and violet smoke grenades would mean that the enemy defenses had been neutralized.

The captain concluded his briefing by reassuring his men that the landing was expected to go smoothly without problems. Apparently, Pratt and his company commander were on an LST carrying elements of the 2nd Battalion, since Pratt was instructed to land with that battalion. Pratt mentioned that each of the three antitank platoons were assigned to each battalion, so at least two of those platoons would have been on other LSTs, although the company headquarters would have been with the commanding officer.

The transports, the landing craft, and the fire support ships moved into their designated areas. Before long, the moon rose, bathing the area in soft, otherworldly light. The divisionary forces prepared for action as the first waves of paratroopers were released over the quiet shoreline. The transports sprang to life as troops made their final preparations.

The Amphibious Assault Force

Vessels*	Transports**	LST	LCI	LCT	LCM	LCC	LCG
TF 84 Alpha Force							
Red Beach		25	46	43	11	7	1
Yellow Beach	Chase, Henrico, Arundel, Thurston	6	9	17	9	3	1
TF 85 Delta Force							
Red Beach	Dickman, Barnett,	10	6	7	1	2	1
Green Beach	Stanton, Marine Robin, Santa Rosa,	5	5	7	2	1	
Yellow Beach	LSI Ascania, 1 LSP	2	2	4	3	1	
Blue Beach	26 LCVPs	1	1	16	3	1	1
Reserve Group		5	20	18			
TF 87 Camel Force							
Red Beach	Squire, Jefferson, Nightingale, Dix, Carroll, 1 LSI, 20 LCVPs	3	5	21	2	3	1
Green Beach	7 LCVPs	14	23	21	2	3	1
Blue Beach		5	1	2			
TOTAL	17 transports & 53 LCVPs	76	118	156	33	21	6

* Does not include all type of command-and-control and fire-support vessels converted from landing craft.

** LCVPs in this column do not include LCVPs carried on transports and LSTs. LCCs (Landing Craft, Control) served as lead navigational craft for landing craft and marked the line of departure. The LCG (Landing Craft, Gun) carried 2 4.7-inch guns, 2 17-pounders, or 2 25-pounders. LSP is a British Landing Ship, Personnel.

CHAPTER 12

Dragoon–The Worst-Kept Secret of the War

Securing the Flanks and the Airborne Operation

For the troops that were to assault south France, the trip was rather longer than it had been in the Normandy invasion. However, the weather was good. At dawn on August 15, 1944, while the troops were still boarding the landing craft, the air force began striking enemy positions. The first phase of the air campaign had actually begun at the end of April 1944, when the Mediterranean Allied Air Force bombed targets all along the coastline in Southern France and beyond. The second phase of the operation started on August 10 with air operations targeting coastal batteries, radar stations, troop concentrations, and bridges over the Rhone, all of which were destroyed or heavily damaged. The final phase, which commenced on the evening of D-1, was directed against all targets in and near the invasion area. When the air attacks ended and the smoke cleared, the naval fire support groups fired some salvos to adjust their fire and seek targets before they began to bombard the invasion beaches in earnest. Since this was a daylight invasion, the Allies had to forgo the element of surprise. The invasion did not come as a surprise anyway, since the Germans were aware of the buildup and even some of the training from agents and air reconnaissance. Security was not as tight as for Overlord, and only the exact day and location in south France were unknown.

Under cover of night, while the main naval forces jockeyed into position off the invasion beaches, the Western Diversionary Group feigned a major landing off the Bay of La Ciotat between Marseille and Toulon. Its reflectors confused the enemy radar, and the Germans fell for the ruse. At the same time, the Eastern Diversionary Group, led by Lt. Comdr. Douglas Fairbanks Jr., launched a similar mission to the southwest of Cannes, while the PT boats traveling with it dropped off Rosie Force, the French Naval Assault Group of sixty-seven commandos, at about 1:00 A.M. Unfortunately, the commandos, who landed in a minefield, failed to reach their objective, and they were eventually captured. Fairbanks carried out the other part of his mission and convinced the Germans, as verified on Radio Berlin, that a landing was taking place in the vicinity of Cannes.

The fast destroyer and British transports of Task Force 86 carried Sitka and Romeo Forces comprising the 2,300 men of the 1st Special Service Force and 800 French commandos. The 1st Special Service Force landed in rubber boats on the islands of Levant and Port Cros by 2:00 A.M. A powerful German battery of 164-millimeter guns on Levant was positioned to cover the main landing beaches. Undaunted, the Allied troops moved quickly forward through a thicket of vegetation and overwhelmed most of the garrison. To their astonishment, the battery turned out to be a collection of dummy positions with pipes simulating guns. A small part of the German garrison held out throughout the day before it finally surrendered. Col. Edwin Walker, commander of the "Black Devils" of the 1st Special Service Force, radioed General Patch that the islands were useless and held nothing of importance for the Allies.

The situation was more troublesome at Port Cros, where about sixty Germans clung to three early-nineteenth-century forts overgrown with vegetation and difficult to spot. The 8-inch guns of the heavy cruiser *Augusta* proved ineffective against the thick stone walls. The German garrisons of two of the forts surrendered the next day, but the third fort held out until the British battleship *Ramillies* fired a couple of salvos from its big 15-inch guns on August 17.

Before 2:00 A.M., the French commandos of Romeo Group and troops of the 1st Special Service Force landed near Cap Nègre. Although they hit the wrong beach, they moved on and established a blocking position. Next, they scaled Cap Nègre and took out a German battery situated there. Shortly before the main landings began, they drove off a German counterattack with the help of navy. Just before 4:00 A.M., one of the covering destroyers also fired on a couple of small German warships off the Hyères Islands, sinking one of the ships. Thus, the flanking operations on the western side of the invasion area met with success.

Late on August 14, the paratroopers of the 1st Airborne Task Force began boarding their transports for the long journey from Central Italy to their drop zones in the Le Muy area several miles behind the Delta and Camel beaches. As in Normandy, they were preceded by C-47s carrying miniature rubber paratroopers, some three hundred of which included explosive charges in addition to an array of firecrackers. The dummies were dropped at 1:55 A.M. near La Ciotat in the area where the naval demonstration was underway. Window tin strips were also dropped to confuse the German radar. At about 3:15 A.M., C-47s began dropping the Pathfinders[1]—ten men from each battalion—who were widely scattered due to enemy fire and fog. Most of the Pathfinders failed to reach and mark their drop zones, except for two of five British Pathfinder groups who had better luck hitting their drop zones north of Le Muy. This was the last major night drop of the European war.

In the meantime, battalions of paratroopers prepared to leave for France. The C-47s of the 50th Troop Carrier Wing carrying the 509th Parachute Battalion lifted off from airfields at Fol-

---

1. The Pathfinders departed from Marcigliana, an airfield just to the north of Rome.

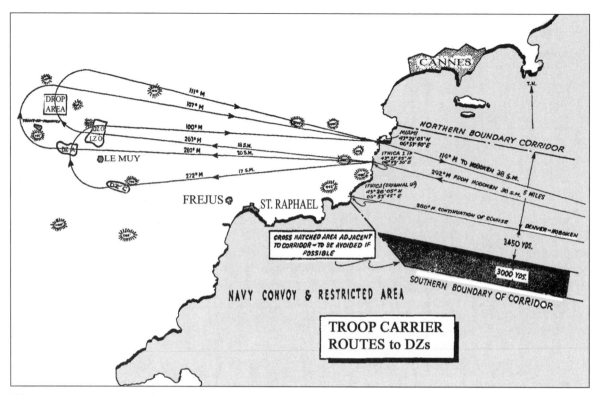

Airborne routes for the invasion of south France.

lonica, Grosseto, Ombrone, and Orbetello; those of the 53rd Wing departed from Montalto and Canino with the 517th Parachute Infantry Regiment,[2] and from Galera and Ciampino with the 2nd British Parachute Brigade. The transports streamed over the northwest tip of Elba and wheeled toward the drop zones on a route that took them over the northern tip of Corsica at Checkpoint Denver. The paratrooper drop phase, code-named Mission Albatross, included 5,000 paratroopers and 32 squadrons numbering about 400 aircraft. When the paratroopers dropped at 5:15 A.M., it was already light, but they made it safely to the ground, protected by a heavy morning fog that shrouded the countryside. Official sources claimed these drops were more accurate than in Normandy.

Some of the pilots managed to identify their drop zones even though they were unmarked and blanketed with mist by using the terrain and their flight time to guide them. Others were far off course because the Pathfinders had not been able to reach and mark the drop zones. The 509th began dropping at 4:20 A.M.; the 517th Parachute Infantry Regiment, which followed at 4:30 A.M. in 180 C-47s, jumped into Drop Zone A just to the southeast of Drop Zone O, set up the western blocking positions, and took up positions to the south of the main road. The 509th Parachute Battalion tried to come down on Drop Zone C and set up blocking positions on the eastern side of the perimeter. The British 2nd Parachute Brigade, the last to arrive, landed at Drop Zone O at 6:00 A.M. to the north of Le Muy. The British paras and members of the 517th Parachute Infantry moved out to secure their objectives and clear the landing zone in their drop zones for the gliders. The 517th was widely scat-

2. The 517th Parachute Infantry Regiment was organized as the 517th Regimental Combat Team. Some battalions, including the 509th Parachute Battalion (509th Battalion Combat Team) and regular infantry units, including those serving as part of an infantry division, used this type of organization, which was often temporary. It generally meant the unit was reinforced for a specific operation or organized to act in a semi-independent role.

Missions for the 1st Airborne Task Force on D-Day

Mission and Arrival at DZ/LZ	Aircraft / Gliders	Unit / Airfield / Troop Carrier (TC) Wing		
Albatross 4:23 A.M.	396 / 0	509th Para. Bn. / Follonica, Grosseto / 50th TC	517th PIR / Ombrone, Orbetello, Montalto, Canino / 50th & 53rd TC	2nd Br. Para. Bde. / Galera, Ciampino / 51st TC
Bluebird 8:15 A.M.*	55 / 35 Horsa 40 Waco			Br. 2nd Para. Bde. Artillery / Tarquinia, Voltone / 53rd TC
Canary 6:10 P.M.	42 / 0	551st Para. Bn. / Montalto / 53rd TC		
Dove 6:19 P.M.	332 / 37 Horsa 295 Waco	550th Glider Bn. / Follonica, Grosseto, Orbetello / 50th TC	A/B Task Force support & HQ / Grosseto, Ombrone, Canino, Galera, Ciampino / 50th, 51st, & 53rd TC	2nd Br. Para. Bde. / Tarquinia, Voltone / 53rd TC

* Only the Wacos were released because of poor ground conditions, and that was after an additional delay of over an hour (after 9:00 A.M.) as the C-47s (each with a double tow) flew around.

tered because twenty planeloads dropped too early. Only about 20 percent of its men landed within two miles of the drop zone. It took most of the day for the 517th to reassemble.

Mission Bluebird began just before 9:30 A.M. as fifty-five aircraft towing the Waco and Horsa gliders loaded with British troops from an artillery unit. By then, the British paratroopers had cleared most of the anti-landing obstacles. However, only the CG-4s landed[3] because some parts of the landing zones were still shrouded in fog, and the tow planes were ordered to return with the Horsas.

Mission Canary started in the afternoon as the 551st Parachute Infantry Battalion boarded its aircraft at the Montalto airport, about a hundred miles north of Rome, and took off at 4:20 P.M. on a relatively uneventful flight with minimal flak interference over France. The battalion jumped unopposed at 6:09 P.M. over Drop Zone A in good weather. The well-executed drop was one of the best-photographed combat jumps of the war. The Pathfinders of the 517th, who had dropped in the wrong place earlier in the morning, had reached and marked Drop Zone A in time for the 551st. The 551st reassembled within an hour and moved into action before dark. It

was followed by the glider infantry and artillery of Mission Dove towed in by 332 C-47s, which cut their tow lines at Landing Zone O and Landing Zone A. According to an army air force official estimate, 85 percent of the troops landed on or near their drop zones, but this was assessment was grossly exaggerated. In reality, about 40 percent landed in or near their drop zones, but only about 230 paratroopers were killed or wounded and 90 percent of the entire 1st Airborne Task Force was ready for action by that evening. The 2,250 men in gliders had a higher rate of success since none died in their landings, but most of the 400 gliders were wrecked.[4] By the end of D+1, Le Muy fell to a combined assault of British and American troops, and 700 German soldiers surrendered.

Veterans of the Air Assault

Sgt. Donald Charles Garrigues had volunteered for the army in June 1942 at age nineteen, done his basic at Camp Roberts in the summer, and attended parachute school at Fort Benning. At the end of that year, he was assigned to the 551st Parachute Battalion, and he went to Panama, where he trained for jungle warfare. His battalion

3. The C-47s were each towing a pair of Waco gliders or a single Horsa. This was the first time a double tow was performed in a European operation.

4. Some paratroopers and pilots died when their gliders came apart over the Mediterranean, but that number was small.

moved by sea to San Francisco in late August 1943 and then by troop train to Camp Mackall. In April, it sailed for Italy via Algeria, reaching Naples in June. It participated in maneuvers and mountain training in Sicily before it moved to the Rome area in July.

Garrigues's stay in Italy seemed to be plagued with mishaps. In Palermo, he came down with dysentery and he was hospitalized for a week with several of his comrades. During training near Rome, a mortar round fell short, killing a forward observer. Another time, the mortars put down a smoke screen that set a wheat field on fire and Garrigues and his fellow paratroopers had to spend two hours putting out the flames. Shortly before the invasion, he heard Axis Sally on the radio telling the paratroopers that there was no need to bring their chutes. "You will be able to just walk down on the flack that will be in the air," she taunted.

When August 15 finally dawned, Garrigues, who was in the light machine-gun platoon of HQ Company,[5] was relieved to go. His platoon consisted of two sections, each of which consisted of four machine-gun squads of four men each. In addition, there were two officers, a platoon sergeant, two section leaders, two messengers, and a medic. Normally Garrigues carried a carbine, but on this occasion, he decided to switch to an M-1 rifle that he carried across his chest in a case under his reserve chute.

On the fateful day, Garrigues's platoon's staff sergeant, who had shot himself in the foot, stayed behind. Morale and tension were high among the men as they boarded their plane. A Frenchman joined their stick just before they embarked. After the paratroopers were settled and their gear was stowed away, the plane's engines roared to life. The plane taxied down the runway, lifted off, and climbed into the blue skies of a perfect Italian summer day. Garrigues and his comrades had about an hour and a half to contemplate their fates. This would be their first combat jump, and pre-jump tension was getting so thick, it could be cut with a bayonet. As they approached the drop zone, the commander barked, "Stand up and hook up!" The Frenchman, who had never jumped before, became tangled in his static line; Garrigues reached out to help him. When his own turn came, there was no place for him to hook his static line. At the go signal, everyone began the shuffle to the door, and Garrigues finally found room to hook up his static line as he pushed the Frenchman ahead.

As we jumped from a fairly low altitude, the descent to the ground didn't take very long. . . . I could see that I was going to land near a small hill, which dropped off to a railroad and a country road below. My first contact with France jarred every bone in my body. I landed on a pile of rocks that formed an old fence line in the midst of brush undergrowth. In the process, a wooden fence post was jabbed in my side. As I recovered from the jolt, I started getting unbuckled from my chute and trying to assemble my M-1 rifle. . . . A fellow paratrooper from another outfit broke through the brush and asked if I was okay. He helped me get from my chute. . . . I hurried to get the equipment bundles containing machine guns and ammunition and join with the other men in my section.

Almost everyone made the landing all right, and soon we were organized. . . . The group that had landed ahead of us had the area pretty well secured, so there was very little enemy resistance at the beginning. The first German I saw was a dead one—his huge form stretched out on the side of the ditch along the road. I wondered if all Germans were that big.

As we were grouped together, reviewing our plans, Sergeant Dean caught a stray bul-

---

5. HQ Company also included a mortar platoon, a commo platoon, and the staff section. Companies A, B, and C had three platoons each. There was also a demolition detachment and a medical detachment. The troops of the service detachment did not jump with the battalion.

let in the leg. He was moved to an accumulation area for eventual evacuation to a hospital. I believe he was the first casualty in our platoon.

As we secured our positions, another wave of C-47s came in over the drop zone and cut loose the gliders they were towing. This was the airborne infantry and small artillery pieces, jeeps, etc., that represented the last group of the First Allied Airborne Army. I shall never forget the sight of these gliders landing. They would only go one way—down. Some of them managed to get to cleared fields and came out all right, but many of them crashed into fences, hedges, and trees. Some of them would touch a wingtip and start cartwheeling. Most of the wooden poles with their sharpened points toward the sky . . . had been removed by the paratroopers. . . . For quite a while, all you could hear was the ripping, tearing, and crashing of the incoming gliders. Sometimes one or two men would stagger out. . . .

That night, we had little opposition from the Germans, but the whole world seemed to be on fire and there were continual explosions as enemy ammunition dumps were destroyed. Our mission of blocking the road networks had been accomplished.

Flight Off. Carson Crabtree from Maupin, Oregon, had enlisted in 1940 and applied for flight training to become a glider pilot after 1942. He arrived in England from Scotland in March 1944 after crossing the Atlantic on the *Queen Mary*. He was assigned to the 306th Squadron, 442nd Troop Carrier Group. After some training in England, he watched D-Day pass him by without a mission.

We were supposed to land behind the German lines, farther in than the beaches. We were all loaded up and ready to go on the mission. The engines were running on the tow planes. I was sitting in the glider with an infantryman in the copilot seat, and someone comes running across the field with his arms waving. Intelligence found that the area we were to land in was occupied by a panzer division, so they scratched the mission about fifteen minutes before takeoff. [After that] we didn't do anything, we just went back to sleep.[6]

After that, we were moved from Fulbeck to Weston Zoyland. We were there when in July most of our outfit was sent to Italy for the invasion of Southern France. We were sent to Follonica, near Elba. We got there in July or the 1st of August, got the gliders ready to go, and did general preparations. We were at a dry lakebed, all sand and dirt. We didn't do any glider flying there prior to the mission. It was in the morning about seven or eight o'clock we got an intelligence briefing, about the same notice as at Normandy. The intelligence sources weren't all that great, either in Normandy or in south France. Our unit took off, headed out over the Mediterranean, and headed north for the Riviera, not too far from Toulon. When we got out there, there was a mix up and we did a 180-degree turn over the Mediterranean. When we were at about 1,500 feet, everybody let loose. There were more gliders than there should have been letting down, and it was difficult to find a place to land. The Germans had put anti-glider stakes in, and some of the people landed in them. I landed in a peach orchard and tore my wings off, but nobody got hurt. There was no German opposition, but there were gliders in every direction. This was the largest operation I had seen. There were a few casualties, but mostly from

---

6. There were no panzer divisions in the vicinity of the landing zones in the American sectors on D-Day and D+1, although some missions were planned and cancelled after D-Day. Crabtree did not give a specific date in June for this event.

cracking up because the landing areas weren't big enough. The anti-glider stakes were put in by conscripted French labor, and they didn't do a very good job. A lot of them fell apart when they got hit.

I had six troops and a trailer with combat equipment. We got out of the glider and there was another glider with a jeep not far away, so we hooked it up and proceeded to look for the command post. We stayed in the bivouac area. The paratroopers were out in the countryside looking for Germans. I was at a medical tent, and some young paratrooper came in. He evidently had his mouth open when he got shot. The bullet went in one side and out the other. They patched him up a little bit and wanted him to go down to the coast to be sent back. He said, "No way—I know where that son of a bitch is, and I am going after him," and he did. We were there about three days and then went back down to the French coast, got an LST, and went to Corsica, where we stayed overnight. Then we were taken by aircraft back to Follonica. From there we got ready to go back to our home base in England.[7]

Lt. William Knickerbocker and Lt. Lambert G. Wilder trained as glider pilots in the United States, and they were sent overseas in 1942. After service in the Mediterranean, Knickerbocker was still awaiting his first combat mission when he was assigned to the 50th Squadron, 314th Group, 52nd Troop Carrier Wing, which was not a glider-towing unit. To fly a mission or even for training, he had to transfer to another wing, despite the fact the 50th had a full complement of gliders and glider pilots.[8]

After landing in Scotland, we went down to the Midlands Saltdy; it is just outside Crampton, between Leicester and Nottingham. We kept on our training. We were transferred to the 435th Group, 76th Squadron, and we mainly flew Horsa gliders.[9]

Then we were sent back to the Mediterranean in July. I went by way of Gibraltar and stopped over there for a very short time. When we stopped in Gibraltar, the beach was off-limits to Americans. We talked our way into town, and we bought gin for eighty cents a bottle and bought five bottles apiece. We hauled them back and took off. We were in Gibraltar just a matter of hours. Then we went on to Italy.

First Lieutenant Wilder, 75th Squadron, 435th Troop Carrier Group, also was sent overseas in 1942.

Our outfit stayed in England on detached service. I was sitting there waiting for another mission to come up. Because I was flight leader, they gave me twelve men and sent me somewhere in Italy. They flew us in C-47s to Gibraltar and then to Italy. I don't know if Knickerbocker was on the same airplane. Then we landed at Follonica. I don't remember the group or squadron I was assigned to there; they kept transferring us. I was assigned to three different squadrons in one day in Italy. We were there a week or two before the invasion. We didn't get a chance to go to Rome.

One thing that stands out in my mind was that there was a Jewish lad, a Catholic lad, and I am Protestant, and we all went to a Catholic church. I carried a camera everywhere I went. The night before we were scheduled to take off, the CO of the squadron said, "You guys are eligible for a liquor ration." He said, "Normally you get it when you come back, but I am going to give it to you tonight because I know a lot

---

7. Crabtree found that this, his first mission, "was an easy mission. It was not as exciting as Market Garden."
8. The only time the 50th Troop Carrier Wing towed gliders was into Wessel, Germany, in 1945.
9. On D-Day in Normandy, Knickerbocker and many of his fellow glider pilots were preparing for missions that never took place.

of you will not be back." So we had three cans of beer apiece. That was the first American beer I had. We took off about noontime for Southern France.

No training [in Italy]. We were supposed to be trained and followed the standard operating procedure. We went through the same method of carrying the operation out as with a Horsa. The gliders were loaded and you were assigned a glider. A pilot and copilot, the plane ahead of you took off and you were on the way. Our base was Follonica.[10]

Lieutenant Knickerbocker was afraid that the war would pass him by without any missions, so he took matters into his own hands.

When we arrived, they told us to go into town, pick out a house, and move in. They were all Fascist at this seaside resort. We were right on the beach; we moved into an all-marble house. We weren't at Follonica; we were north of Rome on the beach for several days. The colonel, who had been a bus driver in the States, wasn't much of a colonel. He wanted to go up the coast and look for damaged vehicles so we would have more transportation. We didn't find any, but that gave me an idea. I had several missions jerked out from under me, and I figured they would jerk this one too. So I got a couple of glider pilots. I was going to go to Pisa. We took off early in the morning; it was ninety miles up to Pisa. We had to walk the last fifteen miles because trucks were exposed to German fire. We got into Pisa and kept out of sight. We heard some mortar fire, we didn't know whose, and we looked over the stone fence and it was Americans. We piled over the fence and said, "Take us to your leader." They took us to this artillery captain. We told him we wanted some combat. He said, "Well, I can sure use you." The

idiot gave us a squad of men apiece and sent us on night patrol. What had happened was the American soldiers had gone out on one of the bridges. We had one side of the river and the Germans the other. This stupid American went out on the bridge to meet this Italian girl and they shot him. They didn't kill him, only wounded him. Some Italians dragged him back to the American side, stripped him of all his clothing, left him there, and told the captain that there was a wounded American up there. What we were supposed to do was get in the buildings looking down the river and open a diversionary action while these remaining troops searched the place for this wounded American. I was supposed to give the signal to start firing. I could see these Germans taking up their night positions laughing and joking. I don't know how many I could have gotten, but it would have destroyed our mission. At seven o'clock, I opened fire across the river. There was quite a firefight, as a matter of fact. . . . They found the American and brought him back. We broke off the action and went back to the HQ. We suffered no casualties, but I did hear two GIs talking in the dark. So we said our farewells the next day and went back to camp. We had actually got to fight the Germans.

I guess maybe a couple days later nothing had happened; the mission still looked iffy so I got a couple of other glider pilots and went back to Pisa. We were welcomed with open arms, and we led another night patrol. We stirred up quite a bit of activity.

We went back to camp, and a couple of days later we loaded up. We didn't get much of a briefing: they said go and we went. We studied the maps one or two days before.

Knickerbocker recorded the events of Monday, August 14, and Tuesday, August 15, in his diary.

---

10. They carried the 550th Glider Battalion, which included an antitank company from the Japanese-American 442nd Infantry (RCT).

August 14: More briefings all morning &
we had to get our equipment ready. Drew
more stuff including combat boots, which I
badly needed. Took a nap during the afternoon then saw a lousy movie after a lousy
meal. Boy! The food is sure rotten here.
Back to have coffee and "shoot the bull."
Hard to get to sleep as the paratroopers
started taking off at 2 A.M. for their drop.
. . . Tomorrow afternoon we leave and I
don't think I've ever looked forward to anything so much. This will be the 13th mission that I have sweated-out, and it looks as
if it will go through.

August 15: Up early to pack baggage,
check glider, & give last minute touches to
my equip. Had a last briefing and we will
take off at 3:45 hitting France about 6 or 7
this date. Yudiski & I split flying time on way
over. Our ships being bombed as we passed
coast. Over valley we cut (it was 30 miles
behind German lines) and headed for C.P.
Lost one wheel & wingtip on landing. Gliders crashing all over & total of 35 pilots
killed on landing out of 822 & many
injured. We unloaded then reported to CP.
No enemy action at landing zone but Le
Muy has 500 Jerries. Had some D ration
then covered area checking on gliders. Fields
full of anti-glider poles. Slept in narrow
ditch, 88 fire during night but I was dead
tired. Had one alert, which I slept through.

Knickerbocker's postwar memories are a little
more detailed. He took off from Canino.

It was the most beautiful sight you ever saw,
the blue sea and the blue sky and a few
white clouds—perfect weather. All these
planes towing these gliders in the air
smooth as glass. You look down and see the
warships and the guns firing. You don't hear

anything. It was just picture perfect. Just like
a navy recruiting poster. The beach was a
beautiful white beach.

I was fortunate, I had my copilot with
me, and I said, "This is where we are going
to land." It was probably the most disagree-
able area on the map, and I said, "There is
enough room to land; there won't be much
competition." We had close to 500 gliders
going into a small valley, and we would
have to fight for landing space. One danger
was not the enemy but your buddies. I
picked out this sorry little field and landed
on it, and it didn't hurt the glider or anything. I had a trailer and no troops. The
jeep was in another glider and was supposed to hook up.

The glider pilots had the option of carrying a
Thompson submachine gun (tommy gun), an M-
1 rifle, or a carbine. Wilder and Knickerbocker
chose the submachine gun despite the heavier
ammunition. They both were issued parachutes
that neither wore after boarding their gliders.
Wilder explained, "We didn't wear them, we sat
on them. My feeling was I got fifteen infantrymen back there, and they don't have chutes. What
am I going to do—bail out and leave them?"[11]
On the way to the landing zone, Wilder ran
into a small amount of enemy fire, while
Knickerbocker did not. For Wilder, the landing
was smooth, the same as on maneuvers, but when
he inspected his glider afterward, he found two
bullet holes in the tail section. He was carrying a
trailer filled with water and possibly one or two
soldiers. "I was the wing man, and the other
glider had the jeep. . . . All they drank in that valley was wine, since we landed in the vineyards
just about the time the grapes were ready to fall."
When his tow was cut, Wilder "lost sight of the
glider with the jeep. . . . You had to watch out
what was going on, it was like driving around at

11. Neither of them was carrying more than one or two troops on this mission, although most glider pilots had the same feeling on wearing parachutes.

Glider Pilots in Action

After his successful landing in the evening of August 15, Lieutenant Knickerbocker looked for more action with three of his friends. He recorded the events of D+1 and D+2 in his diary.

August 16: Went by aid station to get Coe [John W. Coe]; then we met Greenlee & [Leo A.] Morian. Heard airborne inf. would attack Le Muy at 10 a.m., so we joined C Co. & followed creek around & went in on the right flank. Crossed stream & met gunfire at cemetery. Worked way down into edge of town & watched Germans surrendering on outskirts of town—these were front-line troops. Worked on in and caught up w/ first troops. Rounded corner & about 40 Germans rushed out under a white flag. Marquis are really good fighters and we made the rounds w/ one w/ a cockney English accent. Kept taking more prisoners until we had about 200. French really gave us a welcome & we got crocked later on free wine. Captured machine gun & used it on snipers. Hunted snipers until they were cleaned out. Met tanks & 509th paratroopers when they came in from West. Back to sleep in hole & slept like a log.

August 17: We left early as we were going to fight our way down to the 7th Army coming up from coast, but in town we found that they had already broken through. People almost went crazy over us on our way to the beach. Boy did they hate the Germans! The Jerries had really set traps for gliders close to the coast. Finally got down to the beach and saw all the damage of the landings two days before. We were put right on an LST as we had priority over the wounded so we would be available if they called another mission. Hot as hell, starving, dirty, & completely worn out. We got a bath from a bucket, had a sandwich with hot tea and a half hour sleep. We shot the bull for hours & the four of us were the only ones of 822 glider pilots who went into town with the infantry to take the town.

night." As he was coming in for the landing, he faced the same problem as Knickerbocker in the crowded skies.

When you got 500 gliders, you have a problem. The groups for various reasons backed up and stacked up. Instead of releasing at 1,000 feet, we were stacked up to 5,000 feet. All the gliders arrived over the valley at the same time and released at the same time. Can you imagine all 500 gliders landing in a small valley at the same time? We killed thirty-five glider pilots in crashes not counting wounded—most gliders crashing into gliders. You could walk wing to wing from gliders. It was confusion. It was a disaster.

Toting his tommy gun, Wilder climbed out of his glider unscathed with his copilot, and both men wandered around the landing site.

The British were already up there with guns. I remember I saw them make tea the next day. I avoided reporting to the division CP, but our people, as they showed up, reverted to road guards and various sundry duties like guarding POWs, etc.

If you went back to the CP, they were going to give you a job to do. They were going to keep you in the perimeter, and you would have to answer to some son of a bitch who didn't know as much as you did. So I stayed away from the CP; I never reported to it. I joined the paratroopers. [After getting out of the glider] we went out, started looking around, and found this Horsa glider—didn't have a bullet hole in it. The British got there before we did and brought in artillery. The tail section was still on, and it looked like a perfect glider except the pilot and copilot had got out and been shot. They were the only dead people I saw in our landings. There were no troops on it. We messed around, stayed away from the CP, and slept that night. There was a lot of artillery and no small arms. We were just out in the field in a ditch by ourselves.

According to Knickerbocker, they "were expendable in the air, but not on the ground. . . . We were supposed to stay in the perimeter in case we needed to be evacuated and used on a second mission."

Assault from the Sea

Before the Kodiak Force began landing, the German forces in the area had largely been isolated by the Mediterranean Allied Air Forces that had destroyed key bridges on the routes into the invasion areas. Only one of six railway bridges remained over the Rhone south of Lyon, and the coastal rail line to Italy was cut.[12] On D-Day at the crack of dawn, the Mediterranean Allied Air Forces flew over 900 missions, plastering the landing areas to a depth of 400 yards and losing only six aircraft. By the end of the day, the Mediterranean Allied Air Forces' bombers flew 4,200 sorties, 3,936 of which were ground attack missions at the cost of 46 Allied aircraft. At the same time, the *Luftwaffe*'s attempts to bomb the fleet were a dismal failure, and most of its 200 aircraft withdrew to Lyon by the end of the week. The aerial bombings began at 6:50 A.M. on the Alpha beaches and ended at 7:20 A.M. at Camel Red. In the meantime, the fighter-bombers and the warships targeted coastal batteries. The naval fire support ships, within two miles of the coast, had begun earlier at 5:30 A.M., ending at 7:50 A.M., and only ceased long enough to let the aircraft bomb the target areas.[13] The naval gunfire missions shifted to the flanks as the first waves of amphibious forces began to land.

Just before dawn, the troops boarded their landing craft in the dim light of a quarter-moon, marking a shining path to the beach. Off the Camel and Alpha beaches, an LSD (landing ship, dock) released its load of Apex boats from the flooded well deck. At the same time off the Delta beaches, explosive drones with naval combat demolition crews on board were lowered from davits of LSTs. Other naval combat demolition teams boarded landing craft from which they were to guide the Apex boats by radio control into the target area. The teams used two types of Apex boats: male and female. A group of six male control drones led the way, each followed by three female explosive drones. As they closed on the assault area, the crews of the female drones pulled up to the male Apex and jumped aboard, leaving the female to be radio controlled. The naval combat demolition men on the male Apex boats were to use demolition packs to clear the obstacles the female Apex boats had failed to detonate. While the naval combat demolition teams concentrated on their demolition task and shortly before the first wave arrived, the Woofus fired their rockets.

A large number of minesweepers began sweeping operations at 4:40 A.M. and continued their

---

12. The only other rail access from Italy was through Mount Cenis, and that line was sabotaged.

13. According to the actual schedule, fighter-bombers were to hit the Alpha beaches at 5:00 A.M., and the medium and heavy bombers were to strike the beaches and strongpoints at 7:00 to 7:30 A.M. Gunfire support ships were to be ready for counterbattery fire at 6:00 A.M. and bombard the beach areas and other targets from 7:20 to 7:50 A.M.

task during the naval bombardment. Between 7:10 to 7:45 A.M., shallow-water minesweepers joined the Apex units in clearing the approaches to the landing beaches.

Scouts determined that the enemy mine-and-obstacle defenses were relatively weak at their designated landing beaches, except at the Camel Beaches in the Bay of Fréjus where they turned out to be very strong. Early in the morning, navy frogmen successfully removed the water-covered Teller mines at Camel Green in time for the 8:00 A.M. landing of the 141st Infantry. Meanwhile, another team raced up to a submarine net at the entrance to Agay Cove, attached its explosives, and destroyed it.[14] When the minesweepers went to work at Camel Red Beach, where the landings were not scheduled until 2:00 P.M., they were met by enemy artillery fire. The 2nd Battalion of the 765th Grenadier Regiment, 242nd Division, defended these sectors with artillery support; the 3rd Battalion was in reserve; and an *Ost* Battalion from the 148th Division was north of Anthéor Cove. Except for the *Ost* Battalion, most of the German troops put up a spirited resistance.

As the morning mist and smoke from the shelling dissipated, the landing craft formed up for the run to the beaches. Camel Blue, on right flank of the 36th Division, was accessed through an inlet that restricted the deployment of the landing craft. Thanks to the morning bombardment, which had shaken the defenders, the landing craft carrying the 1st Battalion, 141st Infantry, were able to negotiate the inlet and disgorge their passengers on a small, eighty-yard-long beach without difficulty. The 1st Battalion quickly advanced to the road bridge and rail viaduct.[15] However, before the battalion could eliminate enemy resistance, the German gunners, now recovered from their initial shock, started scoring hits on the succeeding wave of landing craft.

Camel Green, the main landing beach for the division, lay further to the west, in the Gulf of Fréjus, where the bulk of the 141st Infantry landed in order to clear Camel Yellow to its right and allow the 143rd Infantry to disembark. The Allied attack started with a barrage of fire laid down by rocket-carrying craft, which failed to stop the Germans from scoring hits with antitank guns on some of the landing craft carrying assault troops. The first wave, which consisted of fifteen LCVPs, carried three companies from the 2nd and 3rd Battalions. The second wave consisted of eight Sherman duplex-drive amphibious tanks. Despite coming under heavy fire, the tanks made it ashore, moved inland for 600 yards, and helped break the resistance, which had not stiffened until after the landings. The third wave included three more companies in fifteen LCVPs, engineers, two more companies, the battalion headquarters, the remainder of the 753rd Tank Battalion, and the 636th Tank Destroyer Battalion. The 2nd Battalion of the 141st moved east to reach the 1st Battalion, and the 3rd Battalion cleared Camel Green.

The 143rd Infantry began landing at Camel Green at 9:45 A.M. and advanced on St. Raphael, relying on tanks and naval gunfire to eliminate the enemy defenses. However, the regiment was delayed at St. Raphael and was unable to assist the planned landing at Camel Red in the early afternoon. Late in the morning, the navy sent rocket ships to clear Camel Red, but the minesweepers were driven off by enemy artillery. The battleship *Arkansas* with her 12-inch guns joined other warships to blast away the defenses. The army air force bombed the area once more, but when the minesweepers returned, they came under fire again. The male Apex control boats, which approached with the LCT(R)s, were rebuffed too and forced to turn back. They made one more attempt, and although they came under fire again,

---

14. According to Angelo Chatas, "At St. Rafael, we frogmen performed almost like in Hollywood the night before blowing up a submarine net. Seeing lights and hearing people and music on shore, so here we were placing explosives." Although he did not mention this in his book, Cmdr. Francis Fane indicated that this action might well have taken place. With other members of his unit, Chatas returned to the United States in September, was assigned to UDT 6, and went back into training.

15. The viaduct was breached by a bombing attack before the invasion so that it could not serve as part of the German line of communications.

they released their drones from 1,000 yards out. Once they were put on radio control, the female Apex boats began to behave erratically. Only three actually exploded, damaging the obstacles, but it was not enough to create the expected breach.[16] German positions for 75-millimeter, 88-millimeter, and 105-millimeter guns covering Camel Red stayed active, and the 7-foot high and 3-foot thick antitank wall and double rows of 240 six-foot-high mined concrete tetrahedrons placed a 5-foot intervals remained relatively intact. Finally, R.Adm. Spencer Lewis, the commander of Task Force 87, cancelled the landing to the chagrin of Gen. Lucian Truscott, commander of the VI Corps. The landing craft of the 142nd Infantry were ordered to land at Camel Green, which became the main beach for the division.

General Truscott, General Patch, Admiral Hewitt, Under Secretary of War Robert P. Patterson, and Secretary of the Navy James Forrestal followed the events of the day from a war room on the *Catoctin*. A wide array of maps, charts, and communications equipment allowed them to maintain contact with all the elements of the armada, the supporting elements of the air force, and the divisional headquarters on other ships. The *Catoctin* began the morning in the vicinity of the Alpha Beaches, where the commanders observed the landings of the 3rd Division. Later in the morning, it steamed toward the Gulf of Fréjus to observe the afternoon landing operation at Camel Red. Truscott watched as almost a hundred B-24s "blasted the beach defenses in a magnificent exhibition of precision bombing." As the smoke began to clear, the gunfire support group "pounded the beach defenses. Could anything live under such a bombardment?" he asked himself. A few German 88s replied and shells fell in front of the leading minesweepers, but all seemed to be moving forward according to plan. Truscott watched some of the Apex boats explode and others go out of control, but he didn't suspect any major problems.

But suddenly, the whole flotilla of landing craft halted just a few thousand yards from the beach. What was wrong? Admiral Hewitt endeavored to communicate with Admiral Lewis. Then while we watched helplessly, to our profound astonishment, the whole flotilla turned about and headed to sea again. Hewitt, Patch, and I were furious. The admiral promised an investigation. But an intercepted message from Admiral Lewis reported that, owing to beach opposition, they were landing RCT 142 over the Agay beaches in accordance with the alternate landing plan.

Truscott was most displeased at what he witnessed at the Camel Red Beach, even though he had already seen the operations of the other two divisions come to fruition. In the Delta sector, the leading waves of the 45th Division assault regiment moved behind a barrage of rocket fire. The scout teams that preceded the Apex boats in their craft found no underwater obstacles, only mines, so they did not use the Apex boats. The 157th Infantry landed on Delta Red and Green beaches. A single battalion of the 765th Grenadier Regiment of the 242nd Division, backed by artillery units, defended the sector. These German troops were so stunned by the bombardment that they did not begin to put up effective resistance until after the 180th Infantry landed at Delta Yellow and Blue Beaches, a short distance from the 157th beaches. The 1st Battalion of the 157th managed to penetrate eight miles inland to Plan de la Tour, while the 3rd Battalion advanced on Ste-Maxime, only to be held up by a bunker and barricades. Eliminating the German strongpoints in the town, the battalion continued westward to link up that evening with the 3rd Division, which had landed on the Alpha beaches. The 1st Battalion of the 180th Infantry lost all four of its supporting duplex-drive tanks to mines on the beach but

16. The Germans likely interfered with the radio signals; the tests at Salerno had been observed by locals, and the Germans may well have learned of the Apex boats and had sufficient time to devise countermeasures.

reached St. Aygulf near the Camel Red Beach. The 3rd Battalion also advanced, taking the high ground overlooking the 45th Division's beaches and driving the Germans back. The division pushed toward Le Muy and made contact with the airborne troops that evening. During the day, the engineers busily cleared the beachhead and laid the pontoons for unloading the LSTs.[17]

Eighteen Apex boats helped clear the underwater obstacles at the Alpha Beaches, but one of them went out of control and turned back toward the fleet, damaging one ship when it exploded. At Alpha Red, ten minutes before H-Hour, six rocket ships—LCT(R)s—and two LCGs fired on the beaches. Next, the first wave with thirty-seven LCVPs, two LCTs that launched Sherman duplex-drive tanks (two each), and two LCMs approached the beaches. As the 7th Infantry landed on Alpha Red, the 15th Infantry with four duplex-drive tanks followed by tank destroyers landed on Alpha Yellow. (One Sherman DD was hit by an erratic rocket and was destroyed by a mine.) Resistance was light because the defenders from the *Ost* battalion of the 765th Grenadier Regiment were still rattled. Nevertheless, the 7th Infantry lost a few landing craft to obstacles with Teller mines. Once ashore, the regiment moved quickly inland, took Cavalaire-sur-Mer, and reached the French commandos at Cape Nègre.

The 15th Infantry, which landed over five miles away from the 7th Infantry, faced elements of the same *Ost* battalion supported by artillery units, but the shaken troops put up little resistance at the beaches. The men of the 15th cleared the beach within forty minutes, allowing the engineers to begin removing the obstacles and laying the pontoons for the LSTs. The 30th Infantry, which landed at H+1, moved swiftly inland toward Grimaud. By this time, the 15th had advanced about a mile inland toward St. Tropez, where misdropped paratroopers had cornered the German troops in the citadel until

6:30 P.M. By evening, the inland advance had reached Collobrière on the Blue Line. The engineers had continued to clear the beach areas throughout the day. In the afternoon, the advancing infantry had pushed the Germans back, freeing the invasion beaches from harassing fire by taking them out of enemy artillery range.

On D+1, the VI Corps reached the Blue Line, completing the relief of the 1st Airborne Task Force and securing the flanks from Cap Bénat to La Napoule. The naval demolition teams continued to clear the obstacles and wrecks at the Camel Red beaches near St. Raphael using explosive packs. At one point, two dozen German troops swarmed out of a bunker to surrender to one of these teams. One of the divers attached explosives to a sunken ship to clear the St. Tropez harbor. The resulting explosion detonated almost all the mines in the harbor. General Aimé Sudre, at the head of the Combat Command, French 1st Armored Division, was told to land at the Delta beaches because they were the most secure. Camel Green was packed because Camel Red, Sudre's intended landing site, and the harbor area at St. Raphael, had not yet been opened. The main body of the French II Corps landed during the next few days and moved west to strike at Toulon and Marseille, while the 3rd Infantry Division swept westward through Aix-en-Provence to Avignon and the Rhone. The 45th and 36th Divisions advanced northward while the 1st Airborne Task Force and the 1st Special Service Force went eastward to secure the Alpine flank with Italy. The reduction of Toulon and Marseille was left to the Free French Army, aided by the Western Naval Task Force. Neither of these large ports could resist very long. The German Nineteenth Army only attempted to delay the Allied advance as it retreated up the Rhone Valley. In the meantime, the Allied forces in Normandy raced toward the Seine and Paris, pushing the German forces toward Germany.

---

17. Camel was one of the beaches with a shallow gradient that prevented LSTs from beaching. Pontoons were required for unloading.

Chronology of a Landing Operation

Most of the regiments that took part in Operation Dragoon at the three beach sectors spread over forty miles[18] of the Riviera coast had similar landing schedules, even though events turned out a bit differently. In the Delta sector, the scout boats with members of the NCDUs aboard, which were sent ahead of the first wave, found no underwater obstructions, so the Apex boats were not used. The following is taken from the journal of the 157th Infantry, which includes radio messages on D-Day.

August 7: Troops load LCIs and LSTs for final rehearsal. The 3rd Division has already prepared to embark for Operation Dragoon.

August 8: In Exercise Thunderbird, the 157th and 180th land near Salerno. In late morning, troops return to ships and sail back to Pozzouli.

August 9: 157th's troops disembark at Pozzouli and march to areas Nevada (for LCIs) and Texas (for LSTs), but the regimental and battalion command groups remain on ships.

August 10: General training.

August 11: 157th boards LCIs and LSTs.

August 12: Convoy sails from Naples area.

August 13: In the early afternoon, Colonel James briefs troops of 157th on *LCI 520* about Operation Dragoon.

August 14: Convoy of LSTs with 157th Infantry passes between Corsica and Sardinia at 7:00 A.M. and at 5:00 P.M. changes direction off northwest coast of Corsica for French invasion coast.

August 15: D-Day

4:00 A.M.: Convoy arrives in Transport Area.

7:00 to 7:30 A.M.: Aerial bombardment of beaches.

7:20 A.M.: Naval gunfire on beaches.

7:45 A.M.: Long-range rocket fire from LCTs.

7:55 A.M.: Short-range rocket fire from Woofus rocket boats.

8:00 A.M.: H–Hour. First wave of 157th's assault troops observed landing on Red and Green Beach. No fire observed on troops.

8:10 A.M.: 3rd Battalion, 157th's first and second waves ashore.

8:23 A.M.: Third wave ashore.

8:27 A.M.: Fourth wave ashore.

8:30 A.M.: Artillery fire on Company B's initial objective lifted.

8:35 A.M.: Company on initial objective.

9:00 A.M.: Regimental Forward CP landed on Red Beach. 3rd Battalion meeting slight resistance.

9:06 A.M.: Fifth wave ashore.

9:10 A.M.: CP group lands on Red Beach.

---

18. The distance from the islands of Levant and Port Cros on the left flank to Antheor on the right flank for this three-division amphibious landing was almost the same as from Utah Beach to the mouth of the Orne River for the five-division Operation Overlord two months earlier.

Chronology of a Landing Operation *continued*

9:20 A.M.: Navy reports slight mortar fire on all beaches.

9:22 A.M.: 1st Battalion takes 12 prisoners.

9:28 A.M.: 3rd Battalion takes 6 prisoners.

9:30 A.M.: 1st Battalion reports no resistance or mines encountered on beach. Companies B & C are in contact. Prisoners state no mines in the area.

9:32 A.M.: 2nd Battalion, third wave has landed.

9:50 A.M.: All of 2nd Battalion landed.

10:00 A.M.: 2nd Battalion has taken total of 51 prisoners from 11th Battery, 1291st Artillery Regiment. 3rd Battalion's Companies I & K on objective.

10:05 A.M.: Rear echelon regimental CP disembarks from *LCI 520* on Green Beach.

10:10 A.M.: Opposition light, all units moving.

10:30 A.M.: 2nd Battalion advances two-phase line with no resistance yet.

10:35 A.M.: 1st Battalion at objective and resistance slight.

10:40 A.M.: Elements of 158th Field Artillery passing CP.

11:20 A.M.: Captain Slayter reports Company I moving to Ste-Maxime. Civilian reports 500 Germans in Ste-Maxime moved out at 6:00 A.M. Casualties 1 KIA, 2 WIA.

1:00 P.M.: Civilian reports a blockhouse, 3 x 155-mm French guns, and a barbed wire and bridge mined on both sides (map reference locations of each given).

1:10 P.M.: 3rd Battalion held up by fire from pillbox on quay at Ste-Maxime and barricaded streets in town.

2:10 P.M.: 3rd Battalion, Company I moving into Ste-Maxime. Roadblock neutralized.

2:15 P.M.: Artillery falling on troops (location included). Pillbox at Ste-Maxime knocked out. Company K fighting for hotel.

3:25 P.M.: 3rd Battalion reports Ste-Maxime cleared out, leaving two squads of Company K.

7:25 P.M.: VI Corps orders to have beaches and Ste-Maxime cleared as soon as possible and advance to Freshia Valley as soon as possible. Expect to land the French combat command on Delta beaches.

8:15 P.M.: 3rd Battalion 1500 yards from final objective and meeting some resistance from pillboxes.

8:20 P.M.: Reports that 36th Division having rough time and has not landed yet.

9:35 P.M.: 3rd Battalion patrol contacted 15th Infantry patrol.

9:53 P.M.: 45th Division G-3 reports 3rd Division 1st Battalion of 30th Infantry in Germany and 36th Division on Blue phase line.

10:45 P.M.: 1st and 3rd Battalion ordered to advance to Vidabuan and then Lorgues by shortest and best routes, and 2nd Battalion at Le Luc.

10:55 P.M.: General Church orders that 2nd Battalion go to Le Luc as fast as possible using stream bed and trails and not the Plan de la Tour road.

CHAPTER 13

Operation Dragoon under Way

Lt. Carl Strom of the 141st Infantry was briefed on the upcoming operation shortly after the ships sailed from the Naples area in a westerly
direction and changed course. The 1st Battalion was to land at the small
beach of Camel Blue, secure the right flank of the 36th Division, and take
the railroad viaduct and coastal road bridge.

Overnight we went around Corsica, between Corsica and Sardinia, and
came up the coast the dawn of the 15th. I could see quite a number of
vessels. They told us our objective on board ship. We were not shocked
because rumors of south France, northern Italy, or Yugoslavia had been
circulating. They unveiled a mockup of the landing beach we were
going to hit; it was taken from aerial photos. It was an exact scale model
of the beach and was very well done and well planned.

We got up and had some breakfast, but I can't remember what it
was. We did go down the side of the ship into the LCVPs and circled
for a while. As we were circling, we could see they were saturating the
beach areas on each side of the landing beach.

Lt. Martin J. Tully's Company C was in the first wave of the 141st landing operation.

It was going to be a scramble beach, everybody on his own more or less. There was only room enough for three LCVPs to go in abreast. The navy and air force came by in the morning and, unlike the lack of support at Salerno, they hammered the area.

Basically, they didn't change the size of the platoon, but made minor changes in the assault teams that would reduce the pillboxes or attack a strongpoint. It took five LCVPs. We were on an LST, and C Company had the bulk of the infantry troops. We were put in command of the troops [on the LST], and we had a run-in with the navy. They told us no smoking on the tank deck. The navy people hollered at them. . . .

Coming into the landing, there were two LCIs [LCTs, not LCIs] that were missile ships; they just went off and kept the Germans down. Between the navy and air force, it would have been impossible without those missile ships and the support of the navy forward observers. It enabled the first wave of C Company to get in there relatively free, and the subsequent waves received the brunt of the defensive fire.

There were no major changes. We had three platoons, company HQ, and weapons platoon—about 300 men—and it was a regular infantry outfit. I was still a first lieutenant. We had special telephones and commo stuff—unauthorized. I didn't get too far like the rest of these people.[1] Lieutenant Everett—he had this navy guy [the naval forward observer] with him—came to a roadblock and the navy guy had it knocked out. Lieutenant Everett was my XO [executive officer]. Everybody used the bangalores— we had no one attached to do it.

Lieutenant Strom's company followed his friend Tully's into the Camel Blue landing area.

At the time, I was executive officer, Company B, and I went ashore in the second wave on Blue Beach, a very narrow, eighty-yard-wide landing site. Company C had landed in the first wave and was ashore, mostly under and past the railroad viaduct. When we got up to the beach and they lowered the ramp, we all took off. We were in water close up to our waist. We started ashore. Lt. Martin Tully of Company C was in the water, shot through the leg, at the time I landed. A very good friend of mine— I asked him if I could help. Typical of the kind of officer and soldier he was, he said, "No, I'll make it back to the ship; get your men in fast, there are snipers on the hills."

We weren't receiving any fire at the time. Apparently, the first couple waves did receive some fire, and some might have been hit. What I deduced from that was that there was a man or two with a MG on the high points on the left-hand side of the railroad viaduct, and he was up high. When he saw C Company had got in and gotten through the arch so they were getting to the rear of them, they decided their position was untenable and pulled out because we were not receiving any fire when we started unloading.

After we got off the beach, we moved our people through the arches of the viaduct and up to a valley, which was clear of any buildings at that time. After we progressed up the valley, perhaps a quarter or

---

1. Tully was wounded on the way in.

eighth of a mile, we discovered on our left flank a fortified position, a German position. We moved over to that, crept up to it, and debated whether or not to use our bangalore torpedoes and blow the wire and attack through there. However, I noticed behind the position, on its north side, there was a high hill almost like a cliff, approximately 100 feet high. I suggested to the company commander that we go around, continue up the valley, and climb the hill. Then we would be on top of the hill looking down on the position. He thought it a good idea, so we did so. When we got to the top of the hill, we could see the mortar emplacements; the Germans had some mortars, MG positions, and the rest of their fortifications pointing toward the beach. It was made of foxholes and trenches, no bunkers. We could see the weapons, but no troops. They were all facing the other direction [to the sea].

I went up, checked the barbed wire, saw the hill, and told the captain we should go around to the hill. From that point, we could see evidence of positions, but could not see the direction their weapons were pointed because we were at ground level [this was his earlier recon]. Three sides were surrounded by wire; the north side against the cliff was not, because they probably felt it safe. We got on top of the hill, set up our MG and mortars facing down into the position, and we moved into the attack down the hill. I don't remember which platoons went first; we went in a column of platoons. We didn't receive any opposition. When we did finally get in the position, we discovered a dugout with twelve to fifteen men in it. They came out and surrendered. They were all enlisted men and there were no officers in it, but there may have been a noncom. We asked where their officers were, and

they said they had all left that morning when they saw the invasion coming. They were all conscripted Poles and ethnic units, but no Germans. The German officers took off. The dugout was like a cave they dug in the ground, which was obviously the HQ. We didn't go in there because you were always wary of booby traps, and we didn't know what they might have done. We could see how much it dominated the position, but I just don't remember how much because I did not have time to evaluate the position. We know it was a flank position because we did not encounter anything to the left of that as we faced the sea.

We sent a detail down into Fréjus and turned the prisoners over to someone there. Either the 1st or 2nd Battalion had swung in from the right. This had to have happened before noon. On the right, the resistance up in that area was light. The POWs didn't have any weapons on them—we checked them all out and looked for important documents, but we found nothing. Their mortars were set up and in position, but they were all in the dugout. There were three mortars and probably three or four machine guns, all abandoned in position. They all had their helmets on and were happy to see us; they were all smiles. After we sent the prisoners away, the objective of the battalion was that C Company would swing to the right down the coastal highway and B Company, after clearing the valley, would swing to the right and go through the hills on the left flank of C Company on the way to Cannes. We didn't have any resistance. However, at one point, we did come to a cave, and we flushed probably twenty or twenty-five Germans, including two officers, out of the cave. They were ready to surrender too. They had their helmets on but again no weapons, but we didn't let any of the fellas go into the cave and we left the cave as it was. We formed a detail to march the Germans back to where we had come from to turn them over to rear area. We continued our advance through the hills toward Cannes.

There were about a half dozen men in the prisoner details, and they did get back. They had a strange way of getting back. They knew what they were supposed to do and had a strange way of doing this. (Later on, during the rapid advance through France toward Lyon, we had situations where companies were totally disconnected by squads, and they would catch trucks to move along. It was the most disorganized thing I ever saw. Just get yourself up toward the front as fast as you can, but that was later on).

I think that last group was real Germans. They were all infantry, but they didn't want to fight. I think they recognized the Normandy forces were pushing east past Paris. They were very happy to give up. We continued on through the hills. After dark, we stopped, and I remember it had been a hectic day. All of us were bushed. I went to sleep—we were out on a side of a hill—by propping my feet against a bush so I didn't slide down. During the night, a German patrol came through, and our guards had a firefight with them; I never heard a thing. The Germans went right through our position with our guards shooting at them and them shooting at our guards and nobody got hurt. They were trying to get away at the time. They were headed basically north.

A Company was in reserve to my knowledge, I honestly don't remember. We were out of contact with battalion HQ; they were back at the rear some place. We knew where we were to go and what to do, but things were moving so fast we didn't know exactly what others were doing. We had one casualty, one man who fell and was hurt and injured when we captured the Germans in the cave. Two Germans carried him on a stretcher.

The next day, we moved across the hills, alongside the coastal highway, eventually arriving at La Napoule, overlooking Cannes.[2] Here the battalion was being held up by SS troops in some houses.

At this point, B Company was detached from the battalion and attached to a special task force to move inland. It relieved some paratroopers trapped in the village of Callian. The company remained attached to what was then designated as Task Force Butler until reassignment to the battalion about September 1.

PFC Arthur P. Rodgers was a machine gunner in the 2nd Platoon, D Company (Weapons Company), 1st Battalion, 141st Infantry.

I guess we got the orders twenty-four hours before we landed. I think we were at sea for about three days, and I think on the morning of the fourth day we hit the beaches. The three platoons and company HQ were on the same LST. The heavy weapons company was larger than the others. The full TO&E [table of organization and equipment] was 253 men and a rifle company was smaller, maybe 180. We were larger and had the vehicles, a jeep, and a trailer, four to each platoon of machine guns and six to a

2. The 1st Battalion was held up by many bunkers along the coast road and did not take Théoule-sur-Mer until late on August 16. They then found the bridges north of it, which led to la Napoule, destroyed. Near this point, they found the few French marines that had survived the diversionary mission that preceded the invasion.

platoon of mortars plus the CO's vehicle. Our company split up for the invasion. When we rendezvoused with the other LSTs, they picked us up. I assume they made the decision at the last moment.

We saw all the ships all around to our left and rear. We got off the LST and on to an LCI [an LCVP, not an LCI] with the company we were attached to. We went over the side on rope ladders. Heading toward the shore on the inlet was a lighthouse, and we went to the right of it. There were mountains behind [the coast]. We got on the beaches and [soon reached the nearby] road and railroad tracks. We got off on the beach with C Company from the LCVPs. The thing I remember most is the lighthouse on the left. We got fire from our left rear in the ravine. The lieutenant from C Company got killed there. We went up to the right. We were on foot, following C Company, and we didn't have time to set up. At one point, the lieutenant came back and said he wanted fire over there and the side, so we set up and fired for ten or fifteen minutes, a couple of belts, and then we disassembled the gun. We initially started firing at about 750 yards and raised it to 900, firing at a general target of two houses where we thought there were some prisoners taken by B and C Company. We saw them and some French civilians who were watching and giving us the high sign. After the initial firing was over, we didn't have any more heavy resistance.

Lt. Ruben D. Parker was with Company E, 2nd Battalion, 141st Infantry, as it landed on the right wing of the first wave at Camel Green Beach in five LCVPs just after 8:00 A.M. Company G and Company I, followed by eight duplex-drive tanks of the 753rd Tank Battalion, formed the remainder of the first wave. Later in the afternoon, this 230-yard beach became the

main landing area for the 36th Division when the 142nd Infantry had to be diverted from its planned Camel Red assault.

I don't remember much about the fleet, but I do remember the day of the invasion. We got up at 4:00 in morning and the invasion was to be at 8:00. At 6:00, we had breakfast, got our packs ready, and got into the small LCVP. I remember these things circled for about an hour before we got word to go into the beach. When we got to the beach, the company was formed into a W, that is, three boats forward and two back. E Company, 2nd Battalion, was in the first assault wave, five companies landing abreast [only three shown on the landing charts]. You could hear the shells going over us hitting the beach. Other than that, it was the sound of the motors. We were coming in and I am surprised when we hit the beach. Instead of sand beaches like Salerno, there were a great number of rocks. We knew to expect an escarpment, and sure enough, twenty-five yards inland there was a little cliff eight to ten feet tall that we had to find footholds to get through. Our mission was to proceed inland about ten yards [actually 100 yards] and turn right.

If they [the Germans] did have any special preparation because of Normandy, it didn't get down to platoon level. I think we had more artillery and air support per unit of beach because we really plastered them. We were scared to death, particularly those soldiers who went into Salerno, which was bloody. They dreaded it more than those of us who never made an invasion. They had seen their buddies decimated [at Salerno]. I think there was relief when we hit the shore and didn't see anybody.

I was in the middle LCVP of the three in front. No resistance on the beach. I had

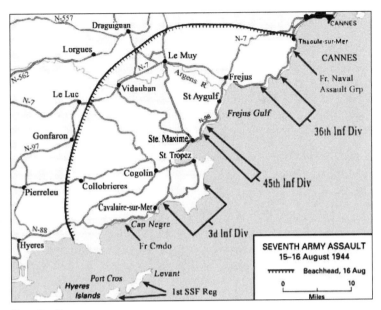

Operation Dragoon.

one casualty, and we don't know to this day what happened to him. He was killed; we don't know if he stepped on a mine or what. We landed and went about fifty to seventy-five yards, turned a ninety-degree angle, found a hill with a little cemetery, and took that. The pillbox on the beach was small and looked like a little dugout with the only German we saw when we hit the beach. He was in the pillbox, and he never saw us because his eyes appeared riveted out to sea and perhaps had no peripheral vision to see us. We took care of him.

I don't think we paid any attention to the *MINEN* signs, and we didn't wait for any engineers. We wanted to get off the beach as quick as we could. After we took that little cemetery, all this was about thirty minutes after landing, we proceeded north cross-country and passed the little village of Le

Drammont, and F Company in the second wave [sixth wave] was supposed to take that.[3] We landed on the right edge of Green Beach. The 143rd was to come in and take St. Raphael. We were the first battalion to come in and take Agay [clear Camel Yellow east of Camel Green]. The 2nd Battalion was to take the high ground behind it, which we did by noon—we were three or four miles inland. The 1st Battalion took the town of Agay,[4] and 2nd Battalion took the little village of Thumont. My company went in three miles inland and took the high ground. We were sort of basking in the sun until about 5:00 in the evening. Then we came back, got on the road, and followed the trail across the massif.[5] The trail wasn't very clear, and many times I had to stop and get under a blanket to decide whether I wanted to go right or left. By midnight, we

---

3. La Drammont and the cape south of it were secured by 10 A.M.

4. Company A, 1st Battalion, coming from Camel Blue, met the 2nd Battalion near Agay.

5. Parker's company was advancing to a secondary road north of Agay. This road became the main axis of advance for the battalion the next day as it moved northeast toward National Road 7 that led to La Napoule and Cannes.

had crossed [the massif] and cut Highway 7 leading from Paris to Cannes.

Within fifteen minutes after reaching Highway 7, a little German roadster came up, and my XO went out with a pistol and stopped him. He yanked the door open, saw this German major, and told him to get out. The German major said to go to hell and gave a signal to his driver who accelerated and got away. About thirty minutes later, a convoy of six trucks came from the same direction, and we knocked out all six with bazooka fire. The last one, which was carrying ammunition, caught fire. It was the Fourth of July.[6] Ammunition was popping all over. The driver was caught and burned in the cab and crawled out into the bushes. His moans and cries were so unnerving that nobody had the guts to go out and put him out of his misery. In the long run, it may have been an advantage because it kept us awake. At daylight, we were counterattacked by a company of German soldiers who had come from Cannes on bicycles. We had a firefight that lasted thirty minutes to an hour and I lost five soldiers and nineteen wounded, but we must have captured forty or fifty bicycles that the men amused themselves with for the next couple days, riding up and down the road. That was the last we saw of the Germans there.

We presumed the major that got away alerted some troops. Nothing [there was no resistance between the beaches and the highway]. The only German was the one they killed on the beach. We were supposed to have been met and led by a French offi-cer, but he didn't show up, so I had to do the best I could with map reading.

T.Sgt. Sammie D. Petty from Lockhart, Texas, was a member of the 141st Infantry, having joined the National Guard at age nineteen in 1940. He served with the 36th Division from the time it trained in the United States through the Italian Campaign as a member of the 1st Platoon, Company F, which was to land at Camel Green in the sixth wave, scheduled for H+30 minutes. During the landings in south France, he was one of the few Texans from the old National Guard division still serving in the frontline infantry unit.

We had a nice trip across the Mediterranean. We knew [or possibly assumed] we were going to invade south France[7] when we got on the ship, and they said the battleship *Texas* was going to support us. It didn't make any difference to us; we were going to hit a beach and that was it. It caused a little excitement because we were the "Texas" Division, but we never did see it.[8] I crossed on a regular troopship with the whole battalion on it. I remember we got up around 2 or 3 in the morning. They fed us steak for breakfast, and we loaded on the LCVPs with about thirty men each, maneuvered around, and landed about daylight. They dropped the ramp [on the LCVP], and we landed on Green Beach.

The only thing that stuck in my mind was that they were using these rocket ships, some kind of a navy vessel that shot fifty or sixty at once. We could see where they hit the beach, and they pulverized it pretty good where we were going to land. I didn't

---

6. According to a situation map in the Seventh Army report, the truck convoy should have arrived about 6:00 A.M. on August 16, so Parker may have remembered the time of the events incorrectly.

7. He added, "I would say a couple days before that they told us where we would land." That indicates they were already aboard ship and at sea.

8. The battleship *Texas* was there, but assigned to the Gun Support Group for TF 85 Delta Force and not TF 87 Camel Force. Thus, it was bombarding the St. Tropez area and not involved with the landings near Fréjus, where the 36th Division went in.

General Patch with Secretary of the Navy James Forrestal aboard a PT boat on D+1 off the coast of south France.

see the air force at all. I wasn't a bit worried about the landing. Normally, you are scared, so I don't know why I was not. As we were going in, I was talking to the boy driving the ship and I told him, "I want you to put me ashore so I don't get my feet wet." He said, "I don't know how to do that," but he put us right up there. It was a rough shore, but we didn't get our feet wet. I told the men on the ship, "When we hit that beach, you hit it running and don't quit. Keep running until you get off it."

We hit the beach running. We were the first wave ashore, nobody ahead of us. There was no resistance; we received no fire.[9] We must have run at least a quarter of a mile till

9. Landing charts show Company F, 2nd Battalion, 141st Infantry, was in the sixth wave. The first wave, followed by the DD tanks, met light opposition, and those that followed met no resistance on the beach.

we reached a little town called Drammont [to the right of the beachhead]. . . . There were Germans in the area because I came face to face with one. I was running along the side of this railroad, which had a deep embankment, and I ran up to this German. I thought I was going to shoot him; something told me I better check. I had a carbine, and I looked down and the clip was out. He was fixing to shoot me too, but I just bailed over the side and got my rifle ready. He had left. He went one way and I went the other. Soon the whole platoon was around him, so I guess he was captured or killed up there. A woman came out of her house with a rifle, and one of the guys killed her. I asked why he shot her and he said she had a rifle and there had been Germans in the house. We went through the town, and behind the town was a high mountain range.[10] We went down the valley and across this mountain. We went—I think—twelve miles to cut the highway over there. We didn't really have any fighting. There was firing around us, but not in our area—no casualties in our platoon.

Cpl. Art John Zalud served as a truck driver in the service battery of a 155-millimeter field artillery battalion.

We had no inkling of our goal. We heard the rumor that this would be the division's last major campaign, and that after the beach was secured, we would go home to the States. We boarded LSTs in Italy, and then we all gathered around the rendezvous area and found out we were going to South France. Everybody was enthused after the stories we had heard about the mademoiselles there. The service battery was on one LST with the firing battery we had to support. They had also waterproofed for landing. It was awfully congested with stuff sitting around. It was smelly. . . . After the whole division gathered at the rendezvous point offshore, they told us where we were going.

Prior to landing, we waterproofed our equipment. All I remember of the landing is that I was surprised we met such little resistance by the time we got on there. I don't know if we were on the third or fourth wave. We landed on Red Beach [actually Green Beach]. I was amazed at all the firing on our side and such little resistance from the German side. We expected it to be like Salerno. I was not there, but those who were told me that is what they expected. We rode right in with little resistance and had a hard time keeping up with the infantry because they moved so fast. The firing batteries went off first and then we came in. Louisiana maneuvers were worse than this. We kept on moving. We supplied C Battery, found out where the ammo dumps were set up, and started supplying them. The dumps were about a mile to a mile and half from the beach. Regular units set up the ammo dumps; they came in after us. Each of our trucks was loaded with ammo and powder. You had to get a requisition from the lieutenant for ammo. We just loaded up one time that day. After the batteries were set up, they had to pack up and start moving again because there was so

---

10. To the south of the town of Le Drammont was a mountain occupying the end of the peninsula. To the north were more mountains. Le Drammont occupied a valley-like position that linked Camel Green with Camel Yellow. The 2nd Battalion, followed by 3rd Battalion, did advance through this corridor to Agay and Camel Yellow and then turned north away from the coastal road into the mountains and a secondary road, which led towards la Napoule. The 1st Battalion at Camel Blue was taking the coast road in the direction of Theoule-sur-Mer and la Napoule. The 142nd and 143rd Infantry Regiments advanced on St. Rapael and Fréjus to the west.

little resistance. It seems in a week's time we were a hundred miles inland. They did do some firing the first day, and we did one resupply. The next day, we moved out and kept moving every day. The ammo supplied to the firing battery stayed with them; we just replenished them. When they were low on ammo, they called and got more.

One night, we were going up to the firing batteries to supply the battery with ammo. It was a light moonlit night. They had us zeroed in and dropped shells behind us. The other fellow in the truck was Rosy and I asked if they were shells, and he said, "Yeah." We kept on going, and the shells followed us but never hit us.[11] There were other times when the road was zeroed in while in Italy and they pinned us in. France was nowhere near as bad as Italy.

Capt. Kenneth P. Stemmons, the commanding officer of Company B, 1st Battalion, 157th Infantry, embarked upon his third campaign. His 45th Division landed on the Delta beaches to the southwest of the 36th Division.

We had no warning before we embarked. We got our equipment on in the morning and marched down to embark on the ships for invasion. Our objective for the invasion was given to us once we were out to sea heading for southern France. Each man was issued an American flag patch to sew on his right shoulder to identify our troops to the French. Any known S-2 intelligence was passed to all troops. This included identification of enemy units and their strength, also that enemy armor had been active in the area.

The 157th Infantry tried to keep the company organization. The landing craft were assigned to landing waves with five minutes between waves. The 1st Battalion beach had five landing craft per wave. The first wave had approx thirty-six soldiers per craft as follows: one soldier from A&P platoon (demolition specialist), two soldiers from Company HQ (either company commander, first sergeant, runners, radio operator, or intelligence specialist), one rifle platoon with a flamethrower and eight-foot scaling ladder. Each rifleman carried a 5-pound block of tetrytol that [after landing] each man was to put in a pile at the seawall as he climbed the ladder and went over the seawall. The man from the battalion A&P platoon was to set the charge off, blowing a large hole in the seawall so that following assault waves of men could go through.

The second wave had the reserve rifle company plus mine detectors, bangalore torpedoes, artillery forward observer teams, and some weapons company personnel. Additional personnel followed in other waves.

An amphibious assault is a very violent and tumultuous time. The adrenalin is pumping; you know not everyone is going to make it off the beach. The new soldiers are looking to the old-timers for advice and knowledge. No one in the first wave is calm, cool, and collected. It's time for soul searching, hope, and a silent prayer.

Fortunately, for Stemmons and his regiment, they met little resistance. The 1st Battalion, 157th Infantry, landed on Delta Green and the 3rd Battalion came in on its left on Delta Red. On the right of the 1st Battalion, the 180th Infantry's 2nd Battalion landed on Delta Yellow, and 1st Battalion, 180th Infantry, disembarked on Delta Blue under ideal conditions, unlike in the other sectors.

---

11. This took place in Italy around San Pietro in the spring of 1944.

The first wave of the 157th Infantry made it to the beach without major problems. The beach in our area was protected by a barbed wire beach and a six-foot seawall. Enemy mortar shells were falling on the beach during the assault. As we moved in over the seawall, we had artillery and mortar fire falling in our area. As we cleared the seawall, I fired my carbine at a small rock building and a sandbag emplacement on the road. Just off the beach, they had some sandbagged positions, not all manned. The defending force had fired until we got close; then they fled to the surrounding hills. As soon as they fell back in the hills, the beach and road area came under mortar fire. We moved inland as fast as possible. As we approached the foothills, we spotted a German unit trying to organize a defense. After a brief firefight, they surrendered and then others that had scattered through the hills came in to surrender.

About the only issued item that was not used for Operation Dragoon was the gas mask. On previous invasions, all of us simply threw the gas masks away at different times as we moved in. However, for Dragoon, HQ passed the word to throw them all in one place as we cleared the beach, so they could be picked up.

According to Sgt. Ralph W. Fink, who led a .30-caliber machine-gun unit in Weapons Company (Company D), 1st Battalion, 157th Infantry, 45th Division, the landing operation and campaign went quite well, with little loss of life. To his great relief, it was not hell, like the Italian campaign was.

I recall being roused before daybreak on August 15th. We must have had cold rations for breakfast because I don't remember going to a galley, and surely this would have messed up our placement on deck. Location was now most important so that we would be in proper sequence for boarding the landing craft.

With the morning light, we were ordered over the side on rope ladder nets and descended into the landing craft. The sea was calm, but it took a while because our heavy machine guns and mortars were lowered to us in slings. When our craft was loaded, it moved away from the ship and started to circle. We could now see that the same thing was happening at the other ships close-by. After circling for approximately half an hour, a flare went up and all landing craft turned shoreward. This was the moment of truth, and the feelings of exhilaration and fear are indiscernible.

Up until this time, we had drawn no fire from shore. As we neared shore, some artillery shells started to hit the water around us, but it soon became obvious that it came from just one small battery and danger was not too great unless we took a direct hit. The craft took us up to about seventy yards off the shore and dropped the front gate, and we plunged into the water about waist deep and made our way toward shore. The sea was calm, the weather was warm, and the beach was almost level, although it slopped up slightly toward the seawall, which was probably eight feet high, fifty yards to our front. At this time, we were hearing small arms fire at a distance to our right and left, but we were drawing no fire at all.

We quickly ran to the seawall and stopped there to see if we were all there and get the individual squads together. As we contemplated scaling the wall, someone on the far left shouted to tell us there was a break in the wall at his point. Now organized squads and sections, we ran to that point and ran through the opening. The

A railroad gun captured during German retreat from south France. JAMES NEWTON

best I can describe the seawall is that it was not a long solid wall, but built like a series of overlapping walls[12] with breaks about every 100 yards or so. I later assumed the wall was constructed to allow any water that washed over the walls to return more gently to the sea. I think the wall was mainly to keep the beach sand from being washed back out to sea during storms. The break in the wall was like a godsend because it let us through easily without the chore of going over the top with our heavy machine guns, etc.

At about this time, men disposed of the ropes and gas masks. I would guess that later it was quite a chore for whoever cleaned up this area because everyone threw away his gas masks. Now again fully in control by officers and noncoms, we headed toward a small wooded area several hundred yards to our front and waited there until orders were received.

On the surface, this whole operation seems like a piece of cake, and in a way, it was. However, considering the rush of preparation on board ship the night before, the sleeplessness, and the intense mental rush of storming the beach left us exhausted. I vividly recall resting there in the trees and my body was trembling. We had carried out our mission once more and were still alive.

As I recall, with the sea to our back, the scene was of gently rolling fields, small wooded areas here and there, and houses

12. He described this as a "baffled-type break in the construction that we were close enough to go right through."

and small farmsteads here and there, but not too close together.

Many of the veterans of the 3rd Division, whose depleted ranks had been filled with many rookies, were somewhat apprehensive about making another landing. For PFC Robert L. Zahradka, company runner, Company D, 7th Infantry, the landing at Red Beach was surprisingly easy. "The boat ride to the invasion area was quiet, but the thought of a daylight [8 A.M.] landing was most unsettling to the older men, who had been on invasions before, always at night or dawn."

First Sgt. Frank Andrews, no longer a frontline combat infantryman, was now in a more administrative position in the headquarters of 1st Battalion, 7th Infantry, 3rd Division. He was relieved to finally be able to go into battle with a reasonable chance of survival. The 7th Infantry landed on Alpha Red several miles to the west of the 15th Infantry, which came ashore on Alpha Yellow. Andrews, whose battalion formed the reserve, watched the 2nd and 3rd Battalions of his regiment forge ahead and saw a few of their LCVPs being hit.

For the actual landing, it was different from what we had done before; we had never made a daylight landing before. I think it was 8:00 in the morning when we stopped milling around and headed for the beach. There was a battleship not too far from us making ready to fire. I guess he did fire before we loaded the boats. He opened up and we got in the small boats [LCVPs] and milled around for a while. At about 8:00 we formed a line and headed for the beach. It was uneventful except for the last little ways. Not much fire, except some machine gun at a point off to our left. When we got

close and reached two minutes from the beach, the front end of the boat in front of us was blown off—I don't think too many killed—just the ramp and front end. A few seconds after, one of the machine-gun bullets hit our boat, came through the side across from me, and hit a young guy name Amundson. He dropped like beef in a slaughterhouse. I didn't give him a second look, thinking he was dead. The ramp was already going down—we made a dash for it—and when we got on the beach, someone hollered, "Mines!" There were these little mounds. It had been mined before and the rain left these little mounds. If you got low and looked, you could pick rows to walk in, and that is what we did. I didn't see any mine set off.[13]

Amundson showed up two months later in the town of Bagney [Bagney-sur-Meuse], France. I went out one day and a trucker came up who said he had a bunch of hospital returnees and replacements for the battalion and I went to check them out. Who steps out, but this kid Amundson?

After Africa, we never saw gas masks anymore. We found big stores of that type of equipment the Germans had on hand, but not on the individual. The big 4.2 chemical mortars were not needed for that and were attached to battalion and regiment. They were a big addition to our firepower, greater than the 60-mm and 80-mm mortar.

After Sicily, we didn't see too much German air force, so the flak wagons [the mobile antiaircraft units] scattered in the rear areas were brought closer to the front, and when we got into Europe, we brought them right up to the front to support advancing infantry.

---

13. The Germans had laid *Schu* mines on part of this beach area. These mines contained a minimal amount of metal; they used wooden boxes, making them difficult to locate with mine detectors.

PFC Isadore L. Valenti, medic, Company K, 3rd Battalion, 7th Infantry, was ready for another campaign. The troops he worked with depended on him in case they got wounded. While he stood at the railing early in the morning, just hours before the invasion, Lt. Paul McGhan, 3rd Platoon leader, approached Valenti to tell him that Captain Syladek's recommendation had been approved and Valenti had been promoted to corporal.

So on the morning of August 15, 1944, we hit the beaches in Southern France in broad daylight. It was a bright, sunny day. The night before the invasion, I asked my platoon leader, 1st Lt. Paul McGhan, why the invasion was scheduled for broad daylight. He said, "The invasion is scheduled for 8:00 A.M. because our air force reconnaissance photos show that the beaches are strewn with French 75-mm, old World War I artillery shells, all connected individually or in clusters by trip wire."[14] He added, "A kick into the wire will detonate individual or clusters of shells."

We hit the beaches exactly at 8:00 A.M. The sun was bright and the day looked promising. We didn't get off the beaches until later afternoon, only to run into additional German reinforcements.

Valenti's landing did not go smoothly, as naval guns boomed and rockets whizzed overhead, methodically pounding the beach area. On its way to the beach, Valenti's little LCVP bobbed like a cork amid the plumes of seawater raised by German shells exploding nearby. Suddenly it lurched, smashed into an underwater obstacle, and its ramp dropped down amid the *rat-a-tat-tat* of an enemy machine gun firing somewhere overhead.

The tension gripped me. I wanted off. . . . I leaped ashore and streaked toward the protection of the fallen trees thirty or forty yards beyond the beach. Everywhere men disappeared into the heavy haze, which was beginning to rise over the beach.

Then it happened! A hundred feet to our right front there was a bright flash and a booming, muffle-like sound. A soldier had tripped a land mine. Sand and the soldier's innards scattered in all directions.

Corporal Valenti set to tending the wounded. In the early morning, PFC Louis Sumien, with the headquarters of the 3rd Battalion, 7th Infantry, clambered down a cargo net from his transport to an LCVP.

We were told to keep our heads down; we weren't squashed-in but still tight. There was smoke, and we got a glimpse of the beach toward the horizon. We began circling along with other craft, waiting for the signal to make toward the beach. A few shells were landing in the water; some craft were hit. Then we got the order to head for the beach. We were wearing lifebelts made of rubber that held CO_2 cartridges to inflate them. I discovered mine didn't work. When we hit the beach, I stepped on dry land, ran across a road as others were doing all down the line, and ran on until falling in a cantaloupe field where ripe cantaloupes were waiting for us. They were delicious. No Krauts were in sight, although we could hear their burp guns. We could see a scattering of artillery fire.

We regrouped. I was with the 3rd Battalion, Forward CP, having been taken out of L company to act as a French interpreter (I was born in northern France). We saw no

---

14. He may have been referring to the explosives attached to the tetrahedron.

German defenses, only unmanned fortifications. I was with the forward CP most of the time, guarding it while listening to Major Flynn giving orders to the rest of the battalion. We had a forward artillery observer from the cruiser *Brooklyn* with us. He was dressed in fatigues, probably a coverall, and wore a green helmet. He had a small crew with him and his radios—about three men.

First Sgt. Sherman Pratt, Anti-Tank Company, 7th Infantry, was on an LST with the 2nd Battalion when he was instructed to locate a site for a command post. His antitank company's platoons were each assigned to a different battalion. On the morning of August 15, he was up early and watched the sunrise from the deck as the naval guns boomed away at the shore targets.

A little after 0700, the waves of smaller landing craft and DWCKs [DUKWs], the boat-like 2½-ton trucks, started for shore in assault formations. Just behind them were the large LSTs and LSIs and other standard amphibious vessels.

When we were about three miles from shore and still too far out to see the beaches very plainly, we came under enemy fire from shore guns. I saw one shell strike an LCI, several hundred yards to our starboard, but in the bouncing waves, it was not possible to see what damage was done. Several other rounds landed in the water, one just to our stern.[15]

A little later on, several rounds churned up the water in front of our boat, and we could hear and feel some slugs plow into or bounce off the steel hull. By now, we could see the beach. . . . There was additional

machine-gun fire, and it seemed to be coming from a pillbox . . . partially hidden in the brush only about two or three hundred yards to our left.

When he reached the shore and proceeded to look for a command post site, Pratt came across two soldiers lying on the ground: one was wounded, the other dead. As the wounded soldier warned him about a sniper, a shot rang out and a bullet grazed his arm without drawing blood. Another volley whizzed past him, and he dived behind a wall. Later, he came across some medics, told them to help the wounded soldier, and warned them and the soldiers with them about the sniper.[16]

Sgt. Harold Taylor, 15th Infantry, 3rd Division, landed on Delta Yellow: "On 15 August, we landed near St. Tropez. At first, we met with sporadic resistance, but our momentum was such that it wasn't long before we established our beachhead. . . . We encountered heavy small arms fire and heavy weapons and mortar fire."

PFC Robert Gehlhoff, 3rd Battalion headquarters, 15th Infantry, who landed on Alpha Yellow, saw many casualties on the beach, mostly due to the mines.

Those Higgins boats were lowered into the water, and then by rope ladders, the troops got over the side of the ship and climbed down. That can be a little tricky with the rising and falling ship and waves. One might be ready to step off the rope ladder into the landing craft only to find the craft had dropped fifteen feet or was coming up to meet you with a backbreaking slam.

When each boat was loaded, it pulled away from the ship and joined others going

---

15. Pratt must have loaded onto an LCVP from the LST, although in his book he states he landed in an LST that dropped its ramp on the beach. The LSTs did not land until hours later and had to use pontoon causeways to unload because of the shallow gradient of the beach.

16. Somehow, he managed to take a photo of the two soldiers hit by the sniper; it appears in his book.

in a large circle. Soon there were many boats and circles. When the signal to hit the beach was given, the circling boats broke formation, formed a straight line, revved up their motors, and headed for the beach. All the ships had opened fire, and the noise was deafening. The air filled with screaming rocket flashes and the thunderous battalion guns. They shelled the beach and hillside for some time and then let up. The first wave broke out from our formation and headed for the beach. Moments later, our formation roared in. We were the second wave.

We tried to get across the sandy beach as fast as we could. The beach was mined with many small foot mines that just blow off your foot and Bouncing Bettys that, when stepped on, would bounce head high and burst. We tried to follow the footprints of the men ahead. Many lay wounded, some dead. We went by one soldier laying on his side with his foot a bloody mess.

For Gehlhoff, the most harrowing part of that morning was getting off Beach Yellow, where it seemed to him that he ran past almost every casualty there was; "the rest of the day was a breeze."

S.Sgt. John Shirley, 3rd Platoon, I Company, 15th Infantry, also landed on Alpha Yellow.

At 6:00 A.M. we were on deck, dressed in woolen ODs, combat boots, and loaded with our gear, including rifle, helmet, field pack, gas mask, ammo belt, canteen, entrenching tool, bayonet, C rations, extra bandoliers of ammo, and extra hand grenades. Some men were armed with BARs, pistols, and carbines. Others carried bazookas, light machine guns, or light mortars.

We were heavily loaded as we climbed over the ship's gunwales and lowered ourselves down cargo nets that hung down the ship's side. We carefully placed our hands

and feet on the rope rungs. To fall, loaded as we were, was to sink to the bottom of the Mediterranean. As we neared the water, we could see the landing craft bob up and down, in and out against the ship. The trick was to let go of the cargo net as the craft moved up towards you, find the thin rail side with your foot, then jump the four to five feet to the deck of the bucking craft. We had practiced several mock invasions off the coast of Italy, so the experience wasn't new, just difficult.

Our LCVP pulled away from the mother ship and joined a group of similar craft circling about two miles offshore. We circled while all the landing craft were loaded and maneuvered into the correct positions. As we circled in the early daylight, we could see hundreds of ships. In every practice invasion, I became deathly seasick within twenty minutes after entering the LCVPs. My helmet served as a catch basin. On this day fear, anxiety, excitement—something—kept me from being seasick. It was a pleasant surprise, and a small plus to what would be a long difficult day. After about an hour of circling, the landing craft moved out of the holding pattern and lined up abreast for the dash to the beach.

The warships softened the beaches with everything from 14-inch shells fired from the battleships to small rockets fired from landing craft. In our practice landings in Italy, several times we had to wade ashore in hip-deep water. On this day, the LCVP ran up on the sandy shore, and we stayed dry as we stormed the beach designated Beach Yellow. I was a squad leader in the 3rd Platoon, I Company. When the front ramp dropped, I led my squad over the soft sand for about seventy-five yards to a coastal road where we took cover from enemy fire coming from a hill to our front. My squad had reached the road without a casualty. If there were mines buried in the sand, we missed them. Our platoon was ordered to attack up the hill where the Germans were resisting our advance.

Light machine guns and riflemen from another platoon set down a base of fire, as we formed a skirmish line along the road. It would be a dangerous attack up the hill covered with trees and low scrub brush. We left our cover and started up the hill, firing our rifles as we moved forward. We moved out without much thought of the consequences. It was a little unreal, more like a training exercise. A half hour later, we stood on the crest of the hill. We had driven the Germans out of their positions. Several Germans soldiers were killed as they tried to escape down the backside of the hill. My twelve-man squad on the beach was now a six-man squad. Two men had been killed and four wounded. Fifty percent casualties in less than an hour was a high price, but we had broken a thin crest of resistance and, fortunately, did not have another firefight the rest of the day.

Our platoon joined the 3rd Battalion Battle Patrol and spent the next seven hours looking for enemy soldiers in the coast gun emplacements that dotted the St. Tropez peninsula. The few we found were taken without a fight. At 6:30 P.M., we sat down by a small stream, washed our feet, changed socks, and ate a can of C rations.

That evening, sometime after 7:00 P.M., Sergeant Shirley's squad joined a patrol of the 3rd Battalion as the 15th Infantry reformed. The regiment moved west to Cogolin on the heels of the 30th Infantry, which had surged northward toward Le Luc and National Route 7 as well as westward toward Collobrières, where it had turned north to Gonfaron to reach the Blue Line,

the objective for securing the beachhead. In its haste, the 30th Infantry, traveling in tanks and other vehicles, had not effectively cleared the sector between Collobrières and the 7th Infantry on the coastal road. It fell to the 15th Infantry to sweep up this area of rough, forested hills, known as the Maures Hills. Fortunately for Sergeant Shirley and his men, whose patrol lasted over twenty hours, they didn't engage in firefights, and his flank patrols came across a lone enemy soldier with an MG42 machine gun.

We had moved parallel to the coast in a westerly direction and had covered nearly thirty miles. We had been up thirty-six hours fighting, scouting, hiking, and sweating under the hot sun, as we marched up and down the hilly coastal roads. Our march was especially hard on flank patrols, as they tried to keep up while scouting out the hilly bush and forestland adjacent to the route of march. My squad took its turn on the flank patrol. It was with great surprise we walked up to the muzzle of a light machine gun pointed at us. A German soldier was lying prone behind the gun. He was alone and, mercifully, surrendered without taking our lives, which he could have easily done.

At about 4:00 P.M. (August 16), we climbed a small, steep hill and dug in. We could not see the town [probably Collobrières], and we did not have to fight for it.

The landings of August 15 generally went as well as could be expected. In the afternoon, General Truscott, the VI Corps' commander, still rankling from the cancellation of the landing at Camel Red, boarded an LCVP of the *Catoctin* and headed for Camel Blue to find Gen. John Dahlquist. He was still convinced that determined troops could force a landing. Truscott was finally appeased when he learned that it was not

Dahlquist who made the decision to cancel the landing, and he was satisfied to know that his T-Patchers would still reach the Blue Line by the next morning. However, shortly after the meeting, the flames of Truscott's resentment were rekindled when the news leaked out that General Dahlquist had seconded the naval commander's decision with a signal. Except for forcing the French armored unit to come ashore on the Delta beaches the next day, the failure to land at Camel Red caused no major reverses for the Allies and very likely averted another needless Bloody Omaha.

CHAPTER 14

The Inland Advance

As D-Day came to a close, over 14,000 troops from the reinforced 36th Division had come ashore on the Camel beaches; 33,000 troops of the 45th Division and supporting units at the Delta beaches; and 12,800 troops of the 3rd Division at the Alpha beaches, for a total of over 60,000 men and about 6,700 vehicles. The next day, another 10,400 men; 8,600 vehicles; and more supplies were unloaded. The losses were light. *LST 282* and two LCVPs were destroyed by a glider bomb off the Camel beaches. German gunners sank two LCVPs and damaged six LCTs. Five LCIs, five LCVPs, one LCT, and one minelayer were damaged by mines; three other LCIs and one LCT were damaged by underwater obstacles. Losses were equally light for the naval, ground, and air forces.

On D+1, the airborne troops consolidated their positions and took the key surrounding towns and cleared Le Muy. The 45th Division secured the central area of the front and advanced to relieve the 1st Airborne Task Force to the north. The 36th Division expanded the beachhead and advanced the right flank of the invasion area and the 3rd Division, the left flank. Additional troops and support units poured out on the beachheads where the first rear area dumps had already been setup on D-Day.

Support

There were many more types of support units than there were combat units. These engineer, transportation, signal corps, quartermaster, and ordnance units' responsibilities included construction, port, maintenance, and various other tasks, which, though not glamorous, were as important to the success of military operations as combat was. In some cases, these units were exposed to as much danger as the frontline units were. For instance, the naval beach battalions, which were critical in operating the beachheads, faced the same hazards as the assault troops. The first elements of the 8th Beach Battalion came ashore with the second wave of the 36th Division on Camel Green, and a full company was on shore operating the beach by that afternoon. These battalions also provided communications and medical evacuation in the early hours.

The most exciting job SN1/C Clifford Leggert had was guarding Italian prisoners when the battalion arrived in Arzew, Algeria, earlier in 1944. For the Riviera invasion, he was reassigned from the Platoon A-2 hydrographic section to the headquarters. "Since D Day," he wrote, "I was assigned to be in charge of my CO's German-held home. I had a dull time and I missed all the fun on the beaches." His battalion busily prepared and operated the beaches for over a month. It was the only beach battalion not to lose men in action, which was unusual for a unit called the "Eight Balls." The 1st and 4th Beach Battalions, which operated the Alpha and Delta beaches, did suffer some casualties.

As in Normandy and other campaigns, unarmed aviation units took part in combat operations in support of the divisional artillery. It was decided during the war to add light aircraft designated L-4 and L-5 to serve as forward observation platforms for the artillery. These liaison aircraft turned out to be so effective that they struck fear in the hearts of the Germans whenever they flew over the battlefields. One of these liaison pilots,

1st Lt. Wilfred Boucher, who came from Hamden, Connecticut, had graduated from Yale as a member of the ROTC. He was commissioned as a lieutenant in the field artillery on June 8, 1942. After serving in a field artillery brigade, he volunteered to become a liaison pilot in April 1943. After completing his training at Pittsburg, Kansas, and Fort Sill, he received his wings in September and was assigned to the 901st Field Artillery Battalion, 76th Division, where he honed his skills until he and a fellow pilot were shipped overseas as replacements in April. He sailed to Africa on a troopship in the company of a dozen other pilots. From there, he went on to Naples, where he reported to a replacement depot. The next day, he and his travel companions were dispersed among different units. Boucher was assigned to the 41st Field Artillery Battalion, 3rd Division, in the Anzio beachhead. On June 1, he reported at the town of Guilanello. From there, he was flown to the front with the division air officer, Lieutenant Schultz. "We saw several tank engagements, and then whammo! The 88s opened up on us and Schultz used our standard evasion tactic and dove for the deck and headed back for the field." Boucher was only in combat for a few days before Rome fell. Next, he and his fellow pilots started to train for Dragoon.

Each of the four field artillery battalions of the division had an air section consisting of two Piper Cubs, two pilots, and two observers, with all these sections under the Division Air Section, which had two more aircraft (a Piper Cub and an L-5 Stinson). Each section also had two mechanics, a 2½-ton truck, and a jeep. Their primary mission was to observe the battle area and report unusual activity and direct artillery fire.

The aircraft was provided with a map, a radio with two channels—battalion and division—and a hand mike (later changed to a throat mike). When flying without an observer, the pilot had a difficult time han-

In preparation for the invasion of south France at Naples, *LST 96* is loaded with L-4 aircraft, which will be launched from its deck during the invasion. WILLIAM BOUCHER

dling the controls, plus the map and radio, but we usually got the job done quite well, and the enemy detested us with a passion because we could pick out enemy artillery positions and direct fire on them.

When Lieutenant Boucher was ordered to Salerno, he concluded that he was going to be asked to direct naval gunfire.

Each of the three divisions involved in the invasion had attached to it a converted LST—in our case *LST 906*—which had a flight deck built on the forward part of the ship. Along the flight deck, which was about sixty feet long, there were two sets of rails, each of which could hold one Piper Cub. The other six Cubs were placed on a platform at the aft

end of the flight deck with one plane positioned at the very end of the runway. Since I was to be the lead airplane, my Cub was in this position. No one had ever used this exact configuration. On July 30, 1944, we flew from Capodichino Airport outside Naples to a Dock H in the Naples harbor. Our planes were hoisted aboard the *LST 906* and put into their proper places. I was in charge of the loading, along with navy personnel. We then stayed on board; the next morning we were just off this village called Lago, and after all planes had taken off successfully (except for one, which caught a wing on an AA battery on the portside of the runway), we returned to Naples.

Although I was a member of 3rd Infantry Division, I was placed on temporary duty

Lt. William Boucher's *Sad Sack II* warming up for takeoff on the LST. WILLIAM BOUCHER

with VI Corps for a few days prior to the actual invasion day, and as a result, I was brought to VI Corps HQ and a map room, where I saw exactly where we were to attack. When we boarded *LST 906*, I was one of the few who knew our destination.

The reason I was on temporary duty with VI Corps was that my Piper Cub had been modified to carry a five-gallon gasoline can, which was strapped to the rear seat and connected by lines through a wobble pump to the fuel tank. The fuel tank in a Piper Cub was placed immediately in front of the pilot's seat and held about eleven gallons. This would allow about three hours in the air and the extra five gallons would extend the flying time. The radio was also modified so that one channel tied into

Corps Naval HQ and the other was our usual division channel. I was issued a rocket pistol with some red flares. The purpose of being attached to VI Corps was that, after taking off, I was to patrol the beaches and report what activity there was. Although I did this for about three hours, I was never sure that I was being received by corps. Though I did send in my reports constantly, I was never able to distinguish return messages, so I simply continued transmitting.

My instructions for the flare gun were that if I saw any enemy activity of interest to our forces on the ground, I was to fire a red flare and switch from corps to division channel. Assuming the ground troops saw my flare, they were to switch to the division channel and I was to describe what I saw.

Boucher's L-4 being recovered on August 15, 1944. WILLIAM BOUCHER

Sometime about two hours after I had begun patrolling, I saw a column of our vehicles and personnel approaching an area where I saw what appeared to be a roadblock. I had never shot a flare from a Piper Cub and I was frankly a bit scared, but I sent the red flare off, leaned across the rear seat, and changed to the division channel. I then described what I had seen, but to this day, I do not know if anything came of this. I had now been up for over two hours, and I returned to patrolling the beaches and reporting the numbers of landing craft and where they were. A short time later, the edge of my left wing hit a barrage balloon, but the plane righted itself. Although I had lost about a foot off the left end of the

wing, I was able to continue. After another thirty or forty minutes, I used the wobble pump to bring fuel from the five-gallon can to the fuel tank. It was not long after this that my propeller simply stopped turning. I was up about a thousand feet and headed toward St. Tropez and landed in the Mediterranean. I had not planned on this. The plane flipped, and I was left hanging from my seat harness while the Piper Cub simply floated on its wings. I was a bit banged up but managed to inflate my Mae West and swim to a small naval vessel that was approaching. I remember little of the rest of the day—I think I was in shock.

I spent the night with a local farmer and the next morning I remembered where our division was located and somehow found my way to our airstrip, which was identified during our briefing.[1]

Sgt. James L. Newton from Dallas, Texas, had joined a National Guard cavalry unit in 1940 and served with the 57th Service Squadron, 332nd Service Group of the Twelfth Air Force, which operated in North Africa in 1943 and then moved to Sicily in July and Italy in September 1943. In May 1944, the unit operated out of Tarquinia. On August 9, he boarded a ship at Naples bound for Operation Dragoon. His 57th Squadron[2] boarded what he called a Liberty ship, which was an anomaly since the unit had previously traveled aboard LSTs.

While waiting in the harbor, we watched the port battalion troops trying to load a landing craft crossways on the deck and then try to put a DUKW into it. The merchant marine could have done this easily, but that "wasn't in their write-up while in port," so they just sat around the dirty ship and snickered at the other guys' efforts.

I understand that the merchant marines' pay went up when they passed through the Straits of Gibraltar and that they got a bonus when in enemy action. That sure beat the pay of the navy men who manned the guns on that ship.

The first time I ever saw a mini-aircraft carrier was there in the harbor, about two ships over from ours. The mini-carrier was adapted from an LST by adding a launching deck above the regular deck. On each side,

it had channel iron tracks welded at an angle from the top deck down to the main deck. They were used to put the spotter planes' wheels in when they were parked over the side, nose first. Those L-4 planes could take off form the LST, but they couldn't land back on it; the pilot had to find a flat place to land once his fuel ran out. And, of course, he hoped our ground forces had landed nearby by then.

We moved out of Naples harbor and on across the Mediterranean toward Southern France. The first we saw of it was just a line of smoke with a frequent burst of fire in it. It was either our artillery on the beach firing or German shells bursting. We thought that this doesn't look like a place to land a bunch of air corps ground troops armed with a carbine and a few rounds of ammo.

The 57th had no actual function in the invasion. Our main purpose was to get ashore as soon as possible and help set up and operate an airstrip. I guess the guy in charge must have figured the same because the lead Liberty ship made a U-turn, and we were to follow him back out to sea. Just as our ship was in the turn, the Jerries came in. I never saw their planes because we were ordered belowdecks. Just as I started down the hatch, I saw a big flash over us. Someone yelled, "They got one!" I think we had just shot down our own barrage balloon.

While we were belowdecks, there was a very loud boom that sounded very close. As it turned out, the LST next to us was hit by a large bomb that buckled it badly. They got

---

1. Boucher continued to fly for his battalion and went through two more L-4s, which he named *Sad Sack II* and *III*. Finally, he was shot down north of Besançon. His observer was badly wounded, and both were taken prisoner for the remainder of the war.

2. The service squadron numbered about 180 men, a dog, and a monkey. It included clerical, mess, supply, tech supply, and motor pool sections. It had four mobile crews that consisted of aviation mechanics and a technician from each of the shops. The shops included a machine shop and instrument shop that operated in large semi-trailers, a prop shop, welding shop, sheet metal shop, paint shop, dope and fabric shop, carpenter shop, electrical shop, and parachute rigger shop. In addition, the unit had a crash crew of several men (with a large boom truck and flatbed trailers) and a refueling unit.

it beached, but I heard that about half the troops on board were killed.[3] I think all twelve Liberty ships got out away from the beach. We went back in about four hours later, near St. Raphael on D-Day.

By the time we got over the side into the landing craft and onto the beach, everything seemed secure. At that time, there was an LCI at the beach, which was already loaded to the gills with prisoners, ready to pull back out. All of those prisoners were from a Russian outfit. They were giving up all over the place. They were coming down to the beach jammed into all kinds of vehicles, even on horseback.

After we got our equipment ashore and parked in some trees, the ship unloading area was moved up the coast a few miles. I suppose to St. Raphael harbor. A day or so later, the German planes came back. Lucky for us, the unloading ships were no longer nearby, so we just stood around and watched from afar. That is until an Me 109 flew down and circled over a couple of times. Somebody was shooting at him, but he probably didn't even know it, because the tracers were missing by about ten or twenty yards.

Several of us machinists were traveling in the machine shop trailer and had set up our cots nearby, about thirty yards from the paved coast road. We had been told right after landing to stay close because the woods were full of collaborators. One totally black night, I was awakened by a scuffling sound on gravel over the road. I couldn't see my own hand. When I heard the sound again, I slipped my .45 out from under the straw sack and was trying to pinpoint the sound. I called out for whomever it was to halt and identify himself. The scuffling started again

with no answer, so I started the trigger squeeze. I decided to call one more time. Then a guy yelled out that he was a drunk GI and had gotten off the pavement. I figured he was facing me, so I told him to back up until he got on the pavement and turned left and kept walking. I never heard from him again. I almost shot an American, at least he sounded like one.

Our first airfield in France was Le Luc, but I don't remember much about it. They were all pretty much alike. The engineers would smooth off a place and lay down a steel mat for the runway and parking stands. Then we would move in and set up the shop tents, park the trailers, set up the living area, and start work. Sometimes the planes were there when we got there. The 29th Bomb Group, which we serviced, had P-47s—about ninety planes. They started out with A-36s but used most of them up and started taking delivery of P-47s in May 1944. I never saw any security around the field at Le Luc.

While the 57th was at Le Luc, it was decided to use napalm, or gel gas as we called it then, on the Germans. Drop tanks were to be utilized by adding a chemical to the gas to jelly it in the tanks. The machine shop drilled holes in the gas tank filler caps to receive a brass fitting on which an incendiary grenade was attached. The grenade was used to ignite the napalm when it struck. Our P-47s used it on a German convoy that was trying to get out of Southern France. There was about five miles of incinerated trucks.

On September 2, we moved to Salon in about ten days—no time to meet the locals. I never got into any seaports except coming

---

3. Newton's estimate of times is not accurate. *LST 282* was hit by a glider bomb at about 8:10 P.M. on August 15, 400 yards off Green Beach. The flaming ship drifted ashore and the battalions treated the survivors, but forty men died.

back through Marseille. The harbor there was a big mess full of sunken hulks.[4]

The Advance Inland

The airborne force was relieved on D+1. Its operation had been largely successful, and it was not treated as an expendable unit like the two airborne divisions dropped in Normandy. Sgt. Donald Garrigues's 551st Parachute Battalion made a picture-perfect drop on the afternoon of D-Day. The next morning, August 16, his battalion received further orders.

> We received orders to hold our present positions with a minimum force and to attack and hold the fairly large town of Draguignan. Using a French guide, we moved through Trans-en-Provence and on to Draguignan [located to the northwest], where we began the attack late that evening.[5] The next day, we took the town and captured over 400 Krauts, including a German major general and his entire staff [German LXII Corps HQ]. There were still some isolated pockets of resistance around the outskirts of the town, and our section took off in support of a rifle platoon to eliminate one of these trouble spots.
>
> With the lieutenant leading the way, we moved out in single file down a drainage ditch, which was about six or seven feet deep and about six feet wide. This provided good protection, but I was concerned about an ambush as we couldn't see over the sides of the ditch and we didn't have any scouts out. Soon there was rifle fire—a skirmish had broken out nearby between some of our riflemen and a group of Germans holed up in a house to our right front. The lieutenant turned to me and said, "Sergeant, get a gun set up to fire at that house!" I turned around to a corporal named Steele and told him to set up his machine gun on the side of the ditch. Steele set his tripod up, and by that time, the Germans spotted us. As he started to place the machine gun on the tripod, a bullet caught him in the shoulder and he fell back into the ditch. Bullets were flying everywhere as the lieutenant said, "Let's get out of here!" and took off running back down the same way we had come.
>
> We retrieved the gun and a couple of men helped Steele as we worked our way back down the ditch. When our group got back to a safe place, the lieutenant was nowhere to be found. I started looking for him, finally leaving the group and working my way back down the streets toward the skirmish we had just left. I couldn't find the lieutenant, but did join with the rifleman and our platoon sergeant, Harold Lawler. We got into the second story of a house only a short distance from the house that the Germans were in. As we fired from the house, one group of riflemen went around to the side and approached the Germans from that direction. Soon the Jerries came out with their hands in the air.
>
> I then returned to the place where I had left the rest of my section—unsuccessful in locating the lieutenant. . . . By that time, the lieutenant was back with the group—red-faced mad—wanting to know where I had been and what the disposition of my men were. I also wondered where he had been during the skirmish. . . . The fact I had been

---

4. In mid-September, the squadron loaded on an LST and moved back to Leghorn, Italy.

5. General Frederick, commander of the airborne task force, was informed on the morning of August 16 that the FFI had taken Draguignan and ordered a company of the 551st to occupy the town.

looking for him and that all of our men were all right and ready to continue except for the one wounded man didn't make any difference to him.

Glider pilot Lt. Lambert Wilder was still with the airborne force, looking for action on the morning of August 16.

I damn near lost a leg there because the next day we were all assembled and told to clean our weapons. We were all carrying tommy guns. This guy, he took his apart and had it laying across his lap. He had left a round in the breach and that round went off and grazed my shin. That is how close I got to being wounded.

When we had to dig foxholes, it was in shale and, boy, was that bad. Otherwise that night, the first night, my copilot and I didn't want to go back to the CP because we knew what it was like from the last time, so we got in a vineyard and dug a narrow slit trench. We slept there till about 3 or 4 o'clock in the morning and all hell broke loose on this crossroads. A few German soldiers had tried to come through, and a few guards on the crossroads opened fire on them.

We were outside the town of Le Muy and joined these paratroopers. There was the 442nd Nissan unit that came in with the gliders—we went in with them. I joined this group of paratroopers; there were a lot of bullets whistling overhead, and we were pinned down. . . . We hadn't had anything to eat, so we started eating breakfast. We ate cantaloupes right off the vine. Then I heard the Frenchman running around chewing our ass out for eating his cantaloupes. After breakfast, we went down toward the RR station just outside town. It was several sto-

ries high. We got down to the RR station and a sniper opened up on us and we dove for shelter. I got behind a post used to stop the train at the end of the track. There was a cockney Englishman who said, "Where have you blokes been? I have been waiting for four years!" He had been living in Le Muy and passed himself off for a Frenchman. Here was a gal running down this dusty road with this big sack on her shoulder. Bullets were hitting around her and she kept running until she got beside us. It was his girlfriend. The sack was full of ammunition. He had a BAR. It was a strange situation. So I left the airborne and went with him. The way we got out of the situation was that some Frenchwoman hung a white sheet out her window and she leaned out and pointed to the apartment above. Then we knew where the sniper fire was coming from. A whole bunch of paratroopers opened fire on him, and that was the end of the sniper. So then we got up and started into town, and I stuck with this Frenchman (British).

We went into town and saw a whole bunch of Germans come out with a white flag. This cockney set this rifle up and was going to open up on these prisoners with his BAR, and I kicked it away so we couldn't fire. . . . That pissed him off and he didn't want any more to do with me. I guess there were about forty to sixty in this one bunch. That was the last action I saw in South France. We walked out, eighteen miles to the beach, got on a boat, went to Corsica, and then took another boat back to our bases.[6]

The 551st Parachute Battalion completed its initial mission when the ground forces of the 36th Division relieved it at Draguignan. The fol-

---

6. Wilder returned to England, where he rejoined his unit at the end of August.

lowing day, Garrigues and his comrades marched back to their original defense sector. From there, "we moved into the town of Puget-sur-Argens, where we rested and cleaned weapons." That night, an air-raid warning rent the air, and "in the darkness, I found an excavation and jumped in just as a lone German plane droned on past us without dropping any bombs."

To my dismay, the ready-made slit trench, which had provided my protection, turned out to be a recently abandoned German latrine.

The next day, trucks transported us along the east side of the Argens River to an area northeast of Fréjus, where we dismounted and began a long hard march through the mountains, eliminating pockets of Germans on the way to Cannes.[7] It was boiling hot and dry as we trudged over the rugged countryside.

As the battalion continued moving along the coastal region, it sent the first American troops into Nice and met with elements of the 1st Special Service Force as they neared the Italian border. Finally, on September 4, the battalion relieved the 1st Special Service Force. The paratroopers and the 1st Special Service Force pushed the remaining German troops located between the coast and Sospel toward the Italian frontier, creating a static front along the mountain barrier of the Maritime Alps.

Meanwhile, the 36th and 45th Divisions advanced northward toward Digne on two different axes of advance heading for the Route Napoléon and the Grenoble Corridor, while the 3rd Division moved into the Rhone Valley. Lt. Ruben D. Parker's 2nd Battalion, 141st Infantry, 36th Division, was involved in this advance.

After Agay, the 1st Battalion started attacking toward the road. I think they got close to Théoule. This had no particular strategic importance I can see; it was a scenic route. Nothing really happened after this. We set up positions on the road itself the first night, and the next day the colonel pulled us back to where we could control the road by observation and fire instead of being down there. We saw no Germans after that. I think there might have been some fighting in this region [another sector on the map].

The paratroopers were thrilled to get the bicycles because they had no transportation. After about D+3 or 4, we left there and got up to Draguignan, where we spent one night in beds in a hospital that had been liberated by that time. Then we got up here on the Route Napoléon [between Nice and Digne heading toward Digne] and almost no resistance. It was a type of leapfrog advance. One unit might be struggling along and the others would be in vehicles, and then they would rotate. All we did was knock out little roadblocks, no real organized resistance.

For PFC Arthur P. Rodgers of Company D, 1st Battalion, 141st Infantry, the first night spent on the ground in France was uncomfortable after the luxury of the pre-invasion training day.

[The first night] we set up [our machine gun] for final protective fires on a rock wall and we slept beside the wall, the other gun set up outside of a storage building area. We had cross covering fires. . . . The next day, we continued and the company took a dozen or more prisoners that came out of this building on the railroad tracks to our

7. Most of the prisoners were of Polish origin, although some sources claim they were Czech. They had been forced into German service, and they were ready to give up at the first opportunity.

left. We were moving southeast at that time (towards Cannes). We never got into Cannes itself.

I guess the biggest thing I remember is that the French people were friendly when no German troops were around; they dug up eggs or a bottle of local wine they had buried and gave them to us. . . . They were very friendly. In the first five days, we captured a lot of German prisoners. We didn't meet a lot of heavy resistance until after the fifth day. The German troops we captured were in good condition. They were not hungry or anything.

Lt. Carl Strom's Company C, 1st Battalion, 141st Infantry, faced a few problems the second day of the landing.

The next morning after I woke up, I found out the Germans had come through us. We resumed our advance toward Cannes at La Napoule, a little town overlooking Cannes. You can see all of Cannes from it. At La Napoule, we came down onto the road, the coastal highway. C Company at that time was held up by some SS troops[8] that were in a house, and we were just suddenly a reserve. We were on the coast road behind C Company and could see the house and the action. At the time, the battalion commander came up and said B Company was going to be detached from the regiment in 2½-ton trucks, and one of the companies from another regiment with us were designated as part of Task Force Butler.[9] It was about a battalion-size unit. We were put in 2½-ton trucks and drove north inland about fifteen to twenty miles to a town called Callian, where they had a report of a group of paratroopers trapped and surrounded by Germans. The mission of the two companies was to break through. We got within a mile of the town itself and sat on the side of a hill. We unloaded from the trucks and moved to the attack across open fields. As we got close to the town, we began to receive scattered fire, nothing really organized, from some Germans in the vineyards, so we attacked the vineyards. We took some prisoners and finally got into town and found there were no Americans there. There was a German hospital unit, some Germans, and German troops in town. It took about half a day to clear the Germans out of town, and we took thirty to thirty-five prisoners. We killed a few in the process. To my knowledge, we only had one casualty; one of our sergeants was shot. By the late afternoon, we cleared the town, taking our objective. That is the end of the second day—one casualty each day.

The only time I saw any aircraft was after Callian; we were in trucks heading north of Route Napoléon. Two low flying Me 109s flew over the column. They didn't fire, so we assumed they were on recon. I can't remember any other aircraft. They were flying very close to the surface. The division was all strung out along Route Napoléon, and it was evident they were looking to see what we had and were bringing up. They were not firing on us.

By the third day, the whole thing was breaking loose. The Germans were fleeing, and we were moving as fast as we could by

---

8. No SS units appear on the German order of battle during this time in this region, so he may have been mistaken or it may have been a small contingent.

9. TF Butler spearheaded the drive north toward Digne and along the Route Napoléon. It consisted of the 117th Cavalry Recon Squadron, 753rd Tank Battalion, 2nd Battalion of the 143rd Infantry, Company C of the 636th Tank Destroyer Battalion, and supporting units. Strom indicates that additional units, including his company, were attached to this force.

any means. We didn't get any resistance until the Montélimar area by going up the Route Napoléon and the Rhone Valley. We were bypassing the German Nineteenth Army. After we bypassed them, we swung left. We were still attached to Task Force Butler. We pulled into a town overlooking the highway, a town north of Montélimar. B Company was in a defensive position there to try to stop the Germans coming up the highway. It amounted to the 36th Division on the right flank of the Nineteenth Army. B Company didn't run into any resistance. . . . We were ahead of them in Task Force Butler while the 36th ran into Grenoble. . . . No more casualties up to Montélimar other than those of the first two days and some Germans giving up.

After the first three days of the invasion, the Germans were moving so fast and we operated individually as far as companies were concerned that we didn't have contact with other units. We would be ordered to go in this direction or that. . . . It was a miracle that we stayed as organized as we did. . . . The fortunate thing is that I had two jeep drivers who were to bring in supplies and could maintain contact with battalion. . . . There were two jeeps assigned to each company; they were for hauling ammo and supplies and occasionally carrying back wounded. It was just rifle, MG, BAR, and mortar ammo, and that was sufficient.

Johnny Witten's weapons platoon was usually assigned to us with its mortar and two MGs. He had a jeep for the mortar.

For Sgt. Sammie D. Petty, Company F, 141st Infantry, the days of the advance became an undistinguished blur, and he could remember clearly only the advance through the mountains to the north.

I remember one incident on the highway [Highway 7 from Cannes to Aix-en-Provence]. There were no troops; there was a truck that had been knocked out, and it had cantaloupes and watermelons. We were all sitting there around a tree eating the cantaloupes and watermelons when a German came pedaling down the road on a bicycle, and someone yelled, "There is a damned German!" We all tried to get our guns, and about the time he pedaled by our squad, a sergeant shot him about eight times right through the side. He walked over and kicked him. . . . Later on that day, we moved off toward the right (Cannes) and had some firefights in a little town. I don't remember too much about it. No major resistance in our company the first few days. Our problems began when we got farther north on the Route Napoléon. Minor skirmishes and roadblocks, but they were nothing. Normally the FFI would clear out the town and everything ahead of us. I don't remember taking any prisoners the first few days. I didn't see any German or American aircraft the first few days. I didn't see much artillery firing, but we weren't hitting resistance or receiving any artillery fire.

The 36th Division crossed to the left of the 45th Division and moved toward Montélimar in the Rhone Valley while the latter continued north on the Route Napoléon to Lyon via Grenoble.

Platoon Sgt. Ralph W. Fink, Company D, 157th Infantry, 45th Division, was relieved to have gone through D-Day without major problems. Only the rapid advance northward stands out in his memory.

The following month [August] or so is like a blur—beautiful weather, very friendly natives, and rapid advancing. The negative aspects were those nerve-wracking motor patrols and the fierce firefights that occurred at roadblocks that the German set up from time to time as delaying tactics. These roadblocks usually consisted of one or two 88s leveled to shoot right down the road at us along with several machine guns and several squads of riflemen. These were always set up behind a bend in the road so they could catch us as we turned—very nasty! Unless we had armor readily at our disposal, a roadblock of this type could delay us for several hours and still let the Germans withdraw without too many casualties. The Germans would withdraw and then set up these vicious roadblocks at opportune places anywhere from five to fifteen miles back, then again withdraw and do it all over again. Our sector was heavily wooded, so the only way was to pursue them was down those blacktop roads through the forests. We had to exercise extreme caution because the next roadblock was usually around a bend in the road, and if we came around that corner, we would get blown away. I don't know how extensively this tactic was used, but I found it excessively nerve-wracking.

It was early on the second day that we encountered the first block on our road north. I fired my machine gun from a flank area as riflemen were inching up to the roadblock. As the Germans were fleeing in two trucks, I had clear shooting at them from about 600 yards. Because there were many roads going through forests, we had to search out the German withdrawals and get people to nullify their roadblocks.

Someone got the idea to organize motor patrols to seek them [roadblocks] out by driving down these roads through the forest until contact was made and then hightail it back with information as to enemy location. A special bracket was made to mount a water-cooled machine gun just above the glove compartment on a jeep. The gunner would ride in the passenger seat, ready to fire directly out over the hood of the jeep to the front. A motor patrol consisted of three jeeps, each with a machine gun and a gunner, a driver, and three or four riflemen. We would then drive through the forest until contact was made with the enemy (by drawing fire) or finding the road clear. The important thing was to get the information back. This sounds so simple, but it was very, very scary! I was involved in several of these patrols, and it was so scary driving down those roads, expecting to be picked off by rifle fire from either side, or rounding a bend and driving directly toward an 88 at zero trajectory. I vividly recall one day we drove approx. eight miles forward and made no contact, but when we returned to the bivouac, I was trembling almost uncontrollably. The guys wondered what the matter was and I told them I was cold because it was raining, but this was a warm day in August. I was scared stiff because of the nervous tension of eight miles out and eight miles back.

I recall often riding on tanks or anything with wheels that was available to try to keep up with the withdrawing Germans. Even DUKWS that were used in the landing were pressed into service for transport. I recall often taking part in a shuttle. Our column would start walking along the road. If any vehicles could be found, they would load as many men as possible and shuttle them fifteen to twenty miles up the road, return, load some more men, take them up, return, and so on. The poor guys at the end of the column walked almost all day. This type of combat was entirely new to us after Italy and was strangely invigorating and exciting.

[During the advance] we were riding on tanks in a very long column. The whole column stopped because a Volkswagen had been abandoned on the roadway, probably out of gas, at a place in the road where the tanks could not get around it. I recall hearing the crackling of the radio from inside our tank as the problem was being discussed. Finally, a command voice came on saying, "Are you going to let a little bug stop this column? Run over the son of a bitch!" That's exactly what the lead tank did, and by the time our tank got there, that Volkswagen was as flat as a pancake! I was never a tanker, but we surely did appreciate their spirit and especially those rides they gave us from time to time. The doughboys were in all their glory riding those tanks.

Things kept going extremely well as we passed through the French Alps near Grenoble and then approached the Vosges Forest. Germans then started to stiffen, and I especially recall a feeling of foreboding as we reached Alsace-Lorraine where the towns all had German names and the speech of the natives took on that guttural German sound. At this point, our worst battle of the war was yet to come in number of KIA, WIA, and POWs. This occurred near Reipertswiller, France, in mid-January 1945.[10]

The first night, Capt. Kenneth Stemmons, Company B, 157th Infantry, advanced about six miles with his company.

We moved up through France via Vidauban, Grimaud, Le Luc, Salernes, Tavernes, Varages, Barjois, Esparron, Rians, and up the Rhone Valley. . . . German resistance stiffened and we suffered many casualties. . . .[11]

We pursued the Germans so fast they never had a chance to organize a defense. As a result, we fought scattered small arms fights the next few days. The Germans would resist a while, then would either give up or retreat and fight again. But they never were able to organize an effective defense until we got farther up in France, and then they were well organized and supplied.

After clearing out St. Tropez and the peninsula on D-Day, the 15th Infantry moved into line through the Maures Hills between the 7th and 30th Infantry Regiments, taking most of the night of August 15–16 to reach its positions on the Blue Line. The next day, August 17, S.Sgt. John Shirley, Company I, 15th Infantry, took part in the breakout of the bridgehead. His company had been on the move the previous night and rested in the evening of August 16–17. The 30th and 15th Infantry Divisions moved on toward Brignoles at 4:00 P.M. On the morning of August 18, the 30th Infantry began the fight for Brignoles, a battle that lasted until the next morning. The two regiments resumed their westward advance on August 19.[12]

I believe on the third day [August 17, but possibly the fifth day, August 19], we loaded up on tank destroyers and tanks and headed towards Marseille.

The French people welcomed us warmly as we liberated one town after another. The village bakery was always our first objective, and we emptied every one on our route. Wine was offered by the civilians; occasionally, a piano was rolled out on the sidewalk

---

10. Sergeant Fink received a Bronze Star and, for wounds to his knee in France and his arm in Germany, Purple Hearts.
11. According to Stemmons, the regiment was at 60 percent strength after the campaign in Alsace. When the Germans attacked it in January 1945, it counterattacked in a seven-day battle.
12. The 7th Infantry had been advancing farther to the south since August 16, but joined the other two regiments.

to serenade us as we marched down the main street. We helped ourselves to fruit, vegetable, and eggs. Looting was strictly forbidden.

The Allied forces ran into the next obstacle on their westward advance, a well-defended German roadblock near Aix-en-Provence, on August 20. After the Germans evacuated the city during the next night, General Patch and Truscott held back the 3rd Division, allowing the French to attack Toulon and Marseille. Finally, on August 23, the generals allowed the American division to advance cautiously up the Rhone Valley. The division reached Avignon by August 25.

Despite his administrative duties, 1st Sgt. Frank Andrews, 1st Battalion headquarters, 7th Infantry, was not spared from frontline action. On the second day, the French underground came to the headquarters and then led the Andrews and his comrades to a cave sheltering maps and other intelligence data they had found.

I was in battalion HQ, and often we were used as a combat team in South France. We had a commo section that was usually scattered stringing wire. We used the old crank phone. There was an AT section usually broken up into groups by gun sections and used on roadblocks and places where armor would move. The small R&R squad used messengers a lot when no other type of communications was possible and for recon work. We had a large ammo detail. As first sergeant, I had to find someone to put in charge of guard duty around the battalion CP, and he usually wound up as corporal of guard himself.

We went up the Rhone. Avignon was the first town, then Montélimar, where we captured a big column of troops and supplies [including heavy rail guns] in a valley there. It was an unbelievable slaughter and the biggest I had ever seen. From there to Besançon.

In south France, I received a Silver Star. It was a fiasco when a bunch of guys got killed and I put out the guard as usual around the battalion CP. This officer heard a rumor that a tank and a good-sized force had broken through on our left. He sent another junior officer out in a jeep, and he grabbed a couple of the guards around the CP to take with him to reconnoiter. It was true: a tank and about twenty men had broken through. Just as he took the guards and jeep, here comes this German force moving in on us. [Meanwhile] four others and I were in a basement breaking down rations when a bunch of men from different platoons came in to collect their rations for the next day. The next thing you know, we heard these German voices, and I told the guys, "Douse your cigarettes and strip down your weapons and ammo, we may have to battle our way out of here." I peeked out. There was a great big old tank, and Germans milling around all over. There was one German in there that lived in the United States because he could speak English as well as any of us. He was walking up the street hollering, "Come out!" He knew there were little groups scattered around; he just didn't know where they were. He was calling out, "Come on out, you yellow-bellied bastards, and fight!" Two or three guys in each place and that tank sitting there; we were not about to come out to satisfy him. The humor of that didn't show up for a few days. We got our way out of there that night. We did lose one of our own tanks that came up that night. An 88 went through the front and came out the back—I have never seen anything like that. I came running back; I was pinned down in this one place and decided to move back a ways when these machine guns opened up. I took a run for it and got back just about where our tank was about the time another shell from an 88 hit the tank and the front sprocket. It flew about forty feet off to one side. I could never believe those 88s could penetrate the big housing on the Sherman tank, cut that shaft off, and pop that big sprocket off as it were a prune pit between your fingers.

The next day, they wanted to know who was in charge of the guard. They were going to court-martial him—me! Somebody higher up knew what was going on because that afternoon a command car from division came along and picked up this one officer, and we never saw him again. The next thing you know, somebody comes up with a story about how these big brave soldiers held off the attack, and they passed out medals. So I never put much stock in this medal thing [because] some are deserved and some are political.

First Sgt. Sherman Pratt witnessed the carnage at Montélimar as the 15th Infantry moved up the Rhone and the 7th and 30th Infantry Regiments approached from the east with elements of the 36th Division to the north of them.

All roads north, and especially Route 7, were clogged with German convoys. We caught up with one of the longest, almost fifteen miles in length, just north of the little town of Montélimar. . . . Fighter planes spotted the convoy about the same time as did our troops, and the planes fired on and destroyed the lead vehicles, which brought the convoy to a halt.

With the bumper-to-bumper, packed, and congested convoy stopped, our battalions went into position from the east almost along its entire length and systematically began to chew it to pieces with every weapon at our disposal.

Most of the enemy soldiers in the convoy fled as we approached. . . . [We] rounded up [Germans] by the hundreds. . . .

When the firing finally came to an end, a scene of mass destruction existed that was rare in war. Burning and destroyed vehicles, tanks, guns, wagons, horses, and other types of rolling stock stretched up and down the highway as far as could be seen and beyond. Over a thousand horses were killed. . . .

On the railroad tracks alongside Route 7, a military freight and troop train rested, also in ruins. . . . Included in the train were two huge, 380-mm railway guns, and four 280-mm guns.

On September 20, 1944, PFC Robert Gehlhoff, 3rd Battalion headquarters, 15th Infantry, described the situation in France in a letter home.

Yesterday I went shopping in a newly liberated town. . . . There isn't too much to buy. Wherever we go it's always the same story: "The Germans took it," or something to that effect.

We're at another French home-just an old man and woman live here. A nice clean little home . . . at the present we're using their living room for the intelligence section headquarters. Tonight the madame made us a nice super, partly from our rations and some from her garden. . . . Our French interpreter is on the ball. Soon as we hit a new area, he takes off in search of a place for the eight of us to eat and sleep. I keep wondering what you folks back home would think if a crowd of dirty soldiers clamored in and asked if you would prepare super and let them use a room to sleep in. . . .

On the Coast

One of the odd events of the European campaign was the U.S. Marines' participation in landing operations. Although there were no amphibious marine units in the theater, there were fleet marines serving on board ships, some of whom were called upon for an operation in Southern France. Thus, 1st Lt. William McDaniel and his men were assigned to one of the ship's antiaircraft batteries of the heavy cruiser *Augusta*. McDaniel had watched the invasion of Normandy from his post on board ship but had a more active role in south France when the *Augusta* served as Admiral Davidson's flagship for the Gunfire Support Group of Sitka Force.

We did not engage in any gunfire missions as far as I can remember on the morning of August 15, but from August 15 through August 31, we did a lot of shooting, more than we did in Normandy. The reason being that the troops we landed—two divisions of French troops outfitted in American uniforms and equipment and one division of American troops [3rd Division] on the left side—drove northward up to the Rhone Valley and westward along the coast, with the mission of capturing the naval base at Toulon and the port of Marseille. Marseille was the finest port in France, and it was desired that we had it to support the war effort. As the troops went westward from the vicinity of St. Tropez, westward to Marseille, we were able to give them gunfire support. Our ships went westward with them. There were some islands off the coast of France that had German positions on them, and we did place gunfire on some of them.

On August 19, a naval force including the *Augusta*, the battleships *Lorraine* (an old French battleship manned by the Free French) and

Nevada, and other cruisers, fired on the defenses of Toulon, particularly targeting Battery Cépet, which mounted 340-millimeter guns from a sister ship of the elderly French *Lorraine*. On August 26, the *Augusta* was further west off Marseille when the ships firing at Battery Cépet made a last pass and moved west. The German commander surrendered Toulon on August 28. The seaward defenses of Marseille were pounded by the naval force beginning August 24 until the city surrendered to the French troops surrounding it on August 28. The German garrisons on three islands at Marseille also decided to surrender, finally giving the marines on the *Augusta* and *Philadelphia* an opportunity to make a landing.

The main problem we ran into as far as the Germans were concerned was some guns that were taken off of the scuttled French fleet at Toulon had been put out on a beach position. There was one particular gun, which was referred to as "Big Willie," that gave us a rather warm reception every time we went past Toulon. I do not know what the caliber of those guns was, but I would guess anywhere from 11 to 14 inches. We had some close misses a time or two that splashed pretty close to us.

The French troops reached the area of Marseille and there were some islands in harbor; Château d'If, Ratonneau, and another, which contained German garrisons. The French army captured the city, but the islands in the harbor held out. They were subjected to a lot of naval gunfire and aerial bombings for several days. Eventually, we sent in a PT boat firing a large flag of truce on it to try to arrange a surrender. Instead of that, they fired on the PT boat with an 88, and it had to beat a hasty retreat. After more shelling and more bombing, we attempted that again, and once again it was repulsed. Eventually, we did made contact with those people and they

German Gen. Botho Elster on September 17, 1944, surrendered 20,000 men of the German First Army after being trapped by the U.S. Third and Seventh Armies.

agreed to surrender to American troops, but not to the French.[13]

No American troops were [in the area] except for the marine detachments of the USS *Augusta* and the USS *Philadelphia*. Normally, we had forty marines [on the *Augusta*], but I think we had an extra dozen or so because the admiral was aboard. It was arranged that we would go in, take these German troops off the island, and arrange for their evacuation to St. Tropez, where we could turn them over to the army.

On August 28, Capt. Francis Schlesinger ordered McDaniel to prepare a marine detach-

ment of fifty-one enlisted men. The small contingent of marines was to be reinforced by a naval party of seven sailors led by a naval lieutenant. (The *Philadelphia* sent thirty men from its marine detachment, giving the force a total of ninety marines and sailors.) After a fitful night, McDaniel woke up on the morning of August 29 prepared to take his men to the island. He arranged for the troop's rations and ammunition, and on a hunch, he decided to take some TNT.

Finally, we were on the well deck of the ship, ready to embark on a minesweeper that came alongside. One of the gunner's mates came up with a box and said, "Sir,

13. This does not match the version presented in Samuel Eliot Morison's *Invasion of France and Germany*. However, Morison only includes a brief statement that the islands wanted to surrender after the commander of Marseille surrendered. The two do not agree on the date, but McDaniel believed it was not the same day as the surrender of Marseille.

French Resistance in the Summer of 1944

As the threat of an Allied invasion of France increased in late 1943, the French resistance forces, which became known as the FFI (French Forces of the Interior), rapidly expanded until the landings took place in the summer of 1944. An estimated 160,000 German police stationed in France failed to stop the rise of the insurgency, and by June 1944, the resistance had reached an estimated strength of 70,000 men south of the Loire River.

The landings in Normandy worsened the situation in the south for the Germans because the main rail and road lines ran through the Rhone Valley to the south of Dijon, where the resistance was most active and the population most hostile to the occupiers. The German lines of communication in southwestern France were blocked by Allied air interdiction, which closed most of the crossings of the Loire and the Seine. Keeping the Seine River open was critical to support the German armies in Normandy. The German forces in the southwest, some of which would have to withdraw, had to rely on the main rail and road routes from Bordeaux through the Carcassonne Gap and along the south coast to the Rhone Valley. By the end of June, about 70,000 German troops (5 divisions) from the 220,000 men of Army Group G in south France had withdrawn, mainly to go to Normandy. Two divisions, a number of *Ost* battalions, and a reserve force equal to another division had to protect the lines of communication. Eventually, one of these divisions also withdrew to the north, while the remaining forces defended the south and west coasts of France. One-fifth of the German forces left south of the Loire were busy securing the lines of communications. At the time of the landings in south France, all the rail routes to the south had been cut. When German units began to withdraw, they were under constant attack.

here is your TNT." I said, "Fine, where are the primers?" He said the primers were in there with the TNT! I had to immediately open the box and take those primers out.

Our troops finally went aboard the minesweeper. It was midday before we got under way for the island of Île d'If. We went in and there was no opposition. There were troops, but I don't know how many.[14] They were scattered out on various places on the island, and we had to send our troops out to bring them in. We marched them to a central location where there were some buildings. There was one large, metal-frame building that had a fence, so we put them there overnight as we disarmed them. Some of the Germans were very unhappy, but others were relieved to become prisoners. There were also eleven Frenchwomen, mostly working in the laundry, but they may have provided other services as well. We were going to send them over to Marseille, but they refused for fear of what would happen to them. So we loaded them

---

14. There were a total of 730 from the three islands.

aboard LCIs and sent them back to St. Tropez with the prisoners the following day.

We found the island had a large supply of wine and champagne, and I think some of the Germans had fortified themselves with that before they surrendered. It was late in the day before we finally got them aboard the LCIs and sailed. It was an all-night journey; we arrived in St. Tropez the following morning and sent them ashore. We turned them over to the army for transportation to North Africa.

I was not on the ship with the French-women, but one of these young women tried to kill herself several times. I am not sure if she made it to St. Tropez since she may have jumped overboard.

We then went back to the *Augusta* [August 31], and after boarding the ship, we soon sailed back for the United States. We went back the same we came in—Corsica, Naples, and on to Philadelphia. It was normally a three-day cruise, but we had to detour south for a hurricane and arrived in Philadelphia early in September. We were in the navy yard until January 1945 since our ship was in bad shape from the weather in the North Atlantic and Arctic from 1943. It had caused a crack all the way across the deck and down the side of the ship that had to be repaired.

As the Sixth Army advanced northward, up the Rhone Valley, the French railway system was put back into service with the help of army engineers. Shortly after Marseille was secured, the 727th Railway Operating Battalion arrived from Italy. Its companies had been pulled back to Naples after operating in Italy for almost a full year. Sgts. Keith Wilson and Fred Buffington, each a conductor in charge of a five-man train crew in Company C, boarded LCIs in Naples for the trip to France in September. The company numbered over 300 men and required two LCIs. When they reached Marseille, they could not dock because the harbor was still filled with sunken ships, so they had to transfer to landing craft to get to shore. Once on terra firma, they went to Lyon in boxcars. On the way, they noticed that many bridges, like the one at Avignon, were still out. Company A went to work at Lyon trying to repair the damage to the rail system there. Wilson was sent into the Jura and Buffington to Épinal, where they were to inspect the trains, advise the French, and report on the situation. The old, worn French engines were replaced with American locomotives, and the French continued to operate their rail system. The 727th soon returned to Marseille to operate the port area through 1945. The logistical support for the 6th Army Group ran quite smoothly and efficiently since it did not face many of the problems encountered in the Normandy campaign.

Chronology of Major Operations and Naval Activity after August 16, 1944

AUGUST 17

French units landed near St. Tropez to relieve the U.S. 3rd Division for the attack on Toulon.

U.S. 3rd Division moves to Brignoles and Sollies Point.

Task Force Butler (from 36th Division) advances toward Digne.

Since August 15, 86,575 men disembark over beaches.

AUGUST 18

French II Corps continues to land in St. Tropez area.

U.S. 3rd Division occupies Brignoles after meeting resistance.

U.S. 45th Division bypassed Barjols and advances into Durance Valley.

U.S. 36th Div reached Grasse, La Bastide, and Chardon, advancing on Route Napoléon toward Digne.

Destroyers fire on two small batteries near Cannes.

AUGUST 19

French II Corps begins attack on Toulon. Allied navy and air forces bombard defenses.

Naval unit bombards enemy batteries north of Cannes.

Since August 15, 106,999 men and 15,695 vehicles disembark over beaches.

Camel Red and half of Camel Red 2 opened. Camel Yellow closed.

AUGUST 20

French army encircles Toulon and advances on Marseille.

Air attacks on Toulon and Nice. Naval bombardment of Toulon.

Port of St. Raphael opened in Camel sector.

Seventh Army takes over evacuation of casualties.

AUGUST 21

Task Force Butler occupied Gap.

Enemy forces defending Aix withdraw at night.

11th Panzer Division reported acting as rear guard.

Bombardment of Toulon continues.

Near Cannes, three destroyers sink three German E-boats off Ile de Lerins.

Delta Red and Green beaches closed.

Since August 15, 118,700 men disembark over beaches,

AUGUST 22

Naval bombardment of Toulon continues.

Naval bombardment of Île de Porquerolles (near Giens, southeast of Toulon).

Porquerolles surrenders to USS *Omaha*.

Cruisers and destroyers engage targets, including 170-mm batteries in Golfe de la Naploue.

Seventh Army CP moves from St. Tropez to Brignoles.

AUGUST 23

Naval bombardment continues from Marseille to Giens.

Since August 15, 130,476 men disembark over beaches.

**Chronology of Major Operations and Naval Activity
after August 16, 1944** *continued*

AUGUST 24

Naval bombardment of Toulon continues.

USS *Nevada* neutralizes Île Pomègues off Marseilles.

Naval bombardment of Nice harbor.

AUGUST 25

Paris taken as Allied forces from Normandy surge across Seine River.

Toulon falls.

Naval bombardment of St. Mandrier (peninsula with heavy gun batteries protecting approaches to Toulon) continues for sixth day.

Naval bombardment of Marseille.

AUGUST 26

Two cruisers and four destroyers provide gunfire support in Nice area.

PT 552 and USS *Livermore* sink eight of ten German explosive boats on eastern flank—the control boats escape.

Since August 15, 147,326 men disembark over beaches.

AUGUST 27

U-boat grounded and scuttled off Toulon and crew captured.

French I Corps disembarks at St. Tropez beaches.

1st Airborne Task Force crossed Var River.

Air attacks against Ratonneau Island (off Marseille).

Port de Bouc prepared to be opened with pontoon causeways towed in.

Patrols of LCVPs set up in Camel area to protect against one-man torpedo attacks.

HMS *Ramillies* bombards St. Mandrier. Two French cruisers target Cap Cepet 340-mm battery.

Since August 15, Seventh Army had taken 40,211 prisoners.

AUGUST 28

Surrender of Toulon (including St. Mandrier and Marseille—about 22,000 prisoners).

Germans on Frioul islands refuse to surrender to French.

U.S. VI Corps advanced on Lyon.

1st Airborne Task Force takes Nice.

French army begins move north.

Since August 15, 150,935 men and 33, 887 vehicles disembark over beaches.

AUGUST 29

Enemy resistance in Montélimar area collapsed.

German 148th Division begins withdrawal from Nice area.

U.S. cruisers send 90 marines to take surrender of 850 Germans on islands off of Marseille.

Carrier aircraft fly last support missions.

AUGUST 30

1st Airborne Task Force moves east of Nice.

1st Beach Battalion detached and directed to Marseille.

Since August 15, 171,907 men disembark over beaches.

**Chronology of Major Operations and Naval Activity
after August 16, 1944** *continued*

AUGUST 31

Germans withdrawing from Southwest France and up Rhone Valley.

Seventh Army in evening reports no further need for gunfire support except in vicinity of Nice–Cannes area.

Since August 15, 184,906 men disembark over beaches.

SEPTEMBER 1

Seabees work with Army Engineers at Toulon and Port de Bouc.

Naval bombardment at Cap Martin and Monaco area continues.

Since August 15, 189,159 men disembark over beaches.

SEPTEMBER 2

Since August 15, Seventh Army takes 61,716 prisoners.

Since August 15, 190,565 men and 41,534 vehicles disembark over beaches.

Port de Bouc limited to cargo.

SEPTEMBER 3

Port de Bouc and Marseille limited to cargo.

Only Delta beaches in use for landing vehicles.

SEPTEMBER 4

1st Airborne Task Force meets resistance at Monaco.

Lyon occupied by French 1st Armored Division.

8, 257 men disembark over Alpha, Delta, and Camel beaches.

SEPTEMBER 5

A human torpedo attack from Menton launched against two destroyers.

No damage and three human torpedos sunk.

Naval bombardment of coastal defenses from Monte Carlo to Menton and positions inland north of Sospel.

First Liberty ships arrive at Toulon and next day unload.

Sandbar formed off Delta Beach 262 from storm.[15] Blasting proved ineffective. LSTs still able to use the beach.

Since August 15, 210,794 men disembark over beaches.

SEPTEMBER 6

B-26s search for human torpedoes in Menton Area.

Alpha and Delta beaches suspend operations because of storm conditions.

SEPTEMBER 7

Two warships attacked by explosive boats. PT boats claim four or five explosive boats sunk.

SEPTEMBER 8

Naval bombardment of batteries, pillbox troops in Sospel area.

SEPTEMBER 9

Naval bombardment of Castillon area.

Alpha beaches closed at noon—a total of 81,573 men and 15,675 vehicles had disembarked there since August 15.

---

15. This was the beach at the head of the Gulf of St. Tropez that was opened after the invasion.

Chronology of Major Operations and Naval Activity
after August 16, 1944 *continued*

SEPTEMBER 10

Attacks by human torpedoes in Menton area. About ten torpedoes sunk—six enemy survivors.

French Army B contacts U.S. Third Army forty-five miles northwest of Dijon.

Since August 15, Seventh Army takes 69,562 prisoners.

Between August 9 and September 25, the Allied naval forces lost one LST, one ML, two YMS, two PT, five LCVP, and two LCM. The Largest ship damaged was a destroyer.

The enemy lost one DD, one TB, thirteen EV, five MAS, five inactive submarines, three minesweepers , sixteen explosive motorboats, thirteen human torpedoes, and a few other craft.

Logistical Support

Comparison of Overlord and Dragoon Invasion Beaches in First Two Weeks

Invasion Beaches	Troops	Vehicles	Supplies	Notes
South France, Aug. 15–28	150,000	33,887	153,607	
Omaha Beach, June 6–19	205,762	29,242	74,563	
Utah Beach, June 6–19	126,507	14,344	49,841	
Mulberries, until June 20			25,000	Total for both Mulberries*
Total	332,269	43,586	123,404*	Not including Mulberry

* Planned 7,000 tons a day reached on July 6 by British Mulberry

Operation Dragoon Logistical Support and Troop Landings

August 15 to Sept. 25	Troops	Vehicles	Tons	Notes
Alpha Beaches	81,573	15,675	67,353	Closed Sept. 9
Delta Beaches	119,954	25,176	121,692	Closed Sept. 16
Camel Beaches	66,888	18,229	14,974	Closed Sept. 25
Total	268,415	59,080	204,019	
Port of Marseille	50,569	6,711	99,171	Opened Sept. 3*
Port of Toulon	5,085	2,628	24,252	Opened Sept. 5*
Port de Bouc	0	0	30,795	Opened Sept. 2*

* Limited facilities for several days after opening.

Marseille and Toulon were of great importance to the Allied logistical situation. The only other major ports the Allies took were Cherbourg in June, Rouen in August, and Antwerp in early September. The approaches to Rouen and Antwerp were cleared. The badly damaged port of Brest fell late in September. All the other French ports the Allies captured had a much smaller capacity.

Logistical Support *continued*

Chart of Coastal Sites Used to Support American Military

Port	Opened / Closed	Average Tonnage	Highest Tonnage	Notes
Omaha Beach	June 6		9,896 on June 12	288,000 tons between June 6 and 30
British Mulberry	June 20 / Oct. 25	6,756		American Mulberry destroyed in June storm
Grandcamp*	June 23 / Sept. 19	675		58,000 tons
Isigny*	June 24 / Oct. 15	740		
St. Vaast*	July 9 / Oct. 16	1,172		
Barfleur*	July / Oct.	803		Operated for 83 days
Carentan*	July 25 / July 31	300		Usually less than 300 tons
Cherbourg**	Aug. 9 Nov. Dec. 10	12,000 14,300 7,000	19,955 on Nov. 4	Badly damaged; Nov. 26 Antwerp opened and soon replaced Cherbourg
Granville	Sept. 15 / Apr. 21	1,244		
St. Malo ***	Sept.	nil		Expected to take 2,400 tons, but port too badly damaged
Morlaix	Sept. 5 / Dec. 14	2,105		Most tonnage from any port restored in Brittany
St. Michel-en-Grevee	Aug. ? / Sept. 1	745		
St. Brieuc	Sept. 15 / Oct. 15	317		
Brest***				Badly damaged
Marseilles	Late Sept.	11,000-plus		Capacity increases
Toulon	Late Sept.	2,000-plus		Capacity increases
Rouen	Oct. 15 / May	4,000 increases after Nov.		Taken Aug. 30 with little damage; required Le Havre to open mouth of Seine
Le Havre	Oct. 2 / May	9,500+		Taken Sept 12, but badly damaged
Antwerp	Nov. 28 / May	40,000 (est.)		Main Allied port replacing Cherbourg in December
Ghent	Jan. 23 / March April	2,500 5,000 9,500		

* Five minor Normandy ports that never reached a total of 12,000 tons daily expected by the U.S. Army. All reverted to French control on November 9.

** Army engineers estimated a daily capacity for 17,900 tons. About 75 percent of the port restored to operation by mid-September.

*** Brittany ports of Brest, Lorient, Quiberon Bay, and St. Malo expected to handle a combined total of 27,000 tons daily in September, but Germans heavily damaged their facilities.

+ Slowly increases and reaches 9,500 tons by end of December 1944.

Note: Liberty ships carried about 7,000 tons, and they could use the Mulberry or major ports.

Logistical Support *continued*

Monthly Tonnages

1944	Normandy Beaches*	Cherbourg	Minor Ports**			Dragoon Beaches	Marseille Pont du Boc Toulon***
June	291,300			Le Havre /	Antwerp		
July	549,400	31,700	40,300	Rouen	*+		
Aug.	536,800	266,600	134,900			174,500	
Sept.	393,700	314,400	175,300			144,800	154,000
Oct.	193,500	365,600	135,500	88,600		Beaches	524,900
Nov.	26,300	433,300	102,800	276,200		Closed	547,600
Dec.	Beaches Closed	250,100	78,000	298,500	427,600		501,600
Total	1,191,000	1,661,700	667,800	663,300	433,400	319,300	1,728,100
Jan. 1945		262,400	44,800	214,500	433,100		385,760

* Utah and Omaha
** In Normandy and Brittany (ports in Brittany no longer used in 1945)
*** Marseille 99,171 tons of Sept. total. *+Antwerp begins operations late in month with 5,873 tons. Rounded off to nearest 100 tons.
In January 1945, Antwerp, whose tonnage increased each month, Cherbourg, and Marseilles remained as the main ports for receiving supplies.

CHAPTER 15

A Joint Effort

As in all the great campaigns of the Second World War, Allied air, ground, and naval forces worked together to break the Axis forces. In addition to the foot soldier who bore the brunt of the fighting, those who maintained the combat troops at the front through support or services played a role in the success of any operation.

The Graves Registration units advanced close on the heels of the army. In each division, a staff officer was assigned the extra duty of grave registration. However, the divisional personnel did not have the skills or training required for handling burials. The Graves Registration officers and their men merely collected the corpses and sometimes prepared temporary graves. The Graves Registration company, on the other hand, was a trained quartermaster unit with trained personnel that handled this very important mission. T.Sgt. Emmett Bailey Jr. from Henderson, a draftee from North Carolina, was assigned to a Graves Registration unit in the United States as soon as he got off a troop train without being given any choice. In April 1944, he was with the 60th Quartermaster Graves Registration Company, which had been put in charge of burying the victims of Exercise Tiger. After that, he was promoted and transferred to the newly formed 3047th Graves Registration Company and became part of its cadre.

We went to Normandy in August 1944, and the 3047th moved to Marigny Cemetery near St. Lô. Another company plus my old company controlled this cemetery.

In Normandy, during a sweeping operation, we collected bodies based on military and civilian information and transported those bodies to a cemetery. Our operations in Normandy were under the supervision of the 1st QM Group under Colonel Witney. However, for administrative purposes, we were under the control of another unit. We had thousands of bodies unburied throughout the Normandy area and many in isolated locations. We were constantly dispatching crews to collect these. We were supplied with 4 x 4 weapons carriers with trailers, 6 x 6 trucks, and jeeps. With the weather conditions in Normandy, from August until March through that winter there were problems with spit and polish conditions to satisfy the Normandy base commander. As a result, thousands of bodies lay rotting in the field because some military alter ego of a small colonel wanted to play stateside politics in battlefield conditions.

There were many temporary cemeteries established by GR units and combat units because of necessity. As a result, we had to conduct sweeping operations to locate these temporary burials and to consolidate them into larger cemeteries. After the war, some of these larger cemeteries were considered inadequate. I use Marigny as an example because it was a very wet location despite the fact it was on a rise. The German cemetery right across the lane did not have the same problem and to this day, it has about 10,000 German burials consolidated in it.

Not everyone can do GR work, and we had this demonstrated very vividly when in the 3045th after we arrived in Normandy.

We had a new CO assigned with no prior training in GR. When we arrived at our location in Marigny, he would like to get in the jeep, ride around, shoot at land mines, and collect souvenirs. He had a habit of having a morning formation. At one formation, he stood before the company, said he was disgusted with our performance, and that he was going to separate the men from the boys. That day, he took me in a jeep and went for a ride with his driver, looking for souvenirs, and continued to shoot at land mines. My response when I came back was to speak to the first sergeant and two other tech sergeants like myself that had been with me in the 605th. We decided he was not a responsible officer. As a result, we went to the adjacent company stationed nearby, I think it was the 603rd GR Company. We asked its CO to speak to Colonel Witney of the 1st QM Group and have this officer relieved of his command, which he promptly did. As a result, we requested that an officer who had been our training officer with the 605th be assigned as our CO. At this time, he was recuperating from an operation in a hospital, but we finally got him as our CO and he remained until our deactivation in 1945.

I remember a man in one of our collection squads. They would put him on guard duty, and at night, he would shoot at the moon and the stars. He was asked what his problem was, and he claimed it was getting on his nerves to be in this unit. The psychiatrist at the hospital kept him a few days. He said he wanted to go home and that he was tired of the war. Between the two of them, they decided the best they could do was to go about their job, do the best they could do, and stop claiming insanity. As a result, this individual turned out to be one of our very reliable and trusted men.

We had no problem with the enemy in Normandy because we were not involved with enemy activity. The only real problem was with land mines and booby-trapped bodies. One particular incident that I recall after Eisenhower moved his HQ to Granville and Coutances was when some Germans came ashore from one of the small Channel Islands and raided the hotel where some of the top brass was billeted. I think there were a couple of casualties, some of them were half scared to death, never having been subjected to enemy activity.[1] We were contacted at our cemetery at Marigny to come down to Granville–Coutances area and provide some security to that HQ after the raid.

At Marigny Cemetery, Sergeant Bailey witnessed the aftermath of a court-martial that involved a GI caught in criminal activity. This was

a GI who had been convicted at St. Lô and was one of many. At the execution, we were lined up with the accuser, a woman he had raped. It was most depressing because the gallows were set along the remaining wall of a house that was burned at St. Lô, and there weren't many houses remaining. While the witnesses and the accused were being brought up to the gallows, the wall collapsed, and if it had not been for the fact that someone happened to see it start, we would have had dozens to bury that day. Nevertheless, after the wall crumbled, everything went according to military plan. The GI was hung, and then myself and a couple of other GR personnel went under the gallows and cut the rope to remove the

body and take him to the Marigny cemetery for internment. The burial was in a criminal part of the cemetery separated from those who had died honorably.

One of the last bad experiences for Bailey also took place long after the Normandy campaign. The war had moved far to the east and only isolated German strongpoints were still holding out on the west coast of France. Late in December 1944, a U-boat torpedoed one of two ships carrying over 2,000 men of the 66th Infantry Division while crossing the Channel to Cherbourg. Although over 700 men died in the incident, the government was vague about it until 1959. Most of these men were left to die because a proper rescue attempt was not made, and the foreign crew abandoned the ship without taking proper measures to help their passengers. Sergeant Bailey knew more about the tragedy than most.

During Christmas, there was a sinking of a small Belgian ship pressed into service as a troopship. It was the *Leopoldville*. While coming from Southampton on Christmas Eve of 1944, within sight of Cherbourg, it was torpedoed with great loss of life. My CO, Louis B. Wiese, and I went to Cherbourg to recover the bodies. We took some to the cemeteries we were operating. Many remained entombed in the ship.

The field hospital, to which the wounded were transported from the battlefield, played an important a role as the Grave Registration units in the rear echelons, however its work was less grim since it ministered to the survivors. The 67th Evacuation Hospital (semi-mobile) serves as an excellent example of the work done by the

---

1. He is referring to the Granville raid of the night of March 8–9, 1945. German forces from the occupied Channel Islands launched a raid on this small supply harbor, sinking several small freighters, seriously damaging the harbor facilities, releasing about fifty German prisoners, and capturing about two dozen Americans. The German raiders lost a single ship, a minesweeper.

Medical Corps. In the annual report of March 15, 1945, 1st Lt. James Woolley recorded the operations of his unit.

The morning of June 16 saw the main detachment of hospital personnel being loaded onto *LCIs 1423* and *1424* in groups of 201 (31 officers, 40 nurses, and 130 enlisted men) and 75 (1 officer and 74 enlisted men). Three officers and thirty-eight enlisted men loaded the remaining vehicles on *LST 1110* later that night.

The crossing of the Channel and the landing of the four detachments into which the 67th Evacuation Hospital had been divided proved entirely uneventful. None of the groups encountered any known enemy action, and the sands of Utah Beach were gained without even a wet foot. One LCI was almost run down by a Liberty ship during the night.

The two main groups of personnel disembarked at 1400 hours [2:00 P.M.], June 17, and proceeded on foot to a temporary transit area a quarter of a mile back from the beach, remaining there for a few hours. Officers and nurses then went to the 91st Evacuation Hospital, several of them going to work soon after arrival. Enlisted men bivouacked in a separate area.

During the morning of the 18th, the detachment with the unit vehicles landed from their LSTs and reached the temporary location of the unit. The first truckload of supplies reached the unit supply office in the early afternoon. On receipt of instructions to open the hospital on the following day, enlisted personnel went to prepare the site and to set up the hospital.

The move to the first site having been completed, the 67th Evacuation Hospital officially opened at 1200 hours in the vicinity of La Fière, about four miles west of Ste-Mère-Église. The front lines were about seven or eight miles away on the north, six miles on the west, and three to four miles on the southwest. The first of the 4,684 patients admitted during twenty-eight-and-a-half days of operation, Pvt. John Micheal, was admitted at three o' clock in the afternoon. Two of the first ten patients were enemy prisoners of war.

The hospital had for its use two large fields bounded by typical Normandy hedgerows. The hospital occupied the larger field, with the pup tents and foxholes of the enlisted men spread along the edges. Tents for officers and nurses were placed in the other and smaller field to the rear, which sloped toward the rearward front line west of Carentan. Adjoining fields were later employed by two attached hospitals. The motor pool had a separate field a few yards away. All fields were nearly level and covered with grass. All in all, the site proved very satisfactory, and it was approached by a fine network of roads.

On the second day of operation, the first of many surgical teams of specialists from the 3rd and other Auxiliary Groups and General Hospitals arrived for duty. Thereafter, the hospital normally functioned with at least two attached surgical teams.

From June 19 until June 27, the hospital had utilized forty prisoners of war, mainly as litter bearers and mess helpers. On this day, the prisoners were returned to a POW enclosure and replaced by some thirty-eight Polish civilians obtained from a civil affairs cage. The men, formerly forced laborers in a German *Todt* battalion in the Cherbourg region, were the first of a group (which for a few days in August numbered sixty-eight) to be employed in an experiment which turned out to be highly successful. The energy and willingness of the Polish workers surpassed all expectations. The hospital benefited from the freedom from the resentment and hostility frequently felt by wounded American soldiers when in the presence of prisoners serving in the hospital. A few of the Polish workers drifted from the hospital during the summer, and nearly half of them left in early November, some to another evacuation hospital and many of the youngest and best workers to join the Polish Army Forces in France and England. Fifteen were still with the hospital at the end of the year in the role of civilian employees—a status which had been attained for them in October.

On the first day of July, Company A of the 91st Medical Gas Treatment Battalion was attached to the hospital and moved into a connecting field. A welcome adjunct, the unit rendered invaluable assistance for a period of slightly more than two weeks. Personnel of the organization worked both in the main hospital and in wards set up in their own tents. A few minor operations were performed at tables in their own operating room. Several officers and nurses from the 77th Evacuation Hospital, which had been assigned a large field near the hospital, were attached also for duty from July 8 to July 16 when their own hospital began to function.

On July 17, the last day of this operation, the hospital was visited by Secretary Henry L. Stimson, accompanied by Lieutenant Generals Bradley and Patton. Secretary Stimson went through the operating room and several wards with General Bradley.

After twenty-eight-and-a-half days of operation, the hospital closed at midnight. The remaining patients were taken over in situ by the 32nd Evacuation Hospital, and attached units were relieved.

Period of operation:
  28½ days, 19 June–17 July 1944
Total admissions:
  4,673 (Informal, 537 in addition)
Total surgical operations: 2,563
Daily average: 89.9
Greatest number of patients in hospital:
  667
Greatest number of surgical operations in
  one day: 137 (July 10)
Greatest surgical backlog: 275 (July 7)
Total deaths 66
Percentage of postoperative deaths to total
  operations: 1.2%

July 18 marked the beginning of a welcome rest period of just under two weeks. Six days were spent in bivouac about a half mile from the site of the operation, followed by a similar stay in the vicinity of Lison, Normandy. At the latter site, the hospital watched from a comfortable distance the bombings of the St. Lô region and the beginnings of the breakthrough.

On the 31st of July, the hospital moved to a site about four miles east of St. Lô, opening at noon on the next day. The hospital set up for Operation 2 in a large field, uneven by nature and now pockmarked by bomb and shell craters of various sizes. Several duds, shells, and mines were removed from the field before occupation. The field was always dry, and before many days of activity, the dust problem became well nigh intolerable. Enlisted men's pup tents and foxholes were spaced along a lane between apple trees which led to a shell of a farmhouse in and about which many dead animals were scattered when the unit arrived. Officers' and nurses' tents were pitched in an orchard and were reached through a path cleared of minefields. Along the sides and at the back of the orchard, on the arrival of the unit, were two unexploded minefields and several bodies of German and American soldiers and civilians.

Early on August 2, the most serious accident of the entire year occurred involving members of the organization. When personnel of the attached 502nd Medical Collecting Company drove their ration truck into the farthest corner of the adjoining field, which had been swept and reported clear by the engineers, a German Teller mine exploded, injuring two sergeants. An ambulance with the personnel train . . . advanced to render medical treatment, thereby setting off another mine. The ambulance, having caught on fire, several officers and men from both the collecting company and the hospital advanced with fire extinguishers and first-aid materials. One of them set off a third mine. At least one dud also went off. Altogether, the accident caused one fatality, while one officer and thirteen enlisted men required medical treatment and hospitalization. In all but three cases, the injuries were sustained by members of the 502nd Medical Collecting Company. Two of the casualties among hospital personnel had to be evacuated and had not been returned at the end of the year. The Purple Heart medals awarded to the men injured in this incident were the only ones awarded to the members of this organization during the year. Engineers again inspected the hospital areas for mines and also gave a demonstration of the mechanism of mines, explaining what had happened.

On the 4th of August, the largest number of operations in any one twenty-four hour period in the year were performed, namely, 145—a figure which no member of the unit would have thought possible during training in England or America. Two days later, 221 patients were evacuated, the largest number in a twenty-four hour period throughout the year.

The stage was thus set for another high-water mark for the hospital. At about four o'clock on August 8, word was received that two hundred casualties were to arrive that evening. Within an hour casualties appeared in an ever-increasing stream until the hospital tents were filled to overflowing. About two hundred of the lesser wounded were placed on litters and blankets under the trees along the entrance. Altogether, nearly five hundred patients arrived in about four hours. In a twelve-hour period between 1800, August 8, and 0600, August 9, the patients actually admitted into the hospital numbered 412, while all the rest had been put under cover.

Naturally enough, therefore, August 8 showed the year's greatest figure for admissions in a day, namely, 476. The next day, August 9, began with the largest surgical backlog of the year, 295. Before midnight, however, all the major operations had been completed, and within another twenty-four hours the surgical backlog had been reduced to nothing—a remarkable achievement for the operative section of the hospital. The hospital closed for admissions at noon on August 10, but continued to evacuate patients until the 27th when the 617th Medical Collecting Company took over the remaining patients.

Bronze Star medals, the first decorations received by members of the 67th Evacuation Hospital, were awarded on August 11 to one ward nurse (post-operative) and two enlisted men (an X-ray and a surgical technician). Second Lieutenant Miller's medal is believed to have been the first awarded to a feminine member of the American armed services during the Western European campaign.

On the sixteenth of August, the hospital moved one hundred miles for Operation 3 at an attractive site on the grounds of a country mansion with an ancient moat just outside Gorron, Mayenne. The hospital proper was set up in fields on one side of a long lane of old beech trees, enlisted and officer's tents were pitched in an orchard on the other side, while the nurses enjoyed a separate garden area behind stone walls. The hospital admitted patients for only four days but remained in its beautiful surroundings for ten more days.

The first and only death among the personnel of the 67th Evacuation Hospital occurred on August 18, when T/5 Earl Seawright died as a result of injuries received when a truck in which he was a passenger overturned while he was on detached service with the 1st Medical Supply Depot.

Thus, as the war raged on the front lines, the men and women of the Medical Corps fought their own battles to save lives in their field hospitals.

Although the end of the war was months away, there was much more fighting ahead, and for some of the soldiers, the worst was yet to come. Sgt. Rosario Calabrese, who served in a PI unit at higher headquarters and occasionally rotated to the front to verify his unit's work, got to witness firsthand the unimaginable horror of Hitler's concentration camps. During the closing days of the war, he was with the 3rd Cavalry Group when it liberated prisoners at the concentration camp of Ohrdsuf. "It was not large, but had all the accoutrements: lots of bodies lying around

and a handful of survivors." The ghastly sight of living skeletons barely clinging to life was etched forever in his memory.

The War Continues

In September, the German fortress position at Brest was reduced while the Allied armies under the British 21st Army Group and the U.S. 12th Army Group raced toward the German border and the Sixth Army Group drove up the Rhone Valley after the invasion of south France. In September, General Eisenhower arrived from England with his SHAEF headquarters. Operation Market Garden, an attempt to find a back door into Germany by crossing the Rhine in the Netherlands accompanied by a massive airborne drop, had failed. In October and November, the Allied forces continued to push forward while the lines of communication behind them kept improving. In some places, like the Hurtegen Forest, the fighting was bloody and vicious. In December, the Germans launched their last major counteroffensive in the West through the Ardennes,[2] which became known as the Battle of the Bulge. The same two airborne divisions—the 82nd and 101st—that had shattered the German defense of the Cotentin Peninsula during the Normandy invasion were dispatched to seal the breach. The Germans launched one last offensive, Operation *Nordwind*, in Alsace in January 1945, but that thrust was blunted after some initial setbacks. After the Germans were finally contained, the war raged for many more weeks until a major Allied offensive breached the Rhine barrier in the spring of 1945 and the German collapse soon followed. Many of the divisions that had fought in Normandy continued to lead the way.

The Information and Education Division published a series of pamphlets, some of which

2. The Germans were using a strategy similar to the one that had defeated the French in 1940 when their main thrusts came through the same lightly defended region.

Why You're Going to France

Most American troops sent to France received *A Pocket Guide to France*, a small booklet that described in about thirty pages the country and its people. In addition to a brief history of how the country came to be occupied by the Germans, the booklet included stereotyped descriptions of the French and their customs and tips on a variety of subjects ranging from etiquette to survival. The guide warned the GI to remember that the French are polite and shake hands frequently, but that they are not "back-slappers." The section on "Security and Health" dealt with safety issues.

You probably won't get mixed up with anything as glamorous as Mata Hari—the Germans have wised up and are sending around much less obvious spies these days. The best thing for you to do is to keep any information of value to the enemy . . . strictly to yourself.

However, the most popular section of the booklet among the GIs was undoubtedly the one that addressed health issues.

Many of the so-called French prostitutes right now have been drawn from the dregs of other occupied countries and are deliberately planted under-cover Nazi Agents. . . . Your outfit might later pay with your lives as a result of you having talked. . . . Or you might merely catch disease and thus make one less good healthy soldier. . . . Make no mistake about this; Nazi propagandists have planned it both ways.

While it is true that the French point of view toward sex is somewhat different than American, it does not follow that illicit sex relations are any safer than in the United States. As a matter of fact there is a greater risk of contracting venereal disease. Before the war the French Government made an attempt to examine and license prostitutes. But don't be fooled. No system of examination has ever made a prostitute safe.

If a girl doesn't carry a prostitute's card, then she is an "irregular" . . . and has not even submitted to a medical examination. You know what that means. It would be a nasty souvenir of Paris for you to take back home.

Other health warnings included a warning against using water in rural area, drinking milk, which "is not safe to drink unless boiled," and overindulging in "French cooking."

Another section of the booklet warned that "sly winks and coy pats on the rear are accepted," and that many young French girls never went out without a chaperone. Furthermore, "France is full of decent women and strict women." In addition, the booklet warned the GIs that marriage to a French girl would lead to bureaucratic complications, that the government would not pay for the transportation of dependents to the United States, and that "in any case you can't marry without permission of your commanding officer."

The guide concluded with a brief reminder that the French were friends, that the Ger-

continued

Why You're Going to France *continued*

mans were enemies, and that the countryside was rife with spies purposely left behind. Once again, it admonished the GI to "keep a closed mouth. . . . Eat what is given you in your own unit. Don't go foraging among the French. . . . Boil all drinking water, no matter where it comes from . . ." unless the Medical Officer had approved it."

The last sentence, "You are a member of the best dressed, best fed, best equipped Liberating Army now on earth," reminded the GI of their blessings and obligations.

came from the Army *Stars and Stripes*, summarizing the achievements of most of the divisions and branches of the army in the European theater of operations. These booklets were printed in Paris in late 1944 and in 1945; some of the summaries from these booklets follow. The Transportation Corps controlled the railway units, the truck units that formed the Red Ball Express, and the port and harbor companies that maintained and operated the logistical lifeline.

Motor Transport moved everything. On June 25, 1944, two 30-ton diesel locomotives were hauled on M-19 tank transporters. On Aug. 11, the M-19 tank transporters were converted to cargo carriers for ammunition, carrying on each 45-ton trailer payloads of supply up to 30 tons.

On July 29, hundreds of thousands of gallons of gasoline were moved in five-gallon cans from the beaches to La Haye du Puits for the Third Army. On July 30, scores of 2,000-gallon semi-trailers moved thousands of gallons of POL from Cherbourg to Beugeville, and a tremendous movement of gas in five-gallon cans from one beach to La Haye-Pesnil for the Third Army was begun.

The daily commitment for hauling POL was raised from 300,000 to 600,000 gallons. An emergency haul of 100,000 gallons of diesel fuel for the French and Armored Division was completed Aug. 10. The figures indicate the tremendous amount of POL devoured by General Patton's and General Hodges's armies. Without motor support, it would have been impossible to exploit General Patton's breakthrough."

Although the Corps of Engineers was also critical in maintaining the rear area, its combat units were in the forefront of any assault.

Engineers do all army construction work except for signal installations, also provide all quartering of troops.

The enemy knocked out bridges again and again with massed artillery. But as fast as he knocked them out, engineer soldiers restored them. Engineers kept the army moving!

They kept highways open, filled in shell craters, blew out enemy pillboxes to keep the Germans from sneaking back at night. They removed mines and booby traps. When the hedgerow country was reached and bitter fighting began, the engineer soldier with his bulldozers and demolitions helped breach tough, century-hardened hedgerows to keep the army moving.

With incredible speed, engineers laid pipelines from beaches to the fighting front to assure gasoline for tanks and trucks where it was needed, when it was needed, and at the same time to ease already choking traffic stretching as far as the eye could reach along the only Allied-held east-west highway in Normandy.

But both the 4th and 6th Armored Divisions had first to move down the single highway leading through Lessay, and they found that town was the most mined and booby-trapped town in France. When the German soldier had failed to stem the surging tide of the Allied assault, mines and booby traps won them time to withdraw and regroup.

The combat engineers played an important role in the reduction of enemy fortifications in late August when the Germans were withdrawing toward the borders of the Reich, leaving behind small garrisons in the French ports of the Atlantic seaboard. Even though they were isolated with no hope of relief, many of these garrisons managed to hold their positions until the end of the war. After the battle for Brest, the Allies largely gave up attempts to reduce these coastal defenses because the advantages of taking them were heavily outweighed by the costs in lives, equipment, and materiel.

A case in point is Fort Montabarray, manned by German elite troops of the 2nd Parachute Regiment, which stood up to the American 29th Infantry Division. The 121st Engineers Battalion played a key role in breaching the antitank ditch, the fort's moat, and minefields on September 13–14. During the afternoon of September 14, the 86th Chemical Mortar Battalion laid smoke. Four British Crocodile flame-throwing tanks attached to a tank destroyer battalion scorched the defenders of the walls with a blast of flame. The tanks were followed by an infantry company. The engineers continued clearing the mines and widening the gaps and improving the path into the moat

while under sniper fire through September 15. The tanks engulfed the fort with flames, but still it held. After the assailants found a tunnel in the moat of the fort, the engineers went in under the cloak of darkness and placed a ton of TNT at a point under the fort's wall. They detonated it in the morning, bringing down the wall and forcing the Germans to surrender on September 16.

The Ordnance Corps, another rear-echelon unit, kept the fighting troops supplied with weapons, ammunition, and equipment.

For every man participating in the invasion, there were 1,500 pounds of ordnance material. What is ordnance? It's the blockbuster and the rocket, which softened up the invasion coast and supported the infantryman as he hit the beach. It's the M-4 tank, which rumbled off an LST and smashed its way into an enemy stronghold. It's the 105-mm howitzer, which helped pave the way for the doughs who carried ordnance in the form of semi-automatic rifles, carbines, machine guns, and every other type of small arms weapons. It's the anti-aircraft gun which brought down Me 109s two miles away; the director which did the gun's thinking. It's the scout car that went out on reconnaissance, the $2\frac{1}{2}$-ton truck hauling supplies from the beachhead. It's everything that rolls, shoots, is shot, and dropped from the air.

It's the story of maintenance crews who put damaged vehicles back into action while sniper bullets zinged nearby and 88s screamed overhead; of ammunition companies fighting off dive-bombers and infiltrating attacks; of tank recovery units and contact teams, depot companies and storehouse workers. It's the story of welders, small arms mechanics, artillery technicians, instrument repairmen, bomb disposal men, foreign materiel experts, and clerks. It's the story of 150,000 officers and men who not only delivered the goods but kept that equipment in fighting condition through France, Belgium, Holland, Luxembourg, and Germany. It's the story of supply and maintenance in five United States Armies.

Ordnance had to supply the following requirements to the army:

The Table of Basic Allowance for an armored division calls for 13,148 small arms weapons, 499 artillery pieces, 879 combat vehicles, and 1,755 other vehicles. This equipment weighs 23,317 tons. For tanks alone, monthly replacements number 8,000 different kinds of parts and assemblies, involving 1,500,000 individual pieces packed in 15,000 containers. The initial equipment of an infantry division calls for 16,843 small arms weapons, 280 artillery pieces, 17 combat vehicles, and 2,072 other vehicles.

To meet these requirements, Ordnance brought 2,000,000 tons of equipment to England before D-Day, including 22,741 combat vehicles, 281,768 general and special purpose vehicles, 1,494,941 small arms weapons, and 19,959 artillery pieces. Since D-Day, Allied troops were supplied with 2,500,000 tons of vehicles and weapons. Artillery supply alone was 1,496,000 tons between D-Day and V-E Day.

Between D-Day and V-E Day, third, fourth, and fifth echelon maintenance shops in the Communications Zone repaired 335,995 vehicles of all types, 407,182 small arms weapons, and 11,182 artillery pieces—a total of 754,259 jobs.

In addition, the Ordnance men were left the cleanup what the engineers did not:

The 20th Bomb Disposal Squad deactivated shells and blockbusters from Normandy to the Cologne Plain.

The Signal Corps was critical in providing and maintaining radio and telephone communications for the forces serving in the European theater. Although signal units generally operated in the rear areas, the combat divisions had their own signal company in addition to their own quartermaster companies, an engineer battalion, and MPs. The military police performed a key security function from the battlefield to the Communications Zone.

Division, Corps, and Army MPs were especially trained amphibious MP companies—the 210th, the 214th, and 449th—normally assigned to Corps but now attached to the famed Engineer Special Brigades. These outfits, experts on beach traffic, were in at the beginning.

D-Day traffic wasn't the only problem. Increasing numbers of PWs jam-packed cages. Immediate help was imperative. Late in the afternoon, June 6, 1944, the 302nd MP Escort Guard Co., composed of 57 percent limited servicemen, came ashore. The unit suffered casualties in men and equipment before relieving 1st Inf. Div. MPs of their stockade responsibility. Several days later, the 595th took charge of three beach evacuation pens while the 301st was busily occupied with PWs in another sector. Supposedly, these were Com. Z units.

Cos. C and D, 783rd MP Bn., directed beach traffic on D+4, and the entire battalion, along with the 713th, followed armies thereafter.

Traffic posts, like Military Police, are everywhere. On the Continent, Com. Z MPs took over or established posts after army MPs had pressed forward into new territories. Before final resistance was crushed, MPs of the 769th and the 707th MP Bns. routed traffic from Cherbourg.

To erect signs and control traffic on the Red Ball Highway was the mission of the

783rd MP Bn., which began working with the Transportation Corps' Motor Transport Brigade Aug. 29, 1944. Every participating service could look with pride on that route as initial convoys roared through without a hitch. An outstanding achievement, it later was extended, with the 783rd getting the toughest job. Because MP strength never was sufficient to provide full-scale control of the Red Ball route, those assigned redoubled efforts, fighting to check pilferage, black market activities, and to curb serious traffic violations.

After the Allies broke out of Normandy,

[the] Cherbourg Peninsula, packed with Germans, began to overflow, but First Army's Provost Marshal was prepared to cope with any sudden influx of prisoners.

A 10,000-man enclosure was established at Foucarville with the 552nd MP EG [Escort Guard] Co. and the 5th Ranger Bn. in charge. In addition, three 1,000-man cages were located on VII Corps' beach. After official notification, a second 10,000-man enclosure, under the 482nd MP EG Co. at Valognes, was built to regulate the flow of prisoners into Foucarville. More than 25,000 prisoners were evacuated in one sweep when the Normandy peninsula collapsed.

These temporary cages were crude affairs, often no more than a strand of barbed wire encircling the field. When time was available, concertina wire was used; carbide floodlights and telephone communications installed.

The Women's Army Corps (WAC) also made a significant contribution to the success of the invasion. These women served in various administrative roles to support the other branches and were even in SHAEF Headquarters.

As casualties were brought in from the beaches in increasing numbers, WACs in the Chief Surgeon's Office in London assisted in loading and moving hospital trains, prepared latest reports on battle casualties.

Flying to Normandy with a group of SHAEF officers on June 22, T.Sgt. Mabel Carney, Camden, New Jersey, became the first WAC to land on the Continent. She took dictation at a beachhead conference, returned to England the same night.

As Allied forces fanned out in Normandy, the first forward echelon of WACs landed on Normandy beaches on D+38, following an urgent call for Headquarters and Communications Zone personnel. Aboard a heavily laden cruiser the loudspeakers blared, "WAC personnel, prepare to disembark." WACs hooked helmet straps, grabbed gear, climbed down the ladder into a bouncing LCI. Ashore, they saw blackened steel skeletons of vehicles, smashed German and American equipment, and mute rows of wooden crosses.

GIs waved from tents hidden under trees as WAC trucks jolted over shelled roads. French peasants looked up from digging in the ruins of bombed villages and smiled an amazed greeting at the American women under pack and helmet.

The 49 EWs and five WAC officers who arrived with Forward Echelon, Communications Zone headquarters, lived under canvas near chateau headquarters outside Valogne. They dug drainage ditches around their tents as Normandy skies poured rain for eight straight days. K and C rations, rationed Lister-bag water, mud and dust, helmet baths, became routine.

The Medical Corps was as indispensable as any of the other rear-echelon units. From the aid man on the front line to the men at aid stations who performed the triage and sent the wounded to field hospitals, to the doctors and nurses, they fought to save lives both their friends and the enemy. Their job may have been one of the hardest in the war since they had to face every day the ultimate consequences of armed conflict.

Finally, there are the combat divisions that took the brunt of the casualties. The established strength of an infantry division between the summer of 1943 and January 1945 was 14,253 men (it was lowered to 4,037 men in 1945), that of an armored division 10,937 men in 1944, and the airborne division was raised to 12,979 men at the end of 1944.[3] Most of the combat divisions suffered heavy casualties between D-Day until V-E Day.

Total American Casualties (Killed, Wounded, and Missing)

Unit	Casualties	Date of arrival
4th Division	22,000	June 6
29th Division	19,794	June 6
9th Division	19,007	June 10
90th Division	18,679	June 6
30th Division	17,166	June 10
80th Division	15,539	August 3
2nd Division	15,524	June 7
1st Division	15,134	June 6
35th Division	14,804	July 5
83rd Division	14,660	June 19
79th Division	14,437	June 14
28th Division	14,138	July 22
8th Division	12,856	July 3
5th Division	11,968	July 11
3rd Arm. Div.	9,809	June 23
101st A/B Div.	8,032	June 6
2nd Arm. Div.	6,795	June 9
82nd A/B Div.	6,580	June 6
4th Arm. Div.	6,475	July 13
6th Arm. Div.	5,549	July 19
5th Arm. Div.	3,290	July 25

Source: *Normandy 1944* by Niklas Zetterling (2000)

The above are casualties during a period of up to eleven months. By comparison, the German casualties between June 6 and August 22 in the Normandy campaign were given at 210,000, including 50,000 lost in the Falaise Pocket. Those German divisions that the Americans faced in Normandy from early June until August 22 suffered losses as shown on the next page.

---

3. The airborne division varied before that because of the number of additional regiments attached and was officially smaller than an armored division in 1944.

Total German Casualties (Killed, Wounded, and Missing)

Unit	Original strength	Casualties	Date of arrival
709th Division	12,320	12,320	June 6
3rd Parachute Division	17,400	11,000	June 12
243rd Division	11,500	10,000	June 6
352nd Division	12,700	9,000	June 6
275th Division	12,000	9,000	June 12
5th Parachute Division	12,250	8,000	July 13
17th SS Pz. Gren. Division	16,100	8,000	June 13
Panzer Lehr Division	13,100	7,000	June 8
363rd Division	11,000	7,000	August 1
2nd Panzer Division	15,900	6,000	June 12
326th Division	11,500	6,000	July 25
1st SS Panzer Division	19,600	5,000	July 4
91st Air Landing Division	7,500	5,000	June 6
77th Division	9,100	5,000	June 11
2nd SS Panzer Division	13,100	4,000	July 1
116th Panzer Division	14,300	3,800	July 24
265th Division	9,700	3,000	June 11
6th Parachute Regiment	4,500	3,000	June 7

Source: *Normandy 1944* by Niklas Zetterling (2000)

APPENDIX

Photos of Veterans

Ray Hood

Earl Duncan

William Biehler

Ed Fabian

Frank Gallagher

Charlie Miller

Graydon Eubank

David Thomas

Joseph Foye

George Gray

Peter Triolo

James Newton

Richard Underwood

Paul Pachowka

A. B. Mirmelstein

Harold Shebeck

Sidney Ulan

Fred Bewersdorf

Francis Steele

Alvin Anderson

William Hart

Bill Bell

Charles Bergeron

Charles Herndon

Richard Johnson

Bill Lewis

John Gregory

Murphy Chustz

Fred Tannery

John McAllister

John Slaughter

Charles Scheffel

Clifford Legerton

Herbert Beatty

Melvin Larson

James Crutchfield

Bonnie Skloss

Douglas McArthur

Byron Cook

David Moore

Jack Sargeant

William McDaniel

John Plonski

Theodore Gaydos

Francis Aleksandrowicz

Wardell Hopper

SERIES BIBLIOGRAPHY

BOOKS AND ARTICLES

The AAF in the Invasion of Southern France: An Interim Report. Washington, DC: Headquarters, Army Air Forces, 1945.

Allied Landing Craft of World War Two. Annapolis, MD: Naval Institute Press, 1989 (reprint).

Anderson, Charles R. *Tunisia*. Washington, DC: Center of Military History, n.d.

Anzuoni, Robert P. *"I'm the 82nd Airborne Division!" A History of the All American Division in World War II after Action Reports*. Atglen, PA: Schiffer Publishing, 2005

AFF: Official World War II Guide to the Army Air Forces. New York: Bonanza Books, 1988 (reprint of 1944 edition).

Archer, Clarke, ed. *Paratroopers' Odyssey History of the 517th PIR*. Hudson, FL: 517th Parachute Regimental Combat Team Association, 1985.

Balkoski, Joseph. *Beyond the Beachhead*. Harrisburg, PA: Stackpole Books, 1989.

Balkoski, Joseph. *Omaha Beach*. Mechanicsburg, PA: Stackpole Books, 2004.

Balkoski, Joseph. *Utah Beach*. Mechanicsburg, PA: Stackpole Books, 2005.

Bando, Mark. *101st Airborne: The Screaming Eagles at Normandy*. Oceola, WI: MBI, 2001.

Basden, Barry, and Charles Scheffel. *Crack! and Thump*. Illano, TX: Camroc Press, 2007.

Beck, Alfred, et al. *Corps of Engineers: The War Against Germany*. Washington, DC: U.S. Government Printing Office, 1985.

Bekker, C. D. *Defeat at Sea*. New York: Ballantine Books, 1955.

Belchem, David. *Victory in Normandy*. Toronto: Clarke Irwin & Co. Ltd., 1981.

Bennett, Gen. Donald V. *Honor Untarnished*. New York: Forge, 2003.

Bennett, Ralph. *Ultra in the West*. New York: Charles Scribner's Sons, 1980.

Bernage, Georges. *Omaha Beach*. Bayeux, France: Heimdal, 2002.

Bernage, Georges, and Dominique Francois. *Utah Beach, Sainte-Mère-Église, Sainte-Marie-du-Mont*. Bayeux, France: Heimdal, 2004.

Bielakowski, Alexander. *African American Troops in World War II*. New York: Osprey, 2007.

Birtle, Andrew. *Sicily*. CMH Pub 72-16. Washington, DC: Center of Military History, 1994.

Black, Robert W. *Rangers in World War II*. New York: Ballantine Books, 1992.

Blumenson, Martin. *Breakout and Pursuit*. Washington, DC: U.S. Government Printing Office, 1984.

Bowman, Martin W. *USAAF Handbook, 1939–1945*. England: Sutton Publishing, 1997.

Bradley, Omar N. *A Soldier's Story*. New York: Popular Library, 1964 (reprint).

Brady, James R. *Invasion B.P.O. A History of the 17th Base Post Office*. N.d.

Brown, Anthony Cave. *Bodyguard of Lies*. New York: Harper-Collins, 1975.

Breuer, William B. *Operation Dragoon*. Novato, CA: Presidio, 1987.

Burton, Capt. David C. "Bombed by Our Own Planes." *Military Magazine* (February 1989).

———. "The Liberator Is Recognized." *Military Magazine* (March 1990).

———. "Our Love Affair with Pratt & Whitney." *Military Magazine* (May 1990).

Butcher, Capt. Harry C. *My Three Years with Eisenhower*. New York: Simon and Schuster, 1946.

Bykofsky, Joseph, and Harold Larson. *The Transportation Corps: Operations Overseas*. Washington, DC: Department of the Army, 1957.

Carell, Paul. *Invasion They're Coming!* New York: Bantam, 1965.

Carter, Kit C., and Robert Mueller. *The Army Air Forces in World War II: Combat Chronology, 1941–1945*. Washington, DC: U.S. Government, 1973.

Callender, Bruce. "The Short Heyday of the Bombardier." *Air Force Times* (9 April 1984).

Casey, William. *The Secret War against Hitler*. Washington, DC: Regnery, 1988.

Chandler, Alfred D. Jr., ed. *The Papers of Dwight David Eisenhower: The War Years*. Vols. 1–5. Baltimore, MD: Johns Hopkins Press, 1970.

Chandler, David, and James Collins, eds. *D-Day Encyclopedia*. New York: Simon and Schuster, 1994.

Chant, Christopher. *World Encyclopedia of the Tank*. Somerset, England: Patrick Stephens Ltd., 1994.

Charles, Roland W. *Troopships of World War II*. Washington, DC: The Army Transportation Association, 1947.

Chazette, Alain. *1940–1944 Les Batteries Allemandes*. Tours, France: Éditions Heimdal, 1988.

Churchill, Winston. *Closing the Ring*. Boston: Houghton Mifflin, 1949.

Clarke, Jeffrey J., and Robert Ross Smith. *Riviera to the Rhine*. Washington, DC: Center of Military History, 1993.

Colley, David P. *The Road to Victory*. Washington, DC: Brassey's, 2000.

Combat Divisions of World War II (Army of the United States). Washington, DC: Army Times, 1946.

Cook, Byron C. *Little Boy Blue: Diary of a B-17 Airman*. Unpublished manuscript, 1991.

Craven, Wesley, and James Cate. *The Army Air Forces in World War II*. Vol 3. Chicago: University of Chicago Press, 1955.

Daniel, Donald C., and Katherine L. Herbig, eds. *Strategic Military Deception*. New York: Pergamon Press, 1981.

D'Este, Carlo. *Decision in Normandy*. New York: Harper Perennial, 1991.

DeNevi, Don, and Bob Hall. *United States Military Railway Service*. Ontario, Canada: Boston Mills Press, 1992.

Devlin, Gerard M. *Paratrooper*. New York: St. Martins Press, 1979.

———. *Silent Wings*. New York: St. Martins Press, 1985.

Dictionary of American Naval Fighting Ships. Vol. 4. Washington, DC: Navy Department, 1969.

Doubler, Capt. Michael D. *Bursting the Bocage: American Combined Operations in France, June 31–July 1944*. Fort Leavenworth, KS: U.S. Army Command & General Staff College, 1988.

Eisenhower, Dwight D. *Crusade in Europe*. New York: Doubleday, 1968 (reprint).

Engineers in the Normandy Invasion. Manuscript. Washington, DC: Society of American Military Engineers, 1991.

Ewing, Joseph H. *29 Let's Go!* Washington, DC: Infantry Journal Press, 1948.

Fahey, James C. *The Ships and Aircraft of the United States Navy*. New York: Ships & Aircraft, 1945.

Fane, Cmdr. Francis D., and Don Moore. *The Naked Warriors*. New York: Appleton Century & Crofts, 1956.

Fifth Army at the Winter Line: 15 November 1943 to 15 January 1944. Washington, DC: Center of Military History, 1990 (reprint of 1945 version).

Forty, George. *U.S. Army Handbook, 1939–1945.* England: Alan Sutton, 1995.

———. *The Armies of George S. Patton.* London: Arms and Armour, 1996.

44th Engineer Combat Battalion. 44th Engineer Combat Association, n.d.

Freeman, Roger A. *The Mighty Eighth.* New York: Orion Books, 1970.

———. *The Mighty Eighth War Diary.* Osceola, WI: Motorbooks, 1990.

Friedman, Norman. *U.S. Amphibious Ships and Craft: An Illustrated Design History.* Annapolis, MD: Naval Institute Press, 2002.

Gabel, Christopher R. *The U.S. Army GHQ Maneuvers of 1941.* Washington, DC: Center of Military History, 1992.

Galland, Adolf. *The First and the Last.* New York: Ballantine Books, 1963.

Garrigues, Donald. *From the Delphus to Destiny.* Unpublished manuscript, 1980.

Gaujac, Paul. *Dragoon: The Other Invasion of France.* Paris, France: Histoire & Collections, 2004.

Gavin, Gen. James M. *On to Berlin.* New York: Bantam Books, 1978.

Gawne, Jonathan. *The Battle for Brest.* Paris, France: Histoire & Collections, 2002.

———. *Finding Your Father's War.* Philadelphia: Casemate, 2006.

———. *Spearheading D-Day: American Special Units in Normandy.* Paris, France: Historie & Collections, 1999.

Goralski, Robert. *World War II Almanac, 1931–1945.* New York: Putman's Sons, 1981.

Greenfield, K. R, et al. *The Organization of Ground Combat Troops.* Washington, DC: U.S. Government Printing Office, 1947.

Guenther, Curt, and Anderson Humphreys. *Semmes America.* Memphis, TN: Humphreys Publishing, 1989.

Guild, Frank H. *Action of the Tiger: The Saga of the 437th Troop Carrier Group.* Tyler, TX: City Publishing Co., 1950.

Harrison, Gordon A. *Cross Channel Attack.* Washington, DC: U.S. Government Printing Office, 1951.

Hartcup, Guy. *Code Name Mulberry.* New York: Hippocrene Books, 1977.

Haswell, Jock. *D-Day Intelligence and Deception.* New York: Times Books, 1979.

Heavey, Brig. Gen. William F. *Down Ramp, The Story of the Amphibian Engineers.* Washington, DC: Infantry Journal Press, 1947.

Hess, William, and Thomas Ivie. *Fighters of the Mighty Eighth.* Osceola, WI: MBI, 1990.

Hoyt, Edwin P. *The Invasion before Normandy.* New York: Stein and Day, 1985.

Huntzinger, Edward J. *The 388th at War.* San Angelo, TX: Newsfoto Yearbooks, 1979.

Ilfrey, Jack. *Happy Jack's Go-Buggy.* Hicksville, NY: Exposition Press, 1979

Impact: The Army Air Forces' Confidential Picture History of World War II. New York: James Parton & Co., 1980 (reprint).

Impact. U.S. Army Air Force (May 1945).

Jacobs, Harry A. "The DUKW." *Ordnance Magazine* (November 1953).

Jaffee, Walter W. *The Liberty Ships from A to Z.* Palo Alto, CA: Glencannon, 2004.

———. *The Victory Ships from A to Z.* Palo Alto, CA: Glencannon, 2006.

Jane's Fighting Aircraft of World War II. New York: Military Press, 1989.

Jensen, Marvin. *Strike Swiftly: The 70th Tank Battalion from North Africa to Normandy to Germany.* Novato, CA: Presidio, 1997.

Johnson, Robert, and Martin Caidin. *Thunderbolt!* New York: Bantam Books, 1990.

Jones, Lloyd S. *U.S. Bombers 1928 to 1980's.* Fallbrook, CA: AeroPub., 1980.

Jones, Lt. Clifford. *The Administrative and Logistical History of the ETO.* Part 6, *Training, Mounting, the Artificial Ports.* Historical Division, U.S. Armed Forces, European Theater, 1946.

Kelly, Everett H. *Angel in My Foxhole.* St. Albans, WV: Miracle Press, 1973.

Knickerbocker, H. R., et al. *Danger Forward.* Washington, DC: Society of the First Division, n.d.

Koskimaki, George. *D-Day with the Screaming Eagles.* Haverstown, PA: Casemate, 2002 (reprint).

Kray, William. *Bluie West One.* Bennington, VT: Merriam Press, 2007.

Lamb, Richard. "The Dieppe Disaster." *War Monthly* 7, No. 4 (May 1979).

Lane, Ronald L. *Rudder's Rangers.* Manassas, VA: Ranger Associates, 1979.

Langdon, Allen. *Ready: A History of the 505th Parachute Infantry Regiment in World War II.* Manuscript. N.d.

Lanier, Lewis, et al. *The Story of Vitamin Baker: We'll Never Go Overseas.* Germany: 741st Tank Battalion, 1945.

Lewis, Nigel. *Exercise Tiger.* New York: Prentice Hall Press, 1990.

Liddell-Hart, B. H. *The Rommel Papers.* New York: Da Capo, 1953.

Lord, William G. *History of the 508th Parachute Infantry.* Washington, DC: Infantry Journal Press, 1948.

Lowden, John. *Silent Wings at War.* Washington, DC: Smithsonian, 1992.

MacDonald, Charles B., et al. *Information about Operations in Southern France, Rear Area Security in Russia 1941–1944, North Africa, and Korea.* Washington, DC: Office of Military History, n.d.

Macksey, Kenneth. *Commando: Hit and Run Combat in World War II.* Chelsea, MI: Scarborough House, 1990.

Majdalany, Fred. *The Battle of Cassino.* New York: Ballantine, 1957.

Marshall, S. L. A. "How the Army is Organized" in *America Organizes to Win the War.* Edited by Erling M. Hunt. Freeport, NY: Books for Libraries Press, 1942.

Masterman, J. C. *The Double-Cross System.* New Haven, CT: Yale University Press, 1972.

Mayo, Lida. *The Ordnance Department: On Beachhead and Battlefront.* Washington, DC: Center of Military History, 1991.

Middlebrook, Martin, and Chris Everitt. *The Bomber Command War Diaries.* London: Penguin Books, 1990.

Morison, Samuel E. *The Invasion of France and Germany.* Boston: Little, Brown & Co, 1984 (reprint).

———. *Operations in North African Waters.* Boston: Little, Brown & Co, 1984 (reprint).

———. *Sicily-Salerno-Anzio.* Edison, NJ: Castle Books, 2001 (reprint).

Mrazek, James E. *The Glider War.* London: Robert Hale & Co., 1975.

Murray, Williamson. *Strategy for Defeat: The Luftwaffe, 1933–1945.* Secaucus, NJ: Chartwell Books, 1986.

"Naval Shore Fire Control Parties in the Southern France Landings." *Field Artillery Journal* (March 1945).

Nordyke, Phil. *All American: All the Way.* St. Paul, MN: Zenith, 2005.

Norman, Albert. *Operation Overlord, Design and Reality.* Westport, CT: Greenwood Press, 1952.

Omaha Beachhead. Washington, DC: Department of the Army, 1946.

Patrick, Stephen. *The Normandy Campaign.* New York: Gallery Books, 1986.

Peek, Clifford H., ed. *Five Years, Five Countries, Five Campaigns with the 141st Infantry Regiment.* Munich, Germany: 141st Infantry Regiment Association, 1945.

Perret, Geoffrey. *There Is a War to Be Won.* New York: Random House, 1991.

Phillips, Henry G. *Heavy Weapons*. Pem Valley, GA: Self-published, 1985.

Pratt, Sherman W. *Autobahn to Berchtesgaden*. Arlington, VA: Self-published, 1991.

Pulver, Murray S. *The Longest Year*. Freeman, SD: Pine Hill Press, 1986.

Rapport, Leonard, and Arthur Northwood. *Rendezvous with Destiny: A History of the 101st Airborne Division*. Washington, DC: Infantry Journal Press, 1948.

Report by the Supreme Allied Commander Mediterranean to the Combined Chiefs of Staff on the Italian Campaign, 8 January 1944 to 10 May 1944. London: His Majesty's Stationery Office, 1946.

The Rise and Fall of the German Air Force, 1933–1945. New York: St. Martin's, 1983.

Robinson, Warren. *Through Combat: 314th Infantry Regiment*. Privately published, circa 1948.

Ross, William F., and Charles F. Romanus. *The Quartermaster Corps: Operations in the War Against Germany*. Washington, DC: Office of the Chief of Military History, United States Army, 1965.

Rottman, Gordon. *Landing Ship Tank (LST) 1942–2002*. Oxford, England: Osprey, 2005.

———. *U.S. Airborne Units in the Mediterranean Theater, 1942–44*. Oxford, England: Osprey, 2006.

Ruppenthal, Roland G. *Logistical Support of the Armies, May 1941 to Sept. 1944*. Washington, DC: Department of the Army, 1953.

Salerno: American Operations from the Beaches to the Volturno. CMH Pub 100-7. Washington, DC: Center of Military History, 1990.

Sayen, John. *U.S. Army Infantry Divisions, 1944–45*. Oxford, England: Osprey, 2007.

Seaton, Albert. *The Russo-German War, 1941–45*. Novato, CA: Presidio, 1971.

Shepperd, G. A. *The Italian Campaign, 1943–45*. New York: Fredrick Praeger, 1968.

Shirley, John. *I Remember: Stories of a Combat Infantryman*. Bennington, VT: Merriam Press, 2005.

Slaughter, J. R. *Wartime Memoirs of J. Robert Slaughter*. Manuscript, 1989.

Small Unit Actions. Washington, DC: War Department Historical Division, 1946.

Speer, Albert. *Inside the Third Reich*. New York: Bonanza Books, 1982.

Stanton, Shelby L. *Order of Battle, U.S. Army, World War II*. Novato, CA: Presidio Press, 1984.

Steiner, Maj. Edward J., ed. *King's Cliff: The 20th. Fighter Group and the 446th Air Group in the European Theater of Operations*. New Braunfels, TX: 20th Fighter Group Association, 1983.

Stonehouse, Frederick. *Combat Engineer! The history of the 107th Engineer Battalion, 1881–1981*. Michigan: 107th Engineer Association, 1981.

To Bizerte with the II Corps. CMH Pub 100-6. Washington, DC: Center of Military History, 1990.

Truscott, Gen. L. K. *Command Missions*. Novato, CA: Presidio, 1954 (1990 reprint).

Tute, Warren, et al. *D-Day*. London: Pan Books Ltd., 1975.

299th Engineer Battalion (Combat: Unit History). Ft. Belvoir, n.d.

U.S. Strategic Bombing Survey. *The Defeat of the German Air Force*. Military Analysis, 1947.

Utah Beach to Cherbourg. Washington, DC: Department of the Army, 1947.

Valenti, Isadore. *Combat Medic*. Tarentum, PA: World Association Publishers, 2006.

Walters, John. "The B-26 Martin Marauder." *Military Magazine* (March 1991).

Wardlow, Chester. *The Transportation Corps: Responsibilities, Organization, and Operations*. Washington, DC: Office of the Chief of Military History, U.S. Army, 1951.

Webster, David K. *Parachute Infantry*. Baton Rouge, LA: Louisiana State University Press, 1994.

Werrel, Kenneth P. *Archie, Flak, AAA and SAM: A Short Operational History of Ground-Based Air Defense.* Maxwell AFB, AL: Air University Press, 1988.

Whitlock, Flint. *The Fighting First.* Boulder, CO: Westview, 2004.

Willoughby, Malcolm F. *The U.S. Coast Guard in World War II.* Annapolis, MD: Naval Institute Press, 1989.

Wood, Alan. *History of the World's Glider Forces.* London: Patrick Stephens Ltd., 1990.

Woolner, Frank. *Spearhead in the West, 1941–1945, The Third Armored Division.* Washington, DC: U.S. Army, 1945.

Zaloga, Steven J. *D-Day 1944 (2): Utah Beach & the U.S. Airborne Landings.* Oxford, England: Osprey, 2004.

———. *Operation Cobra.* Oxford, England: Osprey, 2001.

Zetterling, Niklas. *Normandy 1944: German Military Organization, Combat Power and Organizational Effectiveness.* Winnipeg, Canada: J. J. Fedorowicz Publishing, 2000.

MANUSCRIPTS FROM THE ARMY CENTER FOR MILITARY HISTORY

Becker, Capt. Marshall O. *The Amphibious Training Center.* Study No. 22. Washington, DC: Historical Section, Army Ground Forces, 1946.

Roge, Commandant. *The FFI before and after D-Day (1944).* MS B-035, 1950.

Ziegelmann, Fritz. *352nd Infantry Division.* MS B-722.

———. *352nd Infantry Division—Special Questions (Normandy).* MS B-021.

REPORTS FROM NAVY DEPARTMENT LIBRARY, WASHINGTON NAVY YARD, WASHINGTON, D.C.

Commander, U.S. Naval Forces in Europe. *The Invasion of Normandy: Operation Neptune.* 1948.

NEWS MAGAZINES AND NEWSLETTERS OF VETERANS GROUPS

Dozer Blade, news sheet of the 1121st Engineer Combat Group, 31 March 1945.

Glider Tow Line, Fall 1988.

King's Cliff Remembered: 20th Fighter Group Association.

NEWSPAPERS AND MAGAZINES

London Times, 1944.

New York Times, 1944.

Newsweek, 1944.

Southwestern Journal, 22 February 1990.

Time, 1944.

U.S. News and World Report, 1944.

SPECIAL ITEMS FROM NATIONAL ARCHIVES

Items found in file boxes for various units and with little to no special identification:

1. After-Action Reports for various units found at NARA.

2. Unit Histories such as for the 116th Infantry Regiment with no other bibliographic information.

"Action against Enemy/After Action Reports," HQ Fifth Ranger Infantry Battalion, APO 655, 22 July 1944.

"Action against Enemy/After Action Reports", HQ Fifth Ranger Infantry Battalion, APO 655, 10 October 1944.

"Action against Enemy/After Action Report", HQ 741st Tank Battalion, APO 230, 19 July 1944.

Allied Force Headquarters (AFHQ) Office of Assistant Chief of Staff, G-2, "Intelligence Lessons from North Africa, Operation Torch," March 1, 1943.

Curtin, Cmdr. John F., "Narrative: Second Beach Battalion", 25 July 1944.

Dabney, Col. J. A. (Chief of Staff Allied Forces HQ), "Lessons from Operation Torch," 29 December 1942.

"Digest of Some Notes and Reports from Operation 'Husky'." Combined Operations, London, 1943.

G-2 Reports of 2nd Armored Division from June 1944 from NARA files.

Hewitt, Vice Adm. H. K. *Invasion of Southern France: Report of Naval Commander, Western Task Force.* 15 November 1944.

Historical Record, Operations of 2nd Armored Division, 22 April–25 July 25 1943.

HQ, First U.S. Army, G-2, APO 230, 11 May 1944, "G-2 Estimate No. 2."

HQ, 4th Inf Div, APO 4, 14 May 1944, "Annex #2c to FO #1 Tactical Study of the Terrain and Weather."

HQ, 4th Inf Div, APO 4, 15 May 1944, "Annex #2b to FO #1, Order of Battle."

HQ, 4th Inf Div, APO 4, 28 May 1944, "Amendment #1 to FO #1."

HQ, 5th ESB, n.d. (circa fall 1944), "History of the 5th Engineer Special Brigade."

HQ, 101st A/B Div, APO 472, 22 May 1944, Operational Memorandum #23, "Final Briefing of Division Personnel—Operation Neptune."

HQ, 101st A/B Div, APO 472, 27 May 1944, "Spot Intelligence Report No. 1."

HQ, 101st A/B Div, APO 472, n.d. (circa summer 1944), "Operations of the 101st Division in the Invasion of France."

HQ, 112th Eng Cmbt Bn, APO 230, "Battalion History, June 1944," Appendix 'A' "Diary for June History", July 1944.

HQ, 116th Infantry Regiment, "Unit History," September 1944.

HQ, Southern Lines Communications ETO, U.S. Army. *American Rails In Eight Countries: The Story of the 1st Military Railway Service.* February 1945.

Journal of the 105th Engineer Combat Battalion, 30th Infantry Division, in the European Theater of Operations, 1944–1945. Fort Belvoir, Office of History, n.d.

"Journal—157th Infantry" and "Summary of Operations, August 1944" HQ, 157th Infantry 1944.

Larson, Harold. *The Army's Cargo Fleet in World War II.* Monograph #18. Office of Chief of Transportation Army Service Forces, May 1945.

Learn, 1st Lt. Clinton S. (Historian, 112th Eng.). *Battalion History 112th Engineer Combat Battalion June 1944.* July.

Memorandum No. 1, Armored Notes, published 19 June 1944 by HQ FUSA.

Military Observer, "Notes on the Planning and Assault Phases of the Sicilian Campaign," C.O.H.Q. Bulletin No. Y/1, London, October 1943.

Narrative of Commander Knuepfer, "USS MEREDITH, DD 726 in Normandy Invasion," Recorded 11 June 1944, File No. 240, transcript of May 1945, Office of Naval Records.

"Narrative Report of Engagements of 70th Tank Battalion during the Period 1 to 30 June 1944," July 1944.

"Observer Report, March 29, 1943." HQ Army Ground Forces, Washington DC.

"Report of Operations: Participation 3rd Infantry Division (Reinforced) in Sicilian Operations, July 10–18, 1943." September 10, 1943.

Report of Operations: Seventh United States Army in France and Germany, 1944–1945. 3 vols. Heidelberg, Germany: Aloys Graf, May 1946.

"Report on Operations of 1st Engineer Special Brigade in Normandy," 1944.

Ryder, Gen. Charles, "Lessons from Operation 'Torch'," December 26, 1942.

"Unit History of the Famous 299th Engineer Combat Battalion," Ft. Belvoir, n.d.

Unit Journal 741st Tank Battalion, June 6, 1944, (includes reports of individuals), n.d.

Unit Journal 743rd Tank Battalion, June 6, 1944, (company journals), n.d.

Webb, Wallace (Regimental S-1 Sgt.). *Combat History 137th Infantry Regiment (35th Division)*. August 1944.

Wilson, Gen. Arthur R. "Report of Operations in North Africa," December 12, 1942.

Woolley, Lt. James. "67th Evacuation Hospital," Annual Report for 1944, March 15, 1945.

ITEMS NOT QUOTED BUT USED FOR REFERENCE

HQ, 4th Inf Div, APO 4 12 May 1944 ,"FO #1." 8 pages.

HQ, 4th Inf Div Apo 4, 15 May 1944, "Annex #2 to FO #1, Summary of the Situation." 5 pages.

HQ, 4th Inf Div APO 4, 15 May 1944, "Annex #4 to FO #1, Administrative Order." 7 pages.

HQ, 4th Inf Div APO 4, 15 May 1944, "Annex #9 to FO # 1, Engineer Annex." 4 pages.

HQ, 741st Tank Battalion, APO 230, 21 May 1944, "Administrative Annex to FO #1." 4 pages.

MANUALS, REPORTS, AND ARMY BOOKLETS

I Am a Doughboy. Infantry Replacement Training Center, circa 1943

Messing in the ETO, Office of the Chief Quartermaster. HQ SOS, ETOUSA , circa late 1944

A Pocket Guide to France. 1944.

TM 11-242 Radio Set SCR 300 A. War Department , February 1945

War Department, FM 55-105, *Water Transportation: Ocean Going Vessels* (25 September 1944).

War Department, The Army of the United States, 76th Congress, Senate Document No. 91 (June 1939).

Biennial Report of the Chief of Staff of the United States Army, July 1, 1939, to June 30, 1941, to the Secretary of War. GPO, Washington, D.C., 1941.

Biennial Report of the Chief of Staff of the United States Army, July 1, 1941, to June 30, 1943, to the Secretary of War. GPO, Washington, D.C., 1943.

BOOKLETS FOR THE TROOPS PUBLISHED BY THE EDUCATION DIVISION OF ETOUSA

Destination Berlin: The Transportation Corps. Paris, 1944.

Engineering the Victory: The Story of the Corps of Engineers. Paris, 1945.

The First: The Story of the 1st Infantry Division. Paris, 1944.

Flaming Bomb: The Story of Ordnance in the ETO. Paris, 1945.

MP: The Story of the Corps of Military Police. Paris, 1945.

29 Let's Go: The Story of the 29th Division. Paris, 1945.

Tough Ombres: The Story of the 90th Division. Paris, 1944.

The WAC. Paris, 1945

CORRESPONDENCE

Randy Hill, email, March 29, 2005, concerning his study on the Troop Carrier Command.

George Woodward, correspondence concerning army engineers in the Eureopan theater.

INTERNET SITES

These sites include copies of documents, various types of data, and other reference material mainly from government sources.

Center of Military History Online: www .history.army.mil/reference/Normandy/TS/ index.htm; www.history.army.mil/index.html

État des Lieux: www.6juin1944.com/veterans/ rogers.php

440th Troop Carrier Group: www.440thtroop-carriergroup.org/

History of World War II Medicine: home.att.net/~steinert/wwii.htm

Naval Historical Center, Navy Department Library: www.history.navy.mil/library/index.htm

NavSource Naval History: www.navsource.org/archives/10/03/03idx.htm

Ships of the U.S. Navy, 1940–1945: ftp.ibiblio.org/hyperwar/USN/USN-ships.html#ap

VETERAN ACCOUNTS AND INTERVIEWS

Accounts and interviews from veterans prepared and submitted for this project. Some accounts were written, and others were recorded on audio tape. Some included personal letters, diaries, and citations awarded. The ranks below reflect the individual's rank during the Normandy campaign. The date or dates that the accounts were received are noted. Asterisks indicate a veteran who provided photographs.

Accounts

Cpl. Francis J. Aleksandrowicz (769th Military Police Battalion), 1991

Maj. John A. Allison (30th Division)★ (private unpublished unit history), 1990

T.Sgt. Alvin Anderson (379th Bomb Group), 1990

Flight Off. Eddie Anderson (434th Troop Carrier Group), 1990

1st Sgt. Frank F. Andrews (3rd Division), 1990

Sgt. Vincent A. Angeloni (4th Division), 1990

T.Sgt. Emmett Bailey Jr. (3047th Graves Registration Company), 1990★

PFC Albert J. Bartelloni (29th Division), 1990

PFC Harold Baumgarten (29th Division) (from Slaughter manuscript)

PFC Joseph Bean (82nd Airborne Division), 1990

Tech Sgt. Herbert J. Beatty (445th Bomb Group), 1990

2nd Lt. Charles W. Bell (35th Division), 1990★

RM2/C James J. Bennett (SS *Toltec*), 1990

Sgt. Charles Bergeron (4th Division), 1990

PFC Carl J. Betcher (90th Division), 1991

PFC Frank C. Bettle (1st Division), 1990

PFC Fred Bewersdorf (430th AAA [AW] Battalion), 1990

Pvt. William A. Biehler (90th Division), 1991

Tech 4 Clifton T. Bitgood (29th Division), 1989

1st Sgt. Raus J. Blondo (112th Combat Engineer Battalion) (includes letters to his captain), 1990

Tech 4 Alfred J. Borgman (OSS), 1990

Pvt. William D. Bowell (82nd Airborne Division)

1st Lt. William Boucher (3rd Divison), 1990★

Sgt. Irving A. Bradbury (4th Division), 1990

Lt. Malcolm D. Brannen (82nd Airborne Division), account given at a reunion and provided by Jack Schlegel

PFC Ralph Brazee (4th Division), 1990

Cpl. Floyd E. Brooks (30th Division), 1990

Pvt. Roger L. Brugger (1st Division), 1990

Sgt. William H. Buell (4th Division), 1989

PFC Kenneth Burch (82nd Airborne Division), 1990

PFC Ernest H. Burns (3rd Divison), 1990

Pvt. Sam L. Burns (9th Division), 1990

Capt. David C. Burton (376th Bomb Group, 15th Air Force) (including *Military Magazine* articles), 1990

M.Sgt. Rosario "Zaro" Calabrese (PI Team #45), 1990

Herbert Campbell (5th Engineer Special Brigade), 1990

S.Sgt. Jack W. Carter (4th Division), 1989

Pvt. Frank Catalano (4th Division), 1990★

Shipfitter 2/C Angelos T. Chatas (NCDU-25), 1989

S.Sgt. Murphy Chustz (4th Division), 1989

Ens. Tomas Francis Clark (*LST-507*), 1990

PFC Joseph G. Clowry (82nd Airborne Division), 1990

Pvt. Dalton Coffin (4th Division), 1990

PFC Harper H. Coleman (4th Division), 1990

Tech 5 Walter Condon (29th Division), 1989

S.Sgt. William L. Conrad (4th Division), 1990

S.Sgt. Byron Cook (388th Bomb Group) (including *Little Boy Blue* manuscript), 1990

1st Lt. Thomas Cortright (4th Division), 1990

Maj. X. B. Cox Jr. (101st Airborne Division), 1990

Tech 5 Gerald M. Cummings (82nd Airborne Division), 1989

1st Lt. Arnold N. Delmonico (490th Bomb Group), 1990

Pvt. Howard G. DeVoe (1st Eng. Special Brigade), 1990

1st Lt. Robert S. Dickson (101st Airborne Division), 1990

S/1 Everett Douglas (USS *Meredeth*), 1990

1st Lt. Robert Dove (79th Division), 1990 and 1991

PFC Joseph A. Dragotto (1st Division), 1990

PFC Earl Duncan (9th Division), 1990

Lt. (jg) Eugene E. Eckstam (*LST-597* and *LST-391*), 1990

S.Sgt. John B. Ellery (1st Division), 1990

Pvt. Frederick Erben (1st Division), 1990

Lt(jg). John L. Evans (USS *Augusta*), 1990

T.Sgt. Clarence P. Faria (4th Division), 1990

Sgt. Victor H. Fast (5th Ranger Battalion), 1990

PFC Ralph Fink (45th Division), 1990

PFC Martin M. Finkelstein (82nd Airborne Division), 1989 to 1990

Pvt. William E. Finnigan (4th Division), 1990★

PFC Robert A. Flory (101st Airborne Division), 1990

PFC Joseph M. Foye (9th Division), 1990

Capt. John E. Galvin (4th Division), 1990

Sgt. Don Garrigues (551st Parachute Infantry Battalion) (unpublished memoir), 1990

Capt. Joe Gault (82nd Airborne Division) (unpublished memoir of F Company), 1990

S/2 Theodore Gaydos (*ATA 125*), 1990

PFC Robert M. Gehlhoff (3rd Division), 1990

S.Sgt. Glenn Gibson (70th Tank Battalion), 1990

PFC Raymond Gonzalez (82nd Airborne Division), 1989

Yeoman 2/C George Gray (*LCI-86*), 1989

PFC John D. Gregory (9th Division), 1991

Pvt. Raymond Griffis (4th Division), 1990

Capt. Robert J. Hahlen (312th Air Base Group), 1991

Capt. Charles M. Hangsterfer (1st Division), 1990

Pvt. Robert M. Hardesty (29th Division), 1990

Maj. Harlos V. Hatter (45th Division), 1990

2nd Lt. Nathaniel K. Helman (4th Division), 1989

Sgt. Leonard Herb (4th Division), 1990

S.Sgt. Charles B. Herndon (30th Division), 1990

Col. Gerald J. Higgins (101st Airborne Division), 1990

PFC Ray B. Hood (101st Airborne Division), 1989 to 1994

RM 1/C Carl J. Hummel (USS *Augusta*), 1990

Capt. Jack Ilfrey (20th Fighter Group), 1990

Ens. Donald E. Irwin (*LCT-614*) (including unpublished article from 1984), 1990

1st Lt. Jack Roger Isaacs (82nd Airborne Division), 1990

Lt. Col. Charles Jackson (4th Division) (including personal letters), 1989

1st Lt. Kenneth K. Jarvis (35th Division), 1990

Pvt. Edward Jeziorski (82nd Airborne Division), 1990

PFC Dick Johnson (82nd Airborne Division), 1989

Maj. Robert S. Johnson (56th Fighter Group), 1990

Sgt. Walter Jutkins (741st Tank Battalion), 1990

Capt. Robert B. Kaye (4th Division) (interviewed by Peter Triolo), 1990

PFC Everett H. Kelly (29th and 30th Divisions) (including material from his privately published book), 1990

1st Lt. John A. Kirchner (79th Division), 1990

CWO-2 Larry Knecht (4th Division), 1990★

2nd Lt. William D. Knickerbocker (345th Troop Carrier Group)

S.Sgt. George A. Kobe (29th Division) (from Slaughter manuscript)

Phm3/C Vincent A. Kordack (6th Beach Battalion) (including diary), 1990

Capt. Herbert M. Krauss (4th Division), 1990

Lt. Col. Ralph Maurice Krieger (45th Division), 1990

PFC Allan L. Langdon (82nd Airborne Division) (manuscript on 505th), 1989

Sgt. Melvin F. Larson (388th Bomb Group), 1990

PFC William A. Lawrence (35th Division), 1990

S1/C Clifford L. Legerton (8th Beach Battalion), 1990

PFC Robert Lehmann (35th Division), 1990

1st Lt. Ralph E. Lingert (4th Division), 1989

PFC Albert Littke (299th Engineer Combat Battalion), 1990

Tech 5 Aaron D. Lubin (9th Division), 1990

Lt. Col. William P. Machemehl (101st Airborne Division), 1990

Pvt. Harold Martino (101st Airborne Division) (unpublished memoirs), 1989 to 1990

S.Sgt. Gordon H. Mason (44th Engineer Combat Battalion), 1990★

Col. S. B. Mason (1st Infantry Division), 1989

Floyd M. Matthews (ARS-5, USS *Diver*), 1990

Pvt. Buddy Mazzara (1st Division), 1990

1st Lt. John A. McAllister (29th Division), 1989

1st Lt. Douglas G. McArthur (388th Bomb Group), 1990

PFC John B. McBurney (8th Division), 1991

Capt. Donald McConnell (44th Engineer Combat Battalion), 1990

Lt. William H. McDaniel (Fleet Marine, USS *Augusta*), 1990

PFC John E. McQuaid (29th Division), 1989

Lt. Jay H. Mehaffey (5th Ranger Battalion), 1990★

1st Lt. Leon E. Mendel (1st Division and 82nd Airborne Division)

Sgt. Gino Mercuriali (1st Ranger Battalion), 1989

2nd Lt. Charlie A. Miller (29th Division), 1990★

Pvt. A. B. Mirmelstein (29th Division) (including diary), 1990

Tech 5 Maxwell B. Moffett (29th Division), 1989

Tech 5 Albert Mominee (1st Division), 1990

Pvt. William C. Montgomery (4th Division), 1989

PFC John P. Montrose (29th Division), 1989

Capt. David D. Moore (478th Amphibian Truck Company), 1990

Tech 4 Charles J. Myers (70th Tank Battalion), 1990

S.Sgt. Albert Nendza (1st Division), 1990

S.Sgt. James L. Newton (332nd Service Group), 1990

1st Sgt. Samuel D. Norris (4th Division), 1990

1st Lt. Carlos C. Ogden (79th Division), 1990

PFC Guy E. Overbey (4th Division), 1990

Pvt. James Ousley (1st Engineer Special Brigade), 1990

T.Sgt. Harold E. Owens (82nd Airborne Division), 1990

Pvt. Paul E. Pachowka (82nd Airborne Division), 1991

1st Sgt. Regis J. Pahler (82nd Airborne Division) (correspondence submitted by Mrs. Shipton), 1990

Lt. Roderick Parsch (account submitted by his wife), 1990

S/1 Myron D. Parsons (*LCT-851*), 1991

Sgt. Verl L. Pendelton (3rd Division), 2007

Tech 5 John A. Perry (462nd Amphibious Truck Company), 1990

1st Lt. Henry G. "Red" Phillips (9th Division) (M Company manuscript), 1990

Capt. Ivan G. Phillips (101st Airborne Divison), 1989

1st Lt. Wayne Pierce (82nd Airborne Division) (copy of manuscript), 1989 to 1993

1st Lt. Chester Pietrzak (388th Bomb Group), 1990

PFC John A. Plonski (4th Division), 1990

Sherman Pratt (3rd Division) (including permission to use account from his book *Autobahn to Berchtesgarden*), 1990

1st Lt. Murray Pulver (35th Division) (including permission to use account from his book *The Longest Year*)

Pvt. Gerald Putman (4th Division), 1990

Pvt. Duwaine Raatz (1st Division), 1990

Col. Russell "Red" P. Reeder Jr., 1990

Tech 5 James R. Richards (82nd Airborne Division), 1990

PFC Clinton E. Riddle (82nd Airborne Division), 1989 to 1990

T.Sgt. Jarvis Roberts (388th Bomb Group), 1989

Col. Warren Robinson (79th Division) (including permission to use excerpts from his book), 1990

Pvt. Warren L. Rulien (1st Division), 1990

PFC Robert L. Sales (29th Division) (from Slaughter manuscript)

2nd Lt. Jack R. Sargeant (92nd Bomb Group), 1990

1st Lt. Charles Scheffel (9th Division) (copy of memoirs), 1993

Cpl. Jack W. Schlegel (82nd Airborne Division), 1990

Sgt. Zane D. Schlemmer (82nd Airborne Division), 1990

PFC René A. Schmidt (101st Airborne Division), 1990

Capt. Harold Shebeck (82nd Airborne Division), 1989

1st Sgt. Donald Sherwood (4th Division), 1990

Sgt. John Shirley (3rd Division), 1990 and 2007

Sgt. John Slaughter (29th Division), 1990 to 1991

PFC Raymond G. Sluder (4th Division), 1990

Sgt. Jay B. Smith (463rd AAA AW Battalion), 1990

Staff Sgt. Raymond Smith (101st Airborne Division), 1989

Phm3/C Frank D. Snyder, Jr. (6th Naval Beach Battalion), 1990

Sgt. John Souch (1st Division), 1990

1st Lt. David G. Speer (30th Division), 1990

Sgt. Francis Robert Steele (4th Division) (submitted by his wife Ruth after his death), 1989

Capt. Kenneth P. Stemmons (45th Division), 1990

Sgt. Herbert Stern (9th Division), 1990

Pvt. Richard S. Stewart (35th Division), 1990

PFC Clyde D. Strosnider (1st Division), 1990

Pvt. Stanley Stypulkowski (1st Division), 1990

PFC Louis Sumien (3rd Division), 1990

Sgt. Marcel Galen Swank (34th Division and 1st Ranger Battalion), 1989

Tech 5 Fred R. Tannery (4th Division), 1989 and 1990

Sgt. Harold Taylor (3rd Division), 1990

Pvt. Charles H. Thomas (1st Division), 1990

Ens. Walt Treanor (*LST-58*), 1990

Pvt. Edward A. Trennert (430th Anti-Aircraft Artillery Battalion), 1990

1st Lt. Peter Triolo (4th Division), 1990

PFC John F. Troy (8th Division), 1991

1st Lt. Sidney M. Ulan (441st Troop Carrier Group), 1990

1st Lt. Luther Richard Underwood (21st Finance Disbursing Section), 1990★

Pvt. Richard Weese (82nd Airborne Division), 1990

Pvt. Eldon Wiehe (1st Division), 1990

Pvt. George Lockett Wood (196th Field Artillery Battalion), 1990

Sgt. William Youmans (4th Division), 1990

PFC Robert Lee Zahradka (3rd Division), 1990

Pvt. Sam Zittrer (1st Division), 1990

Interviews

2nd Lt. Fred F. Assmann (86th Chemical Mortar Battalion), April 1990

T.Sgt. Theodore G. Aufort (1st Division), April 1990

Lt. Col. Thomas W. Barfoot 93rd Photo Recon Group), April 1990

1st Lt. L. Benjamin Jr. (86th Chemical Mortar Battalion), April 1990

1st Lt. Sidney Berger (1st Engineer Special Brigade) (including copy of manuscript), October 1990

Sgt. John Birchman (313th Troop Carrier Group), October 1989

PFC Ernest Botella (9th Division), November 1990

1st Lt. Allen Braem (313th Troop Carrier Group), October 1989

Sgt. Fred Buffington (727th Railway Bn), September 1991

Pvt. Otway Burns (1st Engineer Special Brigade), October 1990

Lt. Herman F. Byram (2nd Division), March 1990

Boatswains Mate 2/C Elmer Carmichael (*LCI-85*), November 1989

1st Lt. Don Carroll (8th Armored Division), 1991

2nd Lt. Paul Cody (313th Troop Carrier Group), October 1989

Flight Off. Carson E. Crabtree (442nd Troop Carrier Group), October 1989

1st Lt. James M. Crutchfield (6th Armored Division), May 1990★

PFC Maynard E. Daggett (978th Field Artillery Battalion), September and October 1989★

2nd Lt. John B. Deasy (86th Chemical Mortar Battalion), April 1990

1st Lt. William Denham (452nd Bomb Group), December 1989

Pvt. Howard G. DeVoe (1st Engineer Special Brigade), October 1990

Tech Sgt. Thomas M. Edwards (490th Bomb Group), May 1991

1st Lt. James Eikner (2nd Ranger Battalion), March and April 1990★

GM3/C France L. Enlow (*LCI-326*), November 1989

1st Lt. Graydon K. Eubank (322nd Bomb Group), July 1990

Lt. Ed Fabian (*LCI-86* and *LCI-89*), November 1989★

PFC Robert A. Flory (101st Airborne Division), June 1991

2nd Lt. Lyle Foutz (313th Troop Carrier Group), October 1989

T.Sgt. William F. French (452nd Bomb Group), August 1990

1st Lt. Frank Gallagher (322nd Bombardment Group), July 1990

PFC John P. Gallagher (1st Engineer Special Brigade), Oct. 1990

Sgt. William D. Gammon (101st Airborne Division), June 1991

Chief Quartermaster John Gatton Jr. (*LCI-96*), November 1989

Capt. Joe Gault (82nd Airborne Division), March 1990

CMoMM Ralph W. Gault (*LCI-88*), November 1989

Flight Off. Chas Gauntt (435th Troop Carrier Group), May 1990

Tech 5 Abelardo Gonzales (82nd Airborne Division), January 1990

CWO William Hart (437th Troop Carrier Group), September 1989

S.Sgt. James Henkel (490th Bomb Group), May 1991

PFC A. J. Hester (2nd Division), July 1990

1st Lt. Warren B. Hinchcliff (86th Chemical Mortar Battalion), April 1990

1st Lt. Carl Hobbs (29th Division), October 1989

Cpl. Wardell Hopper (741st Tank Battalion), December 1990

MMM2/C Warren Hotard (*LCI-320*), November 1989

Tech 4 John R. Iggens (720th Railway Operating Battalion), September 1991

Sgt. Walter Jutkins (741st Tank Battalion), July 1990

Tech 4 Dale K. Kearnes (35th Division), March 1990

S.Sgt. George Kerrigan (36th Division), April 1990

2nd Lt. William D. Knickerbocker (345th Troop Carrier Group) (including diary), May 1990

PFC Julius I. Koenig (757th Railway Shop Battalion), September 1991

2nd Lt. William Laahs (490th Bomb Group), May 1991

Sgt. L. R. Langley (727th Railway Battalion), September 1991

1st Sgt. Ernest Lee (29th Division), August 1990

S.Sgt. William Lewis (29th Division), August 1990 and May 1991

1st Sgt. Louis Magnon (Electronics Training Group), April 1990

S/1 Edward Matousek (*LCI-84*), November 1989

S/1 Robert McCrory (*LCI-93*), November 1989

Flight Off. Douglas N. Morilon (490th Bomb Group), May 1991

1st Lt. Rodney Mortensen (6th Armored Division), May 1990

Tech 4 Hyatt Moser (286th JASCO), October 1990

1st Lt Reuben D. Parker (36th Division), April 1990

T.Sgt. Sammie D. Petty (36th Division), April 1990

S.Sgt. Kenneth Potter (490th Bomb Group), May 1991

PFC James D. Purifoy (101st Airborne Division), June 1991

Capt. Elmer D. Richardson (3rd Photo Recon Group), April 1990

S.Sgt. Ralph D. Rickel (490th Bomb Group), May 1991

PFC Arthur Rodgers (36th Division), April 1990

S/1 Leon C. Rodriguez (*LCI-323*), September 1989

Sgt. James C. Ross (490th Bomb Group), May 1991

PFC Chester Saeger (722nd Railway Operating Battalion), September 1991

Flight Off. John F. Schumacher (439th Troop Carrier Group), May 1990

Sgt. Robert B. Seeley (720th Railway Operating Battalion), September 1991

PFC Hyman Shapiro (560th Quartermaster Railhead Company), July 1989

S.Sgt. Bonnie Skloss (388th Bomb Group), June 1990

S.Sgt. Stanley Stout (557th Quartermaster Company), March 1990

1st Lt. Carl Strom (36th Division), April 1990

Tech 5 Henry E. Sunier (286th JASCO), October 1990

Maj. David E. Thomas (82nd Airborne Division), November and Dececember 1989 and April 1990

1st Lt. William M. Thompson (437th Troop Carrier Group), July 1990

1st Lt. Martin Tully (36th Division), April 1990

1st Lt. Ralph Vigliotti (86th Chemical Mortar Battalion), April 1990

1st Lt. Robert Raoul Walsh (379th Bomb Group), September and October 1989

2nd Lt. Ray J. Welty (316th Troop Carrier Group), July 1990

1st Lt. Lambert G. Wilder (435th Troop Carrier Group), May 1990

2nd Lt. James C. Williams (490th Bomb Group), May 1991

Sgt. Keith N. Wilson (727th Railway Battalion), September 1991

Cpl. Art Zalud (36th Division), April 1990

Tech 4 Alex J. Ziese (2nd Division), April 1990

ACKNOWLEDGMENTS

It took the accounts of more than 200 veterans to put this project together. There are too many veterans to list here, but all are listed with their unit in the bibliography (found in volume 3). Here we would simply like to acknowledge some of those who provided additional materials, such as memoirs or books, and gave permission to quote from them. Some veterans, like Larry Knecht and Peter Trioli, even conducted interviews for us early in the 1990s. In addition, we would like to thank the staff at NARA for helping us locate records.

Special thanks go to John "Slim" Stokes, our reader, who spent many hours correcting errors in the manuscript and helping locate veterans with whom we had lost contact during the past fifteen years. We apologize for anyone we may have forgotten to mention.

Sadly, since we began this project in 1989, many of the veterans who contributed their accounts have passed away. It took until 2007 to find a publisher interested in this book, and by that time, many of the contributors had either forgotten about us or assumed the book would never be done. Some, like Robert Dove and Ray Hood, remained in contact and waited patiently, but passed away in the last few years. We regret that they and many other contributors will never see the final product, but we hope that their families and descendants will take the time to read their accounts.

The following is a partial list of those who made contributions to this volume:

Lt. Col. John A. Allison (veteran), who provided a copy of his memoirs.

Steven E. Anders, Ph.D., Command Historian, U.S. Army Quartermaster Center at Fort Lee, who provided information on army rations.

Mark Bando, who provided data on the 101st Airborne Division and gave us additional contacts.

Sidney Berger (veteran), who provided a copy of his manuscript.

Raus Blondo (veteran), who provided a copy of the 112th Engineer Combat Battalion history.

Byron Cook (veterans), who provided a copy of his manuscript, *Little Boy Blue*.

X. B. Cox (veteran), who provided a copy of his memoirs.

Gerard M. Devlin, who provided contacts and additional information on airborne operations not included in his books.

Barbara Donnelly, Reference Librarian at the Naval War College, who provided reference material on naval training.

Col. Robert Dove (veteran), who provided his 79th Recon diary.

Eugene E. Eckstam, who provided additional material on Operation Tiger.

Don Garrigues (veteran), who provided a copy of his unpublished memoir, *From the Delphus to Destiny*, and documents on the 551st Parachute Infantry Battalion.

Ray B. Hood (veteran), who provided a copy of his memoirs in addition to other material, including a piece of his parachute.

Wardell Hopper (veteran), who provided a copy of the history of the 741st Tank Battalion.

Jack Ilfrey (veteran), who provided a copy of part of the 20th Fighter Group's unit history as well as association newsletters.

Larry Knecht (veteran), who provided additional material and contacts for the 4th Division.

Allan L. Langdon (veteran), who provided a copy of his manuscript.

Rev. Melvin Larson (veteran), who provided new details for this book and another project.

William Lewis (veteran), who was always in contact with additional information for this and other projects.

Bernard Lowry, who helped locate sites in England referred to by veterans (who often could not properly spell the names) and clarified many details.

Harold Martino (veteran), who provided a copy of his unpublished manuscript.

Ray Merriam, who contacted veterans and provided copies of now-rare books.

Col. Don Patton, who located former veterans.

Henry Phillips (veteran), who provided a copy of his book, *Heavy Weapons*.

Col. Sherman Pratt (veteran), who provided material from his book, *Autobahn to Berchtesgaden*.

Murray Pulver (veteran), who provided a copy of his book, *The Longest Year*.

Leon J. Renicker, who provided a copy of the 137th Infantry Regiment's combat history.

Gordon Rottman, who providing details on various items of equipment and special units.

Charles Scheffel, who provided a copy of materials about the 1st Battalion, 39th Infantry Regiment, 9th Infantry Division, including memoirs and a report on the German attack at Avranche.

Harold Shebeck (veteran), who provided a copy of his memoirs.

John Shirley (veteran), who provided a copy of his book, *I Remember*, as well as other details.

J. R. Slaughter (veteran), who provided a copy his early manuscript concerning veterans of the 29th Division.

J. B. Smith (veteran), who provided organization information for the of 463rd AAA AW Battalion.

John Stokes, who read this manuscript and helped with research on veterans.

Carl Strom (veteran), who provided additional information.

Lee Unterborn, who helped with general research and loaned books.

Isadore Valenti (veteran), who provided sections from his book, *Combat Medic*.

John Votaw at the 1st Infantry Division Museum at Cantigny, Chicago, who provided veterans' accounts and contacts plus information on the 1st Division.

Andrew Woods at the McCormick Research Center of the 1st Infantry Division Museum, who provided information on training and on General Mason.

INDEX